PHARISAISM *in the* MAKING

SELECTED ESSAYS

by

LOUIS FINKELSTEIN
Chancellor of
THE JEWISH THEOLOGICAL
SEMINARY OF AMERICA

KTAV PUBLISHING HOUSE, INC.
1972

SBN 87068 -178-8

MANUFACTURED IN THE UNITED STATES OF AMERICA
LIBRARY OF CONGRESS CATALOG CARD NUMBER 77-168778

TABLE OF CONTENTS

FOR THE CONVENIENCE OF THE READER, NEW CONSECUTIVE PAGINATION HAS BEEN INTRODUCED AT THE BOTTOM OF EACH PAGE.

Chapter I

INTRODUCTION

The articles included in this volume, written over a span of more than four decades, provide glimpses into the history of Pre-Maccabean and Maccabean Judaism. Their coherence derives, first, from their common subject matter and, second, from the author's point of view. It has been my conviction—a conviction which has grown stronger with the passage of time, and is now confirmed in part by archeological discoveries—that historians have underestimated the immense contributions made to Jewish thought and literature in pre-Maccabean times. More recent textual studies have shown that many passages in the Talmud and in the synagogue liturgy derive from extremely early tradition.[1] Some passages in Rabbinic literature, as I have tried to show elsewhere,[2] probably date back to the Babylonian exile or even earlier. I have not been able to include in this volume my Hebrew studies demonstrating that some passages in the Mishna appear to have been composed in their original form in the fourth century B.C.E., or even earlier.[3] Perhaps they will appear in a subsequent collection.

The purpose of this Introduction is to supplement the studies in this book through reference to additional material which has appeared since the publication of each article. It is also necessary to correct some errors, some inadvertent and others revealed through later research, whether by others or by me.

The thesis of Chapter II dealing with "The Origin of the Synagogue" has been accepted by many scholars.[4] It should now be added that *Sifre* Deut. 343 (p. 395) clearly asserts that an early, germinal version of the Synagogue *amidah* was composed by "the early Prophets." [5] In the Bible and the Talmud, this phrase always signifies pre-exilic Prophets.[6] Documentary evidence is thus available to show that the Synagogue service came into being before the Babylonian Exile. Judgments made about other theses presented in *New Light from the Prophets* do not bear on this fundamental issue. The chapter on "The Origin of the Synagogue" should be read in connection with Chapter VIII of that book.

When the article on "The Oldest Midrash" was first published, many eyebrows were raised. However, the discovery of the Qumran Scrolls, with their clear use of the very midrashic method pursued in the document discussed in Chapter III, facilitates acceptance of an early date for the latter document, for there is ample evidence that some of the Qumran material dates from the latter part of the second century B.C.E.[7]

It may be disturbing for some historians to admit that important parts of the Passover *Haggadah* were composed by Temple priests, under the direction of pre-Maccabean high priests.[8] It may be even more disturbing to observe that the authors of these passages bore in mind the reactions of the Egyptian government which was in control of the Holy Land for a large part of the third century B.C.E. But Jewish liturgy is replete with similar instances of compliance with the prejudices of foreign rulers, and efforts to avoid offending them. Rab Jehudai Gaon did not hestitate to affirm that the *Qedushah* in the *amidah*,[9] as recited by his contemporaries in the Holy Land, was introduced to evade a Roman Imperial decree prohibiting the proclamation of the *Shema* in public. His tradition in this regard is beyond question.

Why should not earlier liturgists living under Egyptian dominion have avoided, particularly on Passover eve, any assertion that Jacob, the ancestor of their people, was "*a lost Aramean*"? That verse, literally understood, might give a semblance of legality to the Seleucid claim to Palestine. And, indeed, at what period other than that of Egyptian rule would anyone dare to misinterpret the biblical verse, in the manner followed by the composers of "The Oldest Midrash"?

The argument made in Chapter III on "The Oldest Midrash" is carried forward and, in my opinion, confirmed by the following chapter, dealing with "Pre-Maccabean Documents in the Passover Haggadah."

The "Introductory Study to the Chapters of the Fathers" (Chapter V), initiated a course of research which led to the analysis of the *Chapters of the Fathers*, and *The Fathers according to R. Nathan*;[10] and finally to a further and perhaps more daring hypothesis, presented in *New Light from the Prophets* (Chapter X, p. 77).

It has long been agreed that the first chapter of *Abot* is one of the earliest portions of the Mishna.[11] It clearly affirms the Pharisaic claim that their teachers alone were authorized interpreters of the Torah, and implicitly negates similar Sadducean claims on behalf of the high priest and their court.

The maxim of the Men of the Great Synagogue, which is discussed in Chapter VI, appeared originally in a form somewhat different from that found in the Mishna that we know. That text was edited for use in the schools and among the general public in the third century C.E., some seven centuries after the maxim had first been formulated. In *Abot d'R. Nathan* the early text has been preserved and is discussed.[12]

A new study (Chapter VII) of the early documents of the Pharisees demonstrates that as early as the fourth century B.C.E. the Pharisaic movement was in full vigor as an effort to establish the authority of the lay scholars. This suggestion runs counter to the theory held by many authorities who date the origin of the Pharisees in the time of the Maccabees and associate them with the Hasideans, without explaining why the name of the group was changed. I, myself, accepted that view, and developed it in *The Pharisees*.[13] However, talmudic and liturgical documents here cited clearly demonstrate the earlier origin of the movement.

It seems evident that Pharisaism originated among a group of lay scholars, the *soferim* or scribes, whose main following was drawn from among the lower classes of Jerusalem, its small traders and artisans.[14] These merchants and workers joined the lay scholars in opposing the authority of the priests and the landed aristocracy.

The Temple priests dubbed the group opposed to them "*Perushim*," meaning "separatists," because the priests considered *themselves* the authoritative interpreters of the Torah. As is shown in *New Light from the Prophets* (pp. 77 ff.), this opposition between the scholar and the lay teacher who drew his following primarily from the marketplace of Jerusalem, existed even before the Babylonian Exile. The Prophet emphasized the individual's direct approach to God through prayer and study, and in this the Prophet was followed by the *sofer* of post-Exilic times. The priest held that the only way to approach the Deity was through sacrifice and the ministry of the Temple, where the non-priestly participant was really only an observer in the audience.

The Pharisees never regarded themselves as a sect, and therefore did not feel it necessary to give themselves a name. For them, their teachings were "Judaism," and their leaders, the *soferim* or *zekenim* ("elders"), were *hakme yisrael,* "the sages of Israel." The rest of the Pharisees were "disciples of the wise." Only when citing the views and doctrines of their opponents did they refer to themselves as "Pharisees."

However, the word *parosh* also signifies "ascetic." Some early scholars who were, in fact, ascetics, therefore may have accepted this title for their group, interpreting the word as referring in a complimentary fashion to their practices.

Chapter VIII shows that one of the underlying principles of early Pharisaism was anonymity. This curious practice was noted and remarked upon by Rab Sherira Gaon who explained that there would have been no point in recording the scholars' names, "as there was no controversy among them."[15] There was no need to seek the authority of particular scholars for one's views, since all agreed regarding the obligations of each Jew. When there were differences, the Scribes and the Pharisees held that each person should follow his tradition.

Anonymity may also have been encouraged by the asceticism which many Pharisees practiced. In any event, not one of the Pharisaic teachers from Ezra until Simeon the Righteous, two and a half centuries later, is known by name. Even more impressively, from the time of Simeon the Righteous, about 200 B.C.E., until that of Shammai and Hillel, two centuries later, we hear primarily of two scholars in each generation, and only of a few others who are mentioned in incidental accounts. This anonymity cannot have been accidental. The chapter dealing with Pharisaic anonymity is intended to indicate the factors which encouraged this custom, its purpose, and the curious stamp it left on later tradition and Hebrew literature, remaining an unconscious element in Jewish culture to this day.

The *halakah* of the Book of Jubilees, discussed in Chapter IX, is most interesting for the light it sheds on the form of the tradition of its time. The article was written in 1918 or 1919 while I was still a student at the Seminary. However, almost all its arguments remain valid. The reader will wish to supplement it with references to further studies on the subject, particularly those reflecting the vast illumination shed on the Book of Jubilees by the discovery of the Qumran Scrolls. Professor Louis Ginzberg's "*Eine unbekannte juedische Sekte*" (published in 1914-1919) remains the standard work on the *halakah* of the Sect of the Jericho Scrolls to this day, and bears heavily on the analysis of the *halakah* of the Book of Jubilees, too. My discussion of the calendar proposed by the author of the Book of Jubilees is now obsolete; Mme. A. Joubert has solved the riddle of the calendar, which was also that of the Sect of the Jericho Scrolls.[16]

Chapter X deals with several norms found in the Book of Jubilees which are implicit, but are not explicitly articulated, in the Rabbinic *halakah*. Perhaps the most interesting of these deals with the obligation of a priest to bathe before each ritual act, then to wash his hands and feet, and again to wash them after the completion of his act of service. The norm is suggested in the Book of Jubilees (21:16), in the commandment given

Abraham, "At all times be clean in thy body, and wash thyself with water before thou approachest to offer on the altar, and wash thy hands and feet before thou drawest near the altar, and when thou art over the sacrificing, wash again thy hands and thy feet." (The word "clean" probably represents an original *tahor*, "pure," meaning levitically pure.) Abraham was thus commanded to be levitically pure at all times. Undoubtedly this was assumed for the priest, so that the requirement to bathe before approaching the altar was not intended to remove any defilement, but to prepare for a particular act of ministry. After bathing, the priest was to wash his hands and feet before offering a sacrifice in accordance with the command given the priests in Exod. 30:20, and after the sacrificial ceremonies, he was again to wash his hands and feet.

The Testaments of the Twelve Patriarchs preserves a slightly different tradition. In Testament Levi 9:11, Levi is commanded (and therefore likewise the priests, his descendants), *"Before entering the holy place*, bathe; and when thou offerest the sacrifice, wash; and again when thou finishest the sacrifice, wash." (It is not entirely clear whether the second washing involved only one's hands and feet, or a second immersion.)

The difference between the two works is that the Book of Jubilees does not suggest that a priest undergo immersion before entering the Temple precincts, as the Talmud requires.[17] He bathed only when "he approached to offer on the altar."

The difference was halakically important. Apparently the requirement imposed by Testament Levi and the Talmud was based on the suspicion that a priest might be defiled, and therefore unfit to enter the Temple courts.[18] Once a priest had bathed to remove a minor impurity he had the status of *tebul yom*.

According to early Pharisaic interpretation of Scripture, a *tebul yom* was prohibited from entering the Temple precincts; but if he did enter, his transgression was minor. He could not defile anything through contact with it.[19] Therefore, a priest suspected of being defiled through contact with the carcass of a dead animal, or through the touch of a woman in her menses (without sexual intercourse), but who had bathed afterward, did not imperil the sanctity of the Temple sacrifices or the holy vessels which he touched.

The Sadducees and, in later times, the Shammaitic wing of the Pharisees (consisting largely of priests), could not agree to the adoption of a ceremonial which, through its existence, proclaimed a suspicion that the priests violated the Law. Therefore, according to them, a *tebul yom* was no less defiled than an impure person who had not undergone immersion.[20] Purification from defilement came only with nightfall, after immersion. Thus priestly tradition held that an Aaronid might not eat the heave-offering until he had bathed, and night had fallen. Priests who were *tebul yom* were denied the right to eat the holy meat, and even to have a part of it set aside for them to eat after dark.

The Book of Jubilees (21:16) apparently rejected the Pharisaic thesis that a priest had to bathe before entering the Temple precincts. But as usual, it offered a compromise between the factions. According to it, the priest prepared for the ritual of offering a sacrifice through immersion, then washed his hands and feet, and washed them again after the sacrifice.

As indicated in this volume, pp. 240 ff., all the Rabbinic works, including Mishna,[21] *Tosefta*[22] and *Sifra*[23], agree that on the Day of Atonement, the high priest bathed before entering the actual Temple precincts (although he had dwelt for seven days in their immediate proximity, and had been "purified" in every possible way). He also washed his hands before and after each act of his ministry on that day—an act of ministry being signified by his change from the high priestly garments to the simple linen ones used when he entered the Holy of Holies; and then by his donning the high priestly garments after leaving the Holy of Holies. Each time he bathed, he washed his hands and feet twice, first before the immersion and then afterward.[24]

The Palestinian *payyetanim* record a further immersion by the high priest at the very end of his ministry on the Day of Atonement—this one outside the Temple precincts themselves. From their record, it seems probable that Testament Levi also referred to an immersion by all priests, following the completion of their participation in the ministry on any particular day.

The basic argument in Chapter XI, dealing with "The Development of the *Amidah*," remains valid in my opinion, despite various criticisms. On the contrary, publication of the many Genizah manuscripts of the *amidah*, and of texts of the Qumran Scrolls, has greatly strengthened the argument. The *baraita* from *Tosefta* and *Yerushalmi Berakot*, cited on p. 125 of this volume, definitely shows that the use of different terms of address to the Deity at the beginning of prayers, involved important theological issues. Therefore, the fact that in some prayers of the *amidah* the Deity was addressed in the opening strophe with the Name, signified by *yod heh*, suggests that they were composed in very early times, when this style alone was considered proper. One who prayed in that way was a *hakam*. If one used the cypher *aleph lamed* (*e-l-o-h-e-n-u*), one was *benoni*, i.e. mediocre. If one substituted *aleph lamed* for *yod heh* at the conclusion of the prayer, in the *hatimah*, one was either a sectarian or ignorant!

We know that the use of the Name *yod heh* outside the Temple ceased in the fourth century B.C.E.[25] It could not be replaced in the petitions of the *amidah* with the title signified by *aleph lamed*, for that would stamp one as *benoni*. Authors of prayers would not include in the central synagogue service (i.e. in the prayers required for the leader), a form marking him as less than a *hakam*. Hence the different types of beginnings used in various paragraphs of the *amidah*. The earliest substitute for *yod heh* was *abinu*, "our Father," a term not interdicted. Later, all terms of address to the Deity were omitted. We can thus determine the order in which the various sections of the daily *amidah* were composed. This has been done conclusively, in my opinion, in Chapter XI.

The development of the *birkat ha-mazon* also requires further examination, and either confirmation or revision of some of the conclusions reached in Chapter XII of this volume. As with the *amidah*, the basic argument of this article has been generally accepted and appears to have been confirmed by the publication of new texts. See, particularly, S. Assaf in *Dinaburg Jubilee Volume*, pp. 129ff.; A. M. Haberman, in *Yediot ha-Makon Le-Heqer ha-Shirah ha-Ibrit* V (1939), pp. 51ff.; Alexander

Scheiber, in the same series, VII (1958), pp. 158ff,; and the text discovered in Dura Europos.[26] The student must now also consult the lengthy discussion of the talmudic passages referring to this prayer, by Professor Saul Lieberman in *Tosefta Kifeshutah, Berakot* pp. 9 ff., and 100 ff.; by G. Allon, in *Mehqarim be-Toledot Yisrael* I, pp. 286ff. and by J. Heinemann, in his comprehensive volume *Ha-Tefillah bi-Tequfat ha-Tannaim* (see there Index, *s.v. Birkat ha-Mazon*). We should further also consider what light, if any, is shed on the Rabbinic *birkat ha-mazon* by the texts discovered in the Qumran caves.

As indicated in this volume, p. 340, the earliest explicit reference to the *birkat ha-mazon* occurs in the Book of Jubilees (22:6 ff.), where Abraham is described as having said a Grace after Meals consisting of three parts, each corresponding to one of the three benedictions of the *birkat ha-mazon* as it was said at the time of the author of that book. Thus we may definitely assume that the three main benedictions of the prayer—the first, thanking God for the food; the second, for the gift of the Land; the third, containing the prayer for Jerusalem—were all pre-Maccabean, and were composed by the Men of the Great Synagogue, perhaps at different dates, but all no later than the early decades of the second century B.C.E. The summons to recite the blessing, later called *birkat ha-zimmum*, was not yet considered a benediction. The fourth benediction, called in the Talmud, "the benediction established by the Sages in Yabneh,"[27] had not yet been composed.

The view that the pre-Maccabean Men of the Great Synagogue actually formulated and promulgated a text for the *amidah*, the *birkat ha-mazon,* and other prayers, has been challenged by some writers on the subject, including, most recently, J. Heinemann in his work *ha-Tefillah bi-Tequfat ha-Tannaim ve-ha-Amoraim*, pp. 10 and 33ff. The discussion of the *amidah*, in Chapter XI, assumes only the existence of a text for the community, recommended by the Men of the Great Synagogue. According to the talmudic authorities of the latter half of the first and the beginning of the second century C.E., this did not preclude improvisation in private or congregational prayer. Individuals in their private devotions, and leaders of congregational prayers were permitted to change the text in the body of the prayer, but generally did not alter the *hatimah*, which remained remarkably constant in the Holy Land from about the fourth century B.C.E. until the destruction of the Jewish community there at the hands of the Crusaders. (The Babylonian authorities introduced changes not only in the body of the prayers, but also in the *hatimot*. But, once the new *hatimot* of the Babylonian Jewish authorities had been promulgated, they, in turn, remained constant.[28])

The composition of prayers formulated for the great mass of Pharisees, who could not be expected to improvise their own prayers and had to have texts which they could memorize, teach their children, and repeat by rote, did not obviate the necessity for norms, such as that found in the *baraita* cited below, p. 175, which guided the creative liturgists in their improvisations. On the other hand, the existence of such norms should not be used as an argument to show that the many different yet closely related versions of the ancient prayers derived from different sources.

The relation of the later texts of the liturgy to one another bears some analogy to the relationship among the normative and aggadic Rabbinic texts. Very often, through scientific study, we can re-create the texts underlying our present Mishna, *Tosefta*, and other sources, as they existed in the third century B.C.E., or even earlier. In those early days there was no edited Mishna, in the sense in which R. Judah the Patriarch created one, but "a disciple was obliged [or, at least, expected] to preserve the language of his teacher"[29] precisely as he had heard it. This did not prevent later scholars from improvising, changing older texts, or formulating new ones.[30] After the time of R. Judah the Patriarch, this was done only with the utmost hesitation, for he had "published" the Mishna.[31] But various *baraitot* in *Tosefta* and elsewhere show clearly that well-known accepted normative texts existed long before R. Judah the Patriarch, and were used by him in his work.

Are we to suppose that because some gifted poets of early

centuries, like Yannai and R. Eleazar ha-Qalir, improvised new versions of the prayers, every Jew was thrown on his own resources to formulate prayers for himself, receiving only vague guidelines from the scholarly authorities? Can we seriously entertain the view that this was the state of the synagogue liturgy until the time of Rabban Gamaliel II?

Abot d'R. Nathan II, chap. 27, 28a (cf. *Yer. Sukkah*, 5, 4, 55b) vividly describes a delightful scene in the Temple courts during the *Sukkot* week when, in the midst of all the frolic, the time had come to pray. The people, we are told, were about to pray, but Hillel, having in mind the injunction against praying when one was light-hearted, interrupted them with the solemn suggestion that God had no need for their prayers since He had myriads of angels paying Him homage. This sermon, doubtless delivered with Hillel-like intensity and persuasiveness, caused the people to burst into tears. Thereupon Hillel added, "But although He has all those myriads of angels, He desires only the prayers of His people." Now that the people were both somber and relieved of sadness, they could pray.

But how could a conglomeration of pilgrims from all parts of the Mediterranean world, or even from all parts of the Land of Israel, pray together at all, if there were no accepted, well-known, respected texts to be followed? There were no prayer-books. The leaders had to say the prayers from memory, and the people had to be able to follow and recognize the prayers as those to which they were more or less accustomed. Thus one must assume the existence of promulgated texts, even though they might not yet have been considered absolutely binding.

The explanation given in the final chapter of this book of the expression *pores et Shema*, as originally meaning "proclaiming the *Shema*" seems to me virtually certain. The evidence adduced shows that the form *pores et Shema* was used in all Palestinian texts. It was changed in the Babylonian tradition to *poreṭ ʿal Shema*, because the meaning of the word *pores* as "proclaim" was either unknown, or rarely used. On the other hand, the term was frequently used for "blessing." Thus the ritual, described by *pores et Shema*, was explained as "reciting the blessings of the

Shema"; the natural form of describing this ritual would be *pores 'al Shema,* "saying the benedictions for the *Shema.*" The interpretation here given has been accepted by Professor Saul Lieberman as "almost certain" (*Tosefta Kifeshutah, Megillah,* p. 1207).[32]

On the other hand the explanation of the word *pros* in such expressions as *pros ha-Pesah,* in the second part of the essay, now seem to me somewhat farfetched and improbable. Most likely, *pros* in those phrases means "before," as it does in the Greek, and refers to the weeks immediately preceding the festivals.

The discussion in these essays, taken as a whole, shows how intellectually and spiritually stirring the period of the Men of the Great Synagogue, beginning with Ezra and ending with Simeon the Righteous, must have been. The synagogue and its services, the home prayers, various Pharisaic norms and *midrashim,* were being formulated. Opposing groups, both Sadducean, i.e. priestly-aristocratic, and peasant dissidents, either Essenes or fore-runners of the Essenes, were thinking through their positions and formulating literary works of surprising merit and endurance. The Maccabean revolt, so remarkable in itself, did not emerge out of a spiritual vacuum, but out of centuries of spiritual indoctrination and thought. The revolt inevitably led to a renaissance of religious life, but the foundations for the great works of the Rabbinic scholars had been laid in earlier generations, the names of whose leaders were deliberately expunged from the historical record, and by their own wish.

NOTES

1. See J. N. Epstein–E. Z. Melammed, *Mebuot le-Sifrut ha-Tannaim* (Jerusalem, Tel Aviv, 1957), pp. 501 ff., and literature there cited. See also below, pp. 13 ff. and pp. 41 ff. Cf. the vast literature on the Qumran Sect, some of which may derive from pre-Maccabean times, and assumes a flourishing *halakah.*
2. See *New Light from the Prophets* (London, 1969).
3. See *Benjamin de Vries Memorial Volume,* pp. 43 ff., where it is demonstrated that Mishna *Sheqalim* 1.5, according to the text preserved in the best manuscripts and underlying the discussion in *Yerushalmi,* derives from a time when some obligatory sacrifices, but not voluntary ones, were accepted from the Gentiles—a view contrary to the post-Maccabean tradition. See also *Ha-Doar,* May 31, 1957, pp. 46 ff., where a section of *Mekilta Bo* is shown to have ante-dated the fall of Carthage in 146 B.C.E., and even more significantly to have ante-dated the Book of Jubilees, itself composed early in the second century B.C.E. at the very latest. (See below, p. 101.) Cf. further, HUCA XXXII (1961), Hebrew section pp. 1 ff.
4. See Salo Baron, *The Jewish Community,* III, p. 9, n. 14, where the literature on the subject is cited. See, however, J. Heinemann, *Ha-Tefillah bi-yeme ha-Tannaim ve-ha-Amoraim,* p. 83.
5. See *New Light from the Prophets,* pp. 35 ff.
6. *Ibid.,* p. 117.
7. The literature on the Dead Sea Scrolls has now become so voluminous, that documentation of any particular point must be suggested only at random. For the earliest date of the writing of some of the manuscripts of the commentaries found in the Qumran Caves, see F. M. Cross, *The Ancient Library of Qumran,* pp. 84 ff. According to Cross, all the manuscripts *of the commentaries* were put into writing in the latter half of the first century B.C.E. and the first half of the first century C.E. However, he holds that the manuscripts of the commentaries which have survived were virtually always the sole copies made, and were based not on earlier written documents but on traditions often two generations older (*op. cit.* p. 85). The midrashic

method, and indeed actual midrashic interpretations found in Rabbinic works, underlies some of the renderings in the Septuagint. See most recently, J. N. Epstein–E. Z. Melammed, *Mebuot le-Sifrut ha-Tannaim,* p. 516, and even some of the views reflected in the Book of Chronicles.

8. Cf. the views of Daniel Goldschmidt in his *Haggadah shel Pesah,* (Jerusalem, 1969), p. 16, n. 10.
9. See *Pirkoi ben Baboi* as quoted in the *Genizah* ms. published by Prof. Louis Ginzberg in *Ginze Schechter,* II, pp. 55-2; B. M. Lewin, in *Tarbiz* II, 1931, p. 398; and cf. further S. Spiegel in *Wolfson Jubilee Volumes,* Hebrew Vol., pp. 244 ff.
10. This analysis is presented in the Hebrew volume, *Mabo le-Mesiktot Abot ve-Abot d'R. Natan* (New York, 1951), hereafter, *Mabo.*
11. D. Z. Hoffman, *Die Erste Mischna* (1881–82), p. 26.
12. See also *Mabo,* pp. 28 ff.
13. See there, *Index,* under *Hasidim.*
14. See below, pp. 175 ff. The early origin of the Scribes and their relationship to Ezra was pointed out, on quite different grounds, by H. H. Schaeder in *Esra der Schreiber,* pp. 39 ff.; his view is adopted by S. Tscherikover, in *Eshkolot* (1954), p. 105. One may assume that as the population of Jerusalem grew, the increased influence of the Scribes on the traders and artisans led to the emergence of a movement known as Pharisaism.
15. *Iggeret R. Sherira Gaon,* ed. B. M. Lewin (Haifa, 1921), p. 8.
16. A. Joubert, *Vetus Testamentum* III (1953), pp. 250 ff. See further S. Talmon, *Mehqarim bi-Megillot Genuzot,* pp. 86 ff. An extremely illuminating discussion of the relation of the *halakah* to the Book of Jubilees was published by Chanoch Albeck under the title *Das Buch d. Jubilaeen and die Halacha* (Berlin 1930); and forms part of the Forty-Seventh Report of the *Hochschule fuer d. Wissenschaft d. Judentums.* (Cf. my review of that work in *Monatsschrift fuer Gesch. u. Wissenschaft d. Judentums* LXXVI (1932), pp. 525ff.).
17. Mishna *Yoma* 3.3. According to *Yer.* and *B., ad loc.,* and the commentaries, the Mishna requires anyone entering the Temple courts (i.e. "the Court of Israelites," which was adjacent to the "Court of the Priests") to undergo immersion; anyone already in the Temple courts, about to participate in the Temple ministry, also had to undergo immersion. These rules apparently did not

apply to those about to enter "the Court of Women" where people underwent the rituals of purification, and assembled for the festive gatherings on *Sukkot* and other occasions. While according to Mishna *Kelim* 1.8, a person known to be a *tebul yom* was forbidden to enter even the Court of Women, it was held that this was not a biblical prohibition, but an ordinance established by King Jehoshaphat and his *Bet Din* (*B. Yebamot* 7b, and parallel passages). On the other hand, according to Mishna *Kelim, loc. cit.,* even a person who entered the Court of Women, while defiled, did not have to sacrifice the sin. offering prescribed for defiled persons who entered the main Courts of the Temple, beginning with the Court of Israel. Therefore, if one was not known to be defiled, it would not be necessary to compel him to undergo immersion in order to enter the Court of Women.

18. No such requirement is mentioned in Scripture, which demands only that the priests wash their hands and their feet when entering the Tabernacle or approaching the altar for their ministry (Exod. 30:17 ff). On the other hand, before the Revelation, the whole people were commanded to purify themselves, and to wash their clothes (Exod. 19:10). In addition, the priests were commanded to "sanctify" themselves because they were to approach the Lord (*ibid.* v. 22). It seems clear that the Rabbinic distinction between immersion "for the sake of purification from defilement" and "purification for the sake of holiness" (*Yer. Yoma* 1.1, 38a) was an ancient one.
19. For a full discussion of the subject, see *The Pharisees,* third ed., pp. 661 ff.
20. This view was adopted in later times by R. Akiba and his school, causing great difficulties for later interpreters. See the view of R. Jonathan in *Sifre* Num. 125, p. 161; and cf. *Sifre Zutta* 19.13, p. 309, but cf. also Mishna *Zabim,* end (5.12), where the various sources of defilement *not* biblically, but Rabbinically commanded, are enumerated—*tebul yom* being among them. (See also Mishna *Negaim* 14.3; *Parah* 11.4.) All agreed that a *tebul yom* at the utmost defiled only the heave-offering and the holy meat. As the Mishna stands, this rule was "Rabbinically ordained," and had no biblical basis. However, in *B. Shabbat* 14b we are told that the words *tebul yom* were to be deleted. (According to *Tosafot, ad loc.,* that was not meant to indicate that the Mishna was to be emended, but that the *tebul yom* was not one of the Rabbinical decrees known as the "Eighteen Decrees.")

The problem needs further discussion, which cannot be included here.

21. Mishna *Yoma* 3.3.
22. *Tosefta Kippurim* 1.20, ed. Lieberman p. 228.
23. *Sifra Ahare, perek* 1.11, 80c; *ibid, perek* 6:3 ff., 82b.
24. See the discussion of the whole subject, and the citations of the *piyyutim* and commentaries by Professor Saul Lieberman, in *Tosefta Kifeshutah, Kippurim,* p. 747.
25. For the evidence, see p. 296 below.
26. See *Syria* XX (1930), pp. 27 ff.; E. L. Sukenik, *Bet ha-Keneset shel Dura Europos ve-Ziyurov,* p. 158; Professor Saul Lieberman, *Midreshe Teman,* pp. 40–41.
27. *B. Berakot* 48b.
28. This can be seen from a review of the texts published below, pp. 304 ff.
29. Mishna *Eduyyot* 1.3.
30. See J. N. Epstein, *Mabo le-Nusah ha-Mishna,* pp. 7 ff.
31. See Professor Saul Lieberman, *Hellenism in Jewish Palestine,* pp. 83 ff.
32. See also, however, I. Sonne, in HUCA XX (1947), p. 299; and Ch. Albeck, Mishna *Moed,* p. 503.

CHAPTER 2

THE ORIGIN OF THE SYNAGOGUE

The beginnings of the synagogue are hidden from us by the mists that gather about the horizon of Jewish history, no matter in which direction we look. When the synagogue rises into view during the Second Commonwealth it is already a well-established institution, and strangely the first mention of it is in a record of persecution, burning and destruction.[1] Some scholars have conjectured that it originated among the Babylonian exiles in response to the need for a house of prayer when there was no longer any Temple for sacrificial offerings. Others have sought to establish a chain of development between the local synagogues of the second commonwealth and the provincial *bamot* of the first.[2] The purpose of the two institutions was manifestly similar,—to enable the Jews in rural districts to have divine communion without resorting to the central sanctuary. But there the similarity ends, for while the *bamot* set themselves up as rivals of the Solomonic Temple, the synagogues always recognized its precedence and never attempted to introduce sacrificial worship.[3] Moreover the synagogue service was conducted entirely in the spirit of the prophetic teachings, while, as we learn from Jeremiah and his contemporaries, the *bamot* were far removed from that point of view.

Many years ago, Leopold Loew,[4] whose work has somehow not received the attention it merits, suggested that we seek the origin of the synagogue in pre-exilic institutions. He may have gone too far, perhaps, in supposing that the *Bet Ha-Am*, People's House, of Jeremiah[5], was the ancestor of the synagogue.[6] But that should not

[1] Ps. 74, 8.

[2] For these and other theories see Krauss, *Synagogale Altertuemer*, pp. 52 ff.; cf. also Wellhausen, *Israel.-Jued. Geschichte*, 7th ed., pp. 184 ff. and Kittel, *Gesch. des Volkes Israel*, pp. 112 and 201.

[3] See below, note 8.

[4] See *Gesammelte Schriften*, Vol. 4, pp. 5 ff.

[5] Jeremiah 39, 8.

[6] And yet one cannot deny the cogency given to Loew's argument by the remarkable statement in the Talmud that the synagogue was called *bet am* by the masses

Reprinted from *Proceedings of the American Academy for Jewish Research*, Volume 1, 1930.

obscure the validity of his remarks that the term *mikra* "assembly, convocation" is frequently used in Scripture so as to suggest a religious gathering, for purposes of worship. We may not be prepared to agree that Isaiah had such prayer meetings in mind when he said: "And the Lord shall create over the whole habitation of Mount Zion, and over all her assemblies (*mikraeha*) a cloud and smoke by day and the shining of flaming fire by night, for over all the glory shall there be a canopy (4, 5)." And yet we cannot miss the reference to some form of synagogue service in the identification of "holy convocations" with festival days which is constantly being made in Leviticus and in Numbers. "These are the appointed seasons of the Lord, even holy convocations (*mikrae kodesh*), which ye shall proclaim in their appointed seasons (Lev. 23, 4)."[7] Modern critics will object, perhaps, that these passages occur exclusively in the so-called Priestly Document, which, according to them, is of late origin. Yet even from that point of view, the expression is significant. For the identification of "holyday" with "synagogue gathering" could only arise if the institution of attending services at prayer meetings had been long and well established.

But more cogent evidence that the prophets conducted prayer meetings on the sabbath day is fortunately available.

The Shunamite woman, we are told, finding her child dead, declared her intention of visiting the prophet. Her husband, ignorant of the catastrophe that had befallen his house, said to her: "Wherefore wilt thou go today, seeing that it is neither new moon, nor sabbath (II Kings 4, 23)." Apparently it was the usage to visit the prophet on holy days. Such visits, we may be sure, did not partake of the nature of social calls; they were made for religious instruction and to obtain heavenly assistance.

Even more significant in regard to prophetic prayer gatherings is the evidence offered by the remarkable prayer which, according to the compiler of the Book of Kings, Solomon recited at the dedication of the Temple. Were we not told otherwise we might have been led by this document to believe that the Temple was merely a cen-

in its day (B. Sab. 32a). Is there not a possibility that as the prayer gatherings grew in size and importance they were transferred from private dwellings into special buildings and frequently into town halls?

[7] See the commentaries *ad loc.*, e. g. Bertholet on Lev. 23, 4.

tral synagogue, and that its offerings were prayers and confessions rather than sheep and bullocks. Throughout the long prayer not a word is uttered about the sacrifices to be offered in the sanctuary. The king asks God to receive graciously the petitions of His people, but says nothing about their holocausts and hecatombs. He bespeaks forgiveness if they confess their sins, but passes over in silence the required sacrifices of atonement.

> "Yet have thou respect unto the prayer of thy servant and to his supplication, O Lord, my God, to hearken unto the cry and to the prayer which thy servant prayeth before thee today:
>
> That thine eyes may be open toward this house night and day, even toward the place of which thou hast said, My name shall be there: that thou mayest hearken unto the prayer which thy servant shall make toward this place.[8]
>
> And hearken thou to the supplication of thy servant and of thy people Israel, when they shall pray toward this place: and hear thou in heaven thy dwelling-place; and when thou hearest, forgive . . .
>
> When thy people Israel be smitten down before the enemy, because they have sinned against thee, and shall turn again to thee, and confess thy name, and pray, and make supplication unto thee in this house:
>
> Then hear thou in heaven and forgive the sin of thy people Israel (I Kings 8, 28ff)."

In this strain the writer of the prayer continues throughout the thirty-one verses composing it. In setting up the new interpretation of the Temple as a unique house of prayer rather than as the center of Israel's sacrificial system, he presumably had before him models of similar institutions, on a smaller scale. If the only known form of public worship had been animal sacrifice, the historian could hardly impute to the founder of the Temple a conception of it so

[8] Apparently even at this early date the synagogue leaders recognized the central position of the Jerusalem Temple to which all prayers must be directed. The windows of Daniel's chamber were open in the direction of Jerusalem (6, 11). The tannaitic sources establish it as a fixed rule that one should recite the principal prayers while facing the Holy City and the Sanctuary (*Mishnah Berakot* 4, 5; *Tosefta, ibid.* 3, 15, ed. Zuckermandel, 7a).

completely at variance with that generally accepted and recognized. Deuteronomy had merely contrasted the authorized sacrifices of the Temple with the prohibited sacrifices of the *bamot*; according to this writer, the Temple was hardly a place of sacrifice at all; the altar occupied, apparently, only a secondary place in it. Its first and most important function was to serve as an avenue through which the prayers of men might come to God. Where had the writer seen such an institution? Where could his readers have become acquainted with so lofty a conception of Divine communion? Surely not in the rural *bamot*, where local priests offered holocausts on their village altars. It seems far more logical to assume that in his time, i. e. about the end of seventh century, the prophetic gatherings of which we catch so fleeting a glimpse in the incident of the Shunamite woman had already developed into well-organized prayer-meetings. With these in mind the compiler of the Book of Kings could naturally speak of the Temple as the center and most sacred of them all, the place toward which the prayers of all Israel were directed.[9]

This suggestion throws light on Jeremiah's peculiar emphasis on prayer. He has preserved in his book several beautiful prayers offered by him on various occasions[10] and he tells us that once he was forbidden to pray for his people,[11] implying that otherwise it was his practice to do so.

If the prayer-gatherings were an established institution in the days of Jeremiah, we may venture the suggestion that the occasion that called them into being was the persecution of the prophetic party under Manasseh. This apostate king had erected in the Temple a graven image of Astarte,[12] and in every way supported the worship of heathen gods and goddesses. The prophetic party was suppressed, so that no word of their activities during his reign has been preserved for us. The Book of Kings records merely the

[9] Compare also the emphasis on prayer in the story of Hezekiah, apparently drawn largely from an ancient biography of Isaiah, II Kings 19, 4 ff., 20, 2. The prophecy of Habakkuk is largely in the form of a prayer, though chapter 3 of the book does not bear on the question, since it probably dates from a later period.

[10] For example Jer. 10, 23 ff.; 12, 1; 14, 7; 17, 12; cf. also Deut. 8, 10; 26, 3; 26, 12.

[11] Jer. 11, 14.

[12] II Kings 21, 7.

one verse: "Moreover Manasseh shed innocent blood very much till he had filled Jerusalem from one end to another (21, 16)." Apparently there was strenuous, though futile, protest made against the king's abandonment of his father's prophetic policies. The king mercilessly destroyed all those who rose against him; and we may even credit the ancient tradition according to which he executed the prophet, Isaiah.[13]

But persecuted and suppressed, the followers of the prophets retained their loyalty to the teachings of God and practised their faith in hiding and in misery. Their loyalty and devotion during the long darkness of Manasseh's reign of more than half a century is attested by the quick rise of a generation of prophets as soon as better days shone. Early in Josiah's reign we meet the four great leaders, Jeremiah, Zephaniah, Habakkuk and Nahum and the prophetess, Huldah. Josiah's conversion and his adoption of the prophetic principles are ample evidence that the party had not died out, but had continued its precarious existence in secret.

Where had these followers of the prophets worshipped during the reigns of Manasseh and Amon, and the first years of Josiah? Not certainly in the polluted Temple, where the second commandment was openly and publicly broken. Nor in the village sanctuaries which they abhorred and whose practices they denounced. They could not have established their own sacrificial sanctuaries for it was one of their cardinal principles that sacrifice could be offered only in the Temple. And besides, sacrificial worship cannot easily be conducted with any regularity in secret. Yet, more devoutly pious than their fellow-citizens, they must have had some place of worship. We are compelled to assume that their services took the form of prayer, and that secret meetings for the purpose of Divine communion grew up among them.

These doubtless were more in harmony with their general spirit and traditions. But in any event the necessity of the first generation would readily become the virtue and piety of the next. So that while the earliest prayer gatherings may have been established as a regular institution to escape the royal persecution, the following generations would tend to retain them as the mode of worship in

[13] *B. Yebamot* 49b. Compare also sources cited in Ginzberg, *Legends of the Jews*, Vol. VI, p. 374, note 103.

which they had been reared. So the modern Maranos in Portugal are said to believe that true prayer can be offered only in secret synagogues.[14] Having never worshipped in a synagogue openly and publicly recognized, they have come to regard what was forced by cruel circumstance on their fathers as normal religious life. Similarly the fifty-five years of Manasseh's reign, added to the short rule of Amon, and the first years of Josiah, would readily make possible the development of a tradition of synagogue and prayer worship to replace that of the defiled Temple.

Josiah could hardly have undertaken to suppress the local *bamot* had he left to the rural population no other method of Divine communion. The Judeans of the seventh century B. C. could not have satisfied their religious wants with the three pilgrimages a year to Jerusalem prescribed in Deuteronomy. What was the peasant whose child was suddenly taken ill to do, in order to obtain Divine mercy and forgiveness? Where was the wife whose husband lay in agony between life and death to shed her tears, where could she find a shrine for her supplications? In an age when religion absorbed almost all the emotional life of man, the concentration of the worship of a whole country in a single edifice, no matter how beautiful and inspiring, must have been impossible. The mere fact of Josiah's reformation indicates the existence of local prayer meetings which could take the place of the suppressed *bamot*.

We must now turn to the linguistic evifience that the synagogue of the second commonwealth had its roots in early prophetic institutions. The Torah itself records how Rebecca, feeling strange and inexplicable pains, went "to seek the Lord (Gen. 25, 22)." She sought him not at a temple or altar, for in that case she would have offered some sacrifices, but at a prophetic oracle, who gave her the famous promise that the result of her sufferings would be the birth of Jacob and Esau.

In describing Rebecca's visit to the oracle, the Scriptures use the term *lidrosh*, "to seek," "to inquire of." This is derived from the root *darash*, which is regularly used by Jeremiah and Ezekiel of the people who come to them for religious instruction and guidance as well as to discover the will of God. Indeed Ezekiel once uses the term in the passive (*iddaresh*) in telling the men who came to him

[14] Samuel Schwarz, in *Menorah Journal* XII (1926) p. 149 and p. 288.

to "inquire of the Lord" that the Lord would not "be inquired of" by them. "And the word of the Lord came unto me saying, son of man, these men have set up their idols in their heart, and put the stumblingblock of their iniquity before their face: shall I be *inquired of* at all by them (14, 2–3)." In this verse the word *iddaresh* is used in a peculiar sense; it means "shall I permit myself to be inquired of by them?" or rather, "shall I commune with them?" For obviously nothing could prevent the men from "inquiring of the Lord;" they had done so by visiting the prophet and asking him to intercede with God for them. The Divine refusal to accept their prayer was in one sense an answer to their inquiry. The words have meaning only if we understand the term *darash* in its derivative, technical sense, of Divine communion. God does not refuse to be asked; that has been done. He declines to make reply to the supplications of the sinful men or to those of the prophet on their behalf. We thus see that in the Babylonian exile *darash* no longer meant "seek the Lord" in its simple primitive form of inquiring at an oracle or prophet; it had come to signify "commune with God."

By the well-known rules of Hebrew noun formation, if the root *darash* means to "seek the Lord," or "commune with God," the place where He is sought is a *midrash*. We must suppose that the word *midrash* originally had this meaning in popular usage, although it has quite a different sense in Scripture. For in Ben Sira (51, 23) and in early tannaitic literature we meet the expression *bet ha-midrash*, meaning lecture hall, and this could be derived only from an earlier, simpler locative *midrash*, just as the late *bet ha-mikdash* is derived from the original *mikdash*. As Hebrew came under foreign influences, the finer significance of some of its word forms and its prefixes was lost, and had to be replaced by whole words. Thus the natural, Hebraic *midrash*, meaning place of Divine communion, gave way to the tautologous *bet ha-midrash* of rabbinic literature.

Some traces of this change can still be found. For while the word *midrash* does not occur in biblical works in a locative sense, it is used for prophetic book. The Chronicler, who alone employs the term, mentions a *midrash* of Iddo, the prophet,[15] and also a *midrash* of the book of kings.[16] In these phrases *midrash* cannot mean com-

[15] II Chron. 13, 22.

[16] *Ibid.* 24, 27.

mentary or interpretation, as is frequently assumed. The prophet Iddo lived long before the day of the commentators, and the Book of Kings did not yet require a commentary in the fourth century B. C. Nor can it be maintained that *midrash* in these passages is to be translated "didactic story." It happens that the later Amoraic midrashim like *Bereshit Rabbah* and *Pesikta d'Rab Kahana* are largely collections of homiletic remarks and aggadic parables. But in the earlier tannaitic sources the word *midrash* is never used in this sense. There it always means authoritative interpretation, what we should call "lecture." Thus R. Eleazar b. Azariah is recorded to have offered a *midrash* to his colleagues by which he proved that fathers cannot be compelled through court action to support their daughters.[17] The Mishnah imputes to Jehoiada, the High Priest, a *midrash* establishing a law about the sacrificial system.[18] In fact the tannaitic sources clearly distinguish between *midrash*, which is the expounding of Scripture or formulated traditions, and the *aggada* which consists of interesting tales, or the *halakah* which denotes the codified law. The tannaitic midrashim are in fact essentially halakic, and are quite different from the late aggadic midrashim.

The usual interpretation of the Chronicler's term *midrash* must therefore be abandoned. The *midrash* of Iddo the prophet is not a series of stories, necessarily, but the collection of his oracles. The *midrash* of the book of kings is probably our Book of Kings, and is called *midrash* because it is an authoritative prophetic production. We may even surmise that the word *sefer* (book) is a scribal interpolation to make clear to a later generation the obsolete meaning of the term *midrash*.

The change from its earlier locative meaning which *midrash* underwent is analogous to similar development in the significance of the term *mishpat*. *Mishpat* should naturally mean "place of judgment," and it still retains that sense in several passages,[19] but generally it stands for "process of judging" or "judicial decision." Perhaps we may also compare to the dual meaning of *midrash* the metonomy by which the Latin *oraculum* and the English *oracle*

[17] *Mishnah Ketubot* 4, 6.

[18] *Mishnah Shekalim* 6, 6.

[19] Deut. 25, 1; Is. 28, 6.

mean both the substance and the place of Divine communication.

The word *midrash*, then, at the beginning of the second commonwealth had these two meanings, the place of prophetic discussion, and the substance of it. But while the locative sense was being taken over by the new term *bet ha-midrash*, and the word *midrash*, itself, was being reserved for the prophetic discussions and books, the whole institution of prophecy, and with it that of prophetic prayer, was undergoing important changes. The prophet of former days, who was in part also an intermediary between God and His people, was fast disappearing. People no longer came to the prophet as had the messengers of Hezekiah to Isaiah, or those of Zedekiah to Jeremiah, to learn the prospects of the immediate future. Men like Malachi and the Second Zechariah contented themselves with visions of a future that was far off, at the end of days: the prophet was losing his hold on reality, and tended to become an apocalyptist. He offered admonition as had his predecessors before him, but neither his threats nor his promises were for to-morrow, they were for the time of the Messiah.[20]

The divine inspiration was disappearing from Israel: prophets were fewer, less eloquent and less deeply moved. The central position in Jewish life was held no longer by the inspired man of God, but by the revealed Law. The student of the law expounded it to his hearers, but he did not necessarily undertake to bring their prayers to God. Another group of saintly pietists, psalmists and hymn writers arose to do that. The work that had been centralized in prophecy, interceding with God and offering instruction in right living, was now becoming specialized. Instruction was confined

[20] Compare for example the apocalypses in Isaiah 24–27, and Joel 3–4, which apparently date from this period. The difficulty which many commentators encounter in interpreting Joel 2, 18, disappears when this change which had overtaken prophecy is considered. Doubtless the older prophets, in discussing a catastrophe like that of the locusts ,would have ventured a prediction of the future. Joel does not do this, he advises merely fasting and praying. An interval must be assumed between 2, 17 and 2, 18, in the course of which the prayers of the priests were heard. The prophet therefore uses the past tense thereafter. Joel takes the disappearance of the locusts as a sign of divine favor, which he believes will further express itself in the end of the drought (2, 22 ff).

to the *bet ha-midrash*, prayer was relegated to the *moed*, the assembly place, the synagogue.

In the synagogue instruction still took part of worship, and perhaps the *savant* might be permitted to read from the Torah or expound the prophets.[21] Particularly on sabbaths and festivals this must have been the central point of the whole service. But the leader of the service, especially in small village communities where he was so much more needed even than in Jerusalem, could not always be an expounder of the law. He would naturally let the congregants give expression to their needs in silent supplication, and then proceed to bespeak God's blessing on them and His acceptance of their petitions. The reasons for believing that this was the actual form of the public prayers before the Maccabean era have been given elsewhere.[22] A critical analysis of our present *amidah* seems to show that at first it was a prayer not of individuals, or indeed for any particular needs, but merely a leader's request that the prayers of his followers be heard. I believe that it must have read approximately as follows:

> "Blessed art Thou, O Lord, the God of our fathers, the God of Abraham, the God of Isaac, and the God of Jacob, the great, mighty and awe-inspiring God, Possessor of Heaven and Earth: Hear our voice and have mercy upon us. Blessed art Thou, O Lord, Who dost hear prayer.[23]

The position of the leader of the congregation when he uttered this prayer is sufficiently akin to that of the early prophet when he "besought the Lord" for those who came to him, to make it likely that the one is an outgrowth of the other.

The various considerations that have been discussed, the evidence that prophetic gatherings took place in early biblical times on

[21] In this manner the ancient prophetic exhortation might give way to an exposition of the law and doctrine. We can thus readily see how the term *midrash* originally applied to the words of a prophet might gradually come to signify the learned interpretation of the Scriptures by a sage. In this manner the rabbinic significance of *midrash* as "interpretation" and finally as "commentary" would naturally arise. Out of this use of the word *midrash*, there doubtless developed the new significance of *darash* "to expound;" a sense entirely unconnected with the biblical meaning "to inquire."

[22] *Jewish Quarterly Review*, n. s., XVI, 1 ff.

[23] *Ibid.*, p. 35.

sabbaths and new moons, the implication in the "prayer of Solomon" at the dedication of the Temple that regular prayer meetings were established in its day, the *a priori* assumption to the same effect necessary to explain the historical events of the reigns of Manasseh and Josiah, and finally the history of the word *midrash*, seem sufficient to establish our thesis; first, that there were prayer gatherings under prophetic guidance even before the fall of Jerusalem in 586 B. C., and second, that out of these gatherings there grew imperceptibly the more definitely institutionalized synagogues that played so important a role in the Maccabean age.

CHAPTER 3

THE OLDEST MIDRASH: PRE-RABBINIC IDEALS AND TEACHINGS IN THE PASSOVER HAGGADAH

THE researches of the last three decades have conclusively shown that toward the end of the third century B.C. a profound change occurred in the spiritual life of the Jews. Literary prophecy, which had been declining since the time of Haggai and Zechariah (ca. 518 B.C.), now definitely came to an end. The noble tradition had been in its death throes for no less than three centuries. In vain did the Joels, the Obadiahs, and the Deutero-Zechariahs seek to save it from complete eclipse. Its hour had passed. In the meantime, new forces were arising to contend for its place in the spiritual leadership of Israel.

A group of poets, who sought to exert an influence through the liturgy and the Temple ritual, composed and collected the larger part of the Psalter. Writers of wisdom literature, influenced in part by Egyptian examples, created the Books of Proverbs, Job, Ecclesiastes, and Ecclesiasticus. Prose writers and novelists undertook to mould the Jewish mind by re-writing the history of the people, and produced the Books of Chronicles, Jonah, Ruth, and Esther, as well as the apochryphal Judith and Tobit. There were individuals, here and there, who combined in themselves various talents and associations, producing Wisdom Psalms, such as Psalms 37, 73, and 139, as well as Lamentations 3; there was one, at least, who attempted to create a direct link between prophecy and psalm-writing, by composing Habukkuk, chapter 3. One gifted novelist, apparently belonging to the class which produced the Books of Jonah and Ruth, transformed the Book of Job from a theological disputation into a religious romance.

In the midst of this struggle for the succession to prophecy we can dimly discern the beginnings of the movement which was actually to supplant the prophetic tradition; the tradition of the Scribes. Refusing to avow themselves the mouthpieces of God, the Scribes achieved even greater influence than had come to Isaiah and Jeremiah, by demanding recognition as

Reprinted from *The Harvard Theological Review*, Volume 31, 1938.

exponents of the Law. For a time, as is clear from Psalm 119, they were persecuted; [1] and for a much longer period, they were unrecognized. Nevertheless, they slowly won a large following among the people, and toward the end of the third century B.C., were apparently strong enough to challenge the supremacy of the High Priesthood itself in the spiritual leadership of Judea.

The final scene which marked the end of Prophecy and the definitive recognition of the Scribes or Scholars, was, doubtless, the Great Assembly, which was convoked by Simeon II, the Righteous, who was High Priest, toward the end of the third century B.C.[2] The confusion which filled the minds of historians regarding the Great Assembly has at last been dissipated through the work of careful and diligent students.[3] We now can say with assurance that there actually was such a meeting; that it consisted of the High Priest, other priests, Levites, and lay scholars; and that its epochal importance lay in the fact that for the first time in the history of the Second Commonwealth, these groups deliberated together.[4]

Among the achievements of the Great Assembly were probably the formulation of daily prayer-services for the Temple and for the synagogues; the establishment of a fixed form for the Grace after Meat; the final closing of the Prophetic Canon; and the transformation of the oligarchic gerousia into a Sanhedrin, in which the lay plebeian scholars sat with the representatives of the priests and other patricians.[5]

The Scribes were distinguished from all the other groups who

[1] See Ps. 119. 161.

[2] Concerning the identity of Simeon the Righteous, see the convincing article of G. F. Moore, in Jewish Studies in Memory of Israel Abrahams, New York, 1927, pp. 348 ff.

[3] G. F. Moore, op. cit., pp. 359 f.; S. Zeitlin, Second Jewish Commonwealth, Philadelphia, 1933, pp. 38–39; and also in Ner Ma'arabi, 1925, pp. 137–142; Henry Englander, The Men of the Great Synagogue, in Hebrew Union College Jubilee Volume, Cincinnati, 1925, pp. 145–161; cf. also Margolis-Marx, History of the Jewish People, Philadelphia, 1927, pp. 131–133.

[4] See S. Zeitlin, op. cit.; and cf. also Abram Menes, Die vorexilischen Gesetze Israels, Giessen, 1928, pp. 90 ff.; and Finkelstein, The Pharisees, Philadelphia, 1938 (hereafter cited simply as Pharisees), pp. 576 ff.

[5] See Pharisees, loc. cit., and below note 42.

struggled to replace the prophets in that they relied primarily on Oral Tradition to preserve their teachings. They were Scribes only insofar as they wrote copies of the Law; they did not in the main compose new works. The material which they gathered and composed is incorporated in the Talmudic tradition, and is almost entirely anonymous. As a result, it has thus far proven quite impossible to separate their early teachings from those of their followers; and we can rarely say with certainty whether a particular norm arose in the second or third century B.C. or in the first or second century of our era. It is this fact which, primarily, accounts for the difficulty in constructing a history of Jewish law and theology, during the Second Commonwealth.

Only within the last century have there been made fully accessible works like the Testaments of the Twelve Patriarchs, the Book of Jubilees, the Books of Enoch, and the Document of the Sect of Damascus (the so-called Zadokite Document) which give us some definite contemporaneous information regarding law and theology in the second century B.C. But each of these books comes from circles which represented special interests, and were apparently of limited influence. None of them is written with the responsibility attaching to authors who had any official position in Judaism.

It is, therefore, a most fortunate chance which enables us to discover in the well-known service for Passover evening an ancient Midrash, which can now be dated as belonging to the last half of the third century or the first half of the second century B.C. The fact that this is three hundred years earlier than the date of the compilation of any similar tract so far identified, would itself make this Midrash significant.[6] It happens, however, that the contents of the Midrash are of singular importance, from an historical as well as from a theological point of

[6] It is probably inaccurate to describe *Megillat Ta'anit*, which was apparently composed during the first century (or at the latest the first half of the second century), as a Midrash. After that work, the oldest compilations are probably those incorporated in our halakic midrashim; concerning which see Ch. Albeck, Untersuchungen ueber die halakischen Midraschim, Berlin, 1927; cf. also my discussion of the Sifre in Proceedings of the American Academy of Jewish Research, 1931–1932, p. 41.

view. They assume an especial significance, as will be shown, because they emanate from the circles of the highest temple ecclesiastics, probably from the High Priest himself, giving us for the first time definite information regarding the views of these distinguished circles of Jewish thought.

The Midrash (hereinafter referred to as M) has been preserved in all the extant rituals for the Passover evening, as well as in a number of Genizah fragments,[7] in practically identical form, so that there can be little question of the original form of the text. In form, it is a running commentary on the following verses from Deuteronomy (26. 5–8), the passage recited by the pilgrims when they brought the first fruits to the Temple: "A wandering Aramaean was my father,[8] and he went down into Egypt, and sojourned there, few in number, and he became there a nation, great, mighty and populous. And the Egyptians dealt ill with us, and afflicted us, and laid upon us heavy bondage. And we cried unto the Lord the God of our fathers, and the Lord heard our voice, and saw our affliction, and our toil, and our oppression. And the Lord brought us forth out of Egypt with a mighty hand, and with an outstretched arm, and with great terribleness, and with signs, and with wonders."

The passage was obviously selected as basis for the Midrash, because it was part of the confession recited each year by the pilgrims, and was, therefore, well known by the people. Even people who could not read every part of Scripture with ease could recall this passage; and those who had no books could recite it by heart.[9]

[7] In addition to the fragments used by I. Abrahams, in J. Q. R., X, 1897, pp. 41 ff.; W. Bacher, ibid., pp. 380 ff.; and J. Greenstone in ZfHB, XV, 1911, pp. 122 ff.; I have consulted the following fragments from the Adler collection in the Library of the Jewish Theological Seminary of America: 2840, 2841, 3214, 3222, 3762, and 3775, all of which contain the part of Passover Haggadah including M.

[8] Heb. *'arami 'obed 'abi*, which is interpreted by the Midrash as though it read *'arami 'ibed 'abi*, "An Aramaean destroyed my father." See below for the discussion of this difference between the received text and the interpretation.

[9] See Deut. 26. 5a; Mishna Bikkurim 1. 1. It is interesting to note that the Karaites also recite the biblical passage, Deut. 26. 5–8 in their Passover Haggadah, though they omit the Midrash (see Ha-Haggadah Shel Pesah 'Im Targum 'Arabi Ke-Minhag Ha-Karaim, Pressburg, 1879, p. 3).

M itself may be translated as follows:

I. 1. Go forth and learn. What did Laban the Aramaean intend to do to our father, Jacob? For Pharaoh decreed the destruction only of the males, while Laban sought to destroy the whole family. Thus it is written, *The Aramaean sought to destroy my father* [10] *and he* (*my father*) *went down into Egypt and sojourned there, few in number, and he became there a nation, great, mighty, and populous.*

II. 1. *And he went down into Egypt;* compelled thereto by the word of God.[11]

2. *And sojourned there.* This teaches us that he did not go down into Egypt to settle there, but only to sojourn, as it is said, "And they said unto Pharaoh: To sojourn in the land are we come; for there is no pasture for thy servants' flocks; for the famine is sore in the land of Canaan. Now therefore let thy servants dwell in the land of Goshen" (Gen. 47. 4).

3. *Few in number,* as it is said, "Thy fathers went down into Egypt with threescore and ten persons; and now the Lord thy God hath made thee as the stars of heaven for multitude" (Deut. 10. 22).

III. 1. *And he became there a nation.* This teaches us that the Israelites were distinguished there.

IV. 1. *Great and mighty,* as it is said, "And the children of Israel were fruitful and multiplied, and waxed exceedingly mighty, and the land was filled with them" (Exod. 1. 7).

[10] See note 8.

[11] The passage "Compelled thereto by the word of God" is omitted in the version of the Haggadah found in the Code of Maimonides and in the ritual of the Yemenite Jews. It was probably also lacking in the text of the Haggadah used by R. Saadia Gaon (882–942 of our era) in composing his famous Seder R. Saadia, since he makes no comment on it. It is also lacking in the version preserved in the Genizah fragment described by I. Abrahams, in J. Q. R., X, 1897, p. 50, fragment no. IX; while the Ms. described by him (ibid., p. 45), as well as that described by J. Greenstone in ZfHB, XV, 1911, p. 123, read *'anush* instead of *'anus,* meaning, "made to suffer through the word of God." Apparently those responsible for this usage had hesitated to delete the ancient passage, and yet felt the need of changing it somewhat so as to reconcile it to their sojourn in Egypt. A similar need apparently led the copyist of Cod. Adler 3222, in the Library of the Jewish Theological Seminary of America (or the group which formulated the version it represents), to add an explanation of the words "compelled thereto by the word of God." Unfortunately, the text is so mutilated that the explanation cannot be reconstructed. It is also to be noted that the phrase, "compelled thereto by the word of God," does not occur in the comment of either the Sifre or the Midrash Ha-Gadol on Deut. 26. 5. With regard to the Sifre, it is possible that its compiler rejected the phrase as he rejected other parts of M, which seemed to him unsupported by Scripture (see below, Appendix II). The omission in the Midrash Ha-Gadol, which transcribes all the rest of M, indicates that, as might be expected, it follows the Yemenite ritual of the Haggadah (see Proceedings of the American Academy of Jewish Research, 1931–1932, pp. 20 ff.).

2. *And populous*, as it is said, "I caused thee to increase, even as the growth of the field; and thou didst increase and grow up, and thou camest to excellent beauty" (Ezek. 16. 7).

V. 1. *And the Egyptians dealt ill with us*, as it is said, "Come let us deal wisely with them lest they multiply, and it come to pass that, when there befalleth us any war, they also join themselves unto our enemies, and fight against us, and get them up out of the land" (Exod. 1. 10).

2. *And afflicted us*, as it is said, "Therefore they did set over them taskmasters to afflict them with their burdens. And they built for Pharaoh store-cities, Pithom and Raamses" (ibid. 1. 11).

3. *And laid upon us heavy bondage*, as it is said, "And the Egyptians made the children of Israel to serve with rigor" (ibid. 1. 13).

4. *And we cried unto the Lord, the God of our fathers*, as it is said, "And the children of Israel sighed by reason of the bondage, and they cried, and their cry came up to God, by reason of the bondage" (Exod. 2. 23).

5. *And the Lord heard our voice*, as it is said, "And God heard their groaning, and God remembered His covenant with Abraham, with Isaac, and with Jacob" (Exod. 2. 24).

VI. 1. *And He saw our affliction*. This refers to the forcible separation from marital intercourse,[12] as it is said, "And God saw the children of Israel and God took cognizance of them" (Exod. 2. 25).

2. *And our toil*. This refers to the children, as it is said, "Every son that is born shall ye cast into the river, and every daughter shall ye save alive" (Exod. 1. 22).

3. *And our oppression*. This refers to the oppression, as it is said, "Moreover I have seen the oppression wherewith the Egyptians oppress them" (Exod. 3. 9).

VII. 1. *And the Lord brought us forth from Egypt*. Not by means of an angel, nor by means of a seraph, nor by means of a messenger; [13] but the

[12] In Cod. Adler 3775, the passage, "This refers to the forcible separation from marital intercourse" is inserted in the comment on the words, "and our toil," instead of on the words, "and our affliction," taking the place of the phrase, "This refers to the children," which is entirely omitted. In Cod. Adler 2841, there is a similar transposition, except that the words, "This refers to the children," are retained so that the passage reads: "*And our toil*. This refers to the forcible separation from marital intercourse. This refers to the children, as it is said, 'Every son etc.'" I. Abrahams cites a Genizah fragment, the reading of which corresponded to that of Cod. Adler 3775 (J. Q. R., loc. cit., p. 45).

[13] Some texts add here, "Nor by the word," referring to Alexandrian doctrine of the Logos (see e.g. I. Abrahams, Some Egyptian Fragments of the Passover Hagada, J. Q. R., X, 1897, p. 47; and Seder R. Saadia, in Frumkin, Seder R. Amram, Jerusalem, 1912, 108b).

Holy One, blessed be He, Himself, in His glory, as it is said, "For I will go through the land of Egypt in that night; and will smite all the first-born in the land of Egypt, both man and beast; and against all the gods of Egypt will I execute judgments: I am the Lord" (Exod. 12. 12). "I will go through the land of Egypt," [14] I, and not an angel; "And I will smite all the first-born," I, and not a seraph; "And against all the gods of Egypt will I execute judgments," I, and not a messenger; "I am the Lord," [15] I am He and no other.

2. *With a mighty hand.* This refers to the murrain, as it is said, "Behold the hand of the Lord is upon thy cattle which are in the field, upon the horses, upon the asses, upon the camels, upon the herds, and upon the flocks; there shall be a grievous murrain" (Exod. 9. 3).

3. *And with an outstretched arm.* This refers to the sword, as it is said, "Having a drawn sword in his hand, stretched out over Jerusalem" (I Chron. 21. 16).

4. *And with great terribleness.*[16] This refers to the visible manifestation of the Divine Presence, as it is said, "Or hath God essayed to go forth to take Him a nation from the midst of another nation, by trials, signs, and by wonders, and by war, and by a mighty hand, and by an outstretched arm, and by great terrors, according to all that the Lord your God did for you in Egypt before thine eyes" (Deut. 4. 34).

5. *And with signs.* This refers to the rod, as it is said, "And thou shalt

[14] The remainder of the passage is omitted according to the version of the Haggadah found in the Seder R. Saadia, the Code of Maimonides, and the ritual of the Yemenite Jews. The view that it is to be omitted is also cited in Shibbale Ha-Leket (ed. Buber, 97a). But it is found in all the other rites; I therefore cannot follow E. D. Goldschmidt, Die Pessach-Haggada, Berlin, 1937, p. 54, in rejecting it. It was doubtless omitted by some rabbis because they were offended by the emphatic denial of the angels, which is implied in it.

[15] It is clear that it is only the words, "I am the Lord," which justify the special interpretation put upon the biblical passage. In all the other phrases the personal pronoun is in no way emphasized. The commentators on the Haggadah have, of course, noticed this and remark that the compiler projects the emphasis on "I am the Lord," into the other phrases.

[16] The compiler obviously read the biblical text *ubemar'eh gadol* "and with a great Vision," rather than *ubemora' gadol* "And with great terribleness," as the Massoretic Text has it. For the evidence that the former was the original reading, see notes 38, 39. The fact that the compiler read *ubemar'eh gadol* was specifically noted by Geiger, Urschrift, pp. 339 ff.; but his view was partially adumbrated by mediaeval writers. Isaac Abravanel in his commentary on the Haggadah, notes that the consonantal text of the biblical verse can still be read *ubemar'eh,* since it omits the *vav* which would naturally follow the *mem,* if the correct reading were *ubemora'*. The remark is repeated by Jacob Emden in his commentary on the Haggadah. Similarly, Mahzor Vitry, ed. Horowitz, p. 293, Siddur Rashi, ed. Buber, p. 193, Orhot Hayyim of R. Aaron Ha-Kohen of Lunel, 83b, and Kol Bo 51, remark that the words *ubemora' gadol* are taken by the compiler of the Haggadah as the equivalent of *ubemar'eh gadol.*

take in thy hand this rod, wherewith thou shalt do the signs" (Exod. 4. 17).

6. *And with wonders.* This refers to the blood, as it is said, "And I will show wonders in the heavens and in the earth, blood and fire and pillars of smoke" (Joel 3. 3).

The numbers prefixed to the sections and the sub-sections have, of course, been added by me; but they reflect, as can be seen from a close examination of the text, a division inherent in M itself. The compiler of M was obviously a systematic thinker who arranged his work according to a clearly recognizable scheme, which can be reduced to the following outline:

I. Introduction, denouncing Laban the Aramaean for seeking to destroy Jacob.
II. Protest against emigration from Palestine to Egypt.[17]
III. Exhortation to the Egyptian Jews to retain their ancestral customs.
IV. Reflections on the rapid increase of the Israelites in ancient Egypt.
V. Citations of parallels to Deut. 26. 6–7, from the relevant verses of Exodus.
VI. Denunciation of the Egyptian bondage.
VII. Enunciation of four propagandist views, of which two concern theology, and two politics.

The transparent lucidity of M is the more remarkable because the Midrashic style necessarily compelled the compiler to arrange his material with a view to the basic Pentateuchal passages which he had chosen as his text. That in spite of this he succeeded in keeping a systematic order for his ideas, marks him as master of rhetorical form.

In the present analysis of M, an effort is made to demonstrate the following propositions:

1. M was composed no later than the Maccabean Age; and probably before that, in the last decades of the third century B.C.
2. It is essentially a propagandist tract, endeavoring to impress the views of its compiler on the many pilgrims who came to Jerusalem for the Passover.
3. Several of the views it inculcates were opposed to those of the great mass of Hasideans and later Pharisees.

[17] Section II, 3, offers, as will be shown below, Appendix I, a reassurance to the Egyptian Jews that the discouragement of immigration to their country will not interfere with their numbers, which depend, after all, on the blessing of God and natural increase.

4. It is the work of a patrician, probably of a High Priest.
5. Several parts of it were addressed to the pilgrims from Egypt, and sought to stem the tide of assimilation in Alexandria and other large Egyptian communities.

I. The Date of M

The date of M necessarily falls between the fourth century B.C. and the third century of our era. These limits are set by the following considerations:

(*a*) The Midrashic style used by M as well as its diction and its concepts all belong to the Second Commonwealth, and a period later than Ezra.

(*b*) It cites the Book of Chronicles, which was certainly put into its present form no earlier than the fourth century B.C.

(*c*) On the other hand, M is itself cited in the tannaitic Midrashim which were compiled in the third century of our era.[18]

Once these limits are recognized, the actual date is fixed more narrowly, in my opinion, by the opening words of M: "Go forth and learn. What did Laban the Aramaean intend to do to our father, Jacob? For Pharaoh decreed the destruction only of the males, while Laban sought to destroy the whole family. Thus it is written, *The Aramaean sought to destroy my father.*"

It would under any circumstances seem peculiar that the story of the Exodus, which deals primarily with Egypt, should open with a denunciation of Laban as having been worse to Israel than Pharaoh. It becomes amazing when we consider that the words on which the compiler of M relies to prove his contention, are simply misinterpreted by him. The Hebrew reads: *'arami 'obed 'abi*, which can only mean, "My father was a lost Ara-

[18] Excerpts from M are incorporated in Sifre Deut. 301, ed. Friedmann 128a, Finkelstein 319; in Mekilta on Deuteronomy, reproduced from the Midrash Ha-Gadol in Midrash Tannaim, ed. Hoffman, pp. 172–173; and in Sifre Numbers 115, ed. Friedmann 35b, Horowitz 128. It certainly provided the basis for the remark that no angel participated in the Exodus, cited in Mekilta Bo, chap. 7, Friedmann 7b, Horowitz-Rabin 23, Lauterbach I, 53; and ibid., chap. 13, Friedmann 13b, Horowitz-Rabin 43, Lauterbach I, 97. It is specifically cited in B. Yoma 74b. For the date of the tannaitic Midrashim, see Ch. Albeck, Untersuchungen ueber die halakischen Midraschim, p. 119 and Finkelstein, Proc. Am. Acad. of Jewish Research, 1931–1932, p. 41.

maean." In order to establish the guilt of Laban, the compiler must read the words, *'arami 'ibed 'abi*, "the Aramaean destroyed my father." But this is a clear distortion of the text.

The daring perversion of the reading of the Scriptures can be explained only on one of two hypotheses. (A) It may have been an expression of Maccabean hostility toward Syria, which was identified with Aram.[19] (B) It may be an effort, made while Palestine was under Egyptian suzerainty, to placate the Egyptian government, by denouncing its rival, Syria. It was particularly necessary to do this before telling the story of the Exodus, which recalled unpleasant relations between Egypt and Israel.

Of the two hypotheses, the second seems to me the more plausible, for several reasons which will soon become apparent. Of these, the most important is the fact that the Septuagint, which was composed by Jews under Egyptian rule, likewise perverts the meaning of the words *'arami 'obed 'abi*. Its texts render the phrase as though it read *'aram y'obed* (or *ye'abed*) *'abi*, which is forced into the sense of "My father forsook Aram." Apparently the authors of the Septuagint, like the compiler of M, hesitated to identify the ancestor of the Jews as an Aramaean. The close relationship between the Septuagint translation and the interpretation put on the phrase *'arami 'obed 'abi* in M is a definite indication that the two works were composed under similar circumstances, that is in the third century B.C., and under Egyptian control.[20]

[19] It is true that the Hellenist kingdoms of Syria and Egypt did not consider themselves identical with the older nations of those countries, but rather part of the Macedonian Empire, which had been divided. Nevertheless, under the stress of the bitter rivalry between the Ptolemies and the Seleucids for the control of Palestine, it is clear that a statement making Jacob an Aramaean would be definitely pro-Seleucid. For the identification of Laban with Syria, see e.g. Sanhedrin 105a, where Laban is identified with Beor the father of Balaam. Elsewhere, he is identified with Balaam himself and declared King of Aram. See Ginzberg, Legends of the Jews, Index, s.v. Laban. The argument presented below remains in general equally valid if the first hypothesis be accepted; the date of M must simply be fixed, in that event, about 150 B.C. instead of between 240 and 220 B.C.

[20] The Rabbinic tradition recalls the fact that the authors of the Septuagint frequently changed their text out of deference to Egyptian sensitivity (see Megillah 9A; Masseket Soferim 1. 8, ed. Higger, p. 101). Similarly, mediaeval copyists and printers

A résumé of the political conditions in Palestine during the third century B.C. will further demonstrate the validity of this hypothesis. The facts are easily summarized.[21] From about the year 301 B.C. to 198 B.C. Palestine was under the control of the Egyptian Ptolemies. The Ptolemies did not, however, govern the country directly. They preferred to entrust as much authority as possible to the High Priests, who thus became the temporal as well as the ecclesiastical rulers of the land.

Under these circumstances, it was altogether natural for the High Priests to look upon themselves as representatives not merely of the Temple but of the Imperial Egyptian Government. They, especially, must have felt that the Passover service ought to begin with a rejection of implication that the Israelites were *kinsmen* of the Aramaeans or Syrians.

It was all the more important to make such a declaration because the Scriptures lay great emphasis on the close relationship of Israel to Aram. Not only does the verse in Deuteronomy 26. 5, which is the subject of the Midrash, describe Jacob as "a wandering Aramaean," but many other passages tell how the patriarchs continually looked toward Syria and Mesopotamia as their home countries.[22] And, on the other hand, the prophets

---

were careful to avoid the use of the word *Romi* for Rome where that might offend the rulers of contemporary Rome, and instead wrote *'aram* or *'Edom* and the words *'abodah zara* "strange worship" are regularly replaced in current editions of the Talmud by *'akum* "the worship of the stars and the planets," so as to avoid giving offense to Christians. In each case, careful consideration of the passages would show that there was no allusion to contemporaries; but there was need of avoiding any possible imputation of giving offense.

[21] For the reconstruction of the history given below, see Eduard Meyer, Ursprung und Anfaenge des Christentums, II, pp. 3 ff., 128–137; Tscherikower, Ha-Yehudim veha-Yevanim, pp. 95, 183; Z. S. Zeitlin, The History of the Second Jewish Commonwealth, Philadelphia, 1933, pp. 11–33; Marx-Margolis, History of the Jewish People, pp. 128–129; E. R. Bevan, The House of Seleucus, London, 1912, pp. 50 ff., 191–234; and Pierre Jouguet, Macedonian Imperialism and the Hellenization of the East, New York, 1938, pp. 189–192.

[22] Abraham insists that Isaac marry a daughter of Aram, rather than one of those of Canaan (Gen. 24. 3 ff.); and similarly Jacob is sent to Aram to seek a wife (ibid., 27. 46; 28. 1 ff.), Elijah and Elisha have close relations with Aram (I Kings 19. 15; II Kings 5. 1 ff.; 8. 7 ff.), and it is well known that the prophets, Isaiah and Jeremiah, as well as the others whose works have been preserved, were always pro-Babylonian and pro-Assyrian in their diplomacy, but definitely anti-Egyptian (see Pharisees, pp. 423 ff.).

never tire of warning Israel and Judah against reliance on Egypt; and the Lawgiver repeats continually the command not to act "after the manner of Egypt." [23]

The rivalry between Egypt and Mesopotamia, which played such an important part in pre-exilic thought, had reached a new climax after the death of Alexander the Great (323 B.C.).

Ptolemy, who had obtained the government of Egypt, had been driven out of Palestine in the year 315 B.C. by his rival, Antigonus. His forces returned three years later, in 312 B.C., when Antigonus was preoccupied with other wars. But they remained for only a very brief period; for Antigonus, having defeated his other enemies, soon turned his attention to Palestine and regained the mastery of it. It was only after Antigonus met his death at the decisive Battle of Ipsus (301 B.C.) that Ptolemy's armies once more seized the land.[24]

But while Ptolemy was now in undisputed possession of Palestine *de facto*, he found himself denied any share in it *de jure*. He had taken no part in the Battle of Ipsus; and the victors, one of whom was his former ally, Seleucus, denied him any share in the spoils. Indeed, the victors of Ipsus had agreed among themselves that Palestine was to be awarded to Seleucus, who had become ruler of Syria.

Just what happened between Egypt and Syria during the next two decades is uncertain. We know only that by the year 280 B.C. Ptolemy Philadelphus was firmly in control of Palestine, although the Seleucids never recognized the Egyptian claim to it. Indeed as late as the year 219 B.C., almost a century after the Battle of Ipsus, Antiochus III, the ruler of Syria, still formally claimed the right to rule Palestine by virtue of the agreements made in the year 301 B.C.

From 274 to 240 B.C., there were sporadic wars between Egypt and Syria. While these were in the main fought far from the land of Israel, the fate of Palestine naturally was continually in the balance. The tension among the people is reflected in the

[23] Lev. 18. 3.

[24] As indicated below, historians disagree regarding the precise status of Palestine between 301 and 281 B.C. We have no definite information as to whether it was under the control of the Seleucids or the Ptolemies during most of these two decades.

curious incidents surrounding the rise of Joseph ben Tobiah, about 240 B.C.[25]

Onias II, the High Priest at the time, had taken advantage of a state of war between Egypt and Syria, to refrain from sending the usual taxes to Ptolemy. When the Imperial Government protested, Joseph ben Tobiah, who was the son of the High Priest's sister, and perhaps the most opulent layman in Judea, interfered to restore peace. In recognition of this service, the Egyptian Government appointed him tax-farmer not only for all Palestine, but also for all the Egyptian possessions in Syria.

The importance attached to this incident may be judged from the legends which surrounded it and which have been fully recorded by Josephus.[26] The rise of this lay family into unprecedented prominence threatened the supremacy of the High Priesthood in Jerusalem, and doubtless was an important factor in the Hellenizing movement which reached such proportions at the beginning of the second century B.C., and which ultimately led to the religious persecutions of Antiochus Epiphanes and the Maccabean Rebellion.

In the year 219 B.C., Antiochus III undertook another effort to gain control of Palestine. He was defeated at the Battle of Raphia (217 B.C.); but this did not prevent him from renewing his efforts when the death of Ptolemy Philopator in the year 204 B.C. left the Egyptian rule in the hands of the regents of the five year old Ptolemy V. This time Antiochus was successful, and after 198 B.C. Palestine passed into the hands of the Seleucids, where it remained until it achieved its independence under the Hasmoneans.

We may well imagine with what care the Egyptian government watched the development of Palestinian sympathies during this period of continuous wars. The Passover celebration which brought pilgrims to the Temple from all parts of Palestine, and also from other countries, was, by its very nature as has already been suggested, reminiscent of an ancient struggle between Egypt and Israel. Clearly it was essential that the High Priests divest the ceremony of any implications which

[25] Ha-Yehudim ve-ha-Yevanim, pp. 170 ff.

[26] Antiquities XII. 3. 3.

could possibly be interpreted as pro-Seleucidean. And it was above all, important, under the circumstances, to place a suitable interpretation on so unfortunate a phrase — from their point of view — as, "A wandering Aramaean was my father." The High Priests had no choice but to transform the significance of the verse; and to interpret it as saying that historically there was even greater bitterness between Israel and Syria, than between Israel and Egypt!

II. The Propagandist Nature of M

The study of the Introduction to M has shown that the work was compiled with a view to the influence it would exert on the people who recited it or heard it. This is further demonstrated by the nature of the rest of the text. The second section supplements the words "And he went down into Egypt," with the phrase, "Compelled thereto by the word of God." Now, the Scriptures nowhere indicate that Jacob was compelled to go to Egypt "by the word of God." On the contrary, he went to Egypt, because he discovered that Joseph was still living there. Genesis 46.3, simply relates that God assured Jacob of His protection during the sojourn in Egypt; but makes not the slightest suggestion that God commanded Jacob to go down to that land.

It is clear that the compiler of M attempts to reinterpret history in the light of contemporaneous conditions; and describes Jacob as being forced to go to Egypt, in order to discourage contemporary Jews from following their ancestor's example.

Absolute proof that this is the correct interpretation of M is offered by the fact that the later Egyptian Jews omitted this passage from their version of the Passover Haggadah.[27] Nat-

[27] See above, note 11. The Genizah fragments naturally represent the Egyptian ritual. That the Seder R. Saadia also represents that ritual is demonstrated by Professor Louis Ginzberg, in Geonica I, p. 167, note 1. It is well known that Maimonides composed his Code in Egypt, and that he followed the ritual of that country. The Yemenite Jews looked to the neighboring Jews of Egypt and especially to Maimonides for guidance in their worship. It must be noted, however, that there are a number of Genizah fragments containing the phrase, "compelled thereto, etc." (See I. Abrahams, J. Q. R., X, 1897, pp. 45, 47, 48, and 49; W. Bacher, ibid., p. 380; and Cod. Adler, in

urally, they could not recite each year a statement which denounced them as sinful, because they lived in Egypt voluntarily![28]

The following passage of M continues in the same vein. It insists that even those Jews who are compelled to reside in Egypt, through force of circumstance, must look on their stay as temporary, and should await the possibility of their return to Palestine.[29] To emphasize this point the compiler of M stresses the fact that Jacob "did not go down into Egypt to settle there, but only to sojourn."

In the third division, the compiler of M denounces the tendency of his contemporary Egyptian co-religionists to assimilate, by reminding them that their ancestors, the Israelites, when they resided in Egypt, were distinguished from the other people.[30]

Library of the Jewish Theological Seminary of America 2840 and 3222.) Possibly these fragments represent the rituals of localities which had come under the influence of Jews of other countries.

[28] It is noteworthy that according to most texts M fails to cite any biblical verse in support of its singular statement. The only verse which is cited in any version is the irrelevant passage, Gen. 46. 3. The famous scholar, R. Elijah Gaon of Wilna, realizing the difficulty of finding some basis for the interpretation in Scripture, explains that Jacob was compelled to go to Egypt in the sense that he was destined to do so. He remarks in his commentary (Wilna, 1818), "The meaning is that he was compelled to go to Egypt because thus was it ordained for him that he should come to Egypt; and God brought it about that he should come to Egypt through a commandment; as our Sages say, 'Jacob, our father, was fated to come to Egypt in iron chains, but his merit liberated him from them' (Shabbat 89b). This is what the author of the Haggadah means by the remark, '*compelled by the word*' — his merit caused him to come through the word, and not in chains." Another commentator (Abraham Danzig, in his commentary, in the same edition) explains that Jacob was compelled to go to Egypt through the famine (Gen. 45. 11), which means, of course, that he was compelled by God. A later rabbinic Midrash, the author of which apparently forgot for the moment the explicit statement of M, maintains that Jacob came to Egypt of his own free will (see Mekilta, Beshallah, Proemium, ed. Friedmann 24b, Horowitz-Rabin 80, Lauterbach I, 181).

[29] For the rapid increase of the number of the Egyptian Jews during this period, see S. W. Baron, A Social and Religious History of the Jews, I, 134 ff.; and III, 33. That many of the Jews who settled in Egypt were compelled to do so by the Egyptian government, is indicated in Josephus, Antiquities XII. 1. 1.

[30] The word *mezuyyanim* as used in this passage of M can only mean "distinguished" in the sense of "distinct." Any attempt to give it an honorific meaning such as "noted" etc., is rendered futile by the fact that the comment is attached to the words, "And he became there a nation." Siddur Rashi and Mahzor Vitry, doubtless reflecting the

But perhaps the clearest evidence of the propagandist nature of M is offered by the final paragraph which deals definitely with questions of theology and politics. The views expressed in that paragraph are definitely partisan, and patrician; and are clearly intended to win the masses of the pilgrims over to the views of the compiler of M.

III. The Theological and Political Views of the Midrash

A. *The Existence of Personal Angels*

The emphatic and repeated denial in VII, I, that the angels participated in the Exodus, is the more remarkable because it directly contradicts the statement of Scripture, "He sent an angel and brought us forth out of Egypt" (Num. 20. 16).[31] Indeed, the story of the Exodus itself implies that it was an angel of the Lord, rather than God, Himself, who smote the

thoughts and circumstances of French Jews of the eleventh and twelfth centuries, explain that the Israelites in Egypt were "distinguished" by being gathered into one locality rather than scattered in many places. Shibbale ha-Leket, however, with far closer approach to the true meaning of M, maintains that the Israelites in Egypt were distinguished by their clothes and their customs. In support of this interpretation of M, Shibbale ha-Leket cites the famous passage of Vayyikra Rabbah, "The Israelites were redeemed from Egypt for four reasons: They had not changed (*a*) their names or (*b*) their language; (*c*) they had spoken no evil of one another; and (*d*) they had refrained from sexual impurity." (Leviticus R. 32. 5.) This interpretation is, in general, also followed by Abravanel and R. Elijah of Gaon of Wilna. The tradition that the Hebrews in Egypt did not "change their name, and did not change their language," is recorded also in Mekilta Bo, chap. 5, Friedmann 5a, Horowitz-Rabin, p. 14, Lauterbach I, p. 34. These passages in the Rabbinic Midrashim are, of course, likewise intended as polemics against the assimilationist tendency of the contemporary Jews of Egypt and the other parts of the Diaspora.

31 The Septuagint to that passage, doubtless under the influence of contemporary exegesis, translates "And having sent an angel, He brought us forth from Egypt." Rashi, attempting to reconcile the biblical passage with M, interprets *mal'ak* in Numbers 20. 16, as meaning a prophet, and makes the word refer to Moses. Targum Ps. Jonathan explicitly states, "And He sent one of his archangels and he brought us forth from Egypt." Apparently with a similar view in mind, the Septuagint translators of Isaiah, rendered Isaiah 63. 8b–9 not as we have it, "so He was their Saviour. In all their affliction He was afflicted, and the angel of His presence saved them"; but rather, "And He became their Saviour from all their affliction. Not a messenger (apparently punctuating *zir* instead of *zar*) nor an angel, but He Himself saved them."

first-born, for the Israelites were warned to observe every detail of the ritual carefully, that the Lord may not "suffer the destroyer to come" into their houses (Exod. 12. 23). In view of this, the insistence of the Midrash that no angel took part in the miracle of the Exodus can have but one purpose. It is, in effect, an emphatic protest against the belief in angels, as God's intermediaries, a belief which was gaining continually wider currency throughout the period of the Second Commonwealth.[32] Not Gabriel, nor Michael, but God Himself, intervened for Israel in the most critical moment in its history. The authority which M gained as part of the Passover Haggadah was ultimately so great, that those who believed in personal angels felt compelled to defend their position against this implication. To achieve this purpose, they inserted, immediately after the passage denying any participation of the angels in the Exodus, the following explanatory statement, still preserved in several versions of the Haggadah:[33]

[32] The denial that the angels participated in the Exodus is cited, with probable reference to the Passover Haggadah, in Yer. Sanhedrin 2. 1, 20a; ibid., Horayot 3. 2, 47a. Interestingly enough Mekilta insists that the destruction of the first-born did not occur through an angel (Mekilta Bo, chap. 7, Friedmann 7b, Horowitz-Rabin 23, Lauterbach 1, 53; see also parallel passage ibid., chap. 13, Friedmann 13b, Horowitz-Rabin 43, Lauterbach I, 97). The commentators on the Passover Haggadah were, of course, disturbed by the passage denying that the angels participated in the Exodus, in view of the statement in Numbers 20. 16, and especially in view of the fact that Moses was clearly the "messenger" of God at the Exodus. They offer various explanations of the difficulty. Abravanel insists that it only means that God redeemed the Israelites, but He made use of "different instruments," in accomplishing His will; R. Yom Tob ben Abraham of Seville maintains that the redemption occurred without any intermediary, and he explains Numbers 20. 16, precisely as does the Septuagint. The same interpretation is cited also in Shibbale ha-Leket. With the various statements denying the use of angels as intermediaries, cf. also Sifre Deut. 325 (Fr. 139a), which comments on the verse, "To Me belongeth vengeance and recompense" (Deut. 32. 35), as follows: "I Myself will punish them; I will not punish them through an angel or an intermediary."

[33] See excerpts from Seder R. Saadia, printed in Frunkin, Seder R. Amram, Jerusalem, 1912, p. 108b; Mahzor Vitry, p. 293; Siddur Rashi, p. 193; according to the rite of Yemen, the Haggadah according to the rite of Bagdad, edds. Calcutta, 1844, and 1889, and Bombay, 1887; and lastly in the appendix to E. D. Goldschmidt, Die Pessach-Haggada, p. 111. The passage is also cited in Midrash Ha-Gadol, on Exodus, 14. 25, ed. Hoffmann, p. 52. But, as Professor Louis Ginzberg surmised (Geonica, 1, p. 167, note 1, and more explicitly in Legends of the Jews, V. p. 433, note 213) this passage is not a genuine part of the Mekilta of R. Simeon. This can now be demonstrated by the

Our teachers,[34] of blessed memory, have said: When the Holy One, blessed be He, descended into Egypt, against the Egyptians, there descended with Him nine thousand myriads of beings. Some of them were angels of fire, some of them angels of hail, some of them angels of fright, some of them angels of trembling, some of them angels of trepidation. Trembling and trepidation seize anyone who beholds them. They said to God, "Master of the Universe, When a human king goes to war, his princes and servants surround him. And Thou art the King of the kings of kings, the Holy One, blessed be He; is it not appropriate [35] since we are Thy servants, and they are the children of Thy covenant, that we should descend, and wage war against the Egyptians." He answered, however, "My feelings will not be assuaged until I, Myself, in My glory, in My greatness, and in My Holiness, descend against them. I am the Lord, I am He, and no other!"

The author of this interpolation apparently did not feel free to contradict the statement of M denying that the angels participated in the Exodus. He simply endeavors to reconcile it with the views of those who believe in the existence of cohorts of angelic intermediaries. The angels might have intervened at the Exodus; but God would not permit them to do so.

This cannot, however, have been the thought in the mind of the compiler of M. On the contrary, *he* obviously wishes to deny that angels can act as intermediaries between God and man. In so doing, he enters into the long controversy about the existence of angels,[36] which beginning with Haggai and Zechariah (ca. 520 B.C.) continued until the compilation of the Mishna (740 years afterwards) and even later. Throughout

---

fact that it is lacking in the Genizah fragments of the Mekilta of R. Simeon to the passage (see Jewish Studies in Memory of George Alexander Kohut, Hebrew section, p. 114). Nevertheless the ascription of the saying to R. Meir may be correct. At any rate it is certain that despite the authority of the Passover Haggadah and the Mekilta of R. Ishmael, many later scholars insisted that God descended to Egypt to redeem Israel, surrounded by hosts of angels. Indeed Shemot Rabbah explicitly states, in the comment on the verse, "For the Lord will pass through to smite the Egyptians" (Exod. 12. 23), "Some say through an angel, and some say the Holy One, blessed be He, Himself" (Shemot Rabbah 17. 5).

[34] With one slight deviation (indicated in the next note) I have followed the text of the interpolation as found in the Passover Haggadah used in the ritual of Bagdad.

[35] Reading *din hu*, with the other texts, rather than *dayyan hu* (He is the Judge) with the ritual of Bagdad.

[36] See Pharisees, pp. 160 ff. The controversy is described in Acts 23. 8, as sectarian, dividing the Pharisees, who accepted the belief in angels, from the Sadducees, who rejected it. But as suggested in Pharisees, pp. 181 ff., the controversy is not mentioned by Josephus or the Rabbinic Sages, because there were a considerable number of Phari-

this time, the patricians of Palestine denied, while the plebeians asserted, the existence of angels as intermediary beings between God and man. No one but a violent partisan would have drawn such a controversial issue into a text intended for universal use. The fact that the author of M did so, stamps him as a patrician, with pronounced factional views.

Moreover, since M, in spite of its partisanship, was adopted by plebeians no less than patricians, for the Passover evening service, the author must have been a person of recognized authority. We may rightly conclude from this alone that he was a distinguished priest, probably a High Priest.

It is improbable, however, that even the authority of a High Priest would have induced the plebeian opposition to accept such a document after the quarrel between John Hyrkan and the Pharisees. It follows, therefore, that the document must have been compiled before that time.

This tentative conclusion is confirmed by more cogent evidence which we will now consider.

B. *The Appearance of God in Visible Form*

The assertion that God appeared in visible form at the Exodus is a second theological statement of great importance. Like the question of the angels, so the question of the possibility of the appearance of the Deity in visible form was long disputed during the Second Commonwealth. In fact, as Leszynsky and Lauterbach [37] have pointed out, the issue was the basis of one of the major controversies between the Pharisees and the Sadducees, that regarding the manner in which the High Priest was to perform the ceremonies of the Day of Atonement. The Pharisees, as is well known, demanded that in accordance with the precise order of the biblical verses, the High Priest enter the

---

sees themselves who opposed the highly developed angelology of later times. Perhaps they found support for their views in M. Nevertheless, it remains true that the Pharisees as a body refused to deny the existence of personal angels; and certainly would not have sanctioned the formulation of a Passover service which implied such a denial.

[37] Leszynsky, Die Sadduzaeer, p. 62; Lauterbach, Hebrew Union College Annual, IV (1927), pp. 185 ff., and see Pharisees, pp. 118 ff.

Holy of Holies, with a censer of fire in one hand and the incense in the other; and that only after he had entered the Holy Chamber should he put the incense on the fire. The Sadducees declared that he should put the incense on the fire before entering the Sacred Chamber.

As the scholars mentioned indicate, the Sadducees were moved to their view by their belief that God appeared in visible form in the Holy Chamber. To protect himself from seeing the Vision, the High Priest was to enter the Chamber behind a cloud of smoking incense. The Pharisees, who denied that God could be seen, insisted that the High Priest bear witness to his acceptance of their teaching, by entering the Holy Chamber, and performing the ceremony there.

In their opposition to anthropomorphism, the plebeian scholars transformed all the passages in Scripture which spoke of "seeing God," into "appearing before God." This involved but a slight change of pronunciation in Hebrew; but it was fundamental to the theology of the plebeians.

In fact, there can be little doubt that as Geiger has pointed out,[38] the verse *ubemora' gadol* which is translated "*and with great terribleness,*" was originally read *ubemar'eh gadol* "*and with a great Vision.*" Only the reading *ubemar'eh gadol* could justify the interpretation, "this refers to the visible manifestation of God." And it is this reading which is reflected in the Septuagint, the Syriac, and most surprisingly of all, the Aramaic, versions.[39]

[38] Geiger, Urschrift, pp. 339 ff.

[39] Similar renderings of *ubemora'* are found also in the Septuagint, Peshitta, and Targumim to Deut. 4. 34, and Jer. 32.21. It is also found in Peshitta and Targumim to Deut. 34. 12. The Vulgate which in all the passages cited follows the Massoretic readings, translates the phrase in Deut. 4. 34, *horribiles visiones*, combining both senses. Geiger's view gains curious support from Sifre Deut. 161, Friedmann 105b, Finkelstein 212, which reads, according to the best texts (Vatican Ms. and commentary of R. Hillel): "*That he may learn to fear the Lord his God.* This teaches us that the Vision leads to reading the Scripture; reading the Scripture leads to translation; translation leads to study of the Mishna; study of the Mishna leads to discussion; discussion leads to deeds; deeds lead to fear (of God)." In ed. pr. as well as in the texts of the Yalkut, and the Mss. of the British Museum and Oxford, the word *she-ha-mar'eh* "for the vision" has been altered to *she-ha-mora'* "for the fear," which makes no sense whatever, since the series begins with "the fear" and ends with "the fear." It seems clear

We do not know the precise date when the reading *ubemora' gadol* (and with great terribleness) was substituted for *ubemar'eh gadol* (and with a great Vision). Certainly, it was before the year 100 of our era, for Aquila, who translated the Scriptures about that time, renders the phrase as though he had our present Massoretic text.

It is evident, however, that no matter how late the change in vocalization was made, the controversy regarding God's appearance in visible form is a most ancient one. Not only was it one of the fundamental controversies between the Pharisees and the Sadducees, but references to it appear in Scripture itself.

Under the circumstances, we must assume that the compiler of M, in interpreting the words *ubemar'eh gadol* as referring to the Visible Appearance of God, had in mind the controversy on the subject, and was endeavoring to clothe his teachings with the authority of an accepted and well-known Midrash.[40] This passage, then, like that regarding the angels, would indicate that the compiler was a patrician, and that he lived before the Pharisaic Order had attained sufficient power to prevent an

---

that the later copyists, recoiling from the implication that God might appear in visible form, changed the original *mar'eh* into *mora'*. This renders it the more likely that a similar development occurred in the biblical texts.

It is interesting to note that the texts of the Sifre in which the reading *mor'a* has been substituted for *mar'eh* belong to the French group (see Proceedings of the American Academy of Jewish Research, 1931–1932, pp. 7 ff.). And curiously enough, as we have seen (note 16), it is in the French school that we find the clearest anticipation of Geiger's theory that *mora'* was originally *mar'eh*.

It must further be noted that apparently the *baraita* in the Sifre, which is now associated as indicated with Deut. 17. 19, really is a comment on the similar verse, Deut. 14. 23, which remarks concerning the tithes and the pilgrimages, "that thou mayest learn to fear the Lord thy God always." The author of the statement in the Sifre indicates the steps by which this fear of God is attained. The pilgrim comes to Jerusalem and sees the Vision of the Glory; this leads him to study, etc.; study leads to deeds; and deeds lead to the fear of God. Perhaps it was an early objection to the association of the Vision of God with the pilgrimage that caused the passage to be transferred in the first place to the verse about the King, where it was considered rather innocuous.

[40] It is probable that as with regard to the question of angels, so with regard to the issue of the appearance of God in visible form, the authority which attached to M as part of the Passover-Haggadah helped to preserve its view among patrician scholars. See Akiba, pp. 195–196; Pharisees, pp. 180 ff.

opinion contrary to the tenets of the majority of its members being introduced into a liturgical service.

IV. Conclusion

We have thus succeeded in showing that M is definitely controversial in its theology, presenting forcefully two patrician doctrines, namely the denial of the angels, and the possibility of God's appearance in visible form. Both of these doctrines were opposed by the main body of the Pharisees, viz. the plebeians, though they received some support from the patrician minority of the Order. It is inconceivable that after the organization of the Pharisaic Order, either doctrine could have been included in a tract intended for universal use on the Passover night. Their inclusion in M indicates that it originated before the rise of the Pharisaic Order, and therefore before the Maccabean period. The subjects of angels and the appearance of God in visible form were already controversial issues, however; and the compiler was trying to use the Passover celebration to foist his opinions on the people.

The patrician character of the teachings points to a priest as the compiler. And the fact that the Pharisees, both the plebeian and the patrician wings,[41] accepted M in the Passover service, indicates that the compiler was a man of the widest possible recognition. This, together with the consideration that Simeon the Righteous is known for other contributions to the liturgy,[42] makes it likely that he was himself the compiler.

This conclusion is supported by a consideration of the historical background which alone can account for the reference to Aram in the Introduction to M.

In the Appendix, further evidence will be presented regarding the propagandist character of M, and for its patrician origin.

[41] Concerning the two factions of the Pharisees, see Professor L. Ginzberg, Mekomah shel ha-halakah be-hokmat yisrael, p. 14. For their views on the issues presented in M, see Akiba, pp. 55, and Pharisees, pp. 118 ff., 160 ff.

[42] He made these contributions either directly or through the Great Assembly. See further regarding this subject, J. Q. R., N. S., XVI, 1925–1926, pp. 41 ff.; and XXI, 1928–1929, p. 229, note 1; as well as Pharisees, pp. 578 ff. For his interest in the study of the Torah, and therefore possibly in the Midrashic form, see Abot 1. 3, and the explanation offered in Pharisees, p. 63.

Appendix I: Other Teachings of M.

Several passages in M which cursorily read seem to have no special significance, turn out on examination to be quite important. One of these is II, 3, which cites in support of the phrase, "Few in number," the verse Deut. 10. 22. There are at least two other verses in the Pentateuch (Gen. 46. 27; Exod. 1. 5) which tell us that Jacob came to Egypt with a family of seventy souls. Either of them would have been in many respects more appropriate to the Midrash than the one cited; for they are direct records of the story rather than citations from the remarks of Moses, as is the verse actually quoted. They are passed over, however, in favor of the verse from Deuteronomy, because the latter stressed what was uppermost in the mind of the compiler: the contrast between the small number of Israelites who came to Egypt, and the large number who were descended from them. So important does this particular point seem to the compiler that he cites two other verses to prove his point. And we note that these other verses, likewise, stress the rapidity of the increase of the Israelites.

Perhaps the compiler is trying to indicate in his Midrashic manner, that while he discourages emigration to Egypt, the Egyptian Jews need have no fear for their numbers. With the Divine blessing on them, their community will grow by natural increase.

The fifth section simply cites Exodus 1. 8–10, as illustrating Deut. 26. 6.

In the sixth section, the compiler of M protests bitterly against the hardships of the Egyptian bondage. This may seem quite appropriate in a Midrash dealing with the Exodus. Yet some parts of the section show that the compiler is thinking of contemporary situations. When he interprets the words, "And He saw our affliction," to refer to "forcible separation from marital intercourse," he cannot be speaking of ancient Egypt, for there is no record that Egyptians inflicted such persecution on the Hebrews. It is a plausible surmise that the compiler of M has in mind the contemporary conscription of Jewish young men into the Egyptian armies, and the consequent interference with their family life. This interpretation is supported by the following passage which reads, "*And our toil.* This refers to the children, as it is said, 'Every son that is born ye shall cast into the river, and every daughter shall ye save alive'" (Exod. 1.22). Once more the compiler is thinking of the seizure of young men in his own time, and comparing it to the even bloodier destruction of male children by the ancient Pharaoh.[43]

The commentators on the Haggadah have found perhaps the greatest difficulty with the following phrase: "*and our oppression,* this refers to the oppression, as it is said, 'Moreover I have seen the oppressions wherewith the Egyptians oppress them'" (Exod. 3. 9).

The compiler apparently adds nothing to the meaning of the text. But for some special reason he substitutes for the biblical word *ha-lahaz* (oppression) the neo-Hebraic *ha-dohak,* yet, peculiarly enough, cites a verse containing the word to support his interpretation!

It was natural for the commentators to suppose that the compiler was referring to some special form of persecution. But if we accept the third century B.C. as the date of the composition of M, the difficulty disappears. The readers and hearers of M knew well what oppression by Egyptian rulers meant; they suffered it every day. Quite aside from any detailed orders which they had to obey, they were conscious of continual petty oppression by the local Egyptian representatives.

The most obscure passages in M are perhaps VII, 2, and VII, 3, explaining the phrases "with a mighty hand," and "with an outstretched arm." The mighty hand is interpreted as the "murrain"; and the outstretched arm as "the sword."

Several questions come to our mind as we read these passages. Why should the compiler refer to the murrain rather than any of the other ten plagues? The question apparently occurred also to the talmudic authorities for they interpret the phrase, *the mighty hand* in Deut. 34. 12 as referring to all the ten

[43] It is also possible that the author wishes to avoid the implication that work as such is degrading or an evil to be avoided. He hesitates, therefore, to interpret "our toil" literally; God, in his opinion, would not have been moved simply by seeing the people at labor.

plagues, and cite in support of their view, Exod. 10. 12 ("And the Lord said unto Moses, 'Stretch out thy hand over the land of Egypt for the locusts'"). Others explain, that the *mighty hand* in that passage refers to the slaying of the first-born.[44]

But even more difficult is the reference to the sword.[45]

There is no record in the story of the Exodus of any battle between the Israelites and the Egyptians. Indeed the sword was conspicuously absent as a means of liberation of the Israelites. Everything happened through the hand of God. It is clearly a forced interpretation of M to suppose that the sword refers to the Divine sword through which the first-born of Egypt were slain. To escape the difficulty, the later sages invented a tale according to which the first-born of Egypt, fearing death because of the threat of Moses, turned in battle against their fathers, and sought to compel Egypt to liberate the Israelites.[46] But that can hardly have been in the mind of the original compiler.

What is perhaps even stranger than the invention of a battle against the Egyptians, is the citation in this connection of a verse recording the punishment of David and Jerusalem! The sword which the angel held in his hand, according to 1 Chronicles 21. 16, was directed against Jerusalem, in punishment for David's sin in counting the people. Why should such a memory

[44] The first interpretation is found in Midrash Tannaim 34. 12, p. 228; the second is found there as an alternative interpretation, and in Sifre Deut. 357, 150b as the only interpretation. The statement of R. Joshua ben Levi that with each of the ten plagues the Egyptians suffered also from pestilence (Shemot Rabbah 10. 1) may be intended as an explanation of this passage. It may be that R. Joshua could only explain the reference to *deber* (murrain) as meaning "pestilence" rather than "murrain," and that since it was mentioned so prominently in M, he presumed that it accompanied each of the ten plagues. This interpretation is supported by R. Aaron Ha-Kohen of Lunel (Orhot Hayyim, I, 83A), and the author of Kol Bo.

[45] It is particularly difficult to explain this passage in view of the fact that the verse cited in support of the interpretation that "arm" means "the sword," does not contain the word "arm" but only the word "hand." To overcome this difficulty several commentators indicate that the word on which the author relies to prove the interference of the "sword" in the Exodus, is *Netuyah* "outstretched," which occurs in both verses.

[46] Pesikta of R. Kahana VII, ed. Buber, 65a; Pesikta Rabbati XVII, ed. Friedmann, 88a. This interpretation is that most generally accepted; see Orhot Hayyim, loc. cit.; Kol Bo, ad loc.; Shibbale Ha-Leket, ed. Buber, 97a; and M. Friedmann, Meir 'Ayyin 'al Seder ve-Hagaddah, 101.

be brought in at the feast of the Exodus; especially as there is no other verse cited from the Hagiographa in the whole comment?

The answers given to these questions can only be tentative. I believe that in these comments the High Priest was indicating as carefully as he could his real purpose in formulating M. He was in fact trying to arouse the people to resistance against the Egyptians; and it was for that very reason that the tale of the ancient Exodus was to be formulated so effectively. The assembled people were to be taught that ancient Egypt had been defeated in two ways: through the murrain which God sent upon their cattle, and through armed battle.[47] That the latter teaching was without support in Scripture was a matter of little concern to an author who did not hesitate to give his own interpretation to an explicit verse.

The verse cited from Chronicles may have been especially attractive to the High Priestly compiler because it recalled a sin of David, and thus reflected ill on the Davidic dynasty. We know from Deutero-Zechariah (12. 12) that the family of David played an important rôle in the second century B.C. and indeed remnants of the family were pointed out centuries later. It suited the interests of the High Priestly dynasty admirably to use the occasion of the Passover to cast reflections on the rival House of David.

Appendix II. The Relation of the Midrash to Rabbinic Literature

The Rabbinic Sages, who accepted M as part of the Passover Haggadah, seem to have felt that it originated in patrician circles. We have noted that M is cited intact by the Mekilta on Deuteronomy,[48] which was the work of the patrician school of R. Ishmael; but is rejected, at least in part, by the Sifre on Deuteronomy, which is the work of the plebeian school of

[47] This interpretation is apparently put on the passage also by E. D. Goldschmidt in his Die Pessach-Haggada, p. 56, note 1.

[48] Preserved in Midrash Ha-Gadol, and printed therefrom in Midrash Tannaim 26. 5–8, pp. 172–173. For the patrician origin of the Mekilta on Deuteronomy see D. Hoffmann, Einleitung in die halachischen Midrashim, Berlin, 1887, pp. 72 ff., and also his introduction to the edition of the Midrash Tannaim.

R. Akiba.[49] Furthermore, its denial that the angels participated in the Exodus is quoted twice in the Mekilta of R. Ishmael on Exodus, another patrician work, but not in the corresponding sections of the Mekilta of R. Simeon on the same book, a plebeian work. The political passages of the seventh section of the Midrash, dealing with the murrain and the sword, are cited in the Sifre on Numbers, also a patrician work.[50] Finally, the expression, "Go forth and learn," clearly a school term at the time of the original of the Midrash, disappeared from the later school vocabulary, and is cited only three times in Rabbinic literature, twice in definitely patrician works,[51] and once by R. Jose ben Halafta,[52] whose Galilean upbringing made him more inclined than others to patrician speech.

[49] See Sifre Deut. 301, Friedmann 128a, Finkelstein 319. (*a*) The Sifre rejects the interpretation that *'arami 'obed 'abi*, means that "the Aramaean sought to destroy my father." Instead of that, it says, "This teaches us that our father Jacob went to Aram in order to be destroyed." The following statement, "And therefore Laban is accounted as though he had destroyed him," clearly contradicts the interpretation that Jacob came to Aram to be destroyed. For why should Laban be accounted guilty for something which he could not control, had it happened; and ultimately did not happen? It is clear that although all the texts have preserved both statements as one, they are really two distinct interpretations. According to the first, Jacob is called a "lost (or *wandering*) Aramaean," because when he came to Aram, he seemed fated for destruction. According to the second, as in the Passover Haggadah, Laban is accounted as though he had destroyed him.

(*b*) The phrase, "this teaches us that Jacob did not go down to Egypt to settle there, but only to sojourn etc.," is found in the French texts of the Sifre, but is omitted in all the better texts, showing as indicated in ed. Finkelstein, loc. cit., that it is not part of the Sifre.

(*c*) The remainder of the Midrash is summarized in the briefest manner.

[50] Sifre Numbers 115, Friedmann 35b, Horowitz 128.

[51] Mekilta Jethro, Bahodesh, chap. 8, Friedmann 70b, Horowitz-Rabin 253, Lauterbach II, and parallel passage, Sanhedrin 86a; and Sifre Numbers 115, Friedmann 35b, Horowitz 128.

[52] Sifra, Vayyikra, parasha 12. 10.

CHAPTER 4

PRE-MACCABEAN DOCUMENTS IN THE PASSOVER HAGGADAH

In an article published in the Harvard Theological Review, XXXI, pp. 291–317, I endeavored to show that the Midrash based on Deuteronomy 26. 5–8, which forms the core of the Passover Haggadah (hereinafter M) was composed in pre-Maccabean times, probably in the third century B.C., when Palestine was ruled by the Ptolemies. I propose in the present article to consider three other parts of the Haggadah, which I believe are likewise pre-Maccabean.[1] They are (1) the opening passage (hereinafter A); (2) the alternative opening (hereinafter B) prescribed by Rab in the third century of the Christian Era, and included in extant rituals after A; and (3) the poem Dayyenu, "it would have been ample for us" (hereinafter D). Evidence will be presented associating B and D particularly with the high priesthood of Jason, the son of Simeon the Righteous, and high priest in Jerusalem from 175 to 172 B.C.[2] In connection with the discussion of these passages, it will be necessary to study also (4) the *Baraita* of the Four Sons (hereinafter E), which has also been incorporated into the Passover Haggadah. (A *baraita* is a formulated, normative statement, originating with the earlier Rabbinic scholars, i.e. those of the Mishnaic or tannaitic period, ending about the year 220 of the Christian Era; but not included in the Mishna itself.)

[1] See pp. 330 ff., where the *sigla* used herein are explained.

[2] The deviations in this article from the usual chronology follow, in general, the results of the researches of F. X. Kugler, Von Moses bis Paulus, 1922, chaps. VI and VII; W. Kolbe, Beitraege z. Syrischen u. juedischen Geschichte, 1926; and E. Bickermann, Der Gott d. Makkabaeer, 1937. The most significant achievement of these studies is the establishment of the year 311 B.C. as the opening date of the Seleucid Era; the fixing of 167 B.C. as that of the profanation of the Temple of Jerusalem by Antiochus IV; and of 164 B.C. as the date of the rededication.

Reprinted from *The Harvard Theological Review,* Volume 35, 1942.

I. The Introduction to the Passover Haggadah (A)

The opening of the Passover Haggadah, according to extant rituals, is essentially a reply to the questions raised by, or put into the mouth of, the child, asking the reasons for the celebration. The father says:

"We were Pharaoh's bondmen in Egypt; and the Lord, our God (Hebrew: *YHWH Elohenu*)[3] brought us forth from there [4] with a mighty hand and an outstretched arm."

This passage is clearly adapted from Deuteronomy 6. 20 ff. which reads as follows:

"When thy son asketh thee in time to come, saying, 'What mean the testimonies, and the statutes, and the ordinances, which the Lord our God hath commanded you?' Then shalt thou say unto thy son: 'We were Pharaoh's bondmen in Egypt; and the Lord brought us out of Egypt with a mighty hand. And the Lord showed signs and wonders, great and sore, upon Egypt, upon Pharaoh, and upon all his house, before our eyes. And He brought us out from thence, that He might bring us in, to give us the land which He swore unto our fathers. And the Lord commanded us to do all these statutes, to fear the Lord our God, for our good always, that He might preserve us alive, as it is at this day. And it shall be righteousness unto us, if we observe to do all this commandment before the Lord our God, as He hath commanded us.'"

The first unmistakable reference to A is that made by Samuel,[5] a Babylonian scholar of the third century of the Christian Era. But the following considerations will show that A originated as the opening of the Passover Haggadah long before the time of Samuel.

Comparing A with the Biblical passage on which it is based, we notice that the compiler of A not only omitted four verses of the five which the Scriptures prescribe as a reply to the inquiring son, but also took liberties in his citation of the one

[3] The reading *adonai* (or YHWH) *elohenu* is found in M, following precisely the text of Scripture. It is altogether probable that this text represents a reading which was "corrected" to agree with that of Scripture; or that the word *elohenu* was omitted in this text by accident.

[4] Heb. *misham*, instead of *mimizraim*, as the Scriptures read in the corresponding passage; see below, p. 295. The words "and an outstretched arm" are found in the Septuagint and in Vetus Latina though they are lacking in all the other versions. This significant agreement between the Passover Haggadah and the Septuagint was first noticed by David Hoffmann, in Magazin f. d. Wissenschaft d. Judenthums 13, 1886, p. 193, note 1. With regard to the significance of the other variant readings to this passage, see Friedmann, p. 51.

[5] Pesahim 116a.

verse which he preserved. Such liberty in dealing with Scripture reflects some impelling necessity, which, when discovered, should give us a clue to the date of the origin of A.

The omission of the last four verses of the Biblical passage and the changes introduced in the verse which was kept, are all clearly prompted by a desire to avoid giving offense to the people of Egypt. In discussing the date and origin of M, I showed [6] that this Egyptophilism is associated with the political conditions of the third century B.C., when Palestine was under the rule of the Egyptian Ptolemies. During all that time, the Seleucids, who were rivals of the Ptolemies, sought to regain the control of Palestine. As the two empires, namely Ptolemaic Egypt and Seleucid Syria, were about equal in power, the friendship of the people of Palestine, which lay midway between them and whose territory was claimed by both, was of vast political importance. Inevitably, the sympathies of the Palestinian Jews were divided.[7] This fact, however, only made it the more necessary for the responsible leaders of the people to avoid any action or public ceremonial which could be interpreted as anti-Egyptian and therefore pro-Seleucid. Unfortunately, the Passover celebration was by its very nature a celebration of the triumph of Israel over Egypt, and therefore anti-Egyptian in character.[8] Added to this was the fact that the Passover celebration, which brought to Jerusalem throngs of pilgrims from all parts of Palestine and even other countries, was in all ages a period favorable to riot and rebellion. As late as the Roman and Herodian rule, Passover

[6] Harvard Theological Review, XXXI, 1938, pp. 300–301.

[7] This is implied in Dan. 11. 14; and is explicitly stated to have been the fact, in Jerome's Commentary to that verse (Patr. Latin. XXV, 562). Reference to Egyptian and Seleucid parties in Coele-Syria is also made by Polybius (Histories V, 86. 10). See further regarding the whole matter, R. H. Charles, A Critical and Exegetical Commentary on the Book of Daniel, 1929, ad loc.; E. Meyer, Ursprung u. Anfaenge d. Christentums, 1921, II, 136; V. Tscherikower, Ha-Yehudim veha-Yevanim, (hereinafter Tscherikower) 1931, pp. 194 ff.; and his Palestine under the Ptolemies in Mizraim, IV–V, 1937 (hereinafter, Tscherikower, Palestine), p. 56; E. Bickerman, in Revue des Études Juives C bis, 1935, p. 24. Regarding the general extent and influence of Egyptian rule in Syria and Palestine, see K. J. Beloch, Griechische Geschichte, IV, 2, pp. 322–323.

[8] Regarding the relationship of Egyptian antisemitism to the story of the Exodus and the Jewish celebration of Passover, see Additional Note.

was a season of trial to the governing and ecclesiastical authorities.[9] It must have been a greater trial to the earlier rulers, the Ptolemies. For these reasons statements which might have been passed over as innocuous at other times, were considered offensive by the Egyptian rulers and their Jewish adherents, when uttered in connection with the Passover celebration. Thus the recital of the Pentateuchal passage, used during the ceremony of the first fruits,[10] must have seemed to the Jews an appropriate formula for the story of the Exodus: "A Syrian, ready to perish, was my father, and he went down into Egypt, and sojourned there with a few, and became there a nation, great, mighty, and populous; and the Egyptians evil entreated us, and afflicted us, and laid upon us hard bondage; And when we cried unto the Lord, God of our fathers, the Lord heard our voice, and looked on our affliction, and our labor, and our oppression; And the Lord brought us forth out of Egypt with a mighty hand, and an outstretched arm, and with great terribleness, and with signs, and with wonders" (Deuteronomy 26. 5–8).[11]

But the Egyptian officials, on the other hand, must have thought that the declaration that the people of Israel were the kinsmen of the Syrians,[12] that Israel was enslaved in Egypt, and that only through the sufferings of the Egyptians did Israel gain its freedom, hardly helped cement the bonds between Palestine and Egypt. The Palestinian authorities were thus virtually compelled to create in M a midrash which made Deuteronomy 26. 5–8 an anti-Syrian document, and purged it at least of its worst anti-Egyptian overtones. Thus the phrase, "A Syrian, ready to perish, was my father," becomes in M, "The Syrian sought to destroy my father." [13]

The shortening of the reply prescribed in Deuteronomy 6. 21 ff. into A is clearly intended to achieve a similar purpose.

[9] Cf. J. Bonsirven, Le Judaïsme Palestinien au Temps de Jésus-Christ, 1935, II, 122.

[10] See Deut. 26. 1 ff.; Mishna Bikkurim 3. 6.

[11] See HTR, loc. cit.

[12] See below, note 56.

[13] See Additional Note B for a discussion of changes in Jewish ritual for apologetic purposes.

Deuteronomy 6. 22 was necessarily omitted from the reply, for its vivid description of the sufferings of the ancient Egyptians at the hands of Israel could not be explained away. Because of the omission of Deuteronomy 6. 22, all the following verses included in the reply, too, had to be omitted.

Even Deuteronomy 6. 21, however, had to be altered somewhat. The substitution of the word *misham* ("from there")[14] for *mimizraim* ("out of Egypt") is apparently intended to clarify a possible ambiguity, which might have been particularly disturbing when Palestine was under Egyptian domination. The word *mimizraim* might mean not only "out of Egypt" but also "from the Egyptians." But obviously the Jews in Palestine of the third century B.C. were still under Egyptian domination. Hence the necessary substitution of *misham* ("from there") to indicate that the redemption of Israel from the land of Egypt is what is meant.

In this changed form, "We were Pharaoh's bondmen in Egypt, and the Lord, our God, brought us forth from there with a mighty hand and an outstretched arm," might, indeed, become an expression of loyalty to the Egyptian empire.[15]

[14] See above, note 4.

[15] The question of the juridical right of Egypt to Palestine was a matter of prime importance in the Hellenistic period. Both the Seleucids and the Ptolemies made amazing efforts to justify their claims to the territories they sought to control by appeals to precedent and right (see CAH, VII, pp. 13; 133 ff.; 161 ff.; E. Bikerman, Institutions des Séleucides, Paris, 1938 (hereinafter Inst. Sel.), pp. 15 ff.). In Additional Note A, evidence will be adduced for the probability that Manetho's story of the origin of "Jerusalem" as a state was part of this tendency to justify might by right. Such appeals to right, as a basis for territorial claims, can of course be duplicated in far higher antiquity. Cf., e.g., the argument between Jephthah and the Ammonites regarding the relative claims of Israel and Ammon to the disputed part of Transjordan (Judg. 11. 12 ff.).

It is interesting to note that the antisemitic writers of a later period, when the question of the juridical right of the Egyptians to Palestine had ceased to be an issue, no longer stressed the Egyptian origin of the Jews. Nevertheless, the older tradition persisted among many writers (cf. e.g. Chaeremon, cited in Jos., Contra Ap. I, 288 ff.; and Apion, ibid. II, 6 ff.). Under the Roman rule, the tradition of Egyptian background became indeed a means of deriding the Jews, denying them any claim to a special and significant place in history (see Bergmann, Jued. Apologetik, p. 146). The Palestinian Jewish scholars, aware of the charges of Egyptian origin, and sensitive to their implications, created a literature of Jewish apologetics, stressing the early origin of Israel (see below, p. 310), and above all denying the charge that the Israelites were born of relations between Egyptian masters and Israelite women. Bergmann, loc. cit. mentions a

The conjecture that this passage was given its present form in the third century B.C. is corroborated by the fact that the word *elohenu* ("our God") is inserted in A after the word *adonai*, "the Lord," of the Biblical text. The third century B.C. witnessed the substitution of the pronunciation *adonai* for the original pronunciation of YHWH.[16] The first substitute pronunciation, introduced at an earlier time, had been *elohim*,[17] as can be seen from the second and third books of the Psalter, as well as from certain passages in Chronicles.[18] The pietists of the third century B.C. felt, however, that the term *elohim* expressed an impersonal philosophical approach to God, and preferred the pronunciation *adonai* for YHWH. As this term has also a secular meaning, "my lord," [19] and might therefore

few references bearing on the general subject. But the insistence on the chastity of the Jewish wives in Egypt is a common motif in Rabbinic literature. Compare e.g. Mekilta, Bo, chap. 5, ed. Friedmann 5a; Horowitz-Rabin 14; Lauterbach I, 34.

[16] Regarding the time when the pronunciation *adonai* was substituted for the original pronunciation of YHWH, see G. Dalman, Der Gottesname Adonai, Berlin, 1889, pp. 63–81; B. Jacob, Im Namen Gottes, Berlin, 1903, pp. 164–176; H. H. Schaeder, Iranische Beitraege I, Halle, 1930, pp. 205–206. Schaeder adduces convincing evidence to show that the original pronunciation ceased to be used in the course of the fifth century B.C. B. Jacob demonstrates that the Chronicler pronounced the tetragrammaton *adonai*, but he also shows that the pronunciation *elohim* was used as a variant. (It may ultimately turn out that the author of the original "Book of Chronicles," i.e., of the older stratum, pronounced YHWH *elohim*, and the later reviser pronounced it *adonai*. In that event the distinction may help the separation of the older from the later material.) In any event it is clear that during the third century B.C., the use of the pronunciation *adonai* was probably not yet sufficiently well established to exclude the meaning of "my lord" in a human sense. The later Sages recalled definitely that the "Men of the Great Assembly" used the original pronunciation of the tetragrammaton (Midrash Tehillim 36. 8, ed. Buber 126a) but we cannot be certain whether they refer to the generation of Ezra or that of Simeon the Righteous; for both are described in Rabbinical literature as belonging to the Great Assembly.

[17] See B. Jacob, Im Namen Gottes, 1903, pp. 16 ff. Passages like Ps. 53. 3, 5, 6, which consistently substitute *elohim* for the YHWH of corresponding verses in Ps. 14; and a passage like Ps. 68. 8, where *elohim* replaces YHWH of Judges 5. 4 amply demonstrate that the compiler of that collection of Psalms at least sometimes writes *elohim* for YHWH.

[18] B. Jacob, op. cit., pp. 165 ff. Cf., also, H. Zimmermann, *Elohim*, Berlin, 1900, pp. 64 ff.

[19] As G. Dalman has noticed (Die Worte Jesu, 1930, p. 268), the expression, *ishi kohen gadol* ("my lord, high priest"), was coined in order to avoid applying the term *adoni*, used for God, to a human superior. *Ishi* in the sense of "my lord" occurs only in this expression (see Mishna Yoma 1. 3, 5; 4. 1; Tamid 6. 3; Parah 3. 8). See, in this connection, also Jewish Quarterly Review, N. S., XXXII, 1942, p. 396, n.

be taken to refer to a human master, it was necessary in oral prayers to add some qualification showing that it referred to the Deity. Hence, prayers and other liturgical formulae originating in the third century B.C. and for some generations thereafter, add the term *elohim* or *elohenu* to *adonai.*[20]

The compiler of the Passover Haggadah intended of course that the word YHWH in the first verse should be pronounced *adonai.* Following the general rule, therefore, he was compelled to add *elohenu* after it.

The evidence that A was formulated in the third century B.C. is completed by the fact that it contains the phrase "and with an outstretched arm." This phrase is omitted in Deuteronomy 6. 21 according to the Massoretic text, as well as the Samaritan, Peshitto, Vulgate and Targumim. In fact, it occurs only in LXX and the Vetus Latina.[21] Quite aside from all

[20] See Jewish Quarterly Review, N. S., XVI, 1925, pp. 8 ff. When I noted these facts, I did not realize their reason or their significance. Clearly, the Men of the Great Assembly who formulated the earliest form of the Amidah and of the Birkat Ha-Mazon, like the compiler of the Haggadah had to use the term *adonai elohenu,* in speaking of the Deity, in order to avoid any misunderstanding. Later authors, recoiling even from the use of the term *adonai,* substituted *abinu* ("our father") or *elohenu* ("our God") for it. It is noteworthy, however, that the call to "bless the Lord" used by the person about to read the Shema in the daily prayers, or the portion of the Law, at services when that is read, says: *bareku 'et 'adonai.* This formula can be traced back to the times of the Temple, but is obviously much older; for it goes back to a time when it was not yet necessary to indicate that one was speaking of the Divine rather than a human Lord; in other words to a time when the tetragrammaton was pronounced in its original form. Now the pronunciation of the tetragrammaton as YHWH continued in the Temple long after it had been abandoned in the synagogue service (Mishna Yoma 6. 2; Sotah 7. 6; Tamid 7. 2). If therefore the call *bareku 'et 'adonai* (YHWH) originated as part of a Temple service, it could only indicate a date about 200 B.C. (Presumably, the pronunciation YHWH in a *call* to the service would not have been used after that date, even in the Temple.) On the other hand, if the call originated in the Synagogue service, it would point to an origin at a much earlier date, perhaps no later than the beginning of the fourth century B.C. As it is probable that the reading of the Torah, at least, originated as a synagogue service; and as the formula *bareku 'et 'adonaie,* is the call used as introduction to that reading, it would seem that this discussion confirms the tradition that the reading of the Torah in public services was introduced by Ezra, toward the middle of the fifth century or, according to the chronology now becoming increasingly prevalent, the beginning of the fourth century B.C. Cf. further my note on the subject in Jewish Quarterly Review, N. S., XXXII, 1942, pp. 394 ff.

[21] See the edition of R. Robert (Pentateuchi Versio Latina Antiquissima) based on the Lyons Manuscript, Paris, 1881, p. 324. This deviation of the text of the Haggadah

other considerations, the fact that A reproduces a reading of the Scriptural text, found otherwise only in LXX and a daughter version would indicate a very early date for the origin of that formula.

The argument for the origin of AM during the period of the Egyptian domination of Palestine is further fortified by a consideration of the pro-Egyptian influences similar to those reflected in AM, which are traceable in other works produced during that period. These works include the Book of Chronicles which apparently received its present form at this time and also the historical Psalms 78 and 105, which must also, I believe, be dated in the third century B.C.

According to the Chronicler, one of the distinguished families of Judah (traced for more than twenty generations to Judah himself) was descended from an Egyptian slave (I Chronicles 1. 35). This is, of course, especially significant in the light of the law set down in Deuteronomy 23. 8. Another Judaite family is said to be descended from the daughter of Pharaoh (ibid., 4. 18). The Chronicler does not hesitate to reproduce the story of Solomon's traffic in horses with the Egyptians (II Chronicles 1. 16; and 9. 28; cf. I Kings 10. 26). The story of the invasion of Shishak is described very sympathetically toward the Egyptians; Judah is to know "My service and the service of the kingdom of the countries" (II Chronicles 12. 8). The incident in which Necho attacked Josiah is described in a manner entirely justifying the Egyptian Pharaoh (II Chronicles 35. 20). This is in contrast to the version given in II Kings 23. 29, which indicates that Josiah was killed by treachery. The sympathy of the Chronicler for the Egyptian Pharaoh in this connection is the more significant because the occasion

from that of the Massoretic text was curiously overlooked by the older commentators. It was noticed, however, and commented upon, by R. Elijah Gaon of Wilna in his commentary (see, J. D. Eisenstein, Ozar Perushim ve-Ziyyurim, New York, 1920, p. 311); by Rabbi Jacob Emden in his commentary (ibid., p. 301); Malbim (in his commentary, published with the text of the Passover Haggadah, Warsaw, 1905); Rabbi Naphtali Z. J. Berlin in his commentary (published with the text of the Passover Haggadah, Warsaw, 1889); by the Yemenite scholar, Rabbi Yahya in his commentary published with the text of the Passover Haggadah (Jerusalem, 1897) by M. M. Krengel, in his commentary, published in Shaare Geulah, Cracow, 1896, see p. 59; and by other even more recent writers.

described is one which had so many parallels in the third century, when the Ptolemies and Seleucids were continually struggling for the possession of Palestine. The treatment of King Joahaz, whom "the people of the land" elected to succeed Josiah is described, too, with an eye to the Egyptian interpreter. Instead of Necho's putting the new king in chains at Riblah (II Kings 23. 34), it is said in Chronicles that Necho simply deposed Joahaz (II Chronicles 36. 3).[22]

With regard to Psalms 78 and 105, it has long been noticed [23] that the enumeration of the plagues inflicted on the Egyptians, according to both of them, varies considerably from the account in the Pentateuch. Psalm 78 omits all reference to the third, sixth, and ninth plagues (lice, boils, and darkness). Psalm 105 mentions the third plague, but omits all reference to the sixth. The author includes a reference to the ninth plague, but curiously enough mentions it before any of the others, obviously in order to separate it from the last plague, the slaying of the first born. There can be no doubt that these deviations from the story as told in Exodus are not due to mere chance; [24] the alterations bear every mark of deliberation.

[22] Regarding the date of the Book of Chronicles, particularly in its final revision, see now R. H. Pfeiffer, Introduction to the Old Testament, pp. 811 ff., who argues for a date about the middle of the third century B.C. Cf. the fascinating theory of W. F. Albright, Journal of Biblical Literature, XL, 1921, pp. 112 ff., according to which the Chronicler was none other than Ezra himself, and also Albright's review of Pfeiffer's work, ibid., LXI, 1942, p. 125. It seems probable that various strains must be distinguished in the work of the Chronicler; the earlier, forming the nucleus of the present work, may well be assigned to a comparatively early date (cf. Rothstein-Haenel, Das erste Buch der Chronik, I, pp. 70–75; 189–195; II, pp. XLIV ff.). If the late date assigned to the final redactor of Chronicles be correct, and the suggestion of Egyptian influence on him be accepted, the story of the war between Asa and the Ethiopians may be associated in some manner with the fact that the Ptolemies found the Ethiopians a source of great trial (see Bouché-Leclerq, Histoire des Lagides, I, 143). Similarly the citation of what is now Ps. 105 in I Chron. 16. 8 ff. is broken off just before the story of the Egyptian enslavement and the Exodus, perhaps to avoid having to emphasize those anti-Egyptian motifs.

[23] Cf. E. Koenig, Die Psalmen, 1927, p. 236; R. Kittel, Die Psalmen, fifth and sixth eds., 1929, pp. 264, 344.

[24] So Koenig and Kittel. A. Jirku, Die aelteste Geschichte Israels, 1917, pp. 106–114, maintains that Ps. 78 follows the enumeration of the Egyptian plagues not in accordance with our present text of the Pentateuch, but with an hypothetical source, which has been woven into the story now included in Exodus. This hypothetical source (Q) he identifies with the Document J of most higher critics; but he disagrees

It is clear that the authors of Psalms 78 and 105 omitted the mention of the sixth plague, "boils" because any reference to this peculiar malady (cf. Deuteronomy 28. 27) of the Egyptians was resented by them.[25] The Egyptians of the third century B.C. might condone the re-telling of the Jewish story of the victory of the ancient Israelites over the early Egyptians, because that, after all, concerned only a particular Pharaoh and his army. They found it more difficult to forgive a reference to a disease still prevalent among themselves.

The hesitation of the author of Psalm 78 to mention the third plague ("lice") is of course due to equally natural sensitivity on this point by the Egyptians.

The authors of both historical psalms encountered difficulty with regard to the ninth plague, that of darkness, for a reason which is perhaps more recondite. As Eduard Meyer and others have shown,[26] the Egyptian antisemites identified the God of

---

with their consensus in rejecting the usual combination of literary criteria for determining the division of the "sources"; and somewhat arbitrarily holds that the story of the plagues should be analyzed solely by the criterion of the agent to whom the plague is ascribed, — those ascribed to God Himself belong to J; those ascribed to Moses belong to E; those ascribed to Aaron belong to P. Through this change of method, Jirku avoids the difficulty that the plague of "darkness" is, according to the usual consensus, included in J, though it is omitted from Ps. 78. He thus comes to the conclusion that Ps. 78 was composed while the original Document J was still in existence as an independent source! Unfortunately for his theory, he cannot possibly make any such claim for Ps. 105, which includes the plague of "lice." He comes to the conclusion therefore that that Psalm is based on some other integration of the sources than our present Pentateuchal text. The evidence given in this article seems to me to dispose both of the possibility of such early origin of these psalms, and also of the need for such a far-fetched hypothesis to explain their deviations from the Pentateuch.

[25] See Cambridge Bible on Exod. 9. 9 for discussion of the Egyptian diseases to which the plague of "boils" might refer. Sifra Emor, parasha 3. 15, ed. Weiss 96c, interprets the word "*garab*" (Lev. 21. 20, "scabbed") as the "Egyptian lichen." So also Babli, Bekorot 41a. It is noteworthy that the Septuagint (both in Exod. and in Ps. 105) renders the word *kinnim* by "gnats" or "fleas" rather than "lice" as do the other versions and in accordance with the meaning of the word in later Jewish tradition.

[26] Ursprung u. Anfaenge d. Christentums II, 35; Tscherikower, p. 369; A. Jacoby, Archiv f. Religionswissenschaft, XXV, 1927, 265 ff. According to the latter, pp. 271 ff., the identification resulted from the confusion of the word IAO, the equivalent of YHWH in Egyptian papyri, with the Coptic word for "ass," which has a similar sound. W. F. Albright's interpretation of *harel* (meaning the altar of the Temple in Jerusalem) as associated with *'r'l* (Archaeology and the Religion of Israel, 1942, p. 151) meaning "denizen of the underworld," suggests the possibility that this fact may have contributed to the identification of the God of the Temple of Jerusalem with Seth. On the

Israel with their own Seth, the god of the wilderness, of eclipses, of storms, and of darkness. It was this identification which led to the development of the incredible, yet widespread Hellenistic myth, to the effect that the Jews worshipped an ass, and that the Innermost Shrine of the Temple in Jerusalem contained as its idol the head of an ass; for the Egyptian god Seth was frequently portrayed as an ass. The reluctance of the psalmists to refer to the plague of darkness indicates that this antisemitic identification had been made in their day. The author of Psalm 78, who is ready to omit the mention of any plague the name of which might be offensive to the Egyptians, simply passes over the ninth plague in silence. The author of Psalm 105, while mentioning the plague, does so in words which indicate that darkness is simply an instrument in the hands of God:

> "He sent darkness and it was dark,
> And they rebelled not against His word."[27] (Psalm 105. 28)

He is also careful to dissociate the plague of darkness from that of the slaying of the first-born, which followed it, according to Exodus. The slaying of the first-born was recognized as a direct visitation of God; and the fact that it was immediately preceded by the plague of darkness was doubtless offered by Egyptian interpreters as evidence that the God of Israel was their god Seth, who manifested himself through darkness. Lest any word he uttered might help give credence to this identification, the psalmist arranges the plagues so that that of darkness comes first, as far as possible from that of slaying the first-born.

The Egyptophilism reflected in these works is possibly to be associated with a more widespread spiritual influence exerted by Egypt on the Palestinian Jews during the third century B.C. Accordingly, the date of Proverbs 22. 17–24. 22 which was so obviously composed under the influence of Egyptian wisdom

---

other hand, the view that the identification of the God of the Jews with Seth was the origin of the charge of ass-worship is challenged by E. Bickermann, Monatsschrift, LXXI, 1927, pp. 171 ff.; 255 ff. See also I. Heinemann, PWRE, Suppl. V, 28 ff.

[27] If we accept the view that v. 28 is an interpolation, the omission of the plague of "darkness" would still lead to the same conclusion as that given in the text.

literature, should possibly be fixed within the period of the Ptolemaic rule over Palestine.[28] That may also apply [29] to the date of Psalm 104.

Of even greater significance is the possibility that the permeation of Egyptian wisdom into the socially higher groups was accompanied by a far different, but typical, reaction, to Egyptian teachings among the scholarly groups. Just as the impact of Aristotelian logic on the Pharisees is said to have produced the system of Rabbinic dialectic with its various rules for the hermeneutic interpretation and advancement of the Law,[30] so the impact of the Egyptian funerary practice and popular concepts may have had a share in the development of the corresponding Hasidean and Pharisaic doctrine of the Resurrection. While the Egyptian doctrine was inherently aristocratic, for only wealthy families could afford the expensive process of embalming and preserving the body, the Hasidean and Pharisaic doctrine was democratic and pietistic, extending the resurrection to the just of all classes.[31] It is usually

[28] H. J. Cadbury, Journal of Religion, IX, 1929, pp. 105 ff.; for bibliography, see ibid., note 2.

[29] See A. M. Blackman, in D. C. Simpson, The Psalmists, 1926, pp. 177 ff.

[30] Cf. W. F. Albright, From the Stone Age to Christianity, 1940, p. 274, and references there given.

[31] Both in The Pharisees, 1938, pp. 145 ff., and in Faith for Today, 1941, pp. 168 ff., I have laid great stress on the aristocratic element in the Egyptian practice, and on the essentially democratic nature of the Hasidean-Pharisaic concept. More recently, I have been led to wonder whether the Egyptian practice of mummification can properly be identified with a doctrine of the Resurrection. Professor A. D. Nock has shown that funerary customs and ideas about the after-life are not necessarily correlated (HTR, XXV, 1932, pp. 335 ff. and Journal of Biblical Literature, LX, 1941, p. 95). Moreover, the Egyptians had, together with their practice of embalming, directed toward the preservation of the body so that it might theoretically enjoy continued existence in the tomb with the offerings there deposited, also entirely different concepts of the dead men riding in the boat of the Sun-god, and being identified with Osiris in an after-life, which is in certain respects the very opposite of the Resurrection. (This dual attitude toward immortality, stressing the Resurrection of the body on the one hand, and also immortality of the soul is, of course, found also in Judaism.) Nevertheless it seems probable that the practice of mummification had its effect on the spread among the Jews, of the doctrine of Resurrection, as well as on the opposition to it, in the following manner. The Jews, impressed with the Persian concept of the Resurrection would tend to relate it to the Egyptian practice. This would have two opposite effects on the people. The purists and rigorists among the religious leaders, including the priests, would reject the Persian belief because they would associate it with the Egyptian practice, to which

assumed that the doctrine of the Resurrection made its first appearance in Judaea in the fourth century B.C.; [32] and the fact that both Palestine and Egypt were then under Persian domination certainly makes the intrusion into Judaea of Egyptian thought (together with that of the Persians) during that period quite likely. But it is more natural to assume that the full impact of Egyptian ideas on the Jews only came with the third century B.C.

In any event, the material presented indicates a widespread reaction in Palestine to the fact of Egyptian suzerainty in the third century B.C. We have already seen how this reaction led to the formulation of M. The facts here presented seem to indicate that the same circumstances led to the formulation of A. Presumably, therefore, A served as introduction to M; and they both were composed at the same time, and by the same men.

---

there had been centuries of objection. On the other hand, there would be double pressure on the populace to accept a doctrine which seems to be worldwide in its recognition. I hope to establish, on another occasion, the theory that the Sadducean negation of the Resurrection preceded the Pharisaic acceptance of the doctrine. This creation of a Sadducean dogma denying the Resurrection, to oppose the Persian doctrine of the Resurrection, might well be associated with the fact that the Persian belief was to some Jewish minds associated with the Egyptian practice. On the other hand, once non-Resurrection had become a dogma of Sadducism, it was only a question of time before the contrary belief, namely the Resurrection, became a dogma of Pharisaism. The belief in angels and demons, stemming, like that of the Resurrection from Persia, never became a really vital issue either for Pharisaism or Sadducism. Indeed except for a passing reference in Acts 23. 8 we could hardly have known that it was a controversial issue. The difference between the great emphasis of both Pharisees and Sadducees on the issue of the Resurrection, and their comparative disinterestedness in the issue of the existence of angels may derive from the fact that the Resurrection was associated with a pagan practice, namely Egyptian preservation and mummification of the body, while the doctrine of angels had no such association. For the instructive fact that the impact of the Persian ideas seems to have been felt in Judaea only after the rise of Graeco-Roman literature, see A. D. Nock in Journal of Roman Studies, XXX (1940), pp. 195–196.

[32] This is the date generally assigned to Is. 24–27; see commentaries of G. H. Box, The Book of Isaiah, 1908, p. 113; J. Skinner, The Book of the Prophet Isaiah (in Cambridge Bible), 1915, p. 217; B. Duhm, Das Buch Jesaia, 1922, p. 172, puts it in the period of John Hyrcan. His view seems, however, to have been generally rejected. W. F. Albright, op. cit., p. 269 considers the sixth century B.C. a possibility. But it seems probable that the apocalypse dates from no earlier than the beginning of the third century B.C. See R. H. Pfeiffer, Introduction to the Old Testament, p. 442.

II. The Alternative Introduction to the Passover Haggadah (B)

As already noted,[33] in using the formula, "We were Pharaoh's bondmen in Egypt," as introduction to the Passover Haggadah, modern Jewish ritual follows the prescription of the famous Babylonian scholar of the third century, Samuel of Nahardea. His contemporary, Rab, held that the recital of the story of the Exodus should begin as follows: [34]

"In the beginning, our fathers were worshippers of strange gods: but now the All-Present has brought us to His service, as it is said: [35] 'And Joshua said unto all the people, Thus saith the Lord God of Israel, Your fathers dwelt of old time beyond the River, even Terah, the father of Abraham and the father of Nahor: and they served other gods. And I took your father Abraham from beyond the River, and led him throughout all the land of Canaan, and multiplied his seed, and gave him Isaac. And I gave unto Isaac, Jacob and Esau; and I gave unto Esau, Mount Seir, to possess it; and Jacob and his children went down into Egypt. (Joshua XXIV. 2–4.)'" [36]

It is clear, however, that this formula did not originate with Rab. It would have been impossible for a scholar of the third century of the Christian Era, no matter how illustrious, to have

[33] See above, p. 292.

[34] B. Pesahim, 116a; Yer., ibid., X, 5, 37d.

[35] The introductory phrase, "In the beginning, etc.," is found as part of B in all the extant versions of the Passover Haggadah, with the exception of those published by I. Abrahams in Jewish Quarterly Review, X, 1898, pp. 44, 48, and 49; and that published by J. Greenstone in Z. f. hebraeische Bibliographie, XV, 1911, pp. 122 ff. The fragment which I. Abrahams numbers VII, on p. 47 of his article, contains the introductory phrase. In those which I. Abrahams numbers II and VII, B opens with the words, "Your fathers dwelt of old, etc." In the fragment which he numbers X, B opens with the words, "And Joshua said unto all the people, etc." According to Rab's view as quoted in Yer. Pesahim, loc. cit., B opens with the words, "Your fathers dwelt of old, etc." The text of Yerushalmi, according to our eds. reads: "Rab said, 'In the beginning one should begin (with the words): Your fathers of old, etc.'" L. Landshuth in his Maggid Mereshit, p. X, has made the interesting suggestion that the passage should be emended by placing the word *mitehilah* ("in the beginning") before the citation from Scripture. The passage as emended would therefore read: "Rab said, 'One should begin (the recital of the Passover Haggadah with the words): *In the beginning* (and then continue) *Your fathers of old*, etc.'" According to Babli, B opens with the words, "In the beginning, etc.," precisely as in our texts. Rab Natronai Gaon, in his responsum, cites a ritual in which B began with, "And Joshua said, etc.," precisely like fragment X published by I. Abrahams. See regarding this ritual, below, p. 327.

[36] For the remainder of the passage in Joshua, chap. 24, and the reason for the failure of the compiler to include it in B, see below, p. 329.

substituted a formula of his own creation for the well-established introduction, "We were Pharaoh's bondmen, etc.," unless his views were fortified by much earlier traditions. Nor can we think of any reason why Rab should have wished to substitute some other introduction for that which is prescribed in Scripture, and which, as we have seen, received its final form in the third century B.C., more than four hundred years before his time.

There is, moreover, definite evidence showing that authorities much earlier than Rab knew of an opening verse to the Haggadah, other than A. Rab's uncle, Rabbi Hiyya transmits a *baraita* [37] which reads as follows (E):

"The Torah (in prescribing the answers to be given the child during the Passover evening service) considers four types of sons: the clever son, the wicked son, the simple son, and the son unable to formulate his questions. (E1) The clever son says, 'What are the testimonies, the statutes, and the ordinances, which the Lord, our God, commanded us?' [38] (Deuter-

[37] Yerushalmi Pesahim, X, 37d, cf. Mekilta Bo, chap. 18, Fr. 22b, Horowitz-Rabin, p. 73, Lauterbach, I, 166. See further regarding this *baraita*, section IV of this article.

[38] The reading *otanu* ("us") instead of *etkem* ("you") gives force to the contrast between the utterance of the wise and the wicked sons. This reading, which is supported by the Septuagint and some texts of the Vulgate, is found in none of the other versions. It is the reading of E according to the text of Yerushalmi, loc. cit.; and the best texts of the Mekilta (see ed. Horowitz, and cf. his notes, ad loc.). It is found in the text of the Passover Haggadah of Maimonides (D); in the Darmstadt Manuscript of the Haggadah, and also in the texts cited by B. Italiener in his Die Darmstaedter Pessach Haggadah, on pp. 176, 182, 192, 194, 209, 212, 218, 228 ("corrected" on margin); (all these are said to be of German origin); p. 254 (Italian); p. 279 (Spanish); and in the edition of Haggadah ke-Minhag Teman (the Yemenite Haggadah) published by W. H. Greenburg, London, 1896, p. 19 as well as in the following texts Sa, O, P, U, Va, X. On the other hand the reading *etkem*, in accordance with the Massoretic text occurs in Siddur R. Saadia, the commentary of R. Isaiah di Trani, (see Shaare Geulah, Cracow, 1896, p. 17) Shibbale Ha-Leket, Orhot Hayyim, Kol Bo, the following Genizah fragments of the Adler collection at the Jewish Theological Seminary 2857, f. 13v.; 2935, f. 4a; 3288, f. 11r.; (there are none with the alternative reading); and the following other texts E, F, G, H, I, J, K (XII, XIII) M, Qa, R, S, Sb, Sc, Sd, T, Ta, Tb, Tc, W, and in the texts cited by B. Italiener, op. cit., pp. 170, 199, 232 (of German origin); p. 249 (Italian); p. 263 (Oriental); p. 269 (French); p. 275 (Spanish). The word is entirely omitted in the manuscript described by Italiener, op. cit., p. 243. See regarding the difference D. Hoffmann, in Magazin f. d. Wissenschaft d. Judenthums 13, 1886, p. 193, and Bet Vaad Lahakamim, I, 1902–03, p. 16; and cf. also S. Lieberman, Hayerushalmi Kifeshuto, I, 1, 1934, p. 520, and other articles, cited below, note 108.

onomy 6. 20). Do thou therefore teach him the laws of the Passover ritual, 'It is forbidden to end the Passover meal with entertainment.'[39] (E2) The wicked son says, 'What mean ye by this service?' (Exodus 12. 26). By saying, 'ye' instead of 'we,' he has withdrawn himself from the community, and has rejected a basic principle of Judaism. Do thou therefore reply to him sharply, 'It is because of that which the Lord did for me, when I came forth from Egypt.' (Exodus 13. 8). (The Scriptures say) *for me*, carrying the implication *not for thee;* for if the wicked son had been there, he would not have been redeemed. (E3) The simple son says, 'What is this?' (Exodus 13. 14). Thou shalt say to him, 'By the strength of hand the Lord brought us out from Egypt, from the house of bondage.' (Ibid.) (E4) As for the son who cannot formulate questions, do thou begin for him, even as it is written, 'And thou shalt tell thy son in that day, saying: It is because of that which the Lord did for me when I came forth from Egypt.'"

It is important to note that Rabbi Hiyya cites all the passages in the Pentateuch which refer to the questions and answers regarding the Passover, except one: namely, Deuteronomy 6. 21, which forms the basis for the answer most commonly used! This omission is astonishing, until we recollect that none of the other explanations of the Passover suggested in the Pentateuch were subject to controversy. Rabbi Hiyya could proceed calmly to discuss their relative merits, and the occasions to which they were especially suitable. Rabbi Hiyya could not use the reply in Deuteronomy 6. 21, apparently, because he held that that reply should *not* be used on any occasion. The aversion to the particular reply constituting A apparently signifies that the use of A was a matter of difference of ritual. Either Rabbi Hiyya declined to take part in the controversy, or he sympathized with those who objected to A. As we know that his nephew and devoted disciple, Rab, objected to A, we may rightly assume that this view was also taken by Rabbi Hiyya himself.

[39] See Additional Note C for the meaning and varying orthography and pronunciation of the word *afikoman* (translated here "entertainment"), according to the different texts of the Mishna, the Passover Haggadah, etc.

We can, however, show that the difference of opinion regarding the use of A arose in ages much earlier than that of Rabbi Hiyya. The Mishna, Pesahim (10. 4) after enumerating the questions to be asked, describes the father's reply in the following words: "According to the understanding of the son, his father instructs him. He begins with the disgrace and ends with the glory; and he expounds from *A wandering Aramaean was my father* . . . until he finishes the whole section."

The discussion between Rab and Samuel regarding the opening of the Haggadah is presented in the Talmud as difference in the interpretation to be placed on the words, "He begins with the disgrace." According to Rab, the disgrace referred to is the idol-worship of the ancestors of the Hebrews; according to Samuel it is their bondage in Egypt. But the question must arise, why was the compiler of the Mishna so inexplicit? He cites verbatim the questions which the son asks. Why, then, did he not specifically quote the reply of the father? The answer must be that the compiler of the Mishna, in this instance as in others, declined to take sides in a controversy regarding different rituals, which were regarded as equally satisfactory. It happens that both A and B might be described as "beginning with the disgrace and ending with the glory." A opens with Israel in bondage, and ends with Israel redeemed by God; B opens with the ancestors of Israel worshipping idols, and ends with their worship of God.

But if the compiler of the Mishna intentionally used an indefinite expression, because he knew of the two variant forms of the Haggadah, A and B, that fact fixes the date of the origin of B much earlier than Rab; for it can be shown that the part of the Mishna containing this passage was compiled before the destruction of the Temple in the year 70.[40]

This argument thus takes us back to Temple times for the origin of B as well as A. We have already seen that there is other evidence pointing to the third century B.C. for the origin of A; the present discussion would seem to make the argument conclusive.

[40] See D. Hoffmann, Die Erste Mischna (Beilage z. Jahresbericht d. Rabbiner-Seminars zu Berlin, 1881–82), p. 8; also Zebi Carl, Pesahim, Lwow, 1925, 93 ff.

For the origin of B, we must now turn to the evidence afforded by literary criticism. The discussion of the origin of AM has shown the importance which was attached in early times to the Passover service as a means to influence popular opinion. The success which attended the use of AM for the purposes it was intended to serve, doubtless strengthened the tendency to use the Passover service for propaganda purposes. In determining the date of B it will be helpful to inquire whether B could have been of any use from this point of view.

B stresses three basic ideas: (1) the antiquity of Israel; (2) its origin in Mesopotamia; (3) its distinctiveness as a religious group. In all three respects, its attitude toward Judaism is, with a varying degree of emphasis, different from that of AM. A might be interpreted at least as associating the Jews with an Egyptian background.[41] As we have seen, M incontinently transforms the verse, "My father was a Syrian," into "The Syrian (i.e., Laban) sought to destroy my father." Opposing both A and M, B reverts to the spirit which animates the literal meaning of Deuteronomy 26. 5, and definitely traces the origins of Israel to the Syrians. The origin of Israel, according to this work, is to be sought, further, not in the Exodus, marking the emergence of the nation from bondage, but in the call to Abraham, by which he turned from idolatry to the worship of the One God. Obviously this is a strange note to strike on the Passover when the Exodus from Egypt, as an historical event, was being celebrated. It is particularly curious to insist that the Passover celebration open on this note. The formulation of such a passage, with its obvious political overtones, bears every mark of deliberate apologetics and propaganda.

Propaganda for what purpose? First, to controvert the Egyptian claim that Israel came into existence only at a comparatively late period; and to insist, in the manner used so emphatically by Josephus in his apologetics of a later age, that Israel was an ancient people.[42] This insistence on the an-

[41] See above, note 15.

[42] Schuerer, III, 546, and references there given; M. Friedlaender, Geschichte der Juedischen Apologetik, 1903, 349 ff.; P. Krueger, Philo u. Josephus als Apologeten d. Judentums, 1906, 62 ff.; J. Bergmann, Jued. Apologetik in Neutestamentlichen Zeitalter, 1908, p. 146; and article, Apologetik u. Apologeten, in Encyc. Judaica (1928).

tiquity of Israel was, of course, nothing more than a particular example of the general tendency of Hellenistic historiography. It was, in fact, the reaction of Jewish writers and thinkers to the propaganda issuing from the court circles of the Ptolemies and the Seleucids. Both of these dynasties were trying to establish some ideational basis for their claim to the loyalty of their subjects; and, in doing so, did not hesitate to re-write history and even foster new philosophical and religious concepts.[43] Thus the Ptolemies endeavored to obtain recognition for themselves as rightful successors of the Pharaohs, and therefore as Pharaohs. Like the Seleucids, they unblushingly invited recognition of themselves as gods.[44] In addition to these efforts to win personal loyalties, the Hellenistic kings had to foster new types of patriotism among their subjects. This was perhaps more difficult for the Seleucids than for the Ptolemies, for unlike Egypt, the Seleucid Empire was a conglomeration of national units, rather than itself a unit. But even in Egypt, national pride had to be stimulated to the utmost, in order to maintain the courage of the people and their willingness to submit to the inevitable burdens of almost continuous warfare.

The eagerness to foment Egyptian patriotism was reflected in the effort of Egyptian historiographers to describe their country as the mother of all culture, including the Jewish and the Greek, and as the most ancient home of all civilization.

The Jewish writers, rendered oversensitive perhaps by the obvious weakness of their people in the face of the vast empires, considered these declarations of the antiquity of the Egyptians and the originality of their culture, a challenge to the dignity of Israel. This sensitivity was emphasized by the Hellenistic tendency to attach great importance to the real or imputed wisdom of Oriental peoples, and to revel in rather fabulous ascriptions of antiquity. It was out of this situation that there

[43] See above, note 15 and references there given.

[44] A. Bouché-Leclerq, Histoire des Lagides, 1907, I, 232; ibid., Histoire des Séleucides, 1913, p. 465; E. Bikerman, Inst. des Séleucides, pp. 236 ff.; E. R. Goodenough, The Political Philosophy of Hellenistic Kingship, in Yale Classical Studies, I (1928), pp. 55 ff.; see also P. Heichelheim, Wirtschaftsgeschichte d. Altertums, I, 651; II, p. 1119.

arose the continuous literary debate regarding the relative antiquity of Jewish and other cultures, as well as of the Jewish and other peoples. This discussion culminated in the endeavor of Josephus to defend the Jews and Judaism through writing his Antiquities and through his bitter diatribe against the Egyptian writers in his Contra Apionem.[45] "In my history of our Antiquities," Josephus writes with emphasis, "I have, I think, made sufficiently clear to any who may peruse that work the extreme antiquity of our Jewish race, the purity of the original stock, and the manner in which it established itself in the country we occupy today. That history embraces a period of five thousand years." He is at great pains to explain to the Graeco-Roman world why, despite the early origin of Israel, none of the earliest Greek writers refers to this people. Now while Josephus is the first writer who so explicitly states his purpose in emphasizing the antiquity of Israel, there can be no doubt that the motif actuated many writers before his day. If, for example, we read the Book of Chronicles *after* studying the fragments of Hecataeus[46] and Manetho,[47] we notice at once why the history of the Temple and its related institutions, which is the main subject of the Chronicler's interest, begins with a list of generations from Adam. The Egyptophilism of the Chronicler, which we have noticed above,[48] did not of course

[45] Contra Apionem, I, 1 ff.

[46] See Reinach, op. cit.

[47] Josephus, Contra Apionem, see above, note 7.

[48] See p. 298. One of the purposes of the historical psalms, 78, 105, and 106 may have been to overcome the tendency toward self-depreciation by the Jews under the stress of the calumnies spread about them in the Egyptian and Hellenistic world by the anti-Jewish writers. Perhaps the fear of self-depreciation by Jews may also be in part responsible for the reference to the Patriarchs at the beginning of the Amidah, the first benediction of which was probably formulated in pre-Maccabean times. (Jewish Quarterly Review, N. S., XVI, 1925, 41 ff.) Ben Sira's "Praise of the Fathers of Old" (Ecclus. Chap. 44) attains a new significance when it is regarded as a reply to detractors of the Israelites as a people of recent origin. The apologetic tendency of the Jewish writers under the Ptolemaic rule is perhaps most clearly to be noticed in Ps. 87. The date of this Psalm seems to be fixed by its reference to Egypt under the cypher *Rahab*, as though the author sought to avoid giving offense to the Imperial rulers. The purpose of the psalmist is to show that Judaea has produced more genuinely great men than any of her neighbors. He says, "Glorious things are spoken of thee, O city of God. Selah. 'I will make mention of Rahab and Babylonia'" (i.e. the Seleucid empire) "'among them that know Me; Behold Philistia and Tyre, with Ethiopia; This one was born there.' But of Zion it shall be said: 'This man and that was born in her; and the

extend to any depreciation of Israel. The Chronicler therefore devotes the first nine chapters of his book to tracing the genealogies of the leading Israelite families. His history begins with the advent of King David; but he demonstrates that the origins of Israel are to be sought in the origin of the human race itself.

This apologetic effort was carried on by other writers, both in Alexandria and in Palestine. The re-formulation of Jewish history by Demetrius and Eupolemus is well-known.[49] Less attention has been given to the equally significant apologetics, which emanated from Palestine, emphasizing the "Jewish contribution to civilization." The author of the Book of Jubilees [50] which, it now seems probable, was composed in the decades immediately preceding the Maccabean uprising,[51] is at great pains to stress the rôle of Abraham in the development of the technical civilization of the world. It was not enough that he was a teacher of monotheism; for to a part of the Jewish world, following in this respect the pagan Hellenists, monotheism did not, apparently, constitute an important factor in human civilization. But everyone knew the value attaching to machines and inventions; and so it became a very significant fact in the historiography of the Book of Jubilees to ascribe to Abraham the invention of a particularly efficient plough; just as the Alexandrian writers tried to increase the stature of Moses by making him the originator of Egyptian culture,[52] and even Philo traces the origin of Greek philosophy to Moses.[53]

In the further effort to increase the self-respect of the Jews, and to evoke reverence for them among the materialistic,

---

Most High Himself doth establish her.' The Lord shall count in the register of the peoples: 'This one was born there.' Selah. And singers, like dancers," (so to be interpreted, in accordance with Kittel and Koenig, ad loc.) "shout: All my fountains are in thee."

[49] E. Schuerer, Gesch. d. jued. Volkes, 1909, III, pp. 472 ff.

[50] Jubilees 11. 19 ff. In Jub. 12. 27, we are told how Abraham learned the Hebrew language, which was obviously foreign to him in Mesopotamia. Cf. I Macc. 12. 21, which claims that the Spartans are descended from Abraham.

[51] See Appendix to this article.

[52] Schuerer, op. cit., pp. 477 ff.

[53] See Quis re. div. heres 43. 214, ed. Wendland-Cohen-Reiter, III, p. 48; Quod omnis probus liber sit 8. 57, ibid., VI, p. 16.

pagan Hellenists, the writer of the Book of Jubilees[54] transforms the Hebrew patriarchs into efficient warriors; and tells how long before their descent into Egypt the Israelites waged wars and won great victories.

This tendency is carried forward in the Testaments of the Twelve Patriarchs,[55] and also in the later Rabbinic midrash.

It was entirely natural that this apologetic tendency should also affect the formulation of the Passover Haggadah.

But the desire to emphasize the antiquity of the Jewish people, clearly reflected in B, is evidently supplemented by another desire, to associate the Jews with the Mesopotamians. This could have only one purpose, pleasing Seleucid rulers.[56]

After the Seleucids came into control of Palestine in the year 198 B.C., it was as necessary to placate them and to induce docility to them in the populace as it had been necessary to placate the Ptolemies and to make the populace subservient to *them* when they were in control. The Seleucids were even more eager than the Ptolemies had been to inculcate in the Palestinian people a sense of loyalty to themselves, and hostility to their enemies and rivals.[57] The Seleucids doubtless looked to

[54] See Jub. 34. 4 ff.; Test. Judah, chaps. 3–7. The wars between Egypt and Canaan, described in Jub. 46. 6 ff., and alluded to in Test. Simeon 8. 2, are strongly reminiscent of those between the Seleucids and the Ptolemies. Much of the material bearing on the apologetic tendencies of the Book of Jubilees and the Testaments of the Twelve Patriarchs, presented by Friedlaender, op. cit., pp. 161–187 remains relevant, though his conception of these books as products of the diaspora can hardly be accepted. The stories of Artapanus, recording the instruction which Abraham gave to the Egyptian rulers in astrology, and making Moses the virtual founder of Egyptian civilization, follows the same line of thought (op. cit., pp. 477–478). The close relationship between the Palestinian and the Egyptian literature of apologetics demonstrates how well the Palestinians, even at an early date, were aware of the nature of the Egyptian polemics against them. It is therefore entirely natural that the leaders of the Jews, doubtless far better acquainted with antisemitic literature than the masses, should seek to counteract it; particularly at the Passover festival, which drew so many Jews from the diaspora to Jerusalem.

[55] Cf. Test. Judah, chaps. 3 ff.

[56] For Syrian traditions associating the Jews with Syrian origin, cf. I. Heinemann, PWRE, Suppl. V, 23. See Reinach, Textes d'auteurs grecs et romains relatifs au Judaïsme, 1895, pp. 79 (Nicholas of Damascus) and pp. 251 ff. (Trogus Pompeius).

[57] The need felt by the Seleucid government for national unity and the jealousy felt regarding Jewish loyalties to Egypt, were doubtless, finally, one of the determining factors in the religious persecution inaugurated by Antiochus IV; concerning which see below. Cf. E. Meyer, II, 143 ff.; 166; Heinemann, PWRE, Suppl. V, 5.

the ecclesiastical leaders of the land to serve them, precisely as the earlier high priests had served the former rulers. The influence of Egypt on Palestine had been profound; there was a strong pro-Egyptian group in the Palestinian community.[58] Palestine was a distant outpost of the Seleucid empire; and so little were the Seleucids able to control Palestine, even after their conquest, that for a number of years the pro-Egyptian landowner, Hyrcan, son of Tobiah, held his estates in Transjordan, openly proclaiming his Egyptian sympathies, and perhaps receiving Egyptian support.[59]

The very weakness of the hold of the Seleucids on Palestine obviously made it the more necessary for the pro-Seleucid Jews to avoid saying or doing anything which might seem to be disloyal; and stimulated the interest of the Seleucids in the position taken by various Palestinian Jewish leaders. The whole situation therefore was one which called for the formulation of an introduction to the Passover Haggadah, containing the ideas inculcated in B, namely that Israel arose in great antiquity; and that it was an offshoot of Syria rather than Egypt.[60]

While it is probable that so fundamental a change in the ritual as the substitution of B for A would have come about, in all probability, only as a measure intended to please the imperial Seleucid government; once the change was made, it is obvious that all self-respecting Jews would prefer B to A, because of B's insistence on the antiquity of Israel. Hence, it came about, doubtless, that long after the Seleucid power in Palestine had disappeared, B was generally recited; and that A was retained only in the most distant outposts of Babylonia, like Nahardea, the home of the teacher, Samuel, where the influence of the change introduced in the Temple service was not

[58] See above, note 7.

[59] For the inherent weakness of the Seleucid kingdom, see E. Meyer, Bluete u. Niedergang d. Hellenismus in Asien, 1925, p. 46, and now M. Rostovtzeff, The Social and Economic History of the Hellenistic World, 1941, I, 473 ff.

[60] It is noteworthy that this relationship with Syria is emphatically stressed in Test. Judah 10. 1; and Jubilees 34. 20, 21; 37. 1. The fact that Levi is described as marrying a daughter of Aram, and Tamar, the ancestress of the Davidic dynasty, is also so described, indicates the significance which these authors attached to the close relationship between Israel and Aram. Marriage with Canaanite women is described in both works as a serious offense (see Jubilees 20. 4; 25. 1–3; 27. 8; Test. Judah 14. 6).

felt.[61] Sura, being nearer Palestine, had apparently adopted the changed form of ritual.[62] Perhaps this was done under the influence of Rab, founder of the Academy of Sura, who rejected A (as we have already noticed) and insisted that B alone was the appropriate beginning for the Passover Haggadah.

While these considerations seem to indicate the period 198–167 B.C. as the time of the origin of B as part of the Haggadah, it is possible to delimit the period more narrowly, by considering carefully the series of epochal events, and the shifting of Seleucid and Jewish policies, which characterized that age.

The first public policy enunciated by Antiochus III after his conquest in 198 B.C. was intended to win the friendship of the people by offering them a larger measure of autonomy.[63] The charter issued by Antiochus III to the Jews [64] recognized the Sanhedrin, as well as the rights of the scribes to be members of the Sanhedrin, and gave important guarantees to the Temple and the community.[65] It seems probable that the High

[61] See note 34.

[62] The customs of Sura frequently followed those of Palestine and opposed those of other parts of Babylonia. Indeed, this distinction was one of the main reasons for the differences between the academies of Sura and Pumbedita in their interpretations of Judaism (see L. Ginzberg, Ginze Schechter, 1929, II, 508, and B. M. Lewin, Methiboth, Jerusalem, 1933, Introduction, pp. i–v).

[63] Cambridge Ancient History, VII, 164; Oesterley and Robinson, A History of Israel, II, 1932, 208–209; Eduard Meyer, Ursprung u. Anfaenge d. Christentums, II, 126; E. Bickermann, Der Gott d. Makkabaeer, 1937, pp. 51 ff.; cf. also his article in Revue d. Études Juives, C, 1935, pp. 4 ff.

[64] Josephus, Antiquities, XII, 129 ff. (3, 3). The edict was, naturally, addressed to Ptolemy, one of the Seleucid officials. For the authenticity of the document, see works of Bickermann, cited in preceding note; as well as the following discussions, H. Willrich, Juden u. Griechen, 1895, 42–43; and his Urkundfaelschung in d. hellenistisch-juedischen Literatur, 1924, 18 ff.; B. Niese, Gesch. d. Griechischen u. Makedonischen Staaten, 1899, II, 579; A. Buechler, Die Tobiaden u. die Oniaden, 1899, pp. 143 ff.; E. R. Bevan, The House of Seleucus, 1902, II, 166, note 4; E. Meyer, Ursprung u. Anfaenge d. Christentums, 1921, II, 127, note 2; Tscherikower, 122 ff. The general trend of modern scholarship seems now to be in favor of the acceptance of the document as genuine.

[65] The privileges granted Jerusalem by Antiochus III were probably from his point of view moderate (see Bickermann, in Revue d. Études Juives, loc. cit., p. 34). But they were of great importance from the point of view of the scholars, in that they recognized for the first time the "scribes of the Temple" and gave a special place, too, to the "sacred singers." Under the first group, we must recognize the *sopherim* or the predecessors of the later Pharisaic Scribes; under the second group, undoubtedly, the Levites (see, further, my discussion of the subject, in The Pharisees, 1938, II, 581). For the

Priest under whom this charter was granted was Simeon the Righteous. Apparently he and the leading scribes of Jerusalem had taken the side of Antiochus in his struggle against the Ptolemies. The charter of liberties which was granted them was more than a token of his gratitude; it was also an effort to obtain their support for the future. The conquest of Palestine was only one step in the expansion of the Seleucid empire; the next step was to integrate the little western country into that empire. It was apparently the belief of Antiochus III, that by granting the Judaites a large measure of autonomy, and by giving recognition to their scribes, he would be able to obtain loyalty and devotion in Palestine for his empire.

After Simeon died, the Syrian government suddenly seems to have realized, however, that it had underestimated the strength of the pro-Egyptian sentiment in Palestine; and that the autonomous powers it had granted the Jewish leaders might interfere with rather than advance, the process of integrating the Jewish community into the Seleucid empire. This apprehension was based on the persistence of the pro-Egyptian faction in Palestine; and the adherence of Onias II, the son of Simeon the Righteous, who became High Priest soon after his father's death, to this pro-Egyptian faction.[66]

The fact is that the Jewish aristocracy was divided in its loyalties between Egypt and Syria; and for urgent reasons. Trade between Palestine and Egypt already considerable in the Persian period, had been vastly stimulated under the Ptolemaic dominion, as the Zenon papyri now show,[67] and as

---

identity of Simeon the Righteous and his date, see G. F. Moore, in Jewish Studies in Memory of Israel Abrahams, 1927, 348 ff. For identical conclusions based on somewhat different materials, see N. Krochmal, More Nebuche Ha-Zeman, ed. Rawidowicz, 1924, p. 65.

[66] The relationship of the Hellenistic movement in Palestine to the international situation has been recognized by a number of writers. Perhaps it has been most emphatically described and most clearly formulated by E. Taeubler, in his essay, Staat und Umwelt: Palaestina in der hellenistisch-roemischen Zeit, in Tyche, historische Studien, 1926, pp. 128–129.

[67] In Cambridge Ancient History, VII, 130 ff.; Rostovtzeff, The Social and Economic History of the Hellenistic World, I, 256, 293, 384 f.; J. Toutain, The Economic Life of the Ancient World, 1930, 160 ff.; and V. Tscherikower; Palestine under the Ptolemies (Mizraim, IV–V, 1937, pp. 15 ff.).

might have been assumed from scattered Talmudic references.[68] For this reason, the leading landowners and the international merchants of Jerusalem in the third century B.C. were as pro-Egyptian as their predecessors in the eighth and seventh centuries B.C. had been.[69] Even after the Seleucid conquest of Palestine, many retained their pro-Egyptian sympathies, and hoped that a restoration of the Egyptian domination would bring about a restoration of the Egyptian export and import traffic, which the conquest of the Seleucids had reduced, if not completely interrupted.

On the other hand, there was apparently a considerable group among affluent Judaites who apparently no longer cherished any hope of the restoration of Egyptian dominion. They, therefore, looked for the expansion of their commerce not to Egypt, but to Palestine itself. They were gravely concerned, therefore, because the political and religious divisions of the country impeded the development of this internal commerce. The chief divisions, which threatened Palestinian commercial unity, were those between the Judaites and the Samaritans, on the one hand; and the Jewish and the Greek cities, on the other.

The conflict between Judaea and Samaria dated back, of course, to the very beginning of the Second Commonwealth.[70] It had become exacerbated under Nehemiah, who, in building the walls of Jerusalem and establishing it as metropolitan trade center, had aroused the opposition not only of the Samaritans, themselves, but also of Tobiah, the Ammonite, and Geshem, the Arab chieftain. These opponents of Nehemiah, it now becomes clear, sided with the Samaritans not because they preferred Samaria to Judaea, but because they feared the effect of any schism in the country on their interests.[71] The situation

[68] Tosefta Makshirin 3. 4, ed. Zuckermandel, p. 675. For the very important historical economic significance of this record, see L. Ginzberg, Mekomah shel ha-halakah behokmat yisrael, 1931, pp. 6 ff.; and cf. S. Lieberman, Tosefet Rishonim, IV, 1939, p. 115.

[69] See L. Finkelstein, The Pharisees, I, p. 424.

[70] Ezra 4. 2, 9, *et al.* For a general discussion of the relations of the Samaritans and the returning Judaites to each other in these early times, see Oesterley and Robinson, A History of Israel, II, pp. 142 ff.; and CAH, VI, pp. 181 ff.

[71] Neh. 2. 19 f.; 3. 33; 4. 1 ff.; 6. 1 ff.; 13. 4 ff. See W. F. Albright, From the Stone

was further aggravated in the course of time, both through the widening schism between Samaria and Judaea, and doubtless also through the economic distress caused by the political dislocation, incidental to the wars of the third century B.C. and the interference with Egyptian trade following on the Seleucid conquest of Palestine.[72]

The second division interfering with Palestinian trade had developed only in Hellenistic times, with the growth of the Greek population in the land. The Ptolemies and the Seleucids[73] had stimulated the development of Hellenistic settlements in Palestine, which by virtue of their status as Greek cities, were separated from the Jewish community, economically, as well as politically, culturally and religiously.[74] V. Tscherikower[75] has shown how important the re-integration of these cities into the Jewish economy was for the leading Palestinian merchants.

Among those who accepted the Seleucid domination of Palestine as an irremediable situation, there might thus be two different approaches to the economic problem resulting from it. The high priestly families, whose social status derived from the Temple, naturally resented any effort to diminish the importance of Jerusalem, though they might welcome whatever steps could be taken to bring about an integration between

---

Age to Christianity, p. 248; Oesterley and Robinson, op. cit., pp. 153 ff. Nehemiah naturally makes the sympathy of so many neighbors of Israel for the Samaritans seem sheer perverseness. But surely the re-establishment of Jerusalem as the religious center of Judaea, and as its metropolis, did threaten the established economic habits of the Transjordanians as well as of the Samaritans, and was a peril against which both groups might be expected to unite. It is interesting to note that the later Tobiads, like the one who was Nehemiah's contemporary, had close relations with the Samaritans (see Josephus, Antiquities, XII, 168 (4. 3); and cf. V. Tscherikower, Ha-Yehudim veha-Yevanim, 1931, pp. 170 ff.).

72 See M. Rostovtzeff, The Social and Economic History of the Hellenistic World, II, 696; cf. ibid., I, 541.

73 For the development of Egyptian-Palestinian commerce under the Ptolemies, see M. Rostovtzeff in Cambridge Ancient History, VII, 191 ff.; Tscherikower, pp. 150 ff.; ibid., Palestine under the Ptolemies, pp. 43 ff.; W. L. Westerman, Upon Slavery in Ptolemaic Egypt, 1929, p. 59; C. C. Edgar, Zenon Papyri in the University of Michigan Collection, 1931, pp. 17 f.

74 Regarding the Greek cities, see Schuerer, Geschichte[4], II, pp. 95 ff.; Tscherikower, pp. 66 ff.; A. H. M. Jones, The Cities of the Eastern Roman Provinces, 1937, pp. 228 ff.; and V. Tscherikower, Palestine under the Ptolemies (Mizraim, IV–V, 1937), pp. 43–45.

75 Ha-Yehudim veha-Yevanim, pp. 205 ff.

Jerusalem and the Greek cities. A much more radical remedy would naturally occur to the great commercial leaders who did not have the high priestly associations and responsibilities, or any special feeling of loyalty to Jerusalem. Their desire would be to bring about not merely a closer association between the Jewish and the Greek settlements, and thus destroy the more recent trade barriers; they would also naturally like to put an end to the ancient quarrel between Jerusalem and Samaria, through some compromise arrangement. It is entirely intelligible that the descendants of Tobiah the Ammonite, the opponent of Nehemiah, should seek to destroy Jerusalem's claim to being the sole sanctuary; and thus to lay the foundation for a rapprochement between Judah and Samaria.

These conflicting interests among the Palestinian aristocrats apparently brought about a series of fraternal conflicts; or perhaps it is more precise to say, that fraternal rivalries and jealousies sought expression in the imperial conflicts between Egypt and Syria, as well as in the divergent interests of the Palestinian traders. Thus while Onias II, the High Priest, was pro-Egyptian, his younger brother, Jason, was pro-Seleucid. Of the members of the leading lay family of Judaea, the Tobiads — the descendants of Tobiah the Ammonite[76] — the elder brothers were pro-Seleucid; the youngest, Hyrcan, pro-Egyptian.

There was apparently this difference, however, between the pro-Seleucid policy of Jason and that of the older Tobiads; Jason wished to adopt a policy which, preserving the sanctity of the Temple of Jerusalem, would destroy the economic barriers between Jewish and Greek cities in Palestine. The Tobiads, as becomes clear from the sequel, really sought to destroy what they considered the basic barrier to Palestinian unity, the claim of the Temple of Jerusalem to a unique status.

There is evidence of a further conflict regarding the status of the Zadokide high priesthood. The claim of the Zadokides to sole hegemony in the Temple is challenged in the Book of Chronicles, which seems to lay the foundation for a demand that a representative of the Ittamar priesthood be made as-

[76] See Additional Note D for further discussion of the associations of the Tobiads, and a bibliography.

sociate to the Zadokide high priest.[77] There is also evidence that long before the rise of Menelaus to the high priesthood, efforts were being made by the Tobiads to seize this office. A reflection of the need felt by the Zadokide to defend their prerogative may be discerned in Ben Sira's passionate plea on behalf of the dynasty;[78] and even more in the account given in the Book of Chronicles of the dire punishment suffered by King Uzziah, who was not an Aaronid, when he dared usurp the high priestly office.[79] The clearest evidence of the conflict is naturally to be found in the course of historical events, which will now be described.

In the first stage of the struggle between the pro-Seleucid and the pro-Egyptian parties in Jerusalem, the pro-Seleucids, including Jason, the brother of Onias, and the elder Tobiads, acted as a unit. They were, doubtless, all as eager as the Seleucids themselves to stress the kinship between the Jews and the Syrians, and to strengthen every possible recollection of the hostility of Israel and Egypt. It was for this reason that the pro-Seleucids so strongly urged that the citizens of Jerusalem be declared Antiochenes, i.e., citizens of the Syrian capital of Antioch; and their city be made into a Greek *polis*, governed after the manner of a Greek city, and having close associations with the various Greek communities in Palestine.[80]

[77] See Van Rad, Das Geschichtsbild d. Chronistischen Werkes, 1930, pp. 85 ff.; and J. W. Rothstein–J. Haenel, Kommentar zum ersten Buch der Chronik, 1927, p. 429. It is noteworthy that the Chronicler does not regard Zadok but Azariah, son of Johanan, as the first priest of the Solomonic Temple (I Chron. 5. 36); and that he places great emphasis on the line of Ittamar and of Ebiatar, the rivals of the house of Zadok.

[78] Cf. the high praise bestowed by Ben Sira on Phineas, the ancestor of the Zadokides (Ecclus. 45. 23 ff.) and the blessing to God for having chosen the "sons of Zadok to be priests" (ibid., 51. 12, Hebrew text).

[79] II Chron. 26. 16 ff.

[80] The precise meaning to be attached to the phrase, "to register (*anagrapsai*) the Jerusalemites as Antiochenes" (II Macc. 4. 10) is not clear (see with regard to it the discussions in Schuerer, Gesch. d. Volkes Israel[4], II, 145, note 205; Tscherikower, pp. 131 ff.; E. Bickermann, Der Gott der Makkabaeer, p. 59, n. 1; Jones, Cities of the Eastern Roman Empire, p. 252; and The Greek City from Alexander to Justinian, pp. 17, 111; Cambridge Ancient History, VIII, p. 503). But the general purpose of the measure was unquestionably to break down the distinction between Jerusalem as a Temple City, and the Greek cities. For a picture of the relation of the Greek cities as they affected the economy of the countries through which they were scattered, see

The dissatisfaction of the Syrian government with Onias II was expressed on a number of occasions; and once almost led to the intrusion of a Syrian general into the Temple itself. It was not until 175 B.C. when Antiochus IV, Epiphanes, became king, that the Syrian government decided to remove Onias II. It took this action on the suggestion and with the encouragement of Jason, the pro-Seleucid brother of Onias, who coveted the high priestly office for himself. II Maccabees (4. 8) records that Jason promised the Syrian government a considerable increase in the annual tax paid by Judaea; but we may be certain that this offer was not the only, or even the primary, consideration in the change of high priests through governmental control.[81] The Seleucid government would not have endangered its domination of so important and so distant an outpost as Palestine through the appointment of an unsatisfactory high priest, no matter what sums were offered it for this purpose. The government did not object, naturally, to receiving payment from the ambitious and covetous Jason for doing what it believed to be to its interest from the general political point of view.

F. M. Heichelheim, Wirtschaftsgeschichte d. Altertums, I, pp. 532 ff.; and also pp. 637 ff. From the point of view of the Hellenists, the recognition of their group in Jerusalem as Antiochenes was simply giving political expression to an existing cultural fact. They were Antiochenes in spirit. As A. D. Nock has shown, in his St. Paul (1938), p. 94, "The notion that the essence of being a Greek was cultural rather than racial had been voiced earlier; but it was now (in the Hellenistic age) translated into effective reality."

[81] It seems to me curious to suppose that nothing more was involved in the appointment of Jason, and later of Menelaus, than an increased tribute or a bribe. It is true that an ancient oriental court would concern itself very seriously with such considerations (E. R. Bevan, The House of Seleucus, II, 169). Nevertheless, on the eve of war with Egypt, the Seleucid king must certainly have taken a careful measure of the need of integrating his dominion; this is especially clear in the light of subsequent events. Perhaps Bevan's failure to recognize this is due to his assumption that the Jews took the initiative in the matter of the Hellenization of Jerusalem. Obviously, this was true, so far as *formal* communication was concerned; it may be assumed, however, that the initiative of the Jews was in this instance, as in other imperialisms, stimulated from above. Cf. Cambridge Ancient History, VIII, pp. 502, 507. For the question of the extent to which the Seleucid government took the initiative with regard to the Hellenization of the Jews, cf. A. Momigliano, in Atti della R. Accademia d. scienze di Torino, LXVII, 1931–32, p. 195; A. D. Nock, Conversion, 1933, p. 35; E. Bickermann, Der Gott d. Makkabaeer, pp. 117 ff.; and the review of the book by I. Heinemann, in Monatsschrift, LXXXII, 1938, 147 ff.

Jason did not, however, remain in office very long. Before he had completed four years of service as high priest he was himself removed, at the instigation of one Menelaus who, though probably not an Aaronid, succeeded Jason as high priest (II Maccabees 4. 24).[82] This removal of Jason is represented, again, as being the result of nothing more than a generous offer of increased taxes to the Syrian overlords. But surely, Menelaus must have used some other arguments, even more potent than a lavish payment to the government, in order to obtain its consent for the removal of the man who had so recently been appointed high priest. We must assume that the real reason for the removal of Jason was the fact that, despite the charges of Hellenization which are brought against him, he was considered by the Tobiads and the Syrian government, too moderate in his efforts to integrate the Jews into the Syrian state.[83] His derelictions, even according to the record of his opponents, consisted only of the introduction of certain externalities of Greek life into Jerusalem (II Maccabees 4. 11). He obviously remained devoted to the Temple service, and observed its regulations and those of Jewish ritual in general, with the utmost care. The failure of II Maccabees to mention any definite derelictions of Jason in Jewish observance offers ample evidence that Jason did not transgress the Mosaic or traditional law, save in his introduction of the Greek gymnasium, and the ways associated with that institution.

The changes introduced by Jason were highly detrimental to the survival of Judaism, and in the end would have meant its destruction. But Jason must have thought that he could proceed with moderate Hellenization of Jerusalem, and still retain Jewish religious worship as the way of life of the people.

The general assumption that Jason was an apostate is, in-

[82] For the ancestry and family connections of Menelaus, see Additional Note E.

[83] So Tscherikower, p. 204, and apparently also E. Meyer, Ursprung u. Anfaenge d. Christentums, II, 146–148. A slightly deviating view of the situation is taken by E. Bickermann, Der Gott der Makkabaeer, pp. 64 ff. According to him, the moderate policy of Jason might have remained acceptable to the Jews, had not Antiochus IV purposely interfered. On the other hand, W. W. Tarn, Hellenistic Civilization, 1927, p. 170, sees no religious import in the quarrel between the Oniads and the Tobiads. His view seems to be shared by E. R. Bevan in Cambridge Ancient History, VIII, 502 ff.

deed, based only on *ex parte* evidence, namely the view taken of him by the Maccabees and their followers, who had every reason to present him in the worst possible colors. He was the last high priest of the ancient family of Zadok. The Maccabees, beginning with Jonathan, had usurped the high priestly dignity. Indeed, the right of the Maccabees to the high priesthood had ultimately to be established through a "great assembly" summoned under the high priesthood of Simeon, which declared (I Maccabees 14. 41) that Simeon was to be "their leader and high priest forever until a faithful prophet should arise." The "faithful prophet," when he appeared, would decide the status of the Hasmonean dynasty, and also that of the family which they had displaced. Since this displacement of the Zadokide high priestly dynasty which had functioned in the Temple for seven centuries and more, could be justified only if the legitimate dynasty was such that its scions could no longer be considered eligible for the office, the historians of the time were thus virtually compelled to make out a strong case against Jason. Jason had to be presented as a man unworthy for the high priesthood, no matter what his ancestry might be. Hence the emphatic declaration in II Maccabees 4. 13, referring to Jason, "No high priest he!"

The report, however, is without corroboration. Indeed, there is some evidence that earlier writers, whatever they may have thought of Jason's action in displacing his brother Onias, and of the assimilation which he either sponsored or permitted, had little to say in especial condemnation of him. Thus the following passage in Daniel seems to indicate that the apocalyptist regarded the year 172–171, that which marked the removal of Jason, as the one which ushered in the worst seven year cycle in Jewish history: [84]

"Seventy weeks are decreed upon thy people and upon the holy city, to finish the transgression, and to make an end of sin, and to blot out iniquity, and to bring in everlasting righteousness, and to seal vision and prophet, and to anoint the most holy place. Know therefore and discern that from the going forth of the word to restore and build Jerusalem unto an anointed one, a prince, shall be seven weeks; and three-score and two weeks it shall be

[84] The translation follows, generally, that of R. H. Charles, in his Commentary on Daniel.

built again . . . ; and after three-score and two weeks shall an anointed one be cut off . . . and the city and the sanctuary shall be destroyed, together with a prince, . . . and a stringent statute shall be issued against the many for one week; and for half of the week, the sacrifice and meat offering shall cease, and in its stead shall be a horror which appalleth" (Daniel 9. 24–27).

The expression, "the anointed one shall be cut off" in this passage is usually interpreted to refer to the murder of Onias,[85] the high priest whom Jason displaced, at the hands of the Syrian Andronicus. But this interpretation is itself based on prejudices deriving ultimately from the story as told in II Maccabees. Considered in its context, and without any pre-judgment based on II Maccabees, the passage is more naturally interpreted as referring to the removal of Jason from the high priesthood.[86] The apocalyptist sees the period of seventy sabbatical cycles divided into three parts. During the first seven sabbatical cycles (i.e. 581–538 B.C.) there is to be neither high priest nor sacrifice. During the succeeding sixty-two sabbatical cycles, into which the author expands the period 538–172 B.C.,[87] the high priestly family will function again, and sacrifices are offered. Then in the last sabbatical cycle, beginning with 172–171 B.C., and expected to end in 165–164 B.C., there will again be no rightful high priest; and in the second half of this sabbatical cycle, the Temple will be profaned through its being dedicated to Baal Shamem, and through the offering of profane sacrifices. The period 172–170 B.C. is thus noteworthy not so much for the death of a displaced, former high priest, but for the removal of the rightful incumbent of the office, and the displacement of the ancient high priestly dynasty — in other words, for the displacement of Jason by Menelaus.

[85] So R. H. Charles, op. cit., p. 247; E. Meyer, II, 150; W. Kolbe, Beitraege z. syrischen u. juedischen Geschichte, p. 101.

[86] So J. Wellhausen, op. cit., p. 239, note. It is not necessary to follow Wellhausen in his rejection of the story of Onias' assassination, as related in II Macc. 4. 34, in order to accept his interpretation of the passage in Daniel. It seems to me probable that the story of the murder of Onias is authentic; nevertheless, the passage in Daniel does not seem to me to refer to it.

[87] See Schuerer, Geschichte des Volkes Israel[4], III, 266 ff. It is interesting to note that the writers of the earlier period expanded the pre-Seleucid period of the Second Jewish Commonwealth, while since the time of R. Jose and his Seder Olam, Jewish tradition has foreshortened that period.

Clearly this contemporary record does not agree with II Maccabees in holding that the appointment of Jason was the beginning of Jewish apostasy.

The same view seems to be reflected in the source on which Josephus drew for the summary of the events leading to the pre-Maccabean crises. In both the War (I, 31) and the Antiquities, XII, 238 (5, 1) Josephus completely omits all reference to the Hellenizing activities of Jason; indeed, in the War, Jason remains quite unmentioned. The assimilationist endeavor is ascribed in the War to the Tobiads, and in the Antiquities to Menelaus. While it is true that both accounts of Josephus are highly confused, it is nevertheless clear that the tradition he used did not record Jason as the arch-apostate, described in II Maccabees.

The account of the proceedings, retained in the Talmudic traditions, likewise appears to attach little blame to Jason. Despite its obviously legendary character, this account is of some importance, for the element of factual history which it recalls. According to this story, preserved in both the Babylonian and Palestinian Talmudim,[88] Simeon the Righteous "at his death told those present that his son, Onias, should succeed him. Onias' brother, Simeon, who was the elder by two and a half years, was moved to jealousy by this. In his indignation, Simeon said to Onias, 'Come, and let me teach thee the manner of the Temple service (by the high priest).' Simeon thereupon dressed his brother Onias in a close-fitting dress and a girdle" (both parts of the usual women's apparel) "and brought him to the altar. There, Simeon said to his fellow-priests, 'Behold the promise which Onias made to his mistress, and how he has kept it! (He promised her) that on the day when he would officiate as high priest, he would wear her garment and girdle!' The other priests hearing this would have slain Onias, but he fled from them to Alexandria in Egypt."

Clearly this tradition confuses[89] Simeon the Benjaminite, who "fell out with the high priest (Onias) over the management of the city market" (II Maccabees 3. 4), with Jason,

[88] B. Menahot 109b; Yer. Yoma 6. 3, 43c.

[89] Zeeb Yavetz, Toledot Yisrael, IV, 1900, Appendix, pp. 15 ff.

the brother of Onias; and hence telescopes the two quarrels, — the original struggle of Simeon the Benjaminite against Onias, regarding the markets, and the later one of Jason, the brother of Onias, for the high priesthood — into one. But it is obvious from the account, that the tradition which the Rabbinical academies preserved, did not recall Jason as an arch-Hellenizer or apostate. Otherwise, something of the sense of outrage that so unworthy a son of Simeon the Righteous should have succeeded to the high priesthood, would doubtless have been reflected even in the legend. This fact is particularly important because the account — perhaps in a somewhat earlier version — seems to have existed in the time of Josephus and to have been used by him.

The realization that Jason was at the utmost a moderate Hellenizer, and that his activities as described in II Maccabees 4. 8 ff. were in the nature of a compromise between the extremists of the two opposing factions, bears profoundly, as we shall presently see, on the dating of the documents preserved in the Passover Haggadah.

Before attempting to demonstrate the bearing of the character of Jason on the problem before us, it is important that we summarize briefly the international events which were bringing the situation in Jerusalem to a crisis between the years 175 and 167 B.C.

In 173 B.C., the reigning Queen of Egypt, Cleopatra, the widow of Ptolemy V, died; and was succeeded by Ptolemy VI Philometor, a youth under the dominance of the violently anti-Seleucid party. One of the leading members of this group was Lenaeus, a native of Coele-Syria, who like his fellow-partisans, had never accepted the cession of Palestine and Coele-Syria to the Syrian government. The new rulers of Egypt almost immediately initiated warlike movements, and only the appearance of Antiochus IV at the head of an army, which came down the Palestinian coast to Joppa, prevented them from attempting an invasion at once.

It was obvious that war would momentarily break out; and under these circumstances, a strong and extreme pro-Seleucid high priest was desirable in Jerusalem. It was apparently by stressing this need, and presenting himself as the person best equipped to fill it, that Menelaus obtained the high priesthood from Antiochus IV. Menelaus' activities, after he became high priest, fully justified Antiochus' expectations. He turned over the Temple treasures to the Seleucids to help them carry on the war; and doubtless proved himself a willing tool in the hands of the Seleucids in all their undertakings.

In the light of these facts, we can hardly attribute the origin of the pro-Seleucid document, B, to the pro-Egyptian Onias II. Before the year 175, it would also not have been urgent to replace A with some other formula of opening the Passover Haggadah. That year, which marks the end of Onias' high priesthood, and also the beginning of the more vigorous policy of imperial integration by Antiochus IV, seems to be the *terminus a quo* for B.

On the other hand, it is inconceivable that any innovation introduced into the Temple by Menelaus would be countenanced by any Temple authorities of later times. Even Alcimus who followed him, would doubtless have rejected a formula which had been introduced by Menelaus.[90]

We may therefore with a high degree of probability attribute the origin of B and its introduction into the Passover Haggadah to the High Priest Jason, 175–172 B.C. Both its pro-Seleucid overtones, on the one hand, and its insistence on the importance of Jewish worship, on the other, would seem to point to this moderate Hellenist as the author. Once introduced by Jason, B would naturally be retained by Menelaus, his successor; and by Alcimus who apparently was, like Jason, a moderate Hellenist. Indeed, as we have seen, the Jews, regarding the description of their origin in B as far more flattering to themselves

[90] It is not clear whether Alcimus belonged to the Zadokide dynasty. In I Macc. 7. 14, he is described as "a priest of the seed of Aaron." But this failure of the historian to refer to any Zadokide antecedents of Alcimus may be due to a desire to avoid giving offense to the Maccabees. It is clear that Alcimus received the office of High Priest as a moderate; this is implied in the sympathy which the Hasideans expressed for him (ibid.). It is noteworthy, in this connection, that Alcimus was a nephew of the famous Jose ben Joezer, a member of the first Pharisaic "Pair" and hence one of the founders of Pharisaism (see Bereshit Rabbah 65. 22, ed. Theodor, pp. 742–743, Midrash Tehillim 11. 7, ed. Buber 52a). According to the Rabbinic tradition, preserved in these Midrashim, Jose ben Joezer was among those whom Alcimus executed (I Macc. 7. 16).

than that in A, would doubtless be inclined to preserve B, even after the rise of the Maccabees to the high priesthood and to independence.

We have seen above that A served as introduction to M.[91] The question must naturally arise whether any change was made with regard to M, when the pro-Seleucid high priest replaced A with B. We have no explicit information on the point. The Mishna, and the interpretation put upon it by Rab,[92] imply that, while B replaced A as introduction to the Passover Haggadah, M was still recited in its original form. But this may reflect the practice of a later period, and not the original action of the Temple authorities in the pre-Maccabean decade.

Fragments recovered from the Genizah, which have preserved a ritual containing B but not A (following therefore the prescription of Rab), usually contain M in a somewhat abbreviated form.[93] But a responsum of Rab Natronai Gaon indicates that he knew of a ritual which, containing B (in a slightly modified form) rejected M entirely, and retained only the recitation of the Scriptural passage on which M is based, namely Deuteronomy 26. 5–8.[94] Rab Natronai, when asked about the propriety of using this ritual for the Passover evening service, unreservedly denounces it. He holds such a ritual, omitting the commentary on Deuteronomy 26. 5–8, heretical. "Thus said Rab Natronai," we are told in Seder Rab Amram,[95] "A person who in the *Kiddush* (the blessing of sanctification) of Passover uses the formula, 'He Who sanctified Israel,' and at the conclusion of the questions of the child does not say, 'We were Pharaoh's bondmen in Egypt,' nor 'In the beginning our ancestors were worshippers of idols,' but simply the passage, '*And Joshua said,*' etc., until '*Jacob and his sons went down into Egypt;*' and then recites the blessing, 'Blessed is He, Who has preserved His promise to Israel,' and reads the passage, '*arami*

[91] Above, p. 303.

[92] See above, p. 307.

[93] See above, note 35.

[94] Siddur Rab Amram, ed. Warsaw, 1865, 37b; ed. Frumkin, II, 103b; B. M. Lewin, Ozar Ha-Geonim, III, p. 89.

[95] Loc. cit.

'obed 'abi ('my father was a wandering Aramaean') until he completes the passage, precisely as it is in Scripture, without adding the Rabbinical commentary; and then recites the statement of Rabban Gamaliel, the blessing for the redemption, and *Hallel,* — I am very much astonished at such a custom. There is no doubt that a person who follows this custom has failed to fulfil his obligation. But beyond that, he who observes this practice must be declared a heretic, a person divided in his loyalty (to Judaism), one who rejects the teachings of the Sages, and holds the words of the Mishna and the Talmud in contempt. All the communities are under obligation to excommunicate him, and to expel him from the congregation of Israel. . . . Such men are the disciples of Anan (i.e., members of the Karaite sect) . . . who said to his followers, 'Forsake the words of the Mishna and the Talmud, and I will create for you a new Talmud of my own.'"

While it was quite natural for the Gaon to identify this ritual, which he so vigorously opposes, with that of the Karaites, we now know that his view could hardly have been correct. No Karaite writer would have included in a ritual a quotation from the Mishna and particularly a statement by Rabban Gamaliel, one of the most famous of the Talmudic Sages, and the grandson of Hillel. No member of that sect would have agreed to retain the blessings introduced by the Rabbinic Sages (to which Rab Natronai refers as parts of the ritual); nor would the sect preserve the questions formulated in the Mishna for the inquiring child. The ritual denounced by Rab Natronai is therefore definitely not of Karaite origin.[96] On the other hand, Rab Natronai is certainly correct in declaring that the ritual runs counter to all the teachings of the Mishna and the Talmud. We must conclude that this ritual in its original form derived from a period earlier than the Mishna; and though it had been supplemented by Rab Natronai's day, with material deriving from the Mishna itself, it had not lost its main distinguishing characteristics: namely the rejection of A, and the use of B as

[96] J. Lewy in Ein Vortrag ueber d. Ritual d. Pesach-Abends, Breslau, 1904, p. 17 is uncertain regarding the Karaite origin of the ritual cited by Rab Natronai. I. Abrahams categorically denies the possible Karaite character of the work (Jewish Quarterly Review, X, 1898, p. 41)

introduction. It may well be, therefore, that this ritual denounced by Rab Natronai, was in its origin, that introduced in the second century B.C. when the first form of the Passover Haggadah was revised. If this surmise is correct, it follows that when B was substituted for A, M also was rejected, and was replaced by the simple reading of Deuteronomy 26. 5–8.

This would be a change entirely in conformity with the substitution of B for A; for M is definitely Egyptophilic, and would doubtless be as objectionable to the pro-Seleucids as A itself.

Whether the pro-Seleucid revisers retained any part of M in their Haggadah, or rejected it completely, it seems obvious that they ended the quotation from Joshua which they used for B precisely where it ends in the current rituals, namely with the words, "But Jacob and his sons went down into Egypt" (Joshua 24. 4). Their unwillingness to retain the remainder of the passage in Joshua as a record of the Egyptian bondage and the Exodus may have been due to the fact that the passage in Deuteronomy 26. 5–8 was so much better known. But it may also have been due to the fact that Joshua 24. 5 specifically makes mention of Moses and Aaron, as the Divine instruments through whom Israel was redeemed from Egypt. The high priests, and the writers who worked under their direction, definitely avoided any mention of either of these two prophets in connection with the Exodus. To stress the importance of Moses would be to assign an importance to the non-priestly Levites, which was, in the opinion of the high priests, undesirable. And even an emphasis on Aaron might give an importance to the non-Zadokide priesthood,[97] which as we have seen was struggling for recognition during this period.

It thus becomes likely that the older form of the Passover Haggadah consisting of AM was basically revised in the early part of the second century B.C., most probably during the high priesthood of Jason, 175–172 B.C., by the substitution of B, plus Deuteronomy 26. 5–8 for AM. We shall presently see that in all probability, the recitation of this revised Haggadah was followed by the recital or singing of the poem Dayyenu, still preserved in the current rituals of the Haggadah.

[97] See above, note 77.

NOTE 1

[1] The text of the Passover Haggadah has been transmitted in a variety of rituals, and is extant in a vast number of manuscripts and printed editions. S. Wiener, Bibliographie der Oster-Haggadah, lists no less than 895 editions which appeared before 1900. His list has been supplemented by A. Jaari in Kiryat Sefer VI, 1929–30, 531–562; and VIII, 1931–32, 122–126; A. Duker, ibid. VII, 1930–31, 574–584; VIII, 1931–32, 100–121; I. Rivkind, ibid. XII, 1935–36, 230 ff., 360 ff.; B. Simches, ibid. XIII, 1936–37, 138; and Rachel Bernstein-Wischnitzer, bibliography to article Haggadah in Universal Jewish Encyclopedia, Vol. VII. Rivkind's bibliography includes an invaluable compilation of discussions of the history of the Haggadah as a whole, as well as of its various sections. For the purposes of this study I have consulted the following texts representing various rituals of the Passover Haggadah. (The letters indicate the *sigla* used in this article for the various texts.)

(A) Seder R. Amram, Warsaw, 1865, 37b, ff.; cf. A. Marx, Untersuchungen zum Siddur d. Gaon R. Amram (offprint. from Jahrbuch d. jued.-literarischen Gesellschaft V) Berlin, 1908, and Seder R. Amram Ha-Shalem, ed. Frumkin, Jerusalem, 1912, II, 103a, ff.;

(B) Siddur R. Saadia Gaon, ed. I. Davidson, S. Assaf, B. I. Joel, Jerusalem, 1941, 134 ff.;

(C) The Haggadah according to the Rite of Yemen, ed. by W. H. Greenburg, London, 1896, cf. (Ca) Tiklal, Jerusalem, 1894, II, 9a, ff. (Yemenite ritual);

(D) Maimonides, Yad Ha-Hazakah, ed. pr. Rome, 1480 (probably Egyptian ritual);

(E) Haggadah Shel Pesah, Bagdad, 1904 (Bagdad ritual, cf. with this text, the descriptions of the manuscripts of the Bagdad ritual given in D. Sassoon, Ohel David, Descriptive Catalogue of the Hebrew and Samaritan Manuscripts in the Sassoon Library, London, 1932, I, pp. 234–236; II, 836–837);

(F) Manuscript from the Enelow Collection, in the Library of the Jewish Theological Seminary of America, written in Bombay, about 1850;

(G) Manuscript of the Haggadah according to a Syrian rite, in the Library of the Jewish Theological Seminary of America;

(H) Manuscript of the Haggadah, in the Library of the Jewish Theological Seminary of America, written in an oriental hand, and containing an Arabic translation;

(I) Manuscript of an Arabic translation of the Haggadah, in the Library of the Jewish Theological Seminary of America, written in Iraq, in the seventeenth century, and marked minhag Babel;

(J) Fragment of a shorthand Haggadah, described in Jewish Quarterly Review, IX, 1897, pp. 520 f.;

(K) Egyptian Fragments of the Passover Haggadah, published by I. Abrahams in Jewish Quarterly Review, X, 1898, pp. 41 ff. (cf. also ibid., pp. 380–382);

(L) A fragment of the Passover Haggadah, described by Julius Greenstone in Zeitschrift f. hebraeische Bibliographie, XV, 1911, pp. 122–123;

(M) Fragment of the Passover Haggadah published by Prof. Louis Ginzberg in Ginze Schechter, II, pp. 259 ff. (reprinted by B. M. Lewin, Ozar Ha-Geonim III, 154 ff.);

(N) Genizah fragments in the E. N. Adler Collection of the Library of the Jewish Theological Seminary of America, cited as follows:

(Na) 696, 1 ff.;
(Nb) 2755, f. 7;
(Nc) 2841, ff. 39–40;
(Nd) 2845, f. 4;
(Ne) 2857, ff. 13–14;
(Nf) 2919, f. 29;
(Ng) 2935, f. 4;
(Nh) ibid., f. 13;
(Ni) 2945, f. 21;
(Nj) 3130, f. 7;
(Nk) 3214, f. 4;
(Nl) 3222, f. 2;
(Nm) 3288, ff. 7, 8;
(Nn) ibid., f. 11;
(No) 3762, ff. 1–4;

(O) Mahzor Romania, Venice, 1526, IIIa, ff. (Balkan ritual);

(P) Mahzor Turin, according to the collated readings prepared by Solomon Schechter from a manuscript in the Library in Turin. (The original manuscript has since that time been destroyed by fire, so that Schechter's collations remain the only witnesses to the text. They are now in the Library of the Jewish Theological Seminary of America.) Cf. A. Schechter, Studies in Jewish Liturgy, Philadelphia, 1930;

(Q) Shibbale Ha-Leket, by R. Zedekiah ben Abraham, ed. S. Buber, Vilna, 1886, 93a, ff. (Italian ritual);

(Qa) Italian Prayer Book, Bologna, 1541 (later Italian ritual);

(R) The Book of Prayer and Order of Service according to the Custom of the Spanish and Portuguese Jews, edited by M. Gaster, London, 1931, V, pp. 24 ff.;

(S) Spanish Prayer Book, Cod. Adler 1337, in the Library of the Jewish Theological Seminary of America, described by Prof. A. Marx in Jewish Quarterly Review, N. S., XIX, 1929, p. 14, note;

(Sa) Spanish Prayer Book, manuscript of the fifteenth century, described in the article by Prof. A. Marx, loc. cit., note 2;

(Sb) Haggadah, according to manuscript of Spanish Prayer Book, 15th century, in 2 vols. in the Library of the Jewish Theological Seminary of America;

(Sc) Text of the Haggadah in Orhot Hayyim of R. Aaron Ha-Kohen of Lunel, I, Florence, 1750, 82a, ff.;

(Sd) Kol Bo, Section 51;

(T) Mahzor Vitry, ed. Hurwitz, Nurenberg, 1923, pp. 291 ff. (Old French ritual);

(Ta) Manuscript of Mahzor Vitry in the Library of the Jewish Theological Seminary of America;

(Tb) Haggadah in manuscript of Siddur Zarfat, dated 1294, described by Prof. Marx, op. cit., p. 10;

(Tc) Sefer Ha-Orah, ed. Buber, pp. 105 ff.;

(U) Ez Hayyim, by R. Jacob ben Judah of London, as transcribed and published by David Kaufmann, in Jewish Quarterly Review, IV, 1892, pp. 550 ff. (ritual of pre-expulsion England);

(V) Manuscript Jewish Theological Seminary, described by Professor Marx, op. cit., p. 10, written in Worms, 1329 (ancient Rhineland ritual, with traces of foreign influence);

(Va) Minhag Ashkenaz, ed. pr., date unknown, probably *ca.* 1490;

(Vb) Mahzor, Minhag Ashkenaz, Soncino, 1486;

(W) Manuscript of the Haggadah service of the Crimean Jews, in the Library of the Jewish Theological Seminary of America;

(X) First ed. of Passover Haggadah, printed separately, Soncino, 1486;

(Z) The text of the Darmstadt Manuscript of the Passover Haggadah, as given by Bruno Italiener in Die Darmstaedter Pessach-Haggadah, Leipzig, 1927, p. 131. (The other texts cited by Italiener are cited by reference to the page on which the particular ritual is described in his book. With further reference to this work see the review of Professor Alexander Marx, Jewish Quarterly Review, N. S., XIX, 1928–29, pp. 1 ff.)

Further light is shed on the text of the Passover Haggadah by reference to the commentaries, particularly those of Abrabanel and of Abudarham (both Spanish rite). Of the Haggadahs published in recent times, the most valuable from the point of view of textual studies are: E. D. Goldschmidt, Die Pessach-Haggada, Berlin, 1936; and Cecil Roth, The Haggadah, a New Edition, with English translation, introduction and notes, London, 1934. A good selection of Rabbinic commentaries has been reprinted together with the text of the Haggadah, by J. D. Eisenstein, Ozar Perushim ve-Ziyyurim, Haggadah shel Pesach, New York, 1920. For discussions of the history of the Passover Haggadah, see, in addition to the works cited in the text of this article, the following: A. Spanier, art. Haggada in Encyclopaedia Judaica, Vol. VII; and articles "Haggadah, Passover," in Universal Jewish Encyclopedia, Vol. V by A. Spanier, I. Elbogen, and Rachel Bernstein-Wischnitzer; M. Friedmann, Meir ayyin al seder vehaggadah shel lele pesah, Vienna, 1901 (herein Friedmann); E. Baneth, Der Sederabend, Berlin, 1904; J. Lewy, Ein Vortrag u. das Ritual d. Pesach-Abends, Breslau, 1904; and introductions of Goldschmidt and Cecil Roth to their editions of the Haggadah already noted. I am under great obligations to Professor Alexander Marx, Librarian of the Jewish Theological Seminary of America, for making available to me the manuscripts and most of the printed works enumerated above, and others, which will be mentioned hereafter. It is a pleasant duty to express my gratitude also to the librarians of Columbia University, Dropsie College, the Jewish Institute of Religion, and Union Theological Seminary for their unfailing helpfulness and courtesy.

III. The Composition, Dayyenu (D)

The composition dayyenu as preserved in the extant rituals consists of two parts — the first a poem in fifteen strophes (Da), the second a prose summary (Db). It reads as follows: [98]

D

How many are the calls of the Almighty upon our thankfulness!

Da

Ia Had He brought us out of Egypt,
And not executed judgment on them
It had sufficed us!

b Had He executed judgment on them,
But not wrought justice on their gods
It had sufficed us!

c Had He wrought justice on their gods,
And not slain their first-born
It had sufficed us!

d Had He slain their first-born,
And not given us their substance
It had sufficed us!

e Had He given us their substance,
And not cleft us the sea
It had sufficed us!

[98] The translation (altered in accordance with the changes suggested by considerations to be presented in the notes immediately following) is that of Cecil Roth (see his ed. and tr. of the Passover Haggadah, London, 1934).

Reprinted from *The Harvard Theological Review*, Volume 36, 1943.

IIa Had He cleft us the sea,
And not brought us through it dryshod
It had sufficed us!

b Had He brought us through it dryshod,
And not sunk our oppressors in its depths
It had sufficed us!

c Had He sunk our oppressors in its depths,
And not satisfied our wants in the wilderness for forty years
It had sufficed us!

d Had He satisfied our wants in the wilderness for forty years,
And not fed us with the manna
It had sufficed us!

e Had He fed us with the manna,
And not given us the Sabbath
It had sufficed us!

IIIa Had He given us the Sabbath,
And not brought us to the Mount of Sinai
It had sufficed us!

b Had He brought us to the Mount of Sinai,
And not given us the Law
It had sufficed us!

c Had He given us the Law,
And not brought us into the Land of Israel
It had sufficed us!

d Had He brought us into the Land of Israel,
And not built us the Chosen Temple
It had sufficed us!

e [Had He built us the Chosen Temple,
And not appointed a High Priest for us
It had sufficed us!] [99]

Db

How much more so, then, hath the Almighty a double, and redoubled, call upon our thankfulness! For He brought us out of Egypt, and executed judgment on them, and wrought justice on their gods, and slew their first-born, and gave us their substance, and cleft us the sea, and brought us through it dry-shod, and sank our oppressors in its depths, and satisfied our wants in the wilderness for forty years, and fed us with the manna, and gave us the Sabbath, and brought us to the Mount of Sinai, and gave us the Law, and brought us into the land of Israel and built us the chosen Temple, [and appointed a High Priest for us] [100] to atone for all our sins.[101]

99 For this addition to the usual text, see Additional Note F.

100 For the correct reading of this passage see Additional Note F.

101 D is omitted from the Passover Haggadah in the ritual prepared by Maimonides.

The date of this work must be earlier than the time of Rab (middle of the third century of the Christian Era), who refers to it. In commenting on Malachi 3. 10: "If I will not open you the windows of heaven, and pour you out a blessing, *that there shall be more than sufficiency*" (*'ad beli dai*), Rab said, the verse means, "Until your lips shall weary from saying, 'it is sufficient'" (*milomar dai*).[102] Clearly, he has in mind the custom of saying *dayyenu* ("It is sufficient") in the Passover service; and predicted that in the future redemption it will be said not fifteen times, but so many times, as to weary the lips.

A tannaitic source, possibly a generation or more older than Rab, likewise indicates an acquaintance with D. Sifre Deuteronomy thrice (sections 9, Fr. 67a, Fi. 17; 337, Fr. 141a, Fi. 387; 339, Fr. 141a, Fi. 338) describes Moses as the "man who brought us forth from Egypt, and sundered the sea for us, and brought us down the manna, and brought us down the quails, and performed miracles and heroic deeds for us." It is apparent that the author of this passage was acquainted with D. Indeed the author's description of Moses is probably intended as a protest against the failure of D to mention the first and greatest of the prophets.

But, as in the case of A, B, and M, it can be demonstrated that D is much more ancient than the third century of the Christian Era.

The poetical portion of D, it is important to note, consists (as indicated in the translation above) of three divisions. The first division is devoted to the mercies shown Israel while in Egypt; the second to those shown Israel during the wandering from Egypt to the Holy Land; the third, to the spiritual goods bestowed on Israel.

The reference to the high priest shows that the work antedates the destruction of the Temple. But even if the text containing that reference be rejected as spurious, it is certain that only a person living during the time of the sanctuary would

---

In that of R. Saadia, it is described as a passage which may be recited, but which is not part of the regular service (see I. Davidson, S. Assaf, B. I. Joel, Siddur R. Saadja Gaon, p. 143).

[102] B. Shabbat 32b; see M. Friedmann, Meir Ayyin, 1895, p. 106.

think of its establishment as the climax of Jewish history; and could fail to refer to it without the customary addition (inserted, indeed, in some rituals) "may it speedily be restored."

The year 70 of the Christian Era is therefore the *terminus ad quem* for this poem. The *terminus a quo* is the year 198 B.C., when Palestine was finally occupied by the Seleucids. The fierce vindictiveness against the Egyptians displayed in the poem contrasts sharply with the manifest Egyptophilism of A and M; and could not have been introduced, or permitted to persist, in a poem recited at the Passover celebration, under the Ptolemaic rule.

Careful analysis enables us to fix the date within more definite limits. D is obviously profoundly influenced by the prayer in Nehemiah 9. 6 ff., as can be seen by comparing the lists of miracles in the two works. Thus, Nehemiah 9. 10 ff. reads: "And Thou didst show signs and wonders upon Pharaoh, and on all his servants, and on all the people of his land . . . (11) and Thou didst divide the sea before them, so that they went through the midst of the sea on the dry land; and their pursuers Thou didst cast into the depths like a stone into the mighty waters . . . (13) Thou camest down also upon Mount Sinai, and spokest with them from heaven, and gavest them right ordinances and laws of truth, good statutes and commandments; (14) and madest known to them Thy holy sabbath, and didst command them commandments, and statutes, and a law, by the hand of Moses Thy servant; (15) and gavest them bread from heaven for their hunger, and broughtest forth water for them out of the rock for their thirst, . . . (20) Thou gavest them also Thy good spirit to instruct them, and withheldest not Thy manna from their mouth and gavest them water for their thirst. (21) Yea, forty years, didst Thou sustain them in the wilderness and they lacked nothing. . . . (22) Moreover Thou gavest them kingdoms and peoples, which Thou didst allot quarter by quarter, so that they possessed the land of Sihon, even the land of the King of Heshbon, and the land of Og, King of Bashan. . . . (24) So the children went in and possessed the land, and Thou didst subdue before them the inhabitants of the land, the Canaanites. . . ."

D also has close relationship with Psalms 135–136, which likewise enumerate the miracles done on behalf of Israel. Yet all of these strongly emphasize the victories of Israel over Sihon and Og, which are unmentioned in D, though the Passover celebration, under an autonomous Jewish government, might seem a particularly appropriate time for referring to these early victories of Israel. The omission of any reference to them, as well as the silence of the poet regarding any military achievements by Israel, seems to indicate a period when the Jews were under the domination of other peoples, and did not dare refer to their early military prowess. The period between 164 and 63 B.C. should therefore be excluded as a possible time for the origin and insertion of this poem in the Passover Haggadah.

Indeed it is quite improbable that D was composed any time after 164 B.C. This follows from the failure of the poet to make any mention of Jerusalem as a holy city. It might have been expected that the five spiritual gifts for which a poet would express thanks to God would be: (*a*) the Sabbath; (*b*) the Torah; (*c*) Palestine; (*d*) Jerusalem; (*e*) the Temple. This poet deliberately omits Jerusalem; though that omission makes it necessary for him to divide the miracle of the Revelation into two parts: the approach to Mount Sinai, and the Giving of the Torah.

The importance of Jerusalem in Judaism was, as indicated above,[103] a subject of controversy during the first part of the second century B.C. At any rate, Ben Sira [104] lays great emphasis on the peculiar sanctity of Jerusalem; whereas the author of Zechariah XII–XIV conceives of a possible eschatological war of Judaea against Jerusalem. Either the son or the grandson of Simeon the Righteous, it must be borne in mind, was actually able to bring himself to establish a Temple at Heliopolis. All these controversies regarding the status of Jerusalem came to an end, however, with the outbreak of the Maccabean war; for that war had for one of its primary purposes freeing the Holy City from Syrian occupation. From that time on, the

[103] See above, Vol. XXXV, pp. 317 f.

[104] Cf. e.g. Ecclus. 36. 17–19.

daily prayers and the blessing after food contained special prayers for Jerusalem.[105] So, too, the various prayers in Daniel lay especial emphasis on Jerusalem. Once gained, this special importance attaching to Jerusalem, as a sacred city, was never lost.[106] The high priestly compiler of D apparently had little feeling for the sanctity of the city. Instead of referring to it as one of the Divine gifts, he preferred to make special mention of the appearance before Mount Sinai. This attitude suggests that he was a pre-Maccabean writer.

The whole tenor of D similarly points to the Hellenistic age as its time of origin. Its spirit is not only un-Rabbinic and un-Pharisaic; it is, in many respects, anti-Rabbinic and anti-Pharisaic. The emphasis on the despoilment of the Egyptians and their sufferings strikes notes alien to the spirit of the Pharisees and the later Rabbinic sages. In the poem no mention is made of Moses or of the dynasty of David. In view of the controversies which surrounded the significance of these men in Jewish history, it is obvious that this omission was deliberate and calculated. Moses is omitted from D for the same reason that he is omitted from M: because the high priestly compilers did not wish to stress the part played in the Exodus by a Levite. Had D been composed after 76 B.C. it would inevitably have become an issue in the controversy between the Pharisees and the Sadducees; and could not have been preserved in the Jewish liturgies. It is obvious from the allusions to D in Rabbinic

[105] Cf. Jewish Quarterly Review, N. S. XVI, 1925, p. 36; XIX, 1929, p. 220. When I wrote the latter article, I still believed that the Book of Jubilees was a product of the latter half of the second century B.C., following in this respect the opinion of R. H. Charles (The Book of Jubilees, 1902, pp. LVIII ff.) and numerous other writers. The belief that the book is really a product of the earlier half of the second century B.C., and is pre-Maccabean, has been supported by E. Meyer, Ursprung u. Anfaenge d. Christentums, II, pp. 45 ff., and W. F. Albright, From the Stone Age to Christianity, pp. 266 ff. A review of the evidence has convinced me that their view is correct. Some of the evidence leading to this conclusion is briefly summarized below, pp. 19 ff.

[106] The curious omission of any reference to Jerusalem or the Holy Temple in the praise of God as the Creator and Deliverer of Israel, in Pss. 135. 3–12 (vv. 1, 2, are obviously an introduction, which is not an integral part of the original psalm; v. 21 is part of the doxology, which is likewise a liturgical addition after the psalm was introduced into the service) and 136. 1–26, may be due to the fact that the essential portions of these psalms were composed during the period of the Maccabean rebellion when the Temple was defiled, and Jerusalem was in the hands of the pagans, so that it would have been blasphemous to mention either as one of God's gifts to Israel.

literature that despite the pointed omission of all mention of it in the Mishna, it was well-known to the Rabbinic sages. Indeed the echoes of it in their casual remarks show that they were in the habit of repeating it frequently. This suggests that D was composed before Pharisaism developed into an organized opposition to the high priesthood, i.e., before the break between the high priesthood and the Pharisees (*ca.* 110 B.C.).

The omissions discussed above show that the date of D cannot possibly be between 167 and 110 B.C.

It follows from this that the poem was composed before 167 B.C.

The conclusion to which these considerations lead us, then, is that D was composed and introduced into the liturgy of the Passover eve during the generation between 198 and 167 B.C. when Palestine was under the rule of the Seleucid government. During the first part of this period Simeon the Righteous served as high priest. In view of the close relations between him and the pre-Pharisaic, Hasidic scribes, it is quite improbable that he was the compiler of this poem. Furthermore, as it is entirely probable that he was the sponsor of the earliest sections of the Passover Haggadah, A and M, it would be strange to find him also responsible for so mundane a work as D.

It is equally improbable that the Egyptophile, Onias II, could have been responsible for so anti-Egyptian a document. We must therefore suppose that D originated under the direction of Jason.

The close relationship between B and D reflected in their common attitude toward Egypt and Syria, as well as in their special emphasis on the Temple ritual, and their common use of the term *Makom* "Place" in referring to God,[107] points to common authorship; and if the suggestion that B was the work of the High Priest Jason be accepted, we may further conjecture that he was also the author of D. It would follow from this that Jason formulated not merely an introduction to the Haggadah to displace that formulated by his father, but also an elaboration of Deuteronomy 26. 5–8, in the form of D, to

[107] Regarding the significance of the use of the terms *Ha-Makom* and *Ha-Kadosh Baruk Hu* in the Passover Haggadah, see Additional Note G.

replace M. The popularity of M̓, however, and its lack of any statement which contemporary Syrians could understand as hostile, prevented its suppression, so that in later times the Temple authorities used as the Passover Haggadah not B, Deuteronomy 26. 5–8, and D, but BM̓.

IV. The *Baraita* of the Four Sons (E)[108]

E has already been cited above (Vol. XXXV, pp. 305 f.). It consists, in its present form, of an introduction and four paragraphs, to which (as indicated above) we may refer as E1 (the wise son), E2 (the wicked son), E3 (the simple son) and E4 (the child unable to ask).

A study of E will show that, unlike A, B, D, and M, it has undergone radical changes; and is no longer in the form originally given it. On the other hand, it is possible to reconstruct that form, and to show that in that original form, E was, like A, B, D, and M, pre-Maccabean in origin. Indeed it is older, in its earliest form, than B or D, dating from the same period as A and M̓, namely the era of Simeon the Righteous, himself.

It is clear that the purpose of E is to explain the four verses in the Pentateuch enjoining upon the father the duty of explaining Jewish ceremonial to his children. Although the passages do not all refer to the ritual of the Passover, they do refer to the Exodus. The compiler of E therefore considers them as redundant, and in accordance with the usual Rabbinic approach

[108] E also occurs in Mekilta Bo, chap. 18, ed. Friedmann 22b, Horowitz-Rabin p. 73, Lauterbach I, p. 166; as well as in Yerushalmi, Pesahim X, 37d. The origin and development of this *baraita* have been widely discussed. See, with regard to it, the notes of Friedmann and Horowitz in the works just cited, and the following: L. Landshut, in Maggid Mereshit, introduction to the Passover Haggadah, Berlin, 1855; Sidon, in Das juedische Literaturblatt, VII, 1878, pp. 110 ff., 114 ff.; the series of articles by David Hoffmann on the subject, in Israel. Monatschrift, 1884, No. 4, pp. 13–14; 1892, No. 4, p. 13; 1894, No. 4, pp. 13–14; Magazin f. d. Wissenschaft d. Judentums, XIII, 1886, pp. 191 ff.; in Bet Vaad La-Hakamim, I, 1902, No. 3, pp. 13 ff.; Ha-Ibri, II, 1911, Nos. 14–15, pp. 164–65; M. Friedmann, in Meir Ayyin al Ha-Haggadah, pp. 42 ff.; A. Marx, in Jewish Quarterly Review, n. s. XIII, 1922–23, p. 517; and XIX, 1928–29, pp. 1 ff.; J. D. Eisenstein, Ozar Perushim ve-Ziyyurim, pp. 9 ff.; A. B. in Ha-Tor, II, 1922, Nos. 24–25, p. 18; S. Lieberman, in Hayerushalmi Kifeshuto, pp. 521 f.; E. D. Goldschmidt, Die Pessach-Haggada, pp. 40 ff.; Cecil Roth, The Haggadah, A New Edition, pp. 14 ff. Hoffmann was the first scholar to recognize the composite character of E, and to show that originally it referred only to three sons.

to the interpretation of Scripture, feels called upon to explain the distinctive significance attaching to each passage. In order to understand E, it is thus necessary to study each of the passages with which it deals. They are Exodus 12. 26 (which we will call A); Exodus 13. 8 (B); Exodus 13. 14 (C); and Deuteronomy 6. 20 (D). The texts of the various passages are as follows:

(A) *Question:* "And it shall come to pass when your children shall say unto you: What mean ye by this service?"

Answer: "Ye shall say, It is the sacrifice of the Lord's passover, for that He passed over the houses of the children of Israel in Egypt, when he smote the Egyptians, and delivered our houses."[109]

(B) *Question:* (lacking).

Answer: "And thou shalt tell thy son in that day, saying: It is because of that which the Lord did for me when I came forth from Egypt."

(C) *Question:* "And it shall be when thy son asketh thee in time to come, saying, What is this?"

Answer: "Thou shalt say unto him, By strength of hand the Lord brought us out from Egypt, from the house of bondage."

(D) *Question:* "When thy son asketh thee in time to come, saying, What mean the testimonies, and statutes, and the ordinances, which the Lord our God hath commanded you?" [110]

Answer: "Then thou shalt say unto thy son, We were Pharaoh's bondmen in Egypt, etc."

Even a cursory examination demonstrates the fact that E is composite. For as it stands now, it fails to fulfil the purpose it sets before itself. To justify the repetition of the commandment that the father recall the exodus to his son, as explanation of the ritual, on the ground that there are various types of sons, who would approach the question differently and would require different forms of reply, the author of E would have to correlate

[109] The four passages do not all deal with the Passover celebration and the question which might be asked concerning it. Indeed, only Exod. 12. 26 ff. and 13. 8 really refer to the Passover ritual. Exod. 13. 14 deals with the redemption of the first-born; and Deut. 6. 20 ff. with the commandments generally. But it was natural that the similarity of the expressions used in all four passages, and the reference to the Exodus, should have convinced the ancient commentator that all of them dealt with the same situation. This is an implied premise, which colors the whole approach.

[110] For the variant reading of the Septuagint and some texts of the Vulgate, see below.

both questions and replies with his classification of the sons. This, however, he fails to do. So far as the question is concerned, A is supposed to deal with the wicked son; but the reply offered in that passage is completely ignored. Answer B is used for both the wicked son and the child unable to ask. Question D is explained as addressed to the wise son, but reply D is not the verse commanded in Scripture, but a citation from the Mishna![111]

Moreover, the very classification of the sons leaves much to be desired. The classification is essentially based on grade of intellectual development. B applies to the child unable to ask; C to the simple child; and D to the wise child. An entirely new standard is introduced when A is made to refer to the "wicked son."

Light is shed on these problems by the discovery that the section dealing with the wicked son occurs also outside of E, in a completely unrelated *baraita*, preserved in Mekilta, on Exodus 13. 8,[112] which reads as follows:

> (*And thou shalt tell thy son in that day saying,*) "*It is because of that which the Lord did for me* (*when I came forth out of Egypt*)."
>
> What purpose is served by this verse? Because the Scriptures say, (above, Exodus 12. 26) "And it shall come to pass when your children shall say unto you, What mean *ye* by this service?" This obviously refers to the wicked son, who has withdrawn from the community. Because he has withdrawn from the community, do thou also reject him from the community, (saying), "It is because of that which the Lord did for me when I came forth out of Egypt." The implication of the phrase *for me* is *not for thee*; that is to say, "Hadst thou been there, thou wouldst not have been redeemed, for thou didst withdraw from the community."

It is clear from a study of this passage that its author was either unacquainted with E or rejected its basic teaching. For according to E, there is no point to the question raised in this passage. Exodus 13. 8 is intended, according to E, to apply to the son who is unable to ask questions, and has to be given an explanation of the Passover without any preliminary inquiry.

[111] This difficulty was noticed by Don Isaac Abrabanel in his commentary on the Passover Haggadah.

[112] Ed. Friedmann 21a, Horowitz-Rabin p. 66, Lauterbach I, p. 149. Mekilta of R. Simeon ben Yohai 12. 26, ed. Hoffmann, p. 21, cites this interpretation in a somewhat abbreviated form.

The passage of Mekilta just cited indicates, however, no awareness of this obligation to explain the Passover to the child who is unable to ask. The author of the passage therefore properly asks what purpose is intended by the verse, Exodus 13. 8, in offering an explanation of the Passover, beyond that given in other verses.

It is equally obvious that the author of E was unaware of or rejected the comment now found in the passage cited from Mekilta. For, had the author of E known and accepted that comment, he would not have said that Exodus 13. 8 is intended as a statement for the son who is unable to ask; the comment in Mekilta would have indicated to him that Exodus 13. 8 is really an extended reply to the question presented in Exodus 12. 26.

These considerations suggest, of course, that the part of E dealing with the wicked son is really an insertion; and that originally E consisted of only three paragraphs dealing with the wise son, the simple son, and the son who cannot ask questions. This suggestion is strengthened by the fact that the paragraph about the wicked son occurs, according to one text of E, after that of the simple son; while in the other two texts, it precedes the paragraph about the simple son. Such difference between texts in regard to the location of a paragraph frequently indicates a later insertion.

It follows from these considerations that E in its present form consists of a combination of two different, and, indeed, opposing traditions.[113] The first is a tradition which knows of *three* sons:[114]

[113] Azulai in his commentary on the Passover Haggadah (Simhat Ha-Regel, Lemberg, 1863) suggests that Exod. 12. 26 deals with two types of children, the good and the wicked, and therefore uses the plural, "your children," while the other passages speak only of "thy son." Similarly, and with a modern approach, Hoffmann in a series of articles indicates his belief that the present form of E has resulted from a combination of two earlier texts, one of which knew of three types of sons, the wise, the foolish, and the one too young to ask; the other dealt with two types of sons, the pious (*tam*) and the wicked (see his articles listed in note 108). As will be seen below, however, the reading *tam*, on which this analysis is based, is a euphemism introduced in the Passover Haggadah, for the word *tippesh* "fool," used in the older forms of E.

[114] It should be noted, perhaps, that another part of the Passover celebration, which at present has four parts, originally had only three. The "four questions" formulated for the child in the extant rituals are an expansion of *three* questions prescribed in the Mishna, according to the best texts (so Mishna Pesahim 10. 4, as printed in Yer. Pesahim 37b.; Mishna, ed. Lowe, p. 48; and other texts cited in ed. Wilna, 1927).

the youngest son, unable to ask, Exodus 13. 8; the simple son, who only asks, "What is this?"; and the wise son of Deuteronomy 6. 20. The author of E, in its original form, did not take Exodus 12. 26 into account because that verse speaks of "children" (in the plural), and therefore may be taken to include the children referred to in the other verses, all of which read "thy son" in the singular. Furthermore, Exodus 12. 26 does not use the word "ask" but "say."

The tradition preserved in Mekilta on Exodus 13. 8 derives from a totally different background. It doubtless reflects the widespread apostasy from Rabbinic Judaism in the latter part of the first and the beginning of the second century. Some of those who rejected the ceremonial law were Christians; others, like Elisha ben Abuyah, were merely Romanophiles.[115] The author of this *baraita* finds a reference to these men "who withdraw from the community" in the question, "What mean *ye* by this service?" (The English rendering hardly can be made to supply the force which can be put into the Hebrew; according to the author of the comment in Mekilta the passage should be interpreted, "What is all this drudgery of yours for?"[116]) The author doubtless notes that in this instance the Scriptures use the word "say," which might be a challenge, rather than "ask," which could only be an inquiry.

A later compiler, knowing both traditions, combined them; and transformed the older *baraita* of three sons into one of four sons.

In addition to recognizing that the whole of E2 is an insertion from another source, it is important to note that E1 is no longer in its original form. This seems obvious from the fact that while the question cites the Scripture according to a reading which seems to have disappeared from the Hebrew text at an early date, the reply cites a passage from the Mishna, and is therefore probably to be dated after the rise of the Schools of Shammai and Hillel in the first century of the Christian Era.[117]

115 See my remarks in Akiba, pp. 254 ff.

116 This excellent rendering is that of Maurice Samuel, in his translation of the Passover Haggadah (New York, 1942).

117 For the date of Mishna Pesahim, chap. X, see D. Hoffmann, Die Erste Mischna, Beilage z. Jahres-Bericht d. Rabbiner-Seminars zu Berlin, pro 1881–82, pp. 16 ff.;

The question reads: "What mean the testimonies, and the statutes, and the ordinances which the Lord our God hath commanded *us*?"[118] As noted above, the reading "commanded us" is found only in the Septuagint and those texts of the Vulgate which appear to be dependent on it.[119] The Massoretic Text, and all the other versions, including the Samaritan, read, "commanded *you*."[120] In view of the agreement of the other versions and the Massoretic Text, this reading must be presumed to be at least as old as the middle of the second century B.C. The passage containing the pre-Massoretic reading must therefore belong to an earlier period.

Further suspicion on the originality of the present text of E1 is cast by the fact that it does not really make sense. The injunction to "teach him the laws of the Passover, etc." cannot be considered a reply to the question asked. The particular rule mentioned is only one of many, and there seems no special reason for its mention. Friedmann, in his notes on Mekilta 22b, suggests therefore, that the particular passage is cited because the compiler of E knew it as the *last* of the rules of the Passover; in other words, the final passage in his text of Mishna Pesahim. Friedmann believes therefore that the correct reading of the passage should be "Teach him the laws of the Passover ritual *until* (the passage) 'It is forbidden to end the Passover meal with entertainment.'" Friedmann states that he recalls seeing the word *'ad* ("until") in some text, but was unable to locate it at the time of his writing the note.[121] I, too, have been unable to locate any such text of E despite my examination of numerous texts of the Passover Haggadah. On the other hand, there are texts where the passage, "It is forbidden to end the Passover meal with entertainment," is replaced by the one

---

Zebi Carl, Pesahim, Introduction, pp. LXXII ff. and Appendix I, pp. 93 ff. This view is also adumbrated, apparently, by M. Friedmann in his edition of Mekilta 22b, note 23.

[118] See above, note 38, for the variant readings of the different texts of the Passover Haggadah.

[119] See variant readings in Biblia Sacra iuxta Latinam Vulgatam Versionem, Rome, 1936, ad loc.

[120] This reading is also found in Vetus Latina, see U. Robert, Pentateuchi Versio Latina Antiquissima, Paris, 1881.

[121] See also Friedmann, pp. 44 ff.

word, *afikoman* ("entertainment") the last word in the sentence, according to the original. This obvious abbreviation of the text suggests the likelihood that the larger citation, which includes the whole passage, "It is forbidden, etc.," is likewise an abbreviation, standing for the whole of the tenth chapter of Pesahim. Accordingly, the text required the father to teach his son *all* the laws of the Passover ritual, ending with the final norm, "It is forbidden, etc." This would mean that at one time E included in itself, at this point, the whole of what now constitutes Mishna Pesahim 10. 1–7; and required that part of the Mishna to be offered as reply to the wise son.[122] For the sake of brevity the transmitters of E omitted everything but the last line of the Mishna in citing it, some going so far as to omit everything but the last word. In any event, it is clear that the passage goes back to a time when the tenth chapter of Mishna Pesahim still did not contain the three last paragraphs of the present text; for in our text, the statement, "It is forbidden to end the Passover meal with entertainment," is paragraph 7, and is followed by several other rules.

But it is also clear that, in its earliest form, E could not have contained either the present abbreviated quotation from Mishna Pesahim, chapter X, or even the older, unabbreviated quotation of the whole chapter. As its purpose is to explain the significance of each passage in the Torah mentioning the inquiring son, E necessarily had to deal with each question and answer, and to show how both applied to distinctive types of children. E1 indicates how question D applies to the wise son; but in substituting a passage from Rabbinic literature for that provided in Scripture, it evades the main issue.[123] It follows therefore that in the original form of E1 the reply to the wise son must have been that provided in D, namely, the passage beginning, "We were Pharaoh's bondmen, etc." This part of E1 had to be changed because in the course of time, as we have seen, the practice changed; and the use of the reply "We were

[122] This interpretation is that given in Friedmann, loc. cit., and notes on Mekilta. It is also implied in the comment of Abrabanel on the passage.

[123] Rabbi Elijah Gaon of Wilna, taking note of this difficulty, explains that E requires both the biblical answer, Deut. 6. 21, "We were Pharaoh's bondmen, etc.," as well as the citation from the Mishna.

Pharaoh's bondmen, etc." fell into desuetude, being replaced by the passage, denominated B, above.

We have seen [124] that the substitution of B for A in the Passover Haggadah occurred, probably, about the year 175 B.C.

This, then, is the *terminus ad quem* for the original formulation of E. After that time, there was no way in which the various passages in Scripture dealing with the inquiring son could be explained in such a way as to harmonize with existing practice; for the most important son, namely the wise one, of Deuteronomy 6. 20, was given another answer than that prescribed.

This explains the fact that the biblical text in E1 follows the reading preserved in the Septuagint. E1 derives from a time when the Hebrew text was still in the form which lay before the authors of the Septuagint, antedating that of all the other versions.

The period 175–172, when B was formulated, is also the *terminus a quo* for the revision of E1, by the substitution of the citation from the Mishna for the original answer, that prescribed in Scripture. It is probable, however, as we have seen, that the adaptation of E to current practice was made much later, in the first generation of the Christian Era.

The text of E as cited in Yerushalmi from the collection of R. Hiyya differs from those in the Passover Haggadah and Mekilta in interchanging the replies of the wise and the foolish sons. According to R. Hiyya's tradition, reply B is offered to the wise son; while as to the foolish son, who asks, "What is this?" the father is instructed, "Do thou therefore teach him the laws of the Passover ritual, *namely that* it is forbidden to end the Passover meal with entertainment."

It is clear that the text of Mekilta and the Passover Haggadah is, in this respect, to be preferred to that of Yerushalmi. For reply B is prescribed in Scripture to the inquiry, "What is this?" which is imputed to the simple or foolish child according to all texts, and not to the longer question, "What are the testimonies, and the statutes, etc.," which all texts agree in imputing to the wise son. Moreover, it is intrinsically more

[124] See above, Vol. XXXV, p. 326.

natural that instruction in the Law should be offered to the wise son, rather than the simple or foolish one. It follows that the present text of Yerushalmi must be the result of either a copyist's or a transmitter's error or editorial revision. On careful consideration, I have come to the conclusion that the change was editorial, probably made by R. Hiyya himself. The reason for the change was the failure of the transmitter or compiler to understand that the phrase, "teach him the laws of Passover, etc.," referred not to the particular rule mentioned, but to the whole chapter, ending with that passage. R. Hiyya could not have guessed this latter meaning, for the Mishna of Pesahim, chapter X, in his day no longer ended with the passage, "It is forbidden, etc." He therefore supposed that this rule was selected by the author of E for some special reason. Why? Because the son was likely to indulge in revelry after the Passover meal. But what type of son was to be warned against such behavior? Certainly not the wise son; but rather the foolish son. Hence, R. Hiyya came to the conclusion that the text he had received ought to be emended, by making reply B that addressed to the wise son (A); and declaring that the suggestion, "Do thou therefore teach him the laws of the Passover ritual, namely that it is forbidden, etc.," was intended as reply to the foolish son.[125]

We may therefore conclude that E passed through the following stages of development:

A. A *baraita* of three sons, which read, "The Torah deals with three types of children, the 'wise son,' the 'foolish son,' and the child who cannot ask. (*a*) The wise son says, 'What mean the testimonies and the statutes, and the ordinances,

[125] Azulai, in his commentary, cited above, quotes a manuscript of the commentary on the Passover Haggadah by R. Isaiah di Trani according to which the reply "Do thou therefore teach him the laws of the Passover ritual, etc.," was given *to the wicked son*. We have no other trace of such a version of E, and it seems probable that the manuscript of the commentary used by Azulai was defective, for in the ed. of R. Isaiah di Trani's commentary on the Passover Haggadah (see M. Krengel, Shaare Geulah, Cracow, 1896, p. 17) the response is assigned to the "wise son" as in other rituals. Azulai, referring to the view of R. Isaiah as recorded in his commentary on the Passover Haggadah, and as cited further in Shibbale Haleket, assumes that R. Isaiah changed his mind regarding the proper text of E (see Simhat Ha-Regel, Lwow, 1782, 100a).

which the Lord, our God, hath commanded us?' Do thou also reply to him, 'We were Pharaoh's bondmen in Egypt, and the Lord brought us out of Egypt with a mighty hand and an outstretched arm.' (*b*) The 'foolish son' says 'What is this?' And thou shalt say unto him, 'By strength of hand the Lord brought us out from Egypt, from the house of bondage.' As for the child who cannot ask, do thou begin for him, even as it is written. 'And thou shalt tell thy son in that day saying: It is because of this which the Lord did for me when I came forth from Egypt.'"

This *baraita* was compiled, as we have seen, either toward the end of the third century or in the first third of the second century B.C. To sum up, the evidence for this derives from the following considerations: (1) it follows the reading of the Scriptures according to the Septuagint, in opposition to all other texts; (2) the reply to the "wise son" was changed between 175 and 172 B.C., and no *baraita* compiled after that date would have assumed the reply to the "wise son" to be that prescribed in the original form of E.

B. Some time between 175 B.C. and the year 70 of the Christian Era (but probably much nearer the latter date than the former) E was revised to conform with current practice, which no longer used the reply prescribed in it for the "wise son." Hence the reply to the "wise son" was changed from the statement "we were Pharaoh's bondmen, etc.," and made into a recitation of the rules of the Passover. Perhaps this was done for the very purpose of inculcating respect among the many pilgrims for the emerging compilations of the Rabbinic tradition. It doubtless was of some importance that one of these compilations should be prescribed as the proper reply to a "wise son" making inquiry about the Passover.

C. In the second century of the Christian Era, the *baraita* was further revised by the interpolation of an extraneous passage, from quite another source, dealing with the "wicked son."

D. Another change was made by R. Hiyya, toward the very end of the second century or early in the third century B.C.; a change, however, which has affected only the text cited from

R. Hiyya's collection in the Yerushalmi, namely the interchange of the replies to the wise and to the foolish son, with each other.

E. A final change was made when the *baraita* itself was introduced into the Passover Haggadah. The reference to the child who asked the simple question, "What is this?" as the "foolish son" seemed inconsistent with the purpose of the Passover celebration, as conceived in later Rabbinic times, to stimulate questions by the children, so that they may learn. Hence the opprobrious term *tippesh* (fool) used in E, according to the versions found in both Mekilta and Yerushalmi, was replaced in the Passover Haggadah by the less objectionable expression *tam*, "the simple son."

The *baraita* was introduced into the Passover Haggadah from some source other than R. Hiyya's collection; since the change, noted under D, was not included in the text of the Passover Haggadah.

APPENDIX

THE DATE OF THE BOOK OF JUBILEES

Eduard Meyer,[126] and, following him, W. F. Albright,[127] have indicated their belief that the Book of Jubilees was composed about the beginning of the second century B.C. The light thrown on the pre-Maccabean struggles between the priests and the laity definitely shows that the preconceptions which led R. H. Charles and others to date the book toward the end of the second century B.C. must now be reconsidered. It appears to me, however, that the *terminus a quo* for the book is provided by its severe denunciation of the Greek habit of appearing naked in the gymnasia. According to the author, Noah commanded his sons, (*a*) "to observe righteousness, and (*b*) to cover the shame of the flesh, and (*c*) to bless their Creator, and (*d*) to honor father and mother, and (*e*) to love their neighbor, and (*f*) to guard their souls from fornication and uncleanness and all iniquity" (Jubilees 7. 20). As I have shown,[128] these six commandments are really a paraphrase of the six Noachic commandments of the Rabbinic tradition. This can be proved from the fact that the commandment "to observe righteousness" is the precise equivalent of *dinim* or "the observance of civil laws" in the Rabbinical form of the Noachic code; and the curious relation of the commandment "to bless their Creator," to that of *birkat ha-shem,* literally, "blessing the Name of God," but used in its own context euphemistically for a prohibition against blasphemy. Either the writer of the Book of Jubilees decided to substitute the positive commandment to bless God for the negative commandment of the Pharisaic code, or the Greek translator misunderstood the meaning of the Hebrew. The sixth, the commandment against fornication, is identical with that of the Rabbinical Noachic

[126] Ursprung u. Anfaenge d. Christentums, II, pp. 45 ff.

[127] From the Stone Age to Christianity, pp. 266 ff.

[128] H. T. R., XVI, 1923, pp. 59 ff.; and Journal of Biblical Literature, XLIX, 1930, pp. 21 ff. Ch. Albeck, Das Buch d. Jubilaeen u. d. Halacha, Berlin, 1930, p. 34 is alone in denying any association between this passage in Jubilees and the Noachic laws of the Talmud. He is right, however, in rejecting E. Schuerer's thesis that the author of the Book of Jubilees could not have known of the Rabbinic code of Noachic laws, and created one which was entirely independent of that known to normative Judaism (see Schuerer[4] III, p. 179). Albeck asserts (p. 59) that "*die Angaben Finkelsteins S. 60 f. wie seine Ausfuehrungen sind unrichtig*" and proceeds simply to refer to the midrashic texts which I cite without further discussion. A re-examination of these texts does not indicate to me any need for the change either of the interpretations I gave, or the conclusions I drew. The view that the passage in Jubilees is closely associated with the Rabbinic tradition regarding the Noachic laws is further upheld by L. Ginzberg, The Legends of the Jews, V, p. 193, note 67; and M. Guttmann, Das Judentum u. seine Umwelt, p. 105.

code. The other three items in the Noachic code of the Book of Jubilees take the place of the prohibitions against idolatry, against homicide, and theft in the corresponding Rabbinic code. It is easy to see that the writer might well have decided to replace the prohibition of murder with the commandment to love one's neighbor; the prohibition of idolatry with the commandment to honor one's father and mother (for there was little danger of idolatry in Israel at the moment); and the commandment against theft seemed included in that to observe righteousness; thus leaving a lacuna which could be filled by the prohibition against appearing naked.

Now we know that one of the worst charges against Jason was his establishment of a gymnasium where the youth of Jerusalem disported themselves naked, after the manner of the Greeks (I Maccabees 1. 14; II Maccabees 4. 11). It is clear that what evoked the denunciation of the zealous author was this situation and not any awareness of the habits of the Greeks in their own cities. The year 175 B.C. when Jason became high priest is thus the *terminus a quo* for this book.

Presumably, however, the book was composed while the issue was still a burning one; for after the Maccabean wars the issue was ended for the Jews, and it would no longer have been necessary to stress the "covering of the flesh" as one of the cardinal ordinances of all human life, revealed by God to Noah.

There is other evidence pointing to the period preceding the Maccabean wars as the date of this book. In the following passage, the author evidently projects the situation of the third century and early decades of the second century B.C. to the period of the patriarchs: "For he (Joseph) knew that the Egyptians would not bring him forth and bury him in the land of Canaan, for Makamaron, king of Canaan, *while dwelling in Assyria*, fought in the valley with the King of Egypt and slew him there, and pursued after the Egyptians to the gates of Ermon. But he was not able to enter, for another, a new king, had become king of Egypt, and he was stronger than he (the king of Canaan) and he returned to Canaan, and the gates of Egypt were closed, and none went out and none came into Egypt" (Jubilees 46. 6 ff.). The reference to the king of Canaan, dwelling in Assyria, seems a direct reflection of the Seleucid conditions; for to the Palestinian the Seleucids were kings of Coele-Syria, primarily, though they sometimes resided in distant Mesopotamia. The closing of the frontiers of Egypt because of the war conditions is an obvious reflection of the situations which developed in the period of Seleucid-Ptolemaic struggle for Palestine. Moreover, the author continues, "And the king of Egypt went forth to war with the king of Canaan in the forty-seventh jubilee . . . and the children of Israel brought forth all the bones of the children of Jacob save the bones of Joseph, and they buried them in the field in the double cave in the mountain. And most (of them) returned to Egypt, but a few remained in the mountains of Hebron." Certainly, this description of an invasion of Palestine by Egypt, in which the Egyptian army included a number of Jewish soldiers who remained in Palestine, seems to be a projection of contemporary conditions. The account of the war ends with the following verses: "And the king of Canaan was victorious over the king of Egypt, and he closed the gates of Egypt. And he devised an evil device against the children of Israel of afflicting them; and he said unto the people of Egypt: 'Behold the people of the children of Israel have increased and multiplied more than we. Come and let us deal wisely with them before they become too many, and let us afflict them with slavery before war come upon us and before they too fight against us; else they will join themselves unto our enemies and get them up out of our land, for their hearts and faces are towards the land of Canaan.'" Here again we note the conditions of the Hellenistic age, though they are projected in a somewhat changed form into that of the patriarchs. Ultimately Palestine falls into the hands of the king of Canaan (the Seleucids); and he closes the frontiers of Egypt. This is doubtless a projection into earlier antiquity of the interruption of trade which so greatly disturbed the Jews, after the conquest of Palestine by Antiochus III (see above notes 67–68). The author is keenly aware, too, of the fear of the imperial government that the Jews of the country might prove disloyal to it. It is in the light of the Seleucid apprehensions regarding the pro-Egyptian party among the Jews and the efforts made to prevent that party from taking the side of Egypt in a war, that the author interprets Exodus 1. 9.

This vivid awareness of conditions as they developed during Syrian-Egyptian wars would itself make it probable that the writer lived in the early part of the second century. It is true that the story of the Egyptian-Canaanite wars of patriarchal times occurs also in the Testaments of the Twelve Patriarchs (Testament of Simon 8 and Testament of Benjamin 12) and that the story in Jubilees may be dependent on that account, or both accounts may come from some earlier source, which has been lost. But the story in the Book of Jubilees has peculiarities of its own, which seem to have been composed by the author of that work, and therefore may be used in fixing his date.

It is further noteworthy that the Book of Jubilees is definitely hostile to Egypt and friendly to Syria. The author considers it meritorious that the patriarchs should marry Aramaean women (Jubilees 34. 20; 41. 1). He records that the "people of Egypt abominated the children of Israel" (Jubilees 46. 16), thus projecting the Egyptian antisemitism of his own time to an earlier age! But in making this projection he is still apparently unaware of the development of Seleucid antisemitism under Antiochus IV.

The period of the author seems further to be determined by his attitude toward the priesthood. Following other writers on the subject I assumed in my earlier discussions [129] that the Book of Jubilees is pro-priestly in its tendencies. A re-examination of the evidence shows that this is an error. It is noteworthy that neither the Book of Jubilees, nor the Testaments of the Twelve Patriarchs which is so closely related to it, mentions Aaron, though both mention Moses, and the Book of Jubilees mentions also Amram (46. 10) and even Miriam (47. 4). The emphasis put on Levi, as high priest, and the ancestor of priests, in both the Book of Jubilees and the Testaments of the Twelve Patriarchs, must therefore be understood as referring to the whole tribe of Levi, rather than to the Aaronids alone.[130] It is noteworthy, in this connection, too, that the halaka of the Book of Jubilees definitely destroys the distinction between the Aaronids and the other Levites with regard to the law of tithes, holding that the tithes are to be given to the sons of Levi who are the priests, and that the tithe of the tithe, which according to the Pentateuch (Numbers 18. 25 ff.) belongs to the Aaronids, is to be consumed by the Levites themselves within the Temple precincts.[131]

In the light of this tendency to obliterate the distinction between the Aaronids and the Levites, the Book of Jubilees must, like the Testaments of the Twelve Patriarchs, derive from circles closely associated with the Chronicler who, like the author of these works, is strongly pro-Levite in his sympathies.[132]

The movement which found literary expression in the work of the Chronicler doubtless had wide ramifications. We must bear in mind that this movement was able to influence the formulation of the charter of liberties granted the Jews by Antiochus III (regarding which, see above, Vol. XXXV, p. 314). In that Charter, the Levitical singers were for the first time given official recognition as exempt from taxation. Undoubtedly this Charter was drawn up only after consultation with Jewish leaders; indeed, John, of the priestly clan of Hakkoz, the father of Eupolemus, who was later sent by Judah the Maccabee as envoy to the Romans, seems to have been one of the most important of these leaders (II Maccabees 4. 11). The recognition granted to the Levitical singers and scribes was thus an achievement of importance

[129] See HTR, loc. cit., p. 53; and Journal of Biblical Literature, XLIX, 1930, pp. 34 ff.

[130] See Ch. Albeck, op. cit., p. 30, whose views in this regard I now completely accept.

[131] See HTR, loc. cit., p. 53; Ch. Albeck, op. cit., pp. 30 ff.

[132] See R. H. Pfeiffer, Introduction to the Old Testament, pp. 794 ff.; G. V. Rad, Das Geschichtsbild d. Chronistischen Werkes, pp. 88 ff.; Rothstein-Haenel, Kommentar z. ersten Buch d. Chronik, II, pp. XXXIII ff.; cf. W. F. Albright, in Journal of Biblical Literature, XL, 1921, p. 119.

not only for the Jews as a people, but for the special group within Judaism which had sought this recognition. In the public reading of the Torah, presumably organized into its present ritual form during the third century B.C., the Aaronid was given precedence, of course; but the status of the Levite, too, was recognized, and he was given the second place.[133] The Sect of Damascus, which is so closely related in its outlook, and probably also in the date of its origin, to the Book of Jubilees, similarly recognizes the Levites as a special group, second only to the Aaronids, and above the other members of the House of Israel.[134]

The Book of Jubilees, like the Testaments of the Twelve Patriarchs, goes further than the other works, in completely obliterating all distinction between Aaronid and Levite. It is hard to believe that any such effort could have been undertaken during the Maccabean period, when the Jews as a whole must have felt so endlessly indebted to the Hasmonean family for their leadership in the war. Nor is it credible that after the great victory for the Torah, signalized in the frustration of the Syrians by the handful of Maccabees, any group of Jews would be willing to accept or to sponsor such deviations from the Law as were proposed in the Book of Jubilees.[135]

It is especially noteworthy that the Book of Jubilees reflects none of the bitterness which was engendered by the break between the Pharisees and the Sadducees. On the contrary, its deviations from normative Judaism are intended consistently as compromises, intended to bring together the extreme wings of *observant* Judaism.[136] The only group to which it is definitely opposed is that of apostates and Hellenizers. The issues with which it deals are thus definitely dated, and are not only earlier than the last years of the high priesthood of John Hyrcan [137] but also earlier than the outbreak of the Maccabean wars. It is only when we realize that the book was written before the time of Hasmonean high priests, in the days of such men as Jason and Menelaus, that we can understand the writer's denunciation of the contemporary high priests for their pollution of the innermost shrine of the Temple, presumably by entering it against the law, and violating the ritual regulations regarding the ceremonial

[133] Mishna, Gittin 5. 8.

[134] See S. Schechter, Documents of Jewish Sectaries, Cambridge, 1910, p. 14, line 3; cf. also ibid., p. 13, line 3; Leonard Rost, Die Damaskusschrift, Berlin, 1933, p. 25; R. H. Charles, Apochrypha and Pseudepigrapha of the Old Testament II, p. 831. For the discussion of the passage, see L. Ginzberg, Eine unbekannte juedische Sekte, 1922, pp. 124 ff.

[135] Cf. Ch. Albeck, op. cit., pp. 35–36; and cf. HTR, XVI, 1923, pp. 42 ff.; as well as Monatsschrift, LXXVI, 1932, pp. 525 ff.

[136] See L. Finkelstein, The Pharisees, pp. 113 f.

[137] So R. H. Charles, The Book of Jubilees, p. LIX.

of the Day of Atonement, when they were commanded to enter it (Jubilees 23. 21).

The book was composed by a writer who revered the sanctuary, but held the men who in his time were at its head, in contempt. He is a writer fierce in his indignation against the high priesthood, and yet sympathetic to views which we find associated with the Temple hierarchy.

The fact that the book contains no reference whatever to the persecution is also significant for its date. The passage Jubilees 23. 12, in which Charles (op. cit., p. LXIII) sees an apocalypse predicting the persecution and the Maccabean war, does not, it seems to me, warrant that interpretation. The passage does, indeed, describe (23. 16) the decay of Judaism under Hellenistic influence, and the rise of bitter conflicts among the Jews (ibid., v. 19). The battle referred to in verse 20, when "they will stand (with bows and) swords and war to turn them (the sinful) back into the way; but they will not return until much blood has been shed" cannot refer to the Maccabean struggle; for it is followed by a prediction of even graver decay of religion (v. 21). On the contrary, the reference must be to an earlier struggle, perhaps an unrecorded civil struggle between the Hellenizers and the Hasids. The last historical reference in the passage seems to be that to Antiochus IV's ravages in Jerusalem on his return from the ill-fated expedition into Egypt in 169 B.C. The author predicts that God "will wake up against them (the sinful in Israel) the sinners of the Gentiles, who have neither mercy nor compassion, and who will respect the person of none, neither old nor young, nor anyone, for they are more wicked strong to do evil than all the children of men (v. 23)." The description of the horrible times continues for several verses, culminating in the announcement of the Messianic age (vv. 27 ff.). The passage seems to prove beyond question that the writer did not witness the profanation of the Temple by Antiochus IV; otherwise, he certainly would not have failed to refer to it.

These considerations make it likely that the Book of Jubilees was composed some time during the turbulent period dividing the appointment of Jason as high priest (175 B.C.) and the final profanation of the Temple by Antiochus (167 B.C.).

ADDITIONAL NOTE A

The Relationship of Egyptian Antisemitism to the Story of the Exodus

The close relationship between Egyptian antisemitism and the Jewish history of the Exodus has been demonstrated by V. Tscherikower in Ha-Yehudim veha-Yevanim, pp. 368 ff. Indeed, in view of the nature of the charges made by the Egyptian writers against the Jews, it is difficult to understand how this relationship can possibly be doubted. In addition to the other evidence heretofore available, it is clear from the discussion of Psalms 78 and 105 (Vol. XXXV, p. 299), that the Egyptians of the third century B.C. were highly sensitive to the suggestion that their ancestors had been punished with the plague of "boils" and that this fact was known, and taken into account, in Palestine. The story of the Exodus as related by Hecateus of Abdera, who certainly was not unfriendly to the Jews, reflects this particular sensitivity, and indeed the unpleasant feeling which Egyptians had regarding the story of the Exodus generally. According to him, the Egyptian population, at the time of the Exodus, suffered from an epidemic, and it was believed popularly that this visitation was due to the anger of the gods at the sufferance granted foreign people to follow their own religious practices, while those of the Egyptian gods were neglected.

Following this development, the strangers were expelled; and the more distinguished among them, led by Danaus and Cadmos, settled in Greece; the mass of them, following a leader by the name of Moses, founded the country known as Judaea. See Reinach, Textes d'Auteurs grecs et romains relatifs au Judaïsme, Paris, 1895 (hereinafter Reinach, Textes), pp. 14 ff.

This is a moderately Egyptophilic reformulation of the Jewish account of the Exodus (see Reinach, op. cit., p. 15, n. 1). Manetho, living apparently a little later than Hecateus, gives another account of the Exodus, definitely less favorable to the Jews. According to him, the men of Jerusalem were descended in part from the Hyksos, and in part from Egyptian lepers and cripples. The discussion of Psalms 78 and 105 shows further, as indicated above, that the charge of "ass-worship," made against the Jews by the Seleucid antisemites of Maccabean times, had sufficiently spread in the third century B.C., under the Ptolemaic rule, to affect the manner in which the Psalmists described the ten plagues. In view of this fact, it is obviously impossible to accept the statement of Josephus (Against Apion, II, 90), whose views are followed by E. Bickermann (Monatsschrift f. Gesch. u. Wissenschaft d. Judentums (hereafter Monatsschrift), LXXI, 1927, pp. 84 ff.; and Der Gott d. Makkabaeer, 1937, pp. 22 ff.) and I. Heinemann (art. Antisemitismus in PWRE suppl. V, 3 ff.; Festgabe z. zehnjaehrigen Bestehen d. Akademie f. d. Wissenschaft d. Judentums, 1929, 76 ff.; and Zion [Hebr. periodical] IV, 1939, p. 279), to the effect that the antisemitic doctrines were only the creations of the Seleucids, in their attempt to justify the atrocities of Antiochus IV. There can, of course, be no doubt that Hellenistic antisemitism entered a new phase, when the older, unofficial and popular misinterpretation of Judaism was replaced by a new antisemitic propaganda, fostered as a political instrument of the Seleucid empire. But it seems certain, in view of the available evidence, that the antisemitic charges themselves originated in Egypt, and were chiefly the response of the Egyptian priests to the story of the Exodus and the doctrine of Jewish monotheism (see further with regard to the origins of antisemitic propaganda, the material assembled in Bousset-Gressmann, Die Religion d. Judentums in Spaethellenistischen Zeitalter, 1926, pp. 75 ff.). Because the early Ptolemies were friendly to the Jews (Fuchs, Die Juden Aegyptens, 5 ff.) and doubtless because Egypt already contained a considerable Jewish population (ibid.), the Egyptian historians of the third entury B.C. were particularly careful to avoid giving offense to *Egyptian* Jews. It is apparently for this reason that Manetho avoids any mention of "Jews" in his story of the Exodus; he deals only with Jerusalem and its inhabitants, the *Solymitai* (Jos., Against Apion I, 90, 241, 248). Heinemann (PWRE, loc. cit.) infers from this, quite correctly, I believe, that Manetho's treatise was "concerned only with the founding of the neighboring state" (i.e. the Temple state of Jerusalem or Judaea), "but not with the origin of the Jewish people." Heinemann fails, however, to draw the correct conclusion from this interesting observation, namely, that Manetho's discussion is intended to lay the juristic basis for the Ptolemaic claim to overlordship of Palestine; and that the author tried to establish this claim in such a manner as to avoid giving any possible offense to the Jews of his own country.

As the antisemitic interpretation of the Exodus spread, the efforts of the Jews to counteract it grew. Thus, the Jews, who had probably originated the identification of the patriarchs with the Hyksos, later tried to obliterate it. Hence the emphasis in M on the fact that Jacob came to Egypt with a small number, and without any desire to remain there. "*And he (Jacob) went down into Egypt,* — compelled by the Divine commandment. *And sojourned there* — this teaches us that he did not go to settle, but to sojourn for a period, as it is said, 'They said moreover unto Pharaoh, To sojourn in the land are we come, for thy servants have no pasture for their flocks, for the famine is sore in the land of Canaan; now, therefore, we pray thee, let thy servants dwell in the land of Goshen (Genesis 47. 4).' *Few in number* — as it is said, 'Thy fathers went down into Egypt with three-score and ten persons; and now the Lord thy God hath made thee as the stars of heaven for multitude (Deuteronomy 10. 22).'" (The italicized passages are from Deuteronomy 26. 5; the rest is the comment of M on the passages.) The passage in M is clearly intended to describe Jacob as coming into Egypt with a small family, in order to escape death by starvation. Significantly enough, no reference is made to Joseph, though such a reference would obviously be flattering to the Jews, and one which they would have liked to make on the occasion of the Passover celebration. The thought implied in this passage is expressed even more clearly in a comment, preserved on the same passage of Deuteronomy, in Sifre 301 (ed. Friedmann, 128a; ed. Finkelstein, p. 319; D. Hoffman, Midrash Tannaim, p. 172): "*And he went down into Egypt* — Lest you think that he went down into Egypt to assume a royal crown, the Scriptures add *and he sojourned there.* Lest you think he came with great hosts, the Scriptures add, *few in number*, as it is said, 'Thy fathers went down into Egypt, three-score and ten.'" While the Sifre in its present form was probably compiled no earlier than the third century of our era, there can be little doubt that this particular passage is of much higher antiquity. There can be no question of the purpose these comments are intended to serve. They are an explicit denial of any association of the Jews or their ancestors, the Israelites, with an invasion of Egypt, "to assume a royal crown" or "with great hosts." It is extremely interesting in this connection to note again the account of the coming of Israel into Egypt, as given in Psalm 105. 16–22; particularly stressing the enslavement of Joseph: "And He called a famine upon the land; He broke the whole staff of bread. He sent a man before them; Joseph was sold for a servant; his feet they hurt with fetters, his person was laid in iron. Until the time that His word came to pass, the word of the Lord tested him. The king sent and loosed him, even the ruler of the peoples, and set him free. He made him lord of his house, and ruler of all his possessions; to bind his princes at his pleasure, and teach his elders wisdom."

It is entirely possible that the same type of resentment which led the Egyptians of the third century B.C. to re-tell the story of the Exodus was in some way responsible for the sufferings visited on the Israelites of Yeb, more than two centuries earlier. Certainly the singular document, referring to the directions given by King Darius for the observance of the Passover at Yeb (see A. Cowley, Aramaic Papyri of the Fifth Century, B.C., Oxford, 1923, pp. 60 ff.), requires further explanation. The interest of the Persian government in such details of Jewish ritual can only be explained if objection was raised to the observances by the Egyptians. One of the reasons for the objection may have been the use of animal sacrifices by the Jews; but in that event it would naturally be expected that the statement of the government would deal with the issue of animal sacrifices specifically. The reference to the Passover celebration seems to indicate that the Egyptians of the period (apparently 519 B.C.) objected to the observance of this festival; and that the imperial Persian government sided with the Israelites, against the Egyptians. Perhaps, the resentment aroused by this victory of the Israelites, through their influence at the Imperial Court, led to the destruction of the Temple, eleven years later, when the power of the central imperial government became weaker (see Cowley, op. cit., pp. 97–109, but cf. A. Vincent, La Religion des Judéo-Araméens d'Elephantine, 1937, pp. 254 ff.).

ADDITIONAL NOTE B

Apologetic Changes in the Jewish Liturgy

Apologetic changes in Jewish ritual and other parts of Jewish literature were made at various times: in antiquity, in the Middle Ages, and even in modern times. The changes were introduced (*a*) perforce under orders of the government; or (*b*) as part of self-censorship to avoid giving offense to the government; or (*c*) out of sheer devotion to the state. An example of a drastic change in the ritual, introduced probably at the behest of the imperial government, is the recorded idolatry of Ahaz and Manasseh, and was intended to indicate their loyalty to their Assyrian suzerain (cf. R. Kittel, Gesch. d. Volkes Israel,[3] 1917, II, 574). The Egyptophilism of the Septuagint is well recognized and was, indeed, known to the Rabbinic authorities (see Mekilta, Bo 14, Friedmann 15b, Horowitz-Rabin 50, Lauterbach, I, 111; B. Megillah 9a; Yer. ibid. i, 71d; Masseket Soferim 1. 7, ed. Higger 101, and parallel passages). Philo and Josephus, following the Septuagint, interpret the law against reviling God (Exodus 22. 28) as prohibiting also the mocking of pagan gods (Philo, Vita Mosis II (26) 205; De Spec. leg. I, 53; Josephus, Contra Ap. II, 257; Ant. IV, 207). In other parts of the ancient diaspora, the law was likewise interpreted in such a manner as to make for better relations with the pagan population. Thus Nahum of Media reduced the prohibition against commerce with idolaters during their festival season (Mishna Aboda Zara I, 1) to one day (B. ibid. 7b); Samuel of Nahardea maintained that in the diaspora the prohibition applied only to the very day of the idolatrous festival (ibid.). Samuel further held that the civil law of the State must be recognized by Jewish religious courts (Baba Kamma 113a). In the Middle Ages, the text of the prayer against sectarians was changed in several rites so as not to give offense to Christians (Elbogen, Der juedische Gottesdienst,[2] 1924, p. 51). Rabbenu Gershom's formal prohibition of plural marriage, long after the practice had disappeared among the Jews of western Europe, was probably influenced in part by a respect for the standards set by the Christian Church (see my remarks in Jewish Self-Government in the Middle Ages, 1924, p. 22). In modern times, many changes in the ritual have been proposed with a view to preventing misunderstanding of Judaism by the general population, as well as out of inner objection to anything which might appear to reflect dual allegiance, or a sense of superiority by Jews. For the changes introduced by Reform Jews, see Elbogen, op. cit., pp. 50, 54, et al., see Index, under Reformbewegung and Reformgebetbuecher; D. Philipson, The Reform Movement in Judaism, revised ed. 1931, pp. 75 ff.; et al., see Index under Prayer-Book.

It is possible that one of the changes in the oldest known synagogue ritual was made because of fear of giving offense to the Egyptian government. The Nash Papyrus (published by Stanley A. Cook, PSBA, XXV, 1903, pp. 34 ff.) is, as is well known, a remnant of an ancient prayer-book, and for this reason contains the Ten Commandments and the beginning of the Shema: i.e., a part of the most ancient liturgy used by the Jews (see Mishna Tamid 5. 1; cf. B. Berakot 12a; Yer. ibid. I, 8, 3c; Elbogen, Der juedische Gottesdienst, 24, 236, 242). As W. F. Albright has demonstrated, this papyrus probably dates from about the middle of the second century B.C. (Journal of Biblical Literature, LVI, 1937, 171 ff.). According to Albright, one of the differences between the text of the Nash Papyrus and that of the Masorah is due simply to apologetics. He explains the deviation between the text of the Nash Papyrus and the Masorah in regard to the fourth commandment as follows: "It is highly improbable that the Egyptian Jews of the Lagide period would dare use the Deuteronomic motivation" (for the observance of the sabbath, viz. "And thou shalt remember that thou wast a slave in the land of Egypt, and the Lord thy God brought thee out thence by a mighty hand and by an outstretched arm; therefore the Lord thy God commanded thee to keep the sabbath day"). Albright continues: "So we may simply regard the substitution of the other motivation (i.e., that of Exodus 20. 11) as a prudent political move."

In his particular instance, however, it seems to me more probable that the Egyptian Jews felt that some other motivation for the observance of the sabbath was needed for themselves. The reason for this was the fact that the benefits of the Exodus had to some extent been lost so far as they were concerned through their resettlement in Egypt. For this reason, as indicated in HTR, XXXI, 1938, p. 295, note 11, the Egyptian Jews omitted, in their version of M, the statement that Jacob came to Egypt "compelled by the Divine commandment." The statement seemed to reflect on the piety of the Jews living in Egypt. On the other hand, the author of the Book of Jubilees (regarding the date of which see Appendix, above), apparently having this passage of M in mind, stresses the fact that God commanded Jacob to go to Egypt (Jubilees 44. 6).

ADDITIONAL NOTE C

Afikoman

The rendering of the word *afikoman* and even the correct reading of the word are in some doubt. Among the recorded variants are: (*a*) *afikoman*, found in the current eds. of Babli, as well as in the Munich Manuscript, and Codex Adler 850 of Babli Pesahim in the

Library of the Jewish Theological Seminary of America, in the text of the Mishna as found in Yerushalmi, in some editions and manuscripts of Aruk, in the Bacher manuscript of Maimonides' Commentary on the Mishna in the Library of the Jewish Theological Seminary of America, in most of the extant rituals of the Passover Haggadah, in Tosefta, ed. pr. and Codex Vienna, as recorded by Zuckermandel in his edition p. 173; in ed. pr. and one manuscript of Mekilta, as recorded by Horowitz; Ca; E; (*b*) *afikmon*, found in Mishna ed. Lowe; in Enelow manuscript 348 of Maimonides' Commentary on the Mishna, in the Jewish Theological Seminary of America; in the reading of Rabbi Yehosef, recorded in Meleket Shelomoh on the Mishna, in Siddur R. Saadia (where, however, it is vocalized *afikemon*, and perhaps should be so read in the other texts), and in Codex Adler 2935, f. 4a (fragment of the Passover Haggadah); (*c*) *afikimon*, found in the Parma and Budapest manuscripts of the Mishna; as well as in the manuscript of the Mishna, Seder Moed, dated 1361, found in the Library of the Jewish Theological Seminary of America; in some editions of Aruk; in Codex Leyden of the Yerushalmi as recorded by S. Lieberman in Hayerushalmi Kifeshuto, p. 521; in Codex Adler 3130, f. 7, verso; in Tosefta, Codes Erfurt as recorded by Zuckermandel, loc. cit.; in C; O; P;Qa (for these sigla see note 1); and manuscripts cited by Italiener, op. cit., pp. 263 (oriental) and 268 (French); cf. also manuscript cited by him on p. 261; (*d*) *afikomin* or *afikomen*, found in Mishna as cited by Meleket Shelomoh; in the manuscript of Maimonides' Commentary on the Mishna, Zeraim and Moed (Miller Collection at the Jewish Theological Seminary of America); in the Constantinople edition of Mekilta; in Yerushalmi Pesahim 37d, line 53, ed. pr.; in F; G; H; M; (vocalized *afikomin*, but spelled without the *yod* before the *nun* in RW; vocalized *afikomen*, and lacking *yod* before *nun* in V; so also in ed. Mantua 1568 and the Darmstadt Manuscript of the Passover Haggadah, see Italiener, op. cit., p. 131, and cf. note 13; as well as p. 218); (*e*) *afikomon*, found in text of Mekilta, according to citation in Midrash Hakamim; in Yerushalmi Pesahim 37d, line 24, according to ed. pr. The meaning of the word has been in doubt at least since the third century of the Christian Era. Authorities of that period rendered it "dessert." But the general tendency among modern writers (including Loew, in his notes to S. Krauss, Griechische u. Lateinische Lehnwoerter s.v., II, p. 107; Ben Yehuda in his Dictionary (Thesaurus Totius Hebraitatis), I, p. 348, note 4; S. Lieberman, Hayerushalmi Kifeshuto, loc. cit., and Z. Carl, Pesahim, p. 89), is to associate the word with the post-prandial revelry, celebrated by going "from group to group" and arranging public entertainment. This practice seems to be referred to in the text of the *baraita*, as recorded in Yerushalmi, and also in the interpretation given to the passage in the Mishna by Rab (Babli Pesahim 119b).

ADDITIONAL NOTE D

The Tobiads

For the older literature regarding the Tobiads, see G. McL. Harper in Journal of American Philology, XLIX, 1928, pp. 7 ff. Other discussions of the Tobiads and their activities are to be found in E. Meyer, Ursprung u. Anfaenge d. Christentums, II, 128 ff.; Tscherikower, pp. 164 ff.; Tarbiz, IV, 1932–33, pp. 242 f. and 354 ff. and his Palestine under the Ptolemies, p. 39; Oesterley and Robinson, A History of Israel, II, 200, 208; Cambridge Ancient History, VII, 160, 193; VIII, 500 ff.; A. Momigliano, in Atti della R. Accademia d. scienze di Torino, LXVII, 1931–32, pp. 165 ff.; S. Zeitlin, Second Jewish Commonwealth (1933), pp. 12 ff.; C. Watzinger, Denkmaler Palaestinas (1935), pp. 13 ff.; S. W. Baron, A Social and Religious History of the Jews (1937), III, p. 33, n. 4; E. Bikerman, Institutions des Séleucides, pp. 171 ff.; F. M. Heichelheim, Wirtschaftsgeschichte d. Altertums (1938), p. 500; B. Meisler, in Tarbiz, XII (1941), pp. 109 ff.; M. Rostovtzeff, The Social and Economic History of the Hellenistic World (see Index, under Tobiads, Tubias). With regard to the extent of the hellenization of the Tobiads, cf. the papyrus cited by Tscherikower, in Palestine under the Ptolemies (Mizraim, loc. cit., p. 53), where Tobias writes a letter to Apollonios and concludes with the usual pagan greeting in the name of "the gods." As Tscherikower remarks, "The plural in the mouth of a Jew" — we may add in the mouth of a Jew named *Tobiah*! — "is most significant; the fact that these words were written by a Greek secretary does not of course change the matter in any way." There are possibly, in addition to the material mentioned in these works, some references to the Tobiads in the later works of Scripture and the earlier Pseudepigrapha. In order to identify these references, it must be borne in mind that Nehemiah, and doubtless the later opponents of the Tobiads, maintained that that family was really of Ammonite descent, and not Judaite at all, though the Tobiads, themselves, appear to have insisted on their own Israelite background, and if we consider Menelaus one of them (see Additional Note E) apparently they considered themselves Benjaminites.

Once this fact is realized a new significance attaches to the remarkable statement in Jubilees 16. 8–9: "And he (i.e. Lot) and his daughters committed sin upon the earth, such as had not been on the earth since the days of Adam till his time. . . . And behold it is commanded and engraven concerning all his seed, on the heavenly tablets, *to remove them and root them out*, and to execute judgment upon them like the judgment of Sodom, and to leave no seed of the man on the earth on the day of condemnation." The fearful judgment would in any event reflect a profound contemporary bitterness against Ammon and Moab (the descendants of Lot); when it is declared to be inscribed on the "heavenly tablets" it becomes particularly significant. For the writer of Jubilees generally described as engraven on the heavenly tablets only subjects which are matters of controversy in his own time (cf. the following passages dealing with subjects of sectarian controversies, Jubilees 3. 10, impurity after childbirth; 6. 17, the date of the Feast of Weeks; 16. 28–29, proper manner of observance of Feast of Tabernacles; etc.). It is especially noteworthy that the writer requires the "children of Lot" to be "removed," as though some of them at least were included within the family of Israel so that they had to be expelled, as a first step to their being "rooted out" and destroyed.

With this passage of the Book of Jubilees in mind, we may also find a special significance in the particular hostility to Ammon and Moab, characteristic of the Chronicles (and already noted by A. Geiger, Urschrift, pp. 49 ff.), as well as in the reference to the "children of Lot," in Psalm 83. 9. The Psalm describes a general attack on the Judaites by their neighbors, and enumerates them in vv. 7 ff. as follows: "The tents of Edom and the Ishmaelites, Moab and the Hagarites; Gebal and Ammon and Amalek; Philistia and the inhabitants of Tyre. Assyria also is joined with them, they have been an arm to the children of Lot." The trend of mind of the Psalmist seems confused, from a first reading of his text, in view of the fact that the Ammonites and Moabites, whom he mentions separately, are the "children of Lot." What he is trying to say becomes clear when we recognize that "Assyria" or *Asshur* is here, as so often in texts of this period, a cypher for the Seleucid empire. If we take the "sons of Lot" to refer to the Tobiad clan, the meaning of the whole passage becomes clear. The Psalmist enumerates the enemies of Israel. He notes with dismay that the Seleucid government has become associated with the ancient enemies of Israel; all these enemies have now become an arm for the Tobiads.

The Psalmist, then, is describing an alliance of the various Palestinian nationalities, which with the assistance of the imperial government "have become an arm for the children of Lot" or the Tobiads. To what time does this psalm refer? It is usually assumed (so Kittel) that this psalm refers to the events described in I Maccabees, chapter 5, when the neighbors of Judaea undertook to attack Judah the Maccabee. But the description of a similar joint attack of Edomites, Ammonites, Moabites, etc., on Jacob and his children in Jubilees chapters 37–38 suggests such alliances of Judaea's neighbors against it were not unusual. Indeed, the Chronicler projects a similar attack on Judah into the days of Jehoshaphat (II Chronicles 20). In view of the growing body of opinion placing the Book of Jubilees in pre-Maccabean times (see Appendix, below) it may be suggested that Psalm 83 also describes a union of the neighbors of Judaea against it preceding that which took place after the initial victories of Judah the Maccabee. Indeed, this would seem likely because of the use of cyphers for the Tobiads and for the Seleucids. If this were a period of open rebellion, presumably a follower of Judah the Maccabee would not need to feel restrained in praying against the enemies of the Jews. We should also expect that a psalmist writing after the profanation of the Temple by Antiochus IV would consider that event the focus of the war, and not simply an incident in the rivalry between the clans and nationalities of Palestine with one another. The tone of the Psalm, with its reference to the support given by Assyria to the "children of Lot," suggests a period before the Maccabean rebellion, and after the conquest of Palestine by the Seleucids.

The Psalmist may well have in mind such a situation as arose when Jason tried to reconquer Jerusalem from its Tobiad masters, and was driven out by the forces of Antiochus IV. As this occasion is described in II Maccabees 5. 5, it may well have seemed to a contemporary a struggle of the surrounding Palestinian nationalities to destroy Judaea, and to enforce on it the government of the Tobiads, who now had the support also of Assyria or Antiochus IV.

ADDITIONAL NOTE E

The Family of the High Priest Menelaus

Menelaus is described as the brother of Simon (II Maccabees 4. 23) and Simon is described as a Benjaminite (ibid. 3. 4). The suggestion (originally made by L. Herzfeld, Geschichte d. Volkes Israel, 1855, I, 218) which has been widely accepted that the word *Beniamein* in the current Greek texts is either a translator's or a copyist's error for *miyamin*, is indeed brilliant and ingenious. According to this, Simon and Menelaus would turn out to be not members of the tribe of Benjamin, and therefore non-priests, but of the family of *Miyamin*, one of the twenty-four priestly families (I Chronicles 24. 9, *et al.*). It is, however, entirely improbable that this theory is correct. Among the reasons which must be urged against it is the fact that one of the sources used by Josephus, in its effort to transform Menelaus into a priest (so as to avoid the suggestion that a non-Aaronid ever served in the capacity of High Priest), is forced to adopt the device of making him a son of Simeon the Righteous, and a bearer of the name Onias (Josephus, Antiquities XII, 239 (5. 1)). Probably this impossible reconstruction of the family background of Menelaus was intended by its perpetrators to prevent Herod or his successors from appealing to the case of Menelaus as a precedent for appointing another non-

Aaronid to the High Priesthood. But if Menelaus had been a priest. this violence to the historical facts would have been quite superfluous, Curiously enough, some texts of II Maccabees try to achieve the same end, of making Menelaus into a priest, by reading *Balgea* (see D. de Bruyne-B. Sodar, Les anciennes Traductions Latines des Machabées, 1932, ad loc.), which was also a priestly family (I Chronicles 24. 14) instead of *Beniamein*. This reading is accepted by E. Bickermann (Der Gott d. Makkabaeer, p. 66), and is given some consideration by A. Kahana in his Hebrew translation of II Maccabees (see A. Kahana, Ha-Sefarim Ha-Hizzonim, ad loc.). But it is probably not to be accepted. The copyists who introduced this change were apparently, like Josephus' source and the modern historians who would emend *Beniamein* into *Miyamin*, disconcerted by the suggestion that a non-Aaronid could have been imposed as High Priest without armed resistance by the Jews. The fact is, of course, that in the pre-Maccabean era the priesthood had become corrupt; and even among those who observed the Law many did so half-heartedly. Hence it happened, for example, that a man who was undoubtedly a direct descendant of Simeon the Righteous — indeed, either his son or his grandson — actually set up a Temple for sacrificial purposes outside of Jerusalem, despite the repeated biblical injunctions prohibiting such a practice. A generation which could see the establishment of a Temple at Heliopolis could also witness the service of a non-Aaronid as priest, without the resentment which would doubtless have been caused through such an appointment in a later age. For a further discussion of the whole subject see, besides the literature already cited, the following: A. Buechler, Die Tobiaden und die Oniaden (VI. Jahresbericht d. israelitisch-theologischen Lehranstalt in Wien) 1899, 9 ff.; Schuerer, I, 195, note 28; J. Klausner, Historia Yisrealit², I (1919), p. 284; E. Meyer, II, 133; W. Kolbe, Beitraege z. syrischen u. juedischen geschichte, 1926, p. 151; Tscherikower, 197; S. Zeitlin, A History of the Second Jewish Commonwealth, 1933, p. 19; A. Kahana's Commentary on II Maccabees (Tel Aviv, 1937, ad loc.); R. H. Charles, A Critical and Exegetical Commentary on the Book of Daniel, 1929, pp. 246 ff. See also J. Wellhausen, who (Israelit. u. jued. Geschichte, 1921, p. 236) suggests that Menelaus and Simon were Tobiads, apparently in the sense that they were sons of Joseph ben Tobiah. This suggestion has won wide acceptance, and is indeed supported by Josephus, War, I, 31 ff. Nevertheless the possibility remains that they were *followers* of the Tobiads or distant members of the clan, rather than sons of Joseph.

ADDITIONAL NOTE F

The Original Text of Dayyenu

The phrase, "and appointed a High Priest for us," occurs only in one text of the Passover Haggadah, so far as I have been able to find, namely a Genizah fragment in the Library of the Jewish Theological Seminary of America, Codex Adler 3214, f. 4 recto. Unfortunately this fragment is torn, so that it contains only the last few lines of Db, beginning with the words "and gave us their substance." But it is obvious that if Db included a reference to the appointment of a high priest, Da must have contained such a reference as well; and we may therefore take it that the manuscript from which this fragment derives, contained such a strophe, as is indicated above under IIIe (above, p. 2). It requires little consideration to realize that although this reading is unique, it represents an older tradition than those of the other texts, which have no reference to the appointment of a high priest. Certainly no one would have added such a reference after the destruction of the Temple; while it may well be argued that communities finding mention of a high priest in their text of D would omit it in view of the fact that no such office now exists. It is possible to express gratitude to God for the establishment of His Temple, even though it is now waste; for the institution rather than any particular building is made the subject of thankfulness. It is not possible to speak of gratitude to God for the appointment of a high priest, when there is no such officer in existence. Moreover, the phrase "to atone for all our sins" follows more logically after such an expression as "appointed a high priest for us" than after mention of the Temple. Finally, it is probable, *a priori*, that Da consisted of fifteen strophes, corresponding to the fifteen steps in the Temple, and to the fifteen pilgrim psalms (120–134). This last argument is strengthened by the observation that in certain rituals, such as those represented by Q, Qa, V, Vb (for these sigla, see Note 1, above) and the text cited by Italiener, in Die Darmstaedter Pessach-Haggadah, p. 280, end Da with two references to the sanctuary. All but the last of these texts read:

> Had He brought us into the land of Israel,
> And not built us the holy Temple,
> It had sufficed us!
>
> Had He built us the Holy Temple,
> And not built us the Chosen House,
> It had sufficed us!

The text cited by Italiener differs from the others only in reversing the order, mentioning the Chosen House before the Holy Temple. This curious redundancy is explained by the commentators (see

Shibbale Ha-Leket, loc. cit.) as an effort to include a reference to the sanctuary at Shiloh (Joshua 18. 1), though that was a temporary sanctuary, before referring to the permanent sanctuary in Jerusalem, which is called "the Chosen Temple." More probably, the redundancy is the result of a conflation of two variant readings, both referring in different terms to the same institution, namely the Temple. Yet the conflation, by its very curiosity, suggests that the persons responsible for it felt the need of adding a fifteenth strophe to Da; and this need may have been felt particularly because of the omission of the older reference to the high priest. It should be noted, however, that many texts seem to have contained only a reference to the *Bet Ha-Mikdash* ("the Holy Temple") and none to the *Bet Ha-Behirah* ("the Chosen Temple"). The "Holy Temple" is mentioned in the texts cited by Italiener on pp. 131, 176, 182, 194, 209, 219, all said to be of German origin; and also in the following E, F, G, H, P, R, Sa, Sb, Sc, Sd, Va, X; the term "Chosen Temple" is found in the texts cited by Italiener on pp. 170, 199, 213, 229, 233, 244, all these being of German origin; 263, (oriental) and B, C, Ca, O, Tb, U, W. At any rate, this seems to have been the reading of Abrabanel, according to his commentary (though the reading of the text has been "corrected" to correspond to that of the usual Passover Haggadah), of Kol Bo, and of Abudarham. The reading *Bet Ha-Behirah* seems, however, to have been the original; for it alone occurs in the final paragraph of D according to *all* texts. This fact indicates that whereever any reference to *Bet Ha-Mikdash* occurs in D, that is the result of some alteration of the text. This suggests that what happened was the insertion of a reference to *Bet Ha-Mikdash* in order to take the place of the omitted reference to the High Priest; and that the redundancy led to the omission of the reference to *Bet Ha-Behirah* according to many texts.

It is further to be remarked that in the fragment containing the reference to the high priest, D ends with the words "May it be rebuilt in our days!" Obviously these words refer to the Temple, which is, however, removed from them by the whole phrase referring to the high priest. Presumably, the words were not inserted immediately after the mention of the Temple because that would have involved an alteration in the traditional text.

ADDITIONAL NOTE G

The Expression *Ha-Kadosh Baruk Hu* ("The Holy One, blessed be He")

The phrase, *ha-kadosh baruk hu*, "The Holy One, blessed be He," should more correctly be read, *ha-kodesh baruk hu*, "The Holiness, blessed be He," and it occurs in that form in most early manuscripts, both of the Passover Haggadah and also in other Rabbinic texts, and sometimes simply as *ha-kodesh*, "The Holiness" (cf. M. Friedmann, note on Sifra debe Rab, 1915, p. 30). This form is analogous to that occurring in *ha-geburah*, "The Power," instead of *ha-gibbor*, "The Mighty One." The Aramaic form *kudsha berik hu* in the *kaddish* is the literal translation of the *ha-kodesh baruk hu*, and thus demonstrates further that that is the correct and original form of the title. Virtually all the rituals agree in reading *ha-makom* in B and D; and *ha-kadosh* (*ha-kodesh*) *baruk hu* in A and M. This is true of all the texts cited by Italiener in Die Darmstaedter Pessach-Haggadah and of the following additional texts: C, Ca (both of which, however, add *baruk hu* after *ha-makom*), D, E, F, G, H, I, O, P, Q, Qa, R, Sa, Sb, V, W, and X (regarding these sigla, see note 1). T contains only the beginning of the Passover Haggadah, and in that part follows the usual text. M contains only passage B, and there follows the usual text. U reads *hamakom* in B and D; and *ha-kodesh*, in abbreviated form (the first two letters, followed by an apostrophe) in A and M. (The use of this abbreviation for *ha-kodesh* is, of course, quite common. See, for example, the reading of *Yalkut* as recorded in my edition of Sifre, Deuteronomy 5, variants to page 13, line 6; and the reading of the Oxford Ms. recorded in the same edition 19, variants to page 31, line 4. In Ginze Schechter I, page 28, Professor L. Ginzberg maintains that this abbreviation stands, in the particular text published there, for *elohim*; but I am not sure that his argument in this respect is cogent. It seems to me probable that the abbreviation in that text, too, stands for *ha-kodesh*). Siddur Rab Saadia Gaon reads, like the other rituals, *ha-kodesh baruk hu* in the following passage of M, "*And the Lord brought us forth from Egypt,* Not by means of an angel, nor by means of a seraph, nor by means of a messenger; but the Holy One, blessed be He, etc." In the appendix to M, which, according to most rituals, reads: "These are the ten plagues which the Holy One, blessed be He, brought upon the Egyptians," Siddur Rab Saadia read *ha-makom baruk hu* instead of *ha-kadosh baruk hu.* It also reads *ha-makom baruk hu* instead of *ha-kadosh baruk hu* in A, where it replaces the usual formula, "Now if the Holy One, blessed be He, had not brought forth our ancestors from Egypt," with the following, "Now if the Omnipresent (*ha-makom*), blessed be He, had not *redeemed* our ancestors from Egypt, etc." (The substitution of *redeemed* for *brought forth* was perhaps intended to meet the needs of the Egyptian Jews who were still in that land, and could not be described as "brought forth" from there.) This reading of A is also found in the following Genizah texts: Nb, Nj, Nn. Genizah text Nf contains the appendix to M in the same form as the Siddur Rab Saadia. The text of J, too, appears to resemble the Siddur Rab Saadia in its reading of A. K XII omits the mention of the Deity in this passage. The other texts published by I. Abrahams in Jewish Quarterly Review, X, 41 ff. do not contain A. So far as they contain the passages found in the extant rituals, they seem to follow the usual differentiation between the use of *ha-kodesh* and *ha-makom.* K IV, VII, X, which contain the appendix to M, all read *ha-makom* there, like Siddur Rab Saadia.

This consistency among all the extant texts is singular indeed, in view of the fact that a study of almost any other Rabbinic text will show endless confusion between the use of *ha-makom* and *ha-kadosh* among the copyists, as though the copyists felt free to use the terms interchangeably. It appears therefore that the usage of the Passover Haggadah regarding these terms of appellation for the Deity was well fixed by tradition. The fact that AM, the earlier parts of the Passover Haggadah, seem to prefer the term *ha-kodesh baruk hu,* while BD, half a century younger, prefer the term *ha-makom* may have some bearing on the history of the development of the two terms and their relation to one another. But this cannot be determined without further study. If the dates given to A, B, D, and M in the present study are accepted, they would constitute the earliest texts containing these terms of appellation for the Deity.

CHAPTER 5

INTRODUCTORY STUDY TO *PIRKE ABOT*

THE treatise *Abot* is doubtless the most popular and best known of the whole Mishna. Recited by observant Jews on Sabbath afternoons during the summer, and thus part of the prayer book, it has been copied and published more frequently than any of its sister tractates; while as an example of Rabbinical ethics and the most easily understood part of the Mishna it has been rendered into many modern languages. Particular interest attaches to it because it has preserved what appear to be among the oldest norms in Rabbinic tradition, some of them going back to the Men of Great Assembly, Simeon the Righteous (circa 220 B.C.E.), Antigonus of Soko (circa 200 B.C.E.), and their immediate successors.

The deserved popularity of the Mishnaic treatise has, however, obscured the fact that it preserves only one form of the Ethics of the Fathers. Another, more expanded form, is to be found in the so-called *Abot d'R. Nathan*,[1] which has, itself, come down to us in two versions, closely related to each other and yet obviously independent.

The valuable studies of the texts of *Abot* and *Abot d'R. Nathan* made by Zunz, Frankel, D. Hoffmann, N. Bruell, Taylor,

[1] I use *ARN* for *Abot d'R. Nathan* generally; *ARN* I for the version denominated *Aleph* by Schechter in his edition; *ARN* II for that which he calls *Bet*. All the references to the *Abot d'R. Nathan* in this paper are to the edition of Solomon Schechter, London—Vienna—Frankfort-a.-M., 1887. The work has been translated into Latin by Francis Tayler, under the title *Tractatus de patribus Rabbi Nathan auctore*, London, 1654; and into German by Kaim Pollak, under the title. *Rabbi Nathans System der Ethik und Moral*, Frankfort-a.-M., 1905.

Reprinted from *Journal of Biblical Literature*, Volume 57, 1938.

Solomon Schechter, and Herford[2] are fundamental, and have shed much light on the history of both treatises. But more remains to be done both in the analysis of the structure of the works, and in the interpretation of the individual passages. I have endeavored in this paper to bring forward some new methods which I hope will be helpful in this further research, and to indicate some of the preliminary results at which I have arrived through the use of them.

The theses which emerge out of the study are as follows:

I. The tradition preserved in *Abot* and *Abot d'R. Nathan* consists primarily of four ancient collections:

A. A series of maxims formulated by scholars who lived between 250 and 20 B.C.E., including the Men of the Great Assembly, Simeon the Righteous, Antigonus of Soko, and the five "Pairs," namely, Jose ben Joezer of Zeredah and Jose ben Johanan of Jerusalem; Joshua ben Perahya and Nittai of Arbel; Judah ben Tabbai and Simeon ben Shattah; Shemayah and Abtalyon; Hillel and Shammai. *This collection was compiled in the School of Shammai, either in his lifetime or soon after his death.* (*Abot* I, 1–15; *ARN* I, 1–13; *ARN* II, 1–27, with additional interpretations by later scholars).

B. A series of maxims formulated by five distinguished disciples of R. Johanan ben Zakkai: R. Eliezer ben Hyrkanos, R. Joshua ben Hananyah, R. Jose Ha-Kohen, R. Simeon ben Nethanel, and R. Eleazar ben Arak. This collection was probably compiled before R. Gamaliel II became Nasi; and certainly before R. Eliezer ben Hyrkanos was expelled from the Academy.[3]

[2] Zunz, *Die Gottesdienstliche Vorträge der Juden*, Second edition, Frankfurt-am-M., 1892, 113 ff.; David Hoffmann, *Die Erste Mischna und Die Controversen der Tannain*, Berlin, 1882, 26 ff.; N. Bruell, *Jahrbücher für jüdische Geschichte und Literatur*, VII, 1–17; Charles Taylor, *Sayings of the Jewish Fathers*, Cambridge, 1877; Solomon Schechter, *op. cit.*; R. T. Herford, *Pirke Aboth*, New York, 1930; see also G. F. Moore, *Judaism*, Cambridge, 1927, I, 157 ff., and the review of Schechter's edition of *Abot d'R. Nathan* in *Monatschrift*, 1887, 374–383.

[3] It seems altogether probable that there was an interim between the death of R. Johanan ben Zakkai about the year 80 C.E. and the appointment of

C. This collection, in some respects the most interesting of all, contains maxims from the four men who "entered the orchard," namely R. Akiba, Ben Azzai, Ben Zoma, and Elisha ben Abuyah.[4] It is probably the only tradition surviving from the discussions which took place in the gatherings of this early philosophical society. It was doubtless compiled before the apostasy of Elisha ben Abuyah; but because of that event, it underwent numerous changes. (*Abot* III, 17–20; IV, 1–2, 25; *ARN* I, 23–26; *ARN* II, 33 and 35).

D. A collection of ethical maxims, probably formulated by R. Akiba, associated together by the similarity of the numerals with which they begin. (*Abot* V, 1–18; *ARN* I, 31–41; *ARN* II, 36–48).[5]

R. Gamaliel II as Nasi or President of the Academy. It was probably necessary to obtain permission from the Roman government for R. Gamaliel to serve as President; and it was during this period that R. Akiba came to the Academy, presenting himself to R. Eliezer and R. Joshua.

[4] *Hagiga*, 14b.

[5] In addition to these main, older collections, there are several younger ones, some of them made, obviously, by the redactor of the Mishna himself, from uncollected traditional material current in his day. Among these we recognize:

(a) The maxims of the descendants of Hillel, before R. Judah I, including those of R. Gamaliel I, R. Simeon ben Gamaliel I, and R. Simeon ben Gamaliel II (*Abot* I, 16–18; *ARN* I, 22, 38a; *ARN* II, 32, 35b, ff.).

(b) The maxims of R. Judah I, and his son, R. Gamaliel III, (*Abot* II, 1–4; *ARN* II, 32, 35b; lacking in *ARN* I).

(c) Supplementary sayings of Hillel, not included in Collection A (*Abot* II, 5–8; *ARN* I, 28, 43b; *ARN* II, 31, 34a. The maxim found in *Abot* II, 7, is attributed to R. Joshua in *ARN* II, 27, 28b).

(d) Sayings of various members of the Patrician faction, including Akabiah ben Mahalalel, R. Haninah Segan Ha-Kohanim, R. Dosa ben Arkenas and some others (*Abot* III, 1–14; *ARN* I, 19–21; *ARN* II, end of 31, 32, 34; in each instance with various later interpolations).

(e) Sayings of various scholars of Yabneh (*Abot* IV, 4–7; uncollected in *ARN* I and II, but found scattered in various parts).

(f) Sayings of the Disciples of R. Akiba (*Abot* IV, 8–17; and scattered in various parts of *ARN* I and II).

(g) Sayings of contemporaries and followers of R. Judah I (*Abot* IV, 18–23; *ARN* II, 33, 37a).

II. The redactors of the Mishna of *Abot*, either R. Akiba, or R. Judah the Patriarch I, took great liberties in recasting the traditions which they received, and which have been preserved in their original form in *ARN*. Thus they changed the order of the norms in the maxim attributed to the Men of the Great Assembly; they transformed a maxim attributed to Akabiah ben Mahalalel from heterodoxy to orthodoxy (this was almost certainly done by R. Akiba); and they placed the maxim of Hillel *before* that of Shammai, rather than after it, as had been the original order.[6]

III. The compilers of *Abot d'R. Nathan* belonged to the Patrician faction, and were favorable to the Shammaites.[7] This tendency is shown both in their preservation of original conservative traditions in unchanged form, and in the manner in which they interpret early liberal traditions so as practically to nullify their significance. It is altogether probable, therefore, that one stage in the redaction of *Abot d'R. Nathan* was completed by R. Nathan the Babylonian, who was a disciple of R. Ishmael,[8] and a member of the Patrician faction.

IV. The two versions of *Abot d'R. Nathan* go back to independent oral traditions, which were put into writing separately.

[6] Apparently the redactor of the Mishna made an effort to conclude each chapter of *Abot* with some statement referring to the reward of merit. For this purpose he added R. Tarfon's saying at the end of Chap. II; R. Eleazar ben Azariah's at the end of Chap. III; and naturally put R. Simeon's statement (IV, 16) at the end of Chapter IV, as it stood in his day.

[7] For the preservation of the patrician tendency after the end of the Shammaitic School, see A. Geiger, *Urschrift*, second edition, Frankfurt, 1928, pp. 150 ff., *et passim*, (see index, under *Halachah, alte*; also Hebrew section of same work, pp. 26 and 30); *Kebuzat Ma'amarim*, first edition, 112 ff.; second edition, pp. 116 ff.; however, in opposition to him, Pineles, *Darkah shel Torah*, Vienna 1861, 168 ff.; and in partial difference L. Ginzberg, notes to the second edition of *Kebuzat Ma'amarim*, 117 ff., and especially, 118; for a further discussion, see A. Epstein, *Mikadmoniot Hayehudim*, Vienna, 1887, 50 ff.; and my *Akiba*, 94 ff.; 177 ff.; and especially 279 ff.

[8] See *Akiba*, 297.

ARN II has, in general, but by no means always, preserved the more original form of the various traditions. Both versions have been deeply influenced in their final form by the wording and structure of the Mishna.[9]

I. The Oldest Collection: the Sayings of the Early Teachers

That Collection A, the oldest collection of apothegms preserved, was made by a Shammaite is sufficiently demonstrated by the fact that in the original form of this Collection, the words of Shammai are given precedence over those of Hillel. This can still be seen in the text preserved in *ARN* II. In our Mishna and in *ARN* I, the text has been altered and the words of Hillel are cited first. But it is clear that in this instance *ARN* II has preserved the original form of the Collection, for it is incon-

[9] Schechter considered *ARN* II the more original version; see his Introduction, p. xx. The reasons he advances for this opinion are as follows: (1) *ARN* II has less numerous interpolations; (2) the fact that *ARN* II has preserved the original order giving the saying of Shammai before that of Hillel in Collection A; (3) the fact that in the latter portions of *ARN*, *ARN* I contains a good deal of obviously late material, and is apparently also stylistically quite late. These arguments must, however, be reconsidered in view of the fact which now becomes apparent, that *ARN* I and *ARN* II were transmitted as separate Oral traditions, which were compiled for memory. It is, therefore, quite understandable that while *ARN* I contains a good deal of material which is late, because those who transmitted it felt more free to add new traditions to the old, and perhaps also put their compilation into writing at a later date (thus having more time for accretions and interpolations), it yet contains in some places the original form of *ARN*, in places where the transmitters of *ARN* II did either alter or add to the traditions they had received. For a further discussion of the late date at which collections of *baraitot* and even the Mishna were officially studied only from memory, see J. N. Epstein's illuminating remarks in his *Der Gaonische Kommentar zur Ordnung Tohoroth*, Berlin, 1915, 48 ff.; in the light of this, the conclusion drawn by Ch. Albeck, *Untersuchungen ueber die halachischen Midraschim*, Berlin, 1927, 119, concerning the late date when the tannaitic Midrashim were put into writing, can hardly militate against the substantial antiquity of most of their material. See further regarding the whole question, *Proceedings of the American Academy of Jewish Research*, 1932, 41.

ceivable that any late editor having received a tradition placing Hillel, the famous Nasi,[10] first, would relegate him to a second place. We must therefore accept *ARN* II as the original in this passage; and assume that either R. Akiba or R. Judah the Patriarch, both ardent adherents of the School of Hillel, intentionally changed the received text so as to mention Hillel first.

Further evidence that Hillel was originally mentioned after Shammai may be found in the fact that in *ARN* (according to both versions), Collection A is immediately followed by a description of Hillel's school. "Hillel the Elder had eighty disciples, etc." While this forms a fine transition to the words of R. Johanan ben Zakkai, according to *ARN* II, it fits in ill with the order of *ARN* I, which mentions the words of Shammai immediately before. The redactor of our Mishna, feeling this incongruity, supplied another transition, "R. Johanan ben Zakkai received the tradition from Hillel and Shammai."[11] In so doing, however, he was sacrificing historical accuracy to the exigencies of rhetoric, for R. Johanan ben Zakkai was an arch-Hillelite, and is not known to have had any connection with Shammai at all.

The full significance of the precedence given to Shammai in this passage can be appreciated only when we bear in mind the facts which have been established concerning the leadership of the Pharisaic sect in Maccabean times. The sect recognized within itself two factions, the patricians and the plebeians, and it was always arranged that the leader of the sect was chosen from one faction, and his associate from the other.[12] The manner in which this was done can be seen best from the following table, giving the list of leaders and their associates during approximately three and a half centuries, from about 170 B.C.E. to about 180 C.E.:

[10] I use the word "Nasi" for the earlier members of the House of Hillel, not in the sense of President of the Sanhedrin, for that position was apparently held by the High Priest; but in the sense of Leader of the Pharisaic faction, a post which they did occupy; see the table of Leaders and Associates below, p. 19.

[11] *Abot* II, 9.

[12] *Akiba*, 294 ff.; the following list is also taken from there.

Leader	*Associate*
Jose ben Joezer of Zeredah*	Jose ben Johanan of Jerusalem
Joshua ben Perahya*	Nittai of Arbel
Judah ben Tabbai*	Simeon ben Shattah
Shemayah	Abtalyon*
Hillel	Shammai*
R. Gamaliel I	(no associate; position offered to Akabiah ben Mahalalel* on certain conditions which he declined)
R. Simeon ben Gamaliel I*	R. Johanan ben Zakkai
R. Gamaliel II* (after the removal of R. Gamaliel II, post given temporarily to R. Eleazar ben Azariah*).	R. Joshua ben Hananyah
R. Simeon ben Gamaliel	R. Nathan the Babylonian*
R. Judah the Patriarch	(no successor appointed to R. Nathan the Babylonian; and system discontinued).

I have marked in each instance the name of the patrician leader with an asterisk; and it is noteworthy that for the first four "Pairs," whom the compiler of *ARN* cites, he conscientiously gives precedence to the duly recognized leader, irrespective of faction. He departs from this rule only with regard to Hillel and Shammai, where he, in opposition to the general tradition, gives Shammai precedence over Hillel, thus declaring the former rather than the latter the true leader of the Pharisaic sect. The change can be attributed only to violent partisanship; and indicates that the compiler lived either during the lifetime of Shammai himself or soon afterward, when feeling ran high regarding his status in relation to Hillel. It had its justification, however, in the fact that Shammai was for a short time actually the leader of the Pharisaic movement — during the rebellion against Rome, which followed Herod's death.[13] Of that time the

[13] *Akiba*, 44.

Talmud records that "Hillel sat bent before Shammai like one of the disciples, and it was as grievous a day for Israel as that when they made the Golden Calf."[14] While the crushing of the rebellion apparently brought about the temporary suppression of the Shammaitic school, and certainly the restoration of Hillel as Nasi, the Shammaites continued to look on the organizer of their School as the rightful Nasi.

It is interesting to note that several other collections of ancient date were made by Shammaites; and that it is therefore entirely probable that the system of arrangement of norms in Mishnaic collections arose in that School. Professor Louis Ginzberg has already shown that a collection of Mishnas, still preserved in Mishna Megillah chapter I, originated with the Shammaites.[15] It is probably this fact that accounts for the custom, which became universal, of mentioning the School of Shammai first in every Collection of Norms. This was naturally done by the Shammaites when they preserved an ancient controversy, and the Hillelites, when they took over these collections, simply followed the established practice.[16]

II. The Origin of Collection B

There can be little doubt that while R. Eleazar ben Arak was a member of the Academy, he outranked all the other disciples of R. Johanan ben Zakkai.[17] Because, however, he left the Academy early, his traditions were not recalled in his name; and he is known only by a few stray references to him. When

[14] *Shabbat* 17a.

[15] *Hoffmann Festschrift*, 311 ff.

[16] The practice may also have been due, of course, to respect paid to the patricians, as such.

[17] *Abot* II, 11; for the most recent discussion of the situation in the Academy immediately after the destruction of the Temple, cf. the stimulating discussion of G. Allon, in *Sefer Klausner* (Klausner Jubilee Volume), Tel Aviv, 1927, 154 ff.

R. Johanan ben Zakkai died, the leadership of the Academy temporarily passed into the hands of the two disciples, who were then foremost, R. Eliezer ben Hyrkanos the patrician, and R. Joshua ben Hananyah, the plebeian.[18] After an interim, permission was apparently obtained to appoint R. Gamaliel II as head of the Academy, and it was then that he replaced R. Eliezer ben Hyrkanos, his brother-in-law, while R. Joshua ben Hananyah retained his position, as second in office.

Any collection of ethical norms by distinguished scholars of the Academy which was made after the appointment of Gamaliel II to head the group would naturally have contained some saying by him. It is true that Collection B purports to transmit only sayings by disciples of R. Johanan ben Zakkai; and R. Gamaliel II apparently was not one of these. But a collection of ethical norms made after R. Gamaliel II's appointment would probably have had a wider basis, out of respect for the President of the Academy. At any rate, since R. Eliezer ben Hyrkanos is mentioned first in the collection, it was clearly made before his expulsion from the Academy, and apparently while he was temporarily the head of it; i. e. before R. Gamaliel's appointment.

[18] That R. Eliezer occupied the position of at least quasi-Leader or President of the Academy after the death of R. Johanan ben Zakkai, seems to me clear from the following considerations. (1) The statement of the famous *baraita*, urging people to attend a recognized Court for litigations, and saying, "After R. Johanan ben Zakkai to Beror Hayyil, after R. Eliezer to Ludd," thus putting R. Eliezer in the same class with R. Johanan ben Zakkai. (2) The fact that he went with R. Joshua and R. Gamaliel II to Rome on the visit of the first Palestinian Rabbinical commission there. (The visit occurred probably about the year 80 C.E. and apparently had as its purpose obtaining permission for R. Gamaliel II to assume the presidency of the Academy). (3) The apparently well authenticated fact that R. Akiba as a prospective student first applied to him for instruction, and then went to R. Joshua (*Yer. Pesahim*, 63, 33b). (4) The several cases on record of people who came to R. Eliezer in the first place for decisions, and then went to R. Joshua, just as they first went to Shammai and then to Hillel (*Shabbat* 30a, *Kiddushin*, 31a). (5) The mention of R. Eliezer, R. Joshua and R. Tarfon as the three leading teachers in *ARN* II, 18, 20a.

III. The Origin of Collection C

Collection C is in some respects perhaps the most interesting of all the constituent parts of *Abot*, for we have here, apparently, a record of the discussions which took place in the "philosophical society" organized by R. Akiba, Elisha ben Abuyah, Ben Zoma, and Ben Azzai, early in their scholarly activity. The only definite record of their work which we have is contained in the famous historical statement: "Four entered a *pardes* (an orchard); R. Akiba, Ben Azzai, Ben Zoma, and Elisha ben Abuyah. Ben Azzai peeped and died; Ben Zoma peeped and became mad; Elisha ben Abuyah cut down the saplings (i. e. became an apostate). R. Akiba, alone, entered in peace and left in peace."[19]

The evil fate which befell three of the members of the group has tended to make readers seek special meanings in the word *pardes*, as used in this connection. It has been allegorized as meaning "hidden" or "mystic" lore; it has been taken to mean simply Paradise. But the most plausible interpretation of the passage, it now seems to me, is that the four scholars made an orchard the center of their studies, just as the Academy itself met in a vineyard; and in later times, Akiba and his diciples foregathered under a fig tree. Any sinister reference, intended by the *baraita*, can have reference only to the fact that the four scholars separated themselves from the general Conclave in the vineyard, and assembled for private discussions in their orchard.

Because of Elisha ben Abuyah's apostasy, which occurred years later, his statements were omitted from the traditions of the Academy, and his very name was expunged from all the records. Whenever mention had to be made of him, he was called simply *Aher*, "another one."[20]

Nevertheless, we find his statements preserved in both *Abot* and *Abot d'R. Nathan*. Clearly there must be some special reason for this exception; and it is provided by an examination of *ARN* I, 23–26. It will be noted that each of these four chapters opens with the name of a member of the Society of the Orchard:

[19] *Tosefta Hagigah* 2.3, ed. Zuckermandel, p. 234; *B. ibid.* 14b, *Yer. ibid.* 21, 77b.

[20] *Loc. cit.*

23, with Ben Zoma; 24, with Elisha ben Abuyah; 25, with Ben Azzai; and 26, with R. Akiba. It is noteworthy that, like the other collections, A and B, this Collection is made the subject of special comment in *ARN* I; but essentially the chapters consist of strings of sayings by each of the four men.

The antiquity and originality of the Collection, as it is cited in *ARN* I, is further demonstrated by the fact that the sayings of R. Akiba are put at the end. It would be altogether in accordance with the humility of that great scholar to cite his colleagues first and himself last. On the other hand, it is quite impossible to suppose that any later redactor finding R. Akiba's statements before those of Ben Azzai and Ben Zoma (as they are in both the Mishna *Abot* and in *ARN* I) would deliberately place them later.[21]

Turning to *ARN* II, however, (33, 36a and b), we note that while it cites R. Akiba, Ben Zoma and Ben Azzai, together, it omits all mention of Elisha ben Abuyah in this connection; and adds his saying only in 35, 39a, after a late compilation including sayings of Eleazar Ha-Kappar, and his son, members of the last generation of tannaim.

Similarly in the Mishna, we find a series of sayings by R. Akiba at the end of Chap. III (III, 17 ff.) and those of Ben Zoma and Ben Azzai at the beginning of Chapter IV (IV, 1, 2)[22] while the saying of Elisha ben Abuyah is relegated to the end, after the sayings of R. Judah I's contemporaries and followers, R. Jannai, R. Jacob, and R. Simeon ben Eleazar.

Taken together, these facts seem to indicate clearly that there was an original collection, approximately similar to that pre-

[21] Naturally the early collection of sayings has been supplemented even in *ARN* I by later material. But that this material is not original is evident from the following facts: (a) the fact that it is lacking in *ARN* II and *Abot*; (b) that it is largely irrelevant to the context; (c) that it derives from later authorities. Clearly it has been added by later redactors, in much the same manner as the comments on Collection A were added.

[22] It seems probable to me that Ben Zoma's saying still opens Chapter IV of the Mishna of *Abot*, because it was placed at the head of a chapter by R. Akiba; and R. Judah I did not feel free to change the chapter heading, as it were. Instead, wishing to place the words of R. Akiba before those of his younger colleagues, he transferred them to Chapter III.

served in *ARN* I, including the statements of all four members of the Society of the Orchard; that the editors of the earlier forms of *ARN* II and Abot elided the name of Elisha ben Abuyah from their collection because of his apostasy, and put the saying of R. Akiba at the beginning where they felt it belonged rather than at the end; and that the final editors of both works, feeling that the words of Elisha ben Abuyah should not be lost, added them to the end of their treatises.[23]

IV. Collection D, Consisting of the Numerical Norms

It is impossible to date this collection with precision. But we know that R. Akiba was fond of such collections; and it is also obvious, especially from the omission of the names of any authorities in this collection, and its occurrence in practically the same form in *Abot* and in *ARN*, that it is quite ancient. We may, therefore, take it that it dates from no later than the time of R. Akiba.

V. The Transition from Collection A to Collection B: The Rival Claims to the Hillelite Succession

There was no doubt of the manner in which the Pharisaic tradition had come down from the Men of the Great Assembly to Hillel and Shammai; all were agreed that the leadership had been in the hands of scholars whose names were well remembered, and who had worked in "pairs," as described above, in each generation. There were, however, two views regarding the manner in which the tradition was being preserved since the time of Hillel and Shammai. The scholars who were engaged in active teaching naturally regarded themselves as the true preservers of the Oral Law. On the other hand, the descendants of Hillel, who had each in his generation held the presidency of the

[23] A development very similar to this possibly took place in the compilation of our present Book of Judges, where an earlier editor apparently ommited what are now Chapters 17–21; and the final editor restored them, *at the end.* See G. F. Moore, *The Book of Judges*, in *International Critical Commentary*, Introduction p. xxx.

Pharisaic Order, believed that it was they, as a family, and as holders of high office, who were maintaining the tradition.

The conflict became embittered, apparently, in the last days of the Commonwealth, when R. Simeon ben Gamaliel I, the great-grandson of Hillel, was Nasi, and R. Johanan ben Zakkai was Ab Bet Din, or Associate.[24] It was universally recognized that while R. Simeon ben Gamaliel had inherited Hillel's office, R. Johanan ben Zakkai was the heir to his spirit. It was also obvious that R. Johanan ben Zakkai, the foremost teacher of his generation, and the master of all the distinguished scholars of the following generation, was actually preserving the Oral Tradition in a sense that R. Simeon ben Gamaliel I could not even pretend to do, for he had no disciples at all. Yet R. Simeon ben Gamaliel I and his adherents felt that his work was the more important, even from the point of view of the preservation of Pharisaism, for they held that "Not the study of the Law but its practice, is fundamental";[25] and surely R. Simeon ben Gamaliel I, as the holder of high office, and the leader of Pharisaism, was contributing as much to the general observance of the Law, as R. Johanan ben Zakkai was to its study.

We have no direct evidence of the controversy as it probably was carried on in the early days, during the lifetime of R. Simeon ben Gamaliel I and R. Johanan ben Zakkai. But it was renewed with even greater vigor a generation later, when R. Gamaliel II became the leader of the Pharisaic Order, and president of the Academy at Yabneh; while R. Akiba, his ardent, young opponent, was the foremost teacher of the time, the successor in spirit, though not in office, to R. Johanan ben Zakkai. In formulating the manner in which the chain of tradition was continued after the time of Hillel, R. Akiba, the redactor of the earliest form of the treatise of *Abot*, apparently wanted to show that after the time of the five earliest "Pairs," the Oral Law was preserved and disseminated by the voluntary teachers and scholars of each generation. It was, therefore, entirely natural for him to add, after the sayings of Shammai and Hillel, "R.

[24] *Midrash Tannaim*, 26.13, p. 176.
[25] *Abot* I, 17.

Johanan ben Zakkai received the tradition from Hillel and Shammai."[26] This was an implicit denial of the claim of the lineal descendants of Hillel that they were the preservers of the great tradition of Pharisaic learning. Not they, but R. Johanan ben Zakkai, the youngest of Hillel's disciples, received the Sinaitic tradition which Shammai and Hillel had received from Shemayah and Abtalyon, and the latter from Judah ben Tabbai and Simeon ben Shattah. This editorial comment, making R. Johanan ben Zakkai the link between the "Pairs" and the later, tannaitic scholars, was followed by a maxim formulated by R. Johanan ben Zakkai, and then by a series of maxims formulated by his disciples, namely, Collection B. This brought the line of tradition down to the time of R. Akiba, himself.

When the Mishna of Abot was re-edited by R. Judah the Patriarch I, who was seventh in descent from Hillel, and very proud both of his lineage and of the part his family had played in the preservation of the Torah, he seems to have decided to interject between the statements of Hillel and the reference to R. Johanan ben Zakkai, a series of maxims deriving from his ancestors, the descendants of Hillel, to indicate, just what R. Akiba had tried to deny, that they were the true transmitters of the Oral Law. Hence, following Collection A, which concludes with the statements of Hillel and Shammai, we find in our Mishna, first a maxim of R. Gamaliel, apparently R. Gamaliel I; after this comes another by his son, Simeon; and

[26] *Abot* II, 9. That this paragraph was originally intended to follow immediately on Collection A, has been recognized already by David Hoffmann (*Die Erste Mischna*, 28) and others. It was impossible, however, to recognize its full implications until the Pharisaic principle of dual leadership, first discovered by Professor Louis Ginzberg, in his *Mekomah shel ha-Halakah be-Hokmat Yisrael*, Jerusalem, 1931, 14, was fully understood. As soon as we realize that R. Johanan ben Zakkai was merely associate to R. Simeon ben Gamaliel I, and a member of a "Pair," we see that the statement that he "received the tradition from Hillel and Shammai," implies a rejection of all competence to R. Simeon ben Gamaliel I. First, the statement makes R. Johanan ben Zakkai the sole bearer of tradition in his day; second, it insists that he was the transmitter of the teachings of the Shammaites, whose opinions he opposed, as well as those of the Hillelites. Perhaps it was with this in mind that he was given the title of *Rabban* by his admirers; a title created, apparently, for R. Gamaliel I, who was the sole leader of his time.

then a third by R. Simeon ben Gamaliel, presumably the Second. This ends the first Chapter of our Mishna; the second Chapter, which was put in its present form after the time of R. Judah the Patriarch I, opens with a maxim attributed to him, continues with another by his son, R. Gamaliel III, and then reverts, suddenly, to a whole series of statements attributed to Hillel. The very confusion which is apparent in this arrangement, separating one group of Hillel's maxims from the other, and placing a whole section of his statements after those of his eighth lineal descendant, proves that we are dealing with the work of successive redactors. Moreover, we have textual evidence that the whole section containing the statements of the descendants of Hillel was lacking in the earliest form of the Mishna, since both *ARN* I and *ARN* II, agree in placing Collection B immediately after the Collection A, without any reference to the descendants of Hillel.

We have, therefore, every reason to believe that R. Judah I, the Patriarch, as redactor of the Mishna, having concluded the list of "Pairs," decided that it was appropriate to follow that with a list of his ancestors who, in his opinion, had been the true preservers of the Mosaic tradition.

In so doing he ignored the associates whom his ancestors had, for as we have seen above, the system of dual leadership was actually continued to his own day. But this, too, was probably intentional. R. Judah the First had apparently decided to destroy the system of "Pairs," and to concentrate the whole formal authority in the hands of one leader. To accomplish this, it was necessary to rewrite the history of tradition since the time of Hillel, and to relegate the associates, who had worked with his ancestors, to the background. Hence no mention is made, in this first list, of R. Johanan ben Zakkai, the associate to R. Simeon ben Gamaliel I, or of R. Joshua, the associate to R. Gamaliel II, or of R. Nathan the Babylonian, the associate to R. Simeon ben Gamaliel II.[27]

[27] Out of loyalty to the received text, and also perhaps to satisfy the opposition, (as well as to pay homage to the founder of his house) R. Judah I opened the second chapter with a series of sayings of Hillel, now found in *Abot* II,

Only one of R. Judah I's ancestors was omitted from the list of Hillel's descendants in Chapter I, namely, R. Gamaliel II, his grandfather. This omission was not caused by the lack of any suitable maxim by him. One of the most touching maxims in the whole Talmud is attributed to him, and might well have been cited in this connection: "He who has mercy on God's creatures will receive mercy from God."[28] The omission was caused, I believe, by a far more astute line of reasoning. R. Gamaliel II, it will be recalled, was removed from the presidency of the Academy, and replaced for a time by R. Eleazar ben Azariah. To have recorded R. Gamaliel II in the line of tradition would have raised the question whether R. Eleazar ben Azariah, too, did not belong there. It was more prudent, therefore, to omit all mention of R. Gamaliel II, and to proceed from R. Simeon ben Gamaliel I, to R. Simeon ben Gamaliel II, without interruption.[29]

We may have in this ignoring of the prerogatives of the Ab Bet Din, the secret to the compilation of the treatise *Abot d'R. Nathan*, as rival to the Mishnaic treatise. R. Nathan was Ab Bet Din, and he might well have been irked, at what must have seemed to him a wanton and insolent omission of all reference to his two or three immediate predecessors in office. Indeed, R. Judah I was practically denying that the office had any significance in the development of Pharisaic tradition since

5 ff. and followed them with the statement formulated by R. Akiba, that R. Johanan ben Zakkai had received the tradition from the Hillel and Shammai. Put in this manner, however, the statement became quite harmless; there was no indication in it that R. Johanan ben Zakkai was the bearer of the tradition of the "Pairs"; it merely described him as a disciple of Hillel and Shammai.

[28] *Tosefta Baba Kamma*, 9.30, p. 366; cf. *B. Shabbat*, 151b. That the reference is to R. Gamaliel II is proven by the fact that R. Judah cites the maxim in the *Tosefta*.

[29] There is the further possibility that Rabbi Judah the Patriarch was prepared to admit the Shammaitic inclinations of his grandfather, and, therefore, felt it proper to omit his name from a list which showed the line of inheritance of Hillelite traditions. That the father of R. Gamaliel II, R. Simeon ben Gamaliel I, too, was a Shammaite, he would hardly have been prepared to admit.

Hillel. What more natural than that this Ab Bet Din, championing the prerogatives of his office against aggression, should compile his own history of the later tradition, and insist, as R. Akiba had insisted a generation earlier, that the tradition descended not from Shammai and Hillel to Hillel's descendants, but to R. Johanan ben Zakkai, the Ab Bet Din, of the last days of Jerusalem, and from him to his disciples? Apparently, however, R. Nathan, who was a patrician, could not persuade himself to assert that R. Johanan ben Zakkai, great teacher that he was, and yet ardent partisan of the plebeian cause, had inherited the traditions of *both Shammai and Hillel*, as R. Akiba had asserted. Hence he indicated rather, that Johanan ben Zakkai had received only the Hillelite tradition, implying that others had preserved the Shammaitic tradition.[30]

VI. The Changes Made in the Tradition by the Editors of the Mishna Abot

If this was the manner in which *Abot d'R. Nathan* came to be compiled, we must indeed be grateful for the conflict; for it is only through *Abot d'R. Nathan* that we can know the original form of many traditions which have been handed down in altered form in our Mishna. One of the maxims changed most fundamentally is the very first one, attributed to the Men of the Great Assembly. As can be seen from *Abot d'R. Nathan*, it read originally:

היו מתונים בדין ועשו סייג לתורה והעמידו תלמידים הרבה

"Be deliberate in judgment; make a hedge about the Torah; and raise many disciples."[31] In our Mishna, the order of the second

[30] Hence the statement that R. Johanan ben Zakkai received the tradition from Hillel and Shammai, occurs in *ARN* II, not *before*, but *after*, Collection B, containing the sayings of his disciples (*ARN* II, 31, 33b). In *ARN* I, it has been placed before that Collection, but as can be seen at once it is entirely out of its place, being quite superfluous in view of the following statement offering a transition between the saying of Hillel and those of R. Johanan's disciples (see *ARN* I, 14, 29a).

[31] This order is implied in that of the comments on the various sayings. The comment on "Make a hedge about the Torah" occurs in both *ARN* I and II, on f. 2a; while that on "Raise many disciples," follows on f. 7a. In citing

and third parts of the maxim is reversed; so that it reads, as is well known, "Be deliberate in judgment, raise many disciples, and make a hedge about the Torah (*Abot* I, 1).

Trivial as this difference is, it made possible an alteration in the fundamental meaning of the statement, "Make a hedge about the Torah." The statement does not mean, as has been assumed for centuries, that scholars are enjoined to add severities to the Law, so as to prevent the infraction of its essential commandments.[32] Such an injunction could not possibly be contained in this maxim for two reasons: first, because the authority of later scholars to add to the Torah was questioned as late as

the statement as a unit, the copyists of *ARN* I, quite naturally, followed our text of the Mishna, while those of *ARN* II, gave only the first third of the maxim, thus avoiding the difficulty.

[32] This interpretation is implied in the later strata of comments on the passage found in *ARN* I and II, and probably compiled by R. Nathan himself (2a ff.). A careful study of the whole passage will show, however, that it is composite, that its different strata definitely contradict one another. Thus *ARN* II says: "Make a hedge about the Torah. For a vineyard which is surrounded by a hedge cannot be compared to one which lacks a hedge. This teaches us that one must not raise a fence beyond the fundamentals (fixed in the Law itself), lest the fence fall and destroy the saplings. For so we find that Adam made a fence beyond the fundamentals, and the fence fell and destroyed the saplings." Then follows a statement, reverting to the fact that "The Holy One, blessed be He, made a hedge about His words; so also Adam, Job, Moses, the Torah, the Prophets, the Holy Writings, and the Sages made a hedge about their words." The examples cited for each of these differ in character from one another. The hedge ascribed to God is an argument to support His decision, as indicated below; that ascribed to Adam consisted in forbidding Eve to touch the tree of Knowledge, whereas God had only forbidden the tasting of it, and as indicated above, the hedge did harm rather than good; the other examples of "hedges" are additional prohibitions in the usual sense. There can be little doubt, I think, that the confusion arose from the fact that the original text mentioned only the "hedge" made by God, as offering an argumentative support for His decision, and calling on the human judges to imitate His example. A later compiler, finding the new interpretation of the phrase, "Make a hedge about the Law," gaining ground, offered an argument against it from Adam; but the final compiler, won over to the new interpretation, wove the older material into a new web, including material supporting the idea of additional prohibitions to protect more ancient ones. The same material can be found in *ARN* I, where, however, editorial activity removed some of the difficulties still apparent in *ARN* II.

the time of the destruction of Jerusalem, and certainly was not recognized early in the second century B.C.E. when this maxim was formulated;[33] second, because the maxim is addressed not to the members of the central Sanhedrin in Jerusalem, who alone could add new prohibitions, even when that power was claimed, but to the local judges and teachers of the various Palestinian villages. Certainly the authority to add new commandments to the Law would not have been delegated to them individually, and mentioned in the same maxim as "be deliberate in judgment," and "raise many disciples." The real meaning of the passage is preserved in our text of *Abot d'R. Nathan*, which, as frequently, gives both the earlier and later interpretation. In explaining the statement, *ARN* says: "The Holy One, blessed be He, made a protection for His words. Whence do we know that the Holy One, blessed be He, made a protection for His words? For it is written, 'And all the nations shall say, "Why did the Lord do thus to this land?"' The creatures of the world began to complain to Moses, saying, 'Because God is omnipotent in His world He slays whom He wishes, and preserves whom He wishes. What did the men of the generation of the Deluge do against Him that He caused them to float like inflated skins on the surface of the water; what did the men of the Generation of the Division do to Him that He scattered them throughout the world; what did the men of Sodom do to Him that He exterminated them with fire and salt; what did His people do Him that He exiled them from His land?' Therefore was Moses commanded to write down, 'Because they have worshipped other gods, For they went and served other gods, and worshipped them, gods whom they knew not, and whom He had not given unto them; . . . And the Lord rooted them out of their land in anger, and in wrath, and in great indignation, and cast them into another land, as it is this day' " (Deut 29 26).

The passage clearly indicates what "a hedge about the Torah" means. In writing the verse cited, God was not adding a new prohibition to the Torah; He was offering a supporting argument for the judgment He was rendering. And it is this that the

[33] See *Menorah Journal*, 1936, 131 ff.; *Jewish Review*, No. IV, 1933, 25–31.

judges were enjoined to do by the Great Assembly. They were to be deliberate in judgment; and when they had reached a decision, they were to give their reasons for it. This was to protect the Torah, by means of a hedge; for it would prevent its being exposed to ridicule and rejection.

It was only as a third part of their task that the local judges were originally asked to raise disciples. That was to be merely a by-product of their work; when they rendered a decision, those who heard it and the arguments supporting it would naturally learn the Law. It is difficult to say whether the change in the maxim, placing the command to raise new disciples second, was made by R. Akiba or R. Judah the Patriarch. R. Akiba, the great teacher, might naturally be expected to put the injunction to teach second; especially, if, as is probable, the words "make a hedge about the Law" had already assumed in his day the meaning of adding new prohibitions to the Law. He might have felt that the increase of students was more important than the legislative function of the Sanhedrin. On the other hand, it is also possible that the change was made no earlier than the time of R. Judah I, and that it was only in his day that a "hedge about the Law" came to have its secondary meaning.

Another statement which the redactors of the Mishna transformed completely was that of Akabiah ben Mahalalel. As preserved in *ARN* I,[34] his maxim reads: "He who takes four things to heart will never fall into sin: whence he came; whither he goes; what he is destined to become; and who is his Judge. Whence does he come? From a place of darkness. Whither does he go? To a place of deep darkness. What is he destined to become? Dust, worms, and creeping things. And who is his Judge? The King of the kings of kings, the Holy One, blessed be He."

It is obvious that for all its beauty and piety this statement must have fallen on the ears of contemporary Pharisees as utter heterodoxy;[35] for they denied that man is to become merely

34 *ARN* I, 19; *ARN* II, 32; 35a.

35 See A. Kaminka in *Sefer Zikkaron*, the Jubilee Volume in honor of A. Z. Rabinowitz (Tel Aviv, 1929), 65. (I owe this reference to the kindness of my friend Mr. I. Rivkind.)

worms and dust.[36] They held, on the contrary, that the body would be raised into eternal life. There can hardly be a doubt, therefore, that this maxim played an important role in the refusal of the scholars to appoint Akabiah as associate to R. Gamaliel I,[37] even though he was one of the foremost scholars of the period; and it may even have led to his expulsion from the Pharisaic Order. Nevertheless, it was not forgotten; and aside from its preservation in its original form by R. Nathan; it has come down to us in slightly changed forms imposed on it by Ben Azzai, who simply interpolated some words to remove the sting of its heterodoxy; and R. Akiba, who is probably responsible for the version preserved in our Mishna: "Consider three things, and thou shalt not fall into sin. Know whence thou comest; and whither thou goest; and before whom thou art destined to give an accounting. Whence dost thou come? From an ill smelling droplet. Whither dost thou go? To a place of earth, worms, and creeping things. And before whom art thou destined to give an accounting? Before the King of the kings of kings, the Holy One, blessed be He" (*Abot* 3.1).[38]

Note how the editor of the Mishna carefully indicates that it is only the physical body which is under discussion, by substituting the sperm for "a place of darkness," as the origin of man; how instead of saying that man is destined to become worms

[36] A similar saying of Ben Sira (7 17) that "the expectation of man is worms" was utterly transformed by his grandson in the Greek translation to read, "the expectation of the *ungodly* man is *fire* and worm." The objection to Akabiah's statement is further obvious from the comment of R. Simeon ben Eleazar who maintained that "man came from a place of fire and returned to a place of fire," rather than from a place of darkness to return to a place of darkness. Patrician loyalty is evidenced in the fact that R. Simeon ben Yohai came to the defence of R. Akabiah repeating his words without change, and citing Job 25 6, in support of the fact that man becomes worms after his death. See *ARN* I, *loc. cit.* So also, apparently R. Leuitas (whose graecized name indicates patrician status) used to repeat Ben Sira's statement in its original form (*Abot* 4.4).

[37] Mishna *Eduyyot* 5.6. It is possible that the refusal to appoint Akabiah as Associate was due to his halakic teachings; while his expulsion from the Academy and the Pharisaic Order followed the accusation of heterodoxy.

[38] Ben Azzai's version is cited in *Derek Erez Rabbah*, chap. 3, M. Higger, *Mesiktot Derek Erez, Pirke Ben Azzai*, chap. 1, p. 155.

and dust, he merely says that he will go "to a place of dust and worms"; and how he definitely asserts the doctrine of a *future* judgment, instead of leaving the matter uncertain, as Akabiah originally did.[39]

[39] In a few instances it is apparent that the sayings of Collection A, both as preserved in *Abot* and in *ARN* are expansions of the original sayings of the "Pairs." This is especially clear in connection with the saying of Simeon ben Shattah, which reads in *Abot*:

> הוי מרבה לחקור את העדים והוי זהיר בדבריך שמא מתוכם ילמדו לשקר
>
> Be very searching in the examination of the witnesses and be heedful of your words lest through them they learn to speak falsehood.

The last (spaced) phrase occurs in *ARN* I in precisely the same form as in the Mishna; in *ARN* II, however, it is cited as follows: (in the name of Judah ben Tabbai)

> והוי זהיר בדבריך מן השומעים שמתוך דבריך ישמעו וילמדו לשקר
>
> And be careful of your words because of your hearers, lest out of your words they understand and learn to speak falsehood.

It is altogether unlikely that any redactor would so completely change the wording of an ancient maxim; and we may, therefore, assume that the original saying contained only the words: והוי זהיר בדבריך "And be careful with your words," and that the final clause was an editorial expansion, the text of which was not fixed, and, therefore, has come to us in two different versions. Similarly, the maxim of Judah ben Tabbai (attributed to Simeon ben Shattah in *ARN* II) reads in *Abot* and *ARN* I:

> אל תעש עצמך כעורכי הדיינין וכשיהיו בעלי דינין עומדין לפניך יהיו בעיניך כרשעים וכשנפטרים מלפניך יהיו בעיניך כזכאין כשקבלו עליהן את הדין
>
> Act not the counsel's part when the parties to a suit are standing before you. Regard them both as guilty and when they leave you regard them both as innocent provided they accept the judgment.

In *ARN* II, however, the spaced portion reads quite differently as is noted in the text below (IJ).

Here it is even more obvious that the spaced portion is a later explanation of the original saying. For there can be little doubt that the occasion of the saying was the entrance of the Pharisaic scholars into the judicial office, when the Pharisees gained power under Queen Salome. Under those circumstances the litigants doubtless had little choice but to accept the judgment rendered, and there was no need for adding that they were to be treated as innocent persons after the trial of their case "if they accepted the judgment." It was only in later times, when the Jewish judges lost their power to enforce their decisions, that this proviso became necessary.

VII. THE PATRICIAN INFLUENCE IN *ARN*

While R. Nathan was probably one of the redactors of *Abot d'R. Nathan*, it is not certain by any means that he was the author of its core, which consists of the comments on the older maxims found in Collections A and B of *Abot*. It is clear, however, that the author of these comments was a patrician who was sympathetic to views otherwise recognized as Shammaitic. Possibly, the comments grew up in the school of R. Ishmael before R. Nathan's time and were simply handed down by him together with additional material.

The patrician bias of the commentator appears in a number of passages. Thus, when Jose ben Johanan, the great plebeian Sage of the middle of the second century B.C.E., remarks, "And let the poor be people of your household" (*Abot* I, 5), the commentator at once explains, "This does not mean that they should be members of your household; but that the poor should tell one another about what they ate and drank in your house" (7a). Another interpretation, in the same spirit, interprets the maxim to mean that "one should teach one's family humility" (7b). The maxim is thus completely transformed; instead of saying, "Let the poor (or humble) be members of your household," it is made to say, "Let the members of your household be humble."

The passage, "Hate office," (I, 10) is interpreted, "A man must not seek greatness, *unless it is offered to him by others*" (*ARN* I, 11; *ARN* II, 22, 23b).

In citing the statement of the Men of the Great Assembly, "Raise many disciples," (*Abot* I, 1) the author finds it necessary to add, at once, the narrowing interpretation of the Shammaites: "The School of Shammai teach that one must offer instruction only to those who are pious, of good parentage, and of good older ancestry. The School of Hillel say, one should teach everyone" (*ARN* II, 4; *ARN* I, 3, 7b).

At the very beginning of the treatise, in commenting on the words, "Moses received the Torah from Sinai" (*Abot* I, 1), the editor takes occasion to deny the existence or effectiveness of intermediary beings. "Moses received the Torah from Sinai;

not from any angel, or any seraph, but from the King of the kings of kings, the Holy One, blessed be He" (*ARN* II, 1, 1b; lacking in *ARN* I). Such emphatic rejection of angels as intermediaries between God and man, was especially characteristic of the patricians. The Sadducees apparently raised it into a dogma;[40] and while the patrician Pharisees did not go quite so far as to declare the belief in angels heterodox, they took frequent occasion to discourage the popular belief in them.[41]

The same spirit of patrician bias is evidenced even in the later strata of the work, which were composed either by R. Nathan or by one of his successors. Thus, the redactor cites with approval a tannaitic statement, rejected by R. Akiba and his school, forbidding a woman to adorn herself during her menstrual period (*ARN* I, 2, 4b; *ARN* II, 3, 6b).[42] Again, in the same stratum, we find a quotation, with approval, from what is apparently a Shammaitic Mishna, reading: "When a man mounts his bed, he should read the Shema; if he is a scholar, he may read the Shema first, and then if he wishes to study, he may do so" (*ARN* II, 3, 7b; in somewhat changed form, *ARN* I, 2, 7b). The statement implies the Shammaitic teaching that the Shema is read properly when one is lying down, at bed time.[43]

[40] Acts 23 8.

[41] Cf. *Akiba*, 197 ff.

[42] This view was vigorously opposed by R. Akiba (*Sifra Mezora*, end). Nevertheless, it was preserved apparently by many Galileans and reappears in Gaonic times (perhaps about the seventh century) in the *Baraita de-Niddah* (published in Horowitz, *Tosefata Atikata*, IV, Frankfurt-am-M., 1890.) This severity of the later Palestinian with regard to Niddah is further illustrated in *Hillufe Minhagim* (ed. B. M. Lewin, published in *Sinai* I, 1937, 353), according to which the "men of the west," i. e., of Palestine, did not permit the Niddah to touch any vessel, or any food which had been moistened, "and only because of the emergency was she permitted to nurse her child."

[43] Mishna *Berakot* 1.3; the habit was so strongly implanted in patrician children that even those of them who became definitely associated with the Hillelites frequently observed it in adult life. Cf. the story of R. Tarfon cited in Mishna, *loc. cit.*, and that of R. Eleazar ben Azariah in *Tosefta Berakot* 1, 4, ed. Zuckermandel, p. 1. Another example of the patrician influence on *ARN* is perhaps to be found in the comment on the words, "Do not converse overmuch with a woman." Jose ben Johanan, who originally made the statement, doubtless was expressing the usual plebeian fear of close association between men and women as possibly leading to sexual license. The patricians, how-

VIII. *ARN* as a Repository of Some Older Traditions

We have already noted how various paragraphs have been preserved in *ARN* in purer form than that found in the Mishna. Perhaps the most notable of those so far examined is the maxim of Akabiah ben Mahalalel. But the redactors of the Mishna for various reasons either abbreviated or expanded the traditional formulae even when no question of heterodoxy was involved. Thus the first Mishna of *Abot* reads in its present form:

משה קבל תורה מסיני ומסרה ליהושע ויהושע לזקנים וזקנים לנביאים ונביאים מסרוה לאנשי כנסת הגדולה

"Moses received the Torah from Sinai, and handed it on to Joshua; who handed it to the elders; they handed it to the prophets; the prophets handed it to the Men of the Great Assembly."

According to *ARN*, however, the chain of tradition included several links omitted in the Mishna. *ARN* II, 1, 1b, reads:

משה קבל תורה מסיני ומסרה ליהושע ויהושע לזקנים וזקנים לשופטים ושופטים לנביאים ונביאים לחגי ולזכריה ולמלאכי חגי זכריה ומלאכי מסרו לאנשי כנה"ג

Moses received the Torah from Sinai and handed it to Joshua; and Joshua to the elders; and the elders to the

ever, were far less fearful of this than the plebeians, and were, therefore, far more liberal in their treatment of women in such matters (regarding this, see B. Bokser, *Pharisaic Judaism in Transition*, 108, note 53; and my *Akiba*, 191; cf. also Professor L. Ginzberg's *Mekomah shel ha-Halakah be-Hokmat Yisrael*, Jerusalem, 1931, 42, which shows how many of the controversies between the Shammaites and Hillelites are apparently based on the different attitudes of various social strata toward women). In view of this, it is not at all surprising to find that the editors of *ARN* explain the saying, "Do not converse overmuch with a woman," as referring to special cases. "If a man comes to the Academy and find himself treated with disrespect, or entering a quarrel with his comrade, he should not go home and report the incident to his wife; for he disgraces himself, disgraces his wife, and disgraces his colleagues" (*ARN*, 18a). It is true that both *ARN* I and *ARN* II also cite the statement of the Mishna that the saying "refers to one's own wife, and how much more to the wife of one's neighbor," and yet it is quite obvious that the general spirit of *ARN* is to limit the applicability of the saying of R. Jose ben Johanan.

> judges; and the judges to the prophets; and the prophets to Haggai and to Zechariah and to Malachi; and Haggai, Zechariah and Malachi handed it over to the men of the Great Assembly.

ARN I, 1, 1b, does not contain this terse form (which was probably compiled in imitation of that found in the Mishna) but gives a more expanded form, as follows:

> על ידי משה נתנה תורה בסיני . . . יהושע קבל ממשה שנאמר ונתת מהודך עליו (במדבר כ"ז כ') . . . זקנים קבלו מיהושע . . . שופטים קבלו מזקנים שנאמר ויהי בימי שפוט השופטים (רות א' א') נביאים קבלו משופטים . . . חגי זכריה ומלאכי קבלו מנביאים אנשי כנסת הגדולה קבלו מחגי זכריה ומלאכי
>
> Through Moses the Torah was given at Sinai . . . Joshua received it from Moses as it is written "and thou shalt put some of thine honor upon him (Num 27 20)". . . The elders received it from Joshua; the judges received it from the elders as it is written, "and now it came to pass in the days when the judges ruled" (1 1). The prophets received it from the judges . . . Then Haggai, Zechariah and Malachi received it from the prophets; the men of the Great Assembly received it from Haggai, Zechariah and Malachi.

The famous statement of Jose ben Johanan of Jerusalem reads, according to our Mishna, as follows:

> יוסי בן יוחנן איש ירושלם אומר יהי ביתך פתוח לרוחה ויהיו עניים בני ביתך ואל תרבה שיחה עם האשה ב א ש ת ו א מ ר ו ק ל ו ח ו מ ר ב א ש ת ח ב י ר ו
>
> Jose ben Johanan of Jerusalem said: "Let thy house be wide open; and let the poor be members of thy household, and engage not in much gossip with a woman. *This applies even to one's own wife, how much more to the wife of one's neighbor.*

But *ARN* I, 7, *ARN* II, 14, 17a, indicate that the final phrase, which is spaced in the above citation, was not part of the original text. In *ARN* it is cited only as a comment at the end of the chapter, which includes a considerable amount of discussion of the original norm (see 18a).

A similar addition to an ancient statement was made by the redactor of the Mishna, in connection with the words of R. Eliezer ben Hyrkanos who said, according to *ARN* I, 15, *ARN* II, 29, 30a,

> יהי כבוד חבירך חביב עליך כשלך אל תהי נוח לכעוס שוב יום אחד לפני מיתתך
>
> Let the honor of thy colleague be as dear to thee as thine own; be not easily moved to anger; repent one day before thy death.

To this, the editor of the Mishna (2.14) added the following comment, which he incorporated in the words of R. Eliezer:

> והוי מתחמם כנגד אורן של חכמים והוה זהיר בגחלתן שמא תכווה שנשיכתן נשיכת שועל ועקיצתן עקיצת עקרב ולחישתן לחישת שרף וכל דבריהם כגחלי אש
>
> And warm thyself by the fire of the wise; but beware of their glowing coals lest thou be burnt; for their bite is the bite of a fox, and their sting is the sting of a scorpion, and their hiss is the hiss of a serpent, and all their words are like coals of fire.

The passage is cited as a comment in *ARN* II, 29, end, 31b; and in *ARN* I, 15, end, 31b, the source of the tradition ascribing it to R. Eliezer ben Hyrkanos is given as R. Jose ben R. Judah, whose grandfather, R. Ilai, had been a favorite disciple of R. Eliezer, and gave the maxim in this elaborate form. There can be little doubt that Rabbi Judah the Patriarch, in editing the Mishna, accepted this longer version as given him either by R. Judah or R. Jose ben Judah, and incorporated it in the Mishna, displacing the older, shorter form.

IX. The Relation of the Two Versions of *ARN* to Each Other

The two versions of *ARN* are independent from one another or from any *written* proto-*ARN*. They were both written down from traditions which had been handed down more or less loosely for a number of generations; the only element of compilation or edition being simply the fact that the names of the authors were arranged in a definite order, though in some instances their very words were handed down. The differences between the two versions are such as could hardly arise after the original form had been reduced to writing, including some ellipses such as would be natural in memorized, partly edited texts.

(IA) Thus in *ARN* I, 1, *ARN* II, 1, 3b, we find a parable given to the story of Adam and Eve, eating of the Tree of Knowledge. The thought which the speaker R. Simeon ben Eleazar, wishes to convey is that Adam prepared the way for Eve's sin by telling her that God had forbidden them to *touch* the Tree of Knowledge whereas the prohibition had extended only to eating of the fruit. The texts read as follows:

ARN I: ר' שמעון בן אלעזר אומר אמשול לך משל למה אדם הראשון דומה לאדם אחד שנשא את הגיורת היה יושב מפקדה אמר לה בתי אל תאכלי פת בשעה שידיך טמאות ואל תאכלי פירות שאינן מעושרין אל תחללי שבתות אל תפרצי בנדרים אל תלכי עם איש אחר הא אם עברת על אחת מהן הרי את מתה. מה עשה האיש ההוא עמד ואכל פת בפניה בשעה שידיו טמאות ואכל פירות שאינן מעושרין וחלל שבתות ופרץ בנדרים והושיט לה בידיו מה אמרה גיורת ההיא בלבה כל הדברים שפקדני בעלי מתחלה שקר הם מיד עמדה ועברה על כולם.

ARN II: ר' שמעון בן אלעזר אומר למה היתה חוה דומה באותה שעה לאחד שנשא אשה גיורת ואמר לה אל תאכלי מן הפת עד שתטילי את ידך ולא מן הפירות עד שתעשרי [אותם] הלכה ואכלה מן הפת ולא נטלה את ידיה ומן הפירות ולא עשרה ומצא הפתח ליכנס בו.

ARN I.: R. Simeon ben Eleazar said: "I will explain this with a parable. To whom may Adam be compared? To a man who married a proselyte. He would sit and admonish her saying to her: 'O my daughter, do not eat bread when your hands are defiled; do not eat fruits which have not been tithed; do not violate the Sabbaths; do not violate your vows; do not go about with another man. For if you will transgress any of these you will die.' Then what did the man do? He arose and ate bread in her presence while his hands were defiled; and he ate fruits which were not tithed; and he violated the Sabbaths; and violated his vows; and gave her (what was forbidden to her) with his own hands. What then did that proselyte think? 'Everything which my husband commanded me at the beginning is false.' And she arose and transgressed them all."

ARN II.: Simeon ben Eleazar says: "To whom may Eve be compared at that moment? To a man who married a proselyte and said to her: 'do not eat the bread before you wash your hands; nor the fruits until you tithe them.' Then she went and ate the bread without washing her hands and the fruits without tithing them, and she found a door in which to enter."

It is clear from an examination of the two forms of the parable that neither of them can be original or correct. As they stand, neither is comparable to the case of Adam and Eve. What has happened is that each version retains part of the original form of the parable. *ARN* I is right in saying that the husband of the proselyte had warned her that eating bread when her hands were impure, eating untithed fruits, would, like violation of the Sabbath, lead to her death. *ARN* II is correct in giving the other half of the story, namely that when she ate the bread without washing her hands and consumed the untithed fruit without harm to herself, she found "the door to enter" the graver sins of violation of the Sabbath.

(IB) On several occasions we find such an ellipsis in *ARN* I, alone, the material being fully supplied in *ARN* II. Thus in *ARN* I, 4, 8a, we find in association with the norm והעמידו תלמידים הרבה "and raise many disciples" the following:

רבי עקיבא אומר כל הנוטל פרוטה מן הצדקה בזמן שאינו צריך אינו נפטר מן העולם עד שיצטרך לבריות

R. Akiba says: "Whoever takes a penny from charity when he does not need it will live to be dependent on others."

The connection of R. Akiba's statement to the main text is quite unintelligible, until we compare *ARN* II, which cites instead the following statement:

> ר' אליעזר אומר בבקר זרע את זרעך [כמשמעו] שאם [בכרת] וזרעת שלא תשב ותאמר דיי . . . רבי עקיבא אומר אם העמדת תלמידים הרבה בנערותך שלא תשב לך ותאמר דיי אלא העמד בזקנותך והרבה תלמוד תורה כי אינך יודע. הוא היה אומר אם בא עני אצלך בשחרית ונתת לו איסר והלך לו ובא אחר במנחה אל תאמר כבר נתתי לראשון [אלא] מוטב תתן לאחרון כי אינך יודע.
>
> R. Eliezer says: "The verse: 'in the morning sow thy seed' (Eccl 11 6), is to be taken literally; namely that if you have sown early do not sit idly and say: 'I have done enough' "... R. Akiba says: "It means rather, if you have raised many disciples when you are young do not sit down and say: 'I have done enough,' but raise more disciples in your old age and increase the study of the Law because you do not know: ('whether shall prosper this or that, or whether both shall be alike good')." He used to say: "If a poor man comes to you in the morning and you have given him an aesarion and he is gone away, and another one comes in the afternoon, do not say I have already given the first, but it is better that you give also the latter since you do not know ('whether shall prosper this or that, or whether both shall be alike good')."

R. Akiba's views in this instance naturally bear very closely on the principle of increasing the number of disciples, and lead quite properly to the other statements cited in his name on f. 8b. The connection has only been obscured in *ARN* I, because R. Akiba's views about the increasing of the number of disciples were somehow placed in the middle of the whole series of his statements, on 8b, bottom. That this is not a scribal displacement is obvious from an examination of the text of *ARN* I, from which it is clear that R. Akiba's statement followed the others given in the original, oral compilation of *ARN* I.

(IC) Again in *ARN* I, 5, 13b, we find the following account of the origin of the Sadducean and Pharisaic sects:

> אנטיגונוס איש סוכו היו לו שני תלמידים שהיו שונין בדבריו והיו שונין לתלמידים ותלמידים לתלמידים עמדו ודקדקו אחריהן אמרו מה ראו אבותינו לומר דבר זה אפשר שיעשה פועל מלאכה כל היום ולא יטול שכרו ערבית אלו היו יודעין אבותינו שיש עולם אחר ויש תחיית המתים לא היו אומרים כך. עמדו ופירשו מן התורה ונפרצו מהם שתי פרצות צדוקין וביתוסין. צדוקין על שום צדוק ביתוסי על שום ביתוס.
>
> Antigonos of Soko had two disciples who were studying his words and were teaching them to disciples. These arose and studied them carefully, and they said: "Why did our ancestors say this? is it possible that the workers should work all day and not receive any reward in the evening? If our ancestors had known that there was another world and there is a resurrection they would not have said this." Thereupon they arose and departed from the Torah and there arose out of them two sects, the Sadducees and the Boethusians. The Sadducees were named after Zadok, the Boethusians after Boethus.

The whole point of the passage, namely that the two disciples were named Zadok and Boethos, is omitted in *ARN* I, by an ellipsis; the material is, however, put quite clearly in *ARN* II, which begins:

> ב׳ תלמידים היו לו צדוק וביתוס
>
> He had two disciples, Zadok and Boethus.

On the other hand, *ARN* II reads:

> ויצאו מהן שתי משפחות צדוקים וביתוסים [צדוקים לשם צדוק ובייתוסים] לשם בייתוס.
>
> And there arose out of them two families, the Sadducees and the Boethusians. The Sadducees after the name of Zadok, and the Boethusians out of the name of Boethus,

which is clearly less precise than the expression of *ARN* I.

(ID) Finally, in *ARN* I, 6, 14b, we find the following:

> דבר אחר הוי מתאבק בעפר רגליהם זה ר' אליעזר, ושותה בצמא את דבריהם זה ר' עקיבא. מה היה תחלתו של ר' עקיבא אמרו וכו'
> Another interpretation is this: the expression, "sit amidst the dust of their feet," refers to R. Eliezer, and the expression, "drink their words with thirst," refers to R. Akiba. What was the beginning of R. Akiba? It is said etc. . . .

We wonder why the case of R. Eliezer is left so summarily, until we turn to 15b, and find a new story beginning with

> מה היה תחלתו של רבי אליעזר בן הורקנוס, בן עשרים וכו'
> What was the beginning of R. Eliezer ben Hyrkanos? He was twenty-two years etc. . . .

In *ARN* II, the matter is put more correctly. The phrase והוי מתאבק בעפר רגליהם (And sit amidst the dust of their feet) is explained with these words, on f. 15a, זה רבי עקיבא שבקש ללמוד תורה (This refers to R. Akiba, who sought to study the Torah) and ושותה בצמא את דבריהם (and drink their words with thirst) is explained as follows on 15b: [אמרו עליו על ר'] אליעזר בן הורקנוס. (It has been said concerning R. Eliezer ben Hyrkanos).

In this instance, too, it is clear that the difference could not have arisen by a copyist's error, but is inherent in the underlying oral tradition.

(IE) Similarly, and even more significantly, we find in *ARN* I, 7, *ARN* II, 14, 17a, the apothegm of Joseph ben Johanan

> ויהיו עניים בני ביתך
> And let the poor be members of your household

interpreted to mean not that the poor should be at home in your home, but that "the people of your home should be humble.' In *ARN* II, however, this is explicitly stated:

> ויהיו עניים בני ביתך ולא עני ממש, אלא מי שהוא עניו ואשתו ענוה ובניו ובני ביתו ענוים אף הכלבים שלו אינם מזיקים
> "And let the poor be members of your household." This does not mean literally the poor, but if a man is humble, and if his wife is humble, and if his children

> and his family are humble, even his dogs will not do any damage.

In *ARN* I, this introduction is omitted. Another interpretation of

> ויהיו עניים בני ביתך
>
> And let the poor be members of your household.

is given first, and then the text suddenly proceeds with

> דבר אחר למוד בני ביתך ענוה
>
> Another interpretation is: "Teach the members of your family humility."

(IF) On the other hand, we find in *ARN* I, 8, 18b, top,

> היה ר' מאיר אומר הלומד תורה מרב אחד למה הוא דומה לאחד שהיה לו שדה אחת וזרע מקצתה חטים ומקצתה שעורים [ונוטע] מקצתה אילנות ונמצא האדם ההוא מלא טובה וברכה.
>
> R. Meir used to say: "He who studies from a teacher may be compared to a man who has one field and sows part of it with wheat, and part with barley, and plants part of it with trees. That man will find himself full of goodness and blessing."

This is reproduced in *ARN* II, 18, 20a, line 15, without the mention of R. Meir as authority, simply as follows:

> הלמד מרב אחד למה הוא דומה למי שהיו לו בבית סאה זרע חטים במקום אחד ושעורים במקום אחר זו מלאה ברכות.
>
> He who studies from one teacher may be compared to a man who has in a single plot the seed of wheat in one place, and barley in another place; such a field is full of blessing.

(IG) Another difference in text pointing to the same fact is that between the comment on ואל תתייאש מן הפורענות, "Do not despair because of suffering" in *ARN* I, 9, 21b, and in *ARN* II, 17, 19a, top. Both cite the verse פחד פחדתי, "For the thing which I greatly fear," from Job 3 25 though in *ARN* I, this is used to prove that one should always fear punishment, and in *ARN* II, this thought is derived from אשרי אדם מפחד תמיד, (Happy is the man that feareth always) (Proverbs 28 14), which is followed by the statement:

> וכן אתה מוצא באיוב שממה שנתיירא בו לקה נתיירא מן השחין בו לקה שנאמר כי פחד פחדתי [וגו']
>
> And so we find in the case of Job that he was punished with that which he feared. He feared boils and was punished with them, as it is written: "for the thing which I greatly fear."

indicating rather that fear of punishment is reprehensible.

(IH) Finally, we note that in two instances, the statements of the oldest Sages, the "Pairs," are interchanged in *ARN* II, the maxim of Joshua ben Perahya (according to Mishna and *ARN* I) being ascribed to his colleague, Nittai of Arbel, and vice versa; and similarly that of Judah ben Tabbai is ascribed to Simeon ben Shattah and vice versa. Curiously enough, the order of the authorities is unchanged, so that Simeon ben Perahya and Judah ben Tabbai lead their pairs in both versions. Such a confusion might easily occur in a memorized text, but could hardly be accounted for in a written one.

(I–I) The same fact is implied in the slight differences in phraseology which are introduced in some of the oldest maxims. *ARN* II, 18a, reads ברח משכן רע, "Run away from an evil neighbor," where *ARN* I, 19b, like the Mishna, reads: הרחק משכן רע, "Keep distant from an evil neighbor."

(IJ) So also *ARN* II, 20, 22a, reads:

> על מנת שיתבעו את הדין ויקבלו את הדין (ויינפנו) [ויצפנו] את הדין
>
> On condition that they should demand judgment and accept judgment and deserve judgment,

whereas the parallel passage in *ARN* I (10, 21b) and Mishna read simply: כשקבלו עליהן את הדין, "When they have accepted the judgment."

(IK) On the other hand, *ARN* II, 20, 21b, is closer to the text of the Mishna in the following maxim:

> שמתוך דבריך ישמעו וילמדו לשקר
>
> Lest out of your words they will understand and learn to speak falsehood.

while the parallel passage in *ARN* I, 10, 22a, reads:

> שמא מתוך דבריך ישמעו השומעין ויוסיפו עליך שקר מפני הרמאין
> Lest out of your words the hearers will hear and speak falsehood because of the deceivers.

The Mishna (1.10) reads:

> שמא מתוכן ילמדו לשקר
> Lest out of them they will learn to speak falsehood.

(IL) The statement of Akabiah ben Mahalalel is given in the two versions as follows (35a):

ARN II (32)

יסתכל אדם בד' דברים ואינו בא לידי עבירה דע מאין באת ולאיכן אתה הולך ומי עתיד להעשות עפר רמה ותולעה ומי הוא דיין לכל המעשים ברוך הוא

Let a man consider four things and he will never come to sin. Know whence you have come, and whither you are going, and what you are destined to become, namely worms and creeping things, and who is the judge of everything, blessed be He.

ARN I (19)

כל הנותן ארבעה דברים אל לבו שוב אינו חוטא מאין הוא בא ולאן הוא הולך ומה עתיד להיות ומי הוא דיינו. מאין הוא בא ממקום חושך, ולאן הוא הולך למקום חושך ואפילה, ומה עתיד להיות עפר רמה ותולעה, ומי הוא דיינו מלך מלכי המלכים הקדוש ברוך הוא.

He who takes four things to heart will never commit a sin: whence he came, and whither he is going, what he is destined to become, and who is his judge. Whence does he come; from a place of darkness. And whither is he going; to a place of deep darkness. And what is he destined to become; dust, worms and creeping things. And who is his judge; the King of the Kings of Kings, the Holy One. blessed be He.

It is clear that in this instance, the text of *ARN* II has been far more definitely influenced by our Mishna and its spirit than *ARN* I. Indeed, the redactor in his anxiety about the maxim's orthodoxy, and his desire to approximate the Mishnaic text, throws grammar to the winds, and, beginning with the third person, suddenly turns to the second person, which is found in the Mishnaic text. He also omits any clearer description of the darkness from which man comes, and to which he goes, citing instead the statement of R. Simeon ben Eleazar, which insists that man comes from a place of fire, and returns to a place of fire.

X. The Influence of the Mishna on the Extant Texts of *Abot d'R. Nathan*

The examples cited are sufficient to show that our present texts of *ARN* are derived from a source which was independent from the Mishna, just as the two versions are independent from each other. Nevertheless, there is evidence that *ARN* I, in great measure, and *ARN* II, in slighter degree, and yet quite noticeably, have been affected by the Mishna, and could therefore not have been reduced to final, written form, until after the redaction of the latter. Examples indicating this are to be found in I J, and I K above. (IIA) Even more significant, however, for the relation of *ARN* I to the Mishna, is the fact that both texts invert the order of Shammai and Hillel, placing Hillel first. This was entirely natural in the Mishna, and is due either to the influence of R. Akiba, who was so complete a follower and admirer of Hillel, or more likely to that of Rabbi Judah the Patriarch, the redactor of the Mishna, who was Hillel's descendant. *ARN* I, naturally, took the order over from the Mishna. In *ARN* II, the older order, which placed Shammai first, is still preserved (cf. *ARN* II, 23, 24a, with *ARN* I, 12, 24b.

(IIB) It is noticeable, moreover, that since *ARN* II, in this instance, differs from the Mishna, it does not repeat the formula קבל, "He received," and simply gives Shammai's views. This indicates that the formulae, ק ב ל משמעון הצדיק etc., "He received from Simeon the Righteous, etc." were not original in the traditional collection, but were added in each instance by the redactor of the Mishna. Its presence in most instances of the relation of the pairs, such as

1) יוסי בן יועזר איש צרדה ויוסי בן יוחנן איש ירושלם קבלו מהן
2) יהושע בן פרחיה ונתאי הארבלי קבלו מהם
3) יהודה בן טבאי ושמעון בן שטח קבלו מהם

1) Jose ben Joezer of Zeredah, and Jose ben Johanan of Jerusalem received the tradition from them.
2) Joshua ben Perahya and Nittai of Arbel received the tradition from them.
3) Judah ben Tabbai and Simeon ben Shattah received the tradition from them.

in both *ARN* I and *ARN* II, shows that they were both influenced by the phraseology of the Mishna. *ARN* I went further, and added the formula even when it was lacking in the Mishna, as in the relation of Joshua to Moses יהושע קבל ממשה, "Joshua received the tradition from Moses," (1b, top), and the Men of the Great Assembly (*ibid.*):

אנשי כנסת הגדולה קבלו מחגי זכריה ומלאכי

The men of the Great Assembly received the tradition from Haggai, Zechariah and Malachi.

(IIC) Finally, in connecting the statements of Johanan ben Zakkai's disciples with those of the "Pairs," the redactor of the early Mishna (i. e. before the time of Rabbi Judah the Patriarch) thought it well to add a statement of R. Johanan himself, and introduced it with the words:

ר' יוחנן בן זכאי קבל מהלל ומשמאי

R. Johanan ben Zakkai received the tradition from Hillel and from Shammai.

An examination of *ARN* II, 28, 29a, shows that its source knew nothing of such a connecting link. Instead it inserted the story of Hillel's eighty disciples, of whom R. Johanan was the youngest, and then followed that with another mentioning R. Johanan's five disciples. Nevertheless, the compiler of *ARN* II, afterward adding the words of R. Johanan ben Zakkai (after those of his disciples) follows the Mishna in using the introductory statement: (31, 33b).

ARN I, more definitely under the influence of the Mishna, puts the phrase introducing R. Johanan ben Zakkai immediately after the statement of Shammai at the beginning of 14, 29a. It is obviously out of place there, however, for it is followed not by any statement of R. Johanan ben Zakkai, but by the story of Hillel's eighty disciples, which was the original form used to introduce R. Johanan ben Zakkai in *ARN*.

(IID) Finally, an examination of *ARN* I and II, 1, 1b–8a, shows as we have seen, that the original form of the statement attributed to the Men of the Great Assembly was as follows:

> הוו מתונים בדין ועשו סייג לתורה והעמידו תלמידים הרבה
> Be deliberate in judgment, make a hedge about the Torah, and raise many disciples.

for this is the order in which the different elements of the maxim are discussed. Nevertheless, in the summary, giving the maxim at the beginning (1b), *ARN* I follows the Mishna in giving the order as follows:

> הוו מתונים בדין והעמידו תלמידים הרבה ועשו סייג לתורה
> Be deliberate in judgment, and raise many disciples, and make a hedge for the Law.

CHAPTER 6

THE MAXIM OF THE *ANSHE KENESET HA-GEDOLAH*

IT IS probable that there were at least two "Great Assemblies" in the pre-Maccabean period of the Second Commonwealth.[1] The first[2] was held in the days of Nehemiah and was responsible for the Covenant still preserved in Neh 10. The second[3] was

[1] Recent discussions of the "Great Assembly" make it increasingly probable that the term did not originally refer to a particular meeting. It was rather an institution which had developed in ancient Israel for bringing together the people in times of crisis. The term is actually used for the gathering which appointed Simeon ruler and high-priest (I Macc 14 28). Presumably the gathering which considered the claim of Rehoboam to succeed Solomon (I Kings 12 1–16), and that which Ahab assembled on Mt. Carmel at the behest of Elijah (ibid. 18 19) were such "great assemblies." (See Abram Menes, *Die vorexilischen Gesetze Israels*, 90). If this be correct, the document preserved in Neh 10 may be presumed to be the work of a "Great Assembly"; and quite another may have been assembled under Simeon the Righteous. The telescoping of the Persian period into a single generation would account for the erroneous identification of the two assemblies. See further with regard to the matter, G. F. Moore, *Judaism*, III, 8–11, and the literature cited by him; L. Ginzberg, *Legends of the Jews*, VI, 447, n. 56; Margolis-Marx, *History of the Jewish People*, 124, 131; S. W. Baron, *A Social and Religious History of the Jews*, III, 41, n. 24; H. Englander, "The Men of the Great Synagogue," *Hebrew Union College Jubilee Volume*, 145–169; and my remarks in *The Pharisees*, 400 and 576.

[2] The tradition describing this first meeting as the "Great Assembly" occurs repeatedly in rabbinic literature. The document in Neh 10, is cited as the work of the "Great Assembly" by R. Joshua ben Levi (*Yer. Berakot*, 4, 11c, line 30); by R. Johanan in *Ruth Rabbah* 4.7 (on Ruth 2 4); by R. Abbahu in *Bereshit Rabbah*, c. 6, 6 ed Theodor, p. 45; and several times anonymously (*Yer. Berakot*, 1, 9, 4a, line 2, *et. al.*).

[3] The evidence for the existence of this "Great Assembly" is to be found in the tradition preserved in *Mishna Abot* 1, 1, and also in *Abot of R. Nathan*, I, chap. 4, and II, chap. 5, ed. Schechter p. 18. As G. F. Moore has demon-

Reprinted from *Journal of Biblical Literature*, Volume 59, 1940.

held toward the end of the third century B.C.E., and was apparently convoked by Simeon the Righteous. It was quite natural for the Talmudic Sages who telescoped the whole Persian period into a single generation (thirty-four years),[4] to identify also the first and second of these national assemblies.[5] This necessitated placing Simeon the Righteous a century before his time, making him the contemporary of Alexander the Great, and therefore (according to this chronology) a younger contemporary of Ezra.[6] Hence it came about that in the Mishnaic

strated, (*Jewish Studies in Memory of Israel Abrahams*, 348–364), Simeon the Righteous of Talmudic tradition was a contemporary of Antiochus III. Only one passage mentions Simeon the Righteous as a contemporary of Alexander the Great (*Yoma*, 69a), but the incident there described is told of the High Priest Jaddua by Josephus (*Antt.* XI, viii, 4). It is certainly reasonable to assume that the Talmudic tradition simply substituted the better known name of Simeon the Righteous for that of the comparatively unknown Jaddua. Even if we accept the Talmudic tradition and assume that the incident occurred to a High Priest named Simeon, that would lead only to the conclusion that the transmitter of the tradition in calling the High Priest Simeon the Righteous, indentified the earlier Simeon of Alexander's generation with the later one of the year 200 B.C.E. Certainly, it can be only the Assembly convoked by the second Simeon which was responsible for the formulation of the liturgy and the final closing of the prophetic canon. See below, notes 7–10.

4 *Seder Olam Rabbah*, c. 30, ed. Ratner 71a; *B. Abodah Zarah*, 9a.

5 It is also possible that the confusion in the chronology of the Persian period was due, at least in part, to the identification of the two "Assemblies," and the assignment to the generation of Ezra of regulations adopted by the Great Assembly which met centuries after his time.

6 This identification of the first Simeon the High Priest with Simeon the Righteous is expressly made by Josephus (*Antt.*, XII, ii, 5; and iv, 1). It is also implied in *B. Yoma*, 69a, cited above. The further telescoping of the period, according to which Zerubabel and Ezra lived at the same time, is not yet envisaged in the description of the chain of tradition preserved in *Abot of R. Nathan*. According to this — doubtless older — version, of the chain of tradition, "The prophets handed down the tradition to Haggai, Zechariah and Malachi. Haggai, Zechariah, and Malachi handed the tradition down to the Men of the Great Assembly." The Men of the Great Assembly, contemporaries of Ezra and Nehemiah are thus explicitly assumed to be removed by a generation or more from the Prophets of the Restoration. On the other hand, according to *Seder Olam Rabbah*, c. 29, ed. Ratner 67b, Zerubabel and Ezra are contemporaries. This tradition is followed by Rabbi Judah the Patriarch, in changing the form of the chain of tradition, and eliminating

tradition, Simeon the Righteous, whose name was inextricably associated with the second of the Great Assemblies, is described as "one of the survivors of the Great Assembly," meaning the first (and for the Talmudic Sages, the only) Great Assembly.

It can be shown, with a high degree of probability, that it was the second of these Great Assemblies which originated the formulae for the main synagogue prayers,[7] and for the Grace after Meat;[8] fixed the canon of the Prophets;[9] and perhaps also the first formula of the Passover Haggadah.[10] It is recorded that it also formulated a maxim of conduct, presumably intended for the local judges appointed under its direction. As preserved in the Mishna (*Abot* 1 2) the maxim reads: היו מתונים בדין והעמידו תלמידים הרבה ועשו סייג לתורה "Be deliberate in judgment; raise

Haggai, Zechariah and Malachi, as a link between the (older) Prophets and the Men of the Great Assembly. According to tradition as expressed in the Mishna (*Abot*, 1, 1), the "Prophets handed down the tradition to the Men of the Great Assembly." Perhaps, the compiler of the Mishna believed that Haggai, Zechariah and Malachi were themselves members of the Great Assembly, and this view seems to be reflected in a number of Amoraic traditions. See the view of R. Johanan recorded in *Megillah*, 17b ("One hundred and twenty elders, among whom were many prophets, established the eighteen benedictions"). Similarly, *Yer. Megillah*, 1, 7, 70d, line 47, speaks of the eighty-five elders (obviously those of Neh 10) and "among them many prophets" who established the festival of Purim. Zerubabel, the contemporary of Haggai and Zechariah is specifically mentioned as a member of the "Great Assembly" in Targum to Cant 7 3; and in the "chain of tradition" incorporated into *Mahzor Vitry*, 481 ff. Malachi is frequently identified with Ezra, and would therefore be a member of the "Great Assembly" (*Targum and Jerome*, Mal 1 1; *Megillah*, 15a).

[7] This view is expressed by R. Johanan, *B. Berakot*, 33a ("The Men of the Great Assembly established benediction, prayers, the forms of *Kiddush* and *Habdalah* for Israel"). For corroboration of this tradition, in a critical study, see *Jewish Quarterly Review*, N.S., XVI (1925), 1 ff.

[8] See *Jewish Quarterly Review*, N.S., XIX (1929), 220 ff. The evidence there presented, showing that the third benediction of the Grace after Meat was added during the Maccabean revolt, seems convincing. That would indicate that the first two benedictions, or at least, the second benediction, was pre-Maccabean. It may probably therefore be properly ascribed to the generation of Simeon the Righteous. There is further evidence for this ascription which I hope to present in another connection.

[9] *Baba Batra*, 15a. See also, Ryle, *The Canon of the Old Testament*, 113.

[10] See *Harvard Theological Review*, XXXI (1938), 300.

many disciples; and make a hedge about the Law." In this form the maxim is cited in the Mishna, also in the *Mekilta*[11] and in the *Sifre*.[12]

I have already indicated[13] that the version of the maxim preserved in the Mishna was not the only one known in Tannaitic times. A parallel version, followed by the compiler of *Abot* of R. Nathan (hereinafter, ARN,), placed the three parts of the maxim in the following order: 1. Be deliberate in judgment; 2. make a hedge about the Law; 3. raise many disciples.

A further study of the text of ARN indicates, however, that this parallel version of the maxim of the Great Assembly, differed even more profoundly from that preserved in our Mishna, and was approximately as follows: "Be deliberate in judgment; make a hedge about *your words*; and *appoint many Sages*."

This ancient form of the maxim can be recovered only through a careful analysis of our present text of ARN.

As is well known, ARN has itself been preserved in two forms, which, following Schechter, we shall indicate as ARN I and ARN II.

The end of chapter II reads as follows:

נוסח א

איזהו סייג שעשו חכמים לדבריהם שחכמים אומרים קריאת שמע של ערבית עד חצות רבן גמליאל אומר עד קרות הגבר. כיצד אדם בא ממלאכתו אל יאמר אוכל קימעא ואשתה קימעא ואישן קימעא ואחר כך אקרא קריאת שמע נמצא ישן כל הלילה ואינו קורא אלא אדם בא ממלאכתו בערב ילך לבית הכנסת או לבית המדרש אם רגיל לקרות קורא ואם רגיל לשנות שונה ואם לאו קורא ק"ש ומתפלל וכל העובר על דברי חכמים חייב מיתה. רב"ג אומר פעמים שאדם קורא אותה שתי פעמים בלילה אחת עד שלא יעלה עמוד השחר ואחת

נוסח ב

מנין שעשו חכמים סייג לדבריהם שאמרו חכמים לקרות ק"ש עד חצות רבן גמליאל אומר עד קריאת הגבר. אלא שלא יאמר אדם הואיל ואני מותר לקרות ק"ש כל הלילה אלך ואישן לי אימתי שארצה אני קורא ק"ש חטפתו שינה ולא קרא (כדי) [הרי] זה מתחייב בנפשו. מכאן אמרו חכמים עלה אדם למטה יקרא

[11] *Mekilta*, *Bo.*, c. 6, Friedmann-Horowitz-Rabin, 19; Lauterbach I, 46.

[12] *Sifre* Deut, 16, Friedmann, 68b; Finkelstein, 25.

[13] *JBL*, LVII, 29.

נוסח א

משיעלה עמוד השחר ונמצא יוצא בה ידי חובתו של יום ושל לילה. עמדו חכמים והרבו ועשו סייג לדבריהם: שבית שמאי אומרים אל ישנה אדם אלא למי שהוא חכם ועניו ובן אבות ועשיר ובית הלל אומרים לכל אדם ישנה שהרבה פושעים היו בהם בישראל ונתקרבו לתלמוד תורה ויצאו מהם צדיקים חסידים וכשרים.

נוסח ב

אם היה ת״ח יקרא את שמע בתחלה ואם רצה לשנות ישנה (כל) [וכל] העובר על דברי חכמים הרי זה מתחייב בנפשו שנאמר חופר גומץ בו יפול [ופורץ גדר ישכנו נחש] (קהלת י׳ ח׳):

Version I

What hedge did the Sages make for their words? For the Sages declared that the time of the reading of the *Shema* in the evening is until midnight. Rabban Gamaliel says until the cock crows. How then (did the Sages make a hedge?). When a man comes home from work, he should not say, "I will eat a little, and drink a little, and then I will read the *Shema*," lest he fall asleep for the night without reading the *Shema*. What, then, shall a person do? When he comes from work in the evening, let him go to the synagogue or the house of study. If he is accustomed to read the Scriptures, let him read them. If he is able to study the oral tradition, let him study it. If not, let him read the *Shema* and pray; and whoever violates the words of the Sages is guilty of a mortal sin. Rabban (Simeon ben) Gamaliel says, "Sometimes a person reads the *Shema* twice in succession in one night, once immediately before the dawn, and once immediately after dawn, and thus he fulfills his obligation both for the day and for the night."... (?) For the School of Shammai say that one should not teach the oral tradition except to a disciple who is wise, meek, of good descent, and rich; while the School of Hillel say, "One should teach everyone, for there were many sinful in Israel who were brought near to the study of the Law, and emerged as righteous, saintly and pious men."

Version II

Whence do we know that the Sages made a hedge about their words? For the Sages said, one should read the *Shema* before midnight. R. Gamaliel said, "Before the crowing of the cock." But a person may not say, "Since I am permitted to read the *Shema* at any time during the night, I will go to sleep, and whenever I desire to do so, I will read the *Shema*." For in that event, sleep may overcome him, and he may fail to read the *Shema*, incurring mortal sin. Hence the Sages said, "When a man goes to bed, he should read the *Shema*. If he is a scholar, he should first read the *Shema*; and then if he desires to engage in study, he may do so. Whosoever transgresses the words of the wise is guilty of mortal sin, as it is written, "He that diggeth a pit shall fall into it; and whoso breaketh a fence a serpent shall bite him" (Eccl 10 8).

It will be noted that in ARN I the controversy between the Schools of Shammai and Hillel which obviously has its basis in the statement "raise many disciples," is not introduced by the citation of the basic norm. Schechter, following most of the commentators, has added the words: והעמידו תלמידים הרבה "And raise many disciples" at the beginning of the passage. But this emendation has no support in any of the Mss. he used, or in that which has become available since his time.[14]

On the other hand, the words עמדו חכמים והרבו ועשו סייג לדבריהם of ARN I, which I have spaced in the citation above, (and have necessarily left untranslated) defy explanation in their present form. R. Elijah Gaon of Wilna deleted them. Schechter, rejecting this *tour de force*, offered a very difficult explanation, which cannot be accepted.

Obviously the text is corrupt. It can, however, be reconstructed by a comparison of that preserved in the Ms. published by Schechter as Appendix II to his edition. According to that Ms. the first three words should read: עמדו חכמים הרבה. With slight emendation, this becomes: העמידו חכמים הרבה "Raise many Sages, and make a hedge about their words." This phrase forms the natural basis for the following comment, "For the School of Shammai say," etc. The compiler is indicating that the School of Hillel, in their insistence that instruction should be given to as many disciples as possible, tended to fulfill literally the command of the Great Assembly.

It is easy to see why this form of the text was misunderstood and distorted by later copyists and authorities. The Mishnaic variant had become so well known that no one would expect to find a parallel form giving the same thought in a somewhat different manner. Nevertheless, there is reason to believe that העמידו חכמים הרבה "Raise many Sages" may be the older form of the text. This seems probable, first because, obviously, the compiler of ARN would not invent a variant form of the saying in opposition to both the Mishna and to the tradition; second, because we know that Rabbi Judah the Patriarch and the earlier compilers of the Mishna felt free to change the wording of the traditions which they included in their Code.

[14] The manuscript of ARN in the Enelow Collection of the Library of the Jewish Theological Seminary of America.

Finally, there is a special reason why Rabbi Judah the Patriarch would wish to substitute the word תלמידים "disciples" for חכמים "Sages," in the current maxim. The original maxim might readily be interpreted as a stimulus to Sages to ordain other Sages. Perhaps indeed that was its original intention. But the later Patriarchs, including apparently Rabbi Judah I, endeavored to centralize the authority to grant ordination in their own office.[15] Rabbi Judah I might therefore be inclined to recast the original maxim in such a way as to leave no doubt that what was intended was the instruction of new *disciples*.

The phrase, עשו סייג לתורה "Make a hedge about the Law," also appears to be the result of an alteration of the original text by Rabbi Judah. In its usual form, it is interpreted to be a command to extend the area of prohibited action, so as to prevent the infringement of the Biblical Law itself. Thus, while Biblical Law declares only marriages with near relatives incestuous, rabbinical tradition made a "hedge about the Law" in adding a considerable number of secondary relatives to the list of those prohibited.

But the compiler of ARN seems to have had quite a different form of the maxim before him. From his comments, it would seem that this phrase was, originally, not "Make a hedge about the Law," but "Make a hedge about your words." His comments consist primarily of examples drawn from the history of Jewish literature. Each example illustrates the principle of making *a hedge about one's own views*. The hedge may consist a. of argument in vindication of the principle; b. of a form of expressing the principle which will help to make it understood; c. of an extension of the principle to cases which might be

[15] Cf. *Yer. Sanhedrin*, I, 19a, line 53; see I. H. Weiss, *Dor Dor ve-Dorshav*, II, 193. The change of text may also have been influenced by Rabbi Judah I's aversion to liberal granting of ordination. His views on this subject are reflected in his refusal to grant Rab full ordination (*B. Sanhedrin*, 5a); and his refusal to ordain several of his disciples, including some of the most eminent, such as Bar Kappara and Levi (see e. g., Yer., *Moed Katan*, 3, 1, 81c, line 66).

overlooked; d. and only in some instances to the suppression of an innocent action lest it lead to serious transgression. It is noteworthy, however, that even in the examples included under the last heading, the serious transgression is not something prohibited by a higher authority, but by the creator of the hedge himself.

The compiler of ARN illustrates these types of hedges by examples drawn from the words of God, Adam, the Torah, Moses, Job, the Prophets, the Hagiographa, and the Rabbinic Sages.

a. "God made a hedge about his words," by anticipating an argument against the theodicy, and refuting it.

b. The Prophets "made a hedge about their words" by expressing the power of God in a form intelligible to human beings.

c. Moses "made a hedge about his words" by separating the Israelites from their wives not for two days, but for three days, before the Revelation. While God had commanded that the Israelites be sanctified only "today and tomorrow" (Exod 19 10), Moses told them, "Be ready against the third day; come not near a woman" (v. 15). This additional severity was explained by the compiler as being intended to guard against a special form of defilement which might occur within three days of marital congress. Similarly Job is said to have "made a hedge about his words," by extending the prohibition against enjoying the beauty of married women to include unmarried ones (Job 31 1). "For Job thought, perhaps I may look on her today, and tomorrow some man will marry her; and it will then turn out that I have looked upon another man's wife (for my enjoyment)."

d. The fourth type of hedge is exemplified by the action of Adam who forbade Eve to touch the tree, when there was, in reality, no prohibition against that. The Book of Proverbs similarly forbids one to enter the street in which an immoral woman resides, lest one be enticed by her. The Sages have, likewise, commanded that one read the *Shema* before midnight, lest one forget to read it at all.

As interpreted by the compiler of ARN, the commandment to "make a hedge" is thus not addressed to a supreme legislative body like the Sanhedrin, which in later times claimed the authority to add restrictions to those mentioned in Scripture. It is addressed to individual scholars, who are urged to follow the examples set in history in fortifying their views in various ways. The individual judge rendering a decision must bear in mind that he should a. anticipate arguments against his judgments; b. make his views clear to those who hear him; c. guard against possible infringements of his decision through unforeseen accidents; d. and make provision against inevitable violation of his decision, through innocent forgetfulness or lack of care.

The phrase, "make a hedge about your words," thus resembles the phrases, "raise many Sages (or disciples)," and "be deliberate in judgment," as the directions of the Great Assembly to local scholars and judges.

Rabbi Judah the Patriarch or one of his predecessors, however, seeking authority for the claim of the Sanhedrin that it could add new prohibitions as "hedges" to the Law, transformed the original maxim to its current form. It was no longer a command to "make a hedge about your words"; it became a command to "make a hedge about the Law."

In this new form, it was quite impossible for the phrase "make a hedge" to stand between the first and third parts of the ancient maxim. The commands, "be deliberate in judgment" and "raise many Sages (or disciples)," were addressed to individual scholars; that to "make a hedge about the Law" was addressed to the Sanhedrin as a whole; for obviously, individual scholars were clothed with no such authority. Hence the arrangement as well as the contents of the maxims was altered. The teaching of the Great Assembly thus assumed the form it has in the Mishna: "Be deliberate in judgment; raise many disciples; and make a hedge about the Law."

The discussion of the maxim, "Make a hedge about your words," will be clarified by a perusal of the full text of ARN's comments on it.

Version I

A.

And make a hedge about the Law. And make a hedge about thy words just as the Holy One, blessed be he, made a hedge about his words; and Adam made a hedge about his words; the Torah made a hedge about its words; Moses made a hedge about his words; and so Job, and the prophets, and the Holy Writings and the Sages, all made a hedge about their words.

What hedge did the Holy One, blessed be he, make about his words? The Scriptures read (Deut 29 23): "Even all the nations shall say, Wherefore hath the Lord done thus unto this land?"

This teaches us that he who spoke, and brought the world into being, knew that the future generations were destined to say this. Therefore, did the Holy One, blessed be he, say to Moses, "Moses, write it down, and preserve it for the future generations, that they may say, that [this happened], "Because they forsook the covenant of the Lord . . . and went and served other gods, and worshipped them, gods that they knew not, and that he had not alloted unto them (ibid. 29 24)."

Version II

A.

And make a hedge about the Law. A vineyard which is surrounded by a fence cannot be compared to one which has no fence. For a man must not make a fence higher than the plant to be protected; lest the fence fall and break the plants. Thus, for example, we find that Adam made a fence higher than the plants, and the fence fell and broke the plants.

The Holy One, blessed be he, made a hedge about his words; likewise Adam; likewise Job; likewise Moses; likewise the Torah; likewise the prophets; likewise the Holy Writings; likewise the Sages made a hedge about their words. Whence do we know that the Holy One, blessed be he, made a hedge about his words? It is written (Deut 29 23): "All the nations shall say, Wherefore hath the Lord done thus unto this land?"

All mankind will begin to say to Moses, "Because God rules the world, he destroys whomsoever he wishes, and preserves whomsoever he wishes. What [evil] did the men of the Deluge do to him, that he caused them to float on the water like leather bottles? Or what did the men of the generation of Division do to him that he scattered them throughout the world? Or what [evil] did the men of Sodom do to him, that he destroyed them with fire and salt? What did his people do to him that he drove them into exile out of his land? Therefore Moses was told, "Write afterward, 'Because they forsook the covenant of the Lord, the God of their fathers, . . . and went and served other gods;' " therefore it is said, "And the Lord rooted them out of their land, in anger, and in wrath, and in great indignation" (ibid.).

The phrase, "with anger", refers to the sword, as it is written (Exod 22 23), "My anger shall wax hot, and I will kill you with the sword." The phrase, "with wrath," refers to the famine, as it is written (Ezek 6 12), "And he that remaineth and is besieged shall die by the famine; thus will I spend my wrath upon them." The phrase, "in indignation" refers to the pestilence, as it is written, (Num 17 11), "For there is indignation gone forth from the Lord, the pestilence is begun."

Version I

B.

What hedge did Adam make about his words? The Scriptures say (Gen 2 16 f.) "And the Lord commanded the man, saying: 'of every tree of the garden thou mayest freely eat; but of the tree of the knowledge of good and evil, thou shalt not eat of it; for in the day that thou eatest thereof thou shalt surely die.'" Adam, however, did not wish to repeat to Eve the precise words of the Holy One, blessed be he. But he told her, rather, that of the "fruit of the tree which is in the midst of the garden, God hath said: Ye shall not eat of it, neither shall ye touch it, lest ye die (Gen 3 3)."

At that moment, the wicked serpent took counsel with his heart, saying, "Since I cannot entrap Adam, I will go and entrap Eve." He, thereupon, went and sat near her, and entered into prolonged conversation with her. He said to her, "If you maintain that the Holy One, blessed be he, forbade you even to touch the tree, I shall show you that I can touch it, and not die. So also, you may touch it, and not die." What did the wicked serpent do thereafter? He stood up, and touched the tree with his hands and with his feet, shaking it, until its fruits dropped to the ground.... Then, he said to her, "If you maintain that the Holy One, blessed be he, forbade you to eat the fruit, I will show you that I can eat of it, without danger. So you too may eat of it, without danger." Thereupon Eve said to herself, "Everything which my master (Adam) commanded me is entirely false."... What caused this touching [of the tree by Eve]? The hedge which Adam made about his words. Hence the Sages taught, "If a man makes a hedge about his words, he cannot uphold his words." Hence the Sages taught, "Let no one add to the words which he has heard". R. Jose says, "Better is a fence of ten hand-breadths, which is standing, than one of one hundred cubits, which has fallen."

Version II

B.

Whence do we know that Adam made a hedge about his words? For the Holy One, blessed be he, commanded him (Gen 2 17): "Of every tree of the garden thou mayest freely eat; but of the tree of the knowledge of good and evil, thou shalt not eat of it."

Hence, from the words of Eve, (Gen 3 3) we learn that Adam made a hedge for her. The serpent argued with himself, "If I go to Adam and speak to him, I know that he will not listen to me. I will, rather go to Eve, for I know that women listen to everyone." He thereupon went and said to her (Gen 3 1), "Yea, hath God said: Ye shall not eat of any tree of the garden?" She said to him, "Yes, of the fruit of the trees of the garden, we may eat. But of the fruit of the tree which is in the midst of the garden, God hath said, Ye shall not eat of it, neither shall ye touch it, lest ye die (ibid. 3 2)." As soon as the serpent heard the words of Eve, he found a door in which to enter.

Version I

C.

What hedge did the Torah make about its words? The Scriptures say (Lev 18 19), "And thou shalt not approach unto a woman to uncover her nakedness, as long as she is impure by her uncleanness."

You might infer from this that he is permitted to embrace her, and kiss her, and engage in vain conversation with her. Therefore, the Scriptures say, "Thou shalt not approach." You might still infer, that she may sleep with him on the bed, so long as she is clothed. Therefore the Scriptures say, "Thou shalt not approach." You might still infer that she is permitted to wash her face or adorn her eyes; therefore the Scriptures say, "and of her that is sick with her impurity." (Lev 15 33), meaning, so long as she is in her uncleanness she shall be held apart. Hence the norm, "She who fails to adorn herself during her uncleanness pleases the Sages; but she who adorns herself during her uncleanness does not please the Sages."...

The Scriptures say, "None of you shall approach to any that is near of kin to him (ibid. v. 6)," From this verse, the Sages have inferred that it is forbidden to anyone to be in private, in an inn, with any woman, even with his sister, or his daughter, or his mother-in-law, lest he incur calumny. Nor should a man engage in conversation with a woman in the market-place, even with his own wife, how much less with another woman, lest she incur calumny. A man should not walk behind a woman, even his own wife, in the street, lest he incur calumny. The Scriptures employ the expression, "approach" in this verse; and they also use the same expession "approach" elsewhere (in Lev 18 19) where not only marital intercourse, but any expression of affection which might lead to transgression is forbidden. [This is to teach us] to shun the unseemly, and what resembles the unseemly. Hence the Sages taught, "Shun light transgression lest it lead to severe transgression; hasten to perform a light commandment, that it may bring you to observe an important commandment."

Version II

C.

Whence do we know that Job made a hedge about his words? For it is written (Job 1 8): "a whole-hearted and an upright man, one that feareth the Lord, and shunneth evil."

Thus Job used to say, "Keep distant from the unseemly, and from that which resembles the unseemly." Thus, too, Job says (Job 31 1): "I made a covenant with mine eyes, how then should I look upon a maiden?"

[This phrase is to be explained as follows:] If I did not look upon a virgin, whom one may take in marriage for oneself, or for one's son, or for one's grandson, or for one's sister's son, and who may marry anyone she desires; how much less would I look on a married woman.... Another interpretation is as follows: "I have made a covenant with mine eyes, how then shall I look upon a maiden?" [This verse means], since a maiden may be married to anyone she chooses, if I were to look upon her, it is as if I looked upon a married woman.

VERSION I

D.

What hedge did Moses make about his words? The Scriptures say (Exod 19 10): "And the Lord said unto Moses, 'Go unto the people and sanctify them today and tomorrow.'"

Moses the Righteous, did not, however, wish to repeat to Israel the precise words of the Holy One, blessed be he. But he told them, rather, "Be ready against the third day; come not near a woman (ibid. v. 15)."

Thus Moses added one day to the command of God. For Moses argued thus, Should a man cohabit with his wife, the semen might be exuded by her on the third day, and they would be impure. The Israelites might then receive the words of the Torah in impurity. I will rather add a third day for them.

VERSION II

D.

Whence do we know that Moses made a hedge about his words? For God said to him (Exod 19 10): "Go unto the people, and sanctify them today and tomorrow."

Only two days of separation were therefore commanded. But Moses argued to himself, "Perhaps a woman may exude the semen, and then come and stand before Mount Sinai, and the people of Israel will receive the Law in a state of impurity." What did he do? He added one day, as it is written (ibid. v. 15), "Be ready against the third day; come not near a woman." Whence do we know that God agreed with him? Because it is said, "And let them be ready against the third day" (ibid. v. 11).

VERSION I

E.

What hedge did Job make about his words? The Scriptures describe Job (Job 1 8) as "a whole-hearted and an upright man, that feareth God and shunneth evil."

This verse teaches us that Job kept himself far from anything which might lead to sin; from the unseemly, and from that which resembles the unseemly. . . .

The Scriptures say [of Job], "I made a covenant with mine eyes; and how then shall I look upon a maiden?" (Job 31 1). This verse teaches us that Job imposed so severe a discipline on himself, as not even to look upon a maiden. And is it not a fair inference, that if he refrained from looking upon a maiden, whom, if he so desired, he might marry, or take in marriage for his son, or for his brother, or for some other relative, he certainly refrained from

VERSION II

E.

Whence do we know that the Torah made a hedge about her words? For it is written (Lev 18 6): "None of you shall approach to any that is near of kin to him." Why do the Scriptures say, "Ye shall not approach"? [To tell us] that a man must not be in private either with his mother-in-law or his daughter-in-law; though he may be in private with them for a brief time, without transgression.

Thus also the Scriptures say, "And thou shalt not approach unto a woman to uncover her nakedness, as long as she is impure by her uncleanness (ibid. 18 19)." How does the injunction apply to him? Because it says, "Thou shalt not approach." You may think that it is permitted for him to play with her when she is impure. Therefore the Scriptures say, "Thou shalt not approach." How then does the injunction apply to her? Because the Scriptures say, "She shall

Version I

E.

looking upon a married woman. But wherefore did Job impose this severe discipline on himself, not even to look upon a maiden? Because Job argued, "Perhaps I may look upon her today; and tomorrow another man may come and marry her; and it will turn out that I was looking upon a married woman [for my enjoyment]."

Version II

E.

not approach."[16] You may think that she is permitted to adorn her garment, or sleep near him, while she is impure, therefore the Scriptures say, "She shall not approach." Whence do we know that she may cook, and wait upon him? Because the Scriptures say, "She shall not approach to uncover her nakedness." Hence the Sages taught, "Any woman who adorns herself during her impurity does not please the Sages."....

Version I

F.

What hedge did the Prophets make about their words? The Scriptures say, "The Lord will go forth as a mighty man, he will stir up jealousy like a man of war. He will cry, yea, he will shout aloud" (Is 42 13). God is to be described, however, not as one man of war, but as [mightier than] all the men of war in the world. Similarly, the verse (Amos 3 8) reads: "The lion hath roared, who will not fear? The Lord God hath spoken, who will not prophesy?" Yet God is to be described not as one lion, but as [mightier than] all the lions in the world. Similarly, the verse (Ezek 43 2) reads: "And behold the glory of the Lord God of Israel came from the way of the east; and his voice was like the voice of many waters; and the earth did shine with his glory." The phrase, "like the voice of many waters," refers to Gabriel, the angel. The phrase, "and the earth did shine with his glory," refers to the appearance of the Divine Presence. Now, if the voice of Gabriel, who is but one of the thousands of thousands of thousands, and myriads of myriads, who minister before God, can be heard from one end of the world to the other; how much more would this be true of the

Version II

F.

Whence do we know that the Prophets made a hedge about their words? For it is written (Amos 3 8): "The lion hath roared, who shall not hear? The Lord God hath spoken, who can but prophesy?" You might infer from this that his voice is merely like that of the lion. But you must consider that it was he who gave the voice to the lion; he is only described in this manner to his creatures so that the ear can rest and be able to comprehend. Thus, too, the Scriptures say (Ezek 43 2): "And behold the glory of the God of Israel came from the way of the east, and his voice was as the voice of many waters." [You might infer from this that his glory is merely like the sound of many waters.] But you must consider that it was he who gave the sound to the waters. He is only described in this manner to his creatures, so that the ear can rest, and be able to comprehend. Thus, too,

[16] The words *lo tiqrab* (of the Hebrew text) may, of course, be translated either "thou shalt not approach" or "she shall not approach." The ancient Sage interprets them in both ways to impose the restrictions equally on the man and the woman.

VERSION I

F.

King of kings of kings, the Holy One, blessed be he. But the eye is shown what it can see; and the ear is permitted to hear what it can hear.

VERSION II

F.

the Scriptures say (Deut 4 11): "And the mountain burned with fire unto the heart of heaven."

VERSION I

G.

What hedge did the Holy Writings make about their words? The Scriptures say (Prov 5 8): "Remove thy way far from her, and come not nigh the door of her house." The phrase, "Remove thy way far from her," refers to sectarianism. We say to a person, "Do not mingle with the sectarians, and do not come into their midst, lest you stumble among them." Lest he should reply, "I am confident that even though I go there, I will not stumble among them," the Scriptures add, (ibid. 2 19) "None that go unto her return, neither do they attain unto the paths of life."

. . . Another interpretation of the passage is as follows. The verse, "Remove thy way far from her" applies to the harlot. We say to a person, "Do not go in this street, nor enter this passage, for a comely, far-famed harlot lives there." If he should reply, "I am confident of myself that even though I go there, I will not be entrapped by her," we answer him, "Even though you are confident in yourself, do not go there, lest you be entrapped;" for the Sages have taught, that a man shall not accustom himself to pass the door of a harlot, as it is written, "For she hath cast down many wounded; yea, a mighty host are all her slain" (Prov 7 16).

VERSION II

G.

Whence do we know that the Holy Writings made a hedge about their words? For it is written (Prov 5 8): "Remove thy way far from her." We say to a person, "Do not walk in this street, and do not enter this passage, for a harlot lives in it, and she is a comely woman, and she entices all men after her with her beauty." He replies, "I am confident that even though I go, I will not look upon her, and not desire her beauty." We answer him, "Even though you are confident, do not go." Another interpretation of the verse is that of R. Joshua ben Korha, according to whom it refers to sectarianism. We say to a person, "Do not go near the sectarians, and do not listen to their words, lest you be entrapped into their actions." He replies, "I am confident that even though I go I will not listen to their words, and will not be entrapped into their actions." We say unto him, "Even though you are confident, do not go, for it is written (Prov 5 8) 'Remove thy way far from her;' and it is also written, 'Yea, a mighty host are all her slain' " (*ibid.* 7 26).

CHAPTER 7

THE ORIGIN OF THE PHARISEES

ALMOST INCREDIBLY the most important text relating to the time of the origin of the Pharisees as a distinct group has thus far been overlooked by all writers on the subject, including myself. Some writers have held that Pharisaism became a defined organization in the time of Jonathan the Maccabean high priest,[1] because it is in that context that Josephus first mentions the Pharisees.[2] Moreover, the earliest "Pair" of Pharisaic leaders apparently flourished at that time.[3] On the other hand, others have maintained that Pharisaism came into being as a party when towards the end of his high priesthood, John Hyrcan quarreled with the Sages of Israel.[4]

However, a passage in *Tosefta Yadaim,* chap. 2, end, (ed. Zuckermandel, p. 684) shows conclusively that the Pharisees existed as a distinct group as early as the beginning of the fourth century B.C.E. For according to it, the Tetragrammaton was still pronounced by the contemporary Pharisees in their prayers. The passage reads: "The Morning-Bathers say to the Pharisees, 'We complain of you, O Pharisees, *because you speak the Name in the morning, before bathing.' The Pharisees reply, 'We complain of you, O Morning-Bathers,* because you speak the Name, with a body containing defilement.'"

(The words italicized are lacking in all editions of *Tosefta,* including Zuckermandel's. This may account in part for the failure of writers on the Pharisees to appreciate the importance of the passage. However, the complete text has survived in the Vienna Ms. of *Tosefta,* and a virtually identical reading is cited by R. Samson of Sens in his Commentary on Mishna *Yadaim,* end. Both texts are cited and discussed by Professor Saul Lieberman in his *Tosefet Rishonim* IV, p. 610.)

The Name to which the Pharisees and Morning-Bathers referred in this argument was certainly the Tetragrammaton. The various ciphers

---

Dr. Finkelstein's The Pharisees (*third edition, Phila.* 1962, 2 *vols.*) *is the standard work on the subject.*

Reprinted from *Conservative Judaism,* Volume 33, 1969.

employed for the Divine Name are never described as "the Name" in Mishna or *Tosefta.*[5] The Morning-Bathers could not object to the Pharisees articulating these ciphers before bathing; nor could the Pharisees pretend to object that the Morning-Bathers pronounced a cipher with a body containing defilement. The norm therefore was composed at a time when the Pharisees articulated the Tetragrammaton in their prayers, and perhaps even in ordinary conversation.[6]

Apparently the Morning-Bathers performed the rite which gave them their name every day after awakening, so as to prepare for Divine worship by removing the contamination supposedly adhering to one through sleep.[7] The term "Morning-Bathers" was applied derisively by some later Pharisaic scholars to members of their own group, who bathed early in the morning, before study or prayer, after marital intercourse.[8] Those later "Morning-Bathers" were not identical with the early sect. They followed the Pharisaic tradition; being censured only for letting the practice interfere with study.

The use of "Morning-Bathers" as a term of contempt in the third century C.E. may well imply that the sect had not disappeared by that time. It would hardly be likely that R. Hanina in that generation would express his objection to the young scholars who acted in opposition to his views, by applying to them the name of a sect which had existed six hundred years earlier. Similarly, the references in the Church Fathers to the Morning-Bathers suggests that some remnants of the ancient sect persisted even in their time (Cf. however, Professor Louis Ginzberg, *Commentary on the Yerushalmi,* II, p. 239).

The Pharisees, who observed the rules of purity, bathed in the morning, before prayers, after marital intercourse.[9] But they did not consider sleep defiling. Thus, they retorted to the taunt of the Morning-Bathers by asking how the latter could get themselves to pronounce the Name with a body which always contains filth in its intestinal tract. The argument of the Pharisees was that the only defilements which could interfere with the enunciation of the Divine Name were those enumerated in the Pentateuch. As the filthiness hidden in the body did not prevent one from offering prayer, so sleep, equally natural and inevitable, should not.

The argument between the Pharisees and the Morning-Bathers did not concern the enunciation of the Name *in the Temple,* for no one was permitted to enter the Temple courts without purification through immersion.[10] The argument between the Pharisees and the Morning-Bathers thus revolved about the question of prayer at home or in the synagogue.

THE EVIDENCE that the Tetragrammaton ceased to be articulated by the Pharisees outside the Temple early in the fourth century B.C.E. is convincing. It has been shown conclusively that in some parts of Chronicles,[11] the Name has been replaced with the cipher called by the Rabbinic scholars *aleph lamed.*[12] In other parts, it was replaced by that known as *aleph dalet.*[13] In the Second Book of Psalms and the first chapters of the Third, the cipher *aleph lamed* is regularly used.

(This fact does not suggest that the psalms included in Books II and III were composed when the Tetragrammaton had ceased to be pronounced. It does not even necessarily suggest that they were collected at that time. It is possible that the levitical guilds, to whom we owe the transmission of these collections, avoided the use of the Tetragrammaton and replaced it with the cipher *aleph lamed.* That is why where the Tetragrammaton occurs in Ps. 14, it is replaced with the cipher *aleph lamed* in the identical text in Book II, Ps. 63. In the same way, the Tetragrammaton of Judg. 5:4 is replaced with the cipher *aleph lamed* in the quotation in Ps. 68:8. As the Tetragrammaton re-appears in the written text of the later chapters of the Third Book, and is used throughout the Fourth and Fifth Books, these parts of the Psalter were probably transmitted by guilds which refused to pronounce the Name, and at the same time preferred the cipher *aleph dalet* to *aleph lamed.*[14])

From the book of Daniel it is evident that by its time, the cipher *aleph dalet* had replaced the Tetragrammaton in prayer.[15]

By the time of the composition of the Septuagint (about 300 B.C.E.), the form *aleph dalet* was generally accepted. That is why, in that version, the Name is rendered, "the Lord".

I have noted elsewhere[16] that in the earliest portion of the Passover *Haggadah* (composed during the third century B.C.E.) the Tetragrammaton had been replaced by the cipher *aleph dalet.* Because that cipher meant literally "my Lord", the authors of the *Haggadah* inserted in the biblical verse "And the Lord brought us out of Egypt with a mighty hand," (Deut. 6:21) the word "our God", so that the simplest peasant might not misunderstand the meaning of the words and be led to suppose that some human lord had brought about the Exodus.

While many scholars have suggested that the Book of Chronicles was composed after Alexander the Great, the evidence presented by W. F. Albright for a much earlier date seems convincing (see *Alexander Marx Jubilee Volume,* pp. 70–72; *Journal of Biblical Literature* XL, 1921, pp. 119–124. See also J. M. Myers, *I Chronicles,* in the *Anchor Bible, Introduction,* p. LXXXVIII). As J. Myers points out, the appearance of fragments of Ezra, Nehemiah, and Chronicles among the Qumran Scrolls virtually rules out a date after the year 300 B.C.E.

As the book of Chronicles and the Psalter were accepted as canonical by the Pharisees, it follows that the use of the ciphers was approved and perhaps even suggested by them. The Septuagint follows the Pharisaic *halakhah* and we must assume that its authors were Pharisees who normally used the cipher *aleph dalet* for the Tetragrammaton. On the other hand, as the Passover *Haggadah* derived from Temple priests, it seems probable that they, too, objected to the use of the Tetragrammaton by the laity, especially in formulae pronounced in unison by large numbers of people, like those gathered in the Temple courts to celebrate the Passover.

THERE IS OTHER EVIDENCE that the early Pharisees spoke the Tetragrammaton in their prayers; and that the use of of the ciphers for the Tetragrammaton was introduced among them at the times mentioned. Part of this evidence may be found in an examination of an ancient Rabbinic norm, requiring the pronunciation of the Tetragrammaton. This *baraita* which is found in *Tosefta Berakot* 6 (7). 20, ed. Lieberman p. 39, and also (with some variations concerning which see below) in *Yer. Berakot* 9.1, 11d, reads:

> *One who speaks the Name* yod heh *[i.e. the Tetragrammaton] in the opening strophe [of one's prayer, i.e. in the petition itself] and also in the closing strophe [the doxology, affirming Gods ability to answer the prayer] is a Sage. One who speaks* yod heh *at the beginning, and* aleph lamed *in the doxology is a* bur *[lit. "ignorant"]. One who begins with* aleph lamed *and ends with* yod heh *is a* benoni *[mediocre]. One who begins with* aleph lamed *and ends with* aleph lamed *is a sectarian.*[17]

As Professor Saul Lieberman has shown,[18] the practice denounced as sectarian was followed by the Sect of the Jericho Scrolls. Perhaps, then, that sect originated earlier than is now generally supposed. More probably, in this instance, as in others implied in the Book of Jubilees,[19] the sect adopted teachings promulgated by non-conformist teachers of earlier times. The word "Sage" (*ḥakham*), in this text connotes more than scholarship.[20] If the practice imputed to the *ḥakham* were simply a matter of erudition, why was it rejected by the *benoni*?[21] The meticulousness and care implied in pronouncing the Tetragrammaton in the closing doxology, while using the term described by *aleph lamed* in the opening phrase of a prayer, suggest anything but mediocrity in thought. On the contrary, they suggest great concern and thoughtfulness. A person following that ritual might be considered a moderate deviationist, but he could hardly be considered semi-ignorant.

Indeed, the person who opened the prayer with a strophe including the Tetragrammaton and ended with a doxology including the term "*aleph lamed*," described in this *baraita* as "ignorant," must have been so only in a very special sense. Apparently the Pharisees considered him "ignorant" because he ignored their tradition. But he certainly must have given considerable thought to his prayers and to the phraseology appropriate to them.

It is surely highly significant that both the "ignorant" and the "mediocre," while objecting to the use of the Tetragrammaton in some part of prayer, pronounced it in other parts. They did not belong, then, to the groups who avoided pronunciation of the Name out of fear, because they imputed danger to it. Their disagreement with the Pharisees and the Sages derived from special views regarding the Deity.

A REASONABLE CONJECTURE regarding this difference may be offered. The issue regarding the Name to be used in prayer may have revolved about the relationship of the God of Israel to the supreme gods of other peoples, particularly to the Zoroastrian Ahura Mazda. Influenced by Persian dualism, some speculative theorists among the Jews, while adhering to Prophetic monotheism, apparently held (as did many Rabbinic Sages in later times,[22] and Philo[23]) that the Tetragrammaton represented one phase of the Deity, and the term represented by *aleph lamed* another. According to them, in His manifestation as merciful Father and Creator, God was *e-l-o-h-i-m*. The Tetragrammaton signified His manifestation as the Ruler of the Universe.

In appealing to Divine mercy, as one did in the opening strophe of a prayer, one should, according to this view, use the term *e-l-o-h-i-m*. In the doxology, when one asserted that God possessed the power to perform His will, one used the Tetragrammaton. Those who held this view were not denounced by the early Pharisees. They were not considered Sages, but they stood midway between the Sages and the "ignorant". Their ascription of a particular significance to the term *e-l-o-h-i-m*, as the manifestation of the Deity in His mercifulness, could not be considered a compromise with Zoroastrian dualism. After all, Scripture did use two appelations for the Deity. Possibly, the term *e-l-o-h-i-m* had been employed in the first Chapter of Genesis because the world was created with mercy.

Quite different from these "mediocre" people, were those who pronounced the Tetragrammaton in the opening strophe of their prayers, but the term *e-l-o-h-i-m* in the doxologies.

These people rejected the notion that Tetragrammaton was in any real sense the Divine Name. Rather, the Tetragrammaton reflected a manifestation of God, while the term *e-l-o-h-i-m* was His proper Name. They belonged to the group which may have included the author of Ecclesiastes,[24] where the term *e-l-o-h-i-m* is always used for God. They were, in fact, philosophers[25] who identified God with the supreme deities of other peoples; at the same time, of course, denying that there were any lesser gods.

They used the Tetragrammaton in the opening strophes of their prayers, because the term suggested the special relationship of God to Israel. But when they said the doxology, ascribing to the Deity power to control the events concerning which one prayed, they preferred the term *e-l-o-h-i-m*.

Their view that the Tetragrammaton was not the proper Name of the Deity certainly marked them as unorthodox. But they were not schismatics or deviationists, for what they said did not suggest any rejection of the Tetragrammaton as representing at least the term through which God signified His special relationship to Israel.

Because these people were widely regarded as masters of wisdom, the early Pharisees felt compelled to describe them somewhat harshly as "ignorant." This denunciation was particularly necessary to offset their claims to wisdom, similar to that of the authors of such works as Ecclesiastes and Job.

The word *"bur"* (ignorant") is thus used in this *baraita* precisely in the sense in which, according to Professor Saul Lieberman, it was applied to the Sages of Alexandria who asked Rabbi Joshua a series of questions, three of them dealing with matters appropriate to a *"bur."* These questions, as Professor Lieberman has shown, were speculative rather than halakhic. The Pharisees, who considered halakhic traditions and discussions to be "wisdom" (*ḥokhmah*), disparaged such abstract speculations as *dibre burot,* empty talk. A person who adopted customs based on such speculations was a *"bur."* They did not consider him a sectarian but he certainly was not a disciple of the wise, not to speak of being wise himself.

One who did not mention the Name at all in prayer but replaced it with a cipher was a sectarian because, apparently, he believed that the pronunciation of the Divine Name in prayer could have harmful or unwelcome results. Perhaps he held that it was forbidden to speak the Name even in prayer, and therefore might be considered to hold a false view of the commandment in Exodus 20.7. He held the Name in a form of awe, which was erroneous and sectarian; for the Pharisees of the time held that the Name should be pronounced in prayer.

Perhaps, too, such a person was considered heretical, because his use of the term *e-l-o-h-i-m* instead of the Tetragrammaton betrayed a schismatic, anti-Pharisaic view of the Deity. The Tetragrammaton was the distinctive Name of the God of Israel, as clearly stated in Exod. 6.3. The use of the word *e-l-o-h-i-m* for the Deity suggested the notion that the God of Israel was in fact identical with the supreme deity of other peoples, all of whom believed in many gods and recognized one among them as being highest of all. Such a doctrine was certainly sectarian.

Ḥakham in this passage, therefore, means a member of the group otherwise known as *ḥakhme yisrael,* "the Sages of Israel". In Maccabean records, the term meant Pharisaic scholars together, perhaps, with their followers: the transmitters of *ḥokhmah* or the Oral Tradition[26] (possibly including some of the Hagiographa).[27] In earlier times, the predecessors of these Sages had insisted on the use of the Tetragrammaton both in the opening petition of their prayers and in the concluding doxologies.

Significantly, the *baraita* makes no reference to the custom, now prevalent, of replacing the *Tetragrammaton* with the cipher called by the Rabbis *aleph dalet.* The authors of the *baraita* did not yet know of this custom. Therefore, they must have lived before the time of the present book of Chronicles, in part of which, as noted above, the cipher *aleph dalet* often replaces the Tetragrammaton of earlier sources.

The practice commended by the *baraita* shows that its authors flourished in the Persian period, probably very early in that period. In later times the term *e-l-o-h-i-m,* rejected in the baraita for the opening strophe of prayers, was adopted for such use in many synagogue services which were presumably composed by disciples of the "Sages" themselves.[28]

The argument tends to confirm the talmudic tradition maintaining that certain Rabbinic norms were composed at the time of Nehemiah.[29] It also confirms the tradition according to which the Men of the Great Synagogue still pronounced the Tetragrammaton.[30] The term "Men of the Great Synagogue" is used for contemporaries of Ezra and Nehemiah, as well as for their successors until the time of Simeon the Righteous.[31] As the cipher *aleph lamed* came into use early in the fourth century, B.C.E., it follows that the Men of the Great Synagogue who pronounced the Tetragrammaton flourished in the early generations of the institution, namely in the latter part of the fifth century B.C.E., in the time of Ezra and Nehemiah.

PRE-MACCABEAN origin of the Pharisees further explains the hitherto enigmatic use of the term "Sadducees" for their main opponents. If the Pharisees had originated at the time of Jonathan the high priest or John Hyrcan, it would be strange indeed for the group centering about the high priesthood to be called Sadducees; for the Hasmoneans could not claim descent from Zadok. The Zadokide high priesthood had come to an end during the wars against the Syrians. The Maccabees were upstarts, not members of the clan of Yedaiah, to which, apparently, the earlier high priests belonged as is clearly stated in Ezra 2:36, but of the clan of Jehoiarib (I Macc. 2:1).

Why then should adherents of the Hasmoneans have been called Sadducees? It has been proposed that the later Maccabees adopted the manner of the former Zadokides, and that therefore their followers would be called Sadducees. But this seems an unnatural explanation, for surely in the first generations of the Maccabees their non-Zadokide origin must have been evident to all.

However, if the Pharisees were an organized group early in the fourth century B.C.E., it would be natural for their opponents, adhering to the teachings of the high priesthood, to be called Sadducees, after the House of Zadok, whose prerogatives they defended.

NOTES

1 Cf. E. Schuerer, *Gesch. d. jued. Volkes,* fourth ed., II, pp. 472 ff.; and my comments in *The Pharisees,* third ed. pp. 595 ff. The origin of the Pharisees in the time of Jonathan suggests their possible identification with the Hasideans (see Schuerer, *loc. cit.*). However, this identification now seems to me unfounded, as I shall undertake to demonstrate elsewhere. Hasideans and Pharisees were apparently different groups, although they may have been related to one another at one time. All the remarks I, following other writers, have made identifying the two, must now be retracted.

2 Josephus specifically states that "*At that time* [i.e. in the time of Jonathan] there were among the Jews three sects" (*Antiquities* XIII 5.9). However, he does not suggest that the different groups *originated* at that time.

3 Jose b. Joezer, the senior of this "Pair" was apparently the uncle of the high priest Alcimus, whom Judah and Jonathan the Maccabees and their followers,

opposed (See I Macc. 7.22 ff.; *Bereshit R.* 65.22, p. 743; and cf. *The Pharisees,* third ed., pp. 594 ff.).

4 See Schuerer, *loc. cit.*, and *The Pharisees, loc. cit.*

5 Cf., e.g. Mishna *Berakot* 9.5, "And they ordained that people should greet one another, mentioning the Name". This obviously refers to the pronunciation of the Tetragrammaton, as the examples cited there show; for surely Boaz pronounced the Name when he greeted the workers. Similarly, Mishna *Sotah* 7.5, discussing the priestly blessing, states that in the Temple the priestly blessing was pronounced "with the Name, as it is written; but in the provinces, a cipher was used." So also Mishna *Sanhedrin* 7.8, maintains that "One who curses his mother and father is not guilty unless he cursed them with the Name." As the discussion in the Talmud shows, this means the pronunciation of the Tetragrammaton. *Tosefta,* too, always used the expression "the Name" when referring to the Deity, to mean the actual pronunciation of the Tetragrammaton. Cf. Ch. J. Kasowski, *Concordance to the Tosefta* under the word *shem.* Particular attention should be paid to *Tosefta Berakot* 5.21, ed. Lieberman p. 28, where we are told that "if a gentile recites a blessing pronouncing the Name, one is required to answer, 'Amen'. If a Samaritan recites a blessing pronouncing the Name, one does not answer 'Amen', unless one hears the whole blessing." As Professor Saul Lieberman explains in *Tosefta Kifeshutah, ad loc.*, the point made by *Tosefta* is that a gentile is not forbidden to pronounce the Name needlessly. Therefore if he pronounced the Name in any blessing, one may say, 'Amen'. A Samaritan is forbidden to do so; therefore, we cannot answer 'Amen' if he mentions the Name, unless one hears the entire blessing, and knows that it is an appropriate one.

6 That the Tetragrammaton was used in ordinary conversation and correspondence in pre-Exilic times is clear from many passages in Scripture. The *Eliashib Archives* discovered in Israel show that it was used in correspondence even toward the end of the Kingdom (see Y. Aharoni, in D. Winton Thomas, *Archaeology and O. T. Study,* p. 399). According to *Yer. Berakot* IX, 13c, one of the ordinances of human courts approved "on high" was that one should pronounce the Tetragrammaton in greeting. It is difficult to determine the time to which the comment refers.

7 See Professor Saul Lieberman in *Tosefet Rishonim,* IV, p. 610, for the mention of this sect in the works of the Church Fathers; see also S. Krauss in *Jewish Quarterly Review,* V (1893), p. 127, n. 2. Professor Louis Ginzberg in his *Commentary on the Yerushalmi* II, pp. 238 f. discusses the nature of the sect at some length, and stresses the fact that they were unrelated to the scholars derisively called by that name in *B. Berakot* 22a, and *Yer. ibid.* 3.4, 6c. R. Samson of Sens (as Professor Ginzberg notes) pointedly remarks that the "Morning-Bathers" of *B. Berakot* 22a were scholars, and therefore quite different from the heretical group mentioned in *Tosefta Yadaim.* See further the discussion of the subject in G. Allon, *Mehqarim be-Toledot Yisrael* I, p. 152.

8 See preceding note. Mishna (*Berakot* 3.4) requires immersion after marital intercourse before praying. However, R. Hanina, as cited in *Yerushalmi, loc. cit.*, objected to the practice of the scholars spending their morning hours bathing and thus interfering with their studies (see Professor Louis Ginzberg, *op. cit.*, II, p. 239).

9 See notes 7 and 8.

10 Mishna *Yoma* 3.3, *Yer. and Babli, ad loc.*, both explain that anyone entering the Temple court, whether intending to perform an act of worship or not, had to bathe; and one inside the Temple courts about to undertake an act of worship had to bathe (so Mishna *Tamid* 1.2). That is also the implication of Mishna *Yoma, ibid.*, according to which the high priest had to bathe before each

act of worship on the Day of Atonement, although he already was within the Temple precincts.

11 Cf. B. Jacob, *Im Namen Gottes* (1903) pp. 165 ff.; H. Zimmermann, *Elohim*, Berlin 1900, pp. 64 ff.; and my discussion of the subject in *Harvard Theological Review* XXXV, 1942, p. 296.

12 This abbreviation stands for the Hebrew word *e-l-o-h-i-m*, which Rabbis of later times hesitated to articulate needlessly.

13 This abbreviation stands for the Hebrew word *a-d-o-n-a-i* which, having become a cipher for the Divine Name, the Rabbis would not needlessly articulate.

14 It cannot be an accident that the cipher *aleph lamed* is employed almost uniformly in Pss. 73-83 of Book III, and the cipher *aleph dalet* in Pss. 84–89. The two groups of psalms derived from different guilds, as indicated by the headings of the individual psalms.

15 It has long been held that the prayer in Daniel chap. 9 is an interpolation. See H. L. Ginsberg, *Studies in Daniel*, pp. 41 and 79. However, see also, more recently, B. W. Jones in *Vetus Testamentum* XVIII, 1968, pp. 488ff. (who considers the prayer part of the original work) and literature cited by both. Accepting the views of H. L. Ginsberg (*op. cit.*) and Frank Zimmerman, *Journal of Biblical Literature* LVII (1938), pp. 258ff. and LVII (1939), pp. 349ff. that the Hebrew portion of Daniel was translated from Aramaic, the original author might naturally cite the prayer imputed to Daniel in Hebrew. Whether the prayer was part of the original work or an interpolation, its author might well assume that someone flourishing during the Babylonian exile would use the Tetragrammaton in prayer. The opening strophe of the prayer, Dan. 9.4, is an exact quotation from the opening strophe of the prayer of Nehemiah (Neh. 1.5), with the substitution of the cipher *aleph dalet* for the Tetragrammaton, and the omission of the words "God of heaven." This would seem to indicate that the author pronounced the Tetragrammaton as *aleph dalet*. He spelled out the Tetragrammaton in other parts of the prayer to emphasize this fact. Possibly he believed that Nehemiah had already done so; and therefore that Daniel, too, would have done so. The author also uses the term *e-l-o-h-e-n-u* in the course of his prayer (vv. 17–18), as well as *e-l-o-h-a-i* (v. 19). But the prayer contains no doxology.

16 *Harvard Theological Review* XXXV, (1942), p. 296.

17 The *baraita* as cited in *Yer. Berakot* 9.1, 11d varies somewhat from that of *Tosefta. According to Yerushalmi*, "One who begins with *aleph lamed* and ends with *aleph lamed* is ignorant," rather than a sectarian. Moreover, in the text of the *Yerushalmi* that passage immediately follows the one describing the Sage. The third category, according to *Yerushalmi*, consists of those who "begin with *aleph lamed* and end with *yod heh*". As in *Tosefta*, they are described as "mediocre." The fourth category in *Yerushalmi* consists of those "who begin with *yod heh* and end with *aleph lamed*". They are sectarians.

18 See his comments on this subject in *Tosefta Kifeshutah, Berakot* p. 123.

19 The relation of the Cave Sect to the Book of Jubilees is most clearly shown in the calendar which they shared. See A. Jaubert, *Le Calendrier des Jubilés et de la Secte d. Qumran*, in *Vetus Testamentum III*, 1953, pp. 250–264; and see also S. Talmon, in *Sukenik Memorial Vol.* (*Mehqarim bi-Megillot ha-Genuzot*), pp. 88 ff.

20 See *B. Qiddushin* 66a, where the term *hakhme yisrael* means Pharisees.

21 For the use of the term *benoni* ("mediocre") to designate a particular type of religiosity or piety, see also *Abot of R. Nathan* II, chap. 26, ed. Schechter 65a.

22 The general Rabbinic view is that the Tetragrammaton represents the Deity in His merciful manifestation; the term *e-l-o-h-i-m* is His manifestation as Judge and Ruler. (See *Sifre* Deut. 26, p. 41 and references there given. See also A.

Marmorstein. *The Old Rabbinic Doctrine of God* I, p. 26; and Professor Louis Ginzberg, *Legends of the Jews* V, p. 4, n. 6, and p. 185, n. 46.) Philo holds that the Tetragrammaton represents the manifestation of God as Lord, Master and Judge, while the term *e-l-o-h-i-m* signifies His mercy (see H. A. Wolfson, *Philo* I, p. 224 and references as there given). However, there is abundant evidence that this view was also held by many Rabbinic authorities. The controversy, which must have originated in very early times, continued as late as R. Ishmael who remarks that the rules regarding illicit sex-relations can be seen to be particularly rigorous, for the Tetragrammaton is used at the beginning of the portion dealing with them and also at the end (*Mekilta d'Arayot*, in *Sifra Ahare, perek* 13.3, 85d.) In the comment on Lev. 18:2, where Scripture says, "I am the Lord [using the Tetragrammaton], your God," *Sifra* (*Ahare, par.* 1.1, 85c) remarks: "I am the Lord, Who spoke and the world came into being; I am a Judge, I am full of mercy." The clear implication of the order of the comments seems to be that the Tetragrammaton signifies the manifestation of the Deity as Judge, while the term *e-l-o-h-i-m* signifies His mercy. That apparently is why in the *Yalkut* the order is reversed.

The Tetragrammaton is interpreted as referring to the manifestation of the Deity in the sterner aspect also in *Sifra Emor, par.* 4.2, where R. Judah holds that the Tetragrammaton refers to the Deity in His manifestation as destroyer.

23 See reference in preceding note and references to Philo in the discussions by A. Marmorstein and Professor Louis Ginzberg, *op. cit.*

24 In Ecclesiastes the term *e-l-o-h-i-m* is used regularly, as it is in the dialogue between Job and his friends in the Book of Job. However, the Tetragrammaton is used in the prologue and the epilogue to Job. The canonicity of the Book of Ecclesiastes was debated by the Schools of Shammai and Hillel, the Shammaites denying its canonicity and the Hillelites affirming it (Mishna *Eduyyot* 5.3). Indeed the disciples of R. Akiba in the second century C. E. still disagreed about it (Mishna *Yadaim* 3.5). However, it is not probable that the question of the Name used in the work played any role in their argument. In Job, the term *e-l-o-h-i-m* may be used because Job and his friends were not Jews, and therefore would not know the Tetragrammaton.

25 See his work, *Siphre Zutta, (The Midrash of Lydda)*, pp. 30ff. As Professor Lieberman points out, the Alexandrians, who discussed various issues with R. Joshua, were great scholars. Nevertheless they are accused of asking some questions which were fit for a *bur* (*dibre burot*). This accusation was based on the fact that the questions related to speculative issues, such as whether the son of the Shunammite woman had actually died (II Kings 4:8 ff).), and whether the future resurrection would apply to the body or only to the spirit (*Niddah* 70b).

Other passages seem to confirm that the word *"bur"* sometimes signifies the variant tradition suggested by Professor Lieberman, rather than the usually accepted meaning of utter ignorance.

Thus, according to *Tosefta Megillah* 3.27, ed. Lieberman p. 361, one who says "Amen" after his own blessings is following "the manner of the *bur*". However, accoring to *Yer. Berakot* 5.4, 9c, while some authorities agree with *Tosefta*, others maintain that on the contrary such a person is a *ḥakham*.

According to *Tosefta Berakot* 1.6, ed. Lieberman p. 3, one may recognize whether a person is a *ḥakham* or a *bur* from the manner of his blessing; for the *bur* will say long blessings when he should be brief, and brief ones when he should pray at length. But the person who prays at length when others think that brevity is appropriate, or briefly when others think prayer at length would be better, cannot be utterly ignorant. He is one who follows his own traditions or his independent opinions.

According to *B. Berakot* 50a, R. Johanan (or, according to one ms., *Rab;* see Professor Saul Lieberman in *Tosefta Kifeshutah Berakot* p. 9, n. 41, and that seems to be the correct reading) held that one who said in the *Birkat ha-Zimmun,* "Let us bless God *for the food which we have eaten*" is a *bur.* But this custom, denounced as that of a *bur* was customary throughout Palestine (see Professor Saul Lieberman, *loc. cit.*).

According to *B. Berakot* 49a, one who includes in the doxology of the blessing for Jerusalem in the *Birkat ha-Mazon* the words, "the Savior of Israel," is a *bur.* But the doxology is actually required by R. Jose b. R. Judah (*ibid.*).

It is clear therefore that the word *"bur"* was frequently applied by some scholars to others who followed opposing traditions.

26 *Hokhmah* in the sense of Rabbinic tradition is used regularly in the Talmud. Cf. Mishna *Baba Mezia* 2.11. See Professor Saul Lieberman in *Tosefta Kifeshutah, Berakot* p. 47, n. 86.

27 The term is interpreted as referring to the Psalms in connection with the norm in *Tosefta Berakot* 3.21, ed. Lieberman p. 17. Thus according to *Yer. Berakot* 5.1, 8d, R. Johanan appears to apply *hokhmah* to a verse from the Psalter. See Professor Louis Ginzberg, *Commentary on the Yerushalmi* IV, pp. 121 ff. It seems clear from the context in *Yerushalmi,* that there were two different interpretations of *hokhmah* as used in the norm cited from *Tosefta Berakot* (see preceding note). According to one school, it meant Rabbinic Torah; according to another, headed by R. Johanan, it meant Psalms.

28 Many of the special prayers for the Sabbath and the festivals inserted in the *Amidah* begin with the cipher *aleph lamed,* which *never* occurs at the beginning of any section of the *Amidah* in the daily prayers.

29 The Talmud maintains that a norm of the Mishna was formulated in the time of Nehemiah (*B. Shabbat* 123b). However, that remark seems to be based on exegesis of a particular verse rather than on tradition.

30 The statement that the Men of the Great Synagogue pronounced the Tetragrammaton is made by R. Abba b. Kahana in *Midrash Tehillim* 36.8, ed. Buber 126a.

31 That the Men of the Great Synagogue included contemporaries of Ezra and Nehemiah is clearly implied in many passages of the Talmud and *Midrash.* See e.g. *B. Yoma* 69b; *Yer. Berakot* 1.9, 4a; 2.4, 4d; 7.4, 10c; *Bereshit R.* 6.5, p. 45; 46.8, p. 465, *et al.* That Simeon the Righteous was counted among them is clearly stated in Mishna *Abot* 1.3. See my discussion of the subject in *Ha-Perushim ve-Anshe Keneset Ha-Gedolah* pp. 40 ff.

CHAPTER 8

THE ETHICS OF ANONYMITY AMONG THE PHARISEES*

A. *The Anonymity of the Individual*

PERHAPS the most remarkable aspect of Hasideanism[1] or Pharisaism is that so little is known about it. Few, if any, other religious movements have left so deep an impress on the human mind. Yet probably none is so little understood. Throughout the world Scripture is avidly read and with veneration. This reverence is, in large measure, due to the activity of those ancient middlemen, the Hasideans, who, when Prophecy ceased, preserved and spread its message. Yet even able and profound scholars have failed to grasp the nature of the Hasidean movement, are confused regarding its relation to Prophecy, and interpret it in a manner totally inconsistent with facts readily established.

Not one of the commentators on Hasideanism has, for example, remarked on its singular durability. Of the forms of Judaism prevalent at various times, Hasideanism alone has resisted time. The Samaritans, once probably as numerous as the Judaites (perhaps, indeed, they were even more numerous than the Judaites) have almost all been assimilated. Only some two hundred individuals survive of a once powerful and influential sect. The Sadducees, the Essenes, and other ancient Judean and Galilean deviationists lack even such vestiges. Karaism, for some centuries a strong rival of rabbinic Judaism, survives as the faith of a few thousand people in Israel, Egypt, perhaps the Crimea and other places, but has lost all vigor. Research into both its history

* This essay may be a chapter in a future book on the Pharisees. One of its readers suggested the incongruity of publishing over my name a discussion of the virtue of anonymity as practised by our ancestors. However, it would be both foolish and presumptuous for me to suppose that this, or anything else I can possibly write, will have such merit that anonymous publication would be anything but a pose. I regard what I write rather as letters, sometimes lengthy, directed to a limited circle of friends, who read them less for content, than out of personal attachment to me. Therefore they must be signed. However, I am very much troubled by the dilemma which the pharisaic and prophetic tradition of anonymity poses for many of us in other aspects of our work. I do not know any clear answer to the challenge of our time, in which to do our work at all, we have almost to assume the pose of ḥasidic Rabbis for whom anonymity was functionally impossible. Yet I realize very well the perils lurking in lack of anonymity, and the wisdom of our ancestors in developing the attitude of mind which made it natural.

[1] I use the words, Hasideanism and Pharisaism, interchangeably in this essay. Pharisee was a name originally given the Hasideans by their enemies, in derision, but ultimately it was, as often happens, adopted by the group itself. I have discussed the question at length in הפרושים ואנשי כנסת הגדולה, p. 33, note 119.

Reprinted from *Conservative Judaism,* Volume 12, 1958.

and literature is pursued almost exclusively by Rabbanite scholars seeking better understanding of their own tradition.

Yet Hasideanism has from its very origin been subject to almost constant persecution. High Priest, Seleucid monarch, Hasmonean prince, Herodian upstart, Roman Conqueror, Christian, Moslem, and in modern times, Communist and Nazi, have in turn tried to extirpate it. Even the occasional blandishments of material well-being have thus far not availed against it.

Hasideanism presents, in fact, a double enigma — its origin, and its power to endure. That so little is recorded about its early exponents is, however, no accident. From the beginning a unique type of selflessness distinguished it. From Ezra the Scribe to Simeon the Righteous, not one figure in Hasideanism is known by name. Its nucleus, the Great Synagogue, included sufficient genius to put its stamp on all later civilization, to establish ritual and pedagogic forms unsurpassed for effectiveness, and to develop to the utmost the vitality and flexibility of Pentateuchal law, enabling it to meet the problems of changing worlds. Yet neither the origin, the constituency, nor the form of organization of this astonishingly effective assembly is anywhere described.

The anonymity of the Men of the Great Synagogue bears no analogy to the oblivion common to primitive authorities in almost every other tradition, such as the creators of the British Common Law. The members of the Great Synagogue did not originate a tradition; they appeared in the midst of it. They were extremely conscious of history and were persuaded of the decisive impact of individuals on the historical process. The oblivion which overtook the founders of the movement can have happened only through deliberate choice.

Apparently, to the ancient Hasideans posthumous fame seemed an irrational goal in life. It was as absurd an aim as contemporary popularity. They had outgrown pagan identification of self and name, and they were unconcerned with epitaphs. Like the Prophets before them, they submitted to the pseudo-immortality of history when necessary for the service of God. Indeed, under such circumstances, they would even accept contemporary fame. But as a goal in life, historical immortality, now so profound a force in human life, seemed to them not only illusory, but sinful. They set their sights above such self-deceptive aims. They sought not appearance of achievement, but achievement; not recognition among mortals, but before God Himself. They wanted Him to accept them as His dedicated servants. Nothing less would do.

Because contempt for fame, contemporary and posthumous, is so rare, anonymity became a distinctive symbol of Hasidean dedication to God.

This urge to anonymity did not originate with the Hasidean. It was a characteristic of Prophecy, virtually unrecognized in modern times. Isaiah, Jeremiah, Ezekiel, and those of the Twelve whose names are known, are the exception rather than the rule. No authors are recorded in Scripture for Joshua, Judges, Samuel, Kings, Ruth, Esther, Lamentations, most of the Psalms, Job, and Chronicles. The Midrash suggests that works ascribed to well known Prophets include anonymous portions.[2] On the other hand, it holds (with apparent justice) that when the name of a Prophet's father is recorded, the latter, too, probably belonged to the prophetic circle.[3] If so, there were many Prophets whose words have either been lost or are included in the works of others.

In at least two instances it can be demonstrated that this oblivion was deliberately chosen. The name of Deutero-Isaiah, presumably a household word in his day, could scarcely have been forgotten, except through his own determination and that of his disciples. Malachi (My messenger) was apparently a title given a Prophet who wished to be anonymous.

One of the sins of the Generation of the Dispersion (the men of the Tower of Babel) was their ambition to make themselves a name.[4] On the other hand, characteristically, the father of Prophecy is known to us not by the name presumably given him by his parents at birth, but by that substituted for it by the Egyptian princess three months later.

To take another example the "monument and memorial" (literally "place and name"), promised by Deutero-Isaiah to the pious among the eunuchs[5] are clearly figurative. The Prophet assures the childless that God will not forget them, and their role in the establishment of His Temple will be recorded *with Him*, and will therefore be an "everlasting memorial that shall not be cut off."[6]

The derogation of fame, either posthumous or contemporary, among these early worthies was such that no objection was raised to the ascription, when desirable, of one's own work to someone else, preferably an earlier figure. Human beings were not considered owners of the inspiration which came to them. All belonged to God. Designation of authorship was a pedagogic device, to be used as helpful to further man's spiritual development.

Just as the Hasidean principle of anonymity originated in Prophecy, so it pervaded talmudic Judaism. From the time of Simeon the Righteous (ca. 200 B.C.E.) until the end of Herod's reign, the names of but one or two scholars are recorded for each generation. A few more are recorded in the period following Hillel and Shammai. But most of the rabbinic tradition was transmitted for centuries with deliberate anonymity. The prayers of the early synagogue liturgy, comparable to the Psalms themselves in beauty and inspiration, are almost all anonymous. Only accidentally do we discover that Rab, in the third century C.E., compiled magnificent special prayers for Rosh ha-Shanah.[7] The great contribution of that scholar and others to the revision of the original texts of the prayers for use in Babylonia has to

[2] Thus according to Rabbi Simon, Beeri the father of Hosea is the real author of Isa. 8.19–20; but because the two verses could not form a book, they were interpolated into the Book of Isaiah. See ויקרא רבה, ו' ו', ed. Margulies p. 162; and *ibid.* 15.2, p. 322.

[3] מגילה ט"ו, א.

[4] Gen. 11.4.

[5] Isa. 56.5.

[6] *Ibid.*

[7] ירושלמי, ראש השנה א:ג, נ"ז, א.

be reconstructed through critical study.[8] We know, for example, neither the date nor the authorship of such a moving work as the prayer, נשמת כל חי recited now on Sabbaths and festivals.

The tradition, as we shall presently see, exerted an almost equally great influence on the legal tradition. While occasionally the name of an editor of an ancient rabbinic work is mentioned, and while Rabbi Joḥanan transmits reliable records concerning the authorship of other texts,[9] almost all compilations of ancient laws and *aggadot* remain anonymous. Only through laborious analysis and research, can we identify, even tentatively, the successive editors of the תוספתא, the מכילתא, the ספרא or the ספרי. When names are attached to particular compilations, they often suggest the schools in which they were transmitted, not primarily the original editors.

In view of this record, it can hardly be doubted that the Founding Fathers of Pharisaism, like various biblical authors, *sought* anonymity precisely as did the חזון איש and the חפץ חיים in our generation. Though the latter seem to have been unaware that they were anticipated in this regard by several millennia, the reason was the same, namely, an expression of supreme and utterly selfless love for God.

In the light of these remarks, it may seem strange that the founder of the Great Synagogue, Ezra himself, is not only recalled by name in history, but is known through the preservation of a portion of his memoirs. But the inconsistency is apparent, rather than real. Ezra himself clearly accepted the principle of anonymity. His memoirs tell us almost nothing about his real achievements, which have to be reconstructed from the talmudic tradition. The book named for him leaves, indeed, the impression that his life was a failure. So little is recorded of him that Ben Sira, rejecting the Hasidean tradition, omitted him from the list of "fathers of old."[10]

The biblical and talmudical references to Ezra's personal life were justified by the function they had to serve. In his native Persia, Ezra occupied positions of high distinction and importance. Even if we reject the hypothesis of H. H. Schaeder[11] that he was a member of the Imperial cabinet, Ezra was still probably one of the two most celebrated Jews in Persia in his time. His memoirs show that he was on terms of intimacy with the Great King himself. We may assume that he might have lived a life of great comfort and even luxury in the Persian capital. All these he rejected in order to cast his lot with his brethren in Jerusalem, to struggle with them, and even against them, so as to bring about their development as a spiritual community, dedicated to Torah.

Ezra's memoirs have been preserved to indicate to future generations the

[8] See *Jewish Quarterly Review*, N. S., XVI, 1925–26, pp. 142 ff. for a comparison of the various texts of the עמידה, and the obvious revisions made by early Babylonian authorities in this prayer.

[9] סנהדרין פ"ו, א.

[10] Ben Sira, 44.1 ff.

[11] *Esra der Schreiber*, Tuebingen, 1930.

source of Hasideanism in the mind and spirit of a man descended from high priests, and a courtier of Artaxerxes. The Hasidean movement, struggling against both high priest and Persian governor, needed the encouragement and stimulus of his example and identity for its very life.

The rule of anonymity was thus, from the beginning, not considered a ritual to be observed under all circumstances. It was an expression of man's dedication to God, to be used when there was no purpose to be served by the recollection of a particular name. Therefore the principle was again relaxed when Simeon the Just became head of the Great Synagogue. The association of the High Priest with Hasideanism was for it a signal triumph necessarily to be proclaimed as widely as possible.

The identification of Simeon the Just with Hasideanism was clearly one of the major arguments used by later Pharisaic scholars to refute the Sadducees. The Sadducees could not reject the teaching and example of so eminent a High Priest as Simeon the Just; yet Pharisaic tradition insisted that that is precisely what they did in rejecting Pharisaism.[12]

But the use of Simeon the Just's name as leader of Hasideanism had other immediate and practical implications. Antiochus III granted the Jews a charter, recognizing the Torah as the law of the land for them and apparently giving the Hasidean scholars legal status as "scribes of the Temple." The High Priest's presidency of the movement was probably indispensable to this arrangement, and almost certainly greatly encouraged it.[13]

Contemporary scholarship, moreover, could for all its wisdom, scarcely have anticipated a time when Simeon's leadership of the Great Synagogue would be far more impressive than his High Priesthood. The Great Synagogue was still a voluntary association of scholars and saints, many without social standing, and almost all poor scribes, artisans, and traders. Its influence was most perceptible in the lower strata of Judea's population. From the viewpoint of the third century B.C.E., Simeon's presidency of the Great Synagogue conferred great distinction on it, but none on him.

However, once a departure from tradition was made, the new custom persisted. Simeon's successor as head of the Great Synagogue could no longer be nameless. He was Antigonus of Socho. After the two wings of Pharisaism became separate schools during the Maccabean crisis, the heads of both were recorded generation after generation. Thus have been preserved the names of five "pairs" of scholars in each period: José ben Joezer and José ben Joḥanan, Joshua ben Peraḥya and Nittai of Arbel, Judah ben Tabbai and Simeon ben Shattaḥ, Shemayah and Abtalyon, Hillel and Shammai. The other scholars mentioned by name during the period of about one hundred and fifty years separating the beginnings of the Maccabean revolt from the end of Herod's reign, are cited mainly in anecdotes and not in relation to norms.

Probably the men called *Ben Bag Bag* and *Ben Hé Hé* in the Talmud, and

[12] For further discussion of this issue, see what I wrote in הפרושים ואנשי כנסת הגדולה, pp. 79 ff.
[13] *Ibid.*, pp. 78 ff.

described as disciples of Hillel, assumed these curious names as pseudonyms to avoid posthumous fame. And it is significant that, recording a number of incidents in which "a certain saint" figures, the Talmud remarks that the term applies always either to Rabbi Judah ben Baba or Rabbi Judah ben Rabbi 'Ilai.[14] Apparently in stories of saintliness, at least, those telling the stories felt it incongruous to identify the central figures. Other circumlocutions, employed in the Talmud to describe nameless scholars, such as "a certain old man," may also be intended to avoid personal identification of particularly saintly people.

The anonymity cultivated by the Hasideans was adopted by fringe groups. Thus the Cave Sect never mentions its founder by name but calls him only "the teacher of righteousness." Indeed, thus far (1958) the name of not a single author of the hymns or other texts, preserved from this sect, has been recovered. They were clearly as community-minded in their spiritual resources, as they were in their material possessions. The authors of such works as the Book of Jubilees, the Enoch writings, the Testaments of the Twelve Patriarchs, Judith, Tobit, all adopted the tradition of anonymity, or sought effectiveness in pseudonymity.

During five centuries, from Ezra until the fall of Jerusalem (70 C.E.), a period of vigorous literary creativeness, only one author is known by name, Jeshua ben Sira, the writer of Ecclesiasticus. Standing wholly outside Hasideanism, opposing its teachings and rejected by it, he apparently sought the name-immortality which it condemned. In the light of this difference between his views and those of the Hasideans, his ode in praise of "the fathers of old"[15] may be particularly significant. It is perhaps intended in part to document the view that immortality in history is consistent with true piety and is properly awarded the good and denied the wicked. There is, for Ben Sira, no other immortality.

B. *Institutional Anonymity*

The Hasidean doctrine of anonymity was not confined to individuals; it applied also to groups and institutions. Just as Hasideanism had no real name, but was the כנסת for its members, and its members were either חסידים or פרושים to outsiders, so the Cave Sect and the Essenes had no name for themselves. In the Damascus Document the sect from which it emanated is called simply "those who entered the covenant," and "those who left the land of Judea to settle in Damascus." Perhaps they were part of the group called by others צנועים, "the modest ones" from the habitual shame they felt for the body, or חשאים, "the chary of speech."

Hence no doubt the Pharisaic Schools which in later times were called those of Shammai and Hillel, had no names in earlier generations. They may each have been identified as the school of the teacher in immediate charge of

[14] בבא קמא ק"ג, ב.   [15] Ben Sira, *loc. cit.*

them, just as the *Midrash* projecting contemporary situations on the remote past speaks of the "School of Shem and Eber." But each faction itself was nameless.

C. *The Talmudic Attitude Toward Anonymity*

The tradition of anonymity was abandoned in some degree in talmudic Judaism after the fall of Jerusalem in the year 70. The destruction of the authoritative center of religious guidance for the community left the individual confused by a welter of contradictory local traditions. "When the scholars entered the Vineyard of Yabneh," records the ancient tradition,[16] "they said, The time is coming when search for the words of Torah or of the scribes will be futile. This is foretold in the verse, 'Behold the days come, saith the Lord, that I will send a famine in the land, not a famine for bread, nor a thirst for water, but of hearing the words of the Lord. And they shall wander from sea to sea, and from the north even unto the east, they shall run to and fro to seek the word of the Lord, and shall not find it.' "[17]

Talmudic exegesis undertook to translate this poetry into prose, and to replace its generalizations with specifics. What "words of the Lord" would be sought in vain, and why? And what does the second verse add to the first? Obviously the Prophet had in mind in the first instance the disappearance of his own calling. But this could not be all. There would scarcely be in this period thirst and hunger for Prophetic exhortations which had been ignored when plentiful. Finally, how could the word of the Lord fail people, so long as the Torah could be studied?

The Talmud replies that the Prophet uses the plural, "words," in the first sentence for a good reason. He anticipates the disappearance of Prophecy; and widespread hunger to know "the time of the redemption." The second verse deals with the Torah. Men will wander from sea to sea and from north to south in search of the word of the Lord, because the teaching of Torah will have become chaotic. "The traditions will not have any resemblance to one another"; there will be utter confusion.

Rabbi Simeon ben Yoḥai[18] interprets the passage with even more explicit reference to the contemporary scene. "The Prophet cannot mean," he said, "that the time will ever come when the Torah will be forgotten, for we have the assurance of Scripture to the contrary, as it is written, 'It will not be forgotten from his seed.'[19] But one scholar will permit what another prohibits; one will declare pure what another holds impure and there will be no clear norm." To prevent such confusion, the talmudic Fathers in Yabneh (on an occasion to be discussed later) began to ascribe norms to specific people. "Let us begin," they said, "with Hillel and Shammai."[20] Thus

[16] תוספתא, עדיות, beginning.

[17] Amos 8.11–12.

[18] שבת קל"ח, ב.

[19] Deut. 31.21.

[20] תוספתא and שבת, *ibid.*

opened an era in which transmission of names in connection with disputed norms became a virtue instead of a vice.

So little weight attached to this innovation that transmitters sometimes deliberately confused the oral record, attributing to one scholar the statement of another.[21] The purpose of such changes was usually to win acceptance for a view which one considered right. From the time of Rabbi Akiba, this practice was denounced as misleading, but traces of it abound in extant Rabbinic literature.[22]

Yet throughout the talmudic period, a clear memory survived of the time when anonymity had been the rule.

Thus we are told that King David once said,[23] "I have a tradition going back to the Academy of Samuel of Ramah, that a scholar who risks his life for the words of the Torah may not be quoted by name." Therefore a decision brought David by his soldiers at the risk of life was transmitted anonymously. "This," the Talmud states, "is what is meant by the words of Scripture, 'But he would not drink thereof, but poured it (the water) out unto the Lord.'[24] 'Water' means Torah; and pouring it out before the Lord means giving it with complete dedication, that is, anonymously."

That this tradition is not a figment of a Babylonian aggadist's imagination but is part of the pharisaic view of life, can be demonstrated from the Mishnah.[25] The Mishnah records a norm brought by Rabbi Ḥaninah of Ono "from prison," i. e. transmitted by Rabbi Ḥaninah from Rabbi Akiba during his imprisonment by the Romans after the rebellion of Bar Kokeba. The curiously oblique reference to Rabbi Akiba in the Mishnah is not a slip or a rhetorical device. Rabbi Akiba is unmentioned in this passage because he had *risked his life* in giving information to Rabbi Ḥaninah for transmission to other scholars. He was no longer alive when the norm was recorded, but violation of the principle of anonymity would, under the circumstances, have been an offense to his memory.

According to Rabbi José ben Ḥalafta, Rabbi Ḥaninah stood in the same peril as Rabbi Akiba. Hence in his discussion of the incident, Rabbi José omits the name of Rabbi Ḥaninah, too. "We told the messenger," begins Rabbi José, recording the argument he gave against the views of Rabbi Akiba.

Despite later association of norms with individuals, anonymity was consciously used by editors of the Mishnah to indicate approval of particular views. "Rabbi Judah the Patriarch accepted such and such an opinion, and therefore taught it anonymously,"[26] the Talmud occasionally remarks.

[21] Cf. S. Liebermann, תוספתא כפשוטה, IV, p. 52, and reference there given.

[22] ספרי דברים, קפ"ח. [23] בבא קמא ס"א, א.

[24] II Sam. 23.16.

[25] גטין פרק ו', end. On the other hand, the simple statement of fact that Rabbi Akiba rendered a decision, in a practical case, while in prison, is transmitted clearly; see יבמות יב:ה, and cf. בבלי and ירושלמי *ad loc.*, from which it is clear that Rabbi Akiba rendered the decision while in prison. Perhaps, however, in this instance, Rabbi Akiba did not risk his life, as he rendered the decision to Rabbi Joḥanan ha-Sandlar in code.

[26] Cf. חולין פ"ה, א.

In the light of this Hasidean commitment to anonymity, the curious story told of the attempted ouster of Rabban Simeon ben Gamaliel II by his colleagues, and the action he subsequently took, becomes intelligible.[27] According to the Talmud, Rabbi Meir and Rabbi Nathan conspired to remove Rabban Simeon ben Gamaliel from office as Patriarch. To achieve their purpose, they planned to raise questions in the Academy concerning the difficult treatise עוקצין, dealing with ritual impurity conveyed to objects through stems, handles and other ancillary parts. As Rabban Simeon was apparently not well acquainted with these laws, he would be embarrassed and leave office. To warn Rabban Simeon (without actually betraying his colleagues) Rabbi Jacob ben Korshai, who got wind of the plan, walked up and back, near Rabban Simeon's dwelling, constantly reciting this treatise. Rabban Simeon, noticing Rabbi Jacob's peculiar concern with עוקצין, understood the hint. He proceeded to master the work in time to meet the emergency. When the questioning began, the following day, he was ready for Rabbi Nathan and Rabbi Meir.

Having thwarted the design, Rabban Simeon expelled his colleagues from the Academy. However, they would write questions, for submission to the Academy; and would also supply answers to questions their colleagues could not answer. Rabbi José finally persuaded Rabban Simeon to let them re-enter the Academy. "But," adds the Talmud, "he (Rabban Simeon) punished them by ordaining that their traditions should not be quoted in their names." For Rabbi Meir, the cypher "others" was employed; for Rabbi Nathan, "some."

The suggestion that Rabban Simeon acted out of vengeance is preposterous, for Rabban Simeon was one of the most self-effacing people in the whole Rabbinic tradition.[28] It is also quite inconceivable that he was unduly concerned about possession of office. He was worried about the action of Rabbi Nathan and Rabbi Meir because it could have disrupted the only surviving organization of Jewish religious life. Authority, attaching to the Academy at Usha, derived largely from the widespread loyalty to the family of Hillel. That is, indeed, why the Patriarchate was retained in the family of Hillel. The Hillelite dynasty was the only link with the glorious past, when the Jews still had had autonomy. Not every peasant or trader could appreciate the significance of Torah as "a portable territory" or an element of continuity in Jewish life. Many might even doubt the authenticity of Rabbinic tradition. But most of the population realized the importance of the institution at the center of which stood a scion of Hillel.

Even more serious consequences than could flow from the removal of Rabban Simeon would have been involved in his intended replacement by Rabbi Nathan. Rabbi Nathan was the son of the Babylonian Exilarch, in effect an office-holder in the Parthian government. It was quite inconceivable that the Romans would permit the son of the Exilarch to become Nasi in

[27] בבלי, הוריות, end.

[28] בבא מציעא פ"ד, ב.

Palestine. The implications of such an election would have been very grave indeed. The Romans might easily suspect a movement to renew the War of Bar Kokeba which had only recently been suppressed. The trend of the Roman government to befriend the Jews might be reversed.

Hence, Rabban Simeon's indignation at the aims of Rabbi Nathan's and Rabbi Meir's conspiracy. Rabban Simeon was alluding to this peril to the community when he said to Rabbi Nathan, after the latter apologized to him, "Your father's girdle may have helped you achieve the headship of the court; but can it lead you to the Patriarchate?"

When Rabbi Meir and Rabbi Nathan were readmitted to the Academy, the Patriarch replaced their names by cyphers. This could scarcely have bothered them even if they were concerned with posthumous fame, since the cyphers were well known and understood. Rabban Simeon did not rob them of their identity; nor did he refuse to have their traditions ascribed to them. He simply proposed to remove their proper names from the halakhic traditions. The purpose of this order was inherently pedagogic. They had risked the interests of Judaism and Torah for the sake of the power and fame attaching to the Patriarchate. From Rabban Simeon's point of view, Rabbi Nathan and Rabbi Meir could scarcely have desired the burdens the office they sought would put on them, or the trials to which its holder was likely to be exposed.

Therefore, they were to be made subject to a rule continuously reminding them and everyone else of the Hasidean doctrine of anonymity. Because the anonymous transmitter of a tradition holds a higher place in the tradition than one who is actually named, the punishment meted out to them was, as is appropriate in wise pedagogics, really a concealed reward.

That this interpretation is correct is shown, I believe, by the sequel to the incident just related. In Rabban Simeon's later years, after the death of Rabbi Meir, his son, later to become famous as Rabbi Judah the Patriarch, encountering a form beginning, "Others say," asked, "Who are these scholars whose waters we drink, but whose names we do not mention?" Rabban Simeon told him. The son remonstrated that the offense ought to be forgiven after so many years. Finally the father agreed that Rabbi Meir's traditions should be cited in the Academy with the formula, "It has been said in the name of Rabbi Meir."

No purpose was served by this circumlocution, except to remind the members of the Academy of the incident, which a less modest man than Rabban Simeon would naturally want to have forgotten, since it reflected very seriously on the limited erudition of his youth. But Rabban Simeon felt that it was necessary to overcome the human tendency to stress unduly the immortality of names; and he thought reference to the incident mentioned, and to the frustration of the plans of conspirators, would be helpful.

In very late tannaitic times, there developed in some circles a belief that the widespread hunger of being remembered by name in the Academies was not inconsistent with belief in man's immortality. Thus Rabbi Joḥanan ben Jehozadak remarked that when David prayed "I will dwell in Thy tent forever"[29] he meant more than the literal sense of the verse suggests. He used the term עולמים, instead of the more natural עולם, to indicate that he wanted to live in two worlds. He desired the immortality of the future life, participating in the Academy on High, and also wanted to be remembered by name in the Academies on earth." Echoing these views, Rabbi Simeon ben Yoḥai remarked that "A dead scholar, whose name is mentioned in connection with an halakhic tradition in this world, will be murmuring the words in his grave."

Rabbi Joḥanan bar Napaḥa attached such importance to recollection of his name as authority for his sayings, that he was offended by the failure of his disciple, Rabbi Eleazar, to give him credit for one of them. Both the Talmud of Jerusalem[30] and that of Babylonia,[31] referring to this story, express astonishment at Rabbi Joḥanan's attitude; but finally conclude that Rabbi Joḥanan shared the view of Rabbi Simeon ben Yoḥai and Rabbi Joḥanan ben Jehozadak, in whose opinion to be remembered by name in the Academy was meritorious. But apparently this view is considered exceptional, and contrary to the accepted opinion.

Anonymity so pervaded Hasidean ethic, that it was not recorded as a formal rule. The selflessness reflected in it extended, as already observed, beyond the individual, to the group itself. The Ḥasid had as little time or desire to describe his institution, as his own life. So far as he was concerned, the way he served, the organization of the Great Synagogue, the history of his movement, and its relationship to Prophecy were relevant only as guides for the future. But this guidance would derive from living Hasidean institutions, rather than descriptions of either the past or present of the society. The struggle between early Hasideanism and the High Priesthood, the achievements of the Great Synagogue, the way Simeon the Just was ultimately drawn to the rising institution, the development of two schools out of the matrix of unified Hasideanism — all this is left to the modern researcher to detect from clues unavoidably left in the literature and institutions of the period.

Rejection of personal fame, basic to Hasideanism, was not a ritual. It was an affirmation, not a negation. It asserted a role for man on earth transcending fame or power. Man is the servant of God. In fact, he may be considered an emanation of Deity. His relation to God is potentially, at least, that of the angels. He has individuality and self-consciousness, but these are means for increased service to God, and should not become instruments for rebellion against Him.

Without the selflessness symbolized in this anonymity, the Men of the Great Synagogue could hardly have proven equal to their task. The wisdom and insight reflected in their decisions, many of which form the basis of all

[29] Ps. 61.5, סנהדרין צ', ב. Cf. ירושלמי, ברכות ב:א, ד', ב.
[30] ירושלמי, ברכות, *loc. cit.*
[31] יבמות צ"ו, ב.

Western religion, have not been duplicated in the centuries since them. The pageant of the Passover eve, the synagogue service and the form of early Hasidean texts, considered merely as pedagogic devices, are astonishing creations. Without paraphernalia of office and often persecuted, the Men of the Great Synagogue preserved for generations and even centuries a movement which, declining to fight its enemies, grew strong enough to take over the leadership of the faith. The miracle of this achievement becomes evident when we consider that the Synagogue, unmentioned in Scripture, opposed by Temple authorities and always insisting on its own secondary place in Judaism, became a cornerstone of Jewish religious life.

But the miracle of the achievement of these ancient sages followed in fact from the miracle of their dedication. They were able to bring to a common task a degree of devotion reserved among other geniuses only for creations bearing their own name. Thus their common creations were greater than any they could have produced as individuals.

This is itself contrary to general experience; for men of supreme gifts are frequently lonely, ego-conscious people, unable to bring their full genius as an anonymous freewill offering to God. The ability of the Men of the Great Synagogue to make this offering explains in part at least, their effectiveness.

No wonder that Hasideanism developed through many centuries without any sign of internal strain. Individuals may have entered with differing views the gardens in which their decisions were to be reached. But in no instance did these differences lead to conflict. There were apparently no votes taken and no victories won. The Hasidean leaders offered the Jewish tradition and human civilization not only rare creations in the product of their mind, but a striking example of cooperation for transcendent goals. The most significant creation of Hasideanism was, in the last analysis, the Hasidean.

CHAPTER 9

THE BOOK OF JUBILEES AND THE RABBINIC HALAKA

LOUIS FINKELSTEIN

Jewish Theological Seminary of America

In spite of the fact that Singer, Epstein,[1] and, somewhat later, Charles,[2] and Schechter have dealt with the Book of Jubilees, no apology is required for attempting to study it from a somewhat new angle.[3] It is well known that much light can be thrown on the Apocrypha and Pseudepigrapha by a comparison with rabbinic sources. It may be true that the Jewish traditions were not compiled till a comparatively late date, and that they were probably put in writing still later, yet much that is contained in them is of very ancient origin, and the authorities in whose names statements are quoted are a help, if not an infallible index, to fixing their date. Especially the Book of Jubilees must be viewed in the light thrown upon it by the Talmud and kindred sources, since it was doubtless written in Hebrew, contains numerous laws and allusions to Agadic statements, and presents generally the appearance of a targum or a midrash.

The book is not of Pharisaic nor yet of Sadducean origin. The former is impossible, as has been shown by Schechter, because the writer has his own views on the calendar and regarding many laws of prime importance to the Pharisees. No Pharisee would ever agree to counting the Omer — the forty-nine days separating the Passover from the Feast of Weeks — from the last day of the festival; nor would any Pharisee have agreed to fixation of the calendar otherwise than by the monthly examination of New Moon. Nor is it of Sadducean origin,

[1] See Revue des études juives, vol. xxii, 8.

[2] Dr. Charles has published the Ethiopic text of the book, and also an English translation with an excellent introduction and copious notes. I assume in the discussion below that the reader has Charles's work before him.

[3] I am indebted to Professor Alexander Marx for many valuable suggestions in the course of writing this article.

Reprinted from *The Harvard Theological Review,* Volume 16, 1928.

since the author believes in immortality and differs from the Sadducees as much as from the Pharisees in regard to the fixation of the Omer and the Feast of Weeks. The book is the product of a sectarian, belonging perhaps to a sect that sought to bring about a compromise between the Pharisees and the Sadducees. But we must beware of permitting our ignorance of the views of the Jewish sects at the beginning of the Christian Era, of which even the names are known in but three or four cases, to blind us to the possibility, nay the certainty, that many other sects existed of which we know nothing. The Book of Jubilees gives us an insight into one of these sects, which must however remain nameless until further discovery may throw more light on the matter.

1. The Calendar

One of Israel's most important institutions in its own land was the fixation of the Calendar. As is well known, the new moon was set each month by the appearance of witnesses before the court to testify that they had seen the new moon. As a lunar month consists of twenty-nine and a half days, the court, a committee of the Sanhedrin, sat during all of the thirtieth day of each month, awaiting any witnesses who might come. If none came, that day was declared to belong to the preceding month, and the following day proclaimed as the new moon of the succeeding month. The ordinary year was thus composed of 354 or 355 days. In order to reconcile this lunar year with the solar year, the Sanhedrin inserted an intercalary month every second or third year. Thus if it appeared that the month Adar, the twelfth month of the Jewish calendar, had arrived too early in the winter, a second Adar was added, so that the Passover might be celebrated in the spring. While the Sanhedrin doubtless had its system of calculations in fixing the calendar, ostensibly everything depended on the testimony of witnesses.

The author of the Book of Jubilees seeks to abolish all this. He proposes a year that shall depend only on solar time. This he intimates in the second chapter, where he informs us that God appointed "the *sun* to be a great sign on the earth for days and for sabbaths and for months and for feasts and for years and for sabbaths of years and for jubilees and for all seasons of the years."[4] This verse contrasts rather sharply with the verse in Genesis which it is meant to paraphrase: "They (the sun and the moon) shall be for signs and for appointed seasons and for days and for years."[5] It is evident that the author deliberately proposes completely setting aside the Jewish lunar year and fixing the calendar on a solar basis.

The details of his scheme are revealed in chapter 6. The year is to consist of 364 days, that is of 52 weeks. It is to be divided into four parts of ninety-one days each. Epstein[6] has attempted to show that the author had in mind a double system, consisting of a civil year of twelve months, of which eight were to have thirty days and four thirty-one, and an ecclesiastical year of thirteen months of twenty-eight days each. He points out correctly that in the Book of Jubilees the Feast of Weeks always occurs on the fifteenth day of the third month, and argues that since the Bible provides that the Feast of Weeks shall be celebrated on the fiftieth day of the Omer, the author must have arranged his months so as to bring the fiftieth day of the Omer always on the fifteenth of the third month. He could only do this by beginning to count the Omer on the day after the Passover (that is, the twenty-second of Nisan), as the Falashas still do today, and by limiting all months to twenty-eight days each. A simple calculation will show that this will cause the fifteenth of the third month always to be identical with the fiftieth day of the Omer.

By his scheme the author doubtless intended to put an end to one of the most bitter points of contention between the Sadducees and the Pharisees. The former held that the Feast of Weeks should always fall on a Sunday, and that the Omer should be counted from the Sabbath occurring in the Passover week. They denied any fixed date to the Feast of Weeks, claiming for it no historical significance. It was to be merely the fiftieth day of the Omer. The Pharisees, on the other hand, claimed that the Feast of Weeks celebrated the giving of the

[4] Jub. 2, 9.

[5] Genesis 1, 16.

[6] See the article referred to above.

Torah to Israel, and hence must be observed on a fixed day. According to them the Omer was to be counted from the first day of Passover, so that the Feast of Weeks would always fall on the sixth of the third month (assuming that of the two months intervening one would have thirty days and the other twenty-nine).

The Book of Jubilees, by establishing months of twenty-eight days each, produced a system by which not only the Feast of Weeks but all festivals (with the exception of the Day of Atonement) would occur on Sundays. Thus if the first of the first month fell on Sunday, the fifteenth day of that month would be a Sunday (Passover), the fiftieth day thereafter would likewise be Sunday (Feast of Weeks), and so would the first day of the seventh month (Rosh ha-Shanah), and the Feast of Booths (the fifteenth of the month).

Thus far we may agree with Epstein's conclusions. It is, however, impossible to follow him in assuming that the Book of Jubilees contemplates a civil year of twelve months, of which eight were to have thirty days, and four thirty-one days. According to him these twelve months are to be divided into four parts, each introduced by a Day of Remembrance, a miniature copy of the traditional Jewish New Year. But, first, it is hardly likely that the author, who evidently is striving to simplify the calendar, would encumber it with a double system. Secondly, Epstein fails to notice that the Day of Remembrance at the beginning of the seventh month would occur in the middle (on the fifteenth) of the ecclesiastical seventh month, that is on Succoth. For in the six months elapsing between the first day of the first month and the first day of the seventh month of the civil year, the ecclesiastical year, with its shorter months, would have fallen behind by two weeks.

It is thus not possible to accept Epstein's hypothesis of a civil year. The fact seems to be that the author contemplates an intercalary week at the end of each quarter of the year. There were to be three months of twenty-eight days each, followed by a week which would complete the thirteen weeks assigned to each quarter of the year. The fourth month would be introduced by a Day of Remembrance, as would also the seventh and the tenth, as well as the first; in every case these Days would be preceded by a week belonging to no month. Thus the year would be divided into four parts of ninety-one days each, insuring absolute regularity of occurrence for the festivals, which would all fall on Sundays.

According to our author this system seems to have come into being only after the deluge. Before that time the months would appear to have consisted uniformly of thirty days. Thus in regard to the deluge we are told, "The water prevailed on the surface of the earth five months, one hundred and fifty days." [7] That this was the belief of the writer of Jubilees is further seen by his story of the creation. Adam is represented as having been created on the sixth day, and taken to the Garden of Eden forty days thereafter, that is on the forty-seventh day of the creation. Now after the completion of seven years, "seven years exactly, and in the second month, on the seventeenth day," [8] Adam committed the sin for which he was expelled from Eden. As the day of his sin was the anniversary of the day of his entrance, he must have entered Eden on the seventeenth day of the second month. As we have seen above, this was the forty-seventh day of creation. Hence it follows that originally the month was to consist of thirty days.

The view that the world was created in the first month is that of R. Joshua in the Talmud.[9] R. Eliezer, however, his colleague, held that it was created in the seventh month. The latter view is the one that has gained widest acceptance in Jewish circles, having been introduced into the liturgy by Rab.[10]

The four Days of Remembrance, which the author of the Book of Jubilees places at the beginning of the first, fourth, seventh, and tenth months, were to be days of judgement, just as is New Year's day in rabbinic literature. This is seen from the fact that while Adam sinned on the seventeenth day of the second month, he was permitted to abide in Eden till the first day of the fourth month,[11] that is till the next Day of Remembrance. We should note that in the liturgy New Year's

[7] Jub. 5, 27.

[8] Jub. 3, 17.

[9] Rosh ha-Shanah 11a.

[10] Additional Prayers for Rosh ha-Shanah.

[11] Jub. 3, 32.

day is regularly called "the Day of Remembrance." In giving that name to these four days, the author is simply raising the dignity of the first days of the first, fourth, and tenth months to that occupied formerly by the traditional New Year's.

It is possible that in creating these Days of Remembrance the author was influenced by the tradition that puts the number of New Year's days at four. The Mishna reads:

There are four New Year's days: on the first of Nisan is the New Year for kings, and for festivals; on the first of Ellul is the New Year in regard to tithes of animals; . . . on the first of Tishri is the New Year for years, for sabbatical years, for jubilees, in regard to planting [the prohibition of the use of the fruit of the first three years], and for [the tithing of] herbs; on the first of Shebat is the New Year for trees according to the school of Shammai, but according to the school of Hillel it is on the fifteenth of that month. At four times in the year is the world judged: on Passover, regarding the grain; on the Feast of Weeks, regarding the fruits; on New Year's all mankind pass before him as in a legion; . . . and on Succoth they are judged concerning the rain.[12]

The early Mishna doubtless did not specify the dates of the New Year's days or of the judgement days, and they may have been identical. There can, however, be no doubt that the author's four Days of Remembrance are in some manner connected with the tradition crystallized in the Mishna.

Roensch tries to find another reference to the four Days of Remembrance in the story that the author tells of Jacob sending gifts to his mother "four times a year, between the times of the months, between ploughing and reaping, and between autumn and rain, and between winter and spring." [13] It looks at first glance as if the author had the four Days of Remembrance in mind. The theory is the more acceptable as New Year's day was of old a time for the interchange of gifts,[14] and our author would naturally transfer that custom to the Days of Remembrance. But even Charles hesitates to subscribe to this explanation. A second reading of the verse sees only three pairs of seasons mentioned, for we cannot assume the words "between the times of the months" to refer to any particular season.

The passage can best be understood in the light of a statement in the Talmud. In an ancient baraita,[15] the year is

[12] Rosh ha-Shanah 1, 1. [13] Jub. 29, 16. [14] Neh. 8, 10. [15] B. M. 105b.

divided into six seasons: Sowing, Autumn, Cold, Reaping, Summer, Heat. It will be noticed that the Book of Jubilees also mentions six seasons: Ploughing, Reaping, Autumn, Rain, Winter, Spring. While these seasons are somewhat different from those of the Talmud, the underlying division of the year into six parts is the same. The reading "four times" is doubtless the error of a scribe who understood the passage as Roensch did, but there can hardly be a doubt that he was mistaken.

In spite of the efforts of the author of the Book of Jubilees to emphasize the equality of the four Days of Remembrance, he seems on one occasion to forget himself and to allude to the first day of the seventh month as a Day of Remembrance for the whole year rather than for three months. Thus he tells us that Abraham sat up all the night of the first day of the seventh month "in order to observe what would be the character of the year in regard to rain." [16] This is of course strongly suggestive of the talmudic story [17] of the man who slept in a cemetery on the eve of Rosh ha-Shanah, and obtained valuable information concerning the weather conditions of the following year by listening to the conversation of spirits. Similarly R. Zebid claims that one may know the character of a coming year by observing weather conditions on New Year's day.[18] Such beliefs must have been so current that the author inadvertently included them in his book even though they conflicted with his own theories. Charles's explanation that Abraham obtained information for only six months is hardly tenable and does not meet the difficulty, for if the author had clung to his four Days of Remembrance, it would not have been possible to discover anything about the future that was more than three months distant.

2. The Sabbath

While, as we have seen, the writer of the Book of Jubilees endeavored to introduce far-reaching changes in the Jewish calendar, his differences from the traditional law in regard to the Sabbath are generally in the nature of undue severities.

[16] Jub. 12, 16.

[17] Berakot 18b. Compare also Abot d'R. Nathan, ed. Schechter, p. 16, chapter 3.

[18] B. B. 147a.

In some cases he seems to echo an ancient halaka that has left only indistinct traces in rabbinic literature. Like many other sectaries, his regulations concerning the sabbath are much more severe than those of the rabbis. He is not satisfied that the violation of the sabbath should be merely a capital offence, but insists that one who desecrates the holy day forfeits his share in the future life. "Whoever does any work thereon shall die eternally,"[19] is plainly a paraphrase of the biblical, "Whoever profanes it shall surely die, for whoever does any work thereon, that soul shall be cut off from the midst of his people."[20] It is noteworthy that while the conclusions of this author often differ from those of the rabbis, his methods are the same. His peculiar interpretation of this verse was doubtless due to his sense of the awkwardness of the redundancy in it. Very little is added by declaring that the soul that profanes the sabbath "shall be cut off from the midst of his people," after it has already been said, "whoever profanes it shall surely die." The rabbis felt the same difficulty, and explained that the offender is to be "cut off from the midst of his people" in cases where there is not sufficient evidence to convict him.[21] They interpret the 'cutting off' to mean premature or childless death. The author of the Book of Jubilees rejects their interpretation — or perhaps he lived before it arose — and explains that the punishment of 'death' relates to this life, that of 'cutting off' to the future life. Such interpretations of redundancies are not uncommon in rabbinic literature. When Isaiah says to Hezekiah, "Set thy house in order, for thou shalt die and not live,"[22] he means according to the rabbis[23] that Hezekiah had forfeited his life in this world, and would not live in the future world.

The author of Jubilees does not tire of sounding the praises of the sabbath. It was celebrated in heaven before it had been

[19] Jub. 2, 27.

[20] Exod. 31, 14.

[21] Mekilta ad loc. In the Talmud the words "he shall be cut off" are interpreted as meaning the forfeiture of future life in the case of one guilty of blasphemy. See Sanhedrin 64b. The cases are however not completely parallel, since in the Talmud it is the repetition of the word that is used as the basis of interpretation. The same interpretation is there given in Ps.-Jonathan to the verse.

[22] Is. 38, 1.

[23] Jer. San. 10, 18; f. 28c.

revealed to man. On earth, however, it is the exclusive possession of Israel. "The Creator of all things did not sanctify all peoples and nations to keep the sabbath on it [*sc.* the seventh day], but Israel alone; them alone did he permit to eat and drink and to keep the sabbath on it on the earth."[24] This view, that the observance of the sabbath was a privilege bestowed on Israel, has its parallel in the Talmud. The Lord is represented as having said to Moses, "A fine gift have I in my treasures, the sabbath is its name, and I desire to give it to Israel. Go and announce it to them." [25] Moreover the rabbis looked upon the sabbath as the bride of Israel. R. Simeon b. Johai gives expression to the common feeling in these words:[26] "Every day has its mate. Sunday is coupled with Monday, Tuesday with Wednesday, Thursday with Friday. The sabbath has no mate among the days. It is espoused to Israel. For one not a Jew to observe it after the manner of the Jews would be equivalent to adultery." In all likelihood this feeling is the basis of the strong aversion of the rabbis to gentile observance of the sabbath.[27] Yet one important distinction is to be observed between the objection of the rabbis to the observance of the sabbath by gentiles and the words of the Book of Jubilees. In this sectarian book only the joy of the sabbath is forbidden to gentiles, nothing is said of abstention from work; but to the rabbis it seemed objectionable that the gentile should observe the sabbath even in abstaining from work. Perhaps the author was thinking of the Babylonian sabbath with its taboo, and expressed his view that the gentiles might observe the sabbath in their own way but should not imitate the Jewish manner of observance.

The author is not content with generalities about the sabbath, he gives in some detail what ought to be the laws of the sabbath. In the last chapter of his book he draws up a list, or rather lists, of actions which are not to be performed on the sabbath. In the first list we read (following Charles's translation):

Whoever desecrates that day, whoever lies with his wife, or whoever says he will do something on it, that he will set out on a journey thereon in regard to

[24] Jub. 2, 31.

[25] Sabbath 11b.

[26] Bereshit R. 11.

[27] Sanhedrin 58b.

buying or selling, and whoever draws water thereon which he has not prepared for himself on the sixth day, and whoever takes up a burden to carry it out of the tent or out of his house, shall die.[28]

Again somewhat later:

And every man who does any work thereon, or goes on a journey, or tills his farm, in his house or in any other place, and whoever lights a fire, or rides on any beast, or travels by ship on the sea, whoever strikes or kills anything, or slaughters any beast or a bird, or whoever catches an animal or a bird or a fish, or whoever fasts or makes war on the sabbath, shall die.[29]

The reason for dividing the prohibited actions into these two groups is not at all clear. The prohibition of marital relations on the sabbath is practically unknown in rabbinic literature.[30] Nor does the author state the grounds for his prohibition. The inclusion of this law sheds no light on the classification of the prohibited actions.

That our author should condemn a man to death for merely saying that he will desecrate the sabbath is inconceivable. Yet the clauses, "whoever says he will do something on it, that he will set out on a journey thereon in regard to buying or selling",

[28] Jub. 50, 8.

[29] Jub. 50, 12.

[30] Perhaps a reference to this prohibition may be found even in the Talmud. In a baraita, quoted Ketubot 3b, we are told that originally it was customary for marriages to take place on Wednesdays. Since the time of the persecution the people developed the custom of celebrating them on Tuesdays, and "the rabbis did not interfere." But "on Monday one should not marry, but if it be because of some compelling reason, it is permitted. And they separate the bridegroom from the bride on the first Sabbath eve because he causes a wound." That the baraita consists of more than one stratum is evident from the expression, "on Monday he may not marry, but if it be because of some compelling reason it is permitted." As a matter of fact only the most compelling of reasons brought about the change from Wednesday to Tuesday. It is therefore clear that this is a later modifying statement, added when Tuesday also had become a dangerous day. The words "because he causes a wound" look very much like a gloss; they can only be explained if they refer to a marriage celebrated on Friday, but no such marriage is contemplated in the baraita. The text seems originally to have had reference to the prohibition of marital relations on the sabbath. In order to make certain that the sabbath would not be violated in this respect, the bride and groom were to be kept apart for the first sabbath eve after their marriage. Similarly in the case of mourning, if the death occur during the course of the married life, the husband and wife are not necessarily separated. But if it occur during the first week of their wedded life, they must be kept apart (Ketubot 4a). If this interpretation of the baraita be correct, the baraita must be very old in its basic form, for already in the days of the schools of Shammai and Hillel the law was obsolete (Niddah 10, 1).

certainly imply that view, if we are to accept the editor's reading. The text, however, as Charles notes, seems not to be in good condition, for two out of the four manuscripts used by Charles omit the word 'thereon' in the second half of the verse. If we take the phrase 'on it' to refer to the act of saying (reading 'whoever says on it that he will do something,' etc.) we have a definite statement which is to some extent in consonance with the rabbinic halaka. For in the Talmud it is clearly forbidden to say on the sabbath that one intends to do such and such work during the week.[31] But in the Mishna the planning of work for a week-day, far from being a capital crime, is considered merely a transgression of a rabbinic injunction. It is true that the prohibition is based on a prophetic verse,[32] but that would not suffice to make it a biblical law.

Charles considers it awkward that the author should prohibit the drawing of water "which one has not prepared for himself on the sixth day." But if we bear in mind the rabbinic law, we see that we have here nothing more than the author's customary extension of the Pharisaic law. In the Talmud it is forbidden to use anything on the sabbath which at the coming of the holy day, that is at nightfall on Friday, was not 'prepared' for use.[33] Apples which fell from their tree on the sabbath or an egg laid on the sabbath may not be eaten till the sabbath has passed. It is not a very serious extension of this rule to consider water which has not been previously drawn as 'unprepared for the Sabbath' and therefore unfit for use.

The last clause of this verse prohibits the taking up of a burden with the intent to carry it out of one's tent or out of one's house. Now taking up a burden with the intention of carrying it is not quite the same as carrying it. It may constitute the necessary preliminary to the performance of the act, but it is not the act itself. According to the Talmud this preliminary is rabbinically prohibited, but no biblical transgression is involved unless the full act is performed by setting down the article that has been taken up.[34]

[31] Sabbath 23, 3. Cf. T. B. ad loc.

[32] Isaiah 58, 13.

[33] See Sabbath, chap. 18.

[34] Sabbath 1, 1.

Turning to the second list we find mention of acts of quite a different character. To go on a journey on the sabbath was even in later times held by some to be biblically prohibited,[35] and in earlier times this opinion may have been held more generally. The verse, "Let no man go forth from his place,"[36] may have been taken literally. Indeed that going on a journey was held to be one of the major prohibited actions we can see from the fact that in the first verse planning to go on a journey is put on the same level as planning to do any other kind of work.

That riding a beast on the sabbath was held to be one of the major prohibited acts follows from the statement in the Talmud that in the Maccabean period a man was stoned for riding a horse on the sabbath.[37] The rabbis who hold that riding an animal is only rabbinically forbidden explain that this was a temporary extension of the law. But there is no reason to doubt the fact which is related; and it is unlikely that any court at any time would have presumed to execute a person for a crime which everyone knew to be slight. It is beyond doubt that originally riding was considered biblically prohibited.

Travelling on board ship on the sabbath was in later times considered wrong.[38] It was not permitted to set sail for three days before the sabbath lest one be compelled to remain aboard on the holy day. It is not unlikely that in earlier times this was counted among the severer classes of prohibited actions.

To kill or wound an animal was held by the rabbis to be one of the thirty-nine classes of prohibited labor.[39] Similarly capturing a living thing was included among the thirty-nine categories. On the other hand fasting on the sabbath, while discouraged, was never looked upon as an infringement of the sabbath law.[40] Indeed under certain circumstances it was considered justified. The earlier view may have been more stringent in this regard. It is, however, noteworthy that it would be against Jewish tradition to execute a person for a transgression

35 Erubin 17b.

36 Exod. 16, 29.

37 Yebamot 90b.

38 Sifrè Deut. ed. Friedmann, 111b; Jer. Sabbath 1, 8.

39 Sabbath 7, 1.

40 Sabbath 11a.

like fasting, which involves no action. Mere inactivity is as a rule not punishable, certainly not in human courts.[41] It is, therefore, reasonable to assume that our author is here inserting what he thinks should be the law rather than what he knows to be the general opinion.

Making war on the sabbath certainly involves the transgression of many sabbath laws, but to make it a category by itself is peculiar. The insertion can be understood only in view of the leniency in this regard introduced by the Maccabeans.[42] Our author is simply protesting against the new usage and is urging a return to the pre-maccabean halaka.

3. Other Festivals

The sabbath is of course the most important Jewish festival; hence in this matter there are more points of contact between the halaka of the Book of Jubilees and rabbinic tradition than at any other, but Jubilees also contains numerous passages regarding the other Festivals that can be better understood in the light of rabbinic sayings. We have seen how the author fixed the date of the Feast of Weeks in such a way as seemed to him to satisfy both the Pharisees and the Sadducees. Another interesting reference to a peculiar regulation concerning the Feast of Weeks occurs in the story of Jacob. The characteristic offering of the Feast of Weeks was that of new grain.[43] It is here said that during the famine Jacob found himself unable to procure new grain for the offering, and therefore brought old grain.[44] Now the question of whether in case of emergency old grain may or may not be used for the offering is a matter of dispute among the rabbis. The Mishna [45] insists that only new grain may be used; a baraita quoted in the Talmud [46] permits the old grain.

In regard to Succoth, the Book of Jubilees seems also to have retained the older halaka. Thus we are told that Abraham built booths for himself "and for his servants." [47] Now accord-

[41] The only cases where punishment is threatened for neglect of duty in Jewish law are those of the paschal lamb and of failure to be circumcised.

[42] 1 Maccabees 2, 41.

[43] Lev. 23, 16.

[44] Jub. 44, 4.

[45] Menahot 8, 1.

[46] T. B. Menahot 83b.

[47] Jub. 16, 21.

ing to later rabbinic law [48] women and slaves are exempt from the law requiring all to live in booths during the festival week. But even in the Talmud there seems to be a recollection of the ancient law, since mention is made of the fact that Queen Helena of Adiabene, who became converted to Judaism about the year 30, had a Succah at Lydda.[49]

4. Tithes, and Fruit of the Fourth Year

Perhaps nowhere does the Book of Jubilees reflect an halaka differing more widely from that of the rabbis than in the matter of Tithes. The various rules about tithes are scattered in the Pentateuch, and their interpretation was difficult.[50] The rabbinical system of tithes was as follows. On the first and second years of the sabbatical cycle, as well as on the fourth and fifth, two tithes were brought from all produce. The first was given to the Levite; the second might be eaten by the owner, but nowhere else than in Jerusalem. In the third and sixth years of the seven-year cycle the first tithe was given to the Levite, and instead of taking the second tithe to Jerusalem it was called 'the tithe of the poor,' and was to be distributed among the needy of the vicinity. The Levites who received the first tithe were obliged by law to give a tithe of their tithe to a priest. During the Second Commonwealth it often happened that the Israelite would give his first tithe to a priest [51] instead of to a Levite. On the propriety of this the talmudic authorities are divided.

The system of tithes in the Book of Jubilees is entirely different. The first tithe is given not to the Levite but to the priest.[52] The latter must then set aside one tithe of this tithe and take it to the temple, where it must be eaten by priests within a definite time, namely before the arrival of the new crop. This 'tithe of the tithe' is called 'the second tithe.'

Practically in the same category with their second tithe the rabbis place the fruits of the fourth year.[53] The fruit of any

[48] Succah 28a. [49] Succah 2a.

[50] The passages to be compared regarding the biblical law of tithes are Lev. 27, 30–33, Num. 18, 21–32, Deut. 14, 22–29; 26, 1–15.

[51] Succah 45a. [52] Jub. 32, 9–11. [53] Maaser Sheni, chap. 5.

tree for the first three years after it is planted is forbidden by the biblical law, and may not be eaten, but that of the fourth year is to be "holy for the giving of praise unto the Lord."[54] The rabbis interpret this as meaning that the fruit is to be eaten by the owners in Jerusalem. In the Book of Jubilees, however, it is decreed that, having been offered at the Sanctuary, it is to be eaten by "the servants of the house of God before the altar."[55] Thus our author, too, treats the fruit of the fourth year in the same way as the 'second tithe' of his special system. As usual Jubilees mentions a specific instance of the application of this law; the biblical personage who is reported to have observed the law of the fruit of the fourth year is Noah. The fruit of the first three years he did not use; that of the fourth year he kept till the new moon of the first month of the fifth year.[56] This would imply that under no circumstances is the fruit of the fourth year to be eaten before the coming of the fifth year. While this is not expressly stated among the laws of the fruit of the fourth year, no objection can be drawn from the omission, as the text there is incomplete. In the Talmud no reference is found to any such law, but R. Aha of Shabha (eighth century), in his Sheeltot,[57] tells us that even if the fruit of the fourth year be redeemed it may not be eaten till the fifth year. A similar view is expressed in the Halakot Gedolot[58] (of the same period), and although R. Samson of Sens (twelfth century)[59] spurns the statement as the gloss of an ignorant copyist, one cannot safely set aside as mere ignorance a law found in two of the oldest codes. It is not impossible that there was a tradition in regard to the matter which for some reason found no expression in the Talmuds.

5. Laws of Sacrifice

In regard to the law of Sacrifice we find another striking parallel between the Book of Jubilees and the accepted rabbinic halaka. According to the law of the Bible the peace-offering

[54] Lev. 19, 24.

[55] Jub. 7, 36.

[56] Jub. 7, 37.

[57] קדושים, No. 100.

[58] Halakot Gedolot, end of laws of ערלה, does not occur in the text published by Hildesheimer.

[59] Commentary on Maaser Sheni 5, 7, cf. Tos. R. H. 10a, catchword ופרות.

may be eaten on the day of the sacrifice and on the morrow.[60] What is left until the third day is to be burned. It is questionable whether the law ought not to be interpreted as permitting the eating of the meat on the night following the second day, for the meat need not be burned till the morning of the third day, and generally in the case of sacrifices the night follows the day. This is, however, denied by the rabbis, who limit the time of eating to the coming of the second night. This is likewise the law in the Book of Jubilees, where we are told: "Eat of its meat on that day and on the second day, and let not the sun on the second day go down upon it till it is eaten, and let nothing be left over till the third day." [61]

6. Soiling the Priestly Garments

An interesting law is that prohibiting priests to permit their clothes to be soiled with blood while they are serving in the sanctuary.[62] In the Talmud we also read: "If his clothes were soiled while he was performing the service, his action is unfit." [63]

7. Covering the Blood

One of the most strongly emphasized commandments in the Book of Jubilees is that which deals with the prohibition of eating blood.[64] According to our author the law requires the covering of the blood of beasts, cattle, and whatever flies. This is in consonance with the Karaite halaka rather than with the rabbinic law, which excludes from the application of this rule domestic cattle, like oxen and sheep, limiting it to the beasts of the field and birds.

8. Laws of Marriage

Our author does not confine himself to mere matters of ceremonial. He deals also with matters social. Thus he holds it to be highly commendable to marry a cousin, especially the daughter of a father's brother. Mahalalel seems to have been the first to introduce this custom,[65] and perhaps this was the

[60] Lev. 7, 16.
[61] Jub. 21, 17.
[62] Jub. 21, 10.
[63] Zeb. 35a.
[64] Jub. 7, 29; 21, 16.
[65] Jub. 4, 15.

reason for his being numbered among the saints.[66] Indeed even in the Bible we frequently find mention of the custom of marrying one's cousin. At the behest of Moses the daughters of Zelophehad marry "the sons of their uncles." [67] It is interesting to note that in the Talmud it is recommended to marry a niece, especially the daughter of a sister.[68] The custom of marrying a cousin probably sprang from the desire of maintaining the family unity and family property, and is therefore likely to be the older view.

That a father may give his daughter in her minority in marriage to anyone of his choice [69] is a well established principle in Talmudic law.[70] But that right does not descend to the sons after the death of the father.[71] Our author, however, writes: "If anyone gives his daughter or his sister in marriage to one of the descendants of Canaan he shall surely die." [72] This implies the right to dispose of a sister in marriage. That this was the older view there can be no doubt. It was only as part of the rabbinic emancipation of woman that it was prohibited. In order to protect the orphan girl, the rabbis ordained that after the death of the father the mother of a girl and her brothers may with her consent give her in marriage to anyone of their choice, but that if on reaching her majority she refuse to remain with him, she is thereby released from him.[73]

9. Cases of Bilhah and Tamar

From the fact that the author of Jubilees makes Jacob appoint Levi to act as priest for him it is clear that he does not regard the patriarchs as priests. Otherwise there would be no meaning in Jacob's giving tithes to Levi. Therefore, according to the accepted halaka, there would have been no reason for Jacob's abstaining from Bilhah because of Reuben's outrage upon her

[66] Jub. 19, 24. [67] Num. 36, 11. [68] Yeb. 62b.

[69] The age of majority for females is given in the Mishna as twelve years; Niddah 5, 9. That this is the case would be implied in Jubilees 30, 2, where it is stated that Dinah was twelve years old at the time of the rape. This seems to be based on the use of the word הנערה, which is always interpreted by the rabbis to refer to a girl for the first six months after reaching her twelfth birthday.

[70] Kid. 41a. [72] Jub. 30, 7.

[71] Kid. 16b. [73] Yeb. 107b.

honor, for in the rabbinic halaka a woman does not become forbidden to her husband merely by reason of rape,[74] and unless he be a priest it is only faithlessness on her part that can compel divorce. Yet our author insists that after that incident Jacob had no relations with Bilhah.[75] This would seem to agree with the Karaite halaka, which forbids marital relations with any woman who has been dishonored against her will.[76] That this was the older custom is attested even in the Bible,[77] where David abstained from his concubines after their defilement by Absalom.[78]

Somewhat analogous to the case of Bilhah is that of Tamar. The rabbis found difficulty in explaining why she should have been ordered to be burned. Even granting that until she was released from her brother-in-law she was considered a married woman, and so liable to capital punishment, yet the penalty for adultery in the case of a married woman is strangling and not burning. The rabbis explain the matter by assuming her to have been the daughter of a priest, identifying Shem with Melchizedek.[79] But the author of the Book of Jubilees does not seem to be acquainted with that genealogy. To him Tamar is "one of the daughters of Aram," [80] which probably means not that she was a Canaanite woman, but one of the descendants of Aram, son of Shem. In order to justify Judah, our author makes Abraham command: If any woman "commit fornication among you, burn her with fire." [81] He knew very well that this was not in accord with Mosaic legislation, and

[74] Ket. 51b et al.; cf. Sifrè Num. 5, 13.

[75] Jub. 33, 9.

[76] Revel, Karaite Halacha, p. 34.

[77] 2 Samuel 20, 3.

[78] In Jer. Sanhedrin 2, 3, there are conflicting opinions as to whether David voluntarily abstained from them or was legally forbidden to have relations with them. But even the authority maintaining the opinion that it would have been prohibited, only holds that view in regard to a king, not in regard to other people. The Babylonian view seems to have been that the concubines were suspected of having acquiesced in the wrong of Absalom against his father. This is at any rate the view of Tosafot, Gittin 6b, catchword עבוב. Professor Ginzberg has called my attention to Ps.-Jonathan, Deut. 22, 26, where the view is expressed: "And unto the maiden shall ye do no harm, the maiden is not to be punished by death, but her husband shall divorce her with a writ." So that here too the plea of compulsion would not save the wife from divorce.

[79] Bereshit R. chap. 85.

[80] Jub. 41, 1.

[81] Jub. 20, 4.

is merely saying that before the revelation a stricter law prevailed.

10. Intermarriage

The rabbis trace Judah's troubles to his sin in having deceived his father by feigning that Joseph had been killed by a wild beast.[82] The writer of Jubilees, however, finds the source of his troubles rather in his transgression of the commandment not to marry a Canaanite woman.[83] For, unlike the rabbis, our author takes the word 'Canaanite' literally, not as meaning simply 'merchant.' The result of this forbidden marriage was that when Judah insisted that his son marry one of the descendants of Aram, the son preferred to marry into the family of his mother.[84] When he was finally induced by his father to marry a woman whom he did not like, he vented his hatred and his anger on her. He was punished by early death. The second son, who performed the levirate marriage at the father's behest, committed a similar sin and was similarly punished.

Now Abraham had warned his children against marrying Canaanite women.[85] Likewise Rebecca was warm in her denunciation of mixed marriages.[86] But it is in connection with the outrage on Dinah that we are finally told that it is one of the laws of the Heavenly Tables that one may not give a daughter to a non-israelite.[87] The punishment for the sin is stoning, and the woman is to be burnt by fire.

The prohibition against this crime is found in an allegorical interpretation of the verse, "And of thy seed thou shalt not give to pass through to Molech."[88] An echo of this verse is found in our book, where it reads, "For of his seed he has given unto Molech."[89] The same interpretation of the verse is found in Ps.-Jonathan to the verse, but it is quoted with condemnation in the Mishna.[90] Since the punishment for "passing one's seed through to Molech" is stoning, that is to be taken as the penalty prescribed in our book for the transgression of marrying a Canaanite woman.

82 Ps.-Jon. Gen. 38, 25.
83 Jub. 41, 2.
84 Jub. 41, 2.
85 Jub. 20, 4.
86 Jub. 25, 1.
87 Jub. 30, 9.
88 Lev. 18, 21.
89 Jub. 30, 10.
90 Meg. 25a.

11. Impurity after Childbirth

Among the first laws referred to in the Book of Jubilees is that declaring a mother ritually unclean after childbirth. This is mentioned in connection with the entrance of Adam and Eve into the Garden of Eden.[91] Adam was created during the first week, Eve during the second week; for this reason a mother is declared to be impure for one week after the birth of a son, and two weeks after the birth of a daughter. Adam did not come into Eden till forty days after his creation, and Eve not until eighty days after she had been created; therefore a woman may not go into the temple for forty days after childbirth if the child be a son, and for eighty if it be a daughter. The connection between the time of the entrance of Adam and Eve into the garden and the permission to a woman to come into the temple is not at all clear. It might be more evident if the child, as well as the mother, were held to be unclean, but in the Talmud this is certainly not the case. Nor does the Book of Jubilees make any reference to the uncleanness of the child. Furthermore, while Eve was presented to Adam in the second week of his existence, yet there were no marital relations between them until the end of the first Jubilee.[92] We are not told the reason for this abstinence; it is certainly contrary to rabbinic tradition, which assumes that both Cain and Abel were born in Eden.

12. Circumcision

Charles believes that when our author insisted that circumcision must be performed on the eighth day, he was declaring his objection to the rabbinic law that permits under certain circumstances the postponement of the performance of the rite for several days.[93] Thus if the child be born on Friday at twilight, the rite is to be performed on Sunday, which would be actually the tenth day after his birth. If that day be a festival, the ceremony is to be observed on the following day, the eleventh of the child's life. If, as might happen even in Palestine in the case of New Year's day, that day, too, be a

[91] Jub. 3, 10. [92] Jub. 3, 34. [93] Jub. 13, 14.

festival, the child is to enter the covenant of Abraham on Tuesday, the twelfth day after his birth.[94] The underlying principle is plainly stated: it is not permitted to violate the Sabbath except when it is certain that the child was born on that day; when the matter is in doubt, the rite must be performed on a week-day. It is unlikely that the author of the Book of Jubilees would protest against that law. If he had had it in mind, he would probably have referred to it clearly. It is far more likely that our author is following the Bible, and is merely emphasizing the importance of the eighth day as the proper time for the observance of the rite.

13. The Law of Retaliation

While we find development in nearly all branches of Jewish law between the times of the Bible and those of the Talmud, perhaps nowhere do we find so radical a change as in regard to the law of Retaliation. The old law of "an eye for an eye, a tooth for a tooth," is practically abolished by the rabbis, and money payments substituted.[95] The only rabbi who insists on the old law is R. Eliezer, but even his words are interpreted by the later authorities so as to agree in principle with the new opinion. In the Book of Jubilees the full rigor of the law is insisted on. Indeed, it is even extended, so that a murderer is to be executed in the same way in which he disposed of his victim. Thus Cain is punished for killing Abel with a stone by having a house fall upon him, for "with a stone did he kill, and with a stone was he killed." [96] While this is accepted by the rabbis as a theological concept — 'measure for measure' — yet it is nowhere affirmed as a legal maxim.

14. The Noachic Laws

We have thus far discussed the laws that apply to Israel alone, but Jewish tradition has also a code of laws that apply to all men, which are generally referred to in the Talmud as the seven laws of the sons of Noah. In the Tosefta we are told that the sons of Noah were given seven commandments. They

[94] Sabbath 19, 5. [95] Baba Kamma 84a. [96] Jub. 4, 31.

are: to institute judgments (civil law), against blasphemy, against illicit sex relations, against murder, against robbery, and against eating the limb of a living animal.[97] We notice that, although we are told that there were seven, on counting those mentioned we find only six. In the Talmud seven are actually mentioned, for beside the prohibition against blasphemy there is a special law against idolatry.[98] In the midrash only six are mentioned and only six are promised in the heading.[99]

In the Book of Jubilees[100] the sons of Noah are commanded to observe six laws; but these are only partly identical with the Noachic regulations of rabbinic literature. "To observe righteousness" might be a fair equivalent to 'dinim,' or civil law. The second of the laws given in the Book of Jubilees is "to cover the shame of the flesh." This is of course considered the basis of morality in the Talmud, but it is nowhere raised to the dignity of a law. Our author, living in days of hellenistic tendencies, with the heathen gymnasia as a thorn in the side of Israel, looked upon this law as one of the highest importance. "To bless the Creator," the third of our author's Noachic laws, may be a mistranslation for the term ברכת השם, which is a euphemistic expression for blasphemy, and the phrase would therefore originally have meant not a positive commandment to bless the Lord but a prohibition of saying anything derogatory against him, which is actually one of the seven Noachic laws of the Talmud. The injunctions to honor one's parents and to love one's neighbor, which are two of the author's six Noachic commandments, are not found in the Talmudic list at all. Yet among the rabbis the universality of these two laws is upheld. Thus we are told that the extent to which one must go in honoring one's parents may be learned from a gentile in Ashkelon who preferred to lose a great profit rather than to disturb his father's sleep.[101] In regard to the commandment to love one's neighbor, attention need but be called to the state-

[97] Aboda Zara, chap. 9, ed. Zuckermandel, p. 473.

[98] Sanhedrin 56a.

[99] Bereshit R. chap. 16; cf. Pesikta, ed. Buber, p. 100b, where some manuscripts read שבע and some שש, but all agree in enumerating only six commandments.

[100] Jub. 7, 20.

[101] Kiddushin 31a.

ment of Ben Azzai that the verse, "This is the book of the generations of man," contains a deeper truth, for it includes all men in a universal brotherhood.[102] The last of the six laws of the Book of Jubilees, "to guard against fornication," is of course merely a paraphrase of the law against illicit intercourse which in the Talmud also is one of the Noachic commandments.

The tone of the six laws as they are set down in the Book of Jubilees seems decidedly older than that of any of the lists in rabbinic literature. There can be no doubt that originally there were only six laws, and that later a seventh was added in order to obtain a round number. In the Tosefta the influence of the current phrase, 'seven Noachic laws,' was strong enough to cause the scribe to insert it in the text, but he could not add commandments which were not before him.

We have thus seen how many of the passages of the Book of Jubilees are made more intelligible by a comparison with the traditions of the rabbis. A comparison of the agadic passages of the book with those of the Talmud would yield even more plentiful fruit. Much has been done in this regard by Charles, but much yet remains. We are handicapped in dealing with this book, since we have it only in the form of a translation; yet it is a well at which the student of the Scriptures and of the development of both Jewish and Christian theology must drink deeply.

[102] Jer. Nedarim, 9, 4.

CHAPTER 10

SOME EXAMPLES OF THE MACCABEAN HALAKA

LOUIS FINKELSTEIN
JEWISH THEOLOGICAL SEMINARY OF AMERICA

THE great and inspiring efforts of talmudic scholars from Geiger till our own day have not sufficed to reconstruct completely the ancient Maccabean halaka. The early, pre-tannaitic teachers and judges did not usually crystallize their opinions into easily remembered maxims, they rather left them to be preserved as fluid custom and vaguely determined precedent. Only in the schools of Shammai and Hillel did the process of reducing the Unwritten Law to fixed, memorized statements become general.[1] And while we know that the mishnaic norms contain laws much older than themselves, the recency of the formulation effectually prevents us from determining the antiquity of the idea.

Our difficulties are increased by the form in which the tannaitic traditions have come down to us. Only rarely do we have the earliest norms in their original state; usually they have suffered alterations and additions which cannot always be separated by

[1] In several instances such as *Mishnah Pesahim* 1, 1; *Mishnah Erubin* 1, 1 the disagreement between the schools of Shammai and Hillel appears to depend on differences of interpretation of older Halakic statements, which had already been formulated. But in general it may be said that the oldest sections of the Mishnah have been traced back no earlier than the first century of the Christian Era, and apparently come from the Shammaitic School. See Hoffmann, *Die Erste Mischna*, pp. 19ff., and Ginzberg in *Hoffmann-Festschrift*, pp. 31ff.

Reprinted from *Journal of Biblical Literature,* Volume 49, 1930.

critical analysis. Scholars like Hoffmann and Ginzberg[2] have succeeded in distinguishing the original bases of some treatises, but in many instances the old and the new are so inextricably intertwined as to defy analysis.

But we can sometimes derive help in fixing the date of a law by a comparison of the rabbinic halaka with the legal references in the apocrypha and pseudepigrapha. True these works were composed not by scholars or legalists, but by sectarians and propagandists, and they were intended not for school study but as popular reading. Hence their statements are not always absolutely accurate, and their authors may even have distorted the extant traditions when that suited their purposes. Yet having before us the rabbinic formulation of a law, as well as the sectarian citation, we are sometimes able to make allowance for the necessary effects of time on the one source, and the conscious schismatic distortion of the other, and thus reconstruct the original with some approach to probability. We propose to utilize this method in attempting to establish the Maccabean form of the following halakas: (1) the Noachic laws; (2) the sabbath law; (3) the law of tithes; (4) the temple regulations regarding priestly ablutions and regarding the preparation of the holy incense. The first three are interesting because of their political-economic implications, the last as an illustration of early Maccabean hermeneutics.

I. The Noachic Laws

According to a *baraita*,[3] cited in several rabbinic sources, the sons of Noah received the following commandments: (1) to establish a system of civil law,[4] (2) not to blaspheme, (3) not to

[2] Journal of Jewish Lore and Philosophy, I (1919), 33ff.

[3] *Tosefta Aboda Zara* 8, 4 (Zuckermandel, 473) and *B. Sanhedrin* 56a.

[4] Guttmann (*Das Judentum u. seine Umwelt*, p. 100, note 1) accepting the interpretation put upon the expression *dinim* by the *Tosefta* (*loc. cit.*), assumes that the Noachic law required the Gentiles to establish courts. This interpretation underlies the description of the commandment in *Pesikta of R. Kahana, Piska 12,* ed. Buber 100b. It is also adopted by Maimonides in his Yad (*hilkot melakim* 9, 14). But in spite of this support it cannot be accepted. The natural expression for a commandment to "appoint judges"

worship idols, (4) not to commit murder, (5) not to commit robbery, (6) not to transgress the laws of chastity, (7) and not to eat the flesh that has been torn from an animal while still alive.

Several writers[5] have endeavored to find a similarity between this tradition and the record contained in the Book of Jubilees, according to which Noah exhorted "his sons (1) to observe righteousness, (2) to cover the shame of their flesh, (3) to bless their Creator, (4) to honor father and mother, (5) to love their neighbor, (6) and to guard themselves against fornication and uncleanness and all iniquity."[6]

Placed side by side in this manner, the two lists may appear to have little in common and the reader may wonder at the readiness of scholars to see in them a fundamental identity. But closer study will show their intimate relationship and also the reasons for their divergence.

We must bear in mind, before proceeding with the study of the texts before us, that the Book of Jubilees which claims for itself Mosaic authorship, was written by a Jew, of Pharisaic leanings, about the year 100 B. C., in order to effect certain purposes of his own. One of these was apparently to bring about greater harmony between the Pharisees and the Sadducees. By announcing the discovery of a document giving Mosaic authority for several distinctly Pharisaic teachings and declaring that they

would be not *dayyanim* as *Pesikta* reads, and certainly not *dinim* as the older sources as well as the Babylonian Talmud reads, but *leha*ᶜ*amid dayyanim.* Clearly the interpretation arose when the original significance of the Noachic laws had been forgotten, and it seemed peculiar that the Gentiles should be asked to observe Jewish civil law. But when we recall that the Noachic laws were established for the Maccabean state, we can readly see why the provision was necessary. The objection that *dinim*, interpreted as the civil code is not a single law but a whole group of them, is hardly to be regarded. In the same manner *gillui* ʿ*arayot*, the prohibition of illicit sex relations, implies a number of separate injunctions and yet for the purposes of the Noachic code it is treated as one law.

[5] Ginzberg, *Legends of the Jews V*, 193, note 67; Guttmann, *Das Judentum u. seine Umwelt*, 103; Finkelstein, *Harvard Theological Review*, XVI, 59ff.

[6] Jubilees 3 21.

had been discovered in a secret document after being hidden for many centuries, this writer imagined he could persuade all groups to unite on a common platform.[7] A second, and incidental purpose, was to strengthen certain institutions for which he had great respect and to denounce objectionable practices. The author, who does not hesitate to attribute his words to Moses, has sufficient daring to cite biblical verses with slight alterations in order to achieve his ends. It is our belief that in formulating the "exhortations" of Noah to his sons, he quoted the widely recognized "commandments of the sons of Noah" in order to emphasize certain favorite teachings.

If we suppose that the Noachic commandments had already been formulated in his day, some of the difficulties about his "exhortations" readily dissolve. His command "to observe righteousness" in its present context is quite meaningless; everything that follows is included under "righteousness." The words become significant if we suppose them to be translated from an original Hebrew, *lishmor et ha-din*, "to observe the civil law," and therefore to correspond exactly to the Talmudic first Noachic commandment, *dinim*, the establishment of civil law.

The third commandment, "to bless their Creator," is likewise peculiarly expressed; we would expect a term more like "to worship," representing an original Hebrew, *laʿabod*, the normal term used in this connection.[8] A commandment, "to bless the Creator," is unnatural unless it is supplemented by an explanation of the occasion for blessing Him, as in Deut. 8 10, where we read: "And thou shalt eat, and be satisfied, and shalt bless the Lord, thy God, for the goodly land which he hath given thee."

In its present context the expression apparently replaces the words *birkat ha-shem* "blessing the Name" the euphemism used in the Hebrew of the Noachic laws to express the prohibition of blasphemy. The ancient Jew could not couple the name of God with a curse, even in a negative commandment, and so he regularly substituted for the word "curse," its opposite, "bless." The

[7] Comp. *Harvard Theological Review*, XXII (1929), p. 246.

[8] Comp. e. g. Deut. 11 13 *et al.*

writer of the Book of Jubilees had no occasion to warn his Jewish readers against blasphemy, but he did want to urge them to "bless their Creator;" and apparently he deliberately took advantage of this use of *birkat ha-shem* in the Noachic laws, to give it positive significance.

The prohibition of unchastity is the same in both lists.

The readers of the Book of Jubilees were in no danger of becoming gross criminals. The author therefore omitted the Noachic commands against murder and robbery, substituting for them the positive ethical injunctions to respect one's parents and love one's neighbor. The one is taken from the third of the ten commandments, the other is a positive expression of the tenth, not to covet the goods of one's neighbor.

Similarly a prohibition of idolatry would have been superfluous in this work, although it had its natural place in the original Noachic laws. The writer puts in its stead a commandment "to cover the shame of the flesh,"—an obvious attack on the custom among the youths of Jerusalem to disport themselves naked in the gymnasium, in complete disregard of older Semitic modesty. The Hellenistic gymnasium, as the author implies, exercised on the Jewish youth of the Greek period the same assimilatory influence that the Canaanite worship had exercised on their ancestors of the first commonwealth.

The Book of Jubilees enumerates only six Noachic "exhortations," but the seventh, kindness to animals, is discussed separately in the following verses. Apparently in the author's day, the commandment not to eat animal flesh before slaughter, was not part of the traditional Noachic laws. The Talmud may have reference to this stage in its statement: "six were given to Adam, and the seventh, that against ill-treating animals, was given to Noah."[9] In their characteristic way the rabbis project the growth of the Noachic laws back from Maccabean times to those of Adam and Noah.

The foregoing analysis leads to the conclusion that the Noachic laws were formulated at the beginning of the Maccabean period.

[9] *Bereshit R.* 16 (ed. Theodor, p. 149); *Pesikta of R. Kahana, loc. cit.*

The occasion for their establishment is then clear. For the first time in four centuries, the Maccabean victory had put Jews in a position of authority in their own land. But Maccabean Palestine contained a large heathen population. Most of these gentiles lived in cities which were not under Hasmonean dominion. But even within the limited Maccabean state, there was a large percentage of them. The scholars of the day were now confronted with the problem of giving these Gentiles a constitutional status in a Jewish state. Were they to be compelled to observe the whole Torah, or any part of it? Ought they to keep the sabbath, for instance, or the dietary laws?

The answer to these questions was given in the Noachic laws. The Maccabean scholars formulated six laws, or rather groups of laws, which were to be binding on Gentiles as well as on Jews. Four of them related to the elementary relations of civil life, being such as in modern life would come within the natural purview of the state, as opposed to the church. The state had to protect its citizens against murder and robbery and the women from violence and betrayal. The civil law, too, had to be uniform for all and the Jewish tradition was naturally adopted.

Beyond this the Noachic laws demanded from the Gentile population, first, that they desist from mocking the dominant religion. The Jews were the more free to make this demand, since their foremost representative in the dispersion, Philo, declared that they were bound by their own law to offer the same minimum of respect even to idol-worship.[10] Second, the Jewish doctrine of monotheism could not tolerate the worship of idols on their soil and within their jurisdiction. In this respect monotheism must necessarily be more intolerant than polytheism; those who believe in the One God cannot permit or sanction by their silence the worship of many gods.

[10] Philo, *Vita Mosis*, II, 204. See also Ritter, *Philo und die Halacha*, p. 131. The same law is cited by Josephus, clearly from Philo, *Ant.* 4, 8, 10 and *Contra Apionem* 2, 33.

II. The Sabbath Law

The newly gained autonomy of the Maccabean state necessitated not only the establishment of a fixed constitutional status for the Gentile population, but also a clearer definition of some laws pertaining to Jews alone. The chief of these was the sabbath law.

The sabbath regulations of the Torah are exceedingly vague. "Work" is prohibited, but little is said of what constitutes work. Only two acts are specifically forbidden, to kindle a fire,[11] and to gather sticks.[12] But nothing is said about buying, selling, writing, weaving, building, sewing and all the industrial arts and crafts.

Some light is thrown on the matter from references to the sabbath in prophetic and hagiographical works. Amos records that in his day the Israelites would not sell grain on the sabbath or the new moon (8 5). The author of Isaiah 58 urges his hearers to desist from business on the sabbath day: "If thou turn away thy foot from the sabbath, from pursuing thy business on my holy day, and call the sabbath a delight, the holy one of the Lord, honorable, and shalt honor it, not doing thine own ways, nor seeking thine own business, nor speaking thine own words, Then shalt thou delight thyself in the Lord; and I will cause thee to ride upon the high place of the earth and feed thee with the heritage of Jacob thy father (58 13–14)."

Nehemiah tells us of his efforts to prevent the violation of the sabbath. He implies that some Judeans were in the habit of "treading winepresses on the sabbath, and bringing in sheaves, and lading asses, as also, wine, grapes and figs, and all manner of burdens which they brought into Jerusalem on the sabbath day (12 15)." In order to prevent this traffic on the holy day, he commanded that gates of Jerusalem which were shut at nightfall on Friday, be kept closed throughout the sabbath. And when some of the merchants remained without the walls of Jerusalem for the whole sabbath, he threatened to take violent measures against them.

On the other hand, we discover from an incidental passage in

[11] Exodus 35 3.

[12] Numbers 15 32ff.

Kings that, at least in early times, riding a beast on the sabbath day was not considered wrong. When the Shunamite woman was preparing to visit the prophet, her husband innocently said to her, "Wherefore wilt thou go today, it is neither new moon nor sabbath (II Kings 4 13)," implying that if it were a festival day he might expect her to undertake the journey.

But the matter of determining what was permitted and what was not permitted, apparently gave the scholars little concern before the Maccabean age. The Jews probably did not have full authority to enforce their law. The observance of the sabbath was largely a matter of private conscience, every man desisting from his individual labor and resting as he thought proper. The only pressure was that of popular custom and public opinion, which probably changed from locality to locality, and perhaps even from generation to generation.

The establishment of a Jewish state brought a new element into the matter. The government undertook to enforce the sabbath law, together with all the other laws of the Torah. For the cornerstone of the Maccabean government was to be the Law, on behalf of which the war had been waged.[13] Under such circumstances, there could be but one law in the country, and diversities of *minhag* could be tolerated only in minor details. Moreover the government was compelled to define in concrete terms what it would regard as punishable violations of the sabbath. Would it be prepared to punish a man for transgressing Isaiah's prohibition of discussing one's business affairs on the sabbath? Would it prohibit riding a beast on the sabbath, though the Bible records that that was practised in the apparently pious Shunamite household?

The Talmud gives us very little information about the action taken by the Maccabean scholars in this matter. R. Eliezer b. Jacob (perhaps the first, who lived at the time of the Fall of the Temple) recalls a tradition that "in the time of the Greeks a man was stoned for riding a horse on the sabbath (*B. Yebamot 90b*)." He, maintaining with all the other Talmudic authorities that riding

[13] Cf. e. g. I Macc. 2 51.

a beast is not biblically prohibited, explains this as an extraordinary measure, beyond the letter of the law. But it is difficult to agree with him that the judges who condemned the man to death took the same view. We can hardly believe that a court would execute a person for an act not legally punishable by death, merely to inspire lawbreakers with fear. Can the death of an innocent man move transgressors to fear? Would it not be far more politic, as well as infinitely more just, to inflict judgment on the wicked. Unless we are to assume that the judges of the "Greek" times were quite blind to the social effects of judicial wrong-doing we cannot accept the Talmudic theorizing as representing actual fact. Far more likely is it that the Maccabean courts[14] considered riding on a horse an offense against the biblical sabbath law and therefore made the man pay the penalty for his transgression.

This conjecture derives additional force from the statement in the Book of Jubilees (50, 12) that riding on a beast is a capital infraction of the sabbath rest.

The Talmud contains no other information about the Maccabean form of the sabbath law. But we can learn something about it from the description in the Book of Jubilees. The author of this work mentions fifteen different forms of prohibited activity, but divides them into two lists, one containing five, and the other ten. items. He says: "And the man that does any work thereon, shall die: whoever desecrates that day, (1) whoever lies with his wife. (2) or whoever says he will do something on it, (3) that he will set out on a journey thereon in regard to buying or selling, and (4) whoever draws water thereon which he has not prepared for himself on the sixth day, and (5) whoever takes up any burden to carry it out of his tent or out of his house shall die (50 8)."

A few verses later, he enumerates other prohibitions: "And every man who does any work thereon, or (1) who goes on a journey, or (2) tills (his) farm, whether in his house or any other place, or (3) whoever lights a fire, or (4) rides on any beast, or (5) travels

[14] The "time of the Greeks" of which the Talmud speaks must have been that of the wars between the Hasmoneans and the Syrians, as all the commentators have understood.

by ship on the sea, and (6) whoever strikes or kills anything or (7) slaughters a beast, or a bird, or (8) whoever catches an animal, or a bird, or a fish, or (9) whoever fasts, or (10) makes war on the sabbath, the man who does any of these things on the sabbath shall die (50 12–13)."

The puzzling division of the prohibited activities into two groups, the one containing five and the other ten members, suggests the utilization of older material. The most satisfactory explanation would seem to be that here, as in his citation of the Noachic commandments, the author employs current traditions, perhaps with slight changes to suit his needs.

Unfortunately we cannot be certain about the extent of these changes, if there were any, because the mishnaic list of thirty-nine prohibited categories of work is of much later origin. The number thirty-nine itself was disputed by some authorities.[15] And even a cursory examination of the tannaitic literature shows that there was no general agreement as to what constituted a major violation of the sabbath. Contrary to the general opinion, the tendency of talmudic law was to make the sabbath law more lenient. Many activities which the older sources called biblically prohibited, were either permitted or declared mere rabbinical prohibitions by the later authorities. Thus in spite of the prophetic support for the rule against discussing one's business on the sabbath (Is. 58 13), the rabbis maintained that there is no biblical prohibition against it.[16] They further asserted that buying and selling on the sabbath is only rabbinically prohibited.[17] They greatly extended the rule, first established in Maccabean times,[18] of setting aside the sabbath law when life is in danger.[19] Again Shammai living toward the

[15] According to *Mekilta* on Exodus 35 1 and *B. Sabbath* 67 b R. Judah the Patriarch was the authority for the statement that there are 39 classes of prohibited work, and that the other authorities do not necessarily agree with him. In fact *B. Sabbath* 97 b clearly indicates that most of them were of a different opinion.

[16] *Maim. Hilkot Shabbat* 6, 1; 24, 1; 4, 5.

[17] Ibid. 23, 12.

[18] 1 Macc. 2 41.

[19] *Mishnah Yoma* 8, 6, comp. Talmud *ad loc.* and Maim. *Yad, Hilkot Shabbat*, Chapter 2.

end of Herod's reign permitted even offensive war on the sabbath,[20] but in the war against Pompey in 63 B. C., Josephus tells us, the Zealots would only strike in actual self-defense, but made no move to prevent the Romans from proceeding with their preparatory activities on the sabbath day.[21]

We may therefore be prepared to find that many of the activities described by the Book of Jubilees as capital offenses against the sabbath, are held by the rabbis not to be such. But that need not deter us from recognizing that the Book of Jubilees is recording the accepted halaka of its own time. With one exception, that of conjugal relations,[22] all of its prohibitions are repeated in Talmudic authorities; although most of them are reduced in status to minor, instead of major violations.

We may surmise that Maccabean scholars, pressed for a definition of the sabbath law, proceeded to enumerate from time to time, as occasion demanded, lists of prohibited classes of labor. They naturally stressed in these lists those prohibitions about which there might be some difference of opinion. Where ultimately the lenient opinion prevailed, the older record, with its more rigorous norms, appears to us antiquated and schismatic.

In the so-called Zadokite Document,[23] we have another attempt to formulate the sabbath law. In the main, as Professor Ginzberg has shown,[24] this compilation is in consonance with the Pharisaic law, and may reflect, to a large extent, the stage reached in the definition of the sabbath law at the time of its writing.

The culmination of these centuries of discussion and study is the series of thirty nine prohibited classes of labor found in our mishna

[20] *Sifre* Deut. 204 (ed. Friedmann, 111b) and *B. Shabbat* 19b.

[21] *Bellum*, 1, 7, 3. Compare the note of Simhoni to the Hebrew translation (Warsaw, 1923), p. 409.

[22] A recollection of the early tannaitic prohibition of marital relations on the sabbath may be found in a *baraita* preserved in *B. Ketubot* 3b, as I maintained in *Harvard Theological Review*, XVI, 48, note 3.

[23] Schechter, *Documents of Jewish Sectaries*, I, 10ff.

[24] *Eine unbekannte jüdische Sekte*, p. 231.

(Sabbath 7, 1). Like the lists in the Book of Jubilees and the Zadokite Document, that of the Mishna does not in fact cover the whole field of prohibited sabbath labor. It can hardly be considered an Aristotelian classification, for the subdivisions that are grouped under the various heads frequently seem far more general and important than some of the items accepted as genera. Sowing and planting are considered two different categories; so are tearing and cutting apart. But extracting the juices of fruit, as in working a winepress, is a subdivision of threshing.[25] Some categcries are so loose that considerable difference of opinion prevailed as to the place to be assigned to many minor forms of labor. The mishnaic formulation, in short, bears all the marks of being the result not of logical analysis, but of organic growth. And this strengthens our conviction that the lists in the Book of Jubilees, and perhaps also in the Zadokite Document, represent stages in its growth.

This explains many peculiar anomalies in the mishnaic law. The prohibition against buying and selling on the sabbath is omitted not because the rabbis held it to be less important than the prohibition against tying a knot, for example, but because the genius of Jewish law, in its organic development preferred to deal with concrete actions rather than abstractions. Buying and selling are legal and technical activities, the manual labor represented by them is the physical transfer of the property. This was forbidden under the category "carrying." Now it is possible to sell and buy without removing the material from its place; that is considered only a secondary prohibition, because it is an abstract, and not a concrete work. Even Nehemiah in denouncing the people who came to sell in the markets of Jerusalem on the sabbath lays particular emphasis on their carrying the burdens and lading them on the beasts.[26] The commercial traffic was technically secondary to the physical acts of removal and carrying. Hence the vehement outburst in Jeremiah 17 21ff. against those who carry on the sabbath. And hence also the peculiar fact that carrying, mentioned

[25] Maim. *Yad*, *Shabbat* 21, 12.
[26] Neh. 13 15.

last among the mishnaic classes of work, nevertheless occupies no less than half of the space devoted to the sabbath in the Talmud.[27]

In a more logically arranged compilation of the sabbath works, we should expect a division primarily into agricultural, pastoral, artisan, commercial, and household activities. But the mishnaic categories are not at all so formulated. The order accepted by the compiler is chronological; he follows the grain of wheat from its origin in the field to its destiny in the baker's oven, enumerating eleven processes that enter into the history, — ploughing, sowing, reaping, gathering into sheaves, threshing, winnowing, selecting, grinding, sifting, kneading, baking. He then takes up the development of the wool, from the time it is shorn from the sheep till it becomes a finished garment, and discovers that thirteen forms of activity are involved, including shearing, bleaching, dyeing, spinning, weaving, tyeing, loosening, sewing and cutting; he then turns to the process of writing, and enumerates nine activities under that head, among them capturing a deer, slaughtering it, tanning its hide, writing upon the parchment, erasing so as to be able to write more correctly. Finally in a miscellaneous group he mentions building, and breaking down for the purpose of rebuilding, kindling a light, extinguishing, striking the anvil and carrying from house into market place.

There is not even an attempt at logical analysis; the order followed is purely mnemonic. The compiler was not worried lest some activity be omitted. For he knew well that those not mentioned as classes find their place in subdivisions. The sabbath laws and prohibitions had been well fixed by custom in his day; only the smallest details were left for rabbinic discussion. What he sought was a convenient method of committing the most important forms of work to memory and this he provided in the list that is contained in our mishna.

III. The Law of Tithes

The Biblical law of tithes, as it was interpreted in the third century B. C., weighed very heavily on the rural population of

[27] This includes the greater part of the treatise *Erubin*, and Chapters 1, of Sabbath.

Judaea. In addition to the Levitical law which assigned one tenth of all the produce to the tribe of Levi,[28] the Deuteronomic law[29] required that a second tenth be consumed annually in Jerusalem. The ordinary peasant thus had to pay an annual income tax of ten percent, and to spend ten percent more of his income in a few days' holiday at the capital city.

We readily surmise that so heavy a tax was evaded by many, and indeed Tobit takes great pride in having observed it. "I used to go to Jerusalem," he tells us, "with the first fruits and the firstlings and the tenth of the cattle and the first shearing of the sheep, and give them to the priests, the sons of Aaron, for the altar; and the tenth of the corn and the wine and the oil and pomegranates and the rest of the fruits to the sons of Levi, who ministered in Jerusalem; and the second tenth I tithed annually for the six years and went and spent it each year at Jerusalem; and gave it unto the orphans and the widows and the proselytes who attached themselves to the children of Israel, I brought it and gave it unto them in the third year."[30]

[28] Nu. 18 21.

[29] Deut. 14 22.

[30] Tobit 1 7ff. We need not concern ourselves here with the controversy between Geiger and Pineles as to whether the older halaka provided also for a "third tithe." If Geiger's thesis be admitted, the tax on the farmer was so much the greater and the need for reform so much the more pressing. But it is doubtful whether the authoritative halaka ever recognized more than two annual tithes. Geiger certainly has shown that Josephus knew of a custom to give a third tithe on the third year (Jos. *Ant.* iv, 8, 22), and possibly this third tithe is presupposed also in Tobit (the passage cited above) and in Targum Ps. Jonathan on Deut. 26 12. But these seem to represent the attitude of the most pious, not the requirements of the savants. But compare Geiger, *Urschrift*, 179ff., and in opposition, Pineles, *Darkah shel Torah*, 173ff. Olitzki in his *Flavius Josephus u. die Halacha*, Berlin, 1885, 16ff. (but see particularly p. 18, note 22) agrees with Pineles in denying that there was a third tithe. He maintains that Josephus, ignorant of the traditional law, was misled into supposing that three tithes were given on the third year, when he noticed that some of the second tithe of the second year was used in Jerusalem also on the third year. It must also be admitted that a comparison of the Sifre Mss. with the printed text, weakens Geiger's thesis. For the Sifre text (Deut. 26 17, section 72, ed. Friedmann, 89b) on which he

The power of the Maccabean government to enforce the tithe as a state law put it in a serious dilemma. It could not refuse to enforce the biblical law, and yet we can realize what difficulties presented themselves against any attempt to compel obedience to it. Both the Talmud and the Book of Jubilees record attempts to deal with this problem realistically.

The author of the Book of Jubilees boldly annuls the law of the second tithe. He maintains that the first tithe is to be given to the priests rather than to the Levites, and that the priests are to separate from their receipts a tithe, which he calls the "second tithe" to be "eaten before the Lord," in the sanctuary at Jerusalem (Jubilees 32 8 ff.). The author thus retains the name "second tithe" which in his day was used familiarly for the additional tenth separated by pious Judaeans for consumption in Jerusalem, but declares that it is not supplementary to the Levitical or Priestly tithe, but one tenth of it.

Quite a different solution to the problem is recorded in the Talmud as having been established in practise. According to its story John Hyrcan,[31] finding that many farmers did not set apart the

relies to show that the rabbis themselves recognized the third tithe, appears in quite a different form in the manuscript sources. I cannot enter into details here, but from the material at present available before me, I believe that the text of the baraita cited by Geiger from ed. pr. arose out of a scribal error.

[31] *Tosefta Sotah* 13, 10 (Zuckermandel, 320) and *Jer. Sotah* 9, 11 and *B. Sotah* 48a. Compare Graetz, iii, note II end (ed. Leipzig 1888, p. 686), who maintains that Hyrcan did not inaugurate the institution of *demai*, but rather enforced the collection of tithes. This view he maintains is supported by *Mishna Sotah* 9, 11 and by the comment in the Talmud of Jerusalem. The mishnah says simply: "In his days (John Hyrcan's) no one had to ask regarding *demai*." And the Talmud of Jerusalem explains that "he appointed pairs." Graetz takes that enigmatic statement to mean that he appointed pairs of overseers to compel payment of the tithe. But Graetz failed to notice that this interpretation is in absolute contradiction to the tradition recorded in Tosefta and cited by R. Johanan in the Talmud of Jerusalem (loc. cit.) that R. Johanan instituted the custom of *demai*. The reading of the *Tosefta*: "He also established the *viddui* and abolished the *demai*" makes no sense. The *viddui* must be the confession recited when

Levitical tithe, ordained that the purchaser of grain should do so, unless he was certain that it had been done by the seller. But having done so, John Hyrcan added, the purchaser was not obliged to give the separated tithe to a priest or Levite, but might use it for his own needs.

This ordinance established the well-known institution of *demai* (the name technically given in the rabbinic sources to grain bought from a farmer or merchant, without definite information as to whether the tithes have already been separated or not). Both the legal theory on which this ordinance is based, and its economic background and purposes, are well worth close attention.

John Hyrcan, acting doubtless on the advice of contemporaneous scholars, apparently held that tithing the grain involved two diverse elements, which might be separated from one another. The first was the purely ceremonial act of setting aside one tenth of the grain for holy purposes.

The second was the civil obligation to transfer the separated tithe to some Levite or priest. There was no ceremonial obligation involved in this transfer, according to John Hyrcan; the original grain which might not be eaten unless the tithes were separated, could be eaten if they were separated but not given away. And the tithe itself could also be eaten — according to purely ritual law — by any Jew, not necessarily by a priest or Levite.

But John Hyrcan went further. He now declared that after all no one could be certain that the proper tithes of any particular

bringing the second tithe to Jerusalem, but this did not have to be established by Hyrcan. It had been ordained in Scripture (Deut. 26 12ff.); nor could Hyrcan have abolished the institution of *demai* for no one maintains that it existed before him. The text must be emended so as to read that "He also established the institution of *demai* and abolished the *viddui*". The tradition that Johanan established the *demai* thus found in the Tosefta, and recorded by R. Johanan, must be accepted in preference to the ambiguous statement in the *mishna*. It is possible nevertheless to reconcile the two statements by supposing that for some time Hyrcan tried to enforce the biblical law, but having failed in that finally established the law of *demai* as a compromise.

3*

grain had not been paid to the priests and the Levites. The burden of proof that it had not been paid rested on the shoulders of the claimants, the priests and the Levites, for the question of ownership was purely a matter of commercial law.

In the absence of any evidence to the contrary, the owner was entitled, so far as the civil obligation was concerned, to take it for granted that the tithe had been paid to the Levite and he could proceed with an easy conscience to consume the grain which he had separated to satisfy the ritual requirement.[32]

This legalistic, almost casuistic, argument must have been worked out by the Maccabean scholars. In view of it, the ordinance of *demai* appears to be no longer a rabbinic law to prevent eating untithed grain, but a statesmanlike interpretation of the ancient law to save purchasers from the theoretical requirement of paying a tithe on bought grain.

Practically the law of *demai* nullified the institution of *maʿaser*, so far as purchasers were concerned. Pious farmers were naturally bound to pay their tithes as before, and many of them did. But as for the majority who did not, they could sell their grain without prejudice and the buyers were relieved of any responsibility of giving away a large part of it. Furthermore, and this doubtless was even more important from the point of view of John Hyrcan, the government was freed from the responsibility of taking energetic steps toward compelling the payment of tithes. The ordinance of *demai* enabled it to call upon each purchaser to protect his own conscience without any great loss to himself.

The value of the record in the Book of Jubilees in this instance is not to bring support to the Talmudic record of the manner of establishment of *demai* as an institution; that is made sufficiently clear in rabbinic sources. But it does show how much difficulty was encountered in the observance of the law of tithes and how restive the common people were under it. The author would hardly have gone to the extent of suggesting a practical abrogation of a clear

[32] See sources mentioned in previous note. The provision that the burden of proof is on the complainant applies not merely to *maʿaser ani*, as might appear from a cursory reading of the *baraita*, but also to the first tithe.

biblical law, if he had not felt that the letter of the law was beyond the willingness or the ability of most people to observe. This strengthens our *a priori* conjecture that John Hyrcan in establishing *demai* had in mind less the observance of the ritual, than the accommodation of the great mass of the people.

IV. Two Temple Regulations

A. Washing the Hands

The Bible provides that before approaching the altar to perform sacrifices the priests "shall wash with water that they die not (Ex. 30 20)." When we turn to the parallel passage in the Book of Jubilees we find that the priests were expected to do much more. In the sacrificial law that Abraham gives to Isaac he says: "And at all times be clean in thy body, and wash thyself with water before thou approachest to offer on the altar, and wash thy hands and thy feet before thou drawest near to the altar, and when thou art over sacrificing, wash again thy hands and feet (21 16)."

This passage does not make clear the distinction between the first "washing" and the following "washing thy hands and thy feet." It is illuminated by a corresponding passage in the Testaments of the Twelve Patriarchs (T. L. 9 11). Where Levi is commanded: "And before entering the holy place, bathe; and when thou offerest the sacrifice, wash; and again when thou finishest the sacrifice, wash."

A comparison of both passages shows that the priests were required to bathe on entering the Temple, then to wash their hands and feet in preparation for sacrifical service, and again to wash their hands and feet at its end. This is made quite clear in the Aramaic and Greek Fragments of the Testament of Levi, which Charles considers to be the source of the law recorded both in the Book of Jubilees and the Testaments of the Twelve Patriarchs. There we are told: "And when thou risest up to enter the house of God, wash thyself with water and then clothe thyself with the garment of the priesthood, and when thou art clothed, again wash thy hands and feet, before thou offer anything on the altar. And when thou takest to offer all that is fitting to offer on the altar, again wash thy h ands and thy feet."[33]

This procedure, nowhere explicitly mentioned in the tannaitic literature, is nevertheless definitely implied by the description of the High Priestly ablutions on the Day of Atonement. The mishna of Yoma tells us that before entering on his duties, at dawn, the High Priest would bathe, don his golden robes of office and then wash his hands and feet in preparation for the morning sacrifice.[34] At the end of the sacrifice he would again wash his hands and feet, remove his golden robes, bathe, and then dress in linen in order to offer the incense in the Holy of Holies.[35] After this ceremony he would once more wash his hands and feet, and bathe. and again assume his golden clothes for the *musaf* service.[36] There were similar ablutions, and another change to linen clothes when. after the *musaf* service, he had to enter the Holy of Holies to remove the remnants of the incense, and finally a last change to golden clothes to offer the afternoon sacrifice. At the end of the whole day's service he would again wash his hands and feet.[37]

The rabbis of the second century, R. Meir and R. Judah were much confused regarding the need of these many bathings and washings.[38] If the High Priest was required to bathe after removing his clothes, why wash his hands and feet before removing them? Purely technical answers, based on difficult hermeneutic derivations, are offered by the Talmud, but these would hardly be acceptable, even if we lacked the clear evidence of the pseudepigraphic works regarding the origin of the custom.

In view of the information in these books, it is clear that the High Priest bathed at dawn before beginning any sacrifice, in

[33] Charles, *Greek and Aramaic Fragments* in his Appendix to *Testaments of the Twelve Patriarchs*, Greek Text, p. 248. Compare also his English Translation of the Testaments, p. 230.

[34] *Mishna Yoma* 3, 4.

[35] *Ibid.* 3, 5.

[36] *Ibid.* 7, 3.

[37] *Ibid.* 7, 4.

[38] *Mishna Yoma* 3, 6; *Tosefta, ibid.*, 1, 16 (p. 182); *baraita*, cited in *B. ibid.*, 32a.

accordance with the rule that "no one may enter the Temple court to offer sacrifice even if he be clean unless he bathe (*Mishna Yoma*, 3, 3)." This bath did not free him from the necessity of washing his hands and feet as he approached the altar, for that was required by the clear biblical statement. At the end of the service the High Priest washed his hands and feet as any other priest might, in accordance with the Pharisaic prescription preserved in the Testament of Levi and the Book of Jubilees.

Having done that, he must proceed to bathe and wash his hands and feet in preparation for the next ceremony and so on throughout the day.[39]

We can hardly expect to find any social need behind these various washings. If they are to be explained at all, we must see in them Maccabean interpretations of the Scriptural verse; the law which requires them is the first sign of the rise of the system of deriving new regulations from superfluous words. In the spirit which in later times so completely animated R. Akiba and his colleagues, these early scholars noted that the root *rahas* (to wash) occurs thrice in the passage commanding the priests to cleanse themselves before approaching the altar (Ex. 30 17 ff.). The divine book could not possibly be redundant and its repetition must be significant. And the natural interpretation which they put on the passage was a requirement of three ablutions, a bath before entering the sanctuary, washing hands and feet before the sacrifice and again after the sacrifice.

B. The Incense Offering

The law of incense offering offers a good example of the development of the halaka. For in this instance we can trace its gradual growth almost as we can follow the annual growth of a tree by the markings on its trunk. The bible requires that the incense to

[39] Definite proof that the washing of the hands and feet, required of the High Priest after the service and before bathing, was not preparatory to the next ceremony, but concluded the first, is to be found in the law demanding that he wash his hands and feet at the end of the whole service (*Mishna Yoma* 7, 4).

be offered on the altar shall consist of "sweet spices, stacte, and onycha, and galbanum; sweet spices with pure frankincense (Ex. 30 34)." In addition to these four spices specified in Scripture, the Book of Jubilees names also nard, myrrh and costum (Jub. 16 24). The Talmudic baraita on the subject adds to the seven of the Book of Jubilees four others: cassia, saffron, sweet flag and cinnamon (*B. Keritot* 6*a*).[40]

In itself it might be possible that the formula for preparing the incense was made more complicated because the priests discovered the value of the new ingredients in preparing the sweet-smelling compound. But we may well doubt whether permission would have been granted them to make these changes, much less that the Pharisees would have advocated them, had they not found biblical support for these additional elements in the repetition of the word *sammim* "spices" in the scriptural verse. The redundancy must have moved the early scholars to suppose that other spices than those mentioned were to be included in the preparation, and they might thereupon have taken the liberty of relying on their own judgment in selecting them.

Conclusion

In the examples of Maccabean law cited we have endeavored to show how the Maccabean scholars approached the task of developing the halaka. The Noachic commandments, the sabbath law, and the law of tithes offer instances of development in response to economic and political conditions; the temple regulations help us to understand the workings of the Maccabean mind where only theoretical questions were involved.

The spirit in which these laws are conceived is that of the Pharisaic scholars, but we are inclined to believe that they antedate the formation of the Pharisaic party. In reconstructing the historical situation in the early Maccabean age, in the years between the acknowledgement of Simeon's practical independence and the break between the Pharisees and the Sadducees, we doubt whether

[40] For a careful identification of these spices see Macht, *The Holy Incense* (Baltimore, 1928).

there were originally recognized party or sectarian divisions. There is no real proof of such division, and everything that has come down to us points to a harmonious working together of all elements during the reign of Simeon and the early years of John Hyrcan.[41] But the social differences which had already existed in pre-Maccabean times, and which we have discussed at length elsewhere,[42] had their influence on the attitude of the people. It would be natural that in the new state of Judea, the priestly nobility and the army officers should concern themselves mainly with diplomatic affairs and the organization of civil government, while the humbler scholars and students would busy themselves with the development of the law. At first such a division of labor might continue in harmony. The urban traders and artisans, represented in the counsels of the government by the scholarship of their sons, might be inclined to look for peace and mutual good will between the Jews and their neighbors, both those within the borders of the state, and those of the neighboring principalities. The nobility, and particularly the soldiers, intoxicated by their victory might be expected to seek the aggrandizement of their small dominions, and the complete control of the heathen population. Hence we find John Hyrcan forcibly proselytizing the Idumeans at the same time that the scholars at home were declaring only seven laws of the Torah applicable to the Gentile world.

We can now understand why a tension developed between the great landowning and priestly aristocracy and the masses of the people. And we can also explain why the differences, hidden at first under a masque of good will, burst out in a flame when at the feast celebrating the victory of the King over the enemies of his people, someone indiscreetly spoke out the suppressed thoughts of

[41] The Wellhausen theory that the antagonism between the groups became bitter as early as the days of Jonathan, cannot be maintained in view of the high praise accorded to the Hasmoneans in the Testaments of the Twelve Patriarchs and the Book of Jubilees. Neither of these come from Sadducean sources; and their enthusiasm for the Hasmoneans shows definitely that even toward the end of the second century B. C. the Pharisees were well-disposed toward the government.

[42] *Harvard Theological Review*, XXII, 198—199.

the pacific masses.[43] Some bitter words were spoken and "the scholars of Israel" as the ancient record puts it, "separated themselves in anger." Thereafter there was a clear breach between the house of the Hasmoneans and the Pharisaic scholars. The savants were doubtless compelled to leave the Sanhedrin and the King and his advisers undertook to legislate for the internal needs of the people as well as to carry on their diplomatic affairs. The Pharisaic writers who had been praising the Hasmonean house and had looked upon the age as almost Messianic were now completely disillusioned and became a bitter and violent opposition. The struggle lasted throughout the remainder of Hyrcan's reign and continued through that of his successors, till in the time of Alexander Jannaeus it broke out into an open rebellion. With the death of Alexander and the succession of Salome, the Pharisees under Simeon b. Shetah returned to power. But now they controlled not only the internal affairs of the community but also its world policy.

This reconstruction of the division between the sects seems to me more plausible than that generally offered. It accounts in a natural manner for the change of the Pharisaic attitude toward John Hyrcan, for the dramatic break between the King and the scholars, and finally is in complete harmony with what we know to have been the respective teachings of the Pharisees and the Sadducees, and what we may assume to have been their social origins.

[43] This story is told in an ancient *baraita*, *B. Kiddushin* 66a, and also in Josephus, *Ant.* xiii, 10, 6. The Talmudic record refers this incident to the reign of Alexander Jannaeus. But for reasons given in *Harvard Theological Review*, XXII, 248, note 140, it seems to me that Josephus's tradition of a break between the two groups during the time of Hyrcan must be accepted.

CHAPTER 11

THE DEVELOPMENT OF THE AMIDAH

INTRODUCTORY*

THE STUDY of the origin and growth of the liturgy of the synagogue has always had a peculiar attraction for scholars. For they saw in it not the expression of individual minds but of the soul of the people. Much of the inner life of the Jew that escaped the volumes of history and even the Argus-eyed Halakic literature, was reflected in the prayers and benedictions which are still recited by the great masses of the people of Israel.

Yet, in spite of the important works that have been written about the Jewish ritual and the remarkable discoveries that have been made regarding its development, it remains true, at least so far as the *Amidah* is concerned, as Dr. Kohler has recently stated,[1] that "the last words have not been spoken". This is largely due to the fact that scholars have not yet sufficiently availed themselves of the important texts of the Palestinian ritual that have come to light as a result of the discovery of the Genizah.

As is well known, the Palestinian Jewish community

* The writer gratefully acknowledges the generous help he received in the course of this study from Professor Louis Ginzberg, who not only read the article in manuscript, making a large number of criticism and suggestions, but called the author's attention to many passages that had been overlooked. His thanks are also due to Doctor Cyrus Adler, Professor Alexander Marx and Professor Israel Davidson, who took a keen interest in this paper. He has also been helped in a number of ways by his friend, Mr. Isaac Rivkind, of the staff of the Library of the Jewish Theological Seminary of America. In view of the fact that in a number of instances his conclusions are at variance with those of Professor Elbogen, he desires to make particular mention of his continual use of the works of that famous scholar, the "*Achtzehngebet*" and "*Der juedische Gottesdienst*", as the basis for his researches.

[1] *Hebrew Union College Annual*, Vol. I, p. 387.

Reprinted from *Jewish Quarterly Review*, New Series, Volume 16, 1925/26.

disappeared during the Crusades. With their disappearance the only traces of their ritual that remained were the random quotations in rabbinic writings that originated in the Holy Land. Fortunately, after seven centuries, Dr. Solomon Schechter recognized on the basis of these quotations several manuscripts of the daily Palestinian *Amidah* among the fragments of the Genizah. These he published,[2] and somewhat later, Dr. I. Elbogen published also some texts of the festival *Amidot*[3] according to the Palestinian ritual from Genizah fragments. It appears that the Palestinian ritual was used by Palestinians in Egypt, and it is from their prayer books that our fragments are derived.[4]

In the course of the study here presented it will be shown that the Palestinian version of the *Amidah* changed but slightly in the thousand years that separated R. Gamaliel II from the twelfth century. It will be further seen that the talmudic tradition,[5] according to which the *Amidah* was established by the men of the Great Synagogue (that is the pre-Maccabean scholars), is true in the sense that there was some form of it in existence in the first half of the second century B.C.E. The rival tradition that R. Gamaliel II formulated the *Amidah*, is true, not in the sense that it had been forgotten and had to be re-established, but that in the time of R. Gamaliel the prayer was finally redacted, and the last benedictions added to it—in Pales-

[2] *Jewish Quarterly Review*, X, 654ff., reprinted by Dalman in *Die Worte Jesu*, pp. 310–3; and by Elbogen, in *Der juedische Gottesdienst*, second edition, pp. 517–8.

[3] *Monatsschrift*, LV, 429ff., 585ff.

[4] That there were two groups of communities in Egypt, the one using the Palestinian, the other the Babylonian ritual, follows from the fact that fragments of both rituals are found in the Genizah. There can be no better proof of the regrettable neglect of the text published by Dr. Schechter of which scholars have been guilty, than the constant reference to the text published by Israel Lévi, in *Revue des Etudes Juives*, 53, 235-7, as a Palestinian ritual. That text is similar to the *Amidah* of the *Seder R. Saadia Gaon* (see below Appendix III) and represents the Egyptian form of the ritual of the Dispersion.

[5] See Berakot 35a; Megillah 17b; and compare *Sifre*, Deuteronomy, 343, ed. Friedmann, f. 142b; and *Midrash Tannaim*, ed. Hoffmann, p. 209. See also Elbogen, *Achtzehngebet*, p. 14.

tine. It will also be possible to fix within reasonable limits the dates of most of the paragraphs of the *Amidah*.

The proofs brought forward are based entirely on a critical study of the received texts of the liturgy of Palestine and the Dispersion, and the references to them in talmudic traditions. On the basis of the arguments presented it has been found feasible to reconstruct, in the case of all but two of the benedictions, the original form. The various versions, together with the reconstructed text, have been brought together in Appendix III.

I. Principal Criteria for Fixing Dates of Paragraphs of the Amidah.

A. *Use of the Tetragrammaton.*

Even a cursory reading of the Palestinian text of the *Amidah* must bring to notice the fact that in some cases the term ה' אלהינו is used to call upon the Deity in the beginning of the paragraph, while in others it is not. At first this phenomenon may strike one as being of little significance, but when we re-read the *Amidah* (in its Palestinian form) we will notice that the Tetragrammaton never occurs in it except either in the first strophe or in the concluding formula[6] (the so-called *eulogy*), and that while it occurs in the concluding formula in every paragraph, it is found in the first strophe only in the following: *Abot* (1), the prayer for Repentance (5), the prayer for Healing (8), the prayer for Prosperous Years (9), the prayer for Jerusalem (14), the prayer for the Acceptance of the *Amidah* (P. 15), *Abodah* (P.16), and *Hodaah* (P.17). In every case but in the prayer for Repentance (5) it is coupled with the word *Elohenu*, "our God."

[6] In this paper the term "concluding formula" will generally be used for the *ulima*, while "body of the prayer" will refer to the whole of it exclusive of the *Ḥatima*.

It is evident that the presence of the term ה' אלהינו in half of the benedictions and its omission in the other half cannot be ascribed to chance. The fact assumes an even greater significance when we examine the formulae of prayer composed by rabbis of different generations. It will be found that the contemporaries of R. Gamaliel II never used the term ה' אלהינו in their prayers, while the rabbis of the following generation (roughly corresponding to the period of the leadership of R. Akiba, 117–135 C.E.) always used it.

The matter is of sufficient importance to justify the citation of the various formulae of prayer composed by rabbis of the two periods.

We are told[7] that on one occasion R. Gamaliel II and some of his colleagues found themselves in a storm at sea, and that being urged by his companions to pray for their safety, R. Gamaliel said: אלהינו רחם עלינו. Thereupon they declared that as the leader in Israel he might use the singular, and he said אלהי רחם עלינו.

More formal are the prayers cited in the name of several contemporaries of R. Gamaliel II. R. Eleazar b. Zadok prescribes the following prayer for a person in danger:[8]

שמע קול צעקת עמך ישראל ועשה מהר בקשתם ברוך[9] (אתה ה') שומע תפלה.

His colleague, R. Eliezer b. Hyrkanos, the brother-in-law of R. Gamaliel II, offers the following formula:[10]

עשה רצונך בשמים ממעל ותן נחת רוח לבריותיך בארץ והטוב בעיניך עשה ברוך (אתה ה') שומע תפלה.

[7] *Midrash Tannaim*, p. 172.

[8] *Tosefta Berakot* 3.7 (ed. Zuckermandel, p. 6). The version of R. Jose (probably R. Jose Ha-Kohen, since he is quoted between R. Eliezer b. Hyrkanos and R. Eleazar b. Zadok) is merely a variant of this, substituting תפלה for צעקה. In the Talmud (29b) it is cited in the name of R. Joshua.

[9] The term אתה ה' I have added as being obviously implied, although I believe it is possible that originally they used only *Elohenu* in these *Ḥatimot*, and that these terms were omitted in accordance with the *baraita* quoted below, which describes the use of *Elohenu* in a *Ḥatima* as being a sign of heresy.

[10] *Tosefta, ibid.*

R. Joshua b. Hananya, the Halakic opponent of R. Eliezer, established this formula:[11]

הושע ה' את עמך את שארית ישראל בכל פרשת העבור יהיו צרכיהם לפניך ברוך אתה ה' שומע תפלה.

It will be noted that in the case of none of these formulae do we find the term ה' אלהינו. In that of R. Gamaliel II, *Elohenu* occurs, but not the Tetragrammaton. In that of R. Joshua the Tetragrammaton is found, but when we recall that the first strophe of his prayer is a citation of a Scriptural verse,[12] we realize that its evidence does not bear on the matter, since his formula is merely a quotation from Scripture.

The intentional omission of the term ה' אלהינו in these formulae becomes even more apparent when we place next to them the prayers formulated by R. Akiba and his contemporaries. R. Akiba who, in opposition to R. Tarphon, insisted on the insertion of a prayer for the future redemption in the benediction for the Exodus on Passover eve, proposed the following formula for it,[13]

כן ה' אלהינו ואלהי אבותינו יגיענו למועדים ולרגלים אחרים הבאים לקראתנו לשלום שמחים בבנין עירך וששים בעבודתך ונאכל שם מן הזבחים ומן הפסחים אשר הגיע דמם על קיר מזבחך לרצון ונודה לך על גאולתנו (ברוך אתה ה' גאל ישראל).

His younger contemporary, Ben Azzai, gives the following as the proper formula to be recited on entering a city:[14]

יהי רצון מלפניך ה' אלהי ואלהי אבותי שתכניסני לכרך זה לשלום.

and he suggests that the following be said when leaving the city:[15]

[11] *M. Berakot* 4.4. This version is that found in the separate editions of the Mishnah and in the Babylonian Talmud (28b). It is to be accepted in preference to that cited in the Talmud of Jerusalem, in view of its similarity to the reading of the Scriptures.

[12] Jeremiah 31.6.

[13] *M. Pesaḥim* 10.6.

[14] *Tosefta Berakot* 7.16, ed. Zuckermandel, p. 16.

[15] *Ibid.*

מודה אני לפניך ה׳ אלהי שהוצאתני מכרך זה לשלום וכשם שהוצאתני לשלום כך תוליכני לשלום ותסמכני לשלום עד שאגיע למקומי.

R. Meir, the pupil of R. Akiba, urges the following substitute for the formulae cited above in the name of R. Eleazar b. Zadok and R. Eliezer b. Hyrkanos:[16]

צורכי עמך מרבים ודעתם קצרה יהי רצון מלפניך ה׳ אלהינו שתתן לכל אחד ואחד כל צורכיו וכל גויה וגויה די מחסורה ברוך (אתה ה׳) שומע תפלה.

In every one of these formulae the term ה׳ אלהי׳ occurs in the body of the prayer.

The meaning of the difference in style between the periods of R. Gamaliel II and R. Akiba can easily be understood in the light of what is known of the sectarian teachings of the day. Ben Azzai in remarking on the fact that the terms *Elohim*, *Shaddai*, and similar Names and Attributes never occur in the Pentateuch in connection with sacrifices, but that the Tetragrammaton alone is used, gives as the reason:

שלא ליתן פתחון פה למינים לרדות.

"to leave no opening for sectarian teachings."[17] Similarly in the following *baraita* the use of the term *Elohim* is associated with sectarianism:[18]

הפותח ביוד ה׳ וחותם ביוד ה׳ הרי זה חכם, באלף ולא בדלת וחותם ביוד ה׳ הרי זה בינוני, ביוד ה׳ וחותם באלף ולא בדלת הרי זה בור, באלף ולא בדלת וחותם באלף ולא בדלת הרי זה דרך אחרת.

"He who begins a prayer with the Tetragrammaton and ends with it is a scholar;

He who begins with *Elohim* and ends with the Tetragrammaton, is one of the average men;

[16] *Tosefta Berakot* 3.7, ed. Zuckermandel, p. 6.

[17] *Sifre* Numbers, 143, ed. Horovitz, p. 191, and compare references there given by the editor.

[18] *Tosefta Berakot* 7.20, ed. Zuckermandel, p. 17. The *baraita* is quoted in *J. Berakot* 9.1 (12d) in an even clearer form, leaving no doubt that באלף ולא בדלת means *Elohim*. See Schwartz, *Tosefta Berakot*, fol. 30a, and note, but compare Geiger, *Urschrift*, p. 179. See also Kohler in *Journal of Jewish Lore and Philosophy*, I, p. 19ff.

He who begins with the Tetragrammaton and ends with *Elohim*, is an ignoramus;
He who begins with *Elohim* and ends with it is under suspicion of being a sectarian."

In the *baraita* the "opening" can refer only to the first strophe of the prayer, and the "ending" to the *Ḥatima*, or closing formula. Now there is no prayer in our rituals in which the *Ḥatima* omits the Tetragrammaton. Whether there ever were any, which were modified in accordance with the rule set down in the *baraita*, can no longer be known. It is interesting to note, however, that there are a number of prayers which begin with *Elohenu*, although that is declared in the *baraita* to be the style of mediocrities. Thus the Sabbath benediction begins with the words: אלהינו ואלהי אבותינו רצה.[19] Similarly the prayer for the coming of the Kingdom of God used in the Babylonian service only on Rosh ha-Shanah and Yom Kippur, but in the Palestinian version on all the festivals,[20] begins with

אלהינו ואלהי אבותינו מלוך על כל העולם

The prayer for the New Moon and the Festivals, which contains no *Ḥatima*, being merely an insertion, is nevertheless of importance in this connection since it begins in the Babylonian version with אלהינו ואלהי אבותינו יעלה ויבא and in the Palestinian with אנא אלהינו.[21] We have also noticed that R. Gamaliel's prayer, consisting of a single strophe, began with *Elohenu*.

It is obvious that in the generation of R. Gamaliel II the use of the form *Elohenu* could have been associated neither with heresy nor mediocrity, and that the *baraita*, dating from a later time, records a change in style due to the rise of sectarian teachings. Which sect it was, whose

[19] The various introductory compositions like ישמח משה, אתה קדשת and אתה אחד are obviously of later date as can be seen from the very fact that they differ for the various services, and in some cases also for the different rituals.

[20] See Elbogen, *Monatsschrift*, 55, 437.

[21] *Ibid.*

teachings would be encouraged by *Elohenu*, and what those teachings were, can only be conjectured, and a discussion of that matter would take us far afield. It is sufficient for our purpose to have established that there were definite reasons why the use of the Tetragrammaton in prayer, which had been abandoned either in the time of R. Gamaliel or before him, was resumed in the generation after his death.[22]

That the term ה' אלהינו had been in use in prayer of earlier times is almost self-evident. We know that the *Amidah* was redacted under R. Gamaliel II, and that in his time the term ה' אלהינו was not used. Hence where it occurs *in the Palestinian version* it must be a remnant of older times. It is not to be assumed that the following generation inserted it in half of the paragraphs and failed to insert it in the other half.

We are thus enabled to designate the oldest paragraphs of the *Amidah*, namely, those containing the term ה' אלהינו. They are *Abot* (1), the prayers for Health (8), for Prosperous Years (9), for Jerusalem (14), for the Acceptance of the *Amidah* (15), *Abodah* (P. 16), and *Hodaah* (P. 17).

We must note, however, that there are two paragraphs

[22] This is practically implied in the statement of R. Abba b. Kahana (*Mid. Tehillim*, ed. Buber, 36.8, f. 126a): שני דורות השתמשו בשם המפורש אנשי כנסת הגדולה ודורו של שמד "Two generations made use of the Tetragrammaton, the generation of the Great Synagogue and that of the Persecution." The first refers of course to the pre-Maccabean leaders and the second to the contemporaries of R. Akiba, who suffered under the Hadrianic persecutions. It is true that the term השתמשו in this connection probably refers to mystical attempts to defeat the enemy by the enunciation of the Divine Name (see *Midrash Tehillim*, *loc. cit.* and *Ekah Zutta*, p. 62). Nevertheless the freedom in pronouncing the Name probably was accompanied by a greater freedom in using it in prayer, at least in its modified pronunciation. The prayer cited in the name of R. Eleazar b. Zadok by his son contains the term ה' אלהינו twice:

מאהבתך ה' אלהינו שאהבת את ישראל עמך ומחמלתך מלכנו שחמלת על בני בריתך נתת לנו ה' אלהינו את יום השביעי הגדול והקדוש הזה באהבה.

This can be explained on either of two grounds. Either the use of the term ה' אלהינו was permissible in private prayer, or the prayer was much older than R. Zadok. We must moreover always envisage the possibility that individuals used their own judgment in matters of private concern.

in the Babylonian *Amidah* which contain the term ה' אלהינו where it does not occur in the corresponding paragraph of the Palestinian ritual. These are the prayers for the Proselytes (13) and for Peace (B. 19). It is obvious that the original form of these paragraphs did not contain the term ה' אלהינו. For if it had, how could we explain the omission of it in the Palestinian *Amidah*? We shall presently see that even when the paragraph *Abodah* (P. 16, B. 17) had to be revised fundamentally because of the destruction of the Temple and the consequent cessation of the sacrifices, the new form retained the term ה' אלהינו as it had occurred in the old formula.[23] Furthermore, even in the Babylonian ritual, the term ה' אלהינו occurs in these paragraphs, not as usual after the first or second word of the paragraph, but in the prayer for Peace (B.19) in the third strophe, and in the prayer for the Proselytes (13) at the end of the first strophe. We are thus justified in assuming that the term ה' אלהינו was added to these paragraphs when they were included in the Babylonian *Amidah*. There is other evidence pointing to the fact that these paragraphs were not added to the Babylonian ritual until a long time after they had been part of the Palestinian.[24] But the use of the term ה' אלהינו definitely fixes the period of their inclusion in the Babylonian *Amidah* as being in the second century, the period of R. Akiba and his followers.

This reveals the important fact that the *Amidah* as fixed under R. Gamaliel II was not at once accepted in Babylonia. We must therefore in our further investigations into the date of the origin of the prayers always keep in mind the possibility that the insertion of any particular paragraph in the Babylonian *Amidah* may not be identi-

[23] See below, Section VI.
[24] See below, Section IV.

cal with the period of its origin in Palestine. We shall, in fact, see that this very often was the case.

B. *The Use of the Term Abinu.*

In connection with the use of the term ה' אלהינו in the older paragraphs of the *Amidah* it is necessary to note that in several paragraphs it is substituted by *Abinu*. This is true of the Palestinian prayers for Wisdom (4) and Forgiveness (6), and of the Babylonian prayers for Repentance (5) and Forgiveness (6).

A little reflection will show that in the case of the prayer for Repentance, the Palestinian text represented by the Genizah fragments is not the original form. It reads

השיבנו ה' אליך ונשובה חדש ימינו כקדם

which is a quotation from Lamentations 5.22. No one would substitute for a well-known verse a prayer-formula made in later times,[25] so that we must assume that the Babylonian form did not displace the Palestinian, but on the contrary, that the Palestinians at some time replaced the old form of the benediction with the verse from the Scriptures. This, we shall see, was part of the tendency to give a nationalist meaning to all the prayers in times of profound patriotic feeling. The verse from Lamentations expressed admirably the feeling of the people about the time of the Fall of the Temple, and so they inserted it

[25] This becomes evident on a little reflection. In early times prayers were not written down, but were memorized. Hence it was with the *Amidah* as with the *Mishnah*, words were changed, added and taken away, but in general the old forms remained the bases for the new. Now if one wanted to remove an old formula and substitute a new one, one had obviously to choose phraseology that was comparatively well known. Otherwise most of the people, finding it difficult to learn a new formula, would adhere to the old. Hence when we find on the one hand a verse of Scripture and on the other a prayer formula independent of the Scriptures, we may be sure that the independent formula is the older, and that in a later time, for one reason or another, the Scriptural verse was substituted for it. This is particularly evident in the case under discussion, where we cannot possibly find any reason for replacing the verse from Lamentations with the formula used in Babylonia; but on the other hand, if we assume that the original form was akin to that used in Babylonia, we may find in the nationalism of the later days of the Commonwealth complete explanation of the change.

instead of the older form of the prayer, which lies at the basis of the Babylonian:

השיבנו אבינו לתורתך (וקרבנו מלכנו לעבודתך)[26] והחזירנו בתשובה שלימה לפניך.

It has been necessary to anticipate some of the conclusions which will be discussed in greater detail below, in order to prove that originally the prayer for Repentance, like that for Wisdom which precedes it and that for Forgiveness which follows it, contained in the first strophe, as term of address to the Deity, the word *Abinu*.

Since we know that the earlier paragraphs use as the term of address the words ה' אלהינו, and the later ones omit it entirely, it seems reasonable to assume that those in which the word *Abinu*, "our Father", is used represent a transitional stage. They date from a time when objection to the use of the Tetragrammaton had developed, but people still felt the need of some word to take its place.

II. Other Criteria for Determining the Dates of Benedictions.

A. *The Seven Word Formula.*

We have now seen that the paragraphs of the *Amidah* may be divided into three groups: (a) those that originally contained the term ה' אלהינו; (b) those where the term *Abinu* was used; and (c) those where no term of address for the Deity was employed. There are a number of other criteria which will enable us to subdivide these groups and also to fix the approximate date of the origin of the various paragraphs.

A study of the Palestinian *Amidah* reveals the fact that the benediction *Kedushat ha-Shem*, as well as the prayers

[26] That this strophe was not part of the original is shown below, Section IIC.

for Wisdom (3), for Repentance (4),[27] and for the Redemption (7) consist of seven words each, not counting the *Hatima*. The matter becomes even more striking when we notice that the prayer for the Gathering of the Dispersed (10), which, in its Palestinian form, consists of eight words, reading:

תקע בשופר גדול לחירותינו ושא נס לקבץ גלויותינו

contained originally only seven words, as can be seen from the fragment of an *Amidah* recovered from the Genizah[28], where it reads

תקע בשופר גדול לחרותנו ושא נס לקבצנו.

This form is substantially that of the *Seder R. Saadia Gaon*. The only difference is that the *Seder R. Saadia Gaon* contains the word מהרה after ושא נס, an obvious insertion. That לקבצנו and not לקבץ גלויותינו was the original reading is evident, since it is altogether unlikely that a reviser would change לקבץ גלויותינו into לקבצנו; while we can well understand how after the fall of Jerusalem לקבצנו might be changed into לקבץ גלויותינו.[29]

We thus have five paragraphs of the *Amidah* which originally consisted of seven words. There can be no doubt that they originated at approximately the same period, a period in which attention was paid to the number of words in the prayer, and in which a mystic power was attached to the number seven.

The rise of mysticism in rabbinic Judaism is traditionally associated with the pupils of Hillel. Thus we are told by a Rabbi of the second century, that R. Akiba

27 While it is true that the present Palestinian text of the prayer for Repentance is not original, it is also true that the original form also consisted of seven words, as can be seen from the text established below, Appendix III, and the argument on which it is based, Section IIC. It is thus seen that both the original form of this benediction and the substitute form grew up during the period of devotion to the mystic number 7.

28 See Appendix III.

29 It is of course true that even before the fall of the Temple one prayed for the gathering of the dispersed. Such prayers occur as early as the Bible (See Elbogen, *Achtzehngebet*, p. 20). Nevertheless it is quite certain that of the two forms לקבצנו must be the older.

derived his mystic learning from R. Joshua, and R. Joshua from R. Johanan b. Zakkai.[30] A famous *baraita* in the Talmud tells of the miraculous powers of Jonathan b. Uzziel, who is said to have been the oldest of Hillel's pupils.[31]

There is thus ground for tentatively referring the five paragraphs which contain seven words to the period of the rise of the pupils of Hillel, that is the period beginning about the year 10–20 of the Common Era.

It is important to note that none of these benedictions contain the term ה' אלהינו; but that two of them, the prayers for Wisdom and Repentance, contain the word *Abinu*. The group is thus seen to fall into two subdivisions, the earlier, consisting of the prayers for Repentance and Wisdom, and the more recent, consisting of the prayers for the Redemption and the Gathering of the Dispersed. The fact that the two prayers of each group are so much akin in content adds to the weight of evidence that the classification is correct.

B. *The Use of Scriptural Expressions.*

The prayers for the Redemption (7) and for the Gathering of the Dispersed (10) are thus shown to belong to the same subdivision, both as to form and obviously as to content. Another striking similarity between them is that each of them is composed of a series of biblical expressions.[32]

Thus the prayer for the Redemption consists of the following phrases:

ראה בענינו	Psalms 119.153	ראה עניי
וריבה ריבנו וגאלנו	*Ibid.* 154	ריבה ריבי וגאלני
גואל ישראל	Isaiah 49.7	גואל ישראל

[30] *Tosefta Ḥagiga* 2.2.

[31] *Baba Batra* 134b.

[32] The facts about the use of Scriptural verses in these paragraphs have, in general, been noticed by Elbogen, in his *Achtzehngebet*, pp. 55 and 57, but he offers no explanation of the phenomenon.

The Scriptural singular is naturally exchanged for a plural since all the prayers in the *Amidah* are in the plural.

The prayer for the Gathering of the Dispersed is even more evidently a group of Scriptural phrases:[33]

תקע בשופר גדול	Isaiah 27.13.	תקע בשופר גדול
ושא נס	*Ibid.* 11.12.	ונשא נס לגוים ואסף נדחי ישראל
מקבץ נדחי ישראל	*Ibid.* 61.8	מקבץ נדחי ישראל

It is noteworthy that in each case the verses referred to deal with the gathering of the dispersed of Israel. It is as if the Deity were reminded of His promise and asked to fulfil it. Of the same character is the use of the biblical expression in the first strophe of the eleventh paragraph, the prayer for the Restoration of Israel's Judges. Its first strophe reads:

השיבה שופטינו כבראשונה ויועצינו כבתחלה

which is of course at once recognized as an echo of Isaiah 1.26; while the concluding formula אהב המשפט occurs in Isaiah 56.8 (אוהב משפט).

The use of the Scriptural expressions in these benedictions [34] is doubtless to be associated with the new interest in the canonical works that developed during the generation preceding the Rebellion of 66–70.[35] We know that a con-

[33] The matter is the more noteworthy in this case as the concluding formula is adopted in spite of the fact that it contains three words, a form found otherwise only in the original text of *Abodah* and *Hodaah*, concerning which see below, Section VI.

[34] So far as the prayer for Redemption is concerned, this necessitates a slight change in Dr. Elbogen's theory that it was merely taken over from the Fast Day Liturgy. (See *Achtzehngebet*, p. 23ff.) The matter is very complicated and requires special treatment, with more space than can be devoted to it here.

[35] The substitution of Lamentations 5.22 for the original form of the prayer for Repentance doubtless took place at the same time as the insertion of the nationalist prayers. The use of the biblical expressions in *Abot* is discussed below, Note 57. In regard to the *Kedushat ha-Shem*, it must be said that the use of Scriptural passages while less striking than in the nationalist prayers, is still discernible. Thus האל הקדוש occurs in the expression והאל הקדוש נקדש בצדקה of Isaiah 5.16. The phrase ואין אלה מבלעדיך seems almost like an answer to the question היש אלה מבלעדי of Isaiah 44.8, and even the words קדוש אתה ונורא שמך may be considered an echo of קדוש ונורא שמו in Psalm 111.9. The expression ואם אמרנו מטה רגלינו of the *Hodaah* (with which compare Ps. 94.18) is certainly not original as it does not occur in the Babylonian text or even in all the Palestinian forms (see texts below, Appendix III). The use of בונה ירושלם (Ps. 148.2) in the prayer for Jerusalem and שומע תפלה (Ps. 65.3) in the prayer for the acceptance of the *Amidah*, do indeed point to the fact that in very early times the

ference about the Canon was held at the home of one of the leaders of the Zealots,[36] and it seems more than likely that the same group, whose nationalist ardor was responsible for the Eighteen Decrees, was also influential in the determination of what were the holy books. The very anxiety to separate the holy books from the secular reveals a devotion to the Scriptures, which might well be carried as far as to prefer Scriptural expressions in all prayers.

Whether or not the reader agree that the use of the Scriptural verses is a definite mark of this period, the content of the three prayers השיבה, ראה, and תקע binds them in a single group. They deal with three aspects of the restoration of Jewish independence: the Redemption, the Gathering of the Dispersed, and the Restoration of the Judges. As such they could only have developed in a time of great nationalist enthusiasm. While the prayer for the Restoration of the Judges does not adhere to the seven-word formula, which is characteristic of the other two paragraphs of this group, it is like them in having no term of address to the Deity.[37]

We know from the Talmud that for about forty years before 70,[38] the jurisdiction of Jewish Courts was limited. We may therefore assign the prayer for the Restoration of the Jewish Judges to that time. We have seen above that all the benedictions containing formulae of seven words probably grew during the period 10–70. I do not believe we shall go far wrong if we assume that the more nationalist prayers were inserted in the latter half of this period, and

attributes of God were expressed in biblical language. On the other hand it is also true that the canon of Hagiographa had not been closed in the Maccabean times, and while the Psalms were doubtless considered sacred words, nevertheless they were probably not classed with the Prophets.

[36] *B. Shabbat* 13b.

[37] The use of the Tetragrammaton in this benediction according to some forms of the ritual of the Dispersion must not mislead us in this connection. The Tetragrammaton is lacking not only in the Palestinian ritual, but also in a number of "Babylonian" versions.

[38] *Sanhedrin* 41a.

the prayers for the abstract goods of Repentance and Wisdom in the first half. That will be consonant not only with the spirit reflected in their contents but also with the fact that the prayers for Wisdom (4) and for Repentance (5) contain the word *Abinu*, which reflects the style of the transitional period.

C. *Emphasis on the Kingship of God.*

We have seen that while the nationalist attitude of certain paragraphs might not be inconsistent with their origin at almost any period, nevertheless there is sufficient evidence associating them with the generation 40–70 C.E. to justify us in stating that they originated in response to the rise of the intense patriotism of the period. It is characteristic of the growth of patriotic emotion that it expresses itself in a number of ways which at first sight seem almost unconnected with it. Thus during the late war, there was a general movement throughout America to make English the universal language and to prohibit or limit the use of the languages even of the allied countries such as French or Italian. We have noticed how the war-animus that was developing in the years 40–70 brought about a feeling that the Jewish sacred literature should be separated and set apart from the profane. This feeling was revived, in connection with the movement of the Bar Kokba rebellion, by R. Akiba, who forbade the reading of any but canonical literature.[39] There are a number of similar outbursts of the nationalist spirit which are slightly evident in the years 40–70, but which were re-emphasized in the generation 117–135 C.E.

Perhaps the most important conception that came to the fore during these periods was that of the Kingdom of God. Of course God was spoken of as King in biblical

[39] *M. Sanhedrin*, 10.1.

times (see Isaiah 33.22, I Samuel 12.12, Psalms 74.12, and numerous other passages). But the feeling of the Kingship of God as a fundamental doctrine seems to have received special attention and to have influenced the liturgy most in connection with the two rebellions.

Mention has already been made of the fact that the prayer for the coming of the Kingdom of God still used on Rosh ha-Shanah and Yom Kippur (א' וא' אבותינו מלוך)[40] developed in the first century. The prayer for the Return of the Judges (11) which, as has just been shown, developed in the period 40–70, contains as its second strophe the words ומלוך עלינו אתה לבדך, "Do thou alone reign over us." Lektor Friedmann has pointed out in a note,[41] that the reading of the *Shema'*, originally merely a reading of the Torah, came to be regarded in these trying days as a declaration of "allegiance to the Kingdom of Heaven," and that it was in this connection that the words ברוך שם כבוד מלכותו לעולם ועד, "Blessed be the name of His glorious Kingdom forever," were inserted after the first verse.

Similarly the preparation for the Bar Kokba rebellion brought about the re-emphasis on the conception of the Divine Kingdom. Thus R. Akiba is said to have established the prayer *Abinu Malkenu*, in which the Kingship of God receives the same emphasis as His Fatherhood.[42] Professor Louis Ginzberg has definitely proved that the *Malkuyot* were inserted in the prayers for Rosh ha-Shanah in the time of R. Akiba.[43]

[40] Above, Section IA.

[41] *Sifre*, Deuteronomy, 31, ed. Friedmann, 72b, note 17.

[42] *Ta'anit* 25b.

[43] This is seen at once on analyzing the *Mishnah Rosh ha-Shanah* 4.5, which gives the order of the prayers of the day:
סדר ברכות אומר אבות וגבורות וקדושת השם וכולל מלכיות עמהן ואינו תוקע קדושת היום ותוקע זכרונות ותוקע שופרות ותוקע ואומר עבודה והודאה וברכת כהנים דברי ר' יוחנן בן נורי אמר לו ר' עקיבא אם אינו תוקע למלכיות למה הוא מזכיר אלא אומר אבות וגבורות וקדושת השם וכולל מלכיות עם קדושת היום ותוקע זכרונות ותוקע שופרות ותוקע ואומר עבודה הודאה וברכת כהנים.

We are justified in holding that any special emphasis on the Kingship of God which is found in the liturgy, is to be associated with either the one or the other of the two periods. By the use of the other criteria that we possess we are enabled in practically every case to state definitely which of the two periods it is which has produced any particular prayer or change in the reading of the prayer.

We have seen that the prayer for Forgiveness (6), while more recent than that for Health (8) or for Prosperous Years (9), is older than that for Repentance (5), since it contains the word *Abinu* as a term of address but does not yet follow the seven-word formula. Now both the prayers for Repentance and for Forgiveness, in the Babylonian *Amidah*, contain the word *Malkenu* in their second strophe. Thus they read:

השיבנו אבינו לתורתך	סלח לנו אבינו כי חטאנו
וקרבנו מלכנו לעבודתך	מחול לנו מלכנו כי פשענו
והחזירנו בתשובה שלמה	
לפניך	

As the term ה' אלהינו was *not* inserted, it is evident that these benedictions were added before the second century; but the use of the word *Malkenu* points to their having been added during the period of the nationalist stress. We may thus definitely state that the prayers for Repentance and for Forgiveness were added to the Babylonian ritual in the period 50–70 C.E.

It will be seen that omitting the reference to the *Malkuyot*, the statements of R. Akiba and R. Johanan b. Nuri are identical. This shows that they had before them an old Mishnah in which no mention was made of the *Malkuyot*. The fact that the *Malkuyot* is very young would in any case follow from its not having any independent benediction like *Zikronot* and *Shofarot*. Finally, it will be noted that in the Fast Day Ritual (*Ta'anit* 2.3) *Zikronot* and *Shofarot* are included but not *Malkuyot*. This is not due, as has been assumed, to an association of *Rosh ha-Shanah* with the kingship of God, for as has been mentioned (Section IA) the prayer for the coming of the Divine Kingdom, which in our rituals is recited only on *Rosh ha-Shanah*, was used in Palestine on every festival. The identification of *Rosh ha-Shanah* as the festival of the Divine Kingdom was a result of the inclusion of the *Malkuyot* and not the cause. The Fast Day Ritual simply remained unchanged, because in later time the omission of the sounding of the *Shofar* obscured the identity of its beginning with the *Rosh ha-Shanah* service.

D. *Evidence from Talmudic Sources.*

1. The Prayers against Heresy and for the Proselytes.

Besides the internal evidence for the date of the origin of the various benedictions, one paragraph is definitely dated in the Talmud, and the date of two others can easily be inferred from Tannaitic sources. We are told explicitly that the prayer against Heresy (12) was added to the *Amidah* under R. Gamaliel II.[44] It is noteworthy that this prayer, which of course does not contain the term ה' אלהינו, differs in style from all the prayers thus far discussed in that it begins with the subject of the prayer. In this it is similar to the paragraph which immediately follows it in the *Amidah*, the prayer for the Proselytes (13).[45] I believe we are justified in assuming that both benedictions were inserted in the same period, and in fact their content strengthens this assumption. A prayer for proselytes could be understood best against the background of Christian missionary activity among the Gentiles. The Jews of course did not recognize conversion to Christianity as true proselytization. Hence at the same time as they condemned those of their own faith who accepted Christianity, they invoked a blessing on "the true proselytes", namely those that accepted Judaism.

2. *Kedushat ha-Shem* and the Prayer for Peace.

A record of an ancient controversy between the schools of Shammai and Hillel in regard to the form of prayer to be used when a festival coincides with the sabbath, enables us to fix definitely the time of the origin of *Kedushat ha-Shem* and the Prayer of Peace. We are told that "the School of Shammai hold that one recites eight benedictions, that for the sabbath being recited separately from that for the festival; the School of Hillel hold that one recites seven

[44] *Berakot* 28b.

[45] See also below Section V.

benedictions, that for the sabbath being combined with that for the festival."[46]

Now we know that the festival and sabbath *Amidah* contains, besides the festival and sabbath benedictions, the first and last three paragraphs of the daily *Amidah*, namely: *Abot*, *Geburot*, *Kedushat ha-Shem*, *Abodah*, *Hodaah*, and the Prayer for Peace. Since the Schools of Shammai and Hillel both assume that normally the sabbath and festival *Amidah* consists of seven benedictions, it is evident that the *Kedushat ha-Shem* had already been established by the time of this controversy.

Although a certain Honi ha-Ḳatan is mentioned in connection with this controversy, it is impossible to date it precisely, since the identity of Honi is not well established. Still from the fact that the members of the School of Shammai are referred to in the passage as the "elders of the School of Shammai", it seems certain that the discussion took place before the fall of the Commonwealth, let us say about 60. Now we have seen that the *Kedushat ha-Shem* is one of the seven-word benedictions, and hence must have originated after the period 10–20 C.E. We are thus enabled to fix the time of the insertion of this benediction as lying between 10 and 60 C.E.

The Prayer for Peace is not one of the seven-word benedictions, but it certainly is younger than the *Kedushat ha-Shem*. This is evident from a consideration of the order of *Rosh ha-Shanah* prayers as given in the Mishnah. We have seen on the basis of Mishnah *Rosh ha-Shanah* 4.5, that the oldest order of prayers for the *Amidah* of *Rosh ha-Shanah* read:[47]

סדר ברכות אומר אבות וגבורות וקדושת השם קדושת היום ותוקע זכרונות ותוקע שופרות ותוקע ואומר עבודה והודאה וברכת כהנים.

[46] *Tosefta Rosh ha-Shanah* 4.11, ed. Zuckermandel, p. 214.

[47] See above, note 43.

Since mention is made in this Mishnah of the *Kedushat ha-Shem*, the Mishnah is younger than the year 10 C.E. Yet no mention is made in it of the Prayer for Peace.[48] On the other hand, we have seen that the controversy between the Hillelites and the Shammaites, which took place approximately about the year 60, implies the existence of the Prayer for Peace. We thus see that the Prayer for Peace belongs to the period 10–60 C.E., but rather to the end of the period than the beginning.

We have noted that the prayers for Redemption (7) and for the Gathering of the Dispersed (10) follow the seven word formula, while the prayer for the Return of the Judges (11) does not. We are now justified in associating with the *Kedushat ha-Shem*, which developed in the first part of the period 10–60 C.E., the prayers for the Redemption and for the Gathering of the Dispersed, while that for the Return of the Judges must be connected with the Prayer for Peace, which like it does not follow the seven-word formula, but which developed toward the end of the period 10–60 C.E.

It should be noted in confirmation of the conclusion just reached that the Palestinian form of the Prayer for Peace asks for peace "for Thy people, Thy city, and Thy heritage, and bless us all as one." The contents point to conditions as they existed about the year 60, when the country was in a state of anarchy, and the people were torn in factions that bitterly hated each other. The men of sound sense and piety could beg for only two things, "Peace" and "Unity".

[48] The usual identification of *Birkat Kohanim* in this passage with the Prayer for Peace is unfounded. *Birkat Kohanim* regularly means the Priestly Blessing, in the Mishnah (see *Sotah* 7.2; *Megillah* 4.10; *Sifre*, Deuteronomy, 62 and 82). The attempt to identify *Birkat Kohanim* in *Tamid* 5.1, with the Prayer for Peace, has been attacked by Asheri (*ad loc.*) and is shown to be untenable, below, note 86. That disposes too of the belief that the Prayer for Peace was part of the early Temple service. Whether it was introduced into the Temple Service at all, even in the last days, cannot be decided without further evidence.

The turmoil of the time explains also the fact, just noted, that while the other nationalist benedictions came to Babylonia at once, the prayer for Peace came there only in the second century. The chaotic conditions made the transfer of the decisions of the Sanhedrin difficult if not impossible.[49]

E. *Anti-heretical Benedictions.*

The prayer against Heresy (12), we have seen, is definitely dated. Associated with it is the prayer for the Proselytes (13). But another benediction that has always been associated with anti-sectarian teachings is *Geburot*.[50] The emphasis on the Resurrection in this benediction is too clear to be missed, and it can only be taken as a confession of faith in Pharisaism as opposed to Sadduceanism. Its importance is the more clearly realized when we bear in mind that the *Amidah* was intended primarily for the Reader (later called *Hazzan*) at the public service. Before he began the prayer he had to declare his faith in the doctrines of the Pharisees.

This benediction must be assigned to the period of the most vigorous controversies between the Pharisees and the Sadducees. This was approximately the generation immediately preceding the opening of the Common Era.

While we may accept the current explanation of the origin of the benediction, there is still need of further elucidation of the fact that the Pharisees chose as the doctrine to be emphasized the Resurrection rather than such a doctrine as the authority of the Oral Law, which would appear to be more fundamental. The matter can best be explained by assuming that the benediction was inserted during a

49 Hence the Babylonian form of the prayer makes no mention of the city. It had been taken before the insertion of the prayer into the Babylonian *Amidah*.

50 See *J. Berakot* 5.4 (9c), and compare Elbogen *Achtzehngebet*, p. 51. The suggestion that the original ending may have been האל הגבור (first made by Blau, *R.E.J*, 19.19) is thus seen to be without foundation.

war or in its aftermath. The death of a number of young men in battle always emphasizes for the bereaved parents the belief in immortality. Again referring to our own experiences as a result of the late war, we have noticed the wide spread of the belief in Spiritualism and kindred doctrines as a result of it. The division of the Pharisees and the Sadducees in regard to the matter of Resurrection was doubtless sharpened during a war period—of which there were many in the century and a half preceding the opening of the Common Era. Hence the benediction begins with the words אתה גבור, "Thou art mighty,"—the power of God is usually associated with war. Hence we may safely assume that the benediction arose in one of the war periods in the latter part of the first century B.C.E.[51]

F. *Summary.*

The conclusion regarding the date of the origin of the various benedictions may perhaps best be summarized as follows:

Group I. Paragraphs containing ה' אלהינו as a term of address.
- *Abot* (1)
- The Prayer for Health (8).
- The Prayer for Prosperous Years (9).
- The Prayer for Jerusalem (14).
- The Prayer for the Acceptance of the *Amidah*, *Shema Kolenu* (P. 15).
- *Abodah* (P. 16).
- *Hodaah* (P. 17).

Group II. Anti-Sectarian confession of faith, requiring no term of address.
- *Geburot* (2).

[51] For the date of the insertion of the anti-heretical benediction in the Babylonian *Amidah* see below, Section III, where the time of the origin of the second half of *Abot* also is discussed.

Group III. Benedictions where *Abinu* was used as a term of address.

The Prayer for Forgiveness (6).

The Prayer for Wisdom (4).

The Prayer for Repentance (5).

Group IV. Prayers containing no term of address.

A. *Kedushat ha-Shem* (3).

B. Nationalist Prayers

1. The Prayer for Redemption (7).

2. The Prayer for the Gathering of the Dispersed (10).

(Characterized by the use of seven word formulae) [Wisdom (4) through Gathering of the Dispersed (10)]

3. The Prayer for the Return of the Judges (11).

4. The Prayer for Peace (P. 18).

C. Prayers that developed after the year 70 (characterized by beginning with subject).

1. The Prayer against Heresy (12).

2. The Prayer for Proselytes (13).

III. The Sabbath Eve Service in Babylonia.

Our study of the development of the first three benedictions of the *Amidah*, particularly as regards the time of their addition to the Babylonian ritual, will be much facilitated by a study of the so-called *Berakah Me'en Sheba* of the Babylonian Sabbath eve service. This benediction, which is usually assumed to be an abbreviated form of the *Amidah*, originated in Babylonia as follows. In communities where wine was scarce and the recitation of the *Kiddush* for that reason impossible, the community would gather in the synagogue and one of them would recite the *Berakah Me'en Sheba* in the place of the *Kiddush*.[52]

[52] *J. Berakot* 8.1 (11d).

The custom spread from these communities to all and became established, so that even when there was wine the *Berakah Me'en Sheba* was nevertheless recited.

As this statement of the origin of the *Berakah Me'en Sheba* is given in the Talmud of Jerusalem, it must be accepted as valid. However, there is no reason for assuming that the *Berakah Me'en Sheba* is a shortened *Amidah*. Indeed there are a number of arguments against this theory. These will become evident from a perusal of its text, which is practically the same in all the rituals:

ברוך אתה ה' אלהינו ואלהי אבותינו אלהי אברהם אלהי יצחק ואלהי יעקב האל הגדול הגבור והנורא אל עליון קונה שמים וארץ.

מגן אבות בדברו מחיה מתים במאמרו האל הקדוש שאין כמוהו המניח לעמו ביום שבת קדשו כי בם רצה להניח להם לפניו נעבוד ביראה ופחד ונודה לשמו בכל יום תמיד מעין הברכות אל ההודאות אדון השלום מקדש השבת ומברך שביעי ומניח בקדושה לעם מדשני עונג זכר למעשה בראשית.

אלהינו ואלהי אבותינו רצה במנוחתנו קדשנו במצותיך ותן חלקנו בתורתך שבענו מטובך ושמחנו בישועתך וטהר לבנו לעבדך באמת והנחילנו ה' אלהינו באהבה וברצון שבת קדשך וינוחו בה ישראל מקדשי שמך ברוך אתה ה' מקדש השבת.

It will be noted that the *Abot* is given in this prayer in a much shorter form than in the regular *Amidah*; that it is followed by the *piyyut*, *Magen Abot*, which contains a summary of the seven benedictions of the Sabbath *Amidah*; and that the prayer closes with the Sabbath benediction, אלהינו וא' אבותינו רצה במנוחתנו, given in full.

Now we have no other example of an abbreviated *Amidah* where the first and last three benedictions are not included *in toto*. Thus the prayer *Habinenu* summarizes the middle benedictions, but not the first and last three.[53] Furthermore one does not see the reason for shortening a public service such as the Sabbath eve prayer. We have no other example of an abbreviated *Amidah* being used

[53] For the Palestinian form see *J. Berakot* 4.2; for the Babylonian, *B. Berakot* 29a.

at a public service. An individual may sometimes find himself pressed for time, but is it to be assumed that when a prayer is fixed for a congregation gathering on Friday nights to welcome the Sabbath, the brief Sabbath *Amidah* would be considered too long, and in need of shortening? Finally, if abbreviation was made, why was the prayer א' וא' אבותינו רצה במנוחתנו recited in full, especially after its contents had been summarized in the words המניח לעמו ביום שבת קדשו?

Only one explanation can answer these questions. That is the assumption that the *Berakah Me'en Sheba* was not at all a summary of the Sabbath *Amidah*, but that it was *the* Sabbath *Amidah* of the time of its origin. The *piyyut Magen Abot* is an insertion from the time when it was felt that the benediction should summarize the seven paragraphs of the Sabbath *Amidah*, but the *Berakah Me'en Sheba* originated before all the seven paragraphs were known in Babylonia.

We can the more easily accept this explanation of the origin of the *Berakah Me'en Sheba*, since we know already that the *Kedushat ha-Shem* (3) developed only after the year 10 C.E., and that the *Geburot*, which arose half a century earlier, was intended as an anti-Sadducean confession of faith and therefore unnecessary in Babylonia, where the controversies between the Palestinian sects seem to have been unknown.

The *Abodah* and *Hodaah*, being part of the Temple service and not yet fully amalgamated with the *Amidah*, were not recited at night, since the Temple held no evening services.[54] The Prayer for Peace was yet unknown.

[54] That the *Abodah* and *Hodaah* were originally a separate service is evident *a priori* from the fact that they were taken over from the Temple service (see below, Section VI). It is, moreover, implied in the text of Mishnah *Rosh ha-Shanah* 4.5, cited above, where, after the order of the prayers is given in full, we are told: עבודה הודאה וברכת כהנים ואומר. The word ואומר can only be used to introduce a new part of the service.

The date of the origin of the *Berakah Me'en Sheba* in Babylonia cannot be definitely fixed. It must, however, have been in the first century, since the Sabbath benediction א' וא' אבותינו רצה במנוחתנו, which, as we have seen, developed in the first century, occurs in its full form.[55]. It is possible that by the time it was adopted in Babylonia the Palestinians were already using the seven Sabbath benedictions, but the benedictions *Kedushat ha-Shem*, *Geburot* and the Prayer for Peace were still unknown in Babylonia, and the prayers *Abodah* and *Hodaah* were still associated with the Priestly Blessing as a separate service.

It must be noted, however, that the benediction *Abot* is incomplete in the *Berakah Me'en Sheba*, ending as it does with the words קונה שמים וארץ. There can be no doubt that this was the original form of this benediction. A comparison of the form of *Abot* in the Palestinian and Babylonian rituals will show that they are alike except that קונה שמים וארץ is changed in the Babylonian into קונה הכל, and that the transitional phrases to the *Ḥatima* are different. This makes it clear that the transitional phrases are late.[56] But on the other hand without them the *Ḥatima* hardly fits the opening benediction. Why should one begin by calling on God as the God of Abraham Isaac and Jacob, and end by referring only to the "Shield of Abraham?" Moreover, while all the expressions used in the benediction occur in the Pentateuch,[57] the attribute *Magen Abraham* occurs only in Ben Sira.[58]

[56] This seems to be implied in the story told of R. Hanina and R Jonathan (***Mid. Tehillim*** 19.2, ed. Buber, 82a, comp. *J. Berakot* 9.5, 14d) who protested against the use in *Abot* of any attributes of God which do not occur in the Pentateuch.

[57] Thus א' אברהם א' יצחק וא' יעקב occurs in Exodus 3.6, 16, האל הגדול הגבור והנורא occurs in Deuteronomy 10.17, אל עליון קונה שמים וארץ occurs in Genesis 14.19. The expression אלהינו ואלהי אבותינו does not occur in Scriptures but in the prayer itself the phrase is not the original one. In the Prayer of Azariah,1.3, as well as in the Song of the Three Children, v.29, we have an opening formula practically identical with *Abot*, but there we read, "Blessed art Thou, O Lord, the God of our Fathers". It seems likely therefore that the word אלהינו was inserted by the purists of the end of the Commonwealth who felt that to say merely the "God of our Fathers," was by implication at least a denial of allegiance to God. אלהי אבותינו of course occurs in Deuteronomy 26.7.

[58] Ben Sira 51.1.

On the basis of these facts there can be no doubt that originally *Abot*, being merely an opening prayer, had no *Ḥatima* at all; the present concluding formula, with its warlike echo, "the Shield of Abraham," dates from the time of the insertion of *Geburot*, which, as we have seen, also dates from a war period.

IV. Additions to the Babylonian Amidah in the Second Century.

It has already been shown that the benedictions regarding the Proselytes (13) and Peace (P. 18, B. 19) were added to the Babylonian ritual in the second century. The same is doubtless true of the prayer against Heresy (12), which developed in Palestine at the same time as the prayer for Proselytes. That the term ה' אלהינו was inserted in the prayer for the Proselytes when it was added to the Babylonian *Amidah* and not in the prayer against Heresy is understandable enough on the principle אין שמו של הקב"ה נזכר על הרעה אלא על הטובה, "The Divine Name must not be pronounced in connection with evil."[59] This doctrine, it is true, is quoted in rabbinic sources only in the name of scholars of the third century, but it is doubtless much older, and has been shown by Professor Louis Ginzberg to be connected with the teachings of Philo.[60]

The Babylonian form of *Geburot* (2) does not contain the term *Elohenu*, but it does contain the Tetragrammaton. In any case it is clear from the discussion regarding the *Berakah Me'en Sheba* that the end of *Abot*, with its insistence on the Redeemer and the Kingship of God, the benedictions, *Geburot* and *Kedushat ha-Shem*, were added to the Babylonian *Amidah*, probably in the second century.

[59] *Tanhuma*, ed. Buber, III, p. 40; compare *Bereshit Rabba*. ed. Theodor, 3.3, p. 73, and notes.

[60] *Legends of the Jews*, V. 5.

A. *Kedushat ha-Shem.*

The development of the Kedushat ha-Shem (3) and the Prayer for Peace (19) in Babylonia presents a number of difficult problems which must now engage our attention.

In the case of both of these paragraphs there are two Babylonian versions, both of which differ radically from that of Palestine. We shall first consider the *Kedushat ha-Shem.*

In the *Seder R. Amram* it reads:

לדור ודור המליכו לאל כי הוא לבדו מרום וקדוש ושבחך אלהינו מפינו לא ימוש לעולם ועד כי מלך גדול וקדוש אתה.

In the *Seder R. Saadia Gaon* it reads:

אתה קדוש ושמך קדוש וזכרך קדוש וכסאך קדוש וקדושים בכל יום יהללוך סלה.

All the other "Babylonian" rituals have the one or the other of these forms with minor variations. The Palestinian version reads:

קדוש אתה ונורא שמך ואין אלה מבלעדיך.

It has already been shown that the Palestinian form arose about the years 10–60 C.E. Like *Geburot* it is clearly a confession of faith in Pharisaic Judaism, directed, however, not against the Sadducees but apparently against the Christians. The statement "There is no God besides Thee," seems to leave no doubt as to that matter; and the emphasis on the holiness of God and the awe-inspiring character of His Name probably is intended to call attention to what the Pharisee regarded as sacrilegious in Christian teachings.

There is nothing mystic in the Palestinian version of this paragraph, nor indeed in the text given in the *Seder R. Amram.* On the other hand the text of R. Saadia Gaon is doubtless an expression of mystic doctrines. Even neglecting the reference to the Heavenly Throne, which does not occur in some of the other versions that are akin to that of R. Saadia Gaon, the statement, "and Holy Beings praise Thee daily," is a declaration of faith in angelology

Mention has been made of the fact that mysticism seems to have become a potent factor in Jewish learning with the rise of the pupils of Hillel. But the movement apparently suffered a set-back after the Fall of Jerusalem, possibly because of the failure of mystical incantations to bring about Jewish victory. Thus R. Joshua, who is said to have derived mystic learning from R. Johanan b. Zakkai, was in his later years incensed when he found Ben Zoma engaged in these hidden studies.[61] R. Eliezer b. Hyrkanos alone of the pupils of R. Johanan b. Zakkai seems to have maintained it,[62] and perhaps it was his continuance of it that was responsible for the harsh action his colleagues took against him.

But like other movements of the early part of the first century that weakened after the fall of Jerusalem, mysticism was revived in the second century under the influence of R. Akiba and his colleagues. Ben Zoma was not the only one of the younger men engaged in these speculations. "Four men entered Paradise," we are told in an ancient *baraita*: "Ben Zoma, Ben Azzai, Elisha b. Abuya and R. Akiba".[63] The pronunciation of the Divine Name, which Abba Saul, living in the second half of the first century, severely condemned,[64] was practised by R. Hanina b. Teradyon, a prominent scholar of the early decades of the second century.[65] The statement of R. Abba b. Kahana,[66] quoted above, to the effect that the Generation of the Persecution "used" the Divine Name, doubtless refers to the attempts to perform miracles through its mystic application.

61 *Tosefta Ḥagiga*, 2.3, ed. Zuckermandel, p. 234.
62 *Sanhedrin*, 68a; compare *Baba Mezia* 59a.
63 *Tosefta*, *Ḥagiga* 215.
64 *Sanhedrin* 10.1.
65 *Abodah Zarah* 18a.
66 *Midrash Tehillim* 36, cited above.

It is out of such an atmosphere, doubtless, that the recitation of the *Kedushah* developed. We first hear of the use of the verses in connection with R. Judah b. Ilai in the middle of the second century.[67] It could not have developed much before his time. For in Palestine the *Kedushah* was recited only on the Sabbath and festivals, while in Babylonia it was used daily. The origin of this difference in practice was doubtless the fact that in Palestine the daily Amidah had been fixed by R. Gamaliel, and no additions could lightly be made, while in Babylonia the prayer remained in a fluid state for some time. We know that the Sabbath and festival *Amidah* had not been fixed in Palestine by R. Gamaliel II.

It was quite natural to add the *Kedushah* to the *Kedushat ha-Shem*, since in a measure both deal with the same subject, the Holiness of God. In Babylonia, however, the mystics were apparently not satisfied with merely adding the *Kedushah*, they introduced with it the *Kedushat ha-Shem* in a completely changed form.

Both texts of the Babylonian form of the *Kedushat ha-Shem* imply the existence of the *Kedushah*. The form *Le-Dor wa-Dor* is obviously a response to the last verse of the *Kedushah*; while the form *Attah Kadosh*, has the mystic implications which are akin to the *Kedushah*. The different communities probably adopted a different form for the benediction, but neither form is older than the second century.

B. *The Prayer for Peace* (19).

Just as there are two forms of the *Kedushat ha-Shem* (3) in the ritual of the Dispersion, so are there two forms of the Prayer for Peace (B.19). In the Ashkenazic ritual,

[67] *Tosefta Berakot*, 1.9, ed. Zuckermandel, p. 2.

the form *Sim Shalom* is used in the morning prayer,[68] and the form *Shalom Rab* for the afternoon and evening prayers. There is nothing, however, in the text of the prayers to make either one more applicable to the one time or the other. There can be no doubt that the arrangement is only a compromise by later authorities, intended to make use of two current versions of the prayer. This is rendered certain from the fact that in the ritual of the Provence[69] the form *Shalom Rab* was used also in the morning service. That the form *Shalom Rab* does not occur in the rituals of the Geonim or Maimonides, does not argue against its early age, since in a number of respects the Western European communities retained early texts of the prayers after they had been superseded in the East.[70]

Shalom Rab like *Le-Dor wa-Dor* is a response, this time to the Priestly Benediction. In fact there are a number of similarities between the text of *Shalom Rab* and *Le-Dor wa-Dor*, which make it probable that both originated in the same circles. Neither uses the Tetragrammaton, both employ the inverted sentence order, beginning with the last significant word of the preceding text, and both are entirely different from the corresponding Palestinian prayer.

What seems likely is that before the communities in the Diaspora learned of the texts of the paragraphs regarding *Peace* and *Kedushat ha-Shem*, they had heard of the names of the benedictions, and some of them arranged their own versions of the prayers; at a later time the Palestinian refugees from the Hadrianic persecutions came, and es-

[68] Compare *Hagahot Maimuni* to the *Seder Tefillah*, in the *Yad* of Maimonides. See, however, Elbogen, *Der jued. Gottesdienst*, p. 59.

[69] Below, Appendix III.

[70] Thus the older form of *Abodah* was retained in the liturgy of the Provence and pre-expulsion England. (See below, Appendix III).

[71] It is also noteworthy that neither *Shalom Rab* nor *Le-Dor wa-Dor* contain the Tetragrammaton. The omission is not accidental as *Le-Dor wa-Dor* used *Elohenu* as term of address. Evidently these formulae developed in circles which resisted as an innovation the common use of the Tetragrammaton.

tablished in some communities forms of the benedictions more nearly akin to those in use in their native land.

V. The Four Oldest Benedictions.

To return to the discussion of the benedictions which contain the term ה' אלהינו, and which, we have seen, are to be considered the oldest in the *Amidah*, they are six in number, but they fall naturally into two groups. The first consists of the prayers for Health, for Prosperous Years, for Jerusalem and for the Acceptance of the Prayers; the second, of the *Abodah* and *Hodaah*. The second group is marked by the fact that the concluding verses have three-word formulae in the place of the ordinary two-word formulae; and that they are mentioned in the Mishnah in connection with the Temple service and independently of the *Amidah*. We will therefore postpone the discussion of them, and confine our attention to the four prayers of the first group.

There are a number of difficulties which we must consider in regard to these benedictions. Of these the foremost is the radical difference between the form of the Prayer for Jerusalem (14) used in Palestine and the forms used in the Dispersion. Moreover we must explain why it is that in the case of the benediction for Jerusalem there is such a variety among the forms used in the Dispersion. The text of the Palestinian *Amidah* for this paragraph is:

רחם ה' אלהינו (ברחמיך הרבים) על ישראל עמך ועל ירושלים עירך ועל ציון משכן כבודך ועל היכלך ועל מעונך ועל מלכות בית דוד משיח צדקך.

This corresponds approximately to the form used in Egypt, as can be seen from Genizah fragments (representing the ritual of the Dispersion)[72] and the *Seder R. Saadia Gaon.*

[72] See below, Appendix III.

But there are two other forms, both of which occur in the various rituals of the Dispersion. The one may be typified by the text found in the *Seder R. Amram*, the other by that found in Maimonides. The three forms found in the rituals of the Dispersion are as follows:[73]

Seder R. Saadia Gaon	*Seder R. Amram*	*Maimonides*
רחם ה' אלהינו עלינו על ישראל עמך ועל ירושלים עירך ועל היכלך ועל מעונך ובנה ברחמים את ירושלים.	על ירושלים עירך ברחמים תשוב ובנה אותה בנין עולם במהרה בימינו.	תשכון בתוך ירושלים עירך כאשר דברת ובנה אותה בנין עולם במהרה בימינו.

The texts of the *Seder R. Amram* and Maimonides agree in that neither of them contains the Tetragrammaton. Both are therefore to be regarded as comparatively late. It is not to be assumed that the Babylonian forms of the prayer were substituted for the Palestinian after the fall of Jerusalem. For there is nothing in the Palestinian text inconsistent with its use after the fall of the Temple. Moreover even if it were felt that a change was necessary, it seems strange that the whole form of the prayer should have been altered. When the *Abodah* had to be recast because of the fact that the sacrifices were no longer offered at the Temple, the use of the Tetragrammaton in it was continued.[74] Why was the prayer for Jerusalem so completely recast in Babylonia and the Tetragrammaton omitted?

The only possible explanation of these facts is that the Babylonian *Amidah* in early times did not contain the prayer for Jerusalem, which therefore can not be considered part of the original *Amidah*. It was doubtless introduced in Palestine at a very early time, but not accepted in Babylonia

[73] The Ashkenazic ritual is a combination of those found in *Seder R. Amram* and Maimonides.

[74] See below, Appendix III.

till such a time as objection had arisen to the use of the term ה' אלהינו in prayer. Hence the Palestinian form contains the term ה' אלהינו, while the Babylonian forms do not. Either the Jews of Egypt adopted the Palestinian form before the Babylonian communities, or, what is more likely, when the prayer was added, the leaders of Egyptian Jewry felt justified in using the term ה' אלהינו because it was used in the corresponding prayer of the Palestinian *Amidah*.

Since it has now been established that the prayer for Jerusalem was not part of the original *Amidah*, we may well doubt whether the prayer for Health (68) or that for Prosperous Years (9) was at first contained therein. Indeed when we recall the nature of the early *Amidah* we shall see that in all likelihood it contained neither of these benedictions, but was in fact limited to what now constitutes the beginning of *Abot* and the earliest form of *Shema Kolenu* (P. 14, B. 15). For the *Amidah* was originally not at all a prayer for the individuals of the community but for the Reader (later the *Hazzan*).[75] The individuals of the Congregation recited their petitions to God in whatever way seemed best to them. After they had made their supplications, the Reader would step forward to pray for them. His prayer was fixed; it was always a request that their supplications might be accepted.

The earliest form of the *Amidah* undoubtedly read somewhat as follows:

ברוך אתה ה' אלהי[76] אבותינו אלהי אברהם אלהי יצחק ואלהי יעקב
האל הגדול הגבור והנורא אל עליון קונה שמים וארץ שמע [ה' אלהינו]
בקולנו ורחם עלינו ברוך אתה ה' שומע תפלה.

It was only a serious national crisis, doubtless a grave

[75] See Elbogen, *Jued. Gottesdienst*, p. 255. It was only under R. Gamaliel II that that *Amidah* was finally made an individual prayer. R. Eliezer, it will be recalled, objected to the fixation of the prayers, and even R. Joshua held that one should recite a prayer "summarizing the eighteen benedictions." *Mishnah Berakot* 4.4.

[76] For the omission of the word *Elohenu* see above, note 57.

peril to the capital and the Temple, that induced the Jewish community to insert into this formula of prayer for the acceptance of the petitions of the people, a request for the safety of their Holy City.

The occasion for this insertion could not have been any of the civil wars of the Hasmonean period, for in none of them was the Temple endangered. Nor could it have been the last revolt against the Romans. For, as we have seen, the prayer for Jerusalem, which in its Palestinian form contains the term ה' אלהינו, is one of the oldest of the paragraphs of the *Amidah*, and is certainly older than the opening of the Common Era.

We can only assume that the prayer was inserted in the Maccabean period, when the Temple had been defiled and the Holy City was in the hands of the Gentiles. Naturally the Jews prayed for mercy "on Thy people Israel, Thy city Jerusalem, Thy holy dwelling-place Zion, and Thy Temple and Thy habitation."

The chaotic conditions which prevailed during the Maccabean wars, as well as the fact that the conservative groups outside of Palestine would naturally resist such an innovation as the prayer for a particular good in what had been a general formula, would sufficiently account for the fact that the prayer was not incorporated in the *Amidah* of the Dispersion.

Once an addition had been made to the *Amidah*, smaller catastrophes might lead to the insertion of new prayers. Thus the occurrence of a famine would be taken to justify the insertion of a prayer for dew and rain; an epidemic would be the occasion of the addition of a prayer for health. It seems that in some parts of Palestine there was also inserted, doubtless in a war period, a prayer for the release of Jewish captives.[77]

[77] See Sifre, 343, and compare *Midrash Tannaim*, *ad loc.*

During the later Maccabean period the authority of the Sanhedrin became more and more widely recognized, so that the additions which they established were accepted throughout the Jewish world. Hence it came about that the prayers for Prosperous Years (9) and for Health (8) were inserted in the Babylonian ritual, while the prayer for Jerusalem, which had not been added in the first place, remained unknown.[78]

We can now understand a matter which has never yet been satisfactorily explained, the fact that the Babylonian *Amidah* devotes a special prayer to the Dynasty of David, while in Palestine that prayer is included in the prayer for Jerusalem.[79] During the years 50–66, as the desire for independence grew among the Jews, there developed also a deep-seated disgust with the later Herodians, and probably also a feeling that the Jewish troubles were due to the assumption of the Kingship by the Hasmoneans. Hence there was a re-awakening of the spirit of loyalty to the Kingdom of David. In Palestine the prayer for David was made part of the prayer for Jerusalem; in Babylonia, where there was no prayer for Jerusalem, a new paragraph was established containing a prayer for the House of David. It will be noted that the Babylonian prayer for David originally consisted of seven words, a form characteristic of the last days of the Commonwealth.[80] On the other hand the fact that it opens with the subject, reflects the new usage in prayer formation.

[78] The prayer for Health in Babylonia shows the influence of the nationalist spirit, in that the verse from Jeremiah which bespeaks the spiritual health of the body politic, has been substituted for the older form where the physical health of the sick was the subject of prayer. A similar development took place in the Palestinian form of the prayer for Repentance (see above, section I B).

[79] The theory that the insertion of the prayer was a compliment to the Exilarchs who claimed descent from the House of David seems to me untenable. For it remains a fact that in the Palestinian *Amidah* a prayer was made for the Davidic dynasty, and even more the term *Elohe David* was inserted into the *Ḥatima*. It was doubtless intended in Palestine to express the feeling that the rebuilding of Jerusalem without the establishment of the Davidic dynasty would be an incomplete achievement.

[80] See above, section II A.

The catastrophic and tragic fall of the Holy City at the hands of the Roman conquerors must have touched the hearts of Jews throughout the world. The rebuilding of the city of God became a matter of anxiety not merely to the Jews who still remained in Palestine, but to their brethren everywhere. Hence one after another the communities outside of Palestine introduced the prayer for Jerusalem in their *Amidah*. Some of them adopted it in the form in which it had been current in Palestine. Others preferred a new form, more in consonance with the style of the period. They established the text תשכון, the style of which is similar to that of the prayers for the Redemption (7), for the Gathering of the Dispersed (10) and for the Restoration of the Judges (11). In other communities a new form was used, which was charateristic of the newer generation, the form in which the prayer began with the subject. They established the form beginning with על ירושלים.[81]

VI. The Ritual of the Priestly Blessing.

We have now traced the development of the *Amidah* proper. The last three benedictions, or more properly *Abodah* and *Hodaah*, are in a class by themselves,[82] being mentioned in the Talmud as part of the Temple ritual. In order to follow their development we must trace the growth of that ritual.

[81] The objection may be raised that the prayer for the Davidic dynasty, which according to the analysis just given originated before the fall of Jerusalem, begins with תשכון. This is not, however, a true exception to the style in vogue before the fall of Jerusalem. In establishing the prayer for the re-establishment of the Davidic dynasty use was made of the benediction of the *Haftarah* praying for the coming of Messianic days. This is shown from the fact that the *Ḥatima* is not אלהי דוד (the words inserted in the Palestinian prayer for Jerusalem for the mention of David), but מצמיח קרן ישועה, the *Ḥatima* of the prayer for the coming of David and Elijah in the benedictions of the *Haftarah*. Since the prayer was built about the *Ḥatima*, as it were, it is natural that it should begin with the words which are the most important in the *Ḥatima*. In any case the earlier date of the prayer for David is sufficiently established by its use of the seven-word formula, not found in the formula על ירושלים. For a further discussion of the origin of the prayer for David in the benedictions of the *Haftarah*, see Appendix I. The origin and development of the prayer for Jerusalem in the *Birkat Ha-Mazon* is discussed in Appendix II.

[82] See above, note 54.

At first it was probably very simple, consisting of the sounding of trumpets, the reading of psalms, and the priestly blessing. By the time of Ben Sira,[83] we find that it had already taken on definite form. Towards the end of the sacrificial offering, the priests sounded their trumpets and all the people prostrated themselves. Thereupon the Levitical songs were chanted, and when these had been completed, "all the people of the land cried in prayer before the Merciful." Meanwhile the priest had completed the altar service and stepped down to pronounce the priestly blessing. Thereupon once more the people prostrated themselves.

In the course of centuries the order of service was changed in a number of important details. The treatise of *Tamid*[84] gives a description of the daily service in the Temple by an eye-witness in a form different from that found in Ben Sira. According to this treatise, after the sacrifices had been slaughtered, but before they had been taken to the altar, the priests assembled for daily services which consisted of the recitation of a benediction, the reading of the Ten Commandments, and the *Shema*ʿ, and the recital of three more benedictions.[85] As is well-known, the treatise of *Tamid* has suffered a number of accretions. One of these attempts to identify the three benedictions, which the original did not specify.[86] But a comparison of the daily

[83] Ben Sira 50.17ff.

[84] See Ginzberg, in *Journal of Jewish Lore and Philosophy*, I, p. 33ff, 197ff., where a detailed discussion of this treatise is given, the older basic text being disentangled from the later accretions.

[85] *M. Tamid* 5.1.

[86] Professor Ginzberg does not point out this passage as an addition. Nevertheless it seems to me certainly to be an accretion. The Mishnah at present reads:
אמר להם הממונה ברכו ברכה אחת והן ברכו וקראו עשרת הדברים שמע והיה אם שמוע ויאמר ברכו את העם שלש ברכות אמת ויציב עבודה וברכת כהנים.
Now it is at once a striking circumstance that the first benediction is not identified and the latter three are. Moreover the Mishnah of Tamid contradicts itself, for here it considers *Birkat Kohanim* one of the three benediction, and later (7.1) it provides for the *Birkat Kohanim* at the end of the sacrificial service. The attempt to identify *Birkat Kohanim* here with the prayer for Peace, *Sim Shalom*. involves insuperable difficulties as has been noticed by Asheri (*ad. loc.*) For how are we to assume that

ritual with that used by the High Priest on the Day of Atonement leaves no room for doubt that the three benedictions were those for the reading of the Torah, for the *Abodah*, and for the *Hodaah*.

The order of these benedictions was as follows. When the priests had completed their reading of the Ten Commandments and the *Shema*ʿ, they naturally recited a benediction for the Torah. They then prayed for the acceptance of the sacrifice that was going to be offered. At the close of this prayer, the people prostrated themselves, and offered words of thanks to God. At the end of this informal praise of the Deity, the priest would recite the benediction "for the Thankfulness" (*ʿal ha-hodaah*). Thereupon the sacrifice was offered, and that was followed by the prescribed Aaronide blessing.

When this service was taken over into the synagogue, the reading of the *Shema*ʿ (and perhaps in early times also the Ten Commandments) had already become matters of private home devotion. There was therefore no occasion for the benediction over the Torah. *Abodah* and *Hodaah* were added immediately to the *Amidah*. For a time they

Sim Shalom was recited before the Priestly Blessing, when it is in fact a response to that Blessing. Moreover, as has been shown above, *Birkat Kohanim* always means the Priestly Blessing. The effort to give it another meaning in *Rosh ha-Shanah* 4.5, is due to a failure to realize that at the time of the origin of the Mishnah, the prayer for Peace had not yet been established (see above, section II D). We must therefore assume that the words אמת ויציב.....כהנים are a later addition by one who did not know the facts. In order to gain a knowledge of which benedictions were recited during the daily service, we must turn to the following argument.

Since *Hodaah* is found in the daily service of the synagogue, immediately after *Abodah*, and is also found in the same position in the order of the priestly service of the Day of Atonement, it seems likely that the two were associated in the daily Temple service. The blessing for the Torah likewise does not appear to have anything characteristic of the Day of Atonement in it. Hence, I believe, we are justified in assuming that the first three benedictions of the service on the Day of Atonement were merely the daily benedictions, after which followed five special benedictions. That the Talmud of Jerusalem (*Berakot* 1.8) identifies the benediction preceding the *Shema*ʿ with the benediction for the Torah does not argue against this conclusion, since by that is meant the benediction before reading the Torah, while from *Yoma* we know that there certainly was a benediction following it. The Babylonian Talmud, as is well known, differs from that of Jerusalem in that some of its authorities identify the benediction preceding the *Shema*ʿ with *Ahabah Rabbah* and others with *Yozer*.

were distinguished from it, but as the years went by the two services coalesced. By the year 50[87] we find that the *Abodah*, *Hodaah* and the Prayer for Peace (which had by that time been established), were all part of the *Amidah*.

The fall of Jerusalem made necessary certain changes in the reading of the benediction *Abodah*, since it was no longer possible to pray for the acceptance of the sacrifices. An attempt to reconstruct the original text has been made by Rashi.[88] It is, however, impossible to establish the early texts with any degree of certainty on the basis of the present versions.

The *Hodaah*, which consisted at first of two parts, the silent prayer of thanksgiving by the multitude, and the benediction by the leader of the congregation or the priest, became a single paragraph, recited both by the individual and by the reader. The old custom, however, is retained in the habit of reciting the מודים דרבנן in a low tone when the *Hazzan* reaches the *Hodaah*.

VII. Conclusion.

We have now traced individually the various benedictions and attempted to fix their dates as far as possible. Gathering together the loose ends of the discussion, it may be stated definitely that the oldest form of the *Amidah* can be proved to have originated as early as the beginning of the second century B.C.E. and that it consisted of a single benediction. This benediction consisted of an introduction, calling upon God in various terms (all taken from the Pentateuch) and of a prayer which asked for the granting of the individual petitions of the congregants. Some time during the course of this century, perhaps during the

[87] That is the time of the discussion between the Schools of Shammai and Hillel referred to above. (See *Tosefta Rosh ha-Shanah* 4.1).

[88] *Berakot* 11b, catchword ועבודה.

Maccabean Wars when the ceremony could not be performed in the Temple, the priestly blessing was established as part of the synagogue ritual. It was preceded by a prayer for the acceptance of the worship of the people, and by a benediction of thanks for the bounties of God.

The Maccabean Wars brought about the insertion of a prayer for Jerusalem into the *Amidah*. This prayer was also added to the *Birkat ha-Mazon*. When times had quieted down, the fact that one benediction had been added led to the insertion of others in far less serious catastrophes. Still, the *Amidah* grew very slowly, only two benedictions being formally added in the course of a century and a half. These benedictions were probably added by an authoritative body, and were therefore adopted throughout the Jewish world. We find them in Babylonia as well as in Palestine. On the other hand, the prayer for Jerusalem, having been established during a period of disorganization, was not used outside of Palestine.

The century preceding the Fall of Jerusalem saw the growth of new movements and the addition of new benedictions with increasing speed. The Pharisees established two benedictions, intended as a confession of their faith in the resurrection and in the unity of God. It is probable that these benedictions were not authorized by the Sanhedrin, since they remained unknown in Babylonia for many years.

The sophisticated character of the period led to the insertion in the *Amidah* of the paragraphs seeking Wisdom, the acceptance of Repentance and Forgiveness. In the form of these prayers one notes the rise of the mystics, who established the formulae of seven words. About the year 50 the nationalists had gained power, and it is to their influence that we must ascribe the insertion of the prayers for the Redemption, the Return of the Judges, and the

Gathering of the Dispersed, as well as the mention of the House of David in the prayer for Jerusalem. About this time there was also added the Prayer for Peace.

After the fall of the Temple the Palestinians added a paragraph in which the extermination of heresy was asked, and another in which divine protection for the "righteous proselytes" was invoked.

The prayers for Wisdom, Repentance and Forgiveness were taken to Babylonia shortly before the fall of Jerusalem, hence their Babylonian text breathes the nationalist spirit that filled the atmosphere during those years. On the other hand, *Geburot* and *Kedushat ha-Shem* were introduced in Babylonia only in the second century, at the same time as the prayers against heresy and for the protection of the proselytes were added to the liturgy of the Dispersion. The prayer for the House of David was added to the Babylonian *Amidah* in the years 50–70, when the mention of it was included in the Palestinian prayer for Jerusalem. The prayer for Jerusalem was added to the *Amidah* in some of the communities of the Dispersion shortly before 70, in others soon after the fall of Jerusalem.

The Babylonian *Amidah* thus developed without the guidance of an authoritative center, such as controlled the growth of the Palestinian *Amidah*. Hence the numerous versions of the *Amidah* of the Dispersion, in which the texts differ from each other not only in matter of words, but sometimes even in the complete content of the paragraphs. Nevertheless the rituals of the Dispersion are sufficiently alike to be recognized as forms of the same prayer; they resemble one another more than any of them resembles the Palestinian *Amidah*. In their varied forms they are all full of the single fervor, the desire of Israel to be re-united with its God.

Appendix I.

The Prayer for the Davidic Dynasty in the Benedictions of the Haftarah

The prayer for the return of David and Elijah in the benedictions of the *Haftarah* presents several difficulties, the solution of which throws light on its origin as well as on the doctrines current in Jewish circles in the first century.

It reads in the current versions practically as it does in the oldest sources, *Masseket Soferim* and Maimonides:

שמחנו ה׳ אלהינו באליהו הנביא עבדך
ובמלכות בית דוד משיחך
3 במהרה יבוא ויגל לבנו
על כסאו לא ישב זר ולא ינחלו עוד אחרים את כבודו
כי בשם קדשך נשבעת לו שלא יכבה נרו לעולם ועד
6 ברוך אתה ה׳ מגן דוד.

It will be noticed that Elijah, who is mentioned in the first strophe, is apparently forgotten after that; the remainder of the benediction concerns itself only with David. Moreover the word יבא in line 3, can refer to nobody. It cannot refer to Elijah, for that name is too far removed, and secondly the pronoun in כסאו refers to the antecedent of יבא, and Elijah had no throne. It cannot refer to David, for in the second strophe it is not David who is expected, but his Dynasty—the House of David. It is true that in later times there developed the belief in the possibility of a personal return of David, but one would hardly expect that the two doctrines of the personal return of David and the coming of a scion of his house as a Messiah should be confused in the same prayer.

The difficulties can easily be met, however, on the assumption that the prayer originally read:

שמחנו ה' אלהינו באליהו הנביא עבדך במהרה יבא ויגל לבנו

It was a prayer for the coming of Elijah, and dates back to the time when Jews had their own kingdom and their independence. Messianic hopes then centered about the return of Elijah. In this form the prayer is at least as old as the beginning of the Common Era. It will be noted that it contains the Tetragrammaton like the oldest prayers of the *Amidah*.

The prayer for the Davidic dynasty was inserted at the time when a similar interpolation was made in the prayer for Jerusalem in the *Amidah i. e.* about the years 50-70. What the original ending was can no longer be stated. It probably was מצמיח ישועה or מצמיח קרן ישועה.

Appendix II.

The Prayer for Jerusalem in the Birkat Ha-Mazon.

The prayer for Jerusalem in the current version of the *Birkat Ha-Mazon* consists of three parts, the first being a prayer for the Holy City and the Temple, the second a prayer for economic prosperity, and the third a transitional phrase referring back to the prayer for Jerusalem, and leading up to the benediction. We know from the Talmud of Jerusalem[89] that the second part is not an integral portion of the prayer. Without it there was probably no need of the final transitional phrase. Hence in dealing with this prayer we need cite only the first part, which reads:

[89] *J. Berakot* Sabbath 15a.

רחם ה' אלהינו על ישראל עמך ועל ירושלים עירך ועל ציון משכן כבודך ועל מלכות בית דוד משיחך ועל הבית הגדול והקדוש שנקרא שמך עליו.

This is not, however, the earliest form of the prayer. In the middle of the first century the rabbis established a shortened form of the *Birkat Ha-Mazon* for use after drinking wine or eating certain products of Palestinian origin, not at the regular meals. This benediction was called the *Berakah Me'en Shalosh*, "the benediction summarizing the three benedictions of the *Birkat Ha-Mazon*".[90]

The prayer for Jerusalem as cited in this *Berakah Me'en Shalosh* reads:

רחם ה' אלהינו על ישראל עמך ועל ירושלים עירך ועל ציון משכן כבודך [91]ועל מזבחך ועל היכלך.

The prayer for Jerusalem as thus quoted is surprisingly like the prayer as found in the Palestinian *Amidah*. The only important difference is the use of the term מזבחך instead of מעונך. But a little reflection will show that the use of מזבחך must be the older. There can be no doubt that after the Fall of Jerusalem when the altar was destroyed, it was felt to be incongruous to pray for it, so that the word מעונך, which really is tautologous when used together with היכלך, was substituted.

There can be no doubt that when the prayer for Jerusalem was added to the *Amidah* in Palestine, *i. e.* during the days of the Maccabean revolt, it was also added to the *Birkat Ha-Mazon*. Hence it is found in the same form in both places. The *Birkat Ha-Mazon* was probably unknown

[90] *Mishna Berakot* 6.1.

[91] The words על מזבחך ועל היכלך are omitted in the Yemenite and Sephardic versions. Yet we must here accept the Ashkenazic version, for how could we otherwise explain the insertion of the words. We can well understand, why they were omitted in some rituals after the fall of Jerusalem. It is interesting to note that the prayer for David had not yet been inserted in the prayer for Jerusalem, when the *Berakah Me'en Shalosh* was established. Some of the rituals added it at a later time, but its omission in the Ashkenazic version, which has in other respects the oldest readings, shows that it was not found in the original form.

in Babylonia at that early date, and when it was introduced, it was accepted with its three benedictions. On the other hand since the *Amidah* had already been established in Babylonia, there was opposition to the addition of the prayer for Jerusalem. Hence the prayer for Jerusalem in the Babylonian *Amidah* shows signs of late origin, while the form in the *Birkat Ha-Mazon* is substantially the same as the Palestinian.

This leads to the interesting conclusion that the *Birkat Ha-Mazon* in Palestine, was pre-Maccabean. A further discussion of that subject, is, however, impossible here.

Appendix III

The Text of the Amidah.

In order to reconstruct the basic text of the various benedictions of the *Amidah*, it is necessary first to present the Palestinian *Amidah* as it is found in the Genizah fragments; second, to classify the various forms of the prayer of the Dispersion with a view to abstracting from them what is fundamental to them all. In order to make the matter clearer the various texts are presented in parallel columns, the various forms of the *Amidah* of the Dispersion, the *Amidah* of the Palestinian liturgy, and finally the hypothetical original text. The period in which each paragraph is supposed to have been added is also indicated.

The Palestinian text (נוסח א"י) is based on the three fragments used by Schechter in his edition (*Jewish Quarterly Review*, X, 656). The text as given is that of the larger fragment, variants from the smaller ones being marked שב and שג respectively. Variants to the first three benedictions, found in the festival *Amidot* published by Professor I. Elbogen in *Monatsschrift*, Vol. 55, are also indicated. Those from the fragment on page 433 are marked נא,

and those from the fragment on page 594, גב, while those from the text of Professor Jacob Mann, in *Ha-Zofeh* VI. 13, are marked גד.

The classification of the forms used in the Dispersion has been much more complicated. Elbogen, following earlier writers, classifies the *Seder R. Saadia Gaon* as a Palestinian liturgy strongly influenced by the Babylonian.[92] It is necessary to note that no matter what the fact may be regarding the rest of the ritual represented by the *Seder R. Saadia Gaon* and kindred forms, the *Amidah* is certainly akin to the Babylonian. This can be seen at once from a comparison of the *Seder R. Saadia Gaon* with the Genizah fragments published by Dr. Schechter. The *Seder R. Saadia Gaon* does indeed contain a prayer for Jerusalem that is almost identical with that of Genizah fragments, but when we consider that its form of *Abot, Geburot, Kedushat ha-Shem*, the prayers for Wisdom, for Repentance, for Forgiveness, for Health, *Abodah*, *Hodaah* and *Sim Shalom* agrees with the Babylonian forms, and furthermore that it contains a special prayer for the dynasty of David, there can be no doubt that it must be classed as a "Babylonian" liturgy. That it retained the prayer for Jerusalem which is found in the Palestinian ritual is no more strange than that the liturgy of Southern France, like that of England before the expulsion, contained a form of *Abodah* practically identical with the Palestinian.

The ritual of the Dispersion grew up in so many different lands, that naturally the differences between the rituals are great, but what is most surprising is not the variation but the basic similarity that exists among them all.

The following rituals have been used in establishing the texts of the Amidah of the Dispersion:

[92] Elbogen, *Jued. Gottesdienst*, p. 361.

Ritual	Source	Notation
Seder R. Amram		סר"ע
	Ed. Warsaw, 1865	סר"ע (נדפס)
	Ms. Sulzberger[93]	סר"ע (ז)
	Bodleian Ms. [94]	סר"ע (א)
Seder R. Saadia Gaon	Bodleian Ms.[95]	רס"ג
Egypt	Genizah fragment[96]	מצרים
Maimonides	*Yad, Hilkot Tefillah, Ms.*[97]	רמבם (כ"י)
	Yad, Hilkot Tefillah, Ed. (Soncino,1490)	רמב"ם (נדפס)
Yemen	*Tiklal* (Jerusalem, 1894)	תימן
Spain	Sephardic Prayer Book (Venice, 1544)	ספרד
Southern France	*Mahzor Avignon* (Avignon,1767)	קלא
Northern France	*Mahzor Zarfat*[98]	צרפת
	Mahzor Vitry (Ms.)	ויטרי (כ"י)
Germany	*Mahzor Vitry* (Berlin, 1889)	ויטרי (נדפס)
	Ashkenazic Prayer Book (ed. Baer)	א
England (pre-expulsion)	*Ez Hayyim*[99]	עץ חיים
Balkan Countries	*Mahzor Kaffa* (Mezyron, 1793)	כפא

[93] The variants from this Manuscript and the Bodleian Ms. have been collected and discussed by Professor Alexander Marx in *Untersuchungen zum Siddur des Gaon R. Amram* in *Jahrbuch der juedisch-literarischen Gesellschaft.* V (1907).

[94] Neubauer 1095.

[95] Neubauer 1096. I used a photograph of the Ms. now in possession of the Library of the Jewish Theological Seminary of America (Cat. Adler, 3396).

[96] Published by Israel Levi, in *Revue des Etudes Juives,* 53, 235ff.

[97] Professor Moses Hyamson was good enough to lend me the photograph of the Bodleian Ms. of the *Yad* now in his possession (Cat. Neubauer 577). It will be borne in mind that this Ms. was corrected on the basis of the original Ms. and is therefore to be accepted as *the* text of Maimonides. The variants from the printed text are nevertheless given for the sake of completeness.

[98] This Ms. and the following are in the library of the Jewish Theological Seminary of America.

[99] I made use of the copy of the Leipzig Ms. XVII, now in possession of the Library of the Jewish Theological Seminary of America (Cat. Adler, 4055–7).

	Mahzor Romania (Constantinople, 1574)	רומניא
	Mahzor Turin[100]	טורין
Italy	Italian Prayer Book[101] (Bologna, 1541)	רומי
Persia	Persian Prayer Book (Mss. Adler 23 and 914)	פרס

Besides these main sources for the various rituals, use has been made of the quotations from the *Amidah* in various works, particularly in the codes. Reference to these has been made in the notes, but mention of one instance must be made here. R. Jacob b. Asher in his *Tur Orah Hayyim*, section 118, says:

ויש בה [בברכת המינים] כ"ט תיבות לפי שמשומד כופר בתורה שיש בה כ"ז אותיות ותורה שבעל פה ובתורה שבכתב. ולפי חשבון זה אין ראוי לומר כל אויבינו אלא ותכניע במהרה בימינו.

(ed. Mantua, 1476). As R. Jacob makes use of the Ashkenazic ritual, it is evident from his statement that the benediction contains 29 words, omitting the words כל אויבינו, that he must have had the following text of the prayer against Heresy:

ולמשומדים אל תהי תקוה וכל עושי רשעה כרגע יאבדו וכל אויבי עמך מהרה יכרתו ומלכות זדון תעקר ותשבר ותמגר ותכניע (כל אויבינו) במהרה בימינו ברוך אתה ה' שובר אויבים ומכניע זדים.

Of equal interest is the following remark of R. Nathan Ha-Yarhi in *Manhig*, 56:

ובמקומות שמכריז החזן בליל השאלה ברך עלינו אינו כלום שהרי בכל גבול ישראל נהגו לפתוח הברכה כך והשאלה היא ותן טל ומטר.

It is evident that the author was not aware of the fact that

100 The variants from this source were collated from the Ms. by the late Dr. Solomon Schechter. As the Ms. had since been destroyed by fire, his notes are probably the only source extant for the readings of this *Mahzor*. My friend, Dr. Jacob Kohn, first called my attention to the fact that this Mahzor represents a Balkan ritual.

101 I have compared the readings from this source with those of Luzzatto. Where they differ, the variants from Luzzatto are marked.

in Spain the summer formula of the prayer for Prosperous Years began with ברכנו, while the winter formula began with ברך עלינו. Hence it was quite appropriate on the evening when the change from the summer formula to that of the winter had to be made to announce the words ברך עלינו.

In addition to the rituals of which the variants are given below, a number of manuscripts have been examined, of which the variants had to be omitted lest the work become too cumbersome. Of these the most interesting perhaps is Ms. Deinard 521, now in the possession of the Library of the Jewish Theological Seminary of America. In some of its benedictions it shows kinship to the Balkan group of rituals, in others to the Spanish group. The prayer for Prosperous Years is in the main according to the Balkan formula, that for Jerusalem follows the formula used in Spain and by Maimonides. Most interesting however is the brief formula of *Sim Shalom* in the Ms. This is the shortest form of that benediction found among the rituals of the Dispersion, and should be given in full.

שים שלום טובה וברכה חן וחסד ורחמים עלינו ועל כל ישראל עמך וברכנו כלנו יחד ברוב עוז ושלום ברוך אתה ה׳ המברך את עמו ישראל בשלום.

No prayer book of Algiers has been available for the complete yearly cycle, but from a Ms. of the prayer book of that country for *Rosh Ha-Shanah* it is evident that it has been influenced by the ritual of Southern France. It does not, however, employ the formula *Shalom Rab* for the prayer for Peace, but *Sim Shalom*. As regards this benediction it follows the Sephardic formula.

It is interesting to note that for one reason or another a number of German communities omitted the sentence ומלכות זדון.... ותשבר ותמגר, "And the kingdom of arrogance mayest Thou destroy speedily in our days," in their prayer books. The words are omitted in the prayer book printed in Amsterdam, 1660, and in other editions. But it is also lacking in some Mss., such as Ms. Adler 558.

Attention must also be called to the fact that the formula for *Kedushat Ha-Shem* according to the rite of Avignon and Algiers for *Rosh Ha-Shanah* was: לדור ודור אתה קדוש ושמך קדוש וקדושים בכל יום יהללוך סלה, a peculiar combination of the formula *Le-Dor va-Dor* and *Attah Kadosh*.

The classification of the various rituals presented a difficult task because so many of them reflect a variety of influences. Thus the rituals of Southern France and Persia are clearly akin to a number of widely varying rituals. Moreover it is probably true that the *Amidot* of the various countries show different alliances than do their *piyyutim*. Thus there are a number of facts regarding the German liturgy which are akin to those of Palestine, but there can be no doubt that the German *Amidah* belongs to the Dispersion. Similarly, the fact that we find in pre-expulsion England and in Southern France a formula for *Abodah* which is remarkably similar to that of Palestine, does not prove that these are connected with the Palestinian *Amidah*. Indeed we find a similar *Abodah* quoted as authoritative by so eminent a Babylonian as R. Natronai Gaon (See Ginzberg, Geonica, II, pp. 119 and 351). Yet it is not found elsewhere in the extant rituals of the Dispersion.

The classification that is attempted here is thus intended to describe only the fundamental kinship groups of the *Amidah* of the Dispersion. The various detailed influences can only be ascertained by further studies of the complete liturgies of the various countries.

The *Seder R. Amram*, of which the original text can only be reconstructed on the basis of the various sources available, represents the ritual of Babylonia proper. The *Seder R. Saadia Gaon* and the Genizah fragment published by Israel Levi in *Revue des Études Juives* (53.235) represent the ritual of Egypt.

This fragment should not be confused with those of the Genizah which represent Palestinian *Amidot*. As has been noticed above, the Palestinian Jews in Egypt maintained their own ritual, but the native Egyptian *Amidah* was a variant of that in use in the Dispersion.

The Amidot of the other rituals mentioned fall into three groups. Maimonides, Yemen, Spain and Southern France are alike in that the prayer for Jerusalem in all of them begins with תשכון בתוך ירושלים. Furthermore in all of them the words וגאלנו מהרה of the prayer for the Redemption (7) have been changed into ומהר לגאלנו. It is true that the Provençal and the Spanish rituals came under other influences, which somewhat obscure their fundamental similarity to those of Maimonides and Yemen, but a careful study of the rituals will show that they belong to the same family.

Within the group, the texts of Maimonides and Yemen are so much alike as almost to form a single ritual, while the text of Southern France is fundamentally similar to that of Spain, although it is true that the former was much influenced by the ritual of Northern France, and the latter by that of Italy and the Balkan countries.

The various influences that helped frame the Spanish ritual can best be seen at work in the peculiar phenomenon which brought it about that the summer form of the prayer for Prosperous Years (9) is similar to that of Maimonides and Yemen, while the winter form resembles that of the Balkan countries. It is noteworthy that while the custom of Southern France agrees with that of Northern France and Germany in having the summer form of the prayer almost identical with the winter form, it differs from them in that it adopted the long Sephardic winter prayer for the whole year (omitting the word ומטר for the summer), while in the north, of course, the short summer form was used with minor changes also in the winter.

A second group of rituals consists of the following: Pre-expulsion England, Northern France and Germany. These rituals are alike in their common use of a very simple form of the ninth benediction both in summer and winter, and in their inclusion of the words ועל זקני עמך בית ישראל, "elders of thy people, Israel," in the prayer for the Proselytes (13). Aside from these outstanding similarities, which are not shared by any other rituals, they have a number of common traits, which have filtered through to the Provençal, Spanish or Italian rituals. In regard to these rituals it should also be stated that while the text of the *Amidah* in Ms. of the *Mahzor Vitry* resembles almost verbatim that of the *Mahzor Zarfat*, the version of the *Amidah* as found in the printed *Mahzor Vitry* is almost identical with that in use in the Ashkenazic prayer book.

The most definite characteristics are those to be found among the Italian-Balkan group of rituals. For instance *Mahzor Romania*, *Mahzor Kaffa*, and the Italian Prayer Book all have את הכל in place of the otherwise universal הכל in *Abot*. *Romania* and *Kaffa* both insert the words אדון הגבורות in the second benediction, and change והחזירנו of the prayer for Repentance into והשיבנו. Similarly המחזיר in the benediction of *Abodah* (B. 18) is changed into המשיב. *Romania*, *Kaffa*, *Turin*, and the Italian Ritual all read כי אל טוב וסלח אתה in the prayer for Forgiveness (6), This is also found in the Sephardic and Provençal rituals but not elsewhere. *Romania* and *Kaffa* insert after the word ראה in the prayer for the Redemption (7) the term ה' אלהינו. The ninth prayer is almost identical in *Kaffa*, *Romania* and *Turin*, but has been considerably shortened and simplified in the Italian ritual. Nevertheless the fact that that ritual also belongs to this group is sufficiently attested by its use of the expression ותן ברכה ורוחה והצלחה במעשה ידינו in this prayer. *Romania* and *Kaffa* add the words אל נוה קדשך in the prayer for the Gathering of the Dispersed (10), and join the Italian ritual in changing the word ומלוך of the prayer for the Restoration of the Judges (11) into ותמלוך. *Romania* and *Kaffa* add at the end of this prayer the words ואל נא תרשיענו בדין. *Romania, Kaffa* and Italy read in the prayer against Heresy (12) ותכניע אותם, while *Turin* has the variant ותכניע אותה. The Italian ritual and *Turin* join the Franco-Germanic group in changing על ירושלים of the prayer for Jerusalem into ולירושלים. *Romania, Kaffa, Turin* and the Italian ritual read חוס וחנינו ורחם in *Shema Kolenu* (B.16). The Italian Ritual and *Turin* have practically the same form of the last strophes of *Shema Kolenu* as is found in *Romania* and *Kaffa*, but have the order inverted. The four rituals also are alike in having resisted the addition of the words צור חיינו מגן ישענו... ונספר תהלתך in the *Hodaah*, an interpolation found in all of the European rituals. On the other hand they contain the expression לא הכלמתנו ה' אלהינו ולא עזבתנו ולא הסתרת פניך ממנו, which is otherwise found only in Southern France and *Seder R. Amram*.

From the examples given it will appear that while the group forms a single family, the rituals of Romania and Kaffa are the most closely related, while the others suffered more or less under foreign influences.

The Persian ritual, which has been described in detail by Elkan N. Adler in the *Jewish Quarterly Review*, X, 601–605, was originally based on a text similar to that of the *Seder R. Saadia Gaon*. It has, however, been strongly influenced by the rituals of the southern European type. Thus the prayer for Jerusalem has the formula רחמנו רחם ה'; the *Kedushat Ha-Shem* contains the sentence זכרך קדוש

כסאך קדוש. In the *Hodaah* occur the words כי יחיד אתה ואין זולתך, characteristic of the *Seder R. Saadia Gaon*. On the other hand there are a large number of variants which recall the Balkan rituals. Thus in the prayer for the Gathering of the Dispersed we find the words אל נוה קדשך, and in the prayer for the Restoration of the Judges ואל תרשיענו בדין.

The relation of the rituals enumerated may be best indicated by the following diagram:

AMIDAH OF THE DISPERSION[102]

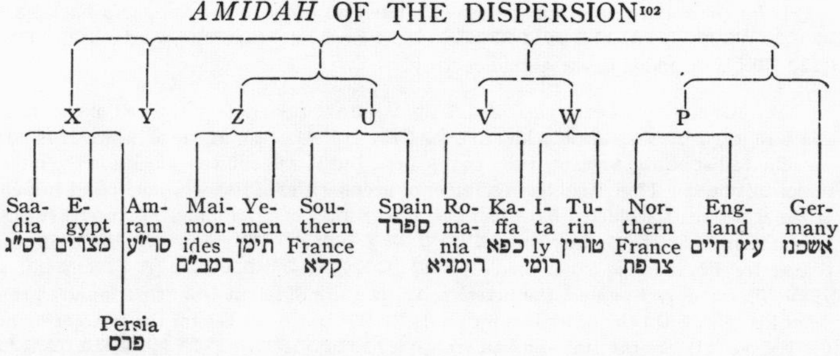

In arranging the text of the *Amidah*, the *Seder R. Amram* is given unless otherwise specified. Wherever the *Seder R. Saadia Gaon* differs materially, its text is placed in parallel column. Similarly where the rituals differ radically, a typical form from each group is given.

In order to save space it was in some cases found necessary to place one of the typical formulae of the ritual of the Dispersion on the same page as the Palestinian ritual. In every case the footnotes belonging to each type are so marked. The name of the ritual which is typical is placed in parantheses, while the names of the other rituals in the group are placed in brackets after it.[103]

[102] In order to simplify the diagram no note is taken in it of the cross influences of which mention has been made. Thus the Persian ritual was strongly influenced by sources of the Balkan-Italian liturgy, and the ritual of southern France was partly influenced by that of the Balkans and also by that of Northern France.

[103] After this article was in press some new material was made available, which can hardly be discussed adequately within the limits of this note, but nevertheless should be mentioned. The Library of the Jewish Theological Seminary of America acquired a copy of the *Facsimiles of the Hebrew Manuscripts* obtained at the Jewish Synagogue in Ka'aefung-foo, printed in Shanghai, 1851, in connection with which there is found

a text of the *Amidah*, which is practically identical with the Yemenite version. The only significant variants from that version are the insertion of the words ומרחם על בניהם after זוכר חסדי אבות in *Abot*, a form found otherwise only in the Persian ritual; the use of לזרעם אחריהם instead of לבני בניהם in the same benediction, resembling the *Seder R. Saadia Gaon* and the liturgies of Kaffa and Persia; the omission of the word והמוסרים in the prayer against heresy (12); the omission of the words בנין עולם in the prayer for Jerusalem (14); and the reading צדקה ורחמים ברכה ושלום instead of the צדקה ושלום which is regularly found in Yemenite liturgies. This version also has the formula *Le-dor va-dor* for the use of the Reader, while the individuals of the congregation recite *Attah Kadosh*, as is done in the Ashkenazic ritual.

Much new light has been thrown on the history of the liturgy by Professor Jacob Mann's article in *Hebrew Union College Annual*, Vol. II, pp. 269–338. I believe that the material furnished by Professor Mann in general corroborates my findings, but some of the points raised by him require fuller discussion than is possible here. I wish, however, to call attention to the fact that fragment 7 (p. 306) published by Dr. Mann, seems definitely to establish the fact that the Palestinian reading of the prayer for the restoration of the judges (11) like that of the *Seder R. Saadia Gaon* was: השיבה שופטים כבראשונה ויועצינו כבתחלה. It is probable that the words ומלוך עלינו אתה לבדך were added in the second century.

My attention has been called also to my failure to take note of the text of the *Amidah* published from an Arabic Ms. in *Ozar Tob*, Vol. I, p. 10, in the article. It is not possible to list all the variants from that source, but it will suffice to mention the more important ones. This ritual has a number of peculiarities of its own, not found in any of the other rituals which I have had the opportunity of examining. It inserts in the benediction *Geburot* (2) the words ומחזיר נשמות לפגרים מתים after לישני עפר; in the prayer for Forgiveness (6) it reads כי אתה ה' טוב וסלח ורב חסד לכל קוראיך after כי פשענו; its prayer against the heretics (12) is quite different from that found in the other liturgies. On the other hand it reads ותמלוך in the prayer for the restoration of the Judges (11) like the Italo-Balkan group; it has כי בשמך בטחנו ועל חסדך הגדול נשעננו at the end of the prayer for the Proselytes (13) which is very similar to the reading of the Spanish and Provencal liturgies, as well as those of Italy and the Balkans. The text of some of the benedictions is sufficiently different from that of the other rituals to be cited completely.

9 ברך עלינו ה' אלהינו את השנה הזאת לטובה ואת כל מיני תבואתה ותן טל ומטר על פני האדמה ותן ברכה והצלחה בכל מעשה ידינו וברכינו וברך שנתינו כשנים הטובות המבורכות כי אל טוב ומטיב אתה. בא"י מברך השנים.

10 תקע בשופר גדול לחירותנו ושא נס לקבץ גליותינו וקבצינו יחד מארבע כנפות כל הארץ לארצנו. ברוך אתה ה' מקבץ נדחי עמו ישראל.

12 והמינים והמלשינים כולם כרגע יאבדו וכל צוררי עמך ישראל ואויביהם וקמיהם וחושבי רעתם ומלשיניהם מהרה מארץ יכרתו וישברו ויאבדו ותכניעם במהרה בימינו. ברוך אתה ה' שובר אויבים ומכניע זדים.

15 אב הרחמן שמע קולנו חוס וחמול ורחם עלינו וקבל ברחמים את תפלתינו והושיענו כי אליך עינינו כי אל מלך שומע תפלה ותחנון אתה ומלפניך מלכינו ריקם אל תשיבנו כי אב מלא רחמים אתה ובידך כח וגבורה לשמוע תפלת כל פה. בא"י שומע תפלה.

17 רצה ה' אלהינו בעמך ישראל ולתפלתם שעה והשב את העבודה לדביר ביתיך ושכון בציון עירך בימינו ויעבדוך בניך בירושלים ואשי ישראל ותפלתם מהרה באהבה תקבל ברצון ותהי לרצון תמיד עבודת ישראל עמך אנא למענך קבלינו ורצינו ורצה נא את תפלתינו ותחזינה עינינו בשובך לציון ברחמים ותרצה בנו כמאז. בא"י המחזיר שכינתו לציון.

18 מודים אנחנו לך לבדך שאתה הוא ה׳ אלהינו על חיינו המסורים בידיך ועל נשמותינו הפקודות לך ועל נסיך ונפלאותיך וטובותיך שבכל עת ערב ובקר וצהרים תעשה עמנו ועל כולם יתברך ויתרומם שמך מלכינו לעולם ועד וכל החיים יודוך סלה האל הטוב כי טוב פעלת לחוסים בך אל ההודאות. בא״י הטוב שמך ולך נאה ולהודות.

נוסח חו"ל

א.

ברוך אתה ה' אלהינו ואלהי אבותינו אלהי אברהם אלהי יצחק ואלהי יעקב האל הגדול הגבור והנורא אל עליון גומל חסדים טובים קונה הכל זוכר חסדי אבות ומביא גואל

רס"ג	סר"ע
לזרעם אחריהם מלך מושיע ומגן	לבני בניהם למען שמו באהבה. מלך עוזר ומושיע ומגן.

ברוך אתה ה' מגן אברהם.

ב.

אתה גבור לעולם ה'

רס"ג	סר"ע
רב להושיע	מחיה מתים אתה רב להושיע

מכלכל חיים בחסד מחיה מתים ברחמים רבים סומך נופלים רופא

א. עליון] פרס. <מלך רם מושל על כל>.

טובים] ויטרי (נדפס) ח'.

קונה] רס"ג. סר"ע (ז) רומניא, רומי, כפא, ויטרי (כ"י ונדפס) עץ חיים, א, פרס, טורין, וקונה.

הכל] רומניא, כפא, רומי, את הכל.

זוכר] רסג, כפא, טורין, פרס, (ר"ה) א. וזוכר.

אבות] פרס <ומרחם על בניהם>.

(סר"ע) [מצרים, רמב"ם, תימן, ספרד, קלא, עץ חיים, צרפת, ויטרי, א. רומניא כפא, טורין, רומי, פרס]

לבני בניהם] כפא, פרס <ולזרעם אחריהם>.

למען... באהבה] רמב"ם (כ"י) ל'.

מלך... מגן] סר"ע (א), ח'. רמב"ם (כ"י) מלך רחמן מושיע ומגן. תימן, מלך רחמן ומושיע ומגן. רומניא, כפא, מלך רחמן אל חי גואל עוזר ומושיע ומגן. ויטרי (כ"י) מלך אל חי עוזר ומושיע ומגן. פרס (ר"ה) אל חי מלך עוזר ומושיע ומגן, פרס (כל השנה) מלך רחמן אל חי גואל עוזר ומושיע ומגן, רומי, מלך גואל עוזר ומושיע ומגן.

ב. (סר"ע) [מצרים, רמב"ם, תימן, ספרד, קלא, עץ חיים, ויטרי (נדפס וכ"י) צרפת, א, רומניא, כפא, טורין, רומי, פרס]. רב] עץ חיים, טורין, ויטרי (כ"י) פרס, ורב.

להושיע] רסג, רמב"ם, תימן, רומי, רומניא, כפא, ספרד, קלא, פרס (בקיץ) מוריד הטל. ובכל הנוסחאות לחורף „משיב הרוח ומוריד הגשם".

סומך... חולים] רמב"ם (כ"י) רופא חולים וסומך נופלים, תימן רופא חולים סומך נופלים.

סומך נופלים] רס"ג, ל'.

רופא] א. ספרד, רומי, פרס, ורופא.

א.

Pre-Maccabean

נוסח ארץ ישראל	הנוסח הקדמון
ברוך אתה ה׳ אלהינו ואלהי אבותינו אלהי אברהם אלהי יצחק ואלהי יעקב האל הגדול הגבור והנורא אל עליון קונה שמים וארץ מגננו ומגן אבותינו מבטחנו בכל דור ודור. ברוך אתה ה׳ מגן אברהם.	ברוך אתה ה׳ [אלהינו ו]אלהי אבותינו אלהי אברהם אלהי יצחק ואלהי יעקב האל הגדול הגבור והנורא אל עליון קונה שמים וארץ. [ברוך אתה ה׳ מגן אברהם].

ב.

First Century B.C.E.

אתה גבור — אתה גבור

מכלכל חיים מחיה משפיל גאים חזק ומדין[שא] ואין כמוך חזק[שב] ואין

א. אלהינו וא׳ אבותינו] עיין בחלק האנגלי, הערה 57.
א׳ אברהם... א׳ יעקב] מ„ברוך" עד „יעקב" מובא במכלתא שמות, הוצאת רמא"ש, י"ט, ע"א.
אל... וארץ] מראשית ברכה זו עד „הארץ" מובא בירושלמי פ"ט ה"א ובמדרש תהלים י"ט (הוצ׳ בובער פ"ב ע"ב), ועיין בחלק האנגלי פרק ג׳.
מגן אברהם] בן סירא נא, א. על דבר החתימה הזאת עיין בחלק האנגלי פרק ג׳.
ב. ומדין] גא. גב. לדין.

נוסח חו"ל

חולים מתיר אסורים ומקיים אמונתו לישני עפר מי כמוך בעל גבורות ומי דומה לך

רס"ג

ממית ומחיה

סר"ע

מלך ממית ומחיה ומצמיח ישועה ונאמן אתה להחיות מתים.

ברוך אתה ה' מחיה המתים.

ג.

רס"ג

אתה קדוש ושמך קדוש וזכרך קדוש וכסאך קדוש וקדושים בכל יום יהללוך סלה.

סר"ע

לדור ודור המליכו לאל כי הוא לבדו מרום וקדוש ושבחך אלהינו מפינו לא ימוש לעולם ועד כי מלך גדול וקדוש אתה.

ברוך אתה ה' האל הקדוש.

חולים] כפא, פרס <עוזר דלים>.

מתיר] רמב"ם (כ"י) רס"ג, ספרד, טורין, א, פרס (ר"ה) ומתיר.

אסורים] רס"ג <ומשען לאביונים>, רומניא, כפא, <משען לאביונים>.

ומקיים] עץ חיים, ויטרי (כ"י) מקיים.

בעל גבורות] רומניא, אדון הגבורות. כפא, אדיר נצח אדון הגבורות. פרס (כל השנה) אב הרחמן אדיר נצח בעל הגבורות.

ומי] פרס, עץ חיים, ויטרי (כ"י) מי.

(סר"ע) [מצרים, רמב"ם, תימן, ספרד, קלא, עץ חיים, צרפת, ויטרי (כ"י ונדפס) א. פרס, רומניא, כפא, טורין, רומי.]

מלך] תימן ל'.

ומחיה] ויטרי (כ"י) מחיה.

ומצמיח ישועה] רמב"ם (כ"י), תימן, ל'. רומי, ויטרי, ומצמיח לנו ישועה. רומניא, כפא, ומצמיח לנו ישועה בקרוב. טורין, מצמיח לנו ישועה בקרוב. פרס, מוריד ומעלה מלך מחיה הכל ברחמים רבים.

אתה] כפא, פרס <הוא>.

ג. אתה קדוש] לנוסחת רס"ג מתאימים נוסחי מצרים, רמב"ם, תימן, ספרד, פרס, ותפלת יחיד של מנהג אשכנז וצרפת. ובעץ חיים, קלא, כפא, רומניא, רומי, טורין, ובחזרת הש"ץ של שבת בסדר רס"ג ובחזרת הש"ץ של מנהג אשכנז וצרפת נמצאה הנוסחא לדור ודור. כתב ר' אהרן הכהן מלוניל בארחות חיים ה' תפלה, סי' כ' (י"ד ע"ג) „ויש אומרים שאין ליחיד לומר לדור ודור נגיד גדלך אלא אתה קדוש", ומובאים דבריו גם בכל בו (סי' י"א).

(רס"ג) וזכרך קדוש וכסאך קדוש] רמב"ם, תימן, ספרד, ויטרי (נדפס) ל'. פרס, זכרך קדוש כסאך קדוש ומשרתיך קדושים. ויטרי (כ"י) ח', ובמקומו „ושבחך אלהינו מפינו לא ימוש לעולם ועד כי אל מלך גדול וקדוש אתה."

יום] פרס <תמיד>.

סלה] אבודרהם <כי אל מלך גדול וקדוש אתה> [וז"ל והמון העם אינם אומרים כי אל מלך גדול וקדוש אתה, ובסדורי הגאונים ישנו ונכון לאמרו כמו שאפרש].

(סר"ע) המליכו] רומי, נמליך [שד"ל, המליכו].

המליכו... וקדוש] רומניא, כפא, טורין, רומי, עץ חיים, ויטרי (נדפס וכ"י) א, רס"ג, נגיד גדלך ולנצח נצחים קדושתך נקדיש.

ושבחך... אתה] קלא, ל'.

ושבחך] כפא, רומניא <ה'>. רס"ג (כ"י אחד) <ועוזך>.

כי] עץ חיים. כפא, רומי, רומניא, טורין, א, ויטרי (כ"י ונדפס) <אל>.

הנוסח הקדמון נוסח א"י

שא שב

מתים. ברוך אתה ה' עריצים חי עולמים מקים זולתך

מחיה המתים. מתים

מכלכל חיים מחיה המתים

שא שב

כהרף עין ישועה לנו ורב להושיע.

תצמיח.

ברוך אתה ה' מחיה המתים.

ג.

10–40 C. E.

קדוש אתה ונורא שמך ואין אלה מבלעדיך ברוך אתה ה' האל הקדוש

קדוש אתה ונורא שמך ואין אלה מבלעדיך ברוך אתה ה' האל הקדוש

מחיה המתים] גב. ומחיה מתים.

כהרף... תצמיח] גא. מלך מו. גב. ואין דומה לך.

ג. קדוש אתה] גב. אתה קדוש. הנוסח „קדוש אתה" מובא בספרי דברים שמ"ג (הוצ' רמא"ש קמ"ב ע"ב).

נוסח חו"ל

ד.

אתה חונן לאדם דעת ומלמד לאנוש בינה חננו מאתך דעה בינה והשכל ברוך אתה ה' חונן הדעת.

ה.

השיבנו אבינו לתורתך וקרבנו מלכנו לעבודתך והחזירנו בתשובה שלמה לפניך. ברוך אתה ה' הרוצה בתשובה.

ו.

סלח לנו אבינו כי חטאנו מחול לנו מלכנו כי פשענו ברוך אתה ה' חנון המרבה לסלוח.

ז.

ראה בענינו וריבה ריבנו

ד. ומלמד] רומניא, כפא, המלמד, ויטרי (כ"י) מלמד.
חנינו] ספרד, ויטרי (כ"י) וחנינו. טורין, חונינו. עץ חיים, וחונינו, פרס, וחנינו ה' אלהינו.
דעה... והשכל] רס"ג, דעה וחכמה בינה והשכל. רמב"ם (כ"י) רומי, דעה ובינה והשכל. רמב"ם (נדפס) דעה חכמה בינה והשכל. עץ חיים, ויטרי (נדפס) בינה דעה חכמה והשכל. ויטרי (כ"י) דעה בינה חכמה והשכל.
והשכל] פרס <כי אל דעות ורחמן אתה>.
ה. לתורתך] רסג, רמב"ם (נדפס) רומניא, כפא, טורין, רומי, <ודבקנו במצותיך>.
מלכנו] רס"ג, ל'.
לעבודתך] רומניא, כפא, והשיבנו. פרס <יחד>.
שלימה] פרס <רצויה>.
לפניך] טורין, <כי אל מקבל שבים אתה>.
ו. מחול] רס"ג, ומחול. א, מחל. פרס, רמב"ם (כ"י) ומחול.
פשענו] רמב"ם (נדפס) טורין, פשענו לך. רמב"ם (כ"י ונדפס) תימן, רומניא, כפא, טורין, רומי, ספרד, קלא <כי אל טוב וסלח אתה>. סר"ע (נדפס) <כי טוב וסלח אתה>. עץ חיים, <כי אל מלך טוב מוחל וסולח אתה>. ויטרי (כ"י ונדפס) צ. <כי אל מלך מוחל וסולח אתה> א. <כי אל מלך חנון ורחום אתה>. פרס <מחה והעבר פשעינו מנגד עיניך כי אל טוב ומטיב וסלח אתה>.
המרבה] רס"ג, מצרים, פרס, רמב"ם (כ"י) ומרבה.
ז. ראה] רמב"ם (נדפס) ספרד, קלא, רומי, כפא, עץ חיים, ויטרי, א, פרס, · <נא>
בענינו] רומניא, כפא, פרס <ה' אלהינו>.
וריבה] רס"ג. וריב.
ריבנו] רס"ג, רמב"ם (נדפס) <ודון דיננו>. פרס, את ריבנו ודון את דיננו.

הנוסח הקדמון	נוסח א"י
ד.	
10–40 C. E.	
חנינו אבינו מאתך דעה ובינה והשכל מתורתך ברוך אתה ה׳ חונן הדעת.	חנינו אבינו מאתך דעה ובינה והשכל מתורתך. ברוך אתה ה׳ חונן הדעת.
ה.	
10–40 C. E.	
השיבנו אבינו לתורתך והחזירנו בתשובה שלימה לפניך. ברוך אתה ה׳ הרוצה בתשובה.	השיבנו ה׳ אליך ונשובה חדש ימינו כקדם. ברוך אתה ה׳ הרוצה בתשובה.
ו.	
20 B.C.E–10 C.E.	
סלח לנו אבינו כי חטאנו. ברוך אתה ה׳ המרבה לסלוח.	סלח לנו אבינו כי חטאנו לך מחה והעבר פשענו מנגד עיניך כי רבים רחמיך. ברוך אתה ה׳ המרבה לסלוח.
ז.	
40–70 C. E.	
ראה בענינו וריבה ריבנו וגאלנו	ראה בענינו וריבה ריבנו וגאלנו

ה. השיבנו] אודות נוסח ברכה זו עיין חלק האנגלי סוף פ"א.
השיבנו... כקדם] איכה ה. כא.
ה׳] שב. <אלהינו>.
ו. מחה והעבר] השוה נוסח „אבינו מלכנו".

נוסח חו"ל

רס"ג	סר"ע
וגאלנו מהרה למען שמך	וגאלנו מהרה למען שמך כי גואל חזק אתה.

ברוך אתה ה' גואל ישראל.

ח.

רפאנו ה' ונרפא

רס"ג	סר"ע
הושיענו ונושעה	הושיענו ונושעה והעלה רפואה שלימה לכל מכותינו כי אל רופא ורחמן אתה.

ברוך אתה ה' רופא חולי עמו ישראל.

וגאלנו] רומי <מלכנו>.

(סר"ע) [רמבם, תימן ספרד, קלא, עץ חיים, צרפת, ויטרי, אשכנז, פרס, רומניא, רומי, כפא, טורין.]

וגאלנו מהרה] רמב"ם (כ"י ונדפס) תימן, ומהר לגאלנו. ספרד, קלא, ומהר לגאלנו גאלה שלמה [קלא <מהרה>]. סר"ע (נדפס), וגאלנו במהרה. סר"ע (ז) ומהרה גאלנו. פרס, והצילנו ווגאלנו.

למען שמך] רמב"ם (כ"י ונדפס) ל'.

כי] ספרד, קלא <אל>. רמב"ם, תימן, עץ חיים, צ, ויטרי (כ"י ונדפס) רומניא, כפא <אל מלך>.

חזק] ויטרי (כ"י ונדפס) עץ חיים, כפא, וחזק.

כי... אתה] פרס, כי מעולם אתה הוא גואלנו ומושיענו אתה.

גואל] רומניא, פרס <עמו>.

ח. רפאנו ה'] סר"ע (ז), עץ חיים, צ, ויטרי (כ"י) רמב"ם (כ"י) <אלהינו>.

(סר"ע) [מצרים, רמב"ם, תימן, ספרד, קלא, עץ חיים, צרפת, ויטרי, א, כפא, טורין, רומניא, רומי].

ונרפא] סר"ע (ז) <לכל תחלואינו>.

(סר"ע) ונושעה] סר"ע (א), כפא, רומניא, טורין, רומי, רמב"ם (נדפס), ויטרי (כ"י ונדפס)

רפואה שלימה] ספרד, ארוכה ומרפא, קלא, ומרפא. פרס <תמימה>.

הושיענו... לכל מכותינו] סר"ע (ז) ל'.

לכל מכותינו] רמב"ם (כ"י ונדפס) תימן, לכל תחלואינו. צ, ויטרי, עץ חיים, רומי, לכל מכותינו ולכל תחלואינו. רומניא, כפא, לכל מכותינו ולכל תחלואינו לחיים ולשלום. ספרד, קלא, לכל תחלואינו ולכל מכאובינו ולכל מכותינו. פרס, לכל מכותינו לחיים ולשלום.

אל] רומניא, כפא, טורין, צ, ויטרי, עץ חיים, א, פרס <מלך>.

ורחמן] רמב"ם (כ"י) רחמן. כפא, רומי, טורין, ספרד, רחמן ונאמן. צ, ויטרי, עץ חיים, א, נאמן ורחמן. קלא, חנם נאמן ורחמן.

הנוסח הקדמון

למען שמך. ברוך אתה ה' גואל ישראל.

נוסח א"י

למען שמך. ברוך אתה ה' גואל ישראל.

ח.

First Century B.C.E.

רפאנו ה' אלהינו ממכאובנו והעלה רפואה למכותינו. ברוך אתה ה' רופא חולים.

רפאנו ה' אלהינו ממכאוב לבנו ויגון ואנחה העבר ממנו והעלה רפואה למכותינו.

שא, שב.

ברוך אתה ה' רופא חולי עמו ישראל.

ירושלמי

ברוך אתה ה' רופא חולים.

ח. ממכאובנו] אולי היתה הגרסא העקרית „מחליינו", בהתאם לנוסחת הביננו בירושלמי ברכות ח' ע"א.

ויגון] שב. יגון.

ואנחה] שב. <ודבר>.

רופא חולים] ירושלמי פ"ב ה"ב.

נוסח חו"ל

ט. (קיץ)

סר"ע

ברך עלינו ה' אלהינו את השנה הזאת לטובה ואת כל מיני תבואתה [רס"ג, מצרים <וברכה כשנים הטובות>].

כפא

ברך עלינו ה' אלהינו את השנה הזאת הבאה עלינו לטובה ואת כל מיני תבואתה ותן ברכה והצלחה והרוחה בכל מעשה ידינו כי אל טוב ומטיב אתה ותברכנו ותברך את שנותינו בברכת השנים הטובות והמבורכות.

ברוך אתה ה' מברך השנים.

ט. נוסחי מצרים ורס"ג משתוים בברכה זאת לנוסח סר"ע, נוסחי רומניא וטורין לנוסח כפא, ונוסח תימן לנוסח הרמב"ם, נוסח ספרד מהאים לנוסח הרמב"ם בתפלת הקיץ. בתפלת החורף יש בנוסח ספרד של ברכה זו שנוי מטבע משאר הנוסחאות, והנוסחא ההיא מובאה גם כן בסר"ע (נדפס) ובמחזור קלא. כנראה השתמשו קהלות קלא בנוסחא זו בקיץ כמו בחורף אלא שבחורף השמיטו המלה „ומטר". בעץ חיים, במחזור ויטרי (כ"י ונדפס), במחזור צרפת, ובסדור אשכנז נמצאה נוסחא פשוטה וקצרה בין לימות החמה ובין לימות הגשמים, אלא שבימות החמה משמיטים המלים „טל ומטר". בסדור רומי יש נוסחא יותר ארוכה מנוסח של אשכנז וצרפת ועץ חיים, אבל יותר פשוטה וקצרה משאר הנוסחאות. נוסח פרס משונה מן הנוסחאות האמורות. מכ"י שלפני נראה שסגנון הברכה שלהם אחד הוא בין לקיץ ובין לחורף.]

לקיץ (סר"ע) ואת כל] רס"ג, בכל.

(כפא) ואת] טורין, את.

תבואתה] רומניא, טורין <וברכה כשנים הטובות>.

ותן... המבורכות] רומניא ל'.

והרוחה] טורין, ל'.

כי... הטובות והמבורכות] טורין, ל'.

בברכת] רומניא, כברכת.

ט.

149–30 B.C.E

הנוסח הקדמון

ברך עלינו ה' אלהינו את השנה הזאת לטובה בכל מיני תבואתה ברוך אתה ה' מברך השנים.

נוסח א"י

ברך עלינו ה' אלהינו את השנה הזאת לטובה בכל מיני תבואתה וקרב מהרה שנת קץ גאולתינו ותן טל ומטר על פני האדמה ושבע עולם מאוצרות טובך ותן ברכה במעשה ידינו ברוך אתה ה' מברך השנים.

נוסח חו"ל (רמב"ם)

[לקיץ] ברכנו ה' אלהינו בכל מעשה ידינו וברך את שנתנו בטללי רצון ברכה ונדבה כשנים הטובות. ברוך אתה ה' מברך השנים.

[לחורף] ברכנו ה'אלהינו בכל מעשה ידינו וברך את שנותינו ותן טל ומטר על פני האדמה ושבע את העולם כלו מטובך ורוה פני תבל מעושר מתנות ידך ושמרה והצילה ה' אלהינו את השנה הזאת ואת כל מיני תבואתה מכל מיני משחית ומכל מיני פורעניות ותן לה אחרית ותקוה שובע ושלום וברבה כשנים הטובות. ברוך אתה ה' מברך השנים.

ט. (נוסח א"י) לטובה] שב. <ולברכה>.
ותן טל ומטר... מאוצרות טובך] שב. ותן גשמי (טללי) רצון על פני האדמה ושבע עולמך מברכותי'.

(נוסח חו"ל) נוסח תימן מתאים לנוסח הרמב"ם בין לקיץ בין לחורף, ונוסח ספרד מתאים לנוסח הרמב"ם רק לקיץ.

(לקיץ) ה' אלהינו] ספרד, אבינו.

ברכה ונדבה] רמב"ם (נדפס) וברכה.

כשנים הטובות] ספרד <ותהי אחריתה חיים ושובע ושלום כשנים הטובות לברכה כי אל טוב ומטיב אתה>.

(לחורף) כלו] רמב"ם (נדפס) ל'.

מטוביך] רמב"ם (נדפס) מברכותיך.

מעושר מתנות ידך... כשנים הטובות] רמב"ם (נדפס) ח'.

וברכה כשנים הטובות] תימן. וברכה ל'.

נוסח חו"ל

ט. (חורף)

סר"ע

ברך עלינו ה' אלהינו את השנה הזאת לטובה ואת כל מיני תבואתה ותן טל ומטר על פני האדמה ושבע את העולם כלו מברכותיך ורוה פני תבל מעושר מתנות ידיך ושמרה והצילה לשנה זאת מכל מיני משחית ומכל מיני פורענות ותהא אחריתה שובע ושלום ותן ברכה במעשה ידינו.

כפא

ברך עלינו ה' אלהינו את השנה הזאת הבאה עלינו לטובה ואת כל מיני תבואתה ותן טל ומטר לברכה על כל פני האדמה ושבע את העולם כלו מברכות טובך ורוה פני תבל מעושר מתנות ידיך שמור והצל את השנה הזאת מכל מיני משחית ומכל מיני פורעניות ותהי אחריתה חיים ושבע ושלום ותן ברכה והצלחה והרוחה בכל מעשה ידינו כי אל טוב ומטיב אתה

ספרד

ברך עלינו ה' אלהינו את השנה הזאת ואת כל מיני תבואתה לטובה ותן טל ומטר לברכה על פני האדמה ורוה פני תבל ושבע את העולם כלו מטובך ומלא ידינו מברכותיך ומעושר מתנות ידיך שמרה והצילה שנה זו מכל דבר רע ומכל מיני משחית ומכל מיני פורענות ועשה לה תקוה ואחרית שלום חוס ורחם עליה ועל כל תבואתה ופירותיה וברכה בגשמי

[המשך על עמוד 315]

לחורף (סר"ע) [רס"ג, מצרים] ואת כל] רס"ג בכל. מצרים ל'.

מברכותיך] רס"ג, מצרים <מברכות טובך>.

לשנה זאת] רס"ג, לשנה הזאת. מצרים ל'.

פורענות] רס"ג <וברכה עלינו כשנים הטובות>. מצרים, <וברכה כשנים הטובות>.

ותהא... ידינו] רס"ג ל'. מצרים, ותהי [והשאר נמחק].

(כפא) [טורין, רומניא] ואת] טורין, את.

לברכה] רומניא, טורין, ל'.

כלו] טורין, ל'.

שמור] טורין, ושמור.

פורעניות] טורין, רומניא <וברכה בשנים הטובות>.

ותהי... ושלום] טורין ל'.

(ספרד) [קלא, סר"ע (נדפס) דבר רע] קלא <ומכל פגע רע>.

והרוחה] טורין ל'.

כי... המבורכות] טורין ל'.

בברכת] רומניא, כברכת.

עליה] סר"ע (נדפס) עלינו. אבודרהם, על כל תבואתה. [וז"ל אבודרהם „והמון העם קורין חוס ורחם עלינו ועל כל תבואתה ואיננו נכון"].

ופירותיה] סר"ע (נדפס) ועל כל פירותיה.

וברכה... ומברך השנים] סר"ע (נדפס) וברכה כשנים הטובות בטללי ברכה וחיים ושובע ושלום. קלא, ותהי לנו אחריתה שנת שובע חיים ברכה ושלום.

נוסח חו״ל

כפא

ותברכנו ותברך את שנותינו בברכת השנים הטובות והמבורכות.

ספרד

רצון ברכה ונדבה ותהי אחריתה חיים ושובע ושלום כשנים הטובות לברכה כי אל טוב ומטיב אתה ומברך השנים.

ברוך אתה ה׳ מברך השנים.

ט. (קיץ וחורף)

רומי

ברך עלינו ה׳ אלהינו את השנה הזאת לטובה ואת כל מיני תבואתה [(לחורף) ותן טל ומטר לברכה על פני האדמה] ושבע את העולם מברכותיך ותן ברכה רוחה והצלחה בכל מעשה ידינו וברך שנותנו כשנים הטובות המבורכות.

עץ חיים

ברך עלינו ה׳ אלהינו את השנה הזאת ואת כל מיני תבואתה לטובה ותן טל ומטר לברכה על פני האדמה ושבענו מטובך וברך את שנתנו כשנים הטובות.

פרס

ברך עלינו ה׳ אלהינו את השנה הזאת הבאה עלינו לטובה ותהי אחריתה ברכה ושבע ושלום ותן ברכה והצלחה בכל מעשה ידינו למען שמך שבענו ושבע את כל העולם כלו מברכות טוביך ורוה את פני תבל מעושר מתנות ידיך שמרה והצילה ה׳ אלהינו את השנה הזאת מכל מיני משחית ומכל מיני פורעניות המתרגשות והמתחדשות המוצאות לבא בעולם חוס וחננו וחמול ורחם עלינו והצליח לנו בכל דרכנו כי אל טוב ומטיב ורחמן וסלח אתה.

ברוך אתה ה׳ מברך השנים.

(עץ חיים) [אשכנז, ויטרי, (כ״י ונדפס) צרפת] מטובך] א, (נוסחאות אחדות) מטובה. [ועיין מה שכתב הגר״א באו״ח סי׳ רמ״א שיש לומר „מטובה״. אבל הרא״ש (שו״ת כלל ד׳ סי׳ כ׳) כתב שנכון לומר „מטובך״ ועיין במגן אברהם או״ח סי׳ קי״ז ס״ק א׳].

את שנתנו] א, ויטרי, שנותינו.

(פרס) על דבר הנוסחא הזאת עיין למעלה בהערה ראשונה לברכה זו.

נוסח חו"ל

י.

תקע בשופר גדול לחירותינו

סר"ע	רמב"ם	א
ושא נס לקבץ גליותינו וקרא דרור לקבצנו יחד מארבע כנפות הארץ.	ושא נס לקבץ את כל גליותינו מארבע כנפות הארץ לארצנו.	ושא נס לקבץ גליותינו וקבצנו יחד מארבע כנפות הארץ.

ברוך אתה ה' מקבץ נדחי עמו ישראל.

יא.

השיבה שופטינו כבראשונה ויועצינו כבתחלה

סר"ע	טורין	רמב"ם
ומלוך עלינו	ומלוך עלינו אתה לבדך בחסד וברחמים בצדק ובמשפט.	והסר ממנו יגון ואנחה ומלוך עלינו אתה לבדך ברחמים בצדק ובמשפט.

ברוך אתה ה' אוהב צדקה ומשפט.

י. (סר"ע) [רומניא, כפא, טורין] לקבץ] רומניא, טורין, לקיבוץ.
יחד] רומניא, א, כפא <מהרה>.
הארץ] ספרד, כל הארץ לארצנו. רומניא, כפא, כל הארץ אל נוה קדשך.
(א) [עץ חיים, צרפת, ויטרי, פרס] לקבץ] פרס, מהרה לקיבוץ.
וקבצנו] פרס, קבצנו.
יחד] פרס, רומי, קלא, צרפת <מהרה>.
הארץ] עץ חיים, ויטרי, כל הארץ. צרפת, כל הארץ ותוליכנו קוממיות לארצנו. פרס <אל נוה קדשך ברינה>.

יא. (סר"ע) [פרס] כבתחלה] פרס <וצדקנו ופדנו במשפט>.
ומלוך עלינו] פרס <בחסד וברחמים ואל תרשיענו בדין>.
(טורין) [רומניא, כפא, רומי, קלא] ומלוך] רומניא, כפא, רומי, ותמלוך.
עלינו] קלא <מהרה>.
אתה] רומי, קלא <ה'>.
בחסד... ובמשפט] קלא, וצדקנו במשפט בחן ובחסד וברחמים.
בצדק ובמשפט] רומניא, כפא, וצדקנו במשפט ואל נא תרשיענו בדין.
(רמב"ם) [תימן, עץ חיים, צרפת, ויטרי, א, ספרד] עלינו] ספרד <מהרה>.
אתה] עץ חיים, צרפת, ויטרי, א, ספרד <ה'>.
(צרפת) ברחמים] רמב"ם (נדפס) א, ויטרי (נדפס) בחסד וברחמים. עץ חיים, ויטרי (כ"י) בחן בחסד וברחמים.
בצדק ובמשפט] ויטרי (כ"י) צדקנו במשפט. א, עץ חיים, צרפת, וצדקנו במשפט.
אוהב] סר"ע (א' ונדפס) מצרים, רמב"ם (נדפס) רומניא, כפא, רומי, קלא, ספרד, תימן, צרפת, ויטרי, (כ"י ונדפס), א, פרס, מלך אוהב.

40–70 C. E.

הנוסח הקדמון	נוסח א"י	נוסח חו"ל (רס"ג)
תקע בשופר גדול לחירותינו ושא נס לקבצנו ברוך אתה ה' מקבץ נדחי ישראל.	תקע בשופר גדול לחירותנו ושא נס לקיבוץ גאליותינו ברוך אתה ה' מקבץ נדחי ישראל.	תקע בשופר גדול לחירותנו ושא נס מהרה לקבצנו ברוך אתה ה' מקבץ נדחי עמו ישראל.

יא.

40–70 C. E.

הנוסח הקדמון	נוסח א"י	נוסח חו"ל (רס"ג)
השיבה שופטינו כבראשונה ויועצינו כבתחלה ומלוך עלינו אתה לבדך ברוך אתה ה' אוהב המשפט.	השיבה שופטינו כבראשונה ויועצינו כבתחלה ומלוך עלינו אתה לבדך ברוך אתה ה' אוהב המשפט.	השיבה שופטינו כבראשונה ויועצינו כבתחלה. ברוך אתה ה' אוהב צדקה ומשפט.

י. (הנוסח הקדמון) ושא נס לקבצנו] עיין חלק האנגלי פרק ב'.

(נוסח א"י) ישראל] גד. עמו ישראל.

(נוסח חו"ל) נוסח מצרים מתאים לרס"ג.

יא. (נוסח א"י) ומלוך] שב. ותמלוך (השוה נוסח ר. כפא, בחו"ל).

אוהב משפט] במדרש פנים אחרים (בובער, ספרי דאגדתא על מגלת אסתר, ל"ד ע"ב) מובאה הגרסא „אוהב צדקה ומשפט", וכן הוא בילקוט שמעוני אסתר ג. ח.

(נוסח חו"ל) נוסח מצרים מתאים לנוסח רס"ג.

אוהב צדקה ומשפט] תהלים לג. ה, בדבר נוסח חתימה זו נחלקו גדולי הפוסקים. הרי"ף והמנהיג (ר"ה, ב') גורסים „האל המשפט". ור' יחיאל בן הרא"ש (מובא בטור סי' קי"ח, ובאבודרהם) כתב „שמעתי שבפרובינציא אין אומרים המלך וישר בעיני. שוב מצאתי בספר הנקרא מחזור ויטרי בפ"ק דברכות כל השנה כולה אומר האל הקדוש האל המשפט", ועיינתי במחזור ויטרי (נדפס וכ"י) ושם הגרסא „מלך אוהב צדקה ומשפט". ובקובץ תשובת הרמב"ם (הוצ' לפסיא צ"ז) כתוב: „נוסח ברכה האחת עשרה בא"י אוהב צדקה ומשפט". וכן נמצא בנוסח התפלה בכ"י המוגה של ספר אהבה ושם היה כתוב המלה „מלך" והעביר המגיה בקולמסו שיטה מלמעלה כזה <u>מלך</u>. ובספרי יד החזקה הנדפסים הגרסא „מלך אוהב". בשבלי הלקט השלם גורס במקום אחד (הוצ' בובער ט' ע"ב) „אוהב צדקה ומשפט", ובמקום **אחר** (קמ"ג ע"ב) „מלך אוהב צדקה ומשפט". ובארחות חיים הל' תפלה (י"ד ע"ג, סי' י"ז) **כ**תוב „ולא תמצא מלכות בכל אלו י"ט ברכות" [והובאו דבריו בכל בו, הלכות תפלה] וגם בסי' כ' (הלכות תפלה י"ד ע"ד) כתב „ואין לחתום בה (בברכת השיבה) מלך אצל משפט אלא מר"ה ועד יה"כ."

נוסח חו"ל

יב.

רס"ג

למשומדים אל תהי תקוה ומלכות זדון תעקר ותשבר בימינו.

סר"ע (ז)

למשומדים אל תהי תקוה והמינים כרגע יאבדו וכל אויבי עמך יכרתו ומלכות זדון מהרה תעקר ותשבר ותכניע בימינו.

ברוך אתה ה' שובר רשעים ומכניע זדים.

יב. (רס"ג) [פרס] למשומדים] פרס <ולמינים ולזדים ולכופרים ולרשעים>.

תהי] פרס <להם>.

תקוה] פרס <ותאוה>.

ותשבר] פרס <תכניע ותאבוד וכל אויבי עמך ישראל וצורריהם במהרה יכרתו ישמדו ויאבדו ואל תתן תקומה לכל אויבי נפשנו>.

(סר"ע) [רמב"ם, תימן, ספרד, קלא, רומניא, רומי, טורין, כפא, עץ חיים, צרפת, ויטרי, א']. למשומדים] קלא, ולמינים. ספרד, ולפושעים. א (נוסחאות אחדות), רומי, ולמלשינים. [וכן הוא ע"ג המחק במ' טורין].

אל] רומי, בל.

תהי] רומניא, כפא, פרס <להם>.

תקוה] סר"ע (א) <אם לא ישובו לבריתך> פרס <ותאוה>.

והמינים] רומניא, כפא, והמינים והמלשינים והכופרים והמוסרים כלם. תימן, כל המינים והמוסרים. רמב"ם (כ"י) כל המינים. רמב"ם (נדפס) וכל המינים כלם. עץ חיים, צרפת, א (נוסחאות ישנות) וכל המינים. א (נוסחאות אחדות) וכל עושי רשעה. [ויטרי (כ"י) טורין, <וכל> והתיבה שלאחריה נמחקה]. ספרד, וכל המינים וכל המלשינים. סר"ע (א) והנוצרים והמינים. קלא, וכל הזדים וכל המלשינים והמוסרות כלם.

וכל... יכרתו] רמב"ם (כ"י ונדפס) תימן, ל'. ספרד, וכל אויביך וכל שונאיך מהרה יכרתו. סר"ע (א) וכל אויבינו וכל שונאינו מהרה יכרתו. רומניא, כפא, וכל אויבינו וכל אויבי עמך [כפא <ישראל>] מהרה מארץ חיים יכרתון [כפא, יכרתו] א, רומי, וכל אויביך מהרה יכרתו. ויטרי (נדפס) וכל אויבי עמך ישראל מהרה יכרתון. עץ חיים ויטרי (כ"י) צרפת, וכל אויבי עמך בית ישראל מהרה יכרתון. קלא, וכל עושי רשעה מהרה יכרתו ותכלם ותכניעם.

ומלכות זדון] ספרד, ומלכות הרשעה. א, (נוסחאות אחדות) והזדים.

ומלכות זדון... ותכניע] קלא, ל'. [בכ"י ויטרי נמחק המשפט „ומלכות זדון... ותשבר"].

מהרה] רמב"ם (כ"י) ל'.

תעקר ותשבר] תימן, תעקור ותשבור.

ותשבר] רמב"ם (כ"י) <מהרה>. ספרד, <ותכלה> צרפת, א, עץ חיים <ותמגר>.

ותכניע] ספרד, ותכניעם. רומניא, כפא, רומי, ותכניע אותם. טורין, ותכניע אותה. עץ חיים, ותכניע ותשפיל את כל אויבינו. ויטרי (כ"י) ותכניע את כל אויבינו. צרפת. ותכניע את כל אויבינו.

בימינו] רומניא, כפא, ספרד, קלא, עץ חיים, ויטרי, צרפת, א, במהרה בימינו. רמב"ם (כ"י ונדפס) תימן, מהרה בימינו.

רשעים] מצרים(?). רמב"ם (נדפס) תימן, ספרד, עץ חיים, ויטרי (כ"י ונדפס), צרפת, א, רומניא, כפא, רומי, טורין, פרס, אויבים. קלא, המינים. [בכ"י הרמב"ם נכתב מראשונה „אויבים" ונמשכה שטה תוך המלה וכתוב למעלה „רשעים". וגם בתשובת ר' נטרונאי גאון הובאה הגרסא „רשעים" (שו"ת הגאונים מן הגניזה, הוצ' גינזבערג, עמ' קי"ט).

יב.

90–117 C. E.

הנוסח הקדמון

למשומדים אל תהי תקוה ומלכות זדון תעקר בימינו. ברוך אתה ה׳ מכניע זדים.

נוסח א״י

למשומדים אל תהי תקוה ומלכות זדון מהרה תעקר והנוצרים והמינים כרגע יאבדו ימחו מספר חיים ועם צדיקים אל יכתבו. ברוך אתה ה׳ מכניע זדים.

יב. למשומדים] על דבר ברכה זו עיין מה שכתב קרויס ברבעון האנגלי, שנה ו׳, עמ׳ קל״ג, ומרקס, בהוספות ושנויים לסדר רב עמרם, (יאהרבוך שנה ה׳, עמ׳ שנ״ג).

תקוה] שב. <אם לא ישובו לתורתך> [השוה גרסת סר״ע (א)].

ימחו מספר חיים] שב. ל׳.

נוסח חז"ל

יג.

על הצדיקים ועל החסידים ועל גרי הצדק יהמו רחמיך ה' אלהינו ותן שכר טוב לכל הבוטחים בשמך באמת

רס"ג	סר"ע
ולא יבושו	ושים חלקנו עמהם ולעולם לא נבוש.

ברוך אתה ה' משען ומבטח לצדיקים.

יד.

סר"ע	רמב"ם
על ירושלים עירך ברחמים תשוב ובנה אותה בנין עולם בימינו.	תשכון בתוך ירושלים עירך כאשר דברת ובנה אותה בנין עולם במהרה בימינו.

ברוך אתה ה' בונה ירושלים.

יג. על... החסידים] רמב"ם, רומי, כפא, טורין, על החסידים ועל הצדיקים.

החסידים] סר"ע (א) <ועל שארית עמך ישראל>. ספרד, <ועל שארית עמך בית ישראל ועל פליטת בית סופריהם>. קלא, <ועל שארית עמך בית ישראל ועל זקניהם ועל פליטת בית סופריהם>. א, ויטרי (נדפס) <ועל זקני עמך בית ישראל ועל פליטת סופריהם>. צרפת, עץ חיים, <ועל זקני עמך בית ישראל ועל פליטת בית סופריהם> [ועיין ברש"י נדרים מ"ט ע"ב ד"ה אמריעי שהביא הגירסא <ועל פליטת סופריהם>].

הצדק] תימן, רמב"ם (כ"י ונדפס) <ועל שארית עמך בית ישראל> פרס <ועל שארית עמך ישראל>. ר, כפא, טורין, ספרד, קלא, עץ חיים, ויטרי (כ"י ונדפס) א <ועלינו>.

יהמו] רומי, פרס, ספרד, עלא ,סר"ע (א' ונדפס) עץ חיים, צרפת, ויטרי, (כ"י ונדפס) א <נא>.

רחמיך] רומניא, כפא <הרבים>.

ותן] רומניא <לה>.

לכל] רומניא, ולכל.

בשמך] ויטרי (כ"י) את שמך.

באמת] רס"ג, ויטרי (כ"י ונדפס) עץ חיים, ל'. רמב"ם (נדפס) באמת הטוב. רומניא, כפא, שד"ל, הטוב באמת.

ושים] לנוסח רס"ג מתאים נוסח מצרים.

(סר"ע) [רמב"ם, תימן, קלא, ספרד, צרפת, ויטרי, א, עץ חיים, רומניא, כפא, רומי, טורין, פרס].

(סר"ע) צרפת, ויטרי (כ"י) ותן.

ולעולם] טורין, רומניא, כפא, רומי, תימן, ויטרי (כ"י) סר"ע (א), א, לעולם. פרס, ל'.

לא] א, פרס, ולא.

ולעולם... נבוש] צרפת, לא נבוש לעולם ועד.

נבוש] סר"ע (א) טורין, ויטרי (נדפס) א, <כי בך בטחנו>. ויטרי (כ"י) <כי בך נשעננו ובשמך בטחנו>. עץ חיים <כי בך בטחנו ובשמך נשעננו>. פרס <כי בשמך הגדול והקדוש בטחנו>. רמב"ם (כ"י) תימן <כי בשמך בטחנו ולישועתך נשענו> רומי <כי בך בטחנו מלך עולמים>. רומניא, כפא, <כי בשמך הגדול בטחנו ועל חסדך נשענו>. ספרד, קלא <כי בך בטחנו ועל חסדך הגדול באמת נשענו [קלא, נשעננו]>. [אבודרהם: הגדול ל']. צרפת <כי בשמך הגדול בטחנו ובחסדך נשעננו>.

יד. (סר"ע) [רומניא, כפא, רומי, טורין, עץ חיים, צרפת, ויטרי, א].

(סר"ע) על ירושלים] עץ חיים, צרפת, ויטרי (כ"י ונדפס) א, רומי, ולירושלים.

תשוב] א, ויטרי (נדפס) <ותשכון בתוכה [נ"א לתוכה] כאשר דברת>. טורין, כפא, צרפת, ויטרי (כ"י) עץ חיים, צרפת <ותשכון בתוכה כאשר דברת וכסא דוד מהרה לתוכה תכין>. סר"ע (נדפס) <ושכון בתוכה כאשר דברת>.

יג.

90–117 C. E.

הנוסח הקדמון

על גרי הצדק יהמו רחמיך ותן לנו שכר טוב עם עושי רצונך. ברוך אתה ה׳ מבטח לצדיקים.

נוסח ה״ז

על גרי הצדק יהמו רחמיך ותן לנו שכר טוב עם עושי רצונך. ברוך אתה ה׳ מבטח לצדיקים.

יד.

168–165 B. C. E.

הנוסח הקדמון

רחם ה׳ אלהינו על ישראל עמך על ירושלם עירך ועל ציון משכן כבודך ועל מזבחך ועל היכלך. ברוך אתה ה׳ בונה ירושלם.

נוסח א״י

רחם ה׳ אלהינו ברחמיך הרבים על ישראל עמך ועל ירושלם עירך ועל ציון משכן כבודך ועל מעונך ועל היכלך ועל מלכות בית דוד משיח צדקך. ברוך אתה ה׳ אלהי דוד בונה ירושלם.

נוסח חו״ל (רס״ג)

רחם ה׳ אלהינו עלינו על ישראל עמך ועל ירושלם עירך ועל היכלך ועל מעונך ועל ציון משכן כבודך ובנה ברחמים את ירושלם. ברוך אתה ה׳ בונה ירושלם.

יג. ותן] שב. תן.

מבטח לצדיקים] עיין תוספתא ברכות ג. כה.

יד. (הנוסח הקדמון) ועל מזבחך] לדעתי יש לנסח כן ע״פ מה שמובא מברכת ירושלים בברכה מעין שלש, ועיין בחלק האנגלי הוספה ב׳.

(נוסח א״י) ברחמיך הרבים על ישראל עמך] שג. עלינו.

ועל... צדקך] שג. ועל מלכות בית דוד משיחך בנה ביתך שכלל היכלך.

(נוסח חו״ל) נוסח מצרים ופרס מתאים לרס״ג.

רחם] פרס. רחמנו רחם.

ועל היכלך ועל מעונך] פרס, ל׳.

ובנה... ירושלם] פרס, ובנה את ירושלים בבנין עולם כאשר דברת.

נוסח חו"ל

טו.

את צמח דוד מהרה תצמיח

רס"ג

וקרנו תרים בישועתך.

עץ חיים

וקרנו תרום בישועתך כי לישועתך
קוינו כל היום.

ברוך אתה ה' מצמיח קרן ישועה.

טז.

שמע קולנו ה' אלהינו ורחם עלינו וקבל ברחמים וברצון את תפלתנו

סר"ע (ז)

כי אל שומע תפלותינו ותחנונינו אתה
מעולם.

רומי

כי אב מלא רחמים רבים אתה הוא
מעולם ולא נשוב ריקם מלפניך כי
אל שומע תפלה ותחנון אתה.

ובנה] כפא, ותבנה.

אותה] א, ויטרי (כ"י ונדפס) <בקרוב בימינו>.

בימינו] א, ויטרי (כ"י ונדפס) ל', רומניא, רומי, במהרה בימינו. א, ויטרי (כ"י ונדפס) <וכסא דוד מהרה לתוכה תכין>.

(רמב"ם) [ספרד, קלא, תימן] דברת] ספרד, קלא <וכסא דוד מהרה לתוכה תכין>.

בנין... בימינו] קלא, בקרוב בימינו בנין עולם.

טו. דוד] עץ חיים, ויטרי (כ"י ונדפס), א, רומי, רומניא, כפא, ספרד, קלא <עבדך>.

מהרה] רס"ג, מצרים, עתה, צרפת, ויטרי (כ"י ונדפס) <אתה> רומי, במהרה.

(רס"ג) [מצרים, סר"ע, תימן] תרים] רמב"ם (נדפס), תימן, תרום. מצרים <בימינו>.

(עץ חיים) [רמב"ם (כ"י), ספרד, קלא, צרפת, ויטרי, א, סר"ע (א' ונדפס), רומניא, כפא, רומי, טורין, פרס] כל היום] סר"ע (א' ונדפס) ח'.

מצמיח] פרס <לנו>.

ישועה] תימן, הישועה, טורין, לישועה. ר. כפא, <לעמו ישראל>.

טז. שמע] ספרד, כפא, אב הרחמן שמע. קלא, אב הרחמן ברחמיך הרבים שמע. פרס, אב הרחמן אנא שמע. [אבודרהם, שמע].

ורחם עלינו] פרס, שמע.

ורחם] רס"ג, תימן, קלא, א, ויטרי (נדפס) חוס ורחם. רומניא, כפא, טורין, רומי, חוס וחנינו ורחם. עץ חיים, ויטרי (כ"י) צרפת, חוס נא ורחם. רמב"ם (נדפס) וחוס ורחם. [ובכ"י היה כתוב „חוס וחמול", והעביר המגיה שיטה על המלה „וחמול" וכתב למעלה „ורחם"].

עלינו] ר, כפא <והושיענו>.

וברצון] רס"ג, ל'. רמב"ם (כ"י) תימן, ורצון.

תפלתנו] רומי <ואת תחנתנו> רומניא, כפא, <ואת תחנתנו כי אליך עינינו>.

(סר"ע) [רומניא, כפא, מצרים] תפלותינו ותחנונינו] רומניא, כפא, תפלה ותחנונים.

אתה] רומניא, כפא, <הוא>.

ולא] רומניא, כפא, לא.

רחמים אתה] רומניא, כפא, רחמים רבים ונאמן אתה ושמע נא אל בקול תפלתינו כאשר שמעת לתפלת אבותינו הצדיקים בימי קדם.

(רומי) [טורין] הוא מעולם] טורין ל'.

ולא] טורין, לא.

אל] טורין <מלך>.

טו.

Pre-Maccabean

הנוסח הקדמון

שמע ה' אלהינו בקולנו ורחם עלינו. ברוך אתה ה' שומע תפלה.

נוסח א"י

שמע ה' אלהינו בקול תפלתינו ורחם עלינו כי אל חנון ורחום אתה. ברוך אתה ה' שומע תפלה.

נוסח חו"ל (רס"ג)

שמע קולנו ה' אלהינו חוס ורחם עלינו וקבל ברחמים את תפלתנו ומלא ברחמיך הרבים כל משאלות לבנו. ברוך אתה ה' שומע תפלה.

טו. (נוסח א"י) שמע... תפלתנו] שנ. שמע בקולנו.

נוסח חו"ל

רמב"ם

[כי אל שומע תפלות ותחנונים אתה ומלפניך] מלכנו ריקם אל תשיבנו.

פרס

ושמע נאקתנו כאשר שמעת את נאקת אבותינו וריקם מלפניך אל תשיבנו מלכנו והעתר לנו מלכנו בתפלתנו טרם נקרא ואתה תעננו למענך ושמע תפלתנו כי אל שומע תפלה ותחנונים אתה שומע תפלה עדיך כל בשר יבאו.

ברוך אתה ה' שומע תפלה.

יז.

רצה ה' אלהינו בעמך ישראל

סר"ע

ובתפלתם והשב עבודה לדביר ביתך ואשה ישראל ותפלתם מהרה באהבה תקבל ברצון ותהי לרצון תמיד עבודת ישראל עמך.

קלא

ושכון בציון מהרה ויעבדוך בניך בירושלים ואתה ברחמיך הרבים תחפוץ בנו ותרצנו.

(רמב"ם) [תימן, ספרד, קלא, עץ חיים, צרפת, ויטרי, א.].

כי... מלפניך] המוסגר לא נמצא ברמב"ם לא בנדפס ולא בכ"י. וגם בתימן חסר עד המלה „ומלפניך".

ומלפניך] ויטרי (כ"י), תימן, ספרד, מלפניך.

חשיבנו] ויטרי (נדפס) <ועניבו>. ויטרי (כ"י) <ועננו אלהינו>. צרפת <ועננו ה' אלהינו>. ספרד <חננו ועננו ושמע תפלתינו>. קלא <ועננו אבינו>.

כל פה] ויטרי (כ"י ונדפס) עץ חיים. צרפת, א, עמך ישראל ברחמים.

יז. ישראל] רס"ג ל'. ויטרי (כ"י) בית ישראל.

(סר"ע) [רס"ג, רמב"ם, תימן, טורין, רומניא, כפא, רומי, ספרד, ויטרי, א'].

ובתפלתם] סר"ע (ז) רומניא, טורין, רמב"ם (נדפס) עץ חיים, ובתפלתם שעה, רמב"ם (כ"י), תימן, ספרד, פרס (ר"ה), ולתפלתם שעה. רומי, ואל תפלתם שעה.

עבודה] רומניא, כפא, עבודת כהנים, רומי, ויטרי (כ"י ונדפס), ספרד, פרס (ר"ה), העבודה. א, את העבודה.

(קלא) [עץ חיים] מהרה] עץ חיים, עירך.

ישראל] רומניא, כפא <בעבודתם>. פרס <היום הוא תפלתם>.

ותפלתם] פרס <ועבודתם>.

מהרה באהבה] רס"ג, ל'. תימן, מהרה, א, באהבה, פרס, במהרה באהבה.

ברצון] פרס, ברחמיך וברצון.

ותהי] כפא <נא>.

ישראל עמך] רס"ג, ישראל. רומניא, עמך כל בית ישראל בימינו. כפא, עמך כל בית ישראל בימינו ותחפוץ בנו ותרצנו. פרס (ר"ה) <ותחפוץ בנו ותרצנו>.

עמך] טורין, בימינו (השוה הגהה הקודמת), תימן, ותרצנו. ספרד, <ותחפץ בנו ותרצנו>. פרס, (כל השנה) <בימינו ותרצה בנו>.

תחפוץ] עץ חיים, תשוב ותחפוץ.

ותרצנו] עץ חיים. <ותערב לפניך תפלתנו כעולה וכקרבן אנא רחום ברחמיך הרבים השב שכינתך לציון עירך וסדר העבודה לירושלים>.

טז.

Pre-Christian; Perhaps pre-Maccabean

הנוסח הקדמון

רצה ה׳ אלהינו........................
....
....?
ברוך אתה ה׳ שאותך נירא ונעבוד.

נוסח א״י

רצה ה׳ אלהינו ושכון בציון
ויעבדוך עבדיך בירושלים [אנא
רחום ברחמיך הרבים השב שכינתך
לציון עירך וסדר העבודה לירושלם]
ברוך אתה ה׳ שאותך נירא ונעבוד.

טז. רצה... בירושלם] מובא בויקרא ו׳ ז. ב. ובפסקתא דר״כ קנ״ח ע״ב, וגם בתשובות הגאונים מן הגניזה (הוצ׳ גינזבערג) עמ׳ קי״ט.

אנא... לירושלם] חסר בכ״י של הגניזה, ומובא במדרש תהלים י״ז (הוצ׳ בובער פ״ד ע״א), ובמדרש שמואל ל״א ומן המדרשים מובא ברוקח סי׳ שכ״ב.

רחום ברחמיך הרבים] רוקח ח׳.

יראו] שג. ביראה, באשכול (עמ׳ י״ט) מביא מירושלמי הגרסא שאותך לבדך ביראה נעבוד.

נוסח חו"ל

ותחזינה עינינו בשובך לציון ברחמים. ברוך אתה ה' המחזיר שכינתו לציון.

יח.

מודים אנחנו לך שאתה הוא ה' אלהינו

סר"ע (ז)

צור חיינו מגן ישענו לדור ודור נודה לך ונספר תהלתך.

מצרים

ואלהי אבותינו

רמב"ם

צור חיינו מגן ישענו אתה הוא לדור ודור נודה לך ונספר תהלתך

עץ חיים

ואלהי אבותינו לעולם ועד צור חיינו מגן ישענו אתה הוא לדור ודור נודה לך ונספר תהלתך

על חיינו המסורים בידיך ועל נשמותינו הפקודות לך

עינינו] פרס (כל השנה) <עין בעין>.

לציון] הימן. לנוך לציון. ויטרי (כ"י), קלא, פרס (ר"ה). לציון ולירושלים עירך. צרפת, עץ חיים, לציון ולירושלים עירך ברחמים כמאז. פרס (כל השנה) לנוך לציון כמו אז.

ברחמים] רס"ג. <ותרצה בנו כמו אז>. רומניא, כפא, <כמאז וכשנים קדמוניות>. ויטרי (נדפס וכ"י) קלא, רומי, טורין, תימן, <כמאז>.

המחזיר] רומניא, כפא, המשיב, רומי, <ברחמיו>, טורין. <מהרה>. פרס. <במהרה>. [ובשבלי הלקט סי' י"ב, הוצ' בובער] ט' ע"ב, הגרסא „המחזיר מהרה שכינתו לציון".

יח. לך] פרס (נוסח אחד) <ומספרים את גדלך ומברכים את שמך כורעים ומשתחווים ומתפללים ומתחננים לפני כסא כבודך באמת>.

שאתה] רס"ג, אתה.

סר"ע (ז) [קלא, רומניא, כפא, טורין, רומי] צור... תהלתך] רומניא, כפא, טורין, רומי, לעולם ועד.

צור] קלא, צורנו צור.

מגן] קלא, ומגן.

לך] טורין <על ניסיך וטובותיך שבכל עת ערב ובקר וצהרים>. קלא <ועל נסיך נפלאותיך וטובותיך שבכל יום עמנו עת ערב ובקר וצהרים> סר"ע (א) רומי <ועל נסיך שבכל יום ויום עמנו ועל נפלאותיך וטובותיך שבכל עת ערב ובקר וצהרים>.

יז.

Pre-Christian; perhaps, Pre-Maccabean.

הנוסח הקדמון

מודים אנחנו לך אתה
הוא ה' אלהינו............
?..............................
ברוך אתה ה' הטוב
לך להודות.

נוסח א"י

מודים אנחנו לך אתה
הוא ה' אלהינו ואלהי
אבותינו על כל הטובות
החסד והרחמים שגמלתנו
ושעשית עמנו ועם אבותינו
מלפנינו ואם אמרנו מטה
רגלינו חסדך ה' יסעדנו.
ברוך אתה ה' הטוב לך
להודות.

נוסח חו"ל (רס"ג)

מודים אנחנו לך אתה
הוא ה' אלהינו ואלהי
אבותינו לעולם ועד על
חיינו המסורים בידיך
ועל נשמותינו הפקודות
לך ועל ניסיך ורחמיך
שבכל עת ערב ובקר
ועל כלם תתברך
ותתרומם כי יחיד אתה
ואין זולתך. ברוך אתה
ה' הטוב שמך ולך נאה
להודות.

יז. שגמלתנו ,שעשית עמנו] שג. [(על הגליון) שגמלת] אשר עשית.
ואם... יסעדנו] שג. כי מלך אל טוב ומטיב אתה.

נוסח חו"ל

סר"ע (ז)

הטוב כי לא כלו רחמיך המרחם כי לא תמו חסדיך כי מעולם קוינו לך לא הכלמתנו ה' אלהינו ולא תעזבנו ולא תסתר פניך ממנו ועל כלם יתברך ויתרומם שמך מלכנו לעולם ועד וכל החיים יודוך סלה ויהללו לשמך הטוב באמת.

מצרים

ועל נסיך שבכל יום עמנו ועל נפלאותיך וטובותיך שבכל עת ערב ובקר ועל כלם יתברך ויתרומם שמך מלכנו לעולם ועד וכל החיים יודוך סלה.

רמב"ם

על נסיך ונפלאותיך שבכל עת ועת ערב ובקר וצהרים הטוב כי לא כלו רחמיך המרחם כי לא תמו חסדיך כל החיים יודוך סלה כי טוב האל הטוב.

עץ חיים

ועל נסיך שבכל יום עמנו ועל נפלאותיך וטובותיך שבכל עת ערב ובקר וצהרים הטוב כי לא כלו רחמיך והמרחם כי לא תמנו חסדיך כי מעולם קוינו לך ועל כלם יתברך

[המשך על עמוד 167]

המרחם] קלא, והמרחם.

כי לא] כפא, וכי לא.

כי מעולם] טורין, מעולם. רומי, ומעולם.

קוינו לך] רומניא, כפא, רבות קוינוך.

תעזבנו] סר"ע (א), קלא, רומניא, כפא, רומי, טורין, עזבתנו.

תסתר] סר"ע (א), קלא, רומניא, כפא, רומי, טורין, הסתרת.

יתברך ויתרומם] רומניא, כפא, יתרומם ויתברך וישתבח. קלא, יתברך ויתרומם ויתנשא תמיד.

מלכנו] טורין, רומי, תמיד.

וכל] רומי, טורין, כל.

ויהללו] רומניא, כפא <ויברכו ויודו>, קלא <ויברכו>.

לשמך] קלא, את שמך.

הטוב באמת] רומניא, חי העולמים ונודה לך.

(מצרים) [פרס] אבותינו] פרס <לעולם ועד>.

נשמותינו] פרס <מלכנו>.

ועל נסיך... ובקר] פרס, נסיך נפלאותיך טובותיך רחמיך וחסדיך אשר בכל יום ובכל עת תעשה עמנו והטוב כי לא כלו רחמיך והמרחם כי לא יתמו חסדיך.

ויתרומם שמך] פרס <וישתבח שמך חסרך לעד>.

לעולם ועד] פרס ל'.

סלה] פרס <באמת חי העולמים בעל הרחמים מלך מלכי המלכים רבון של העולמים יודע הנעלמים כי אל מלא רחמים כי יחיד אתה ואין זולתך ונודה לשמך ואתה חי לבדך הטוב>.

הטוב שמך] פרס, הטוב צדיק שמך.

(רמב"ם) [תימן] ונפלאותיך] תימן, וטובותיך.

יודוך סלה] תימן, יהללו את שמך הגדול [וכן נמצא על הגליון ברמב"ם כ"י].

(עץ חיים) [ספרד, ויטרי, צרפת, א] מגן] ספרד, ומגן. שבכל עת] ויטרי (כ"י) צרפת, שבכל יום עת.

והמרחם] ויטרי (כ"י) צרפת, ספרד, המרחם.

תמנו] א, תמו.

כי מעולם] ויטרי (כ"י) א, מעולם.

נוסח חו"ל

עץ חיים

ויתרומם שמך מלכנו וכל החיים
יודוך סלה ויהללו לשמך האל
ישועתנו ועזרתנו סלה האל הטוב.
ברוך אתה ה' הטוב שמך ולך נאה להודות.

ויתרומם] ויטרי (כ"י) צרפת <תמיד>. ויטרי (נדפס) <וישתבח תמיד>. ספרד <ויתנשא תמיד>.
מלכנו] ספרד, ויטרי (כ"י ונדפס) צרפת, א, <לעולם ועד>.
ויהללו] ספרד <ויברכו>.
לשמך] א, את שמך באמת. צרפת, שמך הגדול. ספרד, את שמך הגדול באמת לעולם כי טוב.
האל ישועתנו... האל הטוב] צרפת, סלה באמת. ויטרי (נדפס) האל הטוב.
האל הטוב] א, ח'.

נוסח חו"ל

יט.

סר"ע

שים שלום טובה וברכה חסד
ורחמים עלינו ועל ישראל עמך
וברכנו אבינו כלנו כאחד באור פניך
כי במאור פניך נתת לנו ה' אלהינו
תורת חיים אהבה חסד צדקה

קלא

שלום רב על ישראל עמך תשים
לעולם ועד כי אתה הוא מלך אדון
על כל השלום וטוב בעיניך לברכנו
ולברך את עמך ישראל בכל יום
ובכל שעה בשלומך.

יט. (סר"ע) [מצרים, רמב"ם, תימן, ספרד, עץ חיים, ויטרי, צרפת, פרס, רומניא, כפא, טורין, ותפלת שחרית באשכנז].

חסד] סר"ע (א), רמב"ם, תימן, רומניא, כפא, ספרד, רומי, ויטרי (נדפס וכ"י) צרפת, א, חן וחסד.

ורחמים] ויטרי (כ"י) ל'. רומניא, כפא, וריוח ורחמים. פרס, בריוח ורחמים ברכה ושלום. צרפת, ורחמים וחיים ושלום.

כל] מצרים, תימן, טורין, ל'.

(קלא) [סר"ע (א) תפלת מנחה, א, מנחה וערבית].

ועד] סר"ע (א), א, ל'.

אל] א, סר"ע (א) ל'.

אדון... השלום] סר"ע (א) ואדון השלום.

וברכנו] רומניא, כפא, טורין, פרס, עץ חיים, ויטרי (כ"י ונדפס) רומי, א, צרפת, ברכנו.

אבינו] סר"ע (א) רמב"ם, תימן, אבודרהם, ל'.

כלנו] פרס, כלם [ולמטה נכתב „כלנו", ועיין בשבלי הלקט סי' כ"ד (הוצ' בובער י"א ע"ב) שגרס גם כן „ברכנו אבינו כלם כאחד".

כאחד] רומניא, כפא, ספרד, יחד.

באור פניך] פרס, רמב"ם (כ"י) ממאור פניך.

כי באור] תימן, רמב"ם (כ"י), כי ממאור. מצרים, כי במאור. פרס, כי ממאור.

ה' אלהינו] רומניא ל'. פרס, ה' אלהינו ואלהי אבותינו.

תורת] מצרים, רמב"ם, תימן, ספרד, תורה וחיים. פרס, תורה וטובה.

אהבה וחסד] רומניא, חן וחסד. כפא, אהבה חן וחסד. ויטרי (כ"י ונדפס) עץ חיים, צ, אהבת חסד. א, ואהבת חסד. פרס, אהבה וחיים חן וחסד.

צדקה ורחמים ושלום] רמב"ם (כ"י), תימן, צדקה ושלום. פרס, צדקה ורחמים ישועה וכבוד ארוכה ומרפא ברכה ושלום. ספרד, צדקה ורחמים ברכה ושלום. ויטרי (כ"י) א, צדקה וברכה ורחמים וחיים ושלום. צרפת, עץ חיים, וצדקה וברכה ורחמים וחיים ושלום יהיה לנו. רומניא, כפא, חן וחסד צדקה ברכה ישועה רחמים רבים ושלום. רומי, צדקה ברכה ישועה ורחמים וחיים ושלום.

וטוב... בשלומך] סר"ע (א) ל'.

לברכנו ולברך] א, לברך.

בכל... עת] א, בכל עת.

יח.

40–70 C. E.

הנוסח הקדמון

שים שלומך על ישראל עמך ועל עירך ועל נחלתך וברכנו כלנו כאחד. ברוך אתה ה׳ עושה השלום.

נוסח א״י

שים שלומך על ישראל עמך ועל עירך ועל נחלתך וברכנו כלנו כאחד: ברוך אתה ה׳ עושה השלום.

יט.

נוסח חו״ל (רס״ג)

שים שלום טובה וברכה עלינו חן וחסד ורחמים וברכנו כלנו כאחד במאור פניך כי ממאור פניך נתת לנו ה׳ אלהינו תורה וחיים אהבה וחסד צדקה ורחמים וטוב בעיניך לברך את עמך ישראל בכל עת, שים שלום בעולם ועל ישראל יהי נא שלום מעתה ועד עולם. ברוך אתה ה׳ המברך את עמו ישראל בשלום.

יח. שים... כאחד] שג. שים שלוהך על ישראל כן תברכנו כלנו בשלום מעון הברכות ועושה השלום.

סר"ע

ורחמים ושלום וטוב בעיניך לברך
את עמך ישראל בכל עת.

ברוך אתה ה' המברך את עמו ישראל בשלום.

וטוב... בכל עת] פרס, אל משים שלום גדול מעתה ועד עולם.
וטוב] רומניא, כפא, רומי <יהיה>.
את] רומניא, כפא, ספרד, את כל.
בכל עת] רמב"ם (כ"י) בשלום. תימן, בכל עת בשלום. רומי, עץ חיים, ויטרי (כ"י ונדפס) א, בכל עת ובכל שעה בשלומך. רומניא, כפא, תמיד בשלומך. ספרד, ברוב עוז ושלום.
את עמו ישראל] פרס <ועדתו>.
על כל] א, לכל.
המברך... בשלום] בעשי"ת אומרים „עושה השלום" לפי מנהג אשכנז, ומשבלי הלקט (י"ח הוצ' בובער ט' ע"א) נראה שכן היתה גרסתו בתפלת כל השנה. וכן הובא בראבי"ה ברכות מ"ג ע"א ועיין הערת העורך שם.

CHAPTER 12

THE BIRKAT HA-MAZON

By Louis Finkelstein, Jewish Theological Seminary of America

I

The command to recite the Grace after Meals (*Birkat Ha-Mazon*) is found by Tradition in the verse "and thou shalt eat and be satisfied and bless the Lord, thy God, for the good land which He hath given Thee" (Deuteronomy 8.10). Without entering into the question whether this interpretation of the passage is literal or midrashic the very ascription of Pentateuchal authority to the *Birkat Ha-Mazon* shows it to be of high antiquity. It throws no light, however, on the age of the text of the Grace. To discover this we must apply to the text the rules of critical and historical study.

A number of scholars[1]—Berliner, Schwab, Mann, Greenstone and Abrahams—have published new texts of the Grace from manuscripts. But no effort has been made to gather the various versions and to establish the original form of the benedictions. So far as fixing the date of the benedictions is concerned, we have hardly advanced beyond

[1] Berliner in *Magazin*, III, 52 (*Ozar Tob*, 1878, p. 016); Israel Abrahams in *JQR*, X (1898), p. 46; J. Greenstone in *ZfHB*, XV, (1911), 122ff.; Moise Schwab in *Le Manuscript Hébreu* No. 1388, p. 13; and Mann in *Hebrew Union College Annual*, II, pp. 335-338. I have greatly benefited by suggestions and criticisms given me in this, as in previous studies, by Professors Louis Ginzberg, Alexander Marx and Israel Davidson. Professor Marx also permitted me to include in this paper a number of suggestions and texts which he had presented in an unpublished article on the same subject. I have also to thank Dr. Cyrus Adler for a number of very helpful suggestions in the preparation of this article.

Reprinted from *Jewish Quarterly Review*, New Series, Volume 19, 1929.

the statement made some sixteen centuries ago by R. Naḥman in Babylonia:[2]

> "Moses formulated the first benediction when the manna came down from Heaven; Joshua the second when Israel entered the Land; David composed the prayer for Jerusalem; Solomon added to it the prayer for the Temple;[3] while the fourth benediction was established by the Sages at Jabneh when permission was granted to bury those slain at Bether."

Yet there can be no doubt regarding the importance of fixing the original texts and the dates of the four benedictions of the *Birkat Ha-Mazon*. In the liturgical service of the Jewish home it occupies much the same outstanding position that the *Amidah* holds in the synagogue service. Together these prayers helped to make possible the continuance of a full and complete Jewish life after the destruction of Jerusalem. Furthermore the *Birkat Ha-Mazon* contains much information which might be utilized in discovering further facts concerning the growth of rabbinic thought and institutions. The universalism of the first, the special mention of the Torah and the Abrahamitic covenant in the second, and the prayer for Jerusalem and the Davidic dynasty in the third benediction are significant as reflecting the state of mind of the generations in which they were composed and developed. It is the purpose of this paper to make an historical study of the *Birkat Ha-Mazon* and to establish what were probably the earliest forms of the benedictions.

[2] Berakot 48b. The general opinion of the commentators is that this refers only to the formulation of the prayers; the injunction that they be recited is biblical. See, for example, R. Yeruḥam, *Sefer Adam ve-Ḥavvah* 16.8.

[3] Literally, David established the phrase: על ישראל עמך ועל ירושלים עירך while Solomon added: ועל הבית הגדול והקדוש.

II

While R. Naḥman, living in the third century, was quite certain of the date of each benediction, the older Tannaitic sources are not so definite. All agree, however, that the first three benedictions are very old and that the fourth was instituted by the Sages.[4] These traditions may be clarified and in part corroborated by external evidence.

Of some importance in this connection is the early Christian prayer of thanks preserved in the *Didache*, Chapter X (Teaching of the Twelve Apostles, ed. Hitchcock and Brown, p. 18).[5] This prayer contains three benedictions, each ending in a doxology. While these benedictions differ in spirit and content from those of the Jewish Grace, it is evident that the deviations were made intentionally and they are such as we might expect early Christian authors to introduce in a Jewish prayer.

The Jewish *Birkat Ha-Mazon* naturally contained in its early forms only an expression of thanks for the food which had been eaten and for the fertile land which had been given Israel. A prayer for Jerusalem and the Temple was also appended. The mention of the Abrahamitic Covenant as something for which one should be thankful, obviously dates from a period of persecution when its practice was prohibited. Similarly we know that the mention of Torah dates from the second century. The Christian prayer evidently expresses the feeling of men who were out of sympathy with those who thanked God for these blessings of

[4] See Berakot, *ibid.* According to J. Berakot 8.1 (11a) R. Ishmael held that the fourth benediction as well as the *Birkat Ha-Zimmum* (to be discussed below) were biblical but it is probable that R. Ishmael's *derashah* was intended originally merely to fortify an argument for the introduction of the fourth benediction.

[5] The close resemblance which this prayer bears to the *Birkat Ha-Mazon* has already been pointed out by Kohler in the *J. E.*, IV, p. 587, article *Didache*. The following translation is taken from Hitchcock and Brown.

everyday life. Partly because of their asceticism, partly because of the fact that the *Birkat Ha-Mazon* was already a long established institution in their day, the authors of the prayer in the *Didache* say: "Both food and drink didst Thou give to men for enjoyment in order that they might give thanks to Thee *but to us Thou hast graciously given spiritual food and eternal life*." The slur upon the Jews is evident. In the second paragraph the Jewish benediction for the land is replaced by the following: "We thank Thee, holy Father, for Thy holy name which Thou hast caused to dwell in our hearts." Again we recognize the emphasis on the spiritual as opposed to the material blessing. And finally the prayer for Jerusalem and the Temple were replaced by a prayer for the well-being of the Church. As a further attempt at spiritualizing the prayer, the words of gratitude for food, which correspond to the first benedictions of the Jewish Grace, were put after the benediction for God's Name and the gift of knowledge, faith and immortality which take the place of the Jewish benediction for the Land (*Birkat Ha-Arez*).

Anyone acquainted with the changes made even by modern revisers[6] in their attempt to give a more spiritual

[6] Thus in most reform prayer books the benediction ברוך אתה ה' מחיה המתים has been replaced by ברוך אתה ה' נוטע בתוכנו חיי עולם. Even more significant are the changes that have been made in the prayer for peace (שים שלום) of the *Amidah*. It may help the reader who is more impressed by the deviations of the Christian prayer from the Jewish than by its similarity to it, to compare the traditional prayer for peace with the form given it in the Union Prayer Book.

Askenazic Prayer Book	*Union Prayer Book*
Grant peace, welfare, blessing, lovingkindness, and mercy unto us and unto all Israel, Thy people. Bless us, O our Father, even all of us together with the light of Thy countenance; for by the light of Thy countenance Thou hast given us, O Lord, our God, the Law of life, lovingkindness and righteous-	Grant us peace, Thy most precious gift, O Thou eternal source of peace, and enable Israel to be a messenger of peace unto the peoples of the earth. Bless our country that it may ever be a stronghold of peace and be its advocate in the councils of nations. May contentment reign within its bor-

and sophisticated tone to ancient prayers, will recognize at once the close relationship between the *Birkat Ha-Mazon* and the Christian prayer of thanks, when the two are put side by side, paragraph by paragraph.

Birkat Ha-Mazon	*Didache*
I	II
Blessed art Thou, O Lord, our God, King of the Universe, Who feedest the whole world with goodness, with grace and with mercy.	Thou, Master Almighty, didst create all things for Thy name's sake; both food and drink Thou didst give to men for enjoyment in order that they might give thanks to Thee, but to us Thou hast graciously given spiritual food and eternal life through Thy servant. Before all things, we thank Thee that Thou art mighty;
Blessed art Thou, O, Lord, Who feedest all.	To Thee be the glory forever.
ness, blessing, mercy, life and peace; and may it be good in Thy sight to bless Thy people Israel at all times and in every hour with peace.	ders, health and happiness within its homes. Strengthen the bonds of friendship and fellowship between all the inhabitants of our land. Plant virtue in every soul and may love of Thy name hallow every home and every heart.
Blessed be Thou, O Lord, who blessest Thy people Israel with peace.	Blessed be Thou, O Lord, Giver of Peace.

It is clear that just as the rejection of Jewish nationalism by Reform Jews led to what is practically a complete rewriting of the prayer, so the new attitude of the early Christians led to a complete rewriting of the Grace. In both instances the outer form has been in a measure retained.

II	I
We thank Thee, O Lord, our God, that Thou hast caused us to inherit a goodly and pleasant land, the covenant, the Torah, life and food. For all these things we thank Thee and praise Thy name forever and ever.	We thank Thee, holy Father, for Thy holy name, which Thou hast caused to dwell in our hearts and for the knowledge and faith and immortality which Thou hast made known to us through Jesus Thy servant;
Blessed art Thou, O, Lord, for the land and for the food.	To Thee be glory forever.
III	**III**
Have mercy, O Lord, our God, on Thy people Israel, and on Thy city Jerusalem, and on Thy Temple and Thy dwelling-place and on Zion Thy resting-place, and on the great and holy sanctuary over which Thy name was called, and the kingdom of the dynasty of David mayest Thou restore to its place in our days, and build Jerusalem soon.	Remember, Lord, Thy church, to deliver it from every evil and to make it perfect in Thy love and gather it from the four winds, it, the sanctified, into Thy kingdom which Thou hast prepared for it;
Blessed art Thou, O, Lord, who buildest Jerusalem.	For Thine is the power and the glory forever.
	Let[7] grace come and this world pass away. Hosanna

[7] Regarding these additional verses see below, p. 234.

to the son of David. Whoever is holy, let him come; whoever is not let him repent. Maranatha. Amen.

Since the eucharistic prayer has only three doxologies, the Jewish prayer after which it was modeled most likely only had three benedictions. The date of the *Didaché* is somewhat uncertain, but it is generally held to belong to the last decades of the first century.[8] Hence the parallel seems to point to the fact that in the generation immediately following the fall of Jerusalem the *Birkat Ha-Mazon* had only three benedictions.

Fortunately more definite evidence of this fact is available from the Talmud itself. R. Gamaliel II, living about the year 100, maintains that after eating certain foods one must recite an abridged *Birkat Ha-Mazon:*[9] "a summary of the three benedictions." It is true that in most versions of this benediction there is contained in addition to the summary of the first three benedictions also a reference to the fourth. But this reference must have been added in later times, for no amount of dialectic reasoning can explain why R.

[8] See Hastings' Dictionary of the Bible, article *Didache.*

[9] M. Berakot 6.8. I examined a large number of texts of this benediction, but find it impossible at the present time to establish its original form. It occurs not only in the Prayer Books, but also in the Talmud as having been given to Abbaye by R. Dimi, one of the rabbis who came from Palestine to Babylonia (*Berakot* 44a). From the Talmud it is quoted in a number of codes and commentaries. But apparently each author gave it the form which he knew from his own rite. The text of the benediction as found in the usual editions of the Babylonian Talmud is reproduced here:

[ברוך אתה ה׳ אלהינו מלך העולם] על העץ ועל פרי העץ ועל תנובת השדה ועל ארץ חמדה טובה ורחבה שהנחלת לאבותינו לאכול מפריה ולשבוע מטובה רחם ה׳ אלהינו על ישראל עמך ועל ירושלים עירך ועל מקדשך ועל מזבחך ותבנה ירושלים עיר קדשך במהרה בימינו והעלנו לתוכה ושמחנו בה כי אתה טוב ומטיב לכל [ברוך אתה ה׳ על הארץ ועל הפירות].

Gamaliel should call a summary of four benedictions "*Berakah Me'en Shalosh*."[10]

What establishes the matter beyond question is the testimony of R. Eliezer b. Hyrkanos, the brother-in-law of R. Gamaliel, who speaks of the fourth benediction[11] as "the benediction established by the scholars at Jabneh." Since R. Eliezer was himself one of the scholars who came to Jabneh with R. Johanan b. Zakkai about the year 70, his words are an irrefutable proof that the fourth benediction was established after the destruction of the Temple.

We must now turn to the task of ascertaining how old the threefold prayer was. Again we are fortunate in having a reference to the *Birkat Ha-Mazon* in an early work. The Book of Jubilees, the date of which can hardly be later than the year 100 B.C.E., attributes to Abraham the recital of a prayer of thanks after he had eaten. The author of the book, who wanted it to be accepted as Mosaic, naturally did not dare commit the gross anachronism of making Abraham repeat the *Birkat Ha-Mazon* in the form which it had in Hasmonean Jerusalem. At the same time he wished to imply that Abraham observed the commandment of reciting the Grace in approximately the same way as his descendants were destined to do. He therefore wrote a prayer which is worded differently from the traditional *Birkat Ha-Mazon*, but, like it, consists of three parts of

[10] The following sources omit the mention of the fourth benediction in the *Berakah me'en Shalosh*: *Maḥzor Vitry*, printed edition p. 53, (Ms. Jewish Theological Seminary of America, f. 25a): *Sefer Ha-Pardes*, ed. Ehrenreich, pp. 176-7; *Ma'aseh ha-Geonim*, p. 57. Meiri also omits the reference to the fourth benediction, but he knows the custom according to which it is inserted (commentary on Berakot chapter VII).

[11] Berakot 48b. The word ביבנה is omitted in the Munich Ms. See below, note 23. But R. Eliezer's statement בברכה שתקנו חכמים even without the word ביבנה would show that it was an accepted fact in his day that this benediction was rabbinical whereas the others were biblical in origin. This could only point to its having been established either in his generation or slightly earlier.

which the first is thanks to God for food and drink, the second addresses Him and praises Him for other blessings, and the third prays for mercy on Israel. The writer tells us[12] that after Abraham ate and drank, he "blessed the Most High God,

> I. Who hath created Heaven and Earth,
> Who hath made all the fat things of the earth
> And given them to the children of men,
> That they might eat and drink and bless their Creator.
>
> II. And now I give thanks unto Thee, my God, because Thou hast caused me to see this day; behold I am one hundred and three score and fifteen years, an old man and full of days, and all my days have been unto me peace. The sword of the adversary hath not overcome me in all that Thou hast given me and my children all the days of my life until this day.
>
> III. My God, may Thy mercy and Thy peace be upon Thy servant and upon the seed of his sons that they may be to Thee a chosen nation and an inheritance from amongst all the nations of the earth from henceforth unto all the days of the generations of the earth unto all the ages."

III

The three benedictions of which the *Birkat Ha-Mazon* consisted at the beginning of the first pre-Christian century were doubtless the earlier forms of the first three benedictions of the present *Birkat Ha-Mazon*. The suggestion has been made elsewhere[13] that the prayer for Jerusalem was

[12] Jubilees 22.6-9.
[13] *JQR.* (N.S.), XVI, 36-7, 128-9.

composed during the Maccabean struggle when the Temple and the Altar, the importance of both of which is emphasized in the earliest form of this prayer, were under the control of the heathen. The term ה' אלהינו was not used in prayers composed during the first century of the Christian era, and at no time before the opening of that era was the Temple in any real danger of destruction.

Additional corroboration of the theory is now available. A comparison of the texts and citations of the prayer proves indisputably that its earliest form was:[14]

רחם ה' אלהינו על ישראל עמך ועל ירושלם עירך ועל ציון משכן כבודך ועל מזבחך ועל היכלך.

This is evidently connected with[15] the following passage in the Book of Ben Sira (36, 17–19)

רחם על עם נקרא בשמך	ישראל בכור כיניתה
רחם על קרית קדשך	ירושלם מכון שבתיך
מלא ציון את הודך	ומכבודך את היכלך.

It follows from this that the prayer for Jerusalem was composed at some time between the Book of Ben Sira and the Book of Jubilees, that is in the second century B.C.E.[16] Certainly within the limits of this century we can find no more appropriate time to suggest for its composition than the days of the Maccabean rebellion when the greatest danger faced the Altar, the Temple, the Holy City and the people of Israel.

[14] See p. 233, below, and *JQR*, (N.S.), *loc. cit.*

[15] This was first pointed out by Professor Louis Ginzberg in the "*Orientalische Studien*," published in honor of Noeldeke, p. 624. There is the possibility that Ben Sira modeled his verses after the prayer. But that I do not consider likely, particularly as we would have to account Ben Sira's omission of מזבחך.

[16] It should be noted that the prayer for Jerusalem as reconstructed here is identical with the earliest form of the prayer for Jerusalem as found in the *Amidah* (*JQR*, N.S., XVI, 159).

IV

Whether the first and second benedictions were formulated at the same time as the third or earlier, and if earlier when, cannot be ascertained at the present time.[17] It is known, however, that the fourth was added in Jabneh, doubtless on the occasion of some great good that befell Israel, for it praises God as "the kind One who dealeth kindly." We have noticed that this benediction is mentioned by R. Eliezer b. Hyrkanos.[18] It was also known to R. Jose the Galilean[19] and R. Ishmael,[20] both somewhat younger contemporaries of R. Eliezer. None of these Tannaitic authorities tells us why the prayer was instituted. It is only the Amoraim of the third century, R. Naḥman[21] and R. Huna,[22] who associate it with the permission that was granted to bury those "who were slain at Bether."

But we know that R. Eliezer b. Hyrkanos died before the outbreak of the rebellion of Bar Kokhba. How then could he mention a benediction that was composed in celebration of the relenting of the government toward those who had taken part in it? It is clear that the Amoraic tradition regarding this benediction cannot be accepted

[17] It is probable, however, that the first two benedictions of the *Birkat Ha-Mazon* are pre-Maccabean. Comp. also S. Klein in *Ha-Zofeh* X 304.

[18] See note 12.

[19] Tosefta Berakot I.7.

[20] Jer. Berakot 8.1 (11a).

[21] Berakot 48b.

[22] Jer. Berakot 11a (7.1): compare also Jer. Ta'anit 69a (5.4). The same tradition is reported in B. Ta'anit 31a. It is to be noted that the tradition found in the Talmud of Jerusalem occurs in the name of R. Huna, the Babylonian Amora. It is probable that it originated with Rab since the three authorities who mention it were his disciples.

although the benediction was doubtless added to the Grace within a half century after the destruction of the Temple.[23]

It is extremely hazardous to guess at the reason of the innovation, since the rabbis who lived a hundred and fifty years after it no longer knew it. Yet with all reserve the suggestion may be ventured that the occasion for the fourth benediction was the granting of permission in the early years of the reign of Hadrian to rebuild the Temple. Certainly the Jews were led to believe that the Temple would be rebuilt, and we can well believe that in their joy they added this new blessing to the Grace.

[23] The question of the date of this benediction is discussed at length by Weiss in his *Dor* II.145, (see especially note 2) and by Halevy in his *Dorot Ha-Rishonim*, I e, p. 742ff. Weiss maintains that the fourth benediction was established not at Jabneh but at Usha, and that the "slain of Bether" were those executed in the persecution rather than those killed in battle. His reasons for this position are: 1. The Sanhedrin could not have met at Jabneh after the fall of Bether. 2. The tradition that the benediction was established after the fall of Bether is found in both the Palestinian and Babylonian Talmud, but only in the latter is there any mention of its having been instituted at Jabneh. 3. The Munich Ms. of the Babylonian Talmud does not read the word ביבנה in the Baraita but merely gives R. Eliezer's words thus: בברכה שתקנו חכמים אומרה (see Strack, Photographic Edition, I, fol. 152b, and *Dikduke Soferim, ad. loc.*).

Halevy insists on the correctness of the Amoraic tradition, and maintains that after the fall of Bether the Sanhedrin met again at Jabneh for a brief period, during which this Takkanah was established.

Neither Weiss nor Halevy, however, have felt the essential difficulty of maintaining their respective positions which lies in the fact that the benediction was known to R. Eliezer, who according to all authorities died before the outbreak of the Bar Kokhba rebellion (Weiss, *Dor*, II, p. 130; Halevy, *Dorot*, I e, p. 617, maintains that R. Ishmael, too, died before the outbreak of the Rebellion, yet he does not seem to have asked himself how R. Ishmael could speak of the benediction which was established *after* the fall of that city).

It is quite evident that the various statements and traditions can be reconciled only on the assumption that the view that associated this benediction with Bether was a third century guess. On the other hand since the benediction was known to R. Eliezer b. Hyrkanos, R. Ishmael and R. Jose the Galilean it was doubtless older than the Hadrianic persecutions, with which Weiss tries to associate it, or even than the Bar Kokhba rebellion.

V

After the discussion of the dates of the benedictions we must now turn to our second task: the reconstruction of the original texts. All of the available versions have been collected in the Appendix but for the purpose of the present discussion only a few typical forms of the benedictions need be cited. We shall choose the Palestinian versions[24] as recovered from the Genizah fragments and those of *Seder R. Amram*,[25] *Seder R. Saadia* and Maimonides.

Palestinian

A

בא"י אמ"ה הזן את
העולם כלו בטוב
בהסד וברחמים נותן
לחם לכל בשר. בא"י
הזן את הכל.

B

בא"י אמ"ה הזן את
העולם כולו בטוב
בהסד וברחמים נותן
לחם לכל בשר כי
לעולם חסדו עמנו וטובו
הגדול לא חסר לנו ואל
יחסר לנו כל טוב
בעבור שמו הגדול כי
הוא זן ומפרנס לכל.
בא"י הזן את הכל.

Amram

בא"י אמ"ה הזן את
העולם כולו בטובו
ובחסד וברחמים נותן
לחם לכל בשר כי הוא
זן ומפרנס לכל והתקין
מזון לכל בריותיו. בא"י
הזן את הכל.

Maimonides

בא"י אמ"ה הזן את העולם כולו
בטוב בחסד ברחמים וטובו הגדול
לא חסר לנו ואל יחסר לנו לעולם
ועד כי הוא זן ומפרנס לכל כאמור
פותח את ידיך ומשביע לכל חי רָצון
ומכין מזון לכל בריותיו אשר ברא.
בא"י הזן את הכל.

Saadia

בא"י אמ"ה הזן את העולם כלו
בטוב בחן בחסד וברחמים. בא"י
הזן את הכל.

[24] For this benediction two Palestinian texts must be presented, the one brief (A), the other somewhat longer (B). The Palestinian texts are characterized by the use of the words בְרית ותורה instead of the longer forms: ועל בריתך שחתמת בבשרנו ועל תורתך שלמדתנו which are found in the rites that follow the Babylonian form. The Palestinian texts always have כי הנחלתנו ארץ חמדה whereas the Babylonian texts generally have שהנחלת את אבותינו. Some have כי הנחלתנו under the influence of either the Egyptian or Palestinian rite.

[25] For the sources of these texts see Appendix.

In attempting to establish on the basis of these later forms, the earliest text of the benedictions we must bear in mind that for many centuries the prayers were not written down but transmitted orally. Under these circumstances new material could be added, but changes or omissions were difficult. It is comparatively easy to issue an edict changing the wording of written prayers, and in an age of printing it is a slight matter to prepare a new edition of a prayer book. But when people recited their prayers from memory, they were willing to learn new verses or phrases, but found it difficult to unlearn what they already knew.

It follows that in dealing with various formulae of prayer we must remember that *in general* these rules hold. 1. The old text is retained as a nucleus of the later formula. 2. Where various versions differ, the part that is common to all of them is the more likely to contain the original form. 3. The briefest form is very often the most akin to the original.

Now taking Palestinian A, Palestinian B, *Seder R. Amram* and Maimonides as the bases we arrive at the following which is common to all:

בא"י אמ"ה הזן את העולם כולו בטוב בחסד וברחמים. בא"י הזן את הכל.

This is practically identical with the version of *Seder R. Saadia*. We thus reach the unexpected conclusion that the earliest of extant forms is not that of Palestine as recovered from the Genizah, but that of *Seder R. Saadia*.[26] This simply means, of course, that the Palestinian version of the *Birkat Ha-Mazon* underwent a number of changes which the Egyptian ritual escaped.

[25] In regard to the *Amidah* it was found that generally the Palestinian version retained the older readings (*JQR*., N.S., XVI, pp. 142-169), but compare *ibid*., p. 12 where it is found that in the case of one benediction *Seder R. Saadia* has retained the oldest reading. It is to be kept in mind that whereas in regard to the *Amidah* the Egyptian community adopted the early forms of the Babylonian version, it seems that its form of the Grace was only slightly influenced by that of Babylonia.

VI

This finding is corroborated and an even older form of the benediction established by the correct interpretation of a passage in the *Tosefta* which in our texts is corrupt. In the Tosefta *Berakot* 1.6, we read:

אלו ברכות שמקצרין בהן מברך על הפירות ועל המצות ברכת הזימון (ד'. הזמן) וברכה אחרונה שבברכת המזון.

"These are the benedictions in which a brief formula[27] is recited: when one pronounces the benediction for fruits, for the commandments, the benediction of *Zimmun*—calling on others to join in the Grace—and the last benediction of the Grace."[28]

By *Birkat Ha-Zimmun* we are to understand the blessing recited by the leader who calls on the company to say the Grace. The usual[29] form for this is: נברך שאכלנו משלו to which the response of the company is: ברוך שאכלנו משלו.

It seems strange that the *Baraita* should put the *Birkat Ha-Zimmun*, which alone among Talmudic benedictions has no mention of the Tetragrammaton, on the same plane as the other benedictions. It is true that a *Baraita*[30] said to represent the view of R. Ishmael finds a reference to the *Birkat Ha-Zimmun* in the Torah and that the term *Birkat Ha-Zimmun*[31] is regularly used for the introductory formula. Nevertheless it is certain that as late as the time of R. Jose the Galilean the text of the *Birkat Ha-Zimmun* was still in a fluid state, and this would seem to indicate that the institution was of recent origin.[32]

[27] "Brief formula" means a benediction consisting of a single sentence like the benedictions for the fruits and the commandments.

[28] One text (Zuckermandel *ad. loc.*) reads שבקריאת שמע instead of שבברכת המזון.

[29] Mishnah Berakot 7.3 and B. Berakot 50a. There different forms are given for larger companies.

[30] Jer. Berakot 8.1 (11a).

[31] *Ibid.* B. Berakot 48b, *Baraita, et al.*

[32] Tosefta Berakot 1.7.

The matter is, however, clarified by the form in which this passage is quoted by Ibn Adret[33] in his commentary to *Berakot* 45b, where for the words ברכת הימון is substituted the term ברכת הן. It is true that Ibn Adret interprets ברכת הן as meaning ברכת הימון, but his interpretation only makes the more certain that he read הן where our texts read הזמון.

For this reading of the Tosefta we have the further authority of a similar citation in an anonymous commentary on *Berakot*, the so-called שטה מקובצת (published in ברכה משלשת, Warsaw 1863). The text[34] as quoted there is sufficiently different from that of Ibn Adret to show that it is an independent citation, and yet here also we find הן instead of הזמון.

It is thus evident that the original reading of the passage was ברכת הן and that, properly interpreted, it means that the first benediction of the Grace originally had no *ḥatimah*, but was a "brief formula" consisting of a only single sentence. The copyists, like the scholars,[35] could not under-

[33] The full text of Ibn Adret's quotation is as follows:
כדתניא בפרק קמא דתוספתא דמכלתין אלו ברכות שמקצרין ואין חותמין בברוך ברכת הפירות וברכת המצות וברכת הן פ' ברוך שאכלנו משלו וברכה אחרונה של ברכת המזון.

[34] Complete text:
ונרסינן בתוספתא אלו ברכות שמקצרין בהן ואין חותמין בהן ברכת הפירות וברכת המצות וברכת הן פירוש ברוך שאכלנו משלו דליכא למימר הן דהא חתמינן בה וברכה אחרונה של ברכת המזון.

It is probable that a similar text underlay that cited by the Provençal Ibn Jarhi in his *Manhig*. In this work, ed. Berlin 1855, p. 40a, the *Baraita* is cited thus:
בתוספתא אלו ברכות שמקצרין בהן וכו' על ברכת המזון שהוא המוציא ובברכה אחרונה שהיא הטוב והמטיב ר' יוסי הגלילי חותם בה ומאריך בה.

The word הן has here been changed to המזון, and interpreted to mean המוציא. The fact that the term never occurs elsewhere in this sense was no obstacle as no other interpretation seemed possible. There would have been no reason for a copyist or a scholar creating such a text as Ibn Jarhi's if his reading had been הזמון, but he had every reason for it if he read הן in his original text.

[35] The Amoraim who cited the Baraita in the Talmudim also emended it by changing הן into הזמון (B. Berakot 46a and Jer. Berakot 3c).

stand how the *Baraita* could speak of the first benediction which in their days had a well-established doxology as a "brief formula" and they were thus led to change ברכת הזן into ברכת המזון. The emendation was so slight that it was almost universally accepted.

We thus arrive at the conclusion that the original form of the first benediction had no *ḥatimah* or doxology and that it merely read:[36]

ברוך אתה ה׳ אלהינו מלך העולם הזן את העולם כלו בטוב בחסד וברחמים.

[36] The development of short into long benedictions is a common phenomenon in the development of Jewish liturgy. The sabbath *ḳiddush* is given in Tosefta Berakot III.7 without any *ḥatimah*:

ועל הכוס אומר אשר קידש את יום השבת ואינו חותם.

But in our liturgies it has developed the long form. We are told that R. Jose the Galilean attempted to add a doxology to the fourth benediction of the Grace ר׳יוסי הגלילי היה חותם בברכה אחרונה שבברכת המזון ומאריך בה (Tosefta, *ibid.*, I.7.). In B. Berakot 11b we are told how R. Johanan developed the benediction for the Torah from the "short" into the "long" form. In B. Sanhedrin 42a we are told how R. Judah established a long benediction for the New Moon instead of the short one which was in use in Palestine. The later theory that every prayer that does not follow immediately after a benediction must begin with a benediction (Berakot 46a), led to the amalgamation of prayers with benedictions so as to make one long benediction (see Tosafot, *ibid.*, catchword כל). An examination of all the benedictions mentioned in the Talmud and found in the liturgy will reveal the fact that practically everyone of the so-called "long formulae," which begin with ברוך and end with a doxology, are either from the period following the fall of the Temple or were short benedictions before the Fall of the Temple. The seeming exceptions are (1) the *Berakah me'en Shalosh* which may or may not in its original form have had the doxology at the end. But even assuming that it had, it antedated the Fall of the Temple by only a decade or two. (2) The first benediction of the *Shema'* in the morning and evening services. I believe it is possible to prove that neither of these is a real exception, but must defer the exposition as it would take us far afield. (3) The first benediction of the Grace, which has been discussed in the text. (4) The first benediction of the *Amidah* which has been discussed in *JQR*, N.S., XVI, 24-27, and proved to have been originally a short formula. The matter requires, however, fuller treatment than can be accorded it here.

VII

In establishing the text of the second benediction we have the important aid of reliable traditions as to the manner of its growth. Before we can apply them, however, we must again compare the available versions. In this case not only do the Palestinian texts agree among themselves, but they are practically identical with that of the *Seder R. Saadia* so that only that version need be quoted to represent both the Palestinian and Egyptian forms. The *Seder R. Amram* represents a purely Babylonian version, while the text of Maimonides is the version of the Dispersion, with strong additional influences from Palestinian or Egyptian sources.

Maimonides

נודה לך ה' א' ונברכך מלכינו כי הנחלתנו (והנחלת) את אבותינו ארץ חמדה טובה ורחבה ברית ותורה (חיים ומזון) ועל שהוצאתנו מארץ מצרים ופדיתנו מבית עבדים על תורתך שלמדתנו על חוקי רצונך שהודעתנו ועל כולם ה' א' אנו מודים לך ומברכים את שמך כאמור ואכלת ושבעת וברכת את ה' א' על הארץ הטובה אשר נתן לך. ברוך אתה ה' על הארץ ועל המזון.

Saadia

נודה לך ה' א' כי הנחלתנו ארץ חמדה טובה ורחבה ברית ותורה חיים ומזון ועל כולם אנו מודים לך ומברכים את שמך לעולם ועד. בא"י על הארץ ועל המזון.

Amram

נודה לך ה' א' ארץ חמדה טובה ורחבה שרצית והנחלת את אבותינו ועל בריתך ששמת בבשרנו ועל תורה שנתת לנו ועל חיים וחסד וחן ומזון שאתה מלוה אותנו בכל עת ועל כלם ה' א' אנו מודים לך ומברכים את שמך יתברך שמך תמיד עלינו לעולם ועד. בא"י על הארץ ועל המזון.

The explanation for the radical differences among these versions must be sought in the history of the growth of the benediction as outlined in the following *Baraita*, (*Berakot* 48b):

תניא ר׳ אליעזר אומר כל שלא אמר ארץ חמדה טובה ורחבה בברכת הארץ ומלכות בית דוד בבונה ירושלם לא יצא ידי חובתו. נחום הזקן אומר צריך שיזכור בה ברית, ר׳ יוסי אומר צריך שיזכור בה תורה.

R. Eliezer says: "One who does not say the words 'A goodly, pleasant and broad land' (in describing the Holy Land) in the second benediction and one who fails to mention the dynasty of David in the third benediction has not fulfilled his duty. Naḥum Ha-Zaḳen says: One must also mention (in the second benediction) thanks for the Covenant. R. Jose says: One must also include the Torah."

The mention of the Torah and the Covenant is made by only a word for each in the *Seder R. Saadia* (ברית ותורה) but in the *Seder R. Amram* it is elaborated into the verses:

ועל בריתך ששמת בבשרנו ועל תורה שנתת לנו.

In the ritual of Maimonides the two customs are combined and in addition to the long verses of thanks, the words ברית ותורה are also added. Since we know from the *Baraita* just cited that the insertion of the mention of the Covenant and the Torah was made by authorities of the second century,[37] we are justified in holding that the insertion of the memory of the redemption ועל שהוצאתנו מארץ מצרים ופדיתנו מבית עבדים in rituals like that of Maimonides, and of thanks for food and life which we find only in the *Seder R. Amram* and *Seder R. Saadia* are likewise later insertions. The final summary of thanksgiving beginning with ועל כלם was added in accordance with the following statement of R. Abba in the *Baraita*[38] quoted above, ר׳ אבא אומר צריך שיאמר בה הודאה תחלה וסוף "One must mention thanksgiving both at the beginning and at the end of the benediction." Obviously R. Abba had in mind the need of some recapitulation of the

[37] The mention of them was probably inserted as a reaction to the persecution to which the Jews were exposed on their account.

[38] B. Berakot 49a. R. Abba is of course Rab.

meaning of the benediction because of the insertions that had been made by earlier scholars.

It is thus clear from the *Baraita* that originally the second benediction consisted of only one verse, thanking God for the gift of the Holy Land. This is exactly what we might expect from the fact that it is intended to fulfil the command: "to bless the Lord, thy God, for the goodly land which He hath given thee."[39]

VIII

The problem of the establishment of the original text of the third benediction has been discussed in part elsewhere.[40] Nevertheless the new material now made available makes a further discussion of the problem desirable. In this instance, too, it will be best to present typical texts from rituals as a basis for the discussion. The text of Maimonides need not be given for this benediction as it is essentially the same as the Palestinian.

[39] R. Eliezer's statement requiring the use of the formula: ארץ חמדה טובה ורחבה naturally arouses speculation as to the rival formula to which he objected. As R. Eliezer is not known as an innovator it is likely that he merely expressed preference for one form over another current form. The form objected to probably was ארץ טובה ורחבה. This seems probable from the fact that in Sifre Deuteronomy 43, ed. Friedmann 81b, there occurs in what seems to be a citation of the *Birkat Ha-Mazon* only the term ארץ טובה ורחבה. The passage in Sifre reads:
כך אמר להם הקב"ה לישראל הכנסתי אתכם לארץ טובה ורחבה לארץ זבת חלב ודבש לאכול מפריה ולשבוע מטובה ולברך שמי עליה
The words ולברך שמי עליה seem to make it clear that the words are taken from the *Birkat Ha-Mazon*. After the article had been written, I found additional confirmation of this hypothesis in the material presented by M. Julien Weill in the Lévi Volume (R.E.J., LXXXII, pp. 129-131). He maintains that the expression ארץ טובה ורחבה was a common liturgical formula in the time of Josephus, so common that Josephus naturally substituted it for the biblical expression ארץ זבת חלת ודבש.

[40] *JQR* (N.S.), XVI, 129.

Palestinian	*Saadia*	*Amram*
רחם ה' א' על ישראל	רחם ה' א' על ישראל	רחם ה' א' על ישראל
עמך ועל ירושלם עירך	עמך ועל ירושלם עירך	עמך ועל ירושלם עירך
ועל מלכות בית דוד	ועל היכלך ועל מעינך	ועל ציון משכן כבודך
משיחך ועל הבית הגדול	ועל ציון משכן כבודך	ועל מלכות בית דוד
והקדוש שנקרא שמך	ועל הבית הגדול	משיחך ועל הבית הגדול
עליו ומלכות בית דוד	והקדוש אשר שמך נקרא	והקדוש שנקרא שמך
מהרה תחזירה למקומה	עליו ומלכות בית דויד	עליו [אבינו מלכנו
בימינו [ובנה ירושלם	תחזיר למקומה בימינו	רועינו זננו מפרנסנו
בקרוב והעלינו לתוכה	ובנה את ירושלם	מכלכלנו הרוח לנו
ושמחינו בה] בא"י בונה	בקרוב. בא"י בונה	מהרה מצרותינו ואל
ברחמיו את ירושלים.	ירושלם.	תצריכנו לידי מתנת
		בשר ודם שמתנתם
		מעוטה וחרפתם מרובה
		בשם קדשך הגדול
		והנורא בטחנו ויבא
		אליהו ומשיח בן דוד
		בחיינו ומלכות בית דוד
		[משיחך] מהרה תחזור
		למקומה ומלוך עלינו
		כי אתה לבדך והושיענו
		למען שמך והעלנו
		לתוכה ושמחנו בה
		ונחמנו בציון עירך.
		בא"י בונה ירושלם.

It is necessary to note that *Seder R. Amram* alone among the oldest versions contains the portion: רענו זונו. That it is not found in the Genizah fragments may seem strange at first sight in view of the well-known fact that the Palestinian Talmud (*Shabbat* 15b) refers to it. It is recorded there that R. Zeira asked R. Ḥiyya b. Abba whether the prayer רענו זונו may be recited on the sabbath in spite of its being a petition for the fulfilment of daily needs. R. Ḥiyya b. Abba replied that it may be recited since it is not a special petition, but part of a fixed formula.[41]

[41] The reading of the Jerushalmi is:
ר' זעירא שאל לר' חייה בר בא מהו מימר רעינו פרנסינו א"ל טופוס ברכות כך הן.

It is a misunderstanding of the passage, however, to assume that it implies that רענו וזוננו was part of the Palestinian *Birkat Ha-Mazon*. Both R. Ḥiyya b. Abba and R. Zeira were Babylonian scholars who had migrated to Palestine. They doubtless preferred to retain—especially in the home services, like the Grace after Meals—the forms of prayer to which they had become accustomed in their youth. But when on coming to Palestine R. Zeira discovered that רענו וזוננו was *not* recited there, he began to have doubts as to whether it ought to be recited on the sabbath, since it evidently was not an essential part of the prayer. He asked R. Ḥiyya b. Abba, who was an older scholar, what his practice was, and was told that there was no objection to the use of the prayer רענו וזוננו since it was kept merely as part of the fixed *Birkat Ha-Mazon* of their native land. Seen in this light, the passage in the Jerushalmi confirms the evidence of the Genizah fragments that the prayer רענו וזוננו was not part of the Palestinian service, while at the same time it shows that it was contained in the Babylonian *Birkat Ha-Mazon* as early as the fourth century.

The mention of the kingdom of David in this prayer is doubtless an early addition. It is not quoted in the

Professor Jacob Mann has already called attention to the parallel passage in Leviticus R. 34.16 (*H.U.C. Annual*, II, 333, note 130), which reads:

ר' זעירא בעי קומי דר' חייא בר אבא א"ל אילין דאמרין רועינו זונינו פרנסינו בשבת מהו א"ל טופס ברכות כך הוא

According to this reading R. Zeira did not at all imply that the portion beginning with רעינו זונינו was part of the Palestinian version of the third benediction. I believe that the interpretation of the passage of the Jerushalmi given here is the correct one. The text of the Jerushalmi is doubtless older and more correct than that of Leviticus R., where not only are the words אילין דאמרין added but also the explanatory statement בשבת. In the Jerushalmi neither was necessary as the whole discussion centers about speaking of weekday needs on the sabbath. The editor who sought to clarify the passage by adding the word בשבת also thought it necessary to add אילין דאמרין because in his Palestinian ritual the passage רעינו זונינו did not occur.

ברכה מעין שלש, but referrred to by R. Eliezer b. Hyrkanos who maintains that its omission necessitated the repetition of the Grace.[42] The words ועל הבית הגדול והקדוש were doubtless added after the destruction of the Temple to replace the earlier ועל מזבחך ועל היכלך which had become obsolete. The Egyptian rite combined both expressions and thus was produced the tautology of the *Seder R. Saadia*: ועל היכלך ועל מעונך ועל ציון משכן כבודך ועל הבית הגדול והקדוש.

The words ובנה ירושלם-בימינו are not found in all the Genizah fragments and were probably added in most versions in order to effect a transition to the benediction בא"י בונה ירושלם.

The earliest formula of this prayer must therefore have read about as follows:

רחם ה' אלהינו על ישראל עמך ועל ירושלם עירך ועל ציון משכן כבודך ועל מזבחך ועל היכלך. בא"י בונה ירושלם.

IX

The fourth benediction which is now quite long was originally extremely brief and merely read: ברוך אתה ה' הטוב והמטיב. This, at any rate, is the view of many early authorities[43] and would appear to follow from the fact that it is usually called the benediction of הטוב והמטיב by the Amoraim. Most of the additional epithets and prayers which were added to it are mentioned in a Midrash[44] which is often cited by mediaeval codifiers. On the other hand the terms אבינו מלכנו occur in all the versions and may have been inserted at a very early time.

[42] B. Berakot 48b.

[43] Tosafot Berakot 46b, catchword הטוב והמטיב; *Shibbale Ha-Leket* 62a; Asheri Berakot 7.22; R. Yeruḥam, *Sefer Adam ve-Ḥavvah* 16.6.

[44] The source for this Midrash is unknown but it is quoted in Asheri Berakot 7.22 and in R. Yeruḥam, *loc. cit.*

X

In all of the versions the fourth benediction is followed by a series of prayers beginning with the word הרחמן. In some rites there are as few as three, in others there are very many. The only reference to such prayers in the Talmud is the statement that a guest should invoke a blessing on his host when reciting the Grace.[45] It is noteworthy that these prayers center about the Redemption and that they are followed by a number of verses dealing with the same thought. It is probable that this custom is very old, for in the Christian prayer of the Eucharist, given in the *Didache*,[46] a similar prayer for the coming of the Kingdom follows the completion of the main benedictions. It seems entirely likely that from the dark days when the Temple fell, Israel always felt the need of comforting herself after the Grace by reading verses in which the future redemption and glory were assured her.

XI

The Karaite version of the *Birkat Ha-Mazon* as printed in the first edition of the Karaite Prayer Book, Venice 1528, contains a number of interesting similarities to some of the Rabbanite versions. For example it begins with ברוך מאכילנו ברוך משביענו ברוך מרוגו, ברוך מַשביע רעבים ברוך מרוה צמאים, expressions which occur in a number of rites. The Grace itself occurs in several forms. The first form consists of two parts of which the first ends with ,ברוך אתה ה׳ הזן את הכל אמן, the second begins with נודה לה׳ חסדו ונפלאותיו לבני אדם and ends with ברוך ה׳ לעולם. As in a number of Rabbanite versions the verse פותח את ידיך ומשביע לכל חי רצון (Ps. 145.16) occurs in the first paragraph and the verse ואכלת ושבעת וברכת

45 Berakot 46a.

46 See above, p. 216.

וכו' (Deut. 8.10) in the second. Moreover the expressions ושלחנך ערוך לכל - כי אתה הוא זן ומפרנס ומכלכל לכל ומכין מזון ומחיה לכל בריותיך are strongly reminiscent of similar expressions that occur in the first benediction according to rabbanite sources.[47]

On sabbaths, new moons and other festive occasions the Grace is appropriately changed. The full significance of the text cannot be determined till more material is available for the study of its history.

[47] The full text of the Karaite Grace for weekdays is here reprinted from the first edition (f. 26b):

ברוך מאכילנו ברוך משביענו ברוך מרונו ברוך משביע רעבים ברוך מרוה צמאים.

(דה"א כ"ט) י. ברוך אתה ה' אלהי ישראל אבינו מעולם ועד עולם. יא. לך ה' הגדולה והגבורה והתפארת והנצח וההוד כי כל בשמים ובארץ לך ה' הממלכה ומתנשא לכל לראש, יב. והעושר והכבוד מלפניך ואתה מושל בכל ובידך כח וגבורה ובידך לגדל ולחזק לכל. ועתה אלהינו מודים אנחנו לך ומהללים לשם תפארתך. ואנחנו נברך יה מעתה ועד עולם הללויה (תהלים קט"ו, י"ח). עיני כל אליך ישברו ואתה נותן להם את אכלם בעתו. פותח את ידיך ומשביע לכל חי רצון (שם קמ"ה. ט"ו–ט"ז). רצון תשביענו ורזון העבר ממנו והטריפנו לחם חקנו ושלחנך ערוך לכל. בארך אפים ובגמילות חסדיך אנו חיים וקיימים ומפתיחת ידיך, כי אתה הוא זן ומפרנס ומכלכל לכל ומכין מזון ומחיה לכל בריותיך אשר בראת. ברוך אתה ה' הזן את הכל, אמן.

נודה לה' חסדו ונפלאותיו לבני אדם (השוה תהלים ק"ז, ח'), כי השביע נפש שוקקה ונפש רעבה מלא טוב (שם ט'). לא יבושו בעת רעה ובימי רעבון ישבעו (שם ל"ז י"ט). ואכלת ושבעת וברכת את ה' אלהיך על הארץ הטובה אשר נתן לך (דברים ח' י'). בית ישראל ברכו את ה' בית אהרן ברכו את ה' (תהלים קל"ה י"ט), בית הלוי ברכו את ה' יראי ה' ברכו את ה' (שם כ'). ברוך ה' מציון שוכן ירושלים הללויה (שם כ"א), ה' עוז לעמו יתן ה' יברך את עמו בשלום (שם כ"ט י"א).

Two other shorter versions also occur, but they throw no further light on the character or derivation of this form of the Grace. The sabbath grace occurs on f. 60a of this volume of the first edition, and differs considerably from the weekday version, mainly, however in the insertion of verses dealing with the sabbath, and verses referring to Jerusalem, and the substitution of Psalm 23 followed by a number of verses for the second paragraph. There are similar and further deviations in the Grace of the Passover eve (II, ff. 31a-33a), Shabu'ot eve (*ibid.* ff. 138a-b), Shabu'ot morning (*ibid.* ff. 161b-162b) etc.

Appendix

The Text of the Four Benedictions

In establishing the text of the four benedictions of the *Birkat Ha-Mazon* an attempt has been made to gather as many versions of it as possible. Of course, the Genizah will continue to offer new readings and it may be that the readings of some of the old prayer books like the *Seder R. Amram* and *Seder R. Saadia* will be corrected by the discovery of new manuscripts. But in general it may be said that the material at present available is sufficient to form a basis for the preceding study. It is the purpose of this Appendix to bring together in one place all the various versions of the benedictions.

No account has been taken of the payyetanic compositions[48] which were sometimes substituted for the standard formulae and more often, especially on festive occasions, added to them. These are many and varied and, like similar compositions that were used in the *Amidah*, throw no light on the development of the ordinary forms. It should be noted, however, that in Palestine the *piyyutim* were permitted to replace the ordinary forms, whereas in the Dispersion they merely supplemented them.[49]

[48] Such have already been published by several scholars (see note 1). Additional material of the same kind is to be found in a number of unpublished manuscripts in Oxford and probably also in other libraries.

[49] This can be seen from the fact that the *piyyutim* published by Greenstone in *ZfHB*, XV (1911), p. 122 from a Genizah fragment where they replace the body of the benediction, are found in the text published by Schwab (*Le Manuscript Hébreu* No. 1388) appended to the body of the benediction. These particular *piyyutim* are also found in a manuscript of *Maḥzor Romania* in the library of the Jewish Theological Seminary of America. Professor Marx informs me that he had the opportunity of examining a copy made by Halberstam of another manuscript of *Maḥzor Romania* (now at Jews College, Hirshfeld 220) and that the same *piyyutim* are also found there appended to the regular forms of the benediction. The *piyyut* begins with אז בפסח גאלת. See regarding it Davidson, *Thesaurus of Mediaeval Hebrew Poetry*, 2116.

The reader will notice that the groups formed on the basis of the similarities in the versions of the *Birkat Ha-Mazon* are slightly different from those which grew out of a study of the *Amidah*.[50] This only proves how complicated a problem it is to determine the method of the spread of the early liturgical formulae. The association of Jewish communities changed from century to century and even from generation to generation. Cross influences are constantly being detected. In view of this it is quite certain that the classification of the various rites which was attempted by early students of the liturgy[51] is in need of revision. Such a revision will enable the historian of mediaeval Judaism to understand, more clearly than is now possible, the relation of the Jewish settlements in Europe to the older communities in Palestine, Babylonia and Egypt, in the centuries before rabbinic literary activity began in Northwestern Africa and Western Europe.

The Spanish text of the *Birkat Ha-Mazon* presents an interesting problem. The text now used by Sephardic Jews and which has been published in their prayer books for hundreds of years is quite different from that found in the early editions of their prayer book and in Abudarham. Much more manuscript material than was available for the present study will have to be consulted to clarify this matter. It seems likely that the two versions represent the *Minhagim* of different communities or provinces. I have called the simple version represented by Abudarham and the early editions Sephardic A and the version at present used by Sephardic Jews Sephardic B.

It is interesting to note how often variant expressions for the same thought were combined in later versions. Mention has already been made of the manner in which rites like

[50] *JQR*, (N.S.), XVI, 132-139.

[51] See Elbogen, *Der Jüdische Gottesdienst*, p. 9.

that of Maimonides adopted both the shorter Palestinian and the longer Babylonian references to the Abrahamitic Covenant and the Revelation. In the same way *Seder R. Saadia* and some other versions retain the old reference to the Temple על מעונך ועל היכלך as well as the newer form ועל הבית הגדול והקדוש.

The text of the *Birkat Ha-Mazon* according to the *Seder R. Amram* is reprinted from Marx, *Untersuchungen zum Seder R. Amram*, and is based on two manuscripts. While it may have suffered slight alterations at the hands of copyists, there is no reason for refusing to accept it as representing as a whole the text used in Babylonia in the time of R. Amram Gaon. It has already been shown that the portion beginning with רענו זוננו was known to rabbis of the fourth century[52] although it is missing in the Genizah fragments, in the *Seder R. Saadia* and in Maimonides. Professor Marx has shown that no importance is to be attached to the omission of the *Birkat Ha-Mazon* from the printed text of the *Seder R. Amram* (*Untersuchungen*, p. 12).

The text of *Seder R. Saadia* presented, is based on two manuscripts, the one found in the Bodleian Library, and the other in the Library of the Jewish Theological Seminary of America.

The texts of the Balkan-Italian-Provençal group are so closely interrelated that it was thought best to treat them as a unit. The text of *Maḥzor Romania* was chosen as typical because it could be better established and because it showed the distinctive characteristics of the group most clearly. Where the other rites of the group differed from it, the variants are noted.

In the same way the English-French-German group is treated as a unit. In this case the text of *Ez Ḥayyim* was chosen as typical because it is not readily accessible and

[52] See above, p. 232.

because it shows individual characteristics of great interest. In the case of both of these groups the reader will find no difficulty in reconstructing any desired text.

Much interest attaches to the ritual of the Persian Jews not only because of its quaintness but also because it has derived so much from other rituals.[53]

The texts and sources of the *Birkat Ha-Mazon* here used are as follows:

Palestine rite (*Genizah* fragments):

1. MS. Jewish Theological Seminary of America (Adler 2017) .... גניזה (ד)
2. MS. Jewish Theological Seminary of America (Adler 2835) .... גניזה (ה)
3. MS. Jewish Theological Seminary of America (Adler 2138) .... גניזה (ו)
4. MS. Dropsie College (Halper 192) .... גניזה (ע)
5. MS. Oxford (Neubauer 2704)[53a] .... גניזה (א)

Non-Palestinian *Genizah* texts:

6. MS. Jewish Theological Seminary of America (Adler 2480) .... גניזה (ז)
7. MS. Oxford (Neubauer 2714) .... גניזה (ב)

Seder R. Saadia:

8. MS. Oxford (Neubauer 1096) f. 78a[54] .... רסג

[53] I have dealt in the following text only with the four benedictions. A comparison of the texts of the remainder of the Grace would have involved too great an expenditure of space and so far as I could see from a study of the various versions did not yield any important results.

[53a] The variants from the Genizah text published by Professor Marmorstein in *Ha-Zofeh* X. 213., which appeared after this article had been sent to press, have been added in proof and are marked גניזה (כ). Attention should also be called to *Bet Ha-Talmud* V. 351 where Lector Friedmann discusses a number of variant readings of the first benediction.

[54] I have had the use for this Ms. of photographs in the Library of the Jewish Theological Seminary of America (Cod. Adler 3396).

9. MS. Jewish Theological Seminary of America (Adler 4036) f. 33b.............רסג (ב)

Seder R. Amram:

10. Marx, *Untersuchungen zum Siddur des Gaon R. Amram*[55]..........................סר"ע

Yemen-Maimonides:

11. *Tiklal* (Jerusalem 1894) f. 167b..........תימן (ד')
12. MS. Jewish Theological Seminary of America (Adler 337)...................תימן (כ"י)
13. *Yad* (Maimonides) MS. Oxford (Neubauer 577)[56].........................רמבם (כ"י)
14. *Yad* (Maimonides) Rome *ca.* 1480......רמבם (ד')

Balkan-Italian-Provençal group:

A. *Romania-Kaffa*:

15. M*aḥzor Romania* (Venice 1526) f. 115a......רומניא
16. MS. (*Maḥzor Romania*) Jewish Theological Seminary of America...........רומניא (כ"י)
17. *Maḥzor Kaffa* (Mezyron 1793) f. 71b.........כפא

B. *Maḥzor Turin*:

18. MS. Jewish Theological Seminary of America[57].............................טורין

[55] Published in *Jahrbuch der jüdisch-literarischen Gesellschaft*, V (1907).

[56] Facsimiles of this Ms. were kindly put at my disposal by Professor Moses Hyamson. The parantheses indicate that the word is crossed out in the manuscript. As is well-known this Ms. was collated with the original Ms. of Maimonides.

[57] At the time of the preparation of this article this Ms., which is a copy made by Dr. Solomon Schechter from the original, was not at the library of the Jewish Theological Seminary of America but had been lent to the library of Cornell University. Through the courtesy of Dr. Abraham Schechter a copy was prepared for me.

C. Italian Prayer Book:

19. Grace and Psalms, Bologna *ca.* 1582[58]..... רומי (א)

20. Prayer Book, Soncino before 1500[59]........ רומי (ב)

21. Luzzatto's Prayer Book, f. 99b[60]............. שדל

D. Provençal Prayer Book:

22. *Maḥzor Avignon*, Avignon 1767, f. 46b ..... קלא (א)

23. *Haggadah Carpentras*, Amsterdam 1759.... קלא (ק)

English-Northern French-German Group:

24. *Ez Ḥayyim*,[61] H. Adler in *Steinschneider Festschrift*, Hebrew part, p. 188........... עץ חיים

25. *Maḥzor Vitry*, Berlin 1889, p. 52......... ויטרי (ד)

26. *Maḥzor Vitry*, MS. Jewish Theological Seminary of America, f. 24a............ ויטרי (כ"י)

27. *Or Zarua'*, Zhitomir 1862, I, section 199.... או"ז (ד)

28. *Or Zarua'*, MS. Jewish Theological Seminary of America, f. 142a, b .... או"ז (כ"י)

29. *Haggadah*, MS. (Worms 1329), Jewish Theological Seminary of America............ הגדה

30. *Mordecai*, *Berakot*, end[61a].................. מרדכי

[58] For this book of which only a unique copy in Parma is known, I have had the use of photographs lent to me by Mr. Moses Marx. At the end of the third benediction which should read:
ובנה את ירושלם עיר קדשך במהרה בימינו [ברוך אתה ה' בונה ירושלם אמן בחיינו במהרה בימינו] ויבא גואל וינאלנו.
The portion indicated by brackets is omitted by *homoioteleuton*.

[59] This unicum is found in the Library of the Jewish Theological Seminary of America.

[60] Most of the early editions of the Italian Prayer Book omit the *Birkat Ha-Mazon*. Where the three texts agree I have used the simple designation רומי. Where they differ, the separate symbols are used.

[61] Adler's text is taken from a copy of Ms. Leipzig XVII (Adler 4055-7) now in the Library of the Jewish Theological Seminary of America.

[61a] Where the readings of the ordinary editions and those of the Riva Edition differ those of the ordinary editions are marked מרדכי (א) and those of the Riva edition מרדכי (ר). After the article was in press, I received, through the kindness of my friend, Dr. Solomon Grayzel, a photograph of Ms. Paris 407 containing this part of the Mordecai.

31. Ashkenazic Prayer Book,[62] (ed. Baer), Roedelheim, 1868, p. 554 .... א

Sephardic Rite (Sephardic A):

32. Spanish Prayer Book, Venice 1544, f. 475a .... ספרד (א)

33. *Birkat Ha-Mazon* found in Spanish Manuscript at the end of *Manhig*, MS. Jewish Theological Seminary of America (written in 1380), f. 150b .... ספרד (כ"י)

34. *Abudraham*, ed. Lisbon, 1489 .... אבודרהם

Sephardic Rite[63] (Sephardic B):

35. Sephardic Prayer Book, ed. Gaster, London 1901, vol. I, p. 60 .... ספרד (ב)

Persian Rite:

36. MS. Jewish Theological Seminary of America (Adler 914), f. 211 .... פרס

Wherever this source offers different readings from the printed editions, I have added them with the symbol מרדכי (כ"י). The Ms. of *Mordecai* in the Library of the Jewish Theological Seminary of America lacks this part.

[62] I have followed the readings of Baer for the text of the Ashkenazic version, but attention should be called to the following variations in the reading of this version, which is at present probably the most widely known of all. Many prayer books read כי הוא אל זן instead of כי הוא זן in the first benediction; הגדושה instead of הקדושה in the third; omit ברחמיו in the *ḥatimah* of the third; and read לעולם אל יחסרנו instead אל יחסרנו in the fourth.

[63] This ritual of the *Birkat Ha-Mazon* is very widespread. It is found in a Genizah fragment (Mann, *H.U.C. Annual*, II.336). From this source it is evident, however, that the poetical portion הזנינו — עלינו was originally intended to be not an addition to the ordinary form but a substitute for it. In some prayer books (e.g. *Seder Berakot*, Amsterdam 1687) the ordinary Spanish form (Sephardic A) is found in the daily service (f.1 3a) and this version (Sephardic B) in the Haggadah (f. 113a). But in many prayer books, like Gaster's, it is found as the standard ritual for the whole year. It is interesting to note also that in some prayer books (for example the Amsterdam edition just referred to) the second benediction begins with the words על ארצנו ועל נחלת אבותינו although otherwise there is no serious deviation from the text as given herein.

I

ברכת הזן

הנוסח המקורי

ברוך אתה ה׳ א׳ מלך העולם הזן את העולם כלו בטוב בחסד וברחמים. [ברוך אתה ה׳ הזן את הכל].

נוסח א״י מן הגניזה

ברוך אתה ה׳ א׳ מלך העולם הזן את העולם כלו בטוב בחסדו[1] וברחמים[2] נותן[3] לחם לכל בשר [כי[4] לעולם חסדו עמנו[5] וטובו הגדול[6] לא חסר[7] לנו ואל[7a] יחסר[8] לנו כל טוב[9] בעבור שמו הגדול כי הוא זן ומפרנס לכל[10]]. ברוך אתה ה׳ הזן את הכל.

נוסח חו״ל מן הגניזה
[ברכת המזון לשבת]

ברוך אתה ה׳ א׳ מלך העולם הזן את העולם כולו בטובו בחסד וברחמים נותן לחם לכל בשר כי הוא זן ומפרנס לכל והתקין מזון לכל בריותיו. ברוך אתה ה׳ הזן את הכל.

Variants I

1 בחסד] גניזה ג, ובחסד, גניזה ה, גני.ה מ, בחן בחסד.
2 וברחמים] גניזה ג, ורחמים. גני.ה מ, ברוח ברחמים הרבים.
3 נותן] גניזה ה, נתן.
4 כי] גניזה א, המוסגר חסר.
5 עמנו] גניזה ו, ל׳. [ובמקומו כתוב „חסדו״ עוד הפעם].
6 הגדול] גניזה ה, <לחם>.
7 חסר] גניזה ג, חִיסַר (כן נקוד בכ״י).
7a ואל-טוב] גניזה מ, כן אל יחסרנו מלכינו מ:ון מעתה ועד עולם.
8 יחסר] גניזה ג, יְחַסֵר (נקוד בכ״י).
9 כל טוב] גניזה ו, מזון וכל טוב.
10 לכל] גניזה ג, <כאמור פותח את ידיך ומשביע לכל חי רצון>. גניזה ו, <ושלחנו ערוך לכל ....(?)>. גני.ה מ, והתקין מ:ון מחיה לכל אשר ברא.

סדר רב עמרם

ברוך אתה ה׳ א׳ מלך העולם הזן את העולם כלו[11] בטובו ובחסד וברחמים נותן לחם לכל בשר כי הוא זן ומפרנס לכל והתקין מזון לכל בריותיו. ברוך אתה ה׳ הזן את הכל.

סדר רב סעדיה גאון [ע״פ שני כ״י]

ברוך אתה ה׳ א׳ מלך העולם הזן את העולם כלו בטוב בחן בחסד[12] וברחמים. ברוך אתה ה׳ הזן את הכל.

רמבם (ד׳ וכ״י) עם שנוים מנוסח תימן (ד׳ וכ״י)

ברוך אתה ה׳ א׳ מלך העולם הזן את העולם כולו [בטוב בחסד][13] ברחמים[14] וטובו[15] הגדול[16] לא חסר לנו ואל יחסר לנו[17] לעולם ועד כי הוא זן[18] ומפרנס לכל כאמור פותח את ידיך ומשביע לכל[19] חי רצון ומכין מזון לכל בריותיו אשר ברא. ברוך אתה ה׳ הזן[20] את הכל.

11 כלו] <בעבור שמו הגדול>.

12 וברחמים] או <נותן לחם לכל בשר כי לעולם חסדו וטובו הגדול לחם לא חסר לנו ואל יחסר לנו תמיד לעולם ועד כי הוא זן ומפרנס לכל>.

13 המוסגר ברמבם כ״י על הגליון. תכלאל, בטוב בחן בחסד. תימן כ״י בטוב בחסד. רמבם נדפס, בטוב בחן ובחסד.

14 ברחמים] תימן כ״י ורמבם נדפס, וברחמים:

15 וטובו] תימן כ״י, ובטובו. רמבם נדפס, וטובו הגדול ... כי הוא זן, ל׳.

16 הגדול] תימן כ״י, <לחם>.

17 לנו] תימן כ״י, <אבינו מזון>.

18 זן] תכלאל, <ומזין>.

19 לכל] תימן כ״י, <ושלחנו ערוך לכל>.

20 הזן] תכלאל, <ברחמיו>.

נוסח ספרד (א) עם שנוים מכ"י ומספר אבודרהם

ברוך אתה ה' א' מלך העולם הזן את העולם כלו[21] בחן בחסד וברחמים נותן לחם לכל בשר כי לעולם חסדו וטובו[22] הגדול תמיד לא חסר לנו[23] ואל יחסר לנו[24] מזון תמיד[25] לעולם ועד כי הוא זן ומפרנס לכל כאמור

נוסח רומניא עם שנוים מכ"י ומנוסחי כפא, קלא, מ' טורין, ומ' רומי

ברוך אתה ה' א' מלך העולם הזננו[26] הזן את העולם כלו[27] בטובו[28] בחן בחסד וברחמיו[29] ובחסדיו[30] הרבים כי[31] הוא נותן לחם לכל בשר כי לעולם חסדו חסדו[32] לעד יהא עמנו ובטובו[33] הגדול ימלא[34] חסרוננו בעבור שמו

נוסח ארץ האי (עץ חיים) עם שנוים מנוסח אשכנז, מחזור ויטרי (ד' וכ"י), או"ז (ד' וכ"י), מרדכי, והגדה (כ"י)

ברוך אתה ה' א' מלך העולם הזן את העולם כלו בטוב[35] בחן[36] בחסד וברחמים[37] נותן לחם לכל בשר כי לעולם חסדו[38] ובטובו[39] הגדול[40] לא[41] חסרנו דבר ואל יחסר לנו מזון[42] לעולם ועד בעבור שמו הגדול כי

21 כלו] אבודרהם, <בטובו> ספרד כ"י <בטוב>.

22 וטובו] ספרד כ"י, ובטובו.

23 לנו] ספרד כ"י, ל'.

24 לנו מזון תמיד] ספרד כ"י, ל'.

25 תמיד לעולם ועד] אבודרהם, (?).

26 הזננו] רומי, קלא (א), קלא (ק), טורין ל'.

27 כלו] רומי, קלא (א), קלא (ק), <בעבור שמו הגדול>.

28 בטובו] טורין, בטוב, רומי (ב), <בטוב>.

29 וברחמיו] רומניא (כ"י), רומי, קלא (א), קלא (ק), טורין, וברחמים.

30 ובחסדיו הרבים] רומניא (כ"י), רומי, קלא (א), קלא (ק), טורין, ל'.

31 כי הוא] רומניא (כ"י), ל'. טורין, רומי, הוא. קלא (א), קלא (ק), כאמור.

32 חסדו לעד יהא] שדל, קלא (א), קלא (ק), ובחסדו הגדול יהיה. רומי (א), וחסדו הגדול יהיה. טורין, ל'

33 ובטובו הגדול] רומי (א), וטובו. רומניא (כ"י) ומטובו הגדול. שדל, רומי (ב), קלא (א), קלא (ק), ל'. טורין, בטובו הגדול.

34 ימלא . . . הגדול] שדל, רומי (ב), קלא (א), קלא (ק), ל'. טורין, לא חסר לנו ואל יחסר לנו מזון לעולם ועד. רומי (א) אל יחסר לנו.

35 בטוב] מרדכי, ל'. אור זרוע (ד' וכ"י), ויטרי (ד' וכ"י), הגדה, א, בטובו.

36 בחן] מרדכי, או"ז (ד' וכ"י) ל'.

37 וברחמים] הגדה, ברחמים. א, <הוא>.

38 חסדו] ויטרי (ד), <עמנו>.

39 ובטובו] הגדה, בטובו. ויטרי (כ"י) <עמנו>.

40 הגדול] או"ז (ד' וכ"י), ויטרי (ד' וכ"י), א, <תמיד>.

41 לא חסרנו דבר] או"ז (ד' וכ"י), ויטרי (ד' וכ"י), הגדה, א, לא חסר לנו. מרדכי (א), הוא לא חיסר. מרדכי (ר וכ"י), לא חסר.

42 מזון] ויטרי (ד), או"ז (כ"י), הגדה, ל'.

פותח את ידיך ומשביע לכל חי רצון.[43] ברוך אתה ה׳ הזן את הכל.

הגדול כי הוא אל[44] זן מרחם[45] ומפרנס[46] ומכלכל[47] ומכין מחיה ומזון לכל בריותיו[48] ולכל מעשה ידיו אשר[49] ברא.[50] ברוך אתה ה׳ הזן את הכל.

הוא[51] זן[52] ומפרנס[53] ומטיב[54] לכל ומכין[55] מזון לכל הבריות.[56] ברוך אתה ה׳ הזן את הכל.

נוסח ספרד (ב)

בא״י אמ״ה הזנו ולא ממעשנו המפרנסנו ולא מצדקותינו המעדיף טובו עלינו הזן אותנו ואת כל העולם כלו בטובו בחן בחסד ברוח וברחמים נותן לחם לכל בשר כי לעולם חסדו וטובו הגדול תמיד לא חסר לנו ואל יחסר לנו מזון תמיד לעולם ועד כי הוא זן ומפרנס לכל ושלחנו ערוך לכל והתקין מחיה ומזון לכל בריותיו אשר ברא ברחמיו וברוב חסדיו כאמור פותח את ידיך ומשביע לכל חי רצון. בא״י הזן את הכל.

נוסח פרס

בא״י אמ״ה האל הזן אותנו ואת כל העולם כלו בטוב בחן בחסד בריוח וברחמים רבים נותן לחם לכל בשר כי לעולם חסדו וחסדו יהא......
הגדול והקדוש כי הוא אל זן ומפרנס לכל ושלחנו ערוך לכל והתקין מחיה ומזון לכל בריותיו ולכל אשר ברא ברחמיו וכרוב חסדיו לקיים פותח את ידיך ומשביע לכל חי רצון רצון תעטרנו ומזון תכלכלנו והוא יכלכלנו והוא יפרנסנו בכבוד ולא בבזוי ואברהם זקן בא בימים וה׳ ברך את אברהם בכל. בא״י הזן את הכל.

43 רצון] ספרד כ״י <ומכין מזון לכל בריותיו אשר ברא>.

44 אל] קלא (א), טורין ל׳.

45 מרחם] רומי, קלא (א), קלא (ק), טורין. ל׳.

46 ומפרנס] רומי, מפרנס.

47 ומכלכל ...ומזון] שדל, קלא (ק), רומי (ב), ומכלכל את הכל ומכין מזון. קלא (א), לכל ושלחנו ערוך לכל ומכין מזון. טורין, לכל ומתקין מזון, רומי (א) ומכלכל לכל ומכין מזון.

48 בריותיו .. ידיו] טורין בריה.

49 ימלא חסרוננו... אשר ברא] רומניא (כ״י), לא חסרנו ואל יחסר לנו מזון לעולם ועד.

50 ברא] רומניא (כ״י), רומי, קלא (א), קלא (ק), <כאמור פותח את ידיך ומשביע לכל חי רצון>.

51 הוא] א, <אל>.

52 זן] מרדכי, <באכילה (?)>.

53 ומפרנס] מרדכי <בשאר צרכים (?)>. או״ז (ד׳ וכ״י) ויטרי (ד׳ וכ״י), הגדה, א, <לכל>.

54 ומטיב לכל] מרדכי(?), או״ז (ד׳ וכ״י), ויטרי (ד׳), ל׳.

55 ומכי, .. הבריות] מרדכי, ויטרי (ד), כאמור פותח את ידיך ומשביע לכל חי רצון.

56 הבריות] הגדה, אשר ברא. א, או״ז (ד׳ וכ״י), ויטרי (ד׳ וכ״י), בריותיו אשר ברא.

II

ברכת הארץ

הנוסח המקורי

נודה לך ה' א' כי הנחלתנו ארץ חמדה [לאכול מפריה ולשבוע מטובה (?)]. ברוך אתה ה' על הארץ ועל המזון.

נוסח א"י מן הגניזה

נודה[1] לך ה' א' כי הנהלתנו[2] ארץ חמדה טובה ורחבה[3] ברית ותורה חיים[4] ושלום[5] ועל כולם[6] אנו מודים לך ומברכים את שמך הגדול[7] והקדוש לעולם ועד. ברוך אתה ה' על הארץ ועל המזון.

נוסח חו"ל מן הגניזה

נודה לך ה' א' ונפאירך מלכינו ונשבחך יוצרנו ונהדרך מושיענו ונמליכך יחיד חי העולמים שהנחלתנו ארץ חמדה טובה ורחבה ברית ותורה [חיים ומזון] [ועל] שהוצאתנו מארץ מצרים ופדיתנו מבית עבדים על בריתך שחתמת בבשרנו ועל תורתך שלמדתנו ועל חקי רצונך שהודעתנו על חיים חן וחסד ומזונות שאתה גומל עלינו בכל עת ובכל שעה. על הכל ה' א' אנו מודים לך ומברכים את שמך תמיד לעולם ועד ונודה לך על נחלת אבותינו והנקם לנו מהרה משונאינו. ברוך אתה ה' על הארץ ועל המזון.

Variants II

1 נודה] גניזה ג, גניזה ה, גניזה ו, על ארצנו ועל נחלת אבותינו נודה.
2 כי הנחלתנו] גניזה ג, שהנחלתנו. גניזה מ, כי הנחלת את אבותינו.
3 ורחבה] גניזה ו, ל'.
4 חיים] גניזה ג, גניזה ה, וחיים.
5 ושלום] גניזה ג, גניזה ה, גניזה ו, גניזה מ, ומזון. גניזה א, (?).
6 כולם] גניזה ו, הכל. גניזה א, <ה' אלהינו>.
7 הגדול ... לעולם ועד] גניזה א, גניזה ג, (?). גניזה ו, יתברך שמך לעולם [ועד]. גניזה מ, ל'.

סדר רב עמרם

נודה לך ה׳ א׳ ארץ חמדה טובה ורחבה שרצית והנחלת את אבותינו ועל בריתך ששמת בבשרנו ועל תורה שנתת לנו ועל חיים וחסד וחן ומזון שאתה מלוה אותנו בכל עת ועל כלם ה׳ א׳ אנו מודים לך ומברכים את שמך יתברך שמך תמיד עלינו לעולם ועד. ברוך אתה ה׳ על הארץ ועל המזון.

סדר רב סעדיה גאון

נודה לך ה׳ א׳ כי הנחלתנו ארץ חמדה טובה ורחבה ברית ותורה חיים ומזון ועל כלם אנו מודים לך ומברכים את שמך[8] לעולם ועד. ברוך אתה ה׳ על הארץ ועל המזון.

רמבם

נודה לך ה׳ אלהינו ונברכך מלכינו כי הנחלתנו (והנחלת)[9] את אבותינו ארץ חמדה טובה ורחבה ברית ותורה (חיים ומזון)[10] ועל[11] שהוצאתנו מארץ מצרים ופדיתנו מבית עבדים על[12] תורתך שלמדתנו על[13] חוקי רצונך שהודעתנו ועל[14] כולם ה׳ א׳ אנו מודים לך ומברכים את שמך כאמור ואכלת ושבעת וברכת את ה׳ א׳ על הארץ הטובה אשר נתן לך. ברוך אתה ה׳ על הארץ ועל המזון.

8 שמך] רס״ג ב, <הגדול והקדוש>.

9 המגיה העביר שיטה על „והנחלת״ ואפשר שהיה בדעתו למחוק את המלה „הנחלתנו״. רמבם נדפס, תכלאל, תימן כ״י, כי הנחלת את אבותינו.

10 חיים ומזון] ברמבם כ״י נמחק, ובנדפס ובתכלאל ל׳, אבל בתימן כ״י איתא.

11 ועל] רמבם נדפס, על.

12 על] תכלאל, ועל.

13 על] תכלאל ותימן כ״י, ועל.

14 ועל] רמבם נדפס, על.

נוסח ספרד (א)	נוסח רומניא	נוסח ארץ האי (עץ חיים)
נודה[15] לך ה' א' על[16]	על[22] ארצנו ועל	נודך[32] ה' א' על
שהנחלת לאביתינו[17]	נחלתנו נודה לך ה' א'	שהנחלת לאבותינו ארץ
ארץ חמדה טובה	נפארך[23] מלכנו[24]	חמדה טובה ורחבה[33]
ורחבה ברית ותורה	נהדרך[25] מושיענו[26]	על[34] שהוצאתנו[35] מארץ
חיים ומזון על שהוצאתנו	ונמליכך מלכנו ומלך[27]	מצרים[36] ופדית' מבית
מארץ מצרים ופדיתנו	יחיד חי העולמים[28]	עבדים ועל[37] בריתך
מבית עבדים על בריתך	שרצית[29] והנחלת את	שחתמת בבשרינו ועל[38]
שחתמת[18] בבשרינו ועל[19]	אבותינו[30] ארץ חמדה	תורתך שלמדתנו ועל[39]
חוקי רצונך שהודעתנו[20]	טובה ורחבה ברית	חקי רצונך[40] שהודעתנו
על[21] חיים ומזון שאתה	ותורה וחיים[31] ומזון	ועל חיים חן[41] וחסד[42]
ו		

15 נודה] ספרד (כ"י), על ארצנו ועל נחלתנו נודה.

16 על] ספרד (כ"י), ל'.

17 שאבותינו] ספרד (כ"י), את אבותינו.

18 שחתמת] ספרד (כ"י) ששמת.

19 ועל] ספרד (כ"י) על.

20 חוקי . . . שהודעתנו] ספרד (כ"י), תורתך שלמדתנו.

21 ועל . . . אותנו] ספרד (כ"י), ל'.

22 על .. נחלתנו] טורין, רומי, קלא (א' וק'), ל'. רומניא (כ"י) <ועל נחלת אבותינו>.

23 נפארך] רומי, קלא (א' וק'), ונפארך.

24 מלכנו] רומי, קלא (א' וק') <ונשבחך יוצרנו>.

25 נהדרך] רומי, קלא (א' וק') ונהדרך.

26 נפארך . . . מושיענו] טורין, ונשבחך מלכינו ונפארך יוצרנו ונהדרך גואלנו ונהללך מושיענו ונקדישך בוראינו.

27 מלכנו ומלך] טורין, מלך. רומי, קלא (א' וק') מלכנו מלך.

28 נפארך . . . העולמים] רומניא (כ"י) ל'.

29 שרצית והנחלת] רומניא (כ"י) על שרצית והנחלת. טורין, שהנחלת. רומי, קלא (א' וק') על שהנחלת.

30 את אבותינו רומי, קלא (א' וק') לאבותינו.

31 ותורה וחיים] קלא (א' וק'), רומניא (כ"י), רומי(ב), ותורה חיים. רומי (א). תורת חיים.

32 נודך] מרדכי (ר), נודה. א, ויטרי (כ"י), נודה לך.

33 ורחבה] ויטרי (כ"י), וברכה. ויטרי (ד' וכ"י) <ברית ותורת חיים ומזון>.

34 על] מרדכי, או"ז (ד'), הגדה, א, ועל.

35 שהוצאתנו] א, <ה' אלהינו>.

36 מארץ מצרים] ויטרי (כ"י) ממצרים.

37 ועל] ויטרי (ד' וכ"י), מרדכי (כ"י), על.

38 ועל תורתך שלמדתנו] הגדה, ל'.

39 ועל . . . שהודעתנו] או"ז (ד' וכ"י), ל'. [וכן ליתא ברש"י ברכות מ"ח ע"ב ד"ה צריך שיקדים].

40 חוקי רצונך] מרדכי (ר' וא'), א, חוקיך.

41 חן] מרדכי (ר' וא'), ל'. [וכן ליתא ברש"י ברכות שם].

42 וחסד] או"ז (כ"י) <ומזון>. [וברש"י ברכות שם ל'.]

זן וכ.פרנס אותנו ועל[22] הכל[23] ה' א' אנו מודים לך ומברכין את שמך כאמור ואכלת ושבעת וברכת את ה' א' על הארץ הטובה אשר נתן לך. ברוך אתה ה' על הארץ ועל המזון.

ועל[24] שהוצאתנו[25] מארץ מצרים ופדיתנו[26] מבית עבדים ועל[27] בריתך שחתמת בבשרנו ועל תורתך שלמדתנו ועל חקי רצונך שהודעתנו ועל חיים חן[28] והסד[29] ומזון[30] שאתה חונן ומלוה[31] אותנו[32] בכל יום בכל עת[33] בכל שעה[34] ובכל זמן.[35] ועל הכל[36] ה'

שחננתנו ועל אכילת[37] מזון[38] שאתה[39] זן ומפרנס אותנו[40] בכל[41] יום ובכל עת ובכל שעה ועל הכל[42] ה' א' אנחנו[43] מודים לך ומברכין אותך[44] יתברך[45] שמך[46] בפה[47] כל חי תמיד לעולם ועד[48] ככתו' ואכלת ושבעת וברכת את ה' א' על הארץ הטובה אשר נתן לך

22 ועל] ספרד (כ"י) על.
23 הכל] אבודרהם, ספרד (כ"י), כלם.
24 ועל] רומניא (כ"י), קלא (ק), רומי (א, ב) על.
25 שהוצאתנו] רומי, קלא (ק), <ה' אלהינו>.
26 ופדיתנו] קלא (א' וק'), רומי (א), רומי (ב), <מלכנו>.
27 ועל] רומניא, קלא (ק), על.
28 חן] טורין, וחן.
29 חן וחסד] קלא (א' וק'), רומי, ל'. ועל חיים . . וחסד, רומניא (כ"י), ל'.
30 ומזון] טורין, ורחמים ומזונות. רומניא (כ"י), ועל אכילת מזון.
31 חונן ומלוה] רומי, קלא (א וק') זן ומפרנס.
32 אותנו] רומי, קלא (א' וק') <תמיד>.
33 בכל עת] רומניא (כ"י), קלא (א), ל'. רומי, טורין, קלא (ק) ובכל עת.
34 בכל שעה] רומניא (כ"י), רומי, קלא (א' וק') ובכל שעה, טורין, ל'.
35 ובכל זמן] רומניא (כ"י), טורין, ל'. רומי, קלא (א' וק'), ובכל רגע.
36 ועל הכל] רומי, קלא (א' וק') על הכל. טורין, ועל כולם.
37 ועל אכילת מזון . . ובכל שעה] או"ז (ד' וכ"י), ל'.
38 אכילת מזון] מרדכי (א וכ"י), אכילה ומזון.
39 שאתה. אותנו] מרדכי, שאתה מזמן לנו ושאתה מפרנסנו.
40 אותנו] א, הגדה, <תמיד>.
41 בכל יום . . . שעה] מרדכי, בכל עת.
42 ועל הכל] מרדכי (א' ור'), או"ז (ד' וכ"י) [ורש"י ברכות מ"ט ע"א ד"ה תחלה וכוף] ועל כולם, ויטרי (ד' וכ"י), מרדכי (כ"י), על כולם.
43 אנחנו] או"ז (ד' וכ"י), ויטרי (ד' וכ"י), מרדכי (ר' וא), אנו.
44 אותך] מרדכי (א', ור') את שמך. או"ז (ד), לך.
45 יתברך] או"ז (ד' וכ"י), ויטרי (ד), ויתברך.
46 יתברך שמך לעולם ועד] מרדכי, ל'.
47 בפה] מרדכי, או"ז (ד' וכ"י), ויטרי (ד), א, בפי.
48 ועד] או"ז (כ"י), ל'.

א׳ אנו[49] מודים לך ומברכים את שמך[50] תמיד אלהי ישענו[51] והנקם[52] לנו[53] מצרינו ובטובך[54] תשביע את נפשנו[55] ונודה לך ה׳ א׳[56] על נחלתנו ועל נחלת אבותינו[57] תושיבנו ותושיענו ותנחילנו[58] ותטעני בגבולנו[59] ככתוב ואכלת ושבעת וברכת את ה׳ א׳ על הארץ הטובה אשר נתן לך.[60] ברוך אתה ה׳ על הארץ ועל המזון.

ונודה[61] לך על הארץ ועל המזונות. ברוך אתה ה׳ על הארץ ועל המזון.

49 אנו] קלא (ק) אנחנו.

50 את שמך] טורין, את שם קודשך. רומניא (כ״י), לשם קדשך.

51 אלהי ישענו] רומניא (כ״י) בפה כל חי תמיד לעולם ועד ... וכתוב ואכלת ושבעת וברכת את ה׳ א׳ על הארץ הטובה אשר נתן לך. טורין, <תתברך בפי כל חי ויתפאר שמך עלינו לעולם ועד כאמור ואכלת ושבעת וברכת את ה׳ אלהיך על הארץ הטובה אשר נתן לך>.

52 והנקם] רומניא (כ״י), וזכור לנו ה׳ אלהינו את ברית אבותינו והנקם.

53 והנקם לנו ... בגבולנו] טורין, וזכור לנו ה׳ אלהינו את ברית אבותינו והנקמנו משונאינו ובישועתך תרום ותוגבה קרנינו והושיענו כל החיים יודוך סלה.

54 ובטובך] כפא, רומניא (כ״י) ומטובך.

55 ובטובך ... נפשנו] רומי, קלא (א׳ וק׳), ל׳.

56 ה׳ א׳] רומי, קלא (א׳ וק׳) ל׳.

57 על ... אבותינו] רומי, קלא (א׳ וק׳), על נחלת אבותינו.

58 תושיבנו ... ותנחילנו] רומי, קלא (א׳ וק׳) ל׳.

59 ותטענו בגבולנו] רומי, קלא (א׳ וק׳), ועל מזונות שחננתנו.

60 תושיבנו ... לך] רומניא (כ״י), ל׳.

61 ונודה לך ... המזונות] ויטרי (כ״י) [על הגליון], ונודה לשמך על הארץ ועל המזונות. הגדה, ונודה לשמך הגדול סלה באמת. או״ז (ד׳ וכ״י), וזכור לנו ה׳ וכ״י <אלקינו>] מהרה את ברית אבותינו ונקמינו מהרה משונאינו ובישועתך תרים ותגביה קרננו וכל החיים יודוך סלה. א, ויטרי (ד), מרדכי, ל׳.

נוסח ספרד (ב)

נודה לך ה׳ א׳ על שהנחלת לאבותינו ארץ חמדה טובה ורחבה ברית ותורה חיים ומזון על שהוצאתנו מארץ מצרים ופדיתנו מבית עבדים ועל בריתך שחתמת בבשרנו ועל חקי רצונך שהודעתנו ועל חיים ומזון שאתה זן ומפרנס אותנו. ועל הכל ה׳ א׳ אנו מודים לך ומברכים את שמך כאמור ואכלת ושבעת וברכת את ה׳ אלהיך על הארץ הטובה אשר נתן לך. בא״י על הארץ ועל המזון.

נוסח פרס

על ארצנו ועל נחלתנו. [על הגליון: ועל נחלת אבותינו] נודה לך ה׳ א׳ כי הנחלתנו והנחלת את אבותינו על ארץ חמדה טובה ורחבה ברית ותורה חיים ומזון ועל שהוצאתנו מארץ מצרים ופדיתנו מבית עבדים ועל בריתך שחתמת [בבשרנו] ועל תורתך תורת משה רבנו שלמדתנו ועל חקי רצונך שהודעתנו ועל חן וחסד ורחמים שאתה חונן ומלוה אותנו בכל רגע ובכל זמן. ועל הכל ה׳ א׳ אנו מודים לך ומברכים את שמך יתברך שמך בפי כל חי תמיד לעולם ועד כאמור ואכלת ושבעת וברכת את ה׳ א׳ על הארץ הטובה אשר נתן לך. בא״י על הארץ ועל המזון.

III

ברכת ירושלם

נוסח א׳י מן הגניזה	הנוסח המקורי
רחם ה׳ א׳[1] על ישראל[2] עמך ועל[3] ירושלים עירך [ועל[3a] מלכות בית דוד משיחך ועל הבית הגדול והקדוש שנקרא שמך עליו ומלכות בית דוד מהרה תחזירה[4] למקומה בימינו [ובנה[5] ירושלים בקרוב והעלינו לתוכה ושמחינו בה] ברוך אתה ה׳ בונה[5a] ברחמיו את ירושלים, אמן. בימינו[6] תבנה.	רחם ה׳ א׳ על ישראל עמך ועל ירושלם עירך ועל ציון משכן כבודך ועל מזבחך ועל היכלך. ברוך אתה ה׳ בונה ירושלם.

Variants III

1 ה׳ א׳] גניזה א, <ברחמיך הרבים ובחסדיך הגדולים ובטוביך הנאמנים>.

2 על ישראל] גניזה א, גניזה ם. עלינו ועל ישראל.

3 ועל . . . עירך] גניזה א, ועל ציון משכן כבודך. גניזה ם, ועל ירושלם עירך ועל ציון משכן כבודך.

3a ועל-משיחך] גניזה ם, ל׳.

4 תחזירה] גניזה א, תחזיר.

5 ובנה] גניזה א, המוסגר ל׳. גניזה ם, בימינו ובנה ירושלם בקרוב בנין עולם והעלנו לתוכה.

5a בונה] גניזה ם, הבונה.

6 בימינו תבנה] גניזה א, ל׳.

סדר רב עמרם

רחם ה׳ א׳ על ישראל עמך ועל ירושלים עירך ועל ציון משכן כבידך ועל מלכות בית דוד משיחך ועל הבית הגדול והקדוש שנקרא שמך עליו [אבינו[7] מלכנו] רועינו זנו מפרנסנו מכלכלנו הרוח לנו מהרה מצרותינו ואל תצריכנו לידי מתנת בשר ודם שמתנתם מעומה וחרפתם מרובה בשם קדשך הגדול והנורא בטחנו ויבא אליהו ומשיח בן דוד בחיינו ומלכות בית דוד [משיחך][7] מהרה תחזור למקומה ומלוך עלינו כי אתה לבדך והושיענו למען שמך והעלנו לתוכה ושמחנו בה ונחמנו בציון עירך. ברוך אתה ה׳ בונה ירושלים.

סדר רב סעדיה גאון

רחם ה׳ א׳ על ישראל עמך ועל ירושלם עירך ועל[8] היכלך ועל מעונך ועל ציון משכן כבודך ועל הבית הגדול והקדוש אשר (אתה)[9] שמך נקרא עליו ומלכות בית דויד[10] תחזיר למקומה בימינו ובנה את ירושלם בקרוב.[11] ברוך אתה ה׳ בונה ירושלם אמן.

רמבם

רחם ה׳ א׳ על ישר[אל] עמך ועל ירושלם עירך ועל ציין משכן כבודך ועל הבית הגדול והקדוש שנקרא שמך עליו ומלכות בית דוד משיחך תחזור[12] למקומה בימינו[13] ובנה את[14] ירושלם[15] בקרוב[16] כאשר דברת.[17] ברוך אתה ה׳ בונה[18] ברחמיו את ירושלם אמן.

7 המוסגר חסר בכ״י א׳:

8 ועל היכלך . . . משכן כבודך] רס״ג ב׳, ל׳.

9 (אתה) שמך נקרא] רס״ג כ״י א, אתה שמך נקרא. רס״ג ב׳, אשר נקרא שמך.

10 דויד] רס״ג ב׳, דוד <מהרה>.

11 בקרוב] רס״ג ב׳, <בנין ב״י [במהרה בימינו] והעלינו לתוכה ושמחינו בה>.

12 תחזור] רמבם נדפס, תכלאל, תימן (כ״י), תחזיר:

13 בימינו] תימן כ״י, במהרה בימינו:

14 את] רמבם נדפס, תכלאל, ל׳:

15 ירושלם] תימן כ״י, תכלאל, <עירך>:

16 בקרוב] תימן כ״י, תכלאל, ל׳:

17 דברת] תימן כ״י, <ובנה אותה בנין עולם במהרה בימינו>.

18 בונה] תימן כ״י, הבונה.

נוסח ספרד (א)

רחם ה' א' עלינו ועל ישראל עמך ועל ירושלם עירך ועל הר[19] ציון משכן כבודך ועל הבית הגדול והקדוש שנקרא שמך עליו אבינו רוענו זונו פרנסנו[20] כלכלנו הרויחנו הרוח[21] לנו מהרה מכל צרותינו ואל[22] תצריכנו ה' א' לידי מתנות בשר ודם ולא[23] לידי הלואתם שמתנתם מעוטה וחרפתם מרובה אלא

נוסח רומניא

ורחם[24] ה' א' עלינו[25] ועל ישראל עמך[26] ועל ציון משכן כבודך ועל מלכות בית דוד משיחך ועל הבית הגדול והקדוש שנקרא שמך עליו ועלינו[27] אבינו[28] רעינו זוננו פרנסנו וכלכלנו הרויחנו הרוח לנו[29] מהרה מכל צרותינו ואל[30] נא תבטיחנו ואל נא[30a] תביאנו לידי מתנת בשר ודם ולא[31] לידי

נוסח ארץ האי (עץ חיים)

רחם ה' א' על[32] ירושלם עירך ועל ציון משכן כבודך ועלינו[33] ועל כל ישראל עמך ועל מלכות בית דוד משיחך ועל[34] הבית הגדול והקדוש[35] מהרה[36] תקימנו[37] למקומו אלהינו[38] אבינו[39] רעינו זונינו פרנסינו וכלכלינו[40] והרויחנו[41] והרוח לנו ה' א' מהרה[42] מכל צרותינו[43] ואל[44]

19 הר] אבודרהם, ל'.

20 פרנסנו וכלכלנו] ספרד (כ"י), מפרנסנו מכלכלנו.

21 הרוח] אבודרהם, והרויח.

22 ואל] ספרד (כ"י), אל.

23 ולא .. והרחבה] אבודרהם, ספרד (כ"י), ל'.

24 ורחם] טורין, רומי, קלא (א' וק'), רומניא (כ"י), רחם.

25 עלינו ועל] רומניא (כ"י) על. טורין עלינו ועל כל. רומי (א), עלינו על.

26 עמך] רומי, קלא (א' וק'), רומניא (כ"י), טורין, <ועל ירושלם עירך>.

27 ועלינו] קלא (א), ל'.

28 אבינו] טורין, ל'. רומניא (כ"י) רומי (א) רומי (ב), <מלכנו>.

29 לנו] רומי, קלא (א' וק') <ה' א'>.

30 ואל נא .... תביאנו] טורין, רומניא (כ"י), ואל תצריכנו ה' א'. שדל, קלא (א' וק') ונא אל תצריכנו ה' א'. רומי (א), ואל תצריכנו ה' א' עוד.

30a נא] רומי (ב), ל'.

31 ולא . . . הלואתם] טורין, רומי (ב), כפא, ל'.

32 על] א, מרדכי, על ישראל עמך ועל. ויטרי (כ"י), או"ז (ד' וכ"י), הגדה, עלינו ועל ישראל עמך ועל. ויטרי (ד'), עלינו ועל כל ישראל עמך ועל.

33 ועלינו . . עמך] א, מרדכי, או"ז (ד' וכ"י), ויטרי (ד' וכ"י), ל'.

34 ועל הבית . . . אבינו] מרדכי, ל'.

35 והקדוש] הגדה, א, או"ז (ד' וכ"י), ויטרי (כ"י) <שנקרא שמך עליו>. ויטרי (ד') <שנקרא שמך עליו ועלינו>.

36 מהרה . . למקומו] א, או"ז (ד' וכ"י), ויטרי (ד'), ל'.

37 תקימנו] ויטרי (כ"י), תחזירנה. הגדה, <ותחזירהו>.

38 אלהינו] או"ז (ד'), ל'.

39 אבינו] ויטרי (כ"י), <מלכנו>.

40 וכלכלינו] או"ז (ד' וכ"י), כלכלינו.

41 והרויחנו והרוח] או"ז (ד' וכ"י), הרויחנו הרויח.

42 ה' א' מהרה] מרדכי, ל'. או"ז (ד'), א, מהרה, ל'.

43 צרותינו] או"ז (ד'), שונאינו.

44 ואל] א, ונא אל. ויטרי (ד') ואל נא.

לידך המלאה והרחבה
שלא[42] נבוש בעולם[43]
הזה ולא נכלם לעולם[44]
הבא ומלכות בית דוד
משיחך במהרה תחזירנה
למקומה ותבנה[45] בית
המקדש בימינו, ברוך
אתה ה' בונה ברחמיו[46]
ירושלם, אמן. בחיינו[47]
תבנה עיר ציון ותכוו
העבודה בירושלם.

הלואתם[48] לפי[49]
שמתנתם מעוטה
וחרפתם מרובה[50] אלא
לידך[51] הטובה[52]
המלאה העשירה
השבעה הפתוחה
הרחבה[53] שלא[54] נבוש
בעולם הזה[55] ולא נכלם
לחיי העולם הבא[56]
כי[57] בשם קדשך הגדול
קוינו[58] הראנו נחמה
ישועה בקרוב בימינו

תצריכנו ה'[59] א'[60] לידי
מתנות[61] בשר ודם ולא
לידי הלואתם[62] ולא
נבוש[63] לעולם ועד
ותבנה[64] ירושלם עיר
הקדש[65] במהרה בימינו.
ברוך אתה ה' מנחם[66]
ציון עירו ובונה ירושלם.

42 שלא] אבודרהם, לא.

43 בעולם הזה] ספרד (כ"י), אבודרהם, ל'.

44 לעולם הבא] אבודרהם, ל'. ספרד (כ"י), לעולם ועד כי בשם קדשך הגדול והנורא בטחנו.

45 ותבנה . . . בימינו] אבודרהם, ספרד (כ"י), ובנה [כ"י <את>] ירושלים עיר קדשך [כ"י <במהרה>] בימינו.

46 ברחמיו] אבודרהם, ספרד (כ"י), ל'.

47 בחיינו . . . בירושלם] ספרד (כ"י) ל'. אבודרהם (?).

48 הלואתם] שדל, רומי (א), קלא (א' וק'), הלואת אדם.

49 לפי] טורין, קלא (ק), ל'.

50 לפי . . . מרובה] רומי, קלא (א), ל'.

51 לידך] רומניא (כ"י), מידך.

52 הטובה...והרחבה] טורין, המלאה והרחבה והנוראה כי בשם קודשך הגדול והנורא בטחנו. רומי (א), המלאה הרחבה והפתוחה והשבעה. רומי (ב), שדל, המלאה הרחבה הפתוחה והשבעה והטובה. קלא (א' וק') המלאה והרחבה הפתוחה והשבעה הטובה.

53 הרחבה] רומניא (כ"י), ל'.

54 שלא] רומי, קלא (א' וק'), אשר לא. טורין, לא.

55 בעולם הזה] טורין, ל'.

56 לחיי העולם הבא] רומניא (כ"י) לעולם הבא. טורין, לא בעוה"ז ולא לעוה"ב.

57 כי בשם . . . ולישועתך קוינו] טורין, רומניא (כ"י), ל'.

58 קוינו . . . קוינו] רומי, [רומי (ב), <והקדוש>] והנורא בטחנו ויבא אליהו הנביא ומשיח בן דוד עבדך במהרה בימינו ויביאו לנו שמועה טובה מארץ מרחק.

59 ה' א' . . לעולם ועד] מרדכי, ל'

60 ה' א'] א, הגדה, או"ז (ד' וכ"י), ויטרי (ד' וכ"י), <לא>.

61 מתנות] א, או"ז (ד'), ויטרי (ד'), מתנת.

62 הלואתם] א, <כי אם לידך המלאה הפתוחה הקדושה והרחבה>. הגדה, <אלא לידך המלאה הרחבה והפתוחה>, או"ז (ד'), <אלא לידך הקדושה והמלאה והרחבה>.

63 ולא נבוש] א, שלא נבוש ולא נכלם. הגדה, ולא נכלם.

64 ותבנה] א, או"ז (ד'), ובנה.

65 עיר הקדש] מרדכי, עירך. או"ז (כ"י), עיר קדשך.

66 מנחם . . ירושלם] מרדכי, או"ז (ד' וכ"י), ויטרי (ד'), בונה ירושלם. א, הגדה, ויטרי (כ"י), בונה ברחמיו ירושלם.

והשב ישראל לנוהו ומלכותך[67] ומלכות בית דוד משיחך תחזירנה למקומה כי לך ה׳ א׳ מיחלות עינינו ולישועתך קוינו ואף על פי שאכלנו ושתינו חרבן ביתך הגדול[68] והקדוש ושאר[69] פיזור גלויותנו לא שכחנו ואל[70] נא תשכחנו גם[71] אתה לנצח כאמור[72] אם אשכחך ירושלם תשכח ימיני תדבק לשוני לחכי אם לא אזכרכי אם לא אעלה את ירושלם על ראש שמחתי ונאמר[73] בונה ירושלם ה׳ נדחי ישראל יכנס. ברוך אתה ה׳ בונה עירו[74] עיר ירושלם, אמן. בחיינו ובמהרה[75] בימינו[76] תבנה[77] עיר ציון[78] וישוכלל[79] אפריון.

67 ומלכותך] כפא, ל׳.

68 הגדול והקדוש] טורין, רומניא (כ״י), ל׳.

69 ושאר פיזור גליותינו] רומי, קלא (א׳ וק׳), ל׳.

70 ואל נא] רומי, קלא (א׳ וק׳), אל. רומי (ב), ואל. רומניא (כ״י), נא אל.

71 גם אתה לנצח] רומי [רומי (ב), <לנצח>] ואל תעזבנו לאורך ימינו. קלא (א׳, וק׳) ואל תעזבנו לאורך ימים. רומניא (כ״י) נא אל תעזבנו נא אל תפר בריתך אתנו. טורין, ה׳ אלקינו ואל תעזבנו מלכינו ואל תטשנו גואלנו ואל תכלימנו בבקשתנו ואל תתננו בנפש אויבנו ואל תפר בריתך אתנו ויבא אליהו הנ׳ ומשיח בן דויד במהרה בימינו.

72 כאמור ... שמחתי] טורין, ובנה ירושלם עירך במהרה בימינו. רומי, קלא (א׳ וק׳) ובנה את ירושלם עיר הקדש [רומי (א) קדשך] במהרה בימינו.

73 ונאמר ... יכנס] רומי, קלא (א׳ וק׳), טורין, ל׳. רומניא (כ״י), ותבנה ירושלם עיר הקודש במהרה בימינו.

74 עירו עיר] רומניא (כ״י), ברחמיו עירו, רומי, קלא (א׳ וק׳) ברחמיו בנין. טורין, ל׳.

75 ובמהרה] רומי, קלא (א׳ וק׳), במהרה.

76 בימינו] רומי, קלא (א׳ וק׳) <ויבא גואל ויגאלנו>.

77 תבנה] רומי, קלא (א׳ וק׳) ותבנה.

78 עיר ציון] טורין, ציון. רומניא (כ״י) עירנו.

79 וישוכלל אפריון] רומי, קלא (א׳ וק׳), טורין, ותכון העבודה בירושלם. רומניא (כ״י) ותכונן היכלנו ויבא גואלנו מהרה ויגאלנו.

נוסח ספרד (ב)

רחם ה' א' עלינו ועל ישראל עמך ועל ירושלם עירך ועל הר ציון משכן כבודך ועל הבית הגדול והקדוש שנקרא שמך עליו אבינו רענו זוננו פרנסנו כלכלנו הרויחנו הרוח לנו מהרה מכל צרותינו ואל תצריכנו ה' א' לידי מתנות בשר ודם ולא לידי הלואתם שמתנתם מעוטה וחרפתם מרובה אלא לידך המלאה והרחבה העשירה והפתוחה שלא נבוש בעולם הזה ולא נכלם לעולם הבא ומלכות בית דוד משיחך תחזירנה למקומה במהרה בימינו ברוך אתה ה' בונה ברחמיו בנין ירושלם, אמן. בחיינו ובחיי כל קהל בית ישראל תבנה עיר ציון ברנה ותכון עבודת הקדש בירושלם וארמון על משפטו ישב בקרוב כבראשונה.

נוסח פרס

רחמנו רחם ה' א' עלינו ועל ישראל עמך ועל ירושלם עירך ועל ציון משכן כבודך על היכלך ועל מקדשך ועל מעונך ועל הבית הגדול והקדוש שנקרא שמך עליו ומלכות בית דוד משיחך מהרה תחזירה למקומה בימינו ובנה את ירושלם בקרוב והעלינו לתוכה ושמחינו בבנינה כי מקדם [צ"ל כמקדם] סלה, בא"י הבונה ברחמיו את עיר ירושלם. ואמרו אמן.

IV

ברכת הטוב והמטיב

הנוסח המקורי

ברוך אתה ה׳ א׳ מלך העולם הטוב והמטיב.

נוסח א׳ כן הגניזה

ברוך אתה ה׳ א׳ מלך העולם אבינו[a] מלכנו[1] הטוב והמטיב אשר[2] בכל יום ויום הוא מטיב עמנו הוא גמלנו הוא[3] יגמלנו [גומלנו ?] הוא יגמלנו לעד חן וחסד ורוח ורחמים [וכל טוב].

סדר רב עמרם

ברוך אתה ה׳ א׳ מלך העולם אבינו מלכנו גואלינו אדירנו יוצרנו אדון נשמתנו קדושנו קדוש יעקב המלך הטוב והמטיב שבכל יום ויום הוא מטיב עמנו [הוא גמלנו] הוא גומלנו הוא יגמלנו לעד חן וחסד ירחמים וכל טוב.

סדר רב סעדיה גאון

בא״י אמ״ה האל[4] אבינו מלכנו בוראנו[5] גואלנו המלך הטוב והמטיב אשר בכל יום ויום הוא מרבה[6] להיטיב עמנו והוא[7] יגמלנו לעד חן וחסד ורוח[8] ורחמים וכל טוב.

רמבם

ברוך אתה ה׳ א׳ מלך העולם האל אבינו מלכנו אדירנו בוראנו[9] קדושנו קדוש יעקב[10] המלך (הרחמן)[11] הטוב והמטיב (אשר) בכל[12] יום ויום (הוא[13] מטיב עמנו) הוא[14] גומלנו[15] חן וחסד ורחמים[16] וכל טוב.

Variants IV

a אבינו] גני.ה מ, האל אבינו.

1 מלכנו] גניזה א, <גואלינו יוצרנו קדושנו קדוש יעקב המלך>. גניזה מ, אדירנו קדושינו קדוש יעקב רועה ישראל המלך הרחמן.

2 אשר . . . ויום] גניזה א, גני.ה מ, שבכל יום.

3 הוא יגמלנו וכו׳] גניזה א, הוא [עתיד] לגומלנו . . . . . (?).

3a ורוח] גני.ה מ, רוח.

4 האל] רס״ג (ב), ל׳.

5 בוראנו גואלנו] רס״ג (ב), יוצרנו קדושנו קדוש יעקב.

6 מרבה להיטיב] רס״ג (ב), מיטיב.

7 והוא] רס״ג (ב) הוא.

8 ורוח] רס״ג (ב) רוח.

9 בוראנו] רמבם (ד׳), <גואלנו>. תימן (כ״י), <גואלנו גומלנו טוב>.

10 יעקב] תימן (כ״י), <רוענו ורועי ישראל עמו האל>.

11 הרחמן] רמבם (ד׳), תימן (ד׳ וכ״י), ל׳.

12 (אשר) בכל] רמבם (ד׳), תימן, שבכל. תימן (כ״י), אשר בכל.

13 הוא מטיב עמנו] רמבם (ד׳), תימן, ל׳. תימן (כ״י), הוא היטיב לנו הוא מטיב לנו הוא ייטיב לנו.

14 הוא] רמבם (ד׳) ל׳.

15 הוא גומלנו] תימן (כ״י), הוא גמלנו הוא גומלנו הוא יגמלנו לעד לנצח.

16 ורחמים] תימן (כ״י), <ופרנסה וכלכלה>.

נוסח ספרד (א)	נוסח רומניא	נוסח ארץ האי (עץ חיים)
בא"י אמ"ה לעד[17]	בא"י אמ"ה[20] תתברך[21]	בא"י אמ"ה[31] האל[32]
האל[18] אבינו מלכנו	האל לעד[22] אבינו	אבינו מלכינו אדירנו[33]
אדירנו בוראנו גואלנו[19]	מלכנו מחסנו[23] אדירנו[24]	גואלינו[34] קדושינו קדוש
קדושנו קדוש יעקב	בוראנו[25] גואלנו[26]	יעקב רועינו רועה
רוענו רועה ישראל	קדושנו קדוש יעקב[27]	ישראל האל[35] המלך[36]
המלך הטוב והמטיב	המלך[28] הטוב והמטיב[29]	החי[37] הטוב והמטיב[38]
לכל שבכל יום ויום	שבכל יום ויום[30] היא	שבכל יום[39] הוא[40]

17 לעד] ספרד (כ"י), ל'.

18 האל] אבודרהם, ל'.

19 גואלנו] ספרד (כ"י), ל'.

20 אמ"ה] רומי, קלא (א' וק') <אלהי אברהם>.

21 תתברך] רומניא (כ"י), טורין, ל'. רומי, קלא (א' וק') יתברך.

22 האל לעד] רומי, קלא (א' וק') לעד האל. טורין, האל.

23 מחסנו] טורין, ל'.

24 אדירנו] רומניא (כ"י), קלא (א' וק'), ל'.

25 בוראנו] טורין, ל'.

26 גואלנו] רומי, קלא (א' וק'), טורין, רומניא (כ"י), <יוצרנו>.

27 יעקב] רומניא (כ"י), רוענו רועה נאמן. טורין, רוענו רועה ישראל. רומי (ב), שדל, קלא (א' וק'), רוענו רועה ישראל רועה נאמן. רומי (א), רוענו רועה נאמן רועה ישראל.

28 המלך] קלא (א), האל המלך. רומניא כ"י, טורין, המלך החי.

29 והמטיב] טורין, קלא (ק), <לכל>. רומניא (כ"י), רומי, קלא (א), <לכל אל>.

30 ויום] רומי, קלא (א' וק'), <עמנו>.

31 אמ"ה] מרדכי, <הטוב והמטיב>.

32 האל] מרדכי, הגדה, ל'.

33 אדירנו] מרדכי, ל'. א, הגדה [ושם נמחק] רש"י [ברכות מ"ט ע"א ד"ה שתי מלכיות] <בוראנו>.

34 גואלינו] א, הגדה, או"ז (ד' וכ"י), <יוצרנו>

35 האל] א, הגדה, ויטרי (ד' וכ"י), או"ז (ד' וכ"י), רש"י [שם], ל'.

36 האל המלך . . . והמטיב] מרדכי, ל'.

37 החי] או"ז (ד' וכ"י), הגדה, ויטרי (ד' וכ"י), א, רש"י [שם], ל'.

38 והמטיב] א, ויטרי (ד' וכ"י [על הגליון]), הגדה, רש"י [שם], <לכל>.

39 שבכל יום] מרדכי, א, או"ז (ד' וכ"י), ויטרי (ד' וכ"י), שבכל יום ויום. הגדה, אל שבכל יום ויום.

40 הוא מטיב . . . ייטיב לנו] מרדכי, טוב ומטיב עמנו. הגדה, הוא מטיב עמנו והטיב לנו. ויטרי (ד'), הוא מטיב עמנו. ויטרי (כ"י) הוא מטיב עמנו והוא הטיב והוא ייטיב עמנו. א, הוא הטיב הוא מטיב הוא ייטיב לנו. או"ז (ד) מטיב עמנו. או"ז (כ"י) מטיב עמנו, והוא ייטיב לנו.

הוא מטיב לנו[41] הוא[42] הטיב לנו[43] הוא ייטיב לנו[44] הוא גומלנו הוא גמלנו הוא יגמלנו לעד חן וחסד ורחמים ורוח וריוח[45] והצלה וכל טוב.

מטיב עמנו[46] הוא[47] ייטיב אחריתנו[48] הוא גמלנו[49] הוא[50] יגמלנו הוא[51] עתיד לגמלנו לעדי[52] עד חיים[53] חן[54] והסד[54a] וריוח[55] ורחמים[56] ובכל[57] טוב נתברך[58] באלהי אמן נשבע באלהי אמן.

מטיב לנו הוא היטיב לנו הוא ייטיב לנו הוא[59] גומלנו הוא גמלנו הוא יגמלנו לעד לריוח[60] והצלה והצלח׳ לחיים ולשלום לכל טוב.

41 לנו] ספרד (כ״י), עמנו.

42 הוא היטיב ... ייטיב לנו] וז״ל אבודרהם, ואמ׳ במדבר שצריך לומ׳ ג׳ הטבות הטוב והמטיב הוא מטיב לנו והראש היה אומר הוא מטיב לנו הוא הטיב לנו הוא ייטיב לנו כמו שאומר גמולות הוא גומלנו הוא גמלנו הוא יגמלנו כנגד הווה ועבר ועתיד].

43 לנו] ספרד (כ״י), עמנו.

44 לנו] ספרד (כ״י), עמנו.

45 וריוח והצלה] אבודרהם, ספרד (כ״י), ל׳.

46 הוא מטיב עמנו] רומניא (כ״י) <הוא הטיב לנו>. שדל, קלא (א׳ וק׳), הוא הטיב לנו הוא מטיב עמנו. רומי, (א), הוא מטיב לנו הוא ייטיב לנו. רומי (ב) עמנו הוא מטיב לנו הוא ייטיב עמנו.

47 הוא ייטיב אחריתנו] רומניא כ״י, רומי (א׳ ב׳), ל׳.

48 אחריתנו] רומי, קלא (א׳ וק׳), עמנו.

49 גמלנו] כפא, רומניא (כ״י), רומי, קלא (ק), <הוא גומלנו>.

50 הוא ... לגמלנו] טורין, הוא עתיד לגמלנו והוא יגמלנו. רומניא (כ״י) הוא יגמלני. רומי (ב), הוא גומלנו הוא יגמלנו ברחמיו לעד.

51 הוא עתיד לגמלנו] כפא, רומי, קלא (א׳ וק׳), ל׳.

52 לעדי עד] טורין, לעד. רומי, קלא (א׳ וק׳) ברחמיו לעד. רומניא (כ״י), כל טוב לעדי עד ולנצח נצחים.

53 חיים] רומי, טורין, קלא (א׳ וק׳), ל׳.

54 חיים ... ובכל טוב] רומניא (כ״י), ל׳.

54a וחסד] רומי (ב), ל׳.

55 וריוח] רומי, קלא (א׳ וק׳), ל׳.

56 ורחמים] טורין, <וברכה והצלחה>. רומי, קלא (א׳ וק׳) <ברכה [רומי (ב) (?) <רפואה>] רוחה והצלחה וחיים ושלום.

57 ובכל טוב] טורין, וכל טוב. רומי קלא (א׳, וק׳), וכל טוב ומכל טוב.

58 נתברך ... נשבע בא׳ אמן] רומי (א), אל יחסרנו הרחמן. שדל, אל יחסרנו לעולם. קלא (א׳ וק׳) רומי (ב), אל יחסרנו אבינו אב הרחמן. טורין, ל׳. רומניא (כ״י), <נושע באלהי אמן>.

59 הוא .. לעד] או״ז (ד׳), ל׳. הגדה, ויטרי (ד׳ וכ״י), או״ז (כ״י), הוא גמלנו הוא גומלנו הוא [הגדה, והוא] ינמול בעדינו. א, הוא גמלנו הוא גומלנו הוא יגמלנו לעד.

60 לריוח .. טוב] מרדכי, ל׳. הגדה, לחן לחסד לרחמים לרוח והצלה והצלחה וברכה וישועה ונחמה פרנסה וכלכלה ורחמים וחיים ושלום וכל טוב. או״ז (ד׳ וכ״י), לחן לחסד ריוח ורחמים הצלחה וברכה וישועה ונחמה וכל טוב. ויטרי (ד׳ וכ״י) לחן לחסד [כ״י <לרחמים>] לריוח והצלה והצלחה וברכה [כ״י <ורחמים>] וחיים ושלום וכל טוב. א, לחן לחסד ולרחמים ולרוח הצלה והצלחה ברכה וישועה נחמה פרנסה ובלכלה ורחמים וחיים ושלום וכל טוב ומכל טוב אל יחסרנו.

נוסח ספרד (ב)

בא"י אמ"ה לעד האל אבינו מלכנו אדירנו בוראנו גואלנו קדושנו קדוש יעקב רוענו רועה ישראל המלך הטוב והמטיב לכל שבכל יום ויום הוא היטיב לנו הוא מטיב לנו הוא ייטיב לנו הוא גמלנו הוא גומלנו הוא יגמלנו לעד חן וחסד ורחמים ורוח והצלה וכל טוב.

נוסח פרס

בא"י אמ"ה יתברך האל לעד אבינו מלכנו מחסנו אדירנו אבירנו יוצרנו גמלנו קדושנו קדוש יעקב ורוענו רועה ישראל האל המלך החי הטוב והמטיב אשר בכל יום מרבה להטיב עמנו הוא גמלנו הוא גומלנו הוא עתיד יגמלנו [!] לעד לחן לחסד ולרחמים המלך [!] הסלחה [צ"ל הצלחה] כל טוב.

CHAPTER 13

THE MEANING OF THE WORD פרס IN THE EXPRESSIONS פורס על שמע, בפרוס עצרת, בפרוס הפסח, AND בפרוס החג

I

THE root פרס as used in the expressions פורס על שמע, בפרוס החג, בפרוס עצרת, בפרוס הפסח means "to promulgate," "to announce." The root has this meaning quite frequently in mishnaic Hebrew,[1] in Aramaic, and in

[1] The phrase וכסיל יפרש אולת (Prov. 13.16) may be an illustration of the use of the root פרש in the sense of "proclaim" even in biblical Hebrew. The meaning "spread" obviously does not apply, and the versions as well as the later translators struggle to give the word פרש a meaning which, retaining the significance of "spread," also includes some other thought. Toy, in his Commentary, renders יפרש "displays," apparently because he feels the inadequacy of the translation "spreads," but he offers no explanation for this rendering. There can be no doubt that the word has the meaning "promulgate" in mishnaic Hebrew. For examples of the use of the word פרס in this sense, see *'Aruk*, ed. Kohut, s. v. פרזדגמא and s. v. דטגמא. To the examples there cited should be added ופרס דיוטגמא in *Abot d'R. Natan*, II, chap. 8, ed. Schechter 12b; and the following passage in *Debarim Rabbah* 5.14: א"ר שמואל בר נחמן מה עשה יהושע היה פ ו ר ש דאטגמא בכל מקום שהיה הולך לכבש והיה כתוב בה מי שמבקש לילך ילך לו [ומי שמבקש לעשות שלום יעשה] ומי שמבקש לעשות מלחמה יעשה "R. Samuel ben Nahman said: 'What did Joshua do? Wherever he went to make battle, he promulgated a decree, in which was written: "Whosoever desires to leave, may leave. Whosoever desires to make peace, may make peace. Whosoever desires to make war, may make war." ' "

In ed. Liebermann, p. 101, the word פורש is replaced by שולח. This substitution for the more common expression occurs also in Yer. Shebi'it 6.1, 36c, where the passage reads: דא"ר שמואל בר נחמן שלש פרסטיגיות ש י ל ח יהושע לארץ ישראל עד שלא יכנסו לארץ מי שהוא רוצה להפנות יפנה להשלים ישלים לעשות מלחמה יעשה "R. Samuel ben Nahman said:

387

Reprinted from *Jewish Quarterly Review*, New Series, Volume 32, 1942.

Syriac.[2] Failure to realize that it has this meaning in the expressions mentioned has resulted in confusion with regard to their significance, and a misconception of the customs and institutions to which they refer.

The expression פרס (על) [את] שמע occurs in the Mishna[3] six times. It is cited quite frequently in other rabbinical sources.[4] Without offering any valid reasons for their decision, ancient and modern writers have assumed that the original form of the expression was פרס ע ל שמע and that פרס א ת שמע was simply a scribal error.[5] A study of the various texts in which the expression occurs indicates, however, (1) that where the form פרס ע ל שמע occurs in extant texts it has frequently displaced an earlier פרס את שמע; (2) that the Palestinian texts generally, if not universally, had the form פרס את שמע;[6] and (3) an authority

'Joshua sent three decrees to the land of Israel, before he entered it. "Whosoever wishes to leave, let him leave. Whosoever wishes to make peace, let him make peace. Whosoever wishes to make war, let him make war." ' "

In *Vayyikra Rabbah* 17.6, the passage likewise reads: א'ר ישמעאל בר' נחמן ג' פרוזדיגמאות ש ל ח יהושע אצלם הרוצה לפנות יפנה להשלים ישלים לעשות מלחמה יעשה. It is unlikely therefore that the שלח is merely a copyist's substitution for פרש; more probably the change was made in the oral tradition. *Debarim Rabbah* has obviously preserved the word פרס originally used by R. Samuel ben Nahman, while the transmitters of the tradition, as preserved in the parallel passages, changed it to שלח, because they no longer understood the meaning of פרש in this connection. The expression is used in precisely the same sense, in *Pesikta Rabbati*, LIII, ed. Friedmann, 151b, in the phrase: פרוסטומא שלו פרושה "his decree was promulgated."

[2] See Payne-Smith, *Thes. Syr.*

[3] Mishna Megillah 4.3, 5, 6 (four times).

[4] Tosefta Megillah 4(3).27 (twice), 28 (twice); *Masseket Soferim* 10.6 (Higger, p. 212); 14.4 (Higger, p. 256); 14.10 (Higger, pp. 264 ff.), five times; 16.9 (Higger, p. 294), twice; Yer. Berakot 5.5, 9c; ibid. Megillah 4.4, 75a (twice); ibid. 4.6, 75b (twice); ibid. 4.7 (thrice); Babli Sotah 30b; *Vayyikra Rabbah* 23.4; *Shir ha-Shirim Rabbah* 2.7 (four times).

[5] See I. Elbogen, *Der juedische Gottesdienst in seiner geschichtlichen Entwicklung*, p. 515; and Kohut, *'Aruk ha-Shalem*, s. v. פרס, VIII.

[6] The evidence for these statements is presented in Appendix A.

as late as R. Amram Gaon preferred the form פרס את שמע to פרס על שמע.

Now while it is universally agreed that the expression פרס (על) [את] שמע refers to the public reading of the Shema,[7] there has been much disagreement regarding the precise meaning of פרס in this expression.

According to a geonic tradition, cited by R. Nissim of Barcelona, in his commentary on Alfasi,[8] the word פרס in this phrase, means "begin." The expression אין פורסים (על) [את] שמע means, therefore, "One must not begin to read the Shema with less than ten people present." The "beginning" refers, according to him, to the benedictions which precede the Shema. This interpretation of the Mishna indicates that it is forbidden for a public reader to "begin" the benedictions preliminary to the Shema until ten people have assembled.

According to another widely cited interpretation of geonic origin, פרס in this connection means "bless."[9] The expression פרס (על) [את] שמע means, according to this interpretation, simply, "One does not say the blessings

[7] This cannot be doubted in the light of Mishna Megillah 4.3.

[8] On Megillah 25b.

[9] See B. M. Lewin, *Ozar ha-Geonim*, V, p. 37. Various writers attempt to prove that פרס has the meaning of "bless" by citing the phrase ארי הוא יפריס נכסתא which they quote from Targum to I Samuel 9.13, כי הוא יברך הזבח (so *'Aruk*, s. v. פרס, VII); marginal note to Yemenite Ms. of Megillah cites the text as follows: הוא יפרוס על מזוניה by citing the Targum to I Samuel 9.13, כי הוא יברך הזבח. According to *'Aruk*, s. v. פרס, VII the passage in Targum reads: ארי הוא יפריס נכסתא. A marginal note to the Yemenite Ms. of the treatise Megillah cites the passage as follows: ארי הוא יפרוס על מזוניה (so in Ms.; J. J. Price, *The Columbia College Ms. of Megilla*, p. 51, erroneously reads הרי). According to Professor Alexander Sperber, the reading of the passage in all the texts he has utilized for his edition is ארי הוא פריס על מזונא. Dr. Sperber writes me, "The only exception is the first Rabbinical Bible, Venice 1515–17, where על is not to be found, so that the reading is כי הוא פריס מזונא."

over the Shema when less than ten male adults are present."[10]

The difference of opinion recorded among these ancient writers has continued to modern times.[11]

This difference of opinion could hardly have arisen had the form פרס את שמע been accepted as valid: for the expression פרס את שמע could only mean "pronounce the Shema" as one pronounces a royal edict. This use of the word in connection with the Shema is particularly appropriate because the Shema is frequently described as a Divine edict.

"The reading of the Shema is (the promulgation) of My edict, said the Holy One, blessed be He," according to a

[10] Rashi's interpretation differs from that of all the older authorities. According to him, the expression פרס על שמע refers to the custom permitting persons who have come late to the service, and have therefore not heard the public recitation of the benedictions of the Shema and the *Kedushah*, to repeat the recitation of those parts of the service, even though these persons do not constitute a quorum by themselves, provided that including them there is a quorum present in the synagogue. (Rashi, Megillah 23b, catchword אין פורסין.) This interpretation has been widely accepted, and is followed by R. Jacob ben Asher in *Tur*, *Orah Hayyim*, 69.1, and also by Caro, in *Shulhan 'Aruk*, *Orah Hayyim* 69.1. The word פרס is, according to Rashi, applied to this custom because only the first benediction (or half the number usually prescribed as introductory to the Shema) is recited in public. According to his interpretation פרס in the phrase פרס על שמע has the meaning of "half" or "part." Rabad, in his strictures on *Yad*, *Hilkot Tefillah* 8.5, holds that פרס in this phrase has its usual meaning of "break," and it is used because it refers to the first of the two benedictions preceding the Shema.

[11] See I. Elbogen, *Studien zur Geschichte des juedischen Gottesdienstes*, Berlin, 1907, pp. 3 ff.; and *Der juedische Gottesdienst in seiner geschichtlichen Entwicklung*, second ed., Frankfort a. M., 1924, pp. 25 ff., 514 ff.; and also in *Revue des Études Juives* (hereafter *REJ*), LVI, 1908, pp. 222–227; L. Blau, *REJ*, XXXI, 1895, pp. 196 ff.; ibid., LV, 1908, pp. 209–220; LIX, 1910, pp. 188 ff.; LXXIII, 1921, pp. 140 ff.; W. Bacher, *REJ*, LVII, 1909, pp. 100–102; M. Liber, ibid., pp. 161–193; LVIII, pp. 1–22; H. Brody, *Monatsschrift*, LIV, 1910, pp. 491 ff.; L. Ginzberg, *REJ*, XCVIII, 1934, p. 80; and my remarks in *REJ*, XCIII, 1932, pp. 23 ff.

passage in *Pesikta d'R. Kahana.*[12] The analogy between the Shema and an edict is further emphasized in the famous passage in which the people are warned not to look upon its words as "an ancient edict, to which no one pays attention, but as a recent edict, which everyone rushes to read."[13]

And, indeed, there can be little doubt that originally the Shema was promulgated to the congregation by the leader as though it were an edict. The verse, "Hear O Israel, the Lord is our God, the Lord is one," readily lends itself to use as such a pronouncement. Because this verse was "promulgated" to the congregation by the leader, who in early times, doubtless, pronounced the Name YHWH in its original form, it was followed by the response of the congregation,[14] customary when that Name was heard,[15] namely, ברוך שם כבודו לעולם ועד "Blessed be His glorious Name forever and aye."

According to the Mishna,[16] the men of Jericho did not use this response, because they did not "promulgate" the Shema. On the contrary, they doubtless all recited it in unison. The expression used to describe their custom is כורכים א ת שמע, an expression coined because כורכים is the opposite of פורסים, as well as because the word כרך suggests action in unison. The use of the accusative את שמע in the phrase כורכים את שמע offers further testimony that the term

[12] Ed. Buber, 77a; similarly *Vayyikra Rabbah* 27.5.

[13] Sifre Deut. 33, Fr. 74a, Fi. 59.

[14] B. Ta'anit 16b, Sotah 40b. Similarly, Elbogen, *Studien*, p. 8. For the relation of this early form of the response to the form ברוך שם כבוד מלכותו לעולם ועד, see Appendix B.

[15] Thus it was used, also, in responding to the mention of the Name by the High Priest on the Day of Atonement (Mishna Yoma 3.8; 4.1, 2; 6.2; and see especially, B. Yoma 37a, Yer. Yoma 3.7, 40d). It is particularly significant that in that connection, as in the case of the Shema, the response is used, though no benediction is recited.

[16] Mishna Pesaḥim 4.8. This interpretation is placed on the Mishna by R. Judah ben Ilai and R. Meir, who both hold that ברוך שם וכו' was not said by the people of Jericho (Tosefta Pesaḥim 2(3).19, p. 160; Yer. Pesaḥim 4.9, 31b; B. ibid. 56a).

describing the alternative form of reading was originally פורס את שמע.

Because the reading of the Shema was looked upon as the promulgation of a royal edict, the ceremony assumed, particularly during the period of the domination of the Romans, the significance of the "acceptance of the Kingdom of God."[17] To listen to the Shema was to hear proclaimed the Divine command to regard God alone as King.

From early times, it was recognized of course that when it was not possible to arrange for a public reading of the Shema, or when an individual could not attend such a public reading, the obligation was fulfilled by reciting the passages privately. This was called קריאת שמע "reading of the Shema."[18]

During the Hadrianic persecutions, when the reading of the Shema was forbidden by the Roman government, the ancient ceremony of "promulgating the Shema" had to be abandoned.[19] Nevertheless, people sought to continue some

[17] See Mishna Berakot 2.5.

[18] See Mishna Berakot 1.1.

[19] There are several references in the talmudic writings indicating that the reading of the Shema was suppressed during the Hadrianic persecutions (cf. Tosefta Berakot 2.13, p. 4; and the fact that so eminent a scholar as R. Judah the Patriarch was accustomed to recite only the first verse of the Shema, because, obviously, he had been reared in a period when reading the Shema was quite unusual, see Berakot 13b, and *REJ*, XCIII, 185, p. 7). But the most explicit references to the effect of the persecutions on the ritual of the Shema occur in the geonic literature. Of these, the most important is the statement of Pirkoi ben Baboi which has been published from Genizah fragments by a number of scholars (see Ginzberg, *Geonica*, II, p. 50; *Ginze Schechter*, II, p. 551; J. Mann, in *REJ*, LXX, pp. 129 ff.; B. M. Lewin, *Tarbiz*, II, 1931, p. 398). The tradition is supported by a responsum of R. Sar Shalom Gaon, cited in *Seder R. Amram*, ed. Frumkin, 139b, and in *Pardes*, ed. Ehrenreich, p. 312. Both of these documents assert that the reciting of the Shema in the *Kedushah* originated in a persecution. Neither document definitely states that this persecution was that of Hadrian. But Pirkoi ben Baboi does state that it occurred five hundred years before his time (*Tarbiz*, ibid., p. 397). This would bring the date of the persecution to about 300. As we have no record of any persecu-

form of public reading of the Shema. Several devices were employed to overcome the vigilance of the Roman soldiery, on guard lest the forbidden ceremony be performed. One of these devices was apparently the recital of the Shema in another part of the service, where the soldier would not expect it, and would, perhaps, be unable to recognize it.[20] Another device, recorded by R. Meir as having been used in the school of his master, R. Akiba, was to recite the Shema in an undertone in unison.[21] The first practice seems to have survived in the form of the *Kedushah*. The second has survived in the form universally used for the public reading of the Shema.

Today the Shema is read in unison by the congregation, rather than promulgated to them by the leader. The first verse is generally read aloud by the whole congregation, and the response, ברוך שם כבוד מלכותו לעולם ועד "Blessed is the name of His glorious Kingdom forever and ever," is said in an undertone (except on the Day of Atonement, when it is said aloud).[22]

tion in the third century, when "a decree was issued forbidding the Jews to study the Torah," but we do know that such decrees were issued during the Hadrianic persecutions, it may be presumed, with good reason, that the persecution to which Ben Baboi refers was that of Hadrian. Other reasons for believing that the persecution which led to the reading of the Shema in the *Kedushah* was that of Hadrian are given in *REJ*, XCIII, pp. 9 ff.

[20] See references cited in preceding note.

[21] Tosefta Berakot 2.13, p. 4. A third device, which also survived in the extant rituals, was to recite the first verse of the Shema privately, at home. Apparently, it was impossible to recite the whole of the Shema even in the privacy of one's home, because of the possibility of betrayal by spies in one's household or among one's neighbors. Hence, as remarked above, note 19, even R. Judah the Patriarch was not taught to recite the whole of the Shema, when he was a child. (See further Appendix C.)

[22] The custom is recorded in *Debarim Rabbah*, *Va-ethanan*, 2.36; see particularly ed. Liebermann, p. 69, and notes ad loc. The remark of R. Jacob ben Asher (*Tur Orah Hayyim*, 619), describing the custom as peculiar to the Jews of Germany, indicates simply that it was not current in Spain where he wrote his work. The record in *Debarim*

While the form of reciting the Shema in public necessarily underwent this fundamental change during the Hadrianic persecution, the term used to describe it remained the same: פורס את שמע. But in its application to the new custom, the expression no longer could apply to the reading of the Shema, for that had ceased to take the form of the promulgation of an edict. Inevitably, the scholars gave it a new interpretation, based on other aspects of the ritual. As it had apparently been the custom from ancient times to begin the service of the Shema, by the announcement: "Bless ye the Lord,"[23] (ברכו את ה'), the

Rabbah shows that the custom was not of mediaeval, but of ancient Palestinian origin. It seems a reasonable conjecture that even during the Hadrianic persecutions the response ברוך שם וכו' was uttered aloud on the Day of Atonement, perhaps with especial reference to the fact that its recital aloud had been such an integral and vivid part of the High Priestly service on that day. Cf. my remarks in *Akiba*, p. 252, and *REJ*, XVIII (1932), p. 8. It is also possible, of course, that when the government relaxed the severity of its decrees, permission was granted to recite the response aloud only on the Day of Atonement, but such permission was refused for the regular daily service.

[23] According to Mishna Tamid 5.1, the priest in charge of the service of the Shema said: ברכו ברכה אחת "Recite one benediction," whereupon the priests recited the benediction (presumably that for the coming of the day). Probably, however, this was substituted for an older formula which read ברכו את ה' ברכה אחת. This surmise is strengthened by the fact that the formula ברכו את ה' opens the service of the Shema in all extant rituals. The formula now used, however, is ברכו את ה' המבורך which is that prescribed by R. Ishmael. R. Akiba disagrees with him, and holds that the formula should read: ברכו את ה' (Mishna Berakot 7.3). While it cannot be said with absolute certainty that the controversy between R. Ishmael and R. Akiba implies the use of the formula ברכו את ה' at the beginning of the service of the Shema, there is every likelihood that it does. For R. Akiba says: מה מצינו בבית הכנסת אחד מרובין ואחד מועטין אומר ברכ' את ה' "Just as in the synagogue, whether there are many or few, he uses the formula ברכו את ה'." Now it is true, that the formula ברכו וכו' is used in the synagogue before beginning to read the Torah. But, if it were used in no other connection, it would have been more natural for R. Akiba to say: מה מצינו בברכת התורה. As the general term "in the synagogue" is used, there is a definite implication that the formula ברכו occurs in several parts of the synagogue service. As the formula

expression פורס את שמע "to promulgate the Shema" might well be applied to this call to enter upon the ceremony. In it the leader of the congregation announced the Shema. Hence when the expression פורס את שמע had lost significance in its original application, because the Shema itself was no longer recited as an edict, the expression came

is known only as introduction to the Shema (morning and evening) and the reading of the Torah, R. Akiba's words imply the use of the formula on these occasions. This argument is strengthened by a consideration of the statement of R. Jose in Sifre Deut. 306, Fr. 132b, Fi. 342. The passage reads: רבי יוסי אומר מנין לעומדים בבית הכנסת ואומרים ברכו את ה' המבורך שעונים אחריהם ברוך ה' המבורך לעולם ועד שנאמר כי שם ה' אקרא הבו גדל לאלהינו. "Whence do we know that if people in the synagogue say ברכו את ה' המבורך those present should respond ברוך ה' המבורך לעולם ועד because, the Scriptures say, 'For I will proclaim the name of the Lord, ascribe ye greatness to our God' " (Deut. 32.3). If R. Jose had known only of the use of the formula ברכו for the reader of the Torah, he would have said מנין למברך על התורה. His use of the general expression מנין לעומדים בבית הכנסת, like the use of a similar expression by R. Akiba, implies that the formula ברכו was used in other connections, i. e., as an introduction to the reading of the service in the morning, and also in the evening.

The fact that both incidents in which the controversy between R. Ishmael and R. Akiba was concerned, and which are recorded in the Talmudim, occurred in connection with the benediction before the reading of the Torah (B. Berakot 50a, and Yer. ibid. 7.4, 11c) is quite irrelevant. In both instances, obviously, visitors used the shorter formula ברכו את ה' to which they were accustomed in their native localities. It was quite natural for a visitor to a synagogue to be called to read the Torah; and it was also natural for him, on his first visit, to use the precise formula to which he was accustomed. But it would hardly be likely that a visitor would be called upon to read the public service of the Shema on the first occasion of his appearance in a new locality!

Nor is there much force in the fact that Yer. (loc. cit.) remarks: היתיבון הרי ברכת התורה הרי הוא אומר ברכו "Why does not the person reciting the benediction over the Torah say, 'Let us bless,' just as the person calling on others to say the Grace after Meat." The contrast between the blessing for the Torah and the blessing for food is quite frequently drawn in talmudic writings (e. g., B. Berakot 48b) and it is therefore natural to ask why a formula applying to one should not be used for the other.

The disagreement between R. Ishmael and R. Akiba concerning the formula derives doubtless from the different traditions they represent. R. Ishmael represents both the priestly and the provincial traditions (see my remarks in *Akiba*, pp. 172 ff.). In these traditions, the for-to be applied, quite unconsciously, to the call for reading the Shema.

In this application, however, it was more natural that the expression should take the form פורס על שמע "to issue a call for the Shema," rather than פורס את שמע "to promulgate the Shema."

Because the Babylonian schools of learning arose after the Hadrianic persecutions, they tended to adopt exclusively the term in the form in which it gained currency

mula ברכו את ה' המבורך was entirely appropriate. The term *adonai* seemed ambiguous to the priests in the Temple, and was also capable of misinterpretation by the provincials. Hence, to make certain that there was no misunderstanding, and that the call had no reference to any human lord, the priests and the provincials would say ברכו את ה' [אדני] המבורך "Bless ye the Lord Who is blessed." There was less likelihood of confusion among the sophisticated laity of Jerusalem, particularly as the institution of human "lordship" was less common among them, than either among the priests or the provincials. Hence, they saw no reason for deviating from the ancient formula.

This concern of the priests regarding the possible ambiguity of the term *adonai* is reflected in other customs, e. g., in the fact that they would not address the High Priest as אדוני כהן גדול, "my lord, High Priest," but invented instead the expression אישי כהן גדול (Mishna Yoma 1.3, 5; 4.1; Tamid 6.3; Parah 3.8). The expression אישי never occurs in early literature in the sense of "my lord," except in the phrase אישי כהן גדול. The expression אדוני כהן גדול occurs in *Vayyikra Rabbah* 3.5, and in the corresponding passage in Midrash *Tehillim* 22.31, ed. Buber, 98b. The expression אדוני הכהן occurs in *Bereshit Rabbah* 71.4, p. 826.

Perhaps it was this fear of misunderstanding which made the priests alter the formula, when used in the Temple service, from ברכו את ה' to ברכו ברכה אחת ברכה אחת, as it occurs in Mishna Tamid, loc. cit.

The earliest specific reference to the use of the call ברכו as introduction to the Shema, occurs in *Masseket Soferim* 10.6, ed. Higger, pp. 30 ff. It is implied likewise in *Sefer Hekalot*, ed. Wertheimer, 31.4, 9b.

The fact that there is no reference to *bareku* in the liturgical fragments published by Schechter (*JQR*, X, 654–55; *REJ*, LIII, 240–1), and J. Mann (*HUCA*, II, pp. 269–338) is not evidence that the formula was unknown in Palestine. All of these fragments were intended for the private reading of the prayers (see Schechter, loc. cit., p. 656; Ginzberg, *Geonica*, I, p. 130). In some fragments, however, it is indicated that an individual, in his private devotions, should recite the verse in the place of *bareku*, which he obviously cannot recite (see J. Mann, loc. cit., p. 286).

after that time. Hence the Babylonians knew the expression primarily as פורס על שמע, while the Palestinians continued to say פורס את שמע.

The new meaning attaching to the term פורס על שמע appears for the first time in a statement of R. Nehemiah, according to whom the people of Israel sang the Song of their Deliverance at the Red Sea, "like people who read the Shema in public." R. Nehemiah explains what he means in the following passage.[24]

בבלי, סוטה ל׳ ע״ב

בו ביום דרש רבי עקיבא בשעה שעלו ישראל מן הים נתנו עיניהם לומר שירה וכיצד אמרו שירה כגדול המקרא את הלל והן עונין אחריו ראשי פרקים משה אמר אשירה לה׳ והן אומרים אשירה לה׳ משה אמר כי גאה גאה והן אומרים אשירה לה׳ רבי אליעזר בנו של רבי יוסי הגלילי אומר כקטן המקרא את הלל והן עונין אחריו כל מה שהוא אומר משה אמר אשירה לה׳ והן אומרים אשירה לה׳ משה אמר כי גאה גאה והן אומרים כי גאה גאה רבי נחמיה אומר כסופר הפורס על שמע בבית הכנסת שהוא פותח תחלה והן עונין אחריו:

ירושלמי סוטה כ׳ ע״ג

בו ביום דרש רבי עקיבה אז ישיר משה וגו׳ לקטן שהוא מקרא את ההלל בבית הספר והן עונין אחריו על כל דבר ודבר משה אמר אשירה והן עונין אחריו אשירה משה אמר עוזי והן אומר׳ עוזי. ר׳ אליעזר בנו של ר׳ יוסי הגלילי אומר לגדול שהוא מקרא את ההלל בבית הכנסת והן עונין אחריו דבר ראשון משה אמר אשירה והן עונין אשירה משה אמר עזי והן עונין אחריו אשירה:

תוספתא סוטה ו׳ ב׳

דרש ר׳ עקיבא בשעה שעלו ישר׳ מן הים שרת עליהן רוח הקודש ואמרו שירה כקטן שהוא קורא את ההלל בבית הסופר ועונין אחריו על כל עינין ועינין משה אומ׳ אשירה לה׳ וישר׳ אומ׳ אשירה לה׳: משה אומ׳ עזי וזמרת יה וישראל אומ׳ עזי וזמרת יה ר׳ אליעזר בנו של ר׳ יוסי הגלילי אומ׳ כגדול שהוא מקרא את ההלל בבית הכנסת ועונין אחריו עינין ראשון משה אומר אשירה לה׳ וישראל אומרים אשירה לה׳ משה אומר עזי וזמרת יה ר׳ נחמיה אומר כבני אדם שקורין את שמע שנ׳ ויאמרו לאמר מלמד שהיה משה פותח תחילה וישראל אומרין אחריו וגומרין משה אומ׳ אז ישיר משה וישראל אומ׳ אשירה לה׳ משה אומר עזי וזמרת יה וישראל אומרים זה אלי ואנוהו משה אומר ה׳ איש מלחמה וישראל אומר ה׳ שמו:

[24] The statement of R. Nehemiah occurs in Tosefta Sotah 6.2, 3, ed. Zuckermandel, p. 303; and B. ibid. 30b. The opposing views, namely those of R. Akiba and R. Eliezer b. R. Jose ha-Galilee, occur also in Yer. Sotah 5.6, 20c.

Tosefta

R. Akiba offered the following interpretation: "When the Israelites came up from the Sea, the Holy Spirit rested upon them, and they recited the Song like a child reading the Hallel at school, with the other children responding to each strophe. Moses said, 'I will sing unto the Lord,' and they said, 'I will sing unto the Lord.' Moses said, 'The Lord is my strength and song,' and the Israelites responded, 'The Lord is my strength and song.' " R. Eliezer b. R. Jose ha-Galilee said, "He was like unto an adult who recites the Hallel in the synagogue, and the congregation responds to him with the first strophe as refrain. Moses said, 'I will sing unto the Lord'; and the Israelites said, 'I will sing unto the Lord.' Moses said, 'The Lord is my strength and my song'; and the Israelites said, 'The Lord is my strength and my song.' " R. Nehemiah said: "(They were) like people who read the Shema, as it is written, 'saying.' This teaches us that Moses began and the Israelites responded to him and completed the passage. Moses said, 'Then Moses sang,' and the Israelites answered, 'I will sing unto the Lord.'

Yerushalmi

On that day, R. Akiba offered the following interpretation of the passage, "Then sang Moses, etc." "It was like unto a child who leads in the recitation of the Hallel, and the congregation responds to each strophe. Moses said, 'I will sing unto the Lord'; and they responded 'I will sing (unto the Lord).' Moses said, 'The Lord is my strength,' and they responded 'The Lord is my strength.' " R. Eliezer b. R. Jose Galilee said: "It was like an adult reciting the Hallel in the synagogue, with the congregation making the first verse its refrain. Moses said, 'I will sing,' and they responded, 'I will sing.' Moses said, 'The Lord is my strength,' and they responded, 'I will sing.' "

Babli

On that day R. Akiba offered the following interpretation: "When the Israelites came up from the Sea, they wished to recite a Song. How did they recite the Song? Like an adult who leads in reciting the Hallel, with the congregation responding with the refrain. Moses said, 'I will sing unto the Lord,' and they said, 'I will sing unto the Lord.' Moses said, 'For He is highly exalted'; and they responded (again) 'I will sing unto the Lord.' " R. Eliezer b. R. Jose ha-Galilee said: "(The Israelites recited the Song) like a boy who leads in the recitation of the Hallel (at school), with the class responding by repeating his words. Moses said, 'I will sing unto the Lord,' and they responded, 'I will sing unto the Lord.' Moses said, 'For He is highly exalted,' and they responded, 'For He is highly exalted.' R. Nehemiah said, '(Moses led them) like a scribe, who recites the Shema in the synagogue, for he begins, and the congregation responds.' "

Tosefta	Yerushalmi	Babli
Moses said, 'The Lord is my strength and my song,' and the Israelites answered, 'This is my God and I shall glorify Him.' Moses said, 'The Lord is a man of war,' and the Israelites answered, 'The Lord is His name.'		

It is noteworthy that according to the text of the *baraita* in Tosefta, the words, "Then Moses and the children of Israel sang," are themselves described by R. Nehemiah as being uttered by Moses.[25] It is usually assumed that the extant texts do not really represent R. Nehemiah's original view in this regard, and that they are the results of a copyist's error. But there is no reason for such an assumption. On the contrary, R. Nehemiah deliberately makes Moses use these words, for, in the Rabbi's reconstruction of the scene, the words correspond to the call to the Shema, issued by the leader of the congregation. Just as the leader of the congregation begins the service of reading the Shema with the words, "Bless ye the Lord," so Moses announced, "Then Moses and the children of Israel sing this song to the Lord," and thus began the service of thanksgiving for the deliverance from the Red Sea.

After the call to enter upon the ceremony of reading the

[25] The two versions of the statement of R. Nehemiah do not of course contradict one another. The version given in Tosefta describes the manner of the reciting of the Song of Moses in detail. The version given in Babli describes the manner of recitation by comparing it to the public recitation of the Shema. It follows therefore that the description of the recitation given in Tosefta is an accurate description of the manner in which the Shema (and its benedictions) were recited in public services. The use of the imperfect ישיר, which may be translated "sing" or "will sing" as well as "sang," perhaps suggested to R. Nehemiah the thought that the phrase was a summons to song, rather than an introductory phrase, describing the event.

Shema, the reader pronounces the benediction for the light, and the congregation responds with the verses from Isa. 6.3, and Ezek. 3.12, "Holy, holy, holy is the Lord of Hosts, the whole earth is full of His glory"; and "Blessed be the glory of the Lord from His place." After the Shema, there are the responses, "Who is like unto Thee, O Lord, among the mighty? Who is like unto Thee, glorious in holiness, fearful in praises, doing wonders?" (Ex. 15.11) and then, "The Lord will reign forever and ever" (ibid. v. 18).

R. Nehemiah imagined that the Song of Moses (from which the last two responses are taken) was recited in a similar responsive manner. According to R. Nehemiah, the Song of Moses was recited as follows:

Moses: Then Moses and the children of Israel sing this song unto the Lord, and speak saying:

Israel: I will sing unto the Lord, for He is highly exalted. The horse and his rider hath He thrown into the sea.

Moses: The Lord is my strength and song,
And He is become my salvation;

Israel: This is my God, and I will glorify Him,
My father's God, and I will exalt Him.

Moses: The Lord is a man of war.

Israel: The Lord is His Name.

R. Akiba maintained that the people simply repeated each verse of the Song of Moses as he recited it. R. Eliezer ben R. Jose the Galilean maintains that the people simply recited the refrain, "I shall sing unto the Lord," while Moses recited the poem itself.

This explanation of the expression פורס (על) [את] שמע enables us to understand more clearly also the expressions בפרוס הפסח, בפרוס עצרת, בפרוס החג.

II

The expression בפרוס הפסח, בפרוס עצרת, בפרוס החג occurs several times in the Mishna and the Tosefta.[26] R. Abbahu, in the third century of the Christian Era, derived the word בפרוס in the expression from the meaning "half" which פרס frequently has.[27] According to him the expression was connected with the well-known rule: שואלים ודורשים בהלכות הפסח קודם לפסח שלשים יום "One discusses the laws of the Passover for thirty days before the Passover.[28] בפרוס הפסח meant therefore half of the thirty-day period, i. e., a fortnight, before the Passover. R. Abbahu's interpretation has been generally accepted by the commentators and lexicographers.[29]

But this interpretation is clearly contradicted by older tannaitic traditions. R. Jose ben Judah, in a statement cited both in Tosefta and in Babli,[30] explains the expression as follows: איזה הוא פרס הפסח ופרס עצרת ופרס החג ר' יוסי]

[26] Mishna Sheḳalim 3.1; Bekorot 9.5; Tosefta Sheḳalim 2.1, p. 175; Ta'anit 2.8, p. 26; Baba Mezi'a 4.18, p. 380; Bekorot 7.9, p. 542; Yer. Sheḳalim 3.1, 47b; Ta'anit 3.2, 33c; B. Ta'anit 19b; Bekorot 58a. For the variant readings בפרס and בפרוס, see Appendix D.

[27] So Babli and Yer., loc. cit.

[28] B. ibid.

[29] R. Israel Lifschitz in his commentary, *Tiferet Yisrael*, both Sheḳalim and Bekorot, explains פרס from the Greek *πρός*, and presumes that it refers to an indefinite period preceding the festival.

[30] Loc. cit. The use of the term בפרוס in several *beraitot* would further demonstrate that it cannot signify any precise date, such as R. Abbahu's view would imply. Thus Tosefta Ta'anit 2.8, p. 217, reads: ומגריעין על האילן בפרוס הפסח על בורות שיחין ומערות בפרוס החג "Petitions are offered for the trees at the announcement of (i. e., during the period immediately preceding) Passover; and for the wells, the pits, and the caves (that they may be filled with water) at the announcement of the festival (of Sukkot)." This *baraita* is cited, with slight variations, in Yer. Ta'anit 3.2, 66c, and Babli ibid. 19b. Rashi, sensing the difficulty of applying R. Abbahu's interpretation of בפרוס to this passage, explains בפרוס הפסח in B. Ta'anit 19b, as בימי הפסח, "in the Passover season." He does not indicate how this interpretation can be reconciled with that of R. Abbahu.

[בר' יהודה אומר] אין פחות מחמשה עשר יום קודם לרגל "the term פרס refers to a period not less than fifteen days." But if, as this statement implies, פרס may mean more than fifteen days, R. Abbahu's explanation of its derivation cannot be accepted. Moreover, in Tosefta Bekorot 7.9, p. 542, R. Akiba, himself, explicitly says: [שלשה ברכות למעשר בהמה בפרס הפסח, ובפרס עצרת, ובפרס החג] אין להם קצבה דברי ר' עקיבא "The period referred to is not fixed." Clearly, R. Akiba's opinion, which is cited in the Tosefta as an alternative to that of R. Jose b. Judah, is implicitly a denial of R. Abbahu's theory; for, according to R. Akiba, the expression בפרס is intended to avoid any such fixed period as R. Abbahu indicates.

This interpretation by R. Akiba's statement in the Tosefta is also accepted by R. David Pardo in his commentary *Hasde David*, ad loc. R. David Pardo realizes, in view of this interpretation, that the transmitter of the *baraita* in the Tosefta gave בפרוס a different meaning from that given it by R. Abbahu. He therefore holds that the view attributed to R. Akiba in the Tosefta represents one tradition, according to which בפרוס does not derive from the root meaning "half" at all. There can be no doubt that R. David Pardo is correct in this conclusion.

In the light of the above discussion, it seems probable that the word בפרוס, in the phrases בפרוס הפסח, בפרוס עצרת and בפרוס החג, means "at the announcement of." Yer. Pesaḥim 1.1, 27b records the fact that the laws of the festivals were discussed at the House of Assembly (i. e., the central *Bet Din*) for thirty days before the festival. שואלין בהילכות הפסח בפסח הילכות עצרת בעצרת הילכות החג בחג בבית וועד שואלין קודם לשלשים יום ר' שמעון בן גמליאל אומר שתי שבתות "The Laws of the Passover are discussed on Passover; those of Shabuot on Shabuot; those of Sukkot on Sukkot. In the 'House of Assembly' the discussions begin thirty days before the festival. R. Simeon ben Gamaliel says, 'Two weeks.' " (Cf. also B. Sanhedrin 101a.)

The *baraita* is cited in variant forms in Babli, Tosefta, and Sifre.[31] In view of this statement, there can be little doubt that the central *Bet Din* took note of the approach of a festival, by devoting the discussions of a whole month to that festival. The beginning of this discussion period may, in all likelihood, have coincided with the announcement of the festival.

It is a significant fact that R. Simeon ben Gamaliel II should have limited this period to a fortnight; and that R. Jose, the son of his contemporary and friend, R. Judah, should likewise suggest that the period covered by the expression בפרוס meant "no less than fifteen days."

Presumably this limitation originated in the fact that the first of Nisan would be an appropriate time to discuss the laws of Passover, and the beginning of Tishri would be an appropriate time to begin the discussion of Sukkot.

Perhaps this change in the time needed for the announcement of the festival was associated with the change which took place in Jewish life through the destruction of Jerusalem. Before the destruction of the Temple, a full month

[31] The parallel passage in Tosefta Megillah 4(3).5, p. 225, reads: ושואלין הילכות פסח בפסח והילכות עצרת בעצרת הילכות החג בחג בבית הוועד ושואלין לעניין הפסח קודם לרגל שלשים יום "The laws of Passover are discussed on Passover; the laws of Shabuot on Shabuot; and the laws of Sukkot on Sukkot. In the House of Assembly, the laws of Passover are discussed thirty days before the festival. R. Simeon ben Gamaliel says, 'Two weeks.' "

According to the version cited in B. Pesaḥim 6a, the *baraita* reads simply: שואלין ודורשין בהלכות הפסח קודם לפסח שלשים יום רשב"ג אומר שתי שבתות "The laws of the Passover are discussed thirty days before the Passover. R. Simeon ben Gamaliel says, 'Two weeks.' " Apparently, this *baraita* deals only with the custom of the בית הוועד. According to the version cited in the tannaitic Midrashim (Sifra, *Emor*, *perek* 17.12, ed. Weiss, 103b; Sifre Numbers 66, ed. Horowitz, p. 62; Sifre Deut. 127, Fr. 100b, Fi. 186) the custom of discussing the laws of each festival during the festival season originated with Moses.

was needed to "announce" the approach of the festival, because the people in distant cities had to prepare themselves for the pilgrimage, particularly through the levitical purification necessary for entering the Temple. To this day, the portion of purification (*Parashat Parah*, i. e., Numbers, chap. 19) is read on the fourth Sabbath preceding Passover. Doubtless some similar notice, perhaps on a less extensive scale, was given to Jews to purify themselves before the other festivals.

When the Temple was destroyed, and the pilgrimages necessarily discontinued, the practice of purifying oneself for the holidays was still retained.[32] But as no pilgrimages could be undertaken, so long a notice as thirty days was quite unnecessary. It was sufficient to inform the people fifteen days before the festival; and it was possible therefore to combine the notice of approach of the festival with the announcement of the New Moon of the month in which the festival occurred.[33] There was thus some economy in making the announcement of the festival only two weeks before the festival.

The Mishna which mentions the announcement of the festivals reads (according to ed. Loewe):
בשלשה פרקים בשנה תורמין את הלשכה בפרס הפסח, בפרס העצרת, ובפרס החג, והן גרנות של מעשר בהמה דברי רבי עקיבה. בן עזאי אומר בעשרים ותשעה באדר ובאחד בסיון ובעשרים ותשעה באב. רבי אלעזר ור' שמעון אומר[ים] באחד בניסן, ובאחד בסיון, ובעשרים ותשעה באלול. It should be translated as follows: "Three times in the year was the offering taken from the shekel-chamber: at the announcement of the Passover, at the announcement of Pentecost, and at the announcement of the Feast of Tabernacles. These are also the seasons for the tithe of

[32] Rosh Hashanah 16b.

[33] Cf. Mishna Rosh Hashanah 1.3.

the cattle. This is the view of R. Akiba.[34] Ben Azzai says: On the twenty-ninth of Adar, and on the first of Sivan, and on the twenty-ninth of Ab. R. Eliezer and R. Simeon[35] say: On the first of Nisan, on the first of Sivan, and on the twenty-ninth of Elul."[36]

According to this interpretation of the Mishna, R. Akiba's remarks, as recorded in the Mishna, correspond precisely to those recorded in his name in the Tosefta, for he declines to fix any specific time for "the announcement of the festival" and consequently for the offering of the shekels, and the tithing of the cattle.

According to Ben Azzai, the periods for the offering of the shekels and the tithing of the animals were fixed, and were independent of the announcement of the festivals. This view was also adopted by R. Eliezer and R. Simeon, who disagreed with Ben Azzai, however, in holding that the dates for the offering of the shekels and the tithing of the animals were the first of Nisan, instead of the twenty-

[34] R. Akiba, in other words, declines to fix the time, beyond the tradition which sets the season at "the announcement of the festival," whenever that should happen to be made.

[35] The view of R. Eliezer and R. Simeon, as expressed in this Mishna, corresponds to that ascribed to them in Mishna Rosh Hashanah 1.1, where they hold that "the first of Tishri is the New Year for the tithes of cattle." The Mishna is compelled to explain that the tithe was actually given on the preceding day, namely, the twenty-ninth of Elul, because the first of Tishri is a festival.

[36] The "announcement of Shabuot" presents certain difficulties of interpretation. Obviously, there was no need, according to rabbinic law, to announce the time of Shabuot. It was fixed as occurring on the fiftieth day after the first day of Passover. The fixing of the New Moon of Sivan had no effect on the day when Shabuot would occur. And, indeed, while, as indicated above, messengers were sent out all over Palestine and even to the Diaspora to announce the precise dates of other festivals, no such messengers were sent to announce the date of Shabuot (Rosh Hashanah 3.1). It may be, however, that in Temple times, the Pharisees "announced" the date of Shabuot, because they observed it at a different time from that of the Sadducees (see my *Pharisees*, I, pp. 115 ff.).

ninth of Adar, and the twenty-ninth of Elul, instead of the twenty-ninth of Ab.

Possibly R. Eliezer and R. Simeon, as well as Ben Azzai, should be interpreted not as disagreeing with R. Akiba, but as explaining him. The periods they define may be simply their interpretations of בפרוס החג, בפרוס עצרת, בפרוס הפסח. R. Akiba reports the tradition in precisely the form in which he received it, because he holds that the period should not be defined any further than was done in the older tradition. His disciples, however, sought to fix a definition, but disagreed regarding the precise definition to be fixed.

If this interpretation of the Mishna is correct, there is a possibility that it reflects an ancient controversy regarding the necessity of a special announcement of the approach of the festivals. Some authorities may have held, even during the time of the existence of the Temple, that no announcement of the approach of the festival had to be made other than the announcement of the New Moon, which determined the date of the festival. Others may have insisted on a special announcement of the festival.

Whatever the facts regarding this difference, there can be no doubt that the expression בפרוס in the phrases בפרוס החג, בפרוס עצרת, בפרוס הפסח means "at the announcement of."

APPENDIX A

The variant readings of the text containing the expression פורס על שמע

For the following analysis of the variant readings of the phrase פורס על שמע, as well as for the variant reading of בפרוס cited in Appendix C, I have had to consult a number of early editions and Mss., most of them belonging to the Library of the Jewish Theological Seminary of America, and courteously placed at my disposal by Professor Alexander Marx. The variant readings of the Midrash *Shir Ha-Shirim Rabbah* were supplied by Professor Mordecai M. Kaplan, and those from *Vayyikra Rabbah* by Professor Saul Lieberman, from their notes.

The Mishna texts which I consulted are as follows: (a) Ed. pr.; (b) ed. Lowe; (c) Ms. Parma; (d) Ms. Budapest; (e) Mishna of the *Yerushalmi*, ed. pr.; (f) Mishna Ms. in the Library of the Jewish Theological Seminary of America, Italian hand, dated 1361; (g) Mishna of *Babli*, ed. pr.; (h) Mishna of *Babli*, Munich Ms.; (i) Mishna of *Babli*, Yemenite Ms., Columbia University Library; (j) Mishna of *Babli*, as cited in Alfasi, ed. pr.; (k) Mishna of *Babli*, as cited in *En Jacob*, ed. pr.; (l) Mishna, as cited in *Midrash Ha-Gadol*, Leviticus 22.32, ed. Rabinowitz, p. 561; (m) Mishna quoted in *Aruk*, s. v. פרס, according to a ms. in possession of Dr. B. M. Lewin, and cited by him in *Ozar Ha-Geonim*.

	4.3	4.5	4.6a	4.6b	4.6c	4.6d
a.	את	את	את	את	את	על
b.	את	את	את	את	את	את
c.	את	את	את	את	את	את
d.	את	את	את	את	את	את
e.	על	את	את	את	את	את
f.	על	את	את	את	את	את
g.	את	על	על	את	את	על
h.	על	על	על	על	על	על
i.	על	על	על	על	על	על
j.	על	על	על	על	על	על
k.	—	—	—	—	על	על
l.	על	—	—	—	—	—
m.	את	—	—	—	—	—

From these variant readings, it is obvious that the form פורס את שמע has ample support as the original reading in the Mishna. Certainly the authority of the Parma and Budapest Mss., and that of ed. Lowe, together with that of ed. pr., and the text as published with the Yerushalmi, is decisive on this point. The tendency to substitute על שמע for את שמע is exemplified in the copy of ed. pr., in the Library of the Jewish Theological Seminary of America, where a Yemenite scribe has written על over את wherever that occurs in the phrase פורס את שמע in the Mishna.

The extant texts of the *Tosefta*, as recorded by Zuckermandel, all read פורס על שמע in each of the four instances in which the phrase occurs in *Tosefta Megillah* 4(3).27, 28 (ed. Zuckermandel, p. 227). However, Professor Saul Lieberman draws my attention to the fact that the current texts of the *Tosefta* are definitely influenced by Babylonian usage. Even, therefore, if Zuckermandel's readings reproduce precisely those of the Mss., it is still possible that the form פורס על שמע appears in the *Tosefta* simply under the influence of the *Babli*.

In the *Gemara* of the *Yerushalmi*, the expression is always cited as פורס את שמע (See *Yer. Berakot* 5.5, 9c; *Megillah* 4.4, 75a, lines 64, 66; 4.6, 75b, lines 63, 65, 70, 74).

Both the current editions of *Babli*, and the Munich Ms. read פורס על שמע in *B. Sotah* 30b, where the expression is cited.

The phrase occurs in *Midrash Rabbah* in the following passage, in *Shir Ha-Shirim Rabbah*, chap. 2.2, referring to Canticles 2.2 (the text is taken from ed. pr.) בנוהג שבעולם עשרה בני אדם נכנסין לבית הכנסת ואין אחד מהן יכול לפרוס על שמע (א) ולעבור לפני התיבה ואחד מהן פורס על שמע (ב) ועובר לפני התיבה למה הוא דומה לשושנה בין החוחים. ר' אלעזר אזל לחד אתה אמרי ליה פרוס את שמע (ג) אמר לון לינא חכם עבר לפני התיבה [אמר לון לינא חכם] אמרין דין הוא ר' אלעזר . . . לבתר יומין אזל

להההוא אתר אמרי ליה פרוס לן את שמע (ד) פרוס לן. "It frequently happens that ten men assemble in a synagogue, and only one of them can lead in the reading of the Shema and the prayers. To what may he be compared? 'To a lily among thorns.' R. Eleazar went to a certain locality. When the people asked him to lead in the reading of the Shema, he replied that he was unable to do so. When they asked him to lead in the reciting of the prayers, he replied that he was unable to do so. Thereupon they said, 'Is this R. Eleazar on whose account we have taken so much trouble? He has no right to be called "Rabbi." ' Embarrassed, R. Eleazar went to his master, R. Akiba. 'Why do you look poorly?' asked R. Akiba. When R. Eleazar told him of the incident, R. Akiba replied, 'Do you wish to learn?' R. Eleazar said, 'Yes.' Thereupon R. Akiba taught him. After the lapse of some time, R. Eleazar again visited that locality. When they said to him, 'Lead us in the reading of the Shema,' he led them. 'Lead us in reciting the prayers'; and again he led them."

The variants of the Mss. are as follows: Ms. Frankfort reads על שמע in all four instances; Vatican Ms. reads על in the first instance, and את for the last three instances. *Vayyikra Rabbah*, ed. pr., citing the anecdote of R. Eleazar Hisma (the second of the passages occurring in *Canticles R.*) reads על שמע both times, according to ed. pr. The whole passage is found in Ms. Oxford 147, where the reading is את in the first two instances, and על in the second two instances. (The copyists who wrote the Vatican Ms. of this Midrash omitted the whole passage, simply referring the reader to the parallel passage in *Shir Ha-Shirim Rabbah.*)

The fact that the printed editions of *Shir Ha-Shirim Rabbah* contain the phrase in the form פורס את שמע in the last two instances, and the Vatican Ms. in the last three instances, gives ground for assuming that originally the form פורס א ת שמע was used throughout the passage. The copyist, being accustomed from the Babli and the works dependent on it, to the form פורס ע ל שמע was inclined to change his text in conformity with this usage, which he naturally deemed correct. Only when he found א ת occurring repeatedly, did he realize that he was dealing with a true variant, which he had no right to suppress. On the other hand the copyist who wrote the Frankfort Ms. (or the text on which that Ms. depends) simply replaced את by על.

The phrase occurs in *Masseket Soferim* as follows: (a) 10.6, p. 212; (b) 14.4, p. 256; (c) 14.10, p. 264; (d, e, f, g, h) 14.12, pp. 264–266; (i) 14.13, p. 267; (j, k) 16.9, pp. 294–5. The variant readings, as recorded by Dr. Michael Higger, in his edition of *Masseket Soferim*, are as follows: (The sigla used below are A, Ms. Oxford 370, 12, Opp. 726; B, Ms. Adler, Library of the Jewish Theological Seminary of America, 3861; C, Munich Ms. of the Babylonian Talmud; D, Ms. Adler, Library of the Jewish Theological Seminary of America, 2237; E, Ms. Oxford 2257, 8a, Mich. 175; F, Ms. Jewish Theological Seminary of America, Enelow Collection 321; G, same collection 270; H, Babylonian Talmud, ed. pr.; I, *Aguddah*, ed. Krakow 1571; J, Mahzor Vitry, ed. Hurwitz; K, *Masseket Soferim*, with comments of R. Elijah Gaon, Sklav 1804).

From the variants cited (p. 34), it is obvious that the reading א ת שמע was more prevalent in the earlier texts of *Masseket Soferim* than may appear from the readings of the ordinary editions. It is noteworthy that whereas all the texts read ע ל in the first occurrence of the phrase, the number reading א ת increases as follows,— one for the second occurrence, eight for the third occurrence, six for the fourth, seven for the fifth (with two omissions); one for the sixth

	A	B	C	D	E	F	G	H	I	J	K
a.	על	על	על	על	על	על	—	את	את	את	את
b.	על	על	על	על	—	על	על	על	על	על	את
c.	על	על	את	את	את	את	על	על	את	על	את
d.	—	על	את	על	את	—	על	—	—	על	את
e.	על	על	את	את	את	—	על	את	את	—	—
f.	על	על	את	את	את	—	על	את	את	את	את
g.	על	על	את	על	את	—	על	את	את	את	את
j.	על	על	את	את	את	—	על	את	את	את	את
k.	על	את	על	את	את	—	את	את	את	—	את
l.	על	על	את	על	—	על	—	—	את	את	את
m.	על	על	את	את	על	—	את	את	את	—	את

(with seven omissions); two for the seventh (with two omissions); seven for the eighth (with two omissions); nine for the ninth (with one omission); five for the tenth (with three omissions); and ten for the eleventh (with one omission). The meaning of this gradually increasing frequency of the reading את is apparent. The copyist when he first found the reading את assumed that it was an error, and tended to "correct" it to על. But as he found את occurring again and again, he gradually came to the conclusion that its appearance represented a genuine variation in the traditional text, and therefore he retained the reading. This explains why in all the various passages so far discussed, the tendency is for על to be found in the first or second occurrence of the phrase, while את occurs more frequently in later repetitions of the phrase.

The expression פורס (על) [את] שמע also occurs in Gaonic writings in both forms. As might be expected the form על occurs with far greater frequency (see Responsum of R. Natronai, in Ginzberg, *Geonica* II, pp. 116–117; another responsum by R. Natronai in *Teshubot Ha-Geonim*, ed. Musafia, Lyck 1864, no. 83; a Gaonic responsum in *Teshubot Ha-Geonim*, ed. Asaf, p. 187; and cf. also B. M. Lewin, *Ozar Ha-Geonim* V, pp. 37 ff.; pp. 42 ff.; and passages cited by L. Blau in REJ LXXIII, 1921, pp. 140–141). But the form את also occurs (see Responsum of Sar Shalom Gaon, cited in *Seder R. Amram*, ed. Warsaw 1865, I, 11a, ed. Frumkin, I, 278, where, Professor Alexander Marx informs me, Ms. Oxford reads על, but Ms. Sulzberger, like ed. Warsaw, reads את, and the responsum ascribed to ריש מתיבתא in ed. Warsaw I, 47a, and R. Natronai in ed. Frumkin II, 342, where ed. Warsaw reads לפרוס את את שמע (sic!); Ms. Sulzberger reads לפרוס שמע, but Ms. Oxford reads לפרוס על שמע. More peculiarly R. Amram Gaon uses the expression למפרס ית שמע (corrupted into למפרס את

שמע in ed. Warsaw I, 3a, but given correctly, according to Ms. Sulzberger, in ed. Frumkin I, 90a). R. Amram Gaon also uses the expression פריסת שמע several times (see ed. Warsaw I, 3a, ed. Frumkin I, 90a), which is more akin to פורס את שמע, than to פורס על שמע.

Doubtless the wide currency of פורס על שמע in the extant Gaonic texts is due to the same influence which led to the substitution of על for את even in works of earlier origin.

It is certainly instructive to find that R. Amram Gaon used the form את, for that would indicate that at least at his time, it was a recognized form and perhaps the only recognized form in the Academy of Sura. This may be due to the great influence exerted on the Gaonim of Sura by the Palestinian academies (see L. Ginzberg, *Ginze Schechter*, II, pp. 515 ff.).

APPENDIX B

ברוך שם כבוד מלכותו לעולם ועד

There can be little doubt that the original form of the response ברוך שם כבוד מלכותו לעולם ועד was the more grammatical ברוך שם כבודו לעולם [ועד] "Blessed be His glorious Name forever." This is the natural response to the mention of the Tetragrammaton, and was doubtless introduced when the use of the Tetragrammaton became associated with especial awe and reverence. The response occurs in this simple form in Ps. 72.19. This ancient form of response was apparently still known in comparatively late times, for it is reproduced in Targum Ps. Jonathan to Deut. 6.4, ed. Ginsburger, p. 313. In that passage, Targum Ps. Jonathan cites the Midrash which attributes the origin of the Shema to the sons of Jacob, and the response to it, to Jacob himself. According to this Midrash, Jacob, about to die, called his sons together, and asked for assurance of their continued loyalty to God. Thereupon they replied, "Hear O Israel (our father), the Lord is our God, the Lord is One." To this Jacob responded (according to the Targum), "Blessed be His glorious Name forever": בריך שום יקריה לעלמי עלמין.

The Midrash occurs in *Sifre* Deut. 31, Fr. 72b, Fi. 52; *B. Pesahim* 56a; *Bereshit Rabbah* 98.3, p. 1252; cf. also ibid. 96, p. 1201; *Debarim Rabbah* 2.35, ed. Lieberman, p. 67; *Pesikta Rabbati* XXI, 105b; *Tanhumah*, old version, *Vayyehi* 8; ed. Buber 9, 109a; *Aggadat Bereshit* 81, p. 155; unknown Midrash, published by Professor L. Ginzberg in *Ginze Schechter* I, p. 122.

From the citation in *Bereshit Rabbah*, *Debarim Rabbah*, ed. Lieberman, and the unknown Midrash published by Professor Ginzberg, it would appear that the author of the homily was R. Eleazar ben Ahavai, a scholar of the latter half of the second and the beginning of the third century. This scholar belonged to the school of R. Ishmael and is therefore rarely cited in the extant rabbinical literature, most of which derives from the School of R. Akiba (see further with regard to him, my remarks in JQR XXXI, 1940–41, p. 234). If R. Eleazar ben Ahavai was really the author, rather than the transmitter of this haggadah, that would indicate that the ancient form was preserved quite unchanged, in conservative circles, as late as the time of the redaction of the Mishna.

Interestingly enough, however, Targum Yerushalmi on Deut. 6.4, translates the response as follows: יהא שמיה רבא מברך לעלם.

Targum Yerushalmi, Genesis 49.2 (lacking in ed. Ginsburger), reproducing the same story, translates the response: יהא שמיה רבא מברך לעלמי עלמין.

This form of the response also occurs in the Kaddish, suggesting, perhaps, that יהא שמיה רבא מברך לעלם is simply the usual ברוך שם כבודו לעולם put in Aramaic as a response to an Aramaic prayer.[37]

The change of the form שם כבודו to שם כבוד מלכותו was doubtless intended to emphasize the Kingship of God, and was a protest against the efforts of earthly kings to replace His dominion. For further discussion of the history of this response, see M. Friedmann, in his notes to *Sifre* Deut. loc. cit.; A. Buechler, *Die Priester und der Cultus*, Vienna 1895, pp. 179 ff.; M. Liber, REJ LVIII, 1909, pp. 18 ff.; I. Elbogen, *Der juedischer Gottesdienst*, pp. 22, 26, 93; 495–7; I. Davidson, *Ozar Ha-Shirah ve-ha-Piut* II, 75; and my remarks in REJ XCIII, 1932, pp. 7 ff.

APPENDIX C

The Private Reading of the Shema in the Morning.

The practice of reading the Shema privately, before the morning service, has been preserved in the extant rituals. The passage containing the verse, opens in the extant rituals, with the curious remark: לעולם יהא אדם ירא שמים בסתר ומודה על האמת ודובר אמת בלבבו. "At all times, let a person fear God in private, and acknowledge the truth, and speak the truth in his heart." In modern prayer books the word ובגלוי "and in public" has been added after בסתר, because the copyists and commentators felt that the literal meaning of the passage might seem to encourage secret Judaism. But obviously the passage originated in a time of persecution, and laid down the rule that when a person could not observe the law in public he should do so in private; but when charged with observing the law, he should confess the truth, and in any event speak the truth in his heart. As early an authority as R. Benjamin, the brother of the author of *Shibbale*

[37] Cf. also Sifre Deut. 306, Fr. 132 b, Fi. p. 342, line 11.

Ha-Leket, maintained that the custom of reciting the first verse of the Shema at the preliminary private service, originated during the Hadrianic persecutions. As quoted in *Shibbale Ha-Leket*, ed. Buber p. 6, he says:

ור' בנימין אחי נר"ו כתב שראוי לומר בסתר שלא אמרו אבא אליהו אלא כנגד דורו של שמד שנזרו שלא לקרוא את שמע ולא היו יכולין להיות יראין בגלוי על כן הזהירם וזרזם לקבל עליהם עול מלכות שמים בסתר. תדע לך שכן הוא שאומר וחייבין אנו לומר לפניך תמיד שמע בכל יום כו' ומיחדים את שמך פעמים באהבה ואומר שמע ישראל וכו'. ועל כן אומר ברוך המקדש שמו ברבים לפי שבשעת השמד אין שמו מקודש ברבים אלא בסתר על כן אין לנו לשנות.

The term דורו של שמד is, of course, the technical expression for the Hadrianic persecution. R. Benjamin's surmise is corroborated by the following evidence:

The whole passage, as preserved in the extant rituals, reads as follows:

לעולם יהא אדם ירא שמים בסתר ובגלוי ומודה על האמת ודובר אמת בלבבו וישכם ויאמר רבון כל העולמים, לא על צדקותינו אנחנו מפילים תחנונינו לפניך כי על רחמיך הרבים מה אנחנו מה חיינו מה חסדנו מה־צדקנו מה ישועתנו מה־כחנו מה גבורתנו מה־נאמר לפניך ה' אלהינו ואלהי אבותינו הלא כל־הגבורים כאין לפניך ואנשי השם כלא היו וחכמים כבלי מדע ונבונים כבלי השכל כי רב מעשיהם תהו וימי חייהם הבל לפניך ומותר האדם מן־הבהמה אין כי הכל הבל: אבל אנחנו עמך בני בריתך בני אברהם אהבך שנשבעת לו בהר המריה זרע יצחק יחידו שנעקד על גב המזבח עדת יעקב בנך בכורך שמאהבתך שאהבת אתו ומשמחתך ששמחת בו קראת את־שמו ישראל וישרון: לפיכך אנחנו חיבים להודות לך ולשבחך ולפארך ולברך ולקדש ולתת שבח והודיה לשמך אשרינו מה־טוב חלקנו ומה־נעים גורלנו ומה־יפה ירשתנו אשרינו שאנחנו משכימים ומעריבים ערב ובקר ואומרים פעמים בכל־יום שמע ישראל ה' אלהינו ה' אחד ברוך שם כבוד מלכותו לעולם ועד אתה הוא עד שלא נברא העולם אתה הוא משנברא העולם אתה הוא בעולם הזה ואתה הוא לעולם הבא קדש את שמך על מקדישי שמך

וקדש את שמך בעלמך ובישועתך תרום ותגבה קרננו ברוך אבה ה'
מקדש את־שמך ברבים:

"At all times let a man fear God as well in private as in public, acknowledge the truth, and speak the truth in his heart; and let him rise early and say: Sovereign of all worlds! Not because of our righteous acts do we lay our supplications before thee, but because of thine abundant mercies. What are we? What is our life? What is our piety? What our righteousness? What our helpfulness? What our strength? What our might? What shall we say before thee, O Lord our God and God of our fathers? Are not all the mighty men as nought before thee, the men of renown as though they had not been, the wise as if without knowledge, and the men of understanding as if without discernment? For most of their works are void, and the days of their lives are vanity before thee, and the preeminence of man over the beast is nought, for all is vanity. Nevertheless we are thy people, the children of thy Covenant, the children of Abraham, thy friend, to whom thou didst swear on Mount Moriah; the seed of Isaac, his only son, who was bound upon the altar; the congregation of Jacob, thy first born son, whose name thou didst call Israel and Jeshurun by reason of the love wherewith thou didst love him, and the joy wherewith thou didst rejoice in him. It is, therefore, our duty to thank, praise and glorify thee, to bless, to sanctify and to offer praise and thanksgiving unto thy name. Happy are we! How goodly is our portion, and how pleasant is our lot, and how beautiful our heritage! Happy are we who, early and late, morning and evening, twice every day, declare: Hear, O Israel, the Lord our God, the Lord is One. Blessed be His name, whose glorious kingdom is for ever and ever. Thou wast the same ere the world was created; thou hast been the same since the world hath been created; thou art the same in this world, and thou wilt be the same in the world to come. Sanctify thy name upon them that sanctify it, yea, sanctify thy name throughout thy world; and through thy salvation let our horn be exalted and raised on high. Blessed art thou, O Lord, who sanctifiest thy name amongst the many."

As noted by various writers on the subject, this passage occurs in the *Seder R. Amram* (ed. Warsaw 2a; ed. Frumkin I, 51a; see also ed. Warsaw 27a, ed. Frumkin II, 38), and is cited in *Seder Eliahu Rabbah*, chap. XIX, ed. Friedmann, p. 118. The recital of the first verse of the Shema, but not of the introductory paragraphs (and of the following prayer in a much modified form) is prescribed in the fragment from a prayer book of the Palestinian ritual, published by J. Mann (HUCA, II, p. 293). The passage seems also to be paraphrased in *Midrash Tehillim* 5.6, 27a, in a statement ascribed to R. Judah:

ר' יהודה פתר לה בארבע מלכיות, אמרי האזינה בבבל, בינה הגיגי במדי, הקשיבה לקול שועי ביון, כי אליך אתפלל באדום, ולמה הוא אומר מלכי ואלהי באדום, אלא אמרו ישראל לפני הקב"ה כמה שמדות וגזירות רעות גזרו עלינו כדי לבטל מלכותך ואדנותך ממנו, ולא בטלנו, אלא בכל יום ויום אנו באים לבתי כנסיות ולבתי מדרשות, וממליכים שם אלהותך פעמים בכל יום, ואומרים שמע ישראל ה' אלהינו ה' אחד (דברים ו ד), ואת עביד דידן, ואנו עבדין דידך, שנאמר דודי לי ואני לו (שה"ש ב' יו):

"The verse, 'For unto Thee will I pray,' refers to the period of subjection to Edom (Rome). Why does the psalmist say, in this connection, 'My King and my God?' Because Israel says unto God, 'Innumerable decrees have been issued to abolish Thy kingdom and Thy dominion from among us; but we have not yielded. On the contrary, twice each day do we assemble into the synagogues and the houses of study, and announce Thy Kingdom as our God; and we say, 'Hear O Israel, the Lord is our God, the Lord is One.' "

Another part of the passage is echoed by R. Jose the Galilean in *Mekilta Shirah*, chap. 10, Friedmann 44a, Horowitz-Rabin p. 150, Lauterbach II, p. 80. The passage in *Mekilta* reads:

ר' יוסי הגלילי אומר אלו אמרו ישראל על הים ה' מלך לעולם ועד לא היתה אומה ולשון שולטת בהן לעולם אלא אמרו ה' ימלוך לעולם ועד לעתִיד לבא על עמך צאן מרעיתיך זרע אברהם אוהבך בני יחידך יצחק עדת יעקב בנך בכורך גפן שהסעתה ממצרים וכנה אשר נטעה ימינך.

"R. Jose the Galilean says: 'If the people of Israel had said at the Red Sea, The Lord reigns forever, no nation or kingdom could have had power over them. But they said, The Lord will reign forever, referring to the future (when Thou wilt reign) *over Thy people, the sheep of Thy pasture, the seed of Abraham, Thy beloved; the children of Isaac, Thine only one; the community of Jacob, Thy first-born son, the vine which Thou didst pluck out of Egypt* (Ps. 80.9) *and the stock which Thy right hand planted*' " (v. 16). (The passage is cited in *Mekilta* of R. Simeon 15.18–19, ed. Hoffmann p. 70, as follows:

י"ח. ה' ימלוך לעולם ועד ר' יוסי אומר אלו אמרו ישראל ה' מלך לעולם ועד לא שלטה בהן אומה ומלכות אלא ה' ימלוך לעולם ועד לעתיד לבוא:

It is clear that the statement of R. Jose the Galilean is derived from the prayer, and not the prayer from the statement of R. Jose the Galilean. The evidence for this is as follows: (a) The part of R. Jose the Galilean's statement which is spaced in the Hebrew, and italicized in the English, is at once recognized as a quotation, from the fact that it is addressed to the Deity, although the whole passage of which it is a part, speaks of the Deity in the third person. (b) The poetical language used by R. Jose the Galilean is quite unlike that which we would naturally expect in a brief haggadic passage, unless it were being cited from a well-known phrase. Moreover, it may be stated as a general rule that it is hardly likely that even a scholarly liturgist would assemble phrases from obiter dicta of various scholars in creating his own work. It is far more probable that when we find such phrases, used in passing by scholars in their addresses, and also in a formal passage of the liturgy, that the liturgical passage is being quoted by the scholars, rather than vice versa.

It is not to be presumed that the phrases זרע אברהם אהבך בני יצחק יחידך עדת יעקב בנך בכורך were added to R. Jose the Galilean's original remarks by the compiler of the *Mekilta*. Clearly the phrase is an integral part of R. Jose's address. Indeed, it is possible from the context, that R. Jose the Galilean used the words as an introduction to a covert recitation of the Shema. In other words, because the formal recitation of the Shema was forbidden, R. Jose began an address by saying that if the people had recognized God's kingdom as present, instead of future, they would never have become subject to alien domination. We may imagine that this led R. Jose to the confession of the Kingdom of God, in the formal *Shema yisrael*. He made the transition, in the manner which had become customary in his day, by beginning to recite the liturgical piece composed for the private recitation of the Shema.

If this argument is correct, there can be no doubt that the private recitation of the Shema before the public service, and the liturgical formulae associated with that recitation, originated during the Hadrianic persecution, in the latter part of the life of R. Jose the Galilean. (For the role of R. Jose the Galilean in meeting the problems of the persecution, see Graetz, *Geschichte* IV, p. 430.) In view of the early origin of this liturgical passage, it is entirely natural to find it cited and paraphrased very frequently. The phrase משכימים ומעריבים "announcing both morning and night," is echoed by R. Eleazar ben Ahavai in *Bereshit Rabbah* 98.3, p. 1252. Another part is obviously referred to in the following passage ascribed to *Yer. Berakot*, IX, in *Yalkut* Deut. sect. 836, to *Yer. Berakot* chap. 9 (but found in the extant texts, *Yer. Berakot* 9.2, 13c, only in briefer form without reference to the prayer):

אליהו ז"ל שאל את ר' נהוראי מפני מה זועות באות לעולם א"ל כתוב אחד אומר תמיד עיני ה' אלהיך בה וכתוב אחד אומר המביט לארץ ותרעד כאן בזמן שאין ישראל עושין רצונו של מקום והזועות באות לעולם א"ל חייך מסתברא מלתא אלא כך הוא עיקרו של דבר בשעה שהקב"ה מביט בעולמו ורואה בתי טרטיאות ובתי קרקסיאות יושבות בטח ושאנן ושלוה ובית מקדשו חרב הוא מסתכ' באפלון עולמו [צ"ל אפלון בעולמו] להחריבו כיון שישראל נכנסים שחרית לבתי כנסיות ולבתי מדרשות ומייחדין שמו ואומרים שמע ישראל ה" וגו' מתקבצין כל מלאכי השרת אצל הב"ה ואומרים לפניו אתה הוא עד שלא נברא העולם אתה הוא משנברא העולם אתה הוא בעולם הזה אתה הוא לעולם קד"ש שמך על מקדישי שמך מיד נוחה דעתו של הב"ה ואינו מחריב עולמו ויישב דעתו בשביל ישראל ה'ה'ד ואתה קדוש יושב תהלות ישראל שמיישב דעתו בשביל תהלות ישראל.

Elijah, of blessed memory, asked R. Nehorai, "Why do earthquakes occur?" He replied, "One verse in Scripture reads, '(A land, which the Lord, thy God, careth for); the eyes of the Lord thy God are always upon it, from the beginning of the year even unto the end of the year' (Deut. 11.12). While another verse reads: 'Who looketh on the earth and it trembleth' (Ps. 104.32). (How then can these verses be reconciled? The first refers to the time when the people of Israel perform the will of God.) The second verse to the time when the people of Israel do not perform the will of God, and for that reason earthquakes occur." He

(Elijah) replied, "By thy life, your argument is reasonable. But the fact of the matter is that when the Holy One, blessed be He, looks at the world, and sees the theatres and circuses secure, prosperous and quiet, while His holy temple is ruins, He looks fiercely at His world, in order to destroy it. As soon as the people of Israel enter their synagogues and schools in the morning, and declare the unity of His Name, saying 'Hear O Israel etc.' the archangels assemble near God, and say to Him, 'Thou were in existence before the world was created; Thou art in existence since its creation. Thou dost exist in this world; Thou wilt exist forever. Sanctify Thy name upon them that sanctify it.' At once His anger is soothed, and He does not destroy the world. Thus His anger is soothed because of Israel, as it is written, 'Yet Thou art holy, O Thou that art enthroned upon the praises of Israel' (Ps. 22.3), for He calms His mind because of Israel." (The root for "calming the mind" being the same as that for "enthroned.")

In the light of these passages the fact that neither the prayer, nor any reference to the recitation of the first verse of the Shema, occurs in the prayer book of R. Natronai, published by Professor Louis Ginzberg, *Geonica* II, p. 114, offers no evidence that the prayer was unknown at the time of R. Natronai. It simply indicates that R. Natronai recognized the custom as the result of a temporary situation, the persecution of Hadrian, and therefore saw no reason for perpetuating it (cf., however, V. Aptowitzer in REJ XCIII, 1932, pp. 179–191).

APPENDIX D

The Orthography of the Word בפרוס.

I have examined the following texts for the orthography of the word בפרוס: I. Mishna, (a) *ed. pr.*; (b) ed. Lowe; (c) Ms. Parma; (d) Ms. Budapest; (e) Mishna of the

Yerushalmi, *ed. pr.*; (f) Mishna Ms. in the Library of the Jewish Theological Seminary of America, described above p. 29 (contains only *Seder Moed*); (g) Mishna of *Babli*, *ed. pr.*; (h) Mishna of Babli, Munich Ms. II. *Tosefta*, variants recorded by Zuckermandel from (a) *ed. pr.*; (b) Ms. Vienna; and (c) Ms. Erfurt. III. *Babli*, *Ta'anit* 19b and *Bekorot* 58a, (a) *ed. pr.*; (b) Munich Ms. (c) Munich Ms. 119, as recorded by Malter for *Ta'anit*. IV. *Yerushalmi*, *ed. pr*. The readings are as follows:

I. Mishna

	Shekalim 3.1,			*Bekorot* 9.5		
	i	ii	iii	i	ii	iii
a.	בפרס	בפרס	ובפרס	בפרס	בפרס	בפרס
b.	בפרס	בפרס	ובפרס	בפרס	בפרס	בפרס
c.	בפרס	בפרס	בפרס	בפרס	בפרס	ובפרס
d.	ביפרס	ביפרס	בפרס	בפרס	בפרס	בפרס
e.	בפרס	בפרס	בפרס	——	——	——
f.	בפרוס	בפרוס	בפרוס	——	——	——
g.	——	——	——	בפרס	ובפרס	ובפרס
h.	בפרו'	בפרו'	בפרו'	בפרוס	ובפרוס	ובפרוס

II. *Tosefta*

	Shekalim 2.1			*Ta'anit* 2.8		*Baba Mezia* 4.18			*Bekorot* 7.9	
	i	ii	iii		i	ii	iii	i	ii	iii
a.	פרס	פרס	פרס	בפרוס	בפרס	בפרס	בפרס	בפרס	ובפרס	ובפרס
b.	פרס	פרס	פרס	בפרס	בפרס	בפרס	בפרס	בפרס	ובפרס	ובפרס
c.	פרי	פרי	פרי	בפרוס	ובפרוס	—	—	—	—	—

III. *Babli*

	Ta'anit 19b	*Bekorot* 58a		
a.	בפרוס	פרס	פרס	
b.	בפרוס	פרס	פורס	
c.	בפרוס	—	—	

IV. *Yerushalmi*

	Shekalim 3.1	*Ta'anit* 3.2	
ed. pr.	פרס	בפרס	בפרס

The variants do not permit any precise determination of the correct spelling of the word. But it may be assumed that the spelling בפרס has been influenced by the statement of R. Abbahu, who was a Palestinian authority.

This assumption is strengthened by the fact that the reading בפרוס occurs principally in *Babli*, and in those probably influenced by it. If this is correct, then there is ground for believing that בפרוס is an older reading than בפרס. Of course, the reading בפרוס would be more natural for expressing the thought, "at the announcement of."

INDEX

INDEX TO PASSAGES

This Index includes references to the Hebrew Scriptures, the New Testament, Apocrypha, Pseudepigrapha, Babylonian and Palestinian Talmuds, Mishna, Tosefta, and other rabbinic works, as well as Josephus and Philo.

The numbers on the right refer to pages.

Numbers

Deuteronomy

Joshua

Judges

I Samuel

II Samuel

I Kings

II Kings

YERUSHALMI

Berakot

Shebi'it

Pesahim

Sheqalim

GOSPELS

Acts

JOSEPHUS

Against Apion

Antiquities

War

PHILO

De Specialibus Legibus